REFINING RUSSIA

REFINING RUSSIA

Advice Literature, Polite Culture, and Gender from Catherine to Yeltsin

CATRIONA KELLY

OXFORD
UNIVERSITY PRESS

OXFORD
UNIVERSITY PRESS

Great Clarendon Street, Oxford OX2 6DP

Oxford University Press is a department of the University of Oxford.
It furthers the University's objective of excellence in research, scholarship,
and education by publishing worldwide in

Oxford New York

Athens Auckland Bangkok Bogotá Buenos Aires Cape Town
Chennai Dar es Salaam Delhi Florence Hong Kong Istanbul Karachi
Kolkata Kuala Lumpur Madrid Melbourne Mexico City Mumbai Nairobi
Paris São Paulo Shanghai Singapore Taipei Tokyo Toronto Warsaw

with associated companies in Berlin Ibadan

Oxford is a registered trade mark of Oxford University Press
in the UK and in certain other countries

Published in the United States
by Oxford University Press Inc., New York

British Library Cataloguing in Publication Data
Data available

Library of Congress Cataloging in Publication Data
Data available
ISBN 0-19-815987-0

1 3 5 7 9 10 8 6 4 2

Typeset in Imprint
by Joshua Associates Ltd., Oxford
Printed in Great Britain
on acid-free paper by
Biddles Ltd., Guildford and King's Lynn

In Memoriam

ALEXANDER KELLY
(30 June 1929 23 October 1996)

Acknowledgements

The composition of acknowledgements is a particularly prickly task for the author of a book about etiquette literature. Fear of failing to express gratitude with sufficient fulsomeness vies with a horror of the conventional phrases of thanks set out in manuals of polite behaviour. I should therefore not only reiterate the time-honoured formula about how the faults here are my own, and its virtues due to others, but also emphasize that the sentiments here, whatever their infelicities of expression, at least have the merit of not being copied straight out of an unctuous letter-writing manual, or a collection of *kumplimenty* meant to be recited on all fours.

I began work on this book some time before moving to New College, Oxford, an institution whose motto is—by a happy coincidence—'Manners Makyth Man'. The fact that I have been able to explore the ramifications of this insight in Russian culture (and also of the no less important insight that 'manners makyth woman') is to a large extent attributable to the excellent conditions for work, congenial atmosphere, and stimulating company that New College offers. Among individuals there, I would particularly like to thank my counterparts in French, German, and Spanish, Ann Jefferson, Karen Leeder, Neil McKinlay, and Wes Williams; and Mark Griffith, who loaned me examples of Victorian advice books from his collection. At the University of Oxford in general, I have been helped (as always) by the staffs of the Taylorian and Bodleian Libraries, and have had amicable and fruitful exchanges about the book's subject matter with the various members of the Sub-Faculty of Russian and other Slavonic Languages. Undergraduate and graduate students at Oxford have fostered the discussions in the book, directly and indirectly, through lively, curious, and sceptical questions and observations about all manner of subjects. I would also like to thank my former comrades-in-arms at the School of Slavonic and East European Studies, University College London, where I was working when I launched myself on the book, particularly Faith Wigzell, another pioneer in the field of 'pulp non-fiction'.

Though some Western libraries, for example the Slavonic Library of the University of Helsinki, and the British Library in London, have amassed a number of how-to manuals (sometimes ones that have disappeared from Russian collections), researching this subject would not have been possible without a good deal of time spent in Russia. Here I was dependent not only upon research grants made by New College, but upon the generosity of the British Academy. The award of a Personal Research Grant in 1996, and of places on the Academic Exchange with the Russian Academy of Sciences in 1997 and 1998, was vital to the completion of the book: my thanks go in particular to Jane Lyddon, and to her counterparts at the Russian Academy of Sciences, I. A. Plyusnin in St Petersburg and V. V. Davydov in Moscow. In Russia, those from whose advice and help I benefited include the staffs of the Russian National Library and Russian State Library, of the Russian State Archive of Literature and Art, and of the Centre for the Preservation of Documents Relating to Youth Organizations (the former Komsomol archive). The employees of these institutions work in conditions that range from the difficult to the appalling: salaries are paid months in arrears, the fabric of buildings deteriorates almost as one watches, and money for book purchasing and conservation grows ever shorter. Nevertheless, they are places where the old intelligentsia traditions of unstinting hard work and devotion to the life of the mind remains largely intact. I also warmly acknowledge the kindness of many friends and colleagues in Russia, in particular N. A. Azhgikhina, A. D. Baiburin, K. A. Barsht, A. I. Blyumbaum, M. L. Gasparov, A. M. Konechnyi, K. A. Kumpan, N. L. Pushkareva, M. A. Robinson, L. I. Sazonova, and B. A. Uspensky. Occasionally, when they learned that I was working on a topic to do with politeness, Russians who were meeting me for the first time seemed to sense some anxiety that they might be about to become the subjects of my research; I hope that these chance acquaintances will be relieved to learn this is not that sort of book, though I fear it will also disappoint still further those who mistakenly assumed me to be an expert source of advice on the table-settings, gestures, and dress favoured by chic British society.

In a broad thematic treatment of this kind, it is as important to grasp what needs to be left out as what should be included. Here, as well as in finding new areas to explore, I was especially helped by the incisive comments on early drafts of Stephen Lovell, Robert Service, and above all Steve Smith. Others who have offered invaluable comments on the manuscript in whole or in part include Robin Aizlewood, Simon Dixon, Barbara Engel, Rebecca Friedman, Barbara Heldt, Isabel de Madariaga, Michelle L. Marrese, Wendy Rosslyn, and Gerry Smith. Those who have supplied material, discussed ideas, and offered encouragement include (besides those already mentioned), Daniel Beer, Tim Binyon, Philip Bullock, Martin Dewhirst, Sheila Fitzpatrick, Peter France, Katya Golynkina, Malcolm Jones, Andrew Kahn, Lyubov' Kiseleva, Eve Levin, Michelle L. Marrese, Susan Morrissey, Arja Rosenholm, Wendy Rosslyn, and participants at seminars and conferences in various parts of Europe and in America: those at 'Gender in Russian History and Culture' at the

University of Birmingham, especially Linda Edmondson and Bill Wagner; Carolyn Jursa Ayers and others at the 'All by Myself' conference on autobiography at the University of Groningen, Netherlands; Hubertus Jahn and other members of the Lehrstuhl Osteuropäische Geschichte at the University of Erlangen; audiences at Bribery and Corruption in Russian Culture, and Reinterpreting Russian History, both held at SSEES, University of London; Christa Binswanger, Gerhard Ritz, Carmen Scheide and other participants at a conference on Gender and Russian Modernism in Zürich; Jostein Børtnes, Knut Grimstad, Astrid Brokke, and others at the Gender and Russian Literature Workshop at the University of Tromsø; Anthony Cross, Simon Franklin, Chris Ward, and others in the Department of Slavonic Languages, University of Cambridge; my fellow-panellists Louise McReynolds and Bob Weinberg and a doughty band of other hurricane-survivors at the AAASS meeting in Boca Raton, Florida; members of the BASEES Russian Revolution Study Group at Durham; Ralph and Oxana Cleminson and the audience of the Russian Circle in Winchester. Thanks also to my editors at Oxford University Press, Sophie Goldsworthy, Matthew Hollis, and Mary Worthington. Nearer home, Ian Thompson has not only made civilized existence possible, but has, as always, contributed far more to my work than I ever will to his researches in the field of neuroscience; the chasing of tail (own), biting of ankles and boxing of ears (mine), and other reprehensible antics of the half-tamed feline who shares our house at least provided distractions when I hit sticky moments at the word processor. Among the rest of my family, I would especially like to mention my father, whose undying enthusiasm for every interesting human activity, from Brahms piano sonatas to scandalous gossip, is, I hope, directly reflected here. Though he, alas, will never read it, I dedicate the book to his memory.

Contents

List of Illustrations

Note on Conventions

Advice books that are listed in the Select Bibliography appear throughout the footnotes in the author-short title form (Fenelon, *O vospitanii devits*, etc.)

Most advice books that are cited in the text or notes are described *de visu*. In the rare cases where I have not been able to locate a publication, but where its intrinsic interest justifies citing it, and it is listed in a major bibliographical source, I have indicated this by an asterisk before the author's name.

Transliteration is according to a modified version of British Standard (Dostoevsky, but Tolstoi, rather than Tolstoy).

Unless otherwise specified, all translations are my own. My own cuts in cited texts are marked by spaced points; unspaced points are as in the original text.

Abbreviations

BE	*Entsiklopedicheskii slovar' izd. Brokgauza i Efrona* (41 + 4 vols., St Petersburg, 1890–1907)
BSE[1]	*Bol'shaya sovetskaya entsiklopediya* (65 vols.; Moscow, 1925–47)
BSE[2]	*Bol'shaya sovetskaya entsiklopediya* (2nd edn.; 51 vols.; Moscow, 1949–65)
BSE[3]	*Bol'shaya sovetskaya entsiklopediya* (3rd edn.; 31 vols.; Moscow, 1969–81)
Chekhov, *PSS*	A. P. Chekhov, *Polnoe sobranie sochinenii i pisem* (18 + 12 vols.; Moscow, 1974–87)
Dostoevsky, *PSS*	F. M. Dostoevsky, *Polnoe sobranie sochinenii v 30 tomakh* (Leningrad, 1972–90)
EK	*Ezhegodnik knigi*
IV	*Istoricheskii vestnik*
KL	*Knizhnaya letopis'*
KP	*Komsomol'skaya pravda*
Mayakovsky, *PSS*	V. V. Mayakovsky, *Polnoe sobranie sochinenii* (13 vols.; Moscow, 1955–61)
O	*Ogonek*
Pushkin, *PSS*	A. S. Pushkin, *Polnoe sobranie sochinenii* (2nd edn.; 19 vols.; Moscow, 1996–8)
Pushkin, *PSS*[2]	A. S. Pushkin, *Polnoe sobranie sochinenii* (10 vols.; Leningrad, 1977)
PSZ	*Polnoe sobranie zakonov Rossiiskoi Imperii*
RGB	Rossiiskaya gosudarstvennaya biblioteka (Russian State Library, formerly Lenin Library, Moscow)
RNB	Rossiiskaya natsional'naya biblioteka (Russian National Library, formerly Saltykov-Shchedrin Public Library, St Petersburg)
RGALI	Russkii gosudarstvennyi arkhiv literatury i iskusstva (Russian State Archive (formerly Central State Archive) of Literature and History, Moscow)
RR	*Russian Review*
SEER	*Slavonic and East European Review*
SK	*Svodnyi katalog russkoi knigi grazhdanskoi pechati XVIII veka, 1725–1800* (5 vols.; Moscow, 1962–7)
SKKIYa:	*Svodnyi katalog knig na inostrannykh yazykakh, napechatannykh v Rossii v XVIII veke* (3 vols.; Leningrad, 1984–7)
SR	*Slavic Review*

Tolstoi, *PSS*   L. N. Tolstoi, *Polnoe sobranie sochinenii* (90 vols.; Moscow and Leningrad, 1928–58)

TsKhDMO   Tsentr khraneniya dokumentov molodezhnykh organizatsii (Centre for Youth Organization Documents, Moscow: from September 2000, will form part of the Russian State Archive of Social and Political History [RGASPI])

VE: *Vestnik Evropy.*

Introduction: How to Read this Book

'After all,' said the Duchess vaguely, 'there are certain things you can't get away from. Right and wrong, good conduct and moral rectitude, have certain well-defined limits.'

'So, for the matter of that,' replied Reginald, 'has the Russian Empire. The trouble is that the limits are not always in the same place.'

(Saki, 'Reginald in Russia', 1904)

A classic study of Russian popular fiction in the nineteenth century goes under the title *When Russia Learned to Read*.[1] In similar style, this analysis of books about refined behaviour, and their links with perceptions of individual and national identity, might have been entitled *How Russia Learned to Behave*. I do not, needless to say, subscribe to the view that there was no such thing as etiquette in pre-Petrine Russian culture (even prejudiced foreign travellers, accusing Russians of being 'a people passing rude, to vices vile inclined', at the same time recorded the existence of intricate and elaborate social ceremonies in the country they mocked).[2] Nor do I propose to add to the numerous books, some excellent, some dreadful, about 'the Russian mind'.[3] The shock effect of arriving to spend a

---

[1] Jeffrey Brooks, *When Russia Learned to Read: Literacy and Popular Literature in Russia, 1861–1917* (Princeton, 1985).

[2] For accounts of this kind (often by foreigners of the 'middling sort', such as merchants, whose contacts with the Russian court elite were in any case limited), see e.g. Lloyd E. Berry and Robert O. Crummey (eds.), *Rude and Barbarous Kingdom: Russian in the Accounts of Sixteenth-Century English Voyagers* (Madison, 1968). More acute and sympathetic visitors, such as Sigmund von Herberstein (*Description of Moscow and Muscovy 1557*, ed. Bertold Picard, trans. J. B. C. Grundy, London, 1969) noted a punctilious observation of etiquette, and medieval documents reveal that a sophisticated vocabulary relating to the ethics and aesthetics of behaviour was in use (I. I. Sreznevsky, *Materialy dlya slovarya drevnerusskogo yazyka*, 3 vols., St Petersburg, 1893–1903 (repr. Moscow, 1958): see e.g. entries under *chin''*, *blagorodnyi*, *chest'*. On the last term, see also Nancy S. Kollmann, *By Honor Bound: State and Society in Early Modern Russia* (Ithaca, NY, 1999).) By lighting only on examples of negative difference, travellers missed information like this, and also failed to note that, for instance, all-over washing was probably commoner among Russians of every social status than it was in Western Europe, where bathhouses had fallen out of use during the Black Death, and where conduct guides of the 16th and 17th cents. stipulated daily hand-washing, but only 'an occasional bath'. (M. von Boehn, *Modes and Manners*, 4 vols. (London, 1932–5), iii 161, quoting a French conduct book of 1640; my thanks to Isabel de Madariaga for bringing this source to my attention).

[3] Among the better studies of the 'Russian mind' are H. Pitcher, *Understanding the Russians* (London, 1964), R. Hingley, *The Russian Mind* (London, 1977), and H. Smith, *The Russians* (London, 1976).

year in a Soviet student hostel during the so-called 'period of stagnation', the end of the Brezhnev era, to find four showers shared between 400 people, and to be greeted by a forgotten pan of omelette falling out of the wardrobe, when my only previous experience of Russian life had been afternoons over tea at Countess N's in Chiswick, with photographs of woodland picnics circa 1910 in the background, was such as to make me suspicious of pretty well any generalizations about national character at a single period, let alone over the course of history. As Norman Douglas enquired in 1915, 'What has the Englishman of today in common with that rather lovable fop, drunkard, and bully who would faint with ecstasy over Byron's *Parisina* after pistolling his best friend in a duel about a wench or a lap-dog?'[4] If one substitutes 'Russian' and 'Pushkin's *Prisoner of the Caucasus*', the sentiments are just as valid. Rather than generalizing about colourful local customs and eternal traits, then, I intend to trace how the spread of literacy, the codification of information about appropriate social relations, and the dissemination of beliefs in the superiority of Western civilization,[5] turned everyday conduct into a controversial and intricately ideologized question, introducing an unprecedented self-consciousness into educated Russians' contemplation of their own behaviour.

The sources upon which the analysis draws are, in the first place, behaviour manuals and how-to books, ranging in size from brochures up to encyclopedias, and with titles such as *House Management*, *The Science of Being Polite*, and even *How to Read a Book*. To date, materials of this kind have been little utilized as a method of understanding Russian history. In his collection of essays, *Conversations about Russian Culture*, Yury Lotman, the most influential cultural historian of Russia in the late eighteenth and early nineteenth centuries, made a plea that cultural history should be as inclusive as possible: 'In the spheres of culture and everyday life, one should never reject this or that element as insignificant on first principles.' Yet literature about appropriate conduct is often considered not only 'in-

---

[4] N. Douglas, *In Old Calabria* (London, 1994), 135.

[5] This term should be understood as carrying invisible quotation marks throughout this book. Any sensible person would agree with N. S. Trubetskoi that 'European culture is not an absolute, it is not a universal human culture, but merely the creation of one, limited, distinct ethnic or ethnographic group of nations sharing a common identity' ('Europe and Mankind', in *The Legacy of Genghis Khan and Other Essays*, ed. A. Liberman (Michigan Slavic Materials 33, Ann Arbor, 1991), 61). As F. Braudel, among others, has shown (*A History of Civilizations*, trans. R. Mayne (London, 1993)), there is no sense in which 'civilization' and 'European' are cognate, nor is the *ideal* of European civilization to be confused with the lamentable failures of European nations to live up to that ideal (on which see further M. Mazower, *Dark Continent: Europe's Twentieth Century* (London, 1998), *passim*.) However, the point is that there has been a long Russian tradition of assuming civilized values to be of universal significance, yet embodied in their most perfect form by Western European societies.

significant on first principles', but absurd. For example, the author of a recent cultural history of the early Soviet Union, having mentioned that two of the authors originally placed on Nadezhda Krupskaya's blacklist of books to be excluded from Soviet libraries were Plato and Samuel Smiles, adds in an aside: 'From the sublime to the ridiculous'.[6] Russian readers of the early twentieth century were a good deal more likely, though, to have read the 'ridiculous' Smiles than the 'sublime' Plato, and at least as likely to have come into contact with the ideas of John Stuart Mill in the diluted form in which Smiles presented them in his self-help books as they were through reading the works of Mill himself. Equally, the works of such forgotten figures as Madame de Lambert, Madame Leprince de Beaumont and Madame Genlis were at least as influential as those of Rousseau in altering attitudes to childhood and the family in late eighteenth-century Russia—though in Lotman's own *Besedy o russkoi kul'ture*, Genlis is mentioned only once (as 'a dreary moralist of the female gender', *skuchnaya moralistka*), while Rousseau figures largely throughout.[7]

The neglect of 'small discourses on pragmatic changes' has been plausibly explained by Oleg Khakhordin, one of the few historians to have considered these in detail, as deriving from the assumptions of 'grand official Marxist discourse'.[8] Undoubtedly, the Marxist–Leninist view that historical change,

---

[6] Yu. Lotman, *Besedy o russkoi kul'ture: Byt i traditsii russkogo dvoryanstva XVIII–nachalo XIX veka* (St Petersburg, 1994); R. Pethybridge, *One Step Backwards, Two Steps Forward: Soviet Society and Politics in the NEP* (Oxford, 1990), 217. Interestingly, Krupskaya herself was later to recognize that 'sublime' materials were not necessarily the most influential: during a fresh round of library purges in 1924, she commented, 'The mass reader will hardly have read Kant' (*Pedagogicheskie sochineniya*, viii (Moscow, 1960); quoted in Evgeny Dobrenko, *The Making of the State Reader: Social and Aesthetic Contexts of the Perception of Soviet Literature*, trans. J. M. Savage (Stanford, Calif., 1997), 194.)

[7] Lotman, *Besedy*, 95. A similar attitude is manifest in the multi-handed history ed. Yu. D. Levin, *Istoriya russkoi perevodnoi khudozhestvennoi literatury*, 2 vols. (St Petersburg, 1995), which mentions Genlis as one among many didactic writers; and in E. O. Putilova, 'Russkaya poeziya detyam', *Russkaya poeziya detyam* (St Petersburg, 1997), i. 14, which contrasts the 'genuine spirit of enlightenment' in Rousseau's *Émile* with the 'tedious moralizing and small-minded didacticism' of Madame Leprince de Beaumont's *Le Magasin des enfants*. In the West, discussion of Russian advice on manners has generally been the province of journalistic ephemera: see e.g. Tobia Frankel, 'Etiquette Line for Russians', *New York Times Magazine*, 16 Nov. 1958, and Anon, 'Graces of Yester: Soviet Union', *Newsweek*, 9 Jan. 1967. (Cited from D. Robertson Hodges, *Etiquette: An Annotated Bibliography of Titles Published in English in the US, 1900 through 1987* (Tanglewood, Mass., 1988).)

[8] O. Khakhordin, *The Collective and the Individual in Soviet Russia: A Study of Practices* (Berkeley, 1999), p. 360. The emphasis upon political literature and upon 'great thinkers' is evident e.g. in S. V. Belov (comp.), *Kniga v Rossii 1850–1917 gg. (Materialy k ukazatelyu sovetskoi literatury. 1917–1982 gg.)* (2nd edn.; Leningrad, 1983); *idem* and M. V. Bezrodnyi (comps.), *Kniga v Rossii 1850–1917 gg. (Materialy k ukazatelyu sovetskoi literatury, 1983–1990 gg.)* (Leningrad, 1991). More than a third of the listings are made up of work on literature produced by the Russian revolutionary movement. Similarly, R. N. Kleimenova, *Knizhnaya Moskva pervoi poloviny XIX veka* (Moscow, 1991) concentrates on 'serious' publications (editions of poetry, philosophy, history, etc.) and mentions advice literature only in passing (21–2, 32, 66–7, 157). Exceptions to the general neglect

where not traceable to underlying socio-economic conditions, is always attributable to the efforts of 'progressive thinkers and activists' (*peredovye mysliteli i deyateli*), has been one reason behind the dismissal of advice literature. Another, though, has been the long-term emphasis, in Russian history, on industrial production, which has meant that everyday life (*byt*) has only recently begun to attract attention (if scholars were likely to disparage a 1947 manual about 'working on the self', or a 1963 instruction on the disciplinary regime in an industrial enterprise, the type of material studied by Khakhordin, their reaction to a 1965 guide to house management was certain to be still more contemptuous). What is more (in another hangover from Marxism-Leninism), everyday life is, where constituted as a possible sphere of enquiry, generally perceived as 'spontaneous' and ideology-free, an inert sphere beyond the realm of 'conscious' thought. For example, in a recent study of gentry upbringing (*dvoryanskoe vospitanie*) in the early nineteenth century, Ol'ga Muranova has argued that behaviour patterns depend on imitation rather than on consultation of 'codified lists of rules' (*svod pravil*). In her words, conduct is to be understood as 'above all a way of life, a style of behaviour that is assimilated in part consciously, in part unconsciously, by means of custom and imitation; it is a tradition that is observed rather than discussed. Therefore, theoretical prescriptions are less important than the principles that actually were exercised in daily life, behaviour, and live social relations [*zhivoe obrashchenie*].'⁹

This argument is suspect not only because of its assumption that 'live social relations' may easily be retrieved from any historical source, but because 'theoretical prescriptions' have, since at least the early eighteenth century, been instrumental in shaping the 'conscious' assimilation of behaviour patterns in Russia. The paradox is that the 'naturalness' seen as proper to good behaviour was learned from absorbing dictates such as the following: 'True politeness should not hamper or burden a person; it should be as natural and unconscious as breathing or the beating of the heart.'¹⁰ And so far from tradition having simply been 'observed' rather

---

of advice literature include, beside Khakhordin's book, J. Toomre's annotated English trans. of E. Molokhovets, *Podarok molodym khozyaikam: Classic Russian Cooking: Elena Molokhovets' A Gift to Young Housewives* (Bloomington, Ind., 1992), though here the advice text is taken as a transparent source of information about actual practices rather than as an expression of ideology. Elena Lavrent'eva, *Svetskii etiket pushkinskoi pory* (Moscow, 1999), is an anthology from selected advice books with popularizing commentary. For an approach close to my own, see Michael S. Gorham, 'From Charisma to Cant: Models of Public Speaking in Early Soviet Russia', *Canadian Slavonic Papers* 38/3–4 (1996), 331–56. R. Bartlett, 'Britain, Russia, and Scurvy in the Eighteenth Century', *Oxford Slavonic Papers* 29 (1996), 23–43; M. David-Fox, 'What is Cultural Revolution?' *RR* 58 (1999), 181–201; and D. Ransel, *Village Mothers: Three Generations of Change in Russia and Tataria* (Bloominghton, Ind., 2000).

⁹ O. S. Muranova, *Kak vospytivali russkogo dvoryanina* (Moscow, 1995), 10.
¹⁰ Anon., *Pravila svetskogo etiketa dlya muzhchin* (1873), p. viii.

than 'discussed' in the last three centuries, the concept itself was the subject of vehement and sometimes embittered disputes; to these advice literature made an important contribution.

To be sure, the intellectual content of advice literature is often scanty, to say the least: the prescriptions offered are predictable, and the sententiae leaden: 'It is possible to be both polite and amiable even if one has little money in one's pocket. Politeness achieves much and costs nothing. It is the cheapest of all commodities.'[11] But there have been eras of history (for instance, the 'long eighteenth century') when people of talent and originality applied themselves to the writing of prescriptive literature, when conduct guidance was a respectable and requisite activity in the authors of fiction and poetry, and when ideas such as the one just cited were novel and challenging. In any case, it would be a mistake to reason from the fatuity or tautology of at least some advice literature to the circumstances of its reception. The persistence of the genre in Russia, the number of titles, the frequent reprinting of some books (from Fénelon's *Traité de l'éducation des filles* in the late eighteenth century to Sarkizov-Serazini's *Let's Cure Ourselves with Sun!* in the 1920s, or *The Book of Tasty and Nutritious Food* in the 1950s and 1960s) all suggest that a lively market for treatises on conduct existed. And the heavy pencil underlinings or marginal annotations in surviving copies indicate that they were not only read, but read with attention and even awe.[12]

The purpose of this study, though, is not simply to note the popularity of authors such as Samuel Smiles or Fénelon, nor to provide a survey of publication data. Rather, this is an exercise in 'the history of books' as defined by one of its most prominent practitioners, Robert Darnton: that is, an attempt not only at 'discovering what books reached readers through an entire society' but also to examine '(at least to a certain extent) how readers made sense of them'. The aim is to 'study literature as part of a general cultural system'.[13]

[11] Iur'ev and Vladimirsky, *Pravila svetskoi zhizni i etiketa* (1889), 8.

[12] See e.g. the marginalia to a passage in Dymman, *Nauka zhizni* (1859) (copy in RGB at T 71/353), 148. Dymman writes: 'Hardly a day goes past without one hearing about someone or other: "He's a wonderful person, very able, but unfortunately he drinks like a fish." It's an astonishing, a mind-boggling human weakness.' A reader has written in purple ink: 'This is all so topical, and thoroughly depressing too. June 1966.' Four others have added (in inks of more conventional colour): 'And 1968.' 'Oct. 1971.' '1973.' '1995.'

[13] R. Darnton, *The Forbidden Best-Sellers of Pre-Revolutionary France* (London, 1996), p. xxi. 'History of the book' in this sense is still a fairly new discipline in Russian studies, though examples to date include, besides Brooks's *When Russia Learned to Read*, G. Marker, *Printing, Publishing, and the Origins of Intellectual Life in Russia* (Princeton, 1985); A. Reitblat, 'Glup li milord?' in *Lubochnaya kniga* (Moscow, 1990), 5–20, and *idem, Ot Bovy k Bal'montu* (Moscow, 1991); F. Wigzell, *Reading Russian Fortunes: Print Culture, Gender and Divination in Russia from 1765* (Cambridge, 1998); B. Holmgren, *Rewriting Capitalism: Literature and the Market in Late Tsarist Russia and the Kingdom of Poland* (Pittsburgh, 1998), ch. 5; S. Lovell, *The Russian Reading*

Of the three aims mentioned, the second and third are more problematic than the first. It is dangerous to argue from the sheer fact of advice literature's presence to a broader cultural meaning, as one commentator has done in the case of Victorian England: 'England was a country in which rules and codes substituted themselves for nature. It was here that social discipline had most succeeded, not so much in conquering as in suppressing whatever was liable to conflict with society. Elsewhere, though the rules may have been stronger than nature, the nature was still there.'[14] Such an assessment would surely have delighted Dostoevsky, since it accords entirely with the drift of his anti-English *Winter Notes on Summer Impressions*; but the association made between the proliferation of rules and the rigidity of 'social discipline' does not stand up to close scrutiny. Advice literature has not gone into a decline in Britain or other parts of Europe, or in America, since the relaxation of 'social discipline' in the 1960s. On the contrary, a visit to any bookshop brings one face to face with a plethora of titles on subjects from the making of knot-gardens to the confection of vegan banquets, from *Little Books of Calm* to Zen guides on skiing, while newspapers and magazines enclose an ever-thickening core of 'lifestyle features' within a thinning veneer of 'hard news'. My own university bombards students and lecturers with advisory material, including guides to Netiquette, admonitions on sexual harassment, and 'alternative prospectuses', not to mention a whole millefeuille of 'study skills' sheets handed out during 'induction week'. New genres of advice literature have proliferated: recent examples include a shrewd and tough-minded guide by Emily Toth, *Ms Mentor's Impeccable Advice for Women Academics* (1997), and Alain de Botton's witty introduction to reading *A la recherche du temps perdu, How Proust Can Change Your Life* (1997).

One should also be careful about pressing the argument in reverse, and suggesting that the large number of advice literature titles published in Russia during the late eighteenth, nineteenth, and twentieth centuries might be an indication of the triumph there of 'social discipline' over 'nature'. To be sure, the prevalence of advisory texts of various kinds, from notices in post offices stating 'It is strictly forbidden to dispatch poisonous snakes by post', to detailed advice on conduct in church (no dogs, no short skirts, no mobile telephones), to the band running across the bottom of NTV's breakfast programme *Segodnyachko* in 1998 ('Have You Turned Off

Revolution: Print Culture in the Soviet and Post-Soviet Eras (London, 2000); and the essays by various hands collected in *Chtenie v dorevolyutsionnoi Rossii: sbornik nauchnykh trudov* (Moscow, 1995). The interpretive drive of these studies contrasts with the emphasis upon publication statistics in the absolute that is evident in some other work: see e.g. A. A. Govorov, M. A. Vinogradov, S. B. Lyublinsky, and E. A. Silant'ev (eds.), *Istoriya knizhnoi torgovli v Rossii* (2nd edn.; Moscow, 1982); and A. Luppov (ed.), *Frantsuzskaya kniga v Rossii XVIII veka: Ocherki istorii* (Leningrad, 1986).

14   A. St George, *The Descent of Manners: Etiquette, Rules and the Victorians* (London, 1993), p. xi.

Your Kettle?' 'Has Your Milk Boiled Over?'), acts as a corrective to the prevalent Western stereotype of the Russians as invariably spontaneous, chaotic, and devil-may-care.[15] What is more, any frequent visitor to Russia during the late twentieth century could testify that advice-giving was common in more informal contexts as well, from the proffering of home remedies to friends stricken with a cold to unsolicited comments on menu choices in canteens ('I wouldn't advise it', said the man behind me in a queue at the Lenin Library in 1991, as I stretched out my hand for a plate of egg mayonnaise). And it was apparently not uncommon for Russian trainees on business management courses in the West during the glasnost and post-Soviet periods to sympathize, in role-playing sessions, with the 'rule-bound manager' rather than with his supposedly more 'creative' and 'flexible' counterparts.[16] But given the popularity of advice literature in all European countries, not to speak of America, at the same period, it would be hard to argue that Russia was exceptional. (And even if its popularity in a comparative sense *could* be established, this would speak less about some essential characteristic of 'the Russian mind' or 'the Russian soul' than about various concrete facts of recent history, most particularly the Soviet government's attempts to impose collective conformity while keeping the populace starved of practical information, or, more recently, the uncertainties caused by the collapse of the Soviet system after 1991.) Moreover, in Russia, as in the West, there is a long-standing tradition of parody advice literature. *Chesterfield Burlesqued* (1811), Daniel Curzun's *Joyful Blue Book of Gracious Gay Etiquette* (1982), or the late 1990s *Little Book of Stress* (whose advice on how to become more stressed includes the suggestion, 'Get in touch with all your ex-lovers once a year and try to restart the relationship'), have counterparts in Strakhov's *Pocket-Book* of sardonic 'advice' to extravagant Russian landowners (1795), Pushkin's joke poem on manners for a friend's son, the *Satirikon* publications of the 1910s, or indeed 1970s playground anecdotes about the grotesquely crude folk hero Stirlitz. And although Russian culture has no precise equivalent of Georges Pérec's genial appropriation of the advice genre in fiction, *La Vie, mode d'emploi*

---

[15] The bard of Russian primness (*chopornost'*, a quality often attributed by unreflective commentators to foreigners, especially 'the English') is of course Nabokov (on which see my 'Nabokov, *snobizm*, and Selfhood', forthcoming in Jane Grayson and Arnold McMillin (eds.), *Nabokov at the Crossroads: International Centennial Conference Papers* (London, 2001)). On the pervasiveness of advice literature in the West, see e.g. Stephen King's melodramatic claim that 'my generation traded God for Martha Stewart. She's this priestess of etiquette who says that when you shovel snow from your drive, you ought to leave an inch or two at the sides, because it looks so nice.' (Peter Conrad, 'Everybody's Nightmare', *Observer*, 9 Aug. 1998, 'Review', 1). Some sense of American publications in the field (including parodies such Daniel Curzun's *The Joyful Blue Book of Gracious Gay Etiquette* (San Francisco, 1982)) is given by Robertson Hodges, *Etiquette: A Bibliography*.

[16] My thanks to Peter Oppenheimer for this information.

(Life, a User's Manual, 1978), writers from A. K. Tolstoi to Chekhov, Nabokov, and Sergei Dovlatov have made their own and zestful uses of such material.

If the popularity of advice literature as a fact in itself must be interpreted with caution, the content of this literature is also not susceptible to the drawing of hasty conclusions. To be sure, domestic manuals—cookbooks, guides to housework—do give some indication of shifts in material culture (for instance, the appearance of new ingredients and techniques, the availability of novel kinds of domestic machinery). Etiquette guides register changes in social practices (for example, the appearance of visiting cards, not mentioned in Russian etiquette books till the 1840s), and the emergence of new forms of gesture (for example, hand-kissing), of prohibition upon emotion (anger, for instance), and of cultural institution (such as the 'American bar').[17] But the gap between the statements made in advice texts and the understanding and practical implication of these by those who read them is potentially vast. As Michel de Certeau reminds us, 'the presence and circulation of a representation . . . tells us nothing about what it is for its users. We must first analyze its manipulation by users who are not its makers. Only then can we gauge the difference or similarity behind the production of the image and the secondary production hidden in the process of its utilization.'[18] A straightforward example of how eccentrically advice texts may be interpreted comes from the collective farm market in Voronezh, the provincial town where I lived as a student in the early 1980s. Here the sellers of dried mushrooms and healing herbs used to display their wares underneath a notice reading 'The selling of dried mushrooms and healing herbs is strictly forbidden', no doubt seeing the prohibition as a convenient advertisement for their activities. There are other cases, too, where negative recommendations have dictated real behaviour in precisely the opposite way to that intended—for instance, by introducing to readers some exotic misdemeanour they had not previously heard of (the regulations against duels introduced by Peter I seem to have been an important *encouragement* to the development in Russia of the practice of

---

[17] On visiting cards, see Sokolov, *Svetskii chelovek* (1847), 155; on hand-kissing, see Metuzala, *Dzhentl'men* (1913), 134; on the 'American bar', ibid. 147–8: 'American bars with high stools, elegant long glasses full of ice and various kinds of extraordinary combinations of sherry, champagne, beaten egg-yolks and all kinds of fruits are becoming more and more popular in Russia.' Another new activity, driving, was the subject of its own advice literature, under titles such as *Avtomobilist* etc. For an exemplary use of how-to material as the basis for understanding of historical evolution, see Herman Roodenberg, 'The "Hand of Friendship": Shaking Hands and Other Gestures in the Dutch Republic', in J. Bremmer and H. Roodenburg (eds.), *A Cultural History of Gesture: From Antiquity to the Present Day* (Cambridge, 1993), 152–89. For a similarly exemplary study in emotionology, see P. N. Stearns, *Jealousy: The Evolution of an Emotion in American History* (New York, 1989).

[18] M. de Certeau, *The Practice of Everyday Life*, trans. S. Rendall (Berkeley, 1988), 12.

duelling).[19] There are of course many other possible shades of appropriation and reinterpretation besides plain subversion, as in the cases just cited:
sincere but failed attempts to implement precept, half-hearted appropriation, or incomplete repudiation of this, or subversively supererogatory
implementation of moral counsels. Whichever way, the point is that
analysis of how written prescription shapes reality is far from straightforward: corroborating material must be retrieved from sources such as letters,
memoirs, and belles-lettres, and compared with the *sententiae* set out in
advice literature texts themselves.

Care is also needed when forming conclusions about the extent to which
advice texts reflect reality: suggestions about desirable modes of behaviour
reflect ideals rather than real-life practices, and sometimes ideals of a rather
idiosyncratic kind. A particularly striking example of the capriciousness and
unreality of some of the advice offered comes from a 1970s Soviet
behaviour book, which instructs visitors to the theatre as follows:

[When taking your seats], the man enters the row first. There is one subtlety to
bear in mind here: before the play begins, you move down the row facing the
other spectators in the row, with your back to the stage. However, once the first
interval is reached, you should (out of respect for the actors) keep your face to the
stage—always provided there is no one you know sitting in the same row as you.[20]

It is extremely doubtful whether many readers can have followed these
instructions to the letter (quite apart from anything else, the possibility of
discovering in retrospect that one has committed a gaffe by failing to
recognize an acquaintance in the same row would discourage the expression of respect to the absent and oblivious actors in the green room).
One senses here the unbuttoned and capricious dogmatism of a cultural
commentator exploiting his captive audience in order to present personal
preferences as universal rules.

Obviously, it is largely when offering negative recommendations that
advice literature reflects reality: the presence of an instruction not to
behave in a certain way is generally some indication that a body of people
exists who do so behave. But even here there are pitfalls. In the case of D. S.
Sokolov's *The Man of the World, or a Guide to Social Rules* (1847), for
instance, there are some places where the counsel offered almost certainly
does reflect undesirable reality. For example, a vivid picture of unlre-
monious behaviour in church emerges from the instruction that 'when
handing over candles that you want lighted [at the icon of a saint], do not

---

[19] Irina Reyfman, 'The Emergence of the Duel in Russia: Corporal Punishment and the
Honor Code', *Russian Review* 54 (1995), 26.

[20] Dorokhov, *Kak ne nado sebya vesti* (1975), 35–6. My thanks to Richard Davies, Leeds
Russian Archive—perhaps the only reader who has ever carried out Dorokhov's instructions!—
for bringing this passage to my attention.

smack your neighbour on the back with them, but politely ask him to pass them over', and the information that 'officers may not attend communion carrying swords or guns'. But when Sokolov advises that, in order to avoid 'discreditable rumours' (*durnye tolki*), a young woman should not go about alone, but in the company of a 'female servant, if there is no manservant', and that 'at public occasions she is accompanied by her mother or some other respectable lady', it would be foolish to take this as meaning that the women of 'middling society' (*obshchestvo srednego kruga*) to whom Sokolov addressed himself customarily went round without male company.[21] In fact, the girls and young women in traditional merchant and gentry families were—as accounts in memoirs and travelogues make clear—supervised with extreme care; the instruction was perhaps mechanically reproduced by Sokolov from a manual in some other language.

Indeed, a process of cutting-and-pasting (or to put it more bluntly, plagiarism), underlay the composition of many etiquette books and household manuals, as described by the author of one of the latter:

Such 'collections' contain a heap of instructions which are mostly extracted from extant books or technical and economic journals with the aid of a pair of scissors or the copyist's pen; the height of effort on the part of a publisher or compiler generally consists in the more or less unthinking addition of little articles translated from foreign books and journals, generally German or French ones.[22]

The result of such unreflective agglutination was cultural inertia: instructions were transferred to a new text irrespective of their relevance to reality, and were as likely to reflect realities and perceptions in the originating culture as those in Russia itself. For example, an instruction given in a manual translated from the English in 1873, 'It is generally customary to speak to titled and prominent persons as one does with anyone else in society,' was not necessarily an adequate description of Russian attitudes *de bas en haut* at the time the book was published—at least if Il'ya Repin's anxiety at having mis-addressed his patron General Pryanishnikov, a Privy Councillor, as though he held the much less impressive rank of State Councillor, is anything to go by.[23] Between 1760 and 1917, advice literature was as much a source of information about

---

[21] *Svetskii chelovek* (1847), 12, 73, [p. iv].

[22] Anon., *Domashnyaya spravochnaya kniga* (1855), vol. i, p. ii. A book that bears out the accusation made here is Anon., *Prakticheskii khozyain* (1838), whose subtitle confesses it is 'selected from the compositions of the best writers'. For a modern example, see A. Galitsky, 'Na chuzhoi karavai rot ne razevai!', *Knizhnoe obozrenie* 52 (1992), 4 (accusing the authors of a brochure on the Russian bathhouse of plagiarizing his book *Fizkul'tura i sport*).

[23] Anon., *Pravila svetskogo etiketa dlya muzhchin* (1873), 23. I. E. Repin, *Dalekoe blizkoe*, ed. K. Chukovsky (Moscow, 1984), 135; on p. 131 Repin describes how, on first meeting Pryanishnikov, 'I durst not sit down' and 'when he stretched out his hand to say goodbye, I rushed to kiss the hem of his satin dressing-gown and fountains of tears started from my eyes'.

the eccentric ways of foreigners as a reflection of local practices: readers were, for instance, more likely to learn about the hour at which the English took afternoon tea than they were about the crucial question of when to address an acquaintance as *ty* (thou, informally) rather than *vy* (you, formally). And after 1917, advice literature, while an excellent guide to the values that the Soviet regime sought to impose upon the 'mass reader' (*massovyi chitatel'*), illuminates the values that actually did prevail in Soviet society haphazardly at best.

My discussion, then, proceeds from the assumption that the relationship of behaviour books to real-life behaviour is complex and oblique. They are treated here primarily as contributions to ideology, rather than contributions to practical life; I anatomize ideas (if that is the right word for the invertebrate formulations in behaviour books) and examine their relation to practices, rather than deriving the latter from the former. In this respect, my approach is quite different to that espoused in the most influential study of advice literature in recent history, Norbert Elias's *The Civilizing Process.*[24] Elias used one specific type of advice text, the etiquette manual, as the basis of wide-ranging assertions about actual changes in French and German society in the late medieval and early modern eras, confidently extrapolating reception from precept, the real-life reader from the in-text one, and manifesting little concern with the production of advice literature—the human beings who wrote or compiled the texts, the methods of their dissemination. He saw the appearance of the prohibitions expressed in etiquette guides upon certain physical activities (spitting, nose-picking, eating with the hands) as linked to the appearance of a code of self-restraint that inhibited violence and encouraged social decorum, inhibiting certain physical activities even in private. And this primary social process was connected by him to two further ones: the emergence of the bourgeoisie (which proceeded, he argued, along different lines in France and in Germany because of the closeness versus distance from the etiquette current in court circles); and a notion of ideal citizenship which required suppression of the self in fulfilment of a disinterested civic ideal. In other words, Elias espouses a variant of modernizing theory which links together the development of a private sphere, the growth of self-restraint in public, and the rise of the rational state.

The Civilizing Process began to attract quite a lot of interest among historians of Russia in the second half of the 1990s,[25] but the extent to

---

[24] N. Elias, *The Civilizing Process*, trans. E. Jephcott (Oxford, 1978).

[25] See e.g. V. Volkov, 'The Concept of *kul'turnost'*: Notes on the Stalinist Civilizing Process', in S. Fitzpatrick (ed.), *Stalinism: New Directions* (London, 2000), 210–30; *idem* and C. Kelly, '*Kul'turnost'* and Consumption' in C. Kelly and D. Shepherd (eds.), *Constructing Russian Culture in the Age of Revolution* (Oxford, 1998), 295 ff.; N. Kozlova, 'On the Cognitive-Normative

which Elias's model may be satisfactorily applied to Russian raw material, even leaving aside interpretative scruples of the kind set out above, is debatable. To be sure, the involvement of the state in publishing conduct literature between 1920 and 1991, as between 1762 and 1783 (the period between Catherine II's accession to the throne and her legalization of private presses), makes the hypothesis about the creation of an ideal citizen carry some weight. The propaganda sponsored by Catherine, like that put out during the Soviet *kul'turnost'* campaign in the 1920s, 1930s, and 1940s, *did* explicitly and self-consciously fuse private behaviour, public order, and social conformity into a coercive model of citizenship as membership of a rational collective. Just as in the Western countries discussed by Elias, this was something fundamentally new. In pre-Petrine culture, bodily restraint was primarily a marker of social prestige, required above all in the protagonists of ritual. The Grand Prince of Muscovy directed the apportionment of food, rather than sating himself at the feast, and at wedding feasts, the bride and groom were supposed to remain perfectly still and contained. Drunkenness and sexual innuendo on the one hand, emotional outbursts on the other, were the prerogative of the wedding guests—for example, those who conducted the newly-weds ('molodye') to the bedchamber and made charivari after the act of consummation took place.[26] Once bodily restraint came to be expected in ever wider sectors of society, departures from customary practices developed a more sinister flavour: they were less likely to be seen as manifestations of ritual 'anti-behaviour' (to borrow the term coined by Boris Uspensky) licensed by context and tradition, than as demonstrations of immorality and of social disorderliness.[27] In eighteenth-century Russia, as in France, the term for 'police' (*blagochinnye*) was related to the concept of 'politeness' (*blagochinie*),[28] while the fact that (as in German and Latin) a single word, *nravy*, came to encompass both 'manners' and 'morals' implied that an offence against the former was also an offence against the latter.

Apart from Elias's thesis of a homogenization in behaviour patterns directed by the elite, another element in *The Civilizing Process* that fits the Russian situation rather well is the hypothesis of the connection between

Mapping of Soviet Civilization: The Space Beneath', in M. Bryld and E. Kulavig (eds.), *Soviet Civilization Between Past and Present* (Odense, 1998), 95–113.

[26] A. D. Baiburin and A. L. Toporkov, *U istokov etiketa: Etnograficheskie ocherki* (Leningrad, 1990), esp. ch. 3.

[27] B. A. Uspensky, 'Antipovedenie v kul'ture Drevnei Rusi', *Problemy izucheniya kul'turnogo naslediya*, ed. G. V. Stepanov (Moscow, 1985), 326–36.

[28] On 'police' and 'politeness' in Western Europe, see e.g. M. de Certeau, *The Writing of History*, trans. T. Conley (New York, 1988), 188–9; Peter France, 'Polish, Police, Polis', in his *Politeness and Its Discontents: Problems in French Classical Culture* (Cambridge, 1992), 53–73. On *blagochinie* see the discussion in Ch. 1 below.

the later stages of the 'civilizing process' and the rise of bourgeois hegemony. As in Germany, so in Russia (though in the latter case about a century later) an 'internal contrast' developed between the 'courtly nobility, predominantly French-speaking and "civilized" on the French model' and a 'middle-class stratum of intelligentsia'.[29] In Russia, estates (*sosloviya*), social categories ascribed at birth, such as *dvoryanstvo* (gentry or nobility), *meshchanstvo* (plebeian town-dweller), or *krest'yanstvo* (peasantry), survived until November 1917 (and lived on, in transmuted form, into the Soviet period).[30] However, this was not specific to Russia: Britain was another country marked by residual estate features—the existence of hereditary peers, the assumption in the armed forces that the upper middle classes were natural 'officer material'—until well into the twentieth century. Nor did the survival of estate features hinder the development of a bourgeois *mentality* in these two countries. Radicals such as Belinsky and Dobrolyubov, rather than being embodiments of the unique character of the Russian intelligentsia, had their counterparts in unconventional, but indubitably bourgeois Western figures such as George Sand, George Eliot, John Stuart Mill, and John Ruskin. The fact that, by the late nineteenth century, the Russian intelligentsia had come to distinguish itself vehemently from the 'bourgeoisie' (*burzhuaziya* or *meshchanstvo*: see Chapter 3) proves, rather than disproves, its bourgeois credentials: one can compare the use by nineteenth- and early twentieth-century British writers, doctors, and lawyers of 'middle class' as a term of abuse. (By extension, it is impossible to translate the German adjective *gutbürgerlich* (bourgeois in the sense, 'of good quality', cf. French *cru bourgeois*) into English or into Russian.) Protean in composition, and liking to think of itself as 'classless', the Russian intelligentsia at the same time espoused a quintessentially bourgeois civilizing mission, at once philanthropic and regulatory: like the efforts of pre-revolutionary intellectuals to bring culture and education to the masses, the Soviet campaign to disseminate *kul'turnost'* was in part an expression of classic middle-class anxieties about the threat of disease and disorder from the lower-class population.[31]

[29] Elias, *The Civilizing Process*, 7.

[30] On the tenacity of estates before 1917, see Gregory L. Freeze's classic article, 'The Soslovie (Estate) Paradigm and Russian Social History', *American Historical Review* 91 (1986), 11–36; on neo-*sosloviya* thereafter, see S. Fitzpatrick, 'Ascribing Class: The Construction of Social Identity in Soviet Russia', in *eadem* (ed.), *Stalinism: New Directions* (London, 2000), 20–46.

[31] On the intelligentsia's view of itself as classless, see Ch. 3; cf. also S. K. Morrissey's observations on the SRs' view of students as *'a group uniquely able to overcome its objective bourgeois origins' (Heralds of Revolution: Russian Students and the Mythologies of Radicalism* (New York, 1998), 73). Such attitudes were attacked in the Soviet Union during the 1920s, when the intelligentsia was understood as a 'forward-thinking bourgeoisie' (*peredovaya burzhuaziya*), but were rehabilitated in the Stalin era (cf. the canonical definition of the Soviet intelligentsia as 'fundamentally different from the bourgeois intelligentsia both in terms of its composition and of its relations

But if post-Petrine Russia (especially during the Enlightenment and the Soviet period) in some respects fits Elias's vision of a 'civilizing process', or indeed Michel Foucault's darker, but equally teleological model of the development of a society of 'universal surveillance',[32] there are important elements in the development of polite culture that are elided by it. The fact that the 'civilizing process' in Russia involved assimilation to behaviour values that were imported from elsewhere and (which is not necessarily the same thing) were understood as foreign, was crucial. To begin with, the sequence of development was idiosyncratic: for example, the cult of the 'natural mother' as propagandized by Rousseau arrived in Russia not much later than Fénelon and Lambert's notion of the 'pedagogical mother', which was the best part of a hundred years older (see Chapter 1), and post-Soviet bookstalls were, in the 1990s, displaying as 'novelties' not only newly written advice literature, but translations of *Parkinson's Law* and of the works of Dale Carnegie (see Chapter 5). A second and more important effect of the 'foreign' character of texts about behaviour was that three quite separate concepts—civilization, modernization, and Westerniza-tion[33]—became entangled, both among foreigners, and among Russians themselves. Differences between native and Western custom were understood as pointing to Russian 'barbarism' and 'backwardness', and thus became a matter for pride on the one side and shame on the other. Among Western Europeans, 'keeping intact European civilizational superiority . . . involved an endless redrawing of mental boundaries',[34] and Russia, at the edge of Europe, was an obvious place where they might be drawn. The allegedly recent arrival of civilized values in Russia prompted a search for evidence that these had been adopted half-heartedly. Commentators might

with the peasantry and working classes', *BSE*[2] xviii; see also Lovell, *The Russian Reading Revolution*, 17–18). For discussions of bourgeois anxieties in the Russian intelligentsia, see L. Engelstein, *The Keys to Happiness: Sex and The Search for Modernity in Fin de Siècle Russia* (Ithaca, NY, 1992), and J. Neuberger, *Hooliganism: Crime, Culture and Power in St Petersburg, 1900–1914* (Berkeley, 1993); S. Frank, 'Confronting the Domestic Other: Rural Popular Culture and its Enemies in Fin-de-Siècle Russia', in *idem* and M. D. Steinberg (eds.), *Cultures in Flux: Lower-Class Values, Practices, and Resistance in Late Imperial Russia* (Princeton, 1994), 74–107.

[32] See particularly *Discipline and Punish: The Birth of the Prison*, trans. A. Sheridan (New York, 1978). Khakhordin, *The Collective and the Individual*, and S. Kotkin, *Magnetic Mountain: Stalinism as a Civilization* (Berkeley, 1995) are thought-provoking and creative adaptations of Foucault to Soviet society. A classic study of the pre-revolutionary era from a Foucauldian perspective is Engelstein, *The Keys to Happiness*.

[33] In his excellent discussion of modernization theory and its applicability to 18th-cent. Russian history, S. Dixon, *The Modernisation of Russia 1676–1825* (Cambridge, 1999), 23, points out that by the 1820s, 'a century of sustained Westernisation had introduced into Russia a hierarchy of rationally ordered government institutions, detailed social regulation, and cultural influences ranging from Italian opera to the political economy of Adam Smith. Yet it had also been responsible for freemasonry, fortune-telling, and Swedenborg's mystical Christianity.'

[34] Mazower, *Dark Continent*, p. xiv. For a case-study of this process, see Larry Wolff, *Inventing Eastern Europe: The Map of Civilization in the Mind of the Enlightenment* (Stanford, Calif., 1994).

remark some falling-off of barbarism in upper-class circles, but were quick to point out its persistence elsewhere. Lady Londonderry, visiting in 1836, was shocked by the filthiness of the Russian peasants whom she encountered on her journey: 'Their great boots, coloured morocco gloves, great folding pelisse of sheepskin, and variegated sash, their long beards and tangled hair, all are covered by a thick crust of dirt.' Such manifestations of unchecked filth were held to mark the superficiality of civilization in Russia: as Stendhal put it aphoristically in his review of Princess Zinaida Volkonskaya's *Tableau slave de l'onzième siècle*, 'Enlevez le jabot bien plissé d'un russe, et vous y trouvez le poil de l'ours' (Lift up the starched cravat of a Russian, and you will find underneath the hairy pelt of the bear). The most brilliant and ambiguous expression of such squeamishness was Heinrich von Kleist's 1808 novella *Die Marquise von O.*, in which the Russian hero or anti-hero is 'devil' and 'angel' at the same time, both the man who commits the supreme offence against military honour and a code of morality enshrining women's sexual purity as supreme symbol of innocence and purity, and the man who redeems himself by superhuman gestures of self-renunciation and acts of courtesy, 'zartes, würdiges und völlig musterhaftes Betragen' (tender, dignified and quite exemplary conduct). The process by which he does this is always unpredictable, shocking, and uninterpretable, both to the characters round him and to the narrator. The story of this new 'rape of Europa' is governed by a polarization between north and south (as well as between 'barbarous' male and 'civilizing' female): in the confessional recollection of her Russian admirer and violator, the Italian heroine becomes a swan spattered by him with the mud of his Northern homeland.[35]

Russian writers shared these perceptions as well: Kleist's *Die Marquise von O* has its counterpart in Pushkin's historical novel *The Captain's Daughter* (1834), in which the contrast between Catherine II and Pugachev is on one level an allegory of 'Russian' barbarism versus 'Westernized' brutality (though here no reconciliation between the two takes place). However, as Western and Russian writers expanded upon the barbarism and incivility to be found everywhere upon the far side of the Russian border, espousing

---

[35] *The Russian Journal of Lady Londonderry, 1836–1837*, ed. W. A. L. Seaman and J. R. Sewell (London, 1973), 58, 91; Stendhal, 'Tableau slave du Vᵉ siècle, par Madame la princesse Volkonsky', in his *Courier anglais*, ed. Henri Martineau, 5 vols. (Paris, 1935–6), ii. 182–3. It would be interesting to trace the lineage of the 'bear' stereotype, which by 1805 was already of sufficient age to be ironized by Princess Dashkova in her memoirs: describing how she was persuaded by Lady Arabella Denny to set to music a hymn written by the latter, Dashkova continues: 'She had it rehearsed several times, and a fortnight later had it sung in church in the presence of a numerous congregation drawn by curiosity to hear what a Russian bear could have composed.' (See *The Memoirs of Princess Dashkova*, trans. K. Fitzlyon (Durham, NC, 1995), 50.) H. von Kleist, *Sämtliche Werke* (Munich, c.1975), 872–908: quote p. 907.

a tradition that went back to Herodotus's horrified fascination with the hairy, wine-bibbing Scythians, a powerful nationalist myth that saw 'coarseness' as 'frankness', 'indiscipline' as 'spontaneity', 'inefficiency' as 'intellectual flexibility', and 'ignorance' as 'a commonsensical response to bogus cultivation', began to rise up in response. Its very different expressions included a late eighteenth-century popular print celebrating the behaviour of a 'shameless man' who, reproved for his failure to use a fork at table in an inn, defecated on the bed slept in by the table-companions who had upbraided him (Fig. 1); the pornographic literature of the late eighteenth century, flourishing the words banned from polite society; the 'anti-salons' of the Russian radicals in the 1860s; the cultivation of 'Northern' sincerity rather than 'French' deviousness by the Slavophiles; the derisive views about '*bon-ton* for toffs' held among avant-garde writers in the 1920s; the flamboyant behaviour of Khrushchev, banging his shoe on the table at international conferences, and labelling modern art as 'dog shit'; and the delight in *mat* ('bad language') among Russian dissidents in the post-Stalin era. The myth of anti-politeness was expressed also in a utopian historical analysis quite different in import to Elias's *The Civilizing Process*, Mikhail Bakhtin's great hymn to carnival culture, *François Rabelais and His World*. It is tempting to see Elias's book (originally published in 1939) as an incentive text as much as a descriptive one, as an ideal picture of European civilization composed at a historical era that called into question any identification between the rise of polite culture and the retreat from violence. Conversely, Bakhtin's book, begun in 1936, at a period when a particularly narrow and repressive ethos of civilization was being disseminated to the Soviet masses, could be at some level interpreted as an ideal representation of the 'anti-civilizing process' enacted through the subversive potential of popular creativity and physical energy.[36]

Rather than *a* (single and unitary) 'civilizing process', then, Russia witnessed a large number of different 'civilizing processes' (and 'anti-civilizing processes'), some of which contradicted each other or ran into dead ends. Moreover, even in periods of rigid state control (let alone those

---

[36] Though Elias's introduction to the 1968 edition of his book (see *The Civilizing Process*, 181–215) makes no reference at all to local circumstances, R. Chartier remarks that 'to read Elias's books properly, they must be read in connection with and in the context of the ages in which they were conceived and written, Weimar Republic Germany for *The Court Society* and exile for *The Civilizing Process*' ('Social Figuration and Habitus', *Cultural History*, trans. L. G. Cochrane (Cambridge, 1988), 76–7). An alternative interpretation of *Fransua Rabele* sees the text as a refraction of Stalinist mythology (see e.g. M. Ryklin, 'Tela terrora: tezisy k logike nasiliya', *Bakhtinskii sbornik* 1 (1990), 60–76). However, Bakhtin's decision to complete and publish his book in the 1960s, when de-Stalinization was in full swing, suggests that, at the very least, the writer's attitude towards this myth was ambivalent.

FIG.1. 'The Shameless Man'. Popular print, after 1750 (taken from a French original by P. N. Chuvaev). The Shameless Man takes revenge on table-companions who have rebuked him for not using a fork by defecating in their bedroom, so that they get a scolding from the inn-keeper ('Get up, you swine! what's this I find? Enough of shitting in the bed! And only yesterday you were, reproaching that good sir . . .')

at which a vigorous commercial book market was in operation), the content of advice literature was concerned with far more areas than that of 'civilizing' the population in the relatively narrow sense defined by Elias, that is, encouraging the repression of the body (a body, in Elias's discussion, always assumed to be gender free).[37] It dictated consumption patterns, encouraging readers to acquire the accoutrements, as well as the habits, of civilization. It sought to mould relationships within the family, with friends, and with strangers, prescribing intimacy, reserve, or a mixture of both. And it propagandized new 'cultivated' activities, such as visiting the theatre, libraries, museums, and also club, restaurants, and other 'autonomous areas of sociability'.[38] In other words, it elaborated a construct of *refinement* that was much broader than civilization as defined by Elias. A *refined* person, as envisaged by etiquette manuals, guides to home economy, and treatises on hygiene, was not simply one who used his or her fork and handkerchief in the right way and avoided kicking the dog or slapping his or her children (at any rate, in public), but also one who was dressed appropriately, ate the right kind of food, decorated and cleaned his or her living space in the right way, took regular exercise, conversed in the prescribed manner with friends, casual acquaintances, servants, and shop assistants, and devoted a proper amount of time to reading, the connoisseurship of the visual arts, and attendance at concerts. The impeccable enactor of willed social conformity, he or she was also a skilled consumer, possessing exactly the right number of the right possessions, and inspiring those with less discrimination (or less money) into idle fantasies of emulation.

Received ideas about the likely audiences of conduct literature notwith-standing, it was not only the upwardly mobile who required its advice, although counsel to the newly moneyed (in particular, on how to recognize the boundary between the discreet communication of wealth and vulgar plutocratic display) was indeed one of its preoccupations. At different periods of history, readers included those who needed advice about the right way of conducting rituals at moments when the consensus about appropriate practices had broken down (see, for example, the advice about christenings discussed in Chapter 3). They included those needing practical information—what books to read in order to educate oneself, where to buy a reasonably priced bed. As Pierre Bourdieu has pointed out, the advice industry offered 'a rationalized form of competence in a class culture' to *all* the literate members of that culture, from whichever social

[37] Cf. the observations of O. Hughes, *The Prospect Before Her: A History of Women in Western Europe*, i (London, 1995), 3: 'the total absence of women from Elias' narrative is not only striking but serves to date the book'.

[38] The phrase is used in R. Friedman, 'In the Company of Men: Student Life and Russian Masculinity, 1825–1855' (Ph.D. thesis, University of Michigan, 2000), 76: chs. 3 and 4 of this work are analyses of the *korporatsiia* (student fraternity) and the tavern as loci of sociability.

stratum they came.[39] At moments of social uncertainty, literate historical subjects turned for reassurance and enlightenment to printed texts, which coached them in appropriate dress, grooming, gesture, and mental attitude. And in Russia, where competence in refined behaviour meant, from the early eighteenth century, comporting oneself as Western Europeans were believed to behave, introductions to translations of advice literature, and advisory texts originally composed in Russian, became places for expressing ideas and concerns about national identity.

This does not mean that advice literature offers a direct route into the essence of Russianness, a guide to the inscrutable workings of the 'Russian mind'. On the contrary: the huge variety of different ideas and concerns expressed serves to undermine 'Grand Cultural Archetypes'. The intricate ordering of domestic detail in the writings of nationalist conservatives in the mid-nineteenth century, for example, makes untenable the idea that the whole of Russian culture has been underpinned by a binary opposition between *byt* and *bytie* (material life and spiritual life).[40] For conservatives of this kind, as I will explain in Chapter 2, *byt* and *bytie* were complementary rather than antagonistic forces, and national character was supposed to be expressed as forcefully in the former as in the latter.

As John Kasson, the author of a recent study of American etiquette manuals, puts it, advice literature 'takes the historian squarely into the dialectics of social classification', showing 'how the categories of refinement and rudeness, appropriate and inappropriate behavior, operate within a culture and illuminate its boundaries'.[41] Boundaries of nationality are by no means the only ones that are important. Differentiation between male and female behaviour patterns has been a crucial element in behaviour modelling in all societies. From the Enlightenment onwards, both foreign and Russian treatises on conduct harped with tedious insistence on the need for men and women to recognize their different roles in society, and dwelt upon the need to inculcate these in children from the very beginning.[42] They contributed to the spread of a belief in women's peculiar

---

[39] P. Bourdieu, *Distinction: A Social Critique of the Judgement of Taste*, trans. R. Nice (London, 1984), 153.

[40] For an instructive assault on 'Grand Cultural Archetypes', see L. Engelstein, 'Paradigms, Pathologies, and Other Clues to Russian Spiritual Culture: Some Post-Soviet Thoughts', *SR* 57 (1998), 864–75, esp. 867. On Russian intolerance to *byt*, see e.g. S. Boym, *Common Places: Mythologies of Everyday Life in Russia* (Cambridge, Mass., 1994), 31: 'Nineteenth-century Westernizers and Slavophiles, Romantics and modernists, aesthetic and political utopians, and Bolsheviks and monarchists all engaged in battles with *byt*. For many of them what mattered was not physical survival but sacrifice, not preservation of life but its complete transcendence, not the fragile human existence in this world but collective happiness in the other world.'

[41] J. Kasson, *Rudeness and Civility: Manners in Nineteenth-Century Urban America* (New York, 1990), 4.

[42] On the face of it, N. I. Novikov's *O vospitanii i nastavlenii detei* (see his *Izbrannye sochineniya* (Moscow and Leningrad, 1954), 417–506) appears to be an exception, but in fact Novikov

role as civilizers, upon their preoccupation with manners, taste, and civilized values—a preoccupation that might be seen positively, as in Karamzin's idealization of women readers in the late eighteenth century, or negatively, as manifested in stereotypes such as the indolent and self-indulgent *zhemanikha* of the eighteenth century, or the grasping *meshchanka* of the post-Stalin era.

The task of tracing the association between women and the arbitration of morality might seem, at first sight, a thankless one: could any historical study go further than recording the process assaulted in Barbara Heldt's pioneering study of women in Russian literature, *Terrible Perfection*, which shows how women's symbolic elevation to positions of moral authority is matched by their disablement as social and cultural agents? Similarly, Marina Warner, whose study of Margaret Thatcher, in *Monuments and Maidens*, emphasizes that its subject has 'tapped an enormous source of female power: the right of prohibition', chooses not to dwell on the power of the negative arbitrator, and describes without enthusiasm the substitution, in John Gibson's monument to Queen Victoria, of the new 'womanly' virtue of Clemency for the traditional attribute of Wisdom.[43] Yet it is possible to see the association of women and refinement that was imported to Russia in the second half of the eighteenth century not only as a repressive mechanism (making it more difficult for women to 'behave badly' than men, and meaning that they were more virulently condemned, and fiercely punished, when they did), but also as a productive one. The association could offer women possibilities of power (albeit of a muted kind, and usually over other women); it also facilitated particular modes of gender expression—whether in memoirs or in literary texts—at different eras of history.[44] The case of Marina Tsvetaeva, remembered by her

assumes that the purpose of education is to produce a 'courageous, industrious boy' and a 'quiet, gentle, charming girl' (428); and the upbringing that he describes (like Locke's) silently assumes the child subject to be male.

[43] B. Heldt, *Terrible Perfection: Women and Russian Literature* (Bloomington, Indiana, 1987); M. Warner, *Monuments and Maidens: The Allegory of the Female Form* (London, 1985/1996), 52, 209. Cf. S. de Beauvoir, *Le Deuxième Sexe* (Paris, 1949); Betty Friedan, *The Feminine Mystique* (New York, 1963); the various contributions in N. Armstrong and L. Tennenhouse (eds.), *The Ideology of Conduct: Essays on Literature and the History of Sexuality* (New York, 1987); and D. Greene, 'Mid-Nineteenth-Century Domestic Ideology in Russia', in R. Marsh (ed.), *Women and Russian Culture: Projections and Self-Perceptions* (New York, 1998), 88: 'Ladies could hardly win autonomy through an ideology which made them dependent on a husband for economic resources, class privilege, social position, self-definition, self-esteem, and the meaning of their lives, which gave them no protection from spousal abuse, which barred them from political power and any serious creative expression, and which effectively divided them from their natural allies, women of other classes and races who faced many of the same constraints.'

[44] Cf. V. Glendinning's observations in her introduction to L. Davidoff, *The Best Circles: Society, Etiquette and the Season* (2nd edn., London, 1986), p. vii: 'We are perhaps too quick to think of all nineteenth- and early twentieth-century women as the oppressed victims of a male-dominated society . . . All the energy and ingenuity of the female sex could be exploited in this

daughter as a dispenser of 'icy politeness' to antagonists in argument, shows a determination to flout convention coexisting with a capacity to exploit propriety when convenient—by no means an unusual pattern in post-Romantic Russian women intellectuals (or, indeed, Western ones).[45]

Of course, one should not exaggerate the power available to women within the ethos of refinement. Women were acceptable as arbiters of morality and taste only if they failed to raise traditional anxieties about obstreperous females as sinful and politically threatening. The suppression of the body that was assiduously propagandized in conduct treatises enhanced the time-honoured sense of the female body as abject, taboo, the source of unmentionable pollution, which is evident in early twentieth-century guides to 'hygiene' as much as it is in eighteenth-century commentaries on women's health.[46] It could even be argued that the anorexic schoolgirl and the obsessive-compulsive housewife are the twin victims of gentility, both locked into a ceaseless struggle to deny the inadmissable aspects of femininity: filth, fertility, loss of physical control. But if the understanding of civilization as 'conquest of nature' was less than helpful to the self-expression of women, the interpretation of refinement as social consensus in performance was more so. The understanding that membership of the cultural elite depended less upon innate characteristics than upon the acquisition of intellectual accomplishments led to a slow expansion of education for women, while the association of refinement with leisure pursuits and the ownership of properly tasteful material possessions led to a concern (on the part of men as well as women) with the domestic environment that in many ways undercut the association of women with private space and men with public space. Certainly, Russia could not boast an equivalent to the 'cot quean', the eighteenth-century 'new man' of whom a lady reader to Addison and

subtle form of social control.' A recent, and exhilarating, recuperation of the potential in gentility for female authority is A. Vickery's *The Gentleman's Daughter: Women's Lives in Georgian England* (New Haven, 1998). M. Poovey, *The Proper Lady and the Woman Writer: Ideology as Style in the Works of Mary Wollstonecraft, Mary Shelley, and Jane Austen* (Chicago, 1984), 23, points out the potential for dissimulation in gentility: 'A woman might well consider chastity her "greatest glory and ornament" because to do so enhanced her social value and promised her the very gratification of the desires that modesty was supposed to deny.'

[45] A. Efron, *Marina Tsvetaeva: vospominaniya docheri* (Moscow, 1989), 34.

[46] See e.g. *Nauka byt' uchtivym* (1774) and Bakherakht, *O neumerennosti v lyubostrastii oboikh polov* (1779), in his *Sobranie raznykh poleznykh lekarstv* (1779), which warns (p. 16) that masturbation in women can bring about tumours. An extreme version of the feminine as extirpation of the female developed in the 19th cent., with the use of ovariotomy as a means of 'exorcis[ing] the organic demons of unladylike behavior': see T. Laqueur, *Making Sex: Body and Gender from the Greeks to Freud* (Cambridge, Mass., 1990), 177. On early 20th-cent. distaste for the female body, see Ch. 3 of the present study. For a bold and sweeping assertion of the connection between abjection and the female body throughout history, see J. Kristéva, *Pouvoirs de l'horreur: essai sur l'abjection* (Paris, 1983).

Steele's *Spectator* lamented, 'He could preserve apricots, and make jellies, before he had been two years out of the nursery . . . He has the whitest hand that you ever saw in your life, and raises paste better than any woman in England.'[47] However, in the work of conservative writers such as Ivan Aksakov and (during the 1870s) Lev Tolstoi, childcare, cooking, and sewing came to be activities in which an educated man could legitimately take a passive interest, if not necessarily ones that he could practise actively.

In the same way that codes of refinement could act to empower as well as to disempower women, and to relax gender boundaries as well as to reinforce these, the 'civilizing process' had ambiguous effects in the area of class differentiation. At one level, the emphasis on cultivation as the end result of hard work, of learning, was inimical to pomposity about ancient lineage. As an eighteenth-century English commentator put it, 'We can have no merit, nor ought we to claim any respect, because our fathers acted well whether we would or no.'[48] This appreciation began to make headway in Russia during the late eighteenth and early nineteenth centuries, and during the second half of the nineteenth century began to alter the attitudes of the privileged to those at the bottom of society too. 'Though delicacy is considered the exclusive property of the higher strata in society', wrote E. N. Akhmatova in 1867, 'it just as often does honour to a simple workman, and in him refinement of feeling is often far better developed than in the descendant of an ancient and wealthy clan.'[49] A result of this recognition of dignity in the plebeian was that the concept of civility could now be used against dominant groups as well as in their favour. Working-class Russians in the early twentieth century were able to turn the rules of polite intercourse to their advantage on some occasions— to advance, for example, the demand that managers and foremen cease to use abusive language when addressing their subordinates on the shop floor.[50] And ambitious individuals from socially abject strata, such as the *meshchanstvo* (urban lower classes) could conceal their origins by emulating the manners espoused by those higher up the social ladder and attacking the behaviour standards in the stratum from which they came (an excellent example of this chameleonization is Chekhov, many of whose writings are at one or another level anti-*meshchanstvo* manifestos, as will be discussed in Chapter 3).

[47] *Spectator* 482 (12 Sept. 1712).

[48] *Spectator* 612 (27 Oct. 1712).

[49] E. N. Akhmatova, 'Dva slova o vezhlivosti i delikatnosti', *Zolotaya zhatva* (St Petersburg, 1867), i. 36.

[50] On refinement as an instrument of working-class politics, see S. A. Smith, 'The Social Meanings of Swearing: Workers and Bad Language in Late Imperial and Early Soviet Russia', *Past and Present* 160 (1998), 183–6.

УДОВЛЕТВОРЕНІЕ ТРЕБОВАНІЙ.

Въ модной мастерской:
Мастерица: — Мы требуемъ вѣжливаго обращенія на „вы"!
Хозяйка: — Ну, хорошо: идите вы къ чорту!
— Ну, вотъ это другое дѣло. Разъ на вы — мы прекращаемъ забастовку.

FIG. 2. 'The Strikers' Demands Fulfilled'. Cartoon by V. Lebedev (1916) satirizing working-class campaigns for courtesy in employers. The seamstresses demand 'polite treatment: we want to be addressed using the formal second person!' The boss replies: 'Fine. Kindly go to hell!' Satisfied, the workers suspend their strike.

Yet at the same time, boundaries of refinement constantly shifted in order to separate the truly refined from those who only seemed refined, those who were 'naturally' well mannered from those who had painfully struggled towards civility.[51] Though the early nineteenth-century Russian term *vospitannost'* places a greater emphasis on training (*vospitanie*) than the English term 'breeding' (it is closer in sense to 'cultivation'), there was in Russia no less than in Britain a sense that those from certain classes were more likely to be 'well-bred' (*vospitany*) than those from others. By the late nineteenth century, the words *intelligentnost'* (behaviour proper to members of the intelligentsia) and *porodistost'* (breeding) made this sense explicit. As concepts of politeness spread wider, naming was transformed to allow members of elite groups to discriminate between 'their' and 'our' politeness: Osip, the servant in Gogol''s *Government Inspector* (1836), who made himself ridiculous by describing the entertainments and citizens of St Petersburg as *politichnye* ('politick'), was in fact employing a term that had been standard in educated speech five decades earlier, but the shift in lexical fashion allowed observers whose own word for what Osip depicted would have been *elegantnye* and *uchtivye* to enjoy Osip's ridiculous pretension. In the same way, the term *kul'turnyi*, a standard epithet of approbation in Russian educated speech from the late nineteenth century to the mid-twentieth, began, in the 1960s, to be seen as characteristic of vulgar usage (much as had earlier been the case with its English equivalents 'genteel', 'cultured', and 'cultivated').

Linguistic discrimination was buttressed by verbal and visual caricature. The figure of the parvenu (a staple of comic plays, novels, and paintings from the seventeenth century in the West, his most famous embodiment being Molière's *Le Bourgeois Gentilhomme*), began figuring in Russia during the late eighteenth century (see Chapter 2), and maintained a central position in cultural consciousness thereafter (as is illustrated by the famous case of Lopakhin in Chekhov's *The Cherry Orchard*). The exercise of taste that allowed a refined person to separate him or herself from 'the vulgar' was supposed to depend not only upon material circumstances, but upon inculcation into appropriate manners during early childhood, as well as upon serene indifference to the outward trappings of privilege. In Russia as in other European countries, refinement was thus kept tantalizingly inaccessible even to

---

[51] On the boundary-creation characteristic of refined behaviour, see especially R. Chartier, 'Distinction et divulgation: la civilité et ses livres', in his *Lectures et lecteurs dans la France d'Ancien Régime* (Paris, 1987), esp. 56–7 (on sensitivity to rank in the 16th and 17th cents.) and p. 81 (on the 19th-cent. understanding of civility as 'bourgeois conformity'). On the ambiguous role of 20th-cent. etiquette books in disseminating greater freedom of manners, but also advocating observance of tradition, see C. Wouters, 'Etiquette Books and Emotion Management in the Twentieth Century', *Journal of Social History* 29 (1995–6), 107–24, 325–40.

those whose socio-economic circumstances made them capable of footing the bill for elegant objects.

During the Soviet period, the dual role of cultivation—at once a challenge to class differentials, and a support to these—persisted, as propaganda championed equality for all, and hymned the importance of self-betterment, but also granted the Soviet intelligentsia some of the status of its pre-revolutionary counterpart. Satire was now targeted at new kinds of parvenu (as in the case of the caricatures aimed at *meshchane*, petits bourgeois, published in humorous magazines throughout the Soviet period). By the 1960s, *intelligentnost'*, or imitation of the intelligentsia, had again become the ideal most commonly disseminated in behaviour literature; by the 1980s, the revival of interest in Russian pre-revolutionary history was accompanied by increasing idealization of *dvoryanskoe povedenie*, or 'gentlemanly behaviour'. This was eventually to lead, in the post-Soviet period, to a full-scale resurgence of a status-linked refinement ethos, as manifested not only in the eccentric efforts of self-nominated Russian 'aristocrats' to revive the gentry assemblies of nineteenth-century Russia, but also, and far more importantly, by a revival of a mass-market etiquette literature emphasizing the need to maintain social distinctions (see Chapter 5).

It is only by considering the development of behaviour ideals over a wide time-span, *longue durée*, that one can gain a sense of such continuities and changes in the understanding of refinement. To date, though, studies of Russian behaviour have concentrated on two specific areas very far apart in time (the 'gentry culture' of the early nineteenth century, and the campaign for *kul'turnost'* in the 1930s).[52] The image that has resulted has been somewhat static: the evolution of *kul'turnost'* from pre-revolutionary Russian behaviour ideals has been obscured, and the relationship between 'gentry culture' and the behaviour patterns of the second half of the nineteenth century barely considered. In particular, the transformation of 'gentry culture' into a sort of timeless paradise of elegant, 'aristocratic' cultivation does not take account of many Russian gentlefolk's warm dislike of *aristokraty*, and the way in which irritation with the excessive consumption attributed to aristocrats prompted a search for alternative modes of behaviour, whether this were socialist asceticism or a 'truly Russian' kind of gentility that eschewed foreign ways as far as possible (see Chapter 2).

[52] On *kul'turnost'* see, apart from the works by Khakhordin, Volkov, and Kozlova mentioned earlier, S. Fitzpatrick, 'Becoming Cultured: Socialist Realism and the Representation of Privilege and Taste', in her *The Cultural Front: Power and Culture in Revolutionary Russia* (Ithaca, NY, 1992); on the Pushkin era, see esp. Lotman, *Besedy o russkoi kul'ture*; W. M. Todd, *Fiction and Society in the Age of Pushkin* (Cambridge, Mass., 1986), ch. 1.

But if a reasonably broad approach is necessary to maintaining a sense of dynamism, a complete history of refinement's ramifications in every period, a sort of *Histoire de la vie privée russe* through etiquette books and domestic manuals, would be beyond the capacity of a single book and of a single person. The numbers of advice texts published run into thousands; many were compilations of, or derivations from, earlier ones, and textological problems are important and illuminating (for example, instances of ellipsis or mistranslation can point to the difference between Western ideologies and their reception in Russia). As Roger Chartier has pointed out, conduct guides are generated by an intricate network of imitation and appropriation; contradictions within individual texts, the nuances of their phrasing, are also extremely important.[53] Attempting to catalogue every textual shift, not to speak of the variable meanings of the different concepts for 'politeness', 'refinement', 'civility', and so on, and to trace the conventions of every genre, would be as thankless a task as compiling a 'key to all mythologies', and would also leave little room for interpretation in a broader sense, for considering the question of what all this meant to the readers of advice literature. Therefore, rather than giving an exhaustive survey of advice publications at a specific era, I have concentrated on what were, so far as I can establish, the most popular, distinctive, or innovative genres at a given date, or those which were most closely linked with social controversies of the time. For instance, pedagogical literature figures most strongly in the discussion of the late eighteenth and early twentieth centuries, material on health and the body most strongly in the treatment of the late imperial and early Soviet periods. Within each section, I concentrate on selected works of advice literature (for example, the pedagogical writings of Lambert, Fénelon, and others in Chapter 1, the household manuals of Katerina Avdeeva in Chapter 2, the self-help books of Samuel Smiles in Chapter 3, key works of Soviet *kul'turnost'* in Chapters 4 and 5) which were reprinted with especial frequency, and use such sources as parodies, reviews, memoirs, belles-lettres, poetry, letters, diaries, and journalism to trace the extent to which the ethos of refinement that they set out succeeded in implanting itself in the Russian public.

Some notable omissions in terms of genre and theme should be made clear. I do not consider religious literature (guides to spiritual exercises,

---

[53] Chartier, 'Distinction et divulgation', 47, 49. *Pace* Darnton—'the advantage of book history as a kind of diffusion study is that one knows precisely what is being diffused' *(The Forbidden Best-Sellers*, 181), 'precision', in the case of popular printed books, is made problematic by the lack of respect for the integrity of the completed text, whether published between hard covers or not, which characterized both authors and publishers. To take a hypothetical instance: is a book that borrows heavily from Della Casa and Erasmus, but adds material of the compiler's own, to be classed as one book, two books, or three?

instruction in how to pray, treatises on the regulation of monasteries). This would make an interesting subject for discussion in itself, but a quite separate one from secular advice literature, even the most moralistic genres of which (such as pedagogical literature) were, since the eighteenth century, remarkably free of material specific to any one Christian denomination; indeed, sometimes even Christianity in the broadest sense was scarcely perceptible.[54] To be sure, it is possible to trace connections of a looser and more abstract kind between religious literature and secular literature (an interesting example of how this may be done is Oleg Khakhordin's analysis of the link between the religious concept of *oblichenie*, 'revelation of sin', and the construction of identity via recognition of one's guilt before the community in Soviet culture).[55] But now that historians of Russia, having neglected religious culture more or less comprehensively for eighty years, are in some danger of forgetting that pre-revolutionary Russia ever had a secular culture, I think that a reconsideration of the advice literature relating to 'life in the world' has at least the justification of restoring historical balance.

Another genre more or less excluded from discussion is advice aimed at small children (though material aimed at adolescents does figure, since it would be foolish to attempt drawing a boundary between books addressed to young adults and books addressed to adolescents). Apart from the sheer bulk of such material, which means that it, like religious literature, ought to be the subject of a separate study, the justification for this omission is that the instruction given here to a large extent overlaps with that set out in advisory literature aimed at the parents of small children.[56] Technical

---

[54] As I. de Madariaga points out (*Catherine the Great: A Short History* (London, 1990), 111, 'Jesus Christ is not mentioned once' in *The Duties of Man and Citizen*, the 1783 conduct book produced at the behest of Catherine II. Piety is of more significance in some other conduct books, such as Fénelon's *Traité de l'éducation des filles*, which outlines the elements of Catholic doctrine that children should be taught in the nursery. However, the fact that instruction in such matters was considered of secondary interest in Russia is suggested by the history of Fénelon translations: the first Russian version of 1763 supplanted the Catholic material by Orthodox material (e.g. 'les préparer doucement contre les discours des calvinistes' becomes 'ikh prigotovit' k razgovoram protiv eretikov'), but another translation of 1794 has 'protiv ukorenii Kalvinov'). (Compare F. Fenelon, *O vospitanii devits*, trans. I. Tumansky (St Petersburg, 1763), 81, with *idem*, *O vospitanii devits*, trans. N. Nikiforova (Tambov', 1794), 112. Equally, a reference to 'indulgences' disappears from the former but is retained in the latter.) Among indigenous books, even those composed by Orthodox priests were not necessarily markedly religious: e.g., Gumilevsky, *Nastavlenie otsa synu* (1866), a brochure aimed at those going into military service, despite being written by a priest, places more emphasis on the need to be faithful to one's oath and avoid drunkenness than on the need to observe the rites of the Church. However, literature aimed at small girls did include exhortations to piety: see Greene, 'Mid-Nineteenth-Century Domestic Ideology in Russia', 84.

[55] Khakhordin, *The Collective and the Individual*: see esp. chs. 2 and 3.

[56] A preliminary study of such material is Greene, 'Mid-Nineteenth-Century Domestic Ideology in Russia', which gives an outline of material published in children's magazines such

manuals (on subjects such as bee-keeping, milking, carpentry, etc.) figure very little, though there is some brief consideration of propaganda for the 'scientific organization of labour' in the early Soviet period.

Something also needs to be said about the authors selected for close study. As is obvious from the quotation about 'cutting and pasting' above, many advice literature texts were produced anonymously, often on the basis of compilation or plagiarism. However, others were the work of specific and named writers. The number of important Russian writers who have expended ink and paper on conduct literature of one kind or another is remarkably high. Catherine II, Novikov, Gogol', Tolstoi, Platon Kerzhentsev, Mayakovsky, and D. S. Likhachev are only some of the prominent figures who have produced actual behaviour tracts. There is also a vigorous and important private tradition of secular sermons on manners intended for relatives (particularly in letters): here Pushkin, Ivan Aksakov, Chekhov, and again Tolstoi and Gogol', all made their mark. And the penchant for didacticism that characterizes Russian literary texts is intimately connected with the provision of prescriptive behaviour models: as Gogol' put it in his notorious conduct book *Selected Passages from Correspondence with Friends* (1847), 'The duty of a writer is not only to supply pleasant entertainment for the mind and taste; he will pay dearly if his works do not disseminate things useful to the soul and if he leaves behind him no moral instruction [*pouchenie*] to others.'[57] The rise of the genre of 'novelized conduct book' that began to be very widespread in the mid-nineteenth century (see Chapter 2) was intimately connected with the desire, among radicals, liberals, and conservatives alike, to push Russian society on to new paths of virtue and to construct models of appropriate behaviour. Conversely, the compulsion to pass on advice on behaviour afflicted even some writers who felt ambivalent or hostile about didactic literature. A key case in point was Nabokov, whose disquisition on 'poshlust' in his study of Gogol', and celebrations of Rembrandt and Picasso, at the expense of Braque and Van Gogh, in *Pnin*, were meant in absolute earnest, and manifest a fusion of aesthetic and ethical categories bearing out the writer's own description of himself as 'a rigid moralist kicking sin, scuffing stupidity, ridiculing the vulgar and cruel—and assigning sovereign power to tenderness, talent, and pride'.[58]

There is of course a danger that the very fame and prominence of the writers just mentioned might make them seem 'untypical'. However, the question of who exactly is or was a 'typical' author of advice literature in

as *Zvezdochka* in the 1840s (83–7). The emphasis on self-restraint and modesty in young girls here is very like that in treatises on maternal education (see my Ch. 1).

[57] N. V. Gogol', *Sochineniya*, iv (Moscow, 1889), 8.
[58] V. Nabokov, *Strong Opinions* (New York, 1990), 193.

Russia is an open one. Professional authors of advisory materials only began to emerge in the mid-nineteenth century, and the tradition was barely established before the Soviet government imposed artificial homogeneity in the form of strict publishing controls (which meant that only those occupying some official role, at the very least a teacher or doctor, were able to exercise their pens as advisory authors). So, while writers such as Isabella Beeton or Emily Post have their Russian equivalents (Ekaterina Avdeeva, Elena Molokhovets, and Kleopatra Svetozarskaya), such figures are less common than it might seem they ought to be on the basis of a straightforward comparison with the West. One could equally well argue for the 'typicality' of the anonymous or pseudonymous plagiarizer or synthesizer (for example 'Uncle Serge', alleged author of *A Manual of Love-Letters*, repeatedly reissued in the late nineteenth century, or 'the blind chef' who published a household manual in 1838), or of the famous and powerful writer whose studied mundanity of tone and impersonal omniscience is faintly but unmistakably overlaid by the glamour of high social status, intellectual standing, or material privilege (or all three: examples here would be Catherine II, Lev Tolstoi, and Nadezhda Krupskaya).[59] In any case, rather than seeing advice authors as 'typical' in the sense of representative of the average, it is perhaps best to see them as *tipici* in the Italian sense, 'characteristic of their kind'. All were part of an educated elite, and those of whom biographical details are available usually belonged to an elite within an elite, either because their books were particularly successful (in the case of Molokhovets), or because their authority as advice authors stemmed from a social position achieved before they began (either through personal eminence—Tolstoi, Catherine II, or through family connections—as in the case of Nataliya Nordman, partner of the painter Il'ya Repin, or of Nadezhda Krupskaya, wife of Lenin). But all of them gave vivid expression to a highly characteristic mission of the Russian intelligentsia, and educated elite more generally, to *vospityvat' narod* (educate the people). Indeed, a central theme of this book is the changing edificatory ambitions of those who saw themselves as bringers of culture

[59] Dyadya Serzh', *Lyubovnyi pis'movnik*; Stepanov, *Poslednii trud sleptsa-startsa Gerasima Stepanova*. The case of millionaire authors of best-selling literature such as Delia Smith in Britain, or Martha Stewart in America, is rather similar, though in Russia the combination of 'common sense' with political and intellectual authority has been more common than the combination of 'common sense' with fortunes made from royalties. Pseudonymous writers are common in the West as well: for example, Francis Gay, whose sententious *Friendship Book* sold 30,000 copies in Britain during 1997, and whose column in the *Sunday Post* was popular for decades with Scottish readers, did not in fact exist: the name was a cover for an ever-changing team of journalists who filed copy on Gay's behalf since at least the early 1940s, though 'there is some suggestion that a Francis Gay-type person did write the column when it was first published in 1938' (Lawrence Donegan, 'Friendship still festive fare', *Guardian*, 27 Dec. 1997, 4).

to the masses, 'in [whose] mind pedagogy and politics were so inter-twined that they could not be examined separately'.[60]

Dealing with 'civilizing processes', not *a* 'civilizing process', this book also seeks to re-examine other orthodoxies of historical change. Though the chapter dates observe customary divisions (1762–1830, 1830–1880, 1881–1917, 1917–1953, and 1953–1998), the broader tendency of the book is to call conventional demarcations into question. For example, the Emancipation of the Serfs in 1861 did not bring about a break in national-conservative celebrations of *byt* (see Chapter 2); so far as behaviour literature was concerned, 1957 and 1961 were much more important dates than 1953, and 1924 than 1917; while the continuities in the early Soviet concept of *kul'turnost'* were such that it is hard to speak, in this context, of a 'Great Retreat' beginning in the mid-1930s. Assumptions about the 'growth of privacy' and the emergence of 'separate spheres' for men and women are replaced by questions such as the following: To what extent was the new idea of woman as moral guide and arbiter of taste accepted in Russian society after 1760? (Chapter 1). How did conserva-tively inclined Russians contrive to mark their distance from the 'wasteful' Westernized aristocracy, and to reconstruct a 'true Russian' identity, yet at the same time to maintain their status as members of the cultural elite? (Chapter 2). How successfully did the individualistic behaviour models of Samuel Smiles implant themselves in Russian popular life, given that collective patterns of behaviour were essential to survival in village and in city? (Chapter 3). What was specifically 'Soviet' about the campaign for *kul'turnost'*, the 'civilizing process' of the first decades of Soviet power, and how successful was it in changing the lives of the Soviet masses, its purported target? (Chapter 4). What were the effects, upon the Soviet population, of the wide-ranging changes in the official *kul'turnost'* cam-paign that were initiated in the late 1950s? (Chapter 5). The chapters are at once separate, 'microhistorical'[61] essays on aspects of polite culture, and sections of a narrative recording the stops and starts of attempted 'Westernization', the modulation of absolutist imperatives about proper conduct in the fluctuating conditions of everyday life.

[60.] Dobrenko, *The Making of the State Reader*, 144. The particular representative of the cultural elite here is Lenin, but the comment applies equally well to Catherine II, Nicholas I, Stalin, and indeed Tolstoi and Dostoevsky.

[61] See David Ransel's defence of 'micro-history' in the Russian context in 'An Eighteenth-Century Merchant Family in Prosperity and Decline', in J. Burbank and D. L. Ransel (eds.), *Imperial Russia: New Histories for the Empire* (Bloomington, Ind., 1998), 257: 'The main point about microhistory is that instead of closing off the generative potential of the evidence by clamping it into a given design, the method explores the latitude actors enjoy for making choices contrary to the normative reality or hegemonic discourse of their time and can, therefore, reveal what is unseen in observations at a macro level.'

Russia is part of Europe
  (Catherine II, *The Grand Instructions*, 1768)

CHAPTER ONE

Educating Tat'yana, Schooling Evgeny: Propaganda for Manners and Moral Education, 1760–1830

> Всему причиной воспитание.
> Moral education's at the root of everything.
>
> Fonvizin, *The Brigadier* (1768)

'Polite society is more or less the same all over Europe,' Élisabeth Vigée Le Brun wrote in the 1830s, after decades of travel that had taken her to Britain and Russia, as well as Italy, Switzerland, and France.[1] This sense of unity through civility is also asserted in one of the most splendid tributes to a Russian aristocrat ever written, Pushkin's epistle 'To a Grandee' (1830).[2] The poem celebrates the life of Prince Nikolai Borisovich Yusupov, courtier to Catherine II, diplomat, and immensely wealthy proprietor of (among other places) Arkhangel'skoe, not far from Moscow (the location at once suggests worldliness, and remoteness from the St Petersburg dependence upon royal favour). Yusupov's life is treated by Pushkin as an *exemplum* of refinement. A connoisseur and 'Grand Tourist' who has conversed with the great men of the age on equal terms, he dispenses lavish hospitality in a palace that is the embodiment of classical grace:

> От северных оков освобождая мир,
> Лишь только на полях, струясь, дохнет зефир,
> Лишь только первая позеленеет липа,
> К тебе, приветливый потомок Аристиппа,
> К тебе явлюся я; увижу сей дворец,
> Где циркуль зодчего, палитра и резец

---

[1] *The Memoirs of Elisabeth Vigée Le Brun, Member of the Royal Academy of Paris, Rouen, Saint-Luke of Rome, Parma, Bologna, Saint Petersburg, Berlin, Geneva and Avignon*, trans. S. Evans (London, 1989), 94. On Vigée Le Brun's European travels, see also Angelica Goodden, *The Sweetness of Life: A Biography of Elisabeth Louise Vigée Le Brun* (London, 1997).

[2] A detailed analysis of 'To a Grandee' is available in V. E. Vatsuro, '"K vel'mozhe"', *Stikhi Pushkina 1820–1830kh godov: Istoriya sozdaniya i ideino-khudozhestvennaya problematika* (Leningrad, 1974), 177–212; C. Kelly, 'Pushkin's Vicarious Grand Tour: A Neo-Sociological Interpretation of "K vel'mozhe" (1830)', *SEER* 77 (1999), 3–27.

Ученой прихоти твоей повиновались
И вдохновенные в волшебстве состязались.

(Pushkin, *PSS* iii. 217)

The moment the airy zephyr breathes on the fields,
Liberating the world from its Northern fetters,
The moment the first lime-tree shows green,
Before you, welcoming descendant of Aristippus,
Before you I shall appear; and I shall see that palace
Where the architect's compasses, the palette and the chisel
Have submitted to your learned whim,
And, bewitched, competed to enchant us.

This is no country estate of the kind later to be portrayed in Gogol''s *Dead Souls*, an anonymous *glush'* stuck in the mud betwixt-and-between the two capitals, but a pavilion of pleasure within a day's carriage ride of the hot city. Just so, Yusupov is the very model of the Europeanized nobleman, his tastes shaped by the 'Grand Tour' that the poem describes, setting out in alternation his visits to people and to places: Voltaire, Versailles, Diderot, London, Beaumarchais, and Seville.[3] The only unexpected omission from the list is Italy, which, however, appears by proxy, in the form of the works of art by 'Canova and Correggio' (line 96) that Yusupov has acquired on his travels.

The portrait of the aristocrat that is given—calm, resilient, disposing sensibly and imaginatively of inherited privilege—is seductive as well as flattering. Yet this apparently extraordinary life also has larger meaning: Pushkin's 'grandee' exemplifies the understanding of taste set out by Voltaire in an article for the *Encyclopédie*: discrimination as the result of a process of cultivation that may be undergone not only by individuals, but by entire nations:

Taste is formed unnoticeably in a nation that lacks it because the wit of good artists contributes to it little by little . . . There are certain vast countries where *taste* has never appeared; these are those in which society has never perfected itself, where men and women are utterly unlike one another, and where certain arts, such as the sculpture and painting of animate beings, are forbidden by religion.[4]

The European visit made by Yusupov had been a crucial step on the road to refinement since the late seventeenth century, when the Russian pioneer 'Grand Tourist', Count Petr Tolstoi, a courtier of Peter the

---

[3] On Russian 'grand tourists' in France (though not including Yusupov), see W. Berelowitch, 'La France dans le "grand tour" des nobles russes au cours de la seconde moitié du XVIIIᵉ siècle', *Cahiers du monde russe* 34 (1993), 193–210.

[4] Voltaire, 'Goût' in *The Complete Works of Voltaire/Œuvres complètes de Voltaire*, xxxiii (Oxford, 1987), 128–32.

Great, was sent on a visit to Italy in 1698. Tolstoi's diary of his visit records admiration of Italian gardens, churches, music (an organ in the church of Santa Giustina in Venice), sculptures, entertainments such as a show with puppets performing a 'comedy just like living people', masquerades, a menagerie. He notes the luxury of his surroundings: 'In women's costume they use colored brocade of silk, and the women folk in Venice are very well formed and upright and politic (*politichen*), tall, thin, and fine in all ways, and they do not willingly do handiwork, but spend their time in idleness', while some women in Bologna kept special 'lap dogs' (*postel'nye sobaki*: literally, 'bed dogs'). Manners were also strangely refined: Venetians he held 'wise, politic and learned', and undemonstrative. Judges in Naples 'speak with great courtesy and do not shout'. Not only the politeness of Italians, but also their cleanliness, was impressive: even the pavements in Bologna were clean, and the Ferrarans themselves 'unnaturally clean, the male and the female sex'.[5]

No Russian gentleman of Yusupov's generation, as Pushkin's poem makes clear, would have spoken with such naive wonderment about his or her impressions of a visit to Europe. By the late eighteenth century, the Russian 'Grand Tour' had become an opportunity to parade Russian refinement in the West, as well as to absorb Western culture. Travel was now an exercise in aesthetic discrimination; phenomena were measured against universal standards and passed through the filter of erudition. Reserve, rather than enthusiasm, was the rule. In *Letters of a Russian Traveller*, Nikolai Karamzin, for example, recorded that a tavern in Königsberg was only 'fairly clean', that Leipzig was 'less picturesquely situated than Dresden', that the Schaffhausen Falls were disappointingly lacking in the sublimity identified there by previous travellers, and that it was impossible to obtain a decent salad in England, where only 'floppy leaves doused in vinegar' were on offer (plus ça change!). A fine prospect or stately building, on the other hand, had become the occasion for recalling the appropriate quotation from Virgil or Horace, Shakespeare, Haller, or Thomson, a parallel moment in Laurence Sterne's *Sentimental Journey*, or an equivalent scene in the painting of Poussin, Salvator Rosa, Correggio, or Claude. Encounters with 'great men' and with travellers from other European countries alike placed the Russian gentleman at the heart of Europe, and demonstrated that Russia's claims to civilization were as valid as those of other Northerners, such as Danes, Swedes, Germans, or Britons. Karamzin's incidental comments upon the French character, which he confidently (and with characteristic lack of originality) declared to be a

[5] *The Travel Diary of Peter Tolstoi: A Muscovite in Early Modern Europe*, trans. and ed. Max J. Okenfuss (DeKalb, Ill., 1987), 94, 100, 152, 154, 310, 76, 149, 196, 317, 320.

combination of *iskusstvo zhit' s lyud'mi* (the art of living with others, *savoir-vivre*) and frivolity, exemplifed the mixture of susceptibility to the values of Western civilization and assertion of national identity that is evident throughout his account. Its purpose is deftly articulated in the closing remarks to his discourse upon the French: 'This is intended both for the lady reader, and for the Frenchwoman, who would exclaim with horror and cry: "Northern barbarian!" if I were to tell her that the French are neither wittier nor more polite than anyone else.'[6]

Fundamental to this sense of self-esteem was the new buying power of some members of the Russian upper classes, which allowed them to domesticate—in the most literal sense of the word—the appointments of Western European polite society. Where Tolstoi had gushed over painted figures that he saw in Olivetano: 'one cannot tell that they are not alive' (p. 197), Russian aristocrats now purchased as well as admired, and bought according to the latest Western fashions. On his visit to Europe, thinly disguised as Le Comte du Nord, the future Paul I commissioned work by the Grand Tourists' favourite portraitist, Pompeo Batoni. Yusupov's admiration for Correggio and Canova was shared by Grand Tourists of his generation everywhere; later, in the late eighteenth and early nineteenth centuries, the Russian royalty and aristocracy began to collect the lyrical landscapes of painters such as Hubert Robert and Joseph Vernet, in order that the picturesque scenes that they had admired on their travels might be translated to the walls of their palaces at home.[7] Smaller-scale souvenirs purchased in France and Italy were also vital status symbols and transmitters of refinement. In the houses of Russian aristocrats, *petits riens*

[6] N. Karamzin, *Pis'ma russkogo puteshestvennika* (Moscow, 1983), 51, 95, 156, 411, 401. Cf. Princess Ekaterina Dashkova's recollections of Versailles: 'As the public was admited to view the King sitting at table, we mingled with the crowd which was anything but fashionable and grand, and entered with it into a room which appeared to me very dirty and very squalid.' Dashkova was also unfavourably impressed by the table manners of those she observed, and in particular by the fact that Princess Adelaide drank soup out of a mug. (See *The Memoirs of Princess Dashkova*, trans. K. Fitzlyon, ed. J. Gheith (Durham, NC, 1995), 128.) This motif was current in the 19th cent. too: for instance, Countess Ekaterina Ignat'eva (née Golitsyna), complained that 'England was a barbarous place compared with Russia', and found Hatfield House 'a vast, cheerless place' (see Michael Ignatieff, *The Russian Album* (London, 1987), 48). On Karamzin's recollections from a different perspective, see A. Kahn, 'Politeness and its Discontents in Karamzin's *Letters of a Russian Traveller*', in J. Renwick (ed.), *L'Invitation au voyage: Studies in Honour of Peter France* (Oxford, 2000), 263–72.

[7] On Paul's Grand Tour, see Louis Ducros, 'The Grand Duke Paul and his Retinue in the Forum Romanum', A. Wilton and I. Bignamini (eds.) *Grand Tour: the Lure of Italy in the Eighteenth Century* (exhibition catalogue; Tate Gallery, London, 1996), pl. 95. On the passion for Correggio and Canova, see ibid., esp. p. 27 and note to plate 32. On Robert and Vernet, see Charles Sterling, *Great French Paintings in the Hermitage* (New York, 1958), 55. Apart from Yusupov, other major collectors included A. S. Stroganov, D. M. Golitsyn, and A. A. Kushelev-Bezborodko. See R. P. Gray, 'The Golitsyn and Kushelev-Bezborodko Collections and their Role in the Evolution of Public Art Galleries in Russia', *Oxford Slavonic Papers* 31 (1998), 51–67.

(*bezdelushki*) such as jewelled snuff-boxes ornamented boule-work desks and side-tables; gilded chairs were set out along the painted and wall-papered sides of reception rooms and antechambers. As Madame Vigée Le Brun recalled, Prince Bezborodko's house held 'salons crammed with furniture he had bought in Paris from the studios of the famous cabinet-maker Daguère', while Count Buturlin 'owned a huge library in Moscow, composed of many rare and precious books in various languages'. Vigée Le Brun, who had frequented Versailles in its last days, felt quite at home among the aristocrats of Catherine II's Russia.[8]

As the eighteenth century drew to a close, the Westernized manners of the aristocracy began to be widely imitated by provincial gentlefolk as well. Sergei Aksakov's memoir *The Childhood Years of Grandson Bagrov* (1858), closely based on the writer's own childhood in the Urals during the last years of Catherine II's reign and the first years of Paul I, emphasizes the role of the narrator's Muscovite mother in communicating ideals of refinement quite new to the locality. Revolted by the 'dirt' and 'stench' of the local Tatars and Chuvashes, uninterested in housekeeping or estate management, reluctant to communicate with the local peasantry except through a window, detesting 'the presence and society of servants', Bagrov's mother occupied her days in genteel pursuits such as jam-making, the confection of almond biscuits, visits to neighbours (carefully donning her best city finery in order to impress a neighbour whom she considered a parvenu), and conducting a war of emotional attrition with her children (thereby giving them an induction in the self-scrutiny requisite to 'civilized manners'). Nor were Bagrova's interventions merely repressive: they were striking demonstrations of how refinement might be constructed in a positive sense. Her reorganization of the interior of the Bagrov manor house in order to separate private rooms from public rooms illustrated the need to contrive intimate spaces designed for the entertainment of a family's inner circle. And her recondite tastes (not content with the produce of the manorial vegetable gardens and orchards, she demanded lemons, a fruit of which no one in the district had ever heard) underlined the importance of preferring the rare, the expensive, and the exotic to the cheap and the familiar.[9]

Not all families, of course, were able to rely on blood relations or marital connections as cultural informants in this way, but foreigners (French, and by the early nineteenth century also English, tutors and governesses or

[8] *Memoirs*, 220. See also Priscilla Roosevelt, *Life on the Russian Country Estate: A Social and Cultural History* (New Haven, 1995), chs. 2 and 4. On the taste for fine English goods, such as Wedgwood and clocks, for English horses, and for parks in the English manner, see A. Cross, *By the Banks of the Neva: Chapters from the Lives and Careers of the British in Eighteenth-Century Russia* (Cambridge, 1997), 17–20, 233–9, 262–328.

[9] Sergei Aksakov, *Detskie gody Bagrova-vnuka* (1858), in *Semeinaya khronika* (Moscow, 1975). See esp. 90, 91, 93, 113, 132, 159, 179, 208, 213–14, 300.

companions) could also supply information about the way that things ought to be done, as could impoverished Russian nobles. The parvenu Durasov visited by the Bagrov family, who held opulent banquets accompanied by serf choirs in a rural palace filled with costly furniture, had modelled his style of life on the households of Moscow aristocrats whom he had visited, supplemented by tutorials from a decayed nobleman, 'practically a prince', whom he had engaged as an adviser on how to live.[10]

But by far the most important role in diffusing refinement was played by that royal *Kulturträgerin* extraordinary, Catherine II. As Pushkin put it in 1833, she disseminated a 'new etiquette . . . founded upon good sense and a politeness comprehensible to all'.[11] In a memoir which itself was an exemplary work of propaganda for cultivated values, Catherine described how she had herself experienced the 'civilizing process'. Neglected by her mother and left, as an infant, to the care of empty-headed and ill-educated young women, Catherine had been rescued by a governess, Babette Kardel, who had imposed upon her the self-control and grasp of morality that others had signally failed to instil. Saved from herself by the benevolent strictness of her governess, and answering thereafter only to 'gentleness and reason', Catherine had been able to continue civilizing herself in late childhood and adolescence, broadening both her intellectual education and her moral education by private reading.[12] Having attained the Russian throne thanks to an act of violence that definitely did not fit the paradigm of self-improvement, and so had to be represented to herself and others as a desperate measure provoked by the extreme barbarism of Peter III, her husband, Catherine turned her considerable intelligence and energy to the Russian state. Her *mission civilisatrice* would not have been realizable without the cultural changes achieved under Peter I and his successors, most particularly Elizabeth; but it had an intensity and coherence not previously evident in Russia. In the Russian capital, granite embankments along the Neva symbolized the taming of the natural world, and 'came to serve as a stone ribbon binding the city together'.[13] Urban space was also controlled through new regulations which forbade unseemly displays of crude behaviour such as drunkenness, and appointed *blagochinnye* ('order-

[10] See Aksakov, *Detskie gody*, 304.

[11] 'Puteshestvie iz Moskvy v Peterburg', *PSS* xi. 265. For a fuller discussion of this essay, see Ch. 2.

[12] See Catherine II, *Zapiski Imperatritsy Ekateriny Vtoroi: perevod s podlinnika, izdannogo Imperatorskoi Akademiei Nauk* (St Petersburg, 1907), 1–7. This volume assembles the various fragments of Catherine's memoirs, written at different times for different readers, including the self-justifying account of the palace coup that brought down Peter III (Variant 4), that was to become her best-known piece of autobiography.

[13] See B. A. Ruble, 'From Palace Square to Moscow Square: St Petersburg's Century-Long Retreat from Public Space', in W. C. Brumfield (ed.), *Reshaping Russian Architecture: Western Technology, Utopian Dreams* (Cambridge, 1990), 11.

lies', i.e. policemen) to uphold decorum.[14] The use of architecture intended to impress the citizens with the might of the state was, of course, something that Catherine had learned from Peter I's programmes of reform. But where Peter was particularly concerned with the external regulation of behaviour via public ceremony and punitive legislation,[15] Catherine was at least as eager to promote the internal mechanisms of behaviour regulation. The Russian population was to police itself as well as to be policed.

One important way of ensuring that it did was through education. The Imperial Foundling Homes, set up in 1764 and 1770, were supposed to offer their inmates not merely shelter but also a programme of general education common to both sexes. In the 1780s, a network of state-run schools began to be set up in Russian cities and towns, providing pupils not only with tuition in the three Rs, but also in the behaviour proper to citizenship. *On the Duties of Man and Citizen* (1783), a reader to be used in these schools, exhorted readers not only to be orderly, economical, and polite, but also to love labour and to be contented. Above all, two

---

[14] The First Supplement to the Grand Instructions, 'Of Good Order, otherwise termed Police', sections 527–66, envisaged a very wide range of duties for the *blagochinnye*, including the supervision of agriculture, building, accident prevention, and weights and measures as well as of 'whatever is necessary to repress Luxury, to deter from Drunkenness, to put a Stop to the Progress of prohibited Games', etc. See *The Grand Instructions*, 201 ff. The Statute on the Police (Ustav o blagochinii) of 1782 proceeded along similar lines: police were mandated to control hygiene and luxury as well as public order, and prohibitions were placed on gambling, swearing, worldly conversations in church, squabbling and abuse in public, drunkenness and mixed bathing as well as on public assemblies and the vandalism of official notices. See 15.379, *PSZ* xxi. 462–88.

[15] Laws introduced by Peter to foster the transformation of private life included—besides the notorious decrees on dress of 1700 and 1705—the stipulation that the interiors of houses should be plastered and a regular life led therein (1705). See E. V. Anisimov, *The Reforms of Peter the Great*, trans. J. Alexander (Armonk, NY, 1993), 217–20. Catherine's successors were as disinclined as Peter to enter the field of behaviour discourse. Alexander I's contributions to conduct included the sponsorship of the Tsarskoe Selo Lyceum (see below), as well as the disastrous plan to set up 'Arakcheev villages', model military settlements, based on the Interior Minister's estate village, all over Russia. The settlements soon became the focus of riots, and their only long-lasting offshoot was the model Russian village at Potsdam (which still stands), with impeccably neat wooden houses set in well-kept vegetable gardens along a figure-eight gravel track, topped by a church in icing-sugar pink—a curious instance of the reimportation of a Prussianized Russian settlement *back* into Prussia. Under Nicholas I, there was also emphasis on the institutional regulation of behaviour—e.g. the *Dvoryanskaya Opeka*, or Trusteeship of the Nobility, which in the second quarter of the nineteenth century 'sometimes on the slenderest of pretenses sought to wrest control of settled estates from nobles suspected of conduct unbefitting their station' (see M. L. Marrese, 'Gender, Morality, and the Limits of Private Property in Russia' (unpublished paper, 1999), 5). The conduct of university students was regulated through an inspectorate which enforced observation of disciplinary codes dictating sexual propriety, obedience, order, neatness and good grooming, and correct attire, on the pain of confinement in the student prison (*karttser*). See R. Friedman, 'In the Company of Men: Student Life and Russian Masculinity, 1825–1855' (Ph.D thesis, University of Michigan, 2000), 50–60.

principles were stressed: the need to be patriotic, and the need to accept innovation. An economic argument was used to link the two together:

Common people show themselves to be sons of the fatherland when they do not cling to old-fashioned habits, but try as much as possible to borrow whatever is useful from other countries and use it for the benefit of the fatherland, or when they plant and cultivate foreign products on their own fields, or when they imitate their neighbours' manner of farming, or when they are as diligent as their neighbour in manufacturing their own products. This is in order that there should be no need for foreign produce and manufacturers, and so that the money paid out [for these] should be kept in the fatherland.[16]

Despite the use of the term 'fatherland', and the stress in parts of *The Duties of Man and Citizen* upon citizenship as primarily a male role, Catherine also envisaged that women of the 'common people' would make an important contribution to the well-being of the nation, albeit primarily through their roles as housewives.

For all the emphasis that she laid on homilies of virtue addressed to 'the common people', Catherine was, however, conscious that these could only be expected to recognize the ideals of efficiency and orderliness that she hoped to plant in them if they were set a suitable example by the powerful. So far as the imperial succession was concerned, she made sure that nothing would be left to chance. Though prevented from bringing up her son, who later ruled as Paul I, she provided her grandsons with the best education available, ensuring Russia's character as a superannuated enlightened autocracy until the mid-nineteenth century.[17] Her capacity for expedient ruthlessness did not prevent her from posing as the embodiment of refinement, the figure whom she described thus in an undated manuscript note: 'Be gentle, philanthropic, accessible, sympathetic and generous; do not let your greatness prevent you from condescending to little people and putting yourself in their position, though making sure that your kindness does nothing to injure your power, or the respect they have for you.'[18]

[16]   *O dolzhnostyakh cheloveka i grazhdanina*, 127–8; translation adapted from J. L. Black, *Citizens for the Fatherland: Education, Educators, and Pedagogical Ideals in Eighteenth-Century Russia* (Boulder, Colo., 1979), 249–50. On the foundling hospitals, see D. Ransel, *Mothers of Misery: Child Abandonment in Russia* (Princeton, 1988). On Catherine's educational policy, see, besides Black, I. de Madariaga, *Russia in the Age of Catherine the Great* (London, 1981), ch. 31; M. J. Okenfuss, 'Education and Empire: School Reform in Enlightened Russia', *Jahrbuch für Geschichte Osteuropas* 27 (1979), 41–68.

[17]   Catherine's plan for the education of the boys was a characteristically 18th-cent. mixture of sensible hygiene, morals, and manners with reading in the humanities. (See Madariaga, *Russia in the Age of Catherine the Great*, 567–8).

[18]   ['Nravstvennye idealy Ekateriny II'], in Catherine II, *Zapiski* (St Petersburg, 1907), 655. Cf. the description of Catherine by L. F. Segur as 'a majestic ruler and an amiable lady' (*Rossiya XVIII veka glazami inostrantsev* (Leningrad, 1989), 318). From the perspective of the late 18th cent., the contribution made by Peter to 'civilization' seemed highly questionable: see e.g. the comments

Catherine's stress upon the fact that those occupying high office must behave in accordance with the principles of refinement was another difference between her and Peter.[19] Peter's primary requirement of the Russian upper classes had been loyal service, a requirement enforced by the twin means of punishment and reward. Savage penalties were imposed upon *dvoryane* who avoided military duty, and education for all 10 to 15-year-old boys was made compulsory in 1714. And in 1722, the 'Table of Ranks', a new hierarchy for the civil and military service, substituted a meritocratic service ladder for the old system of *mestnichestvo*, or the awarding of posts according to family status.[20] The Table (in theory, at least) favoured those *dvoryane* who worked assiduously over those who did not; and it made it possible for able young men of low birth to rise by service into the *dvoryanstvo* estate (personal membership of the *dvoryanstvo* was conferred upon all holders of posts in the civil service, and hereditary membership of the *dvoryanstvo* upon holders of the top eight civil ranks, while all officers in the armed forces enjoyed hereditary nobility). Further, exceptionally distinguished individuals might be rewarded with the titles of count or baron, or very occasionally prince, as was the case with Peter's henchman and perhaps lover Aleksandr Men'shikov. The conferral of titles had analogues in other European countries, but the custom of awarding 'personal' and 'hereditary *dvoryanstvo*' is difficult to match. It made the boundaries of the *dvoryanstvo* more porous than those of the Adel in Prussia and the Holy Roman Empire, or than those of the *noblesse* in France. The situation in Britain was more closely analogous, but even here there was—at least until the system of life peerages introduced by Harold Macmillan's government in the 1960s—nothing similar to the notion of the 'personal *dvoryanin*'.[21] And in Britain, it is difficult to think of an equivalent to, say, Mikhail Chulkov (*c.*1734–1792), a gifted and astute actor and writer from plebeian

upon Peter's character in the memoirs of Princess Ekaterina Dashkova, President under Catherine of the Academy of Sciences: 'He had genius, energy, and zeal for improvement, but his total lack of education had left him with unbridled passions which completely swayed his reason; quick-tempered, brutal, and despotic, he treated all people without distinction as slaves who must bear with everything; his ignorance did not allow him to see that many reforms being introduced by him through violence were being introduced quietly and peacefully by trade, exchange, the passage of time, and the example of other nations' (*The Memoirs of Princess Dashkova*, 181).

[19] Though the difference was one of emphasis, since official publications during Peter's reign included a number of advice books aimed at public servants, most notably the *Honest Mirror of Youth* (see below). It would be reasonable to suppose that Catherine could be more demanding because Peter had so effectively propagandized the elements of Enlightenment civilization to the court elite.

[20] See L. Hughes, *Russia in the Age of Peter the Great* (New Haven, 1998), 172–4, 180–5.

[21] On life peerages see David Cannadine, *The Decline and Fall of the British Aristocracy* (New Haven, 1990), 680–1.

origins, who had managed, by the mid-1770s, to acquire an estate, to which he was able to retire in late middle age (in 1789 of all years), by now elevated to the *dvoryanstvo* as a reward for service.[22]

As this last example indicates, Catherine retained the meritocratic principle behind the Table of Ranks; she was also notably prodigal in awarding the title of count—as is shown by Yakov Knyazhnin's comedy *The Boaster*, in which a self-serving imposter can plausibly pass himself off as a new count because there are so many of these around. However, at the same time, she also encouraged a quite different view of the social elite, one based on the notion of *noblesse oblige*. The *dvoryanstvo*, legally liberated from service in 1762, during the short reign of Catherine's husband, Peter III, was now reconstructed as a 'nobility' along Western European lines, its privileges enhanced, and its honorific status emphasized. As the official English translation of Catherine's *Nakaz* put it: 'Nobility is an Appellation of *Honour*, which distinguishes all those who are adorned with it from every other Person of Inferior Rank.'[23] The *dvoryanstvo* was marked out, in Catherine's phrasing, not only from the toiling serfs, but also from a 'working class' of another kind—the *meshchanstvo* or plebeian town-dwellers. This, in her definition, was a group made up of those 'who are neither *Gentlemen*, nor *Husbandsmen*, but employ themselves in *Arts, Sciences, Navigation, Commerce* or *Handicraft Trades*'[24]—in design, that is, a European 'third estate', *Bürgertum*, or *bourgeoisie*. Though there was no direct statement to the effect that a gentleman was a person who did not engage in commerce, handcraft, arts, sciences, or trades, that was one interpretation that could be placed upon the definitions of rank. And in 1785, the 'Declaration of the Rights, Freedom and Privileges of the Well-Born Russian *Dvoryanstvo*' underlined the practical advantages of the estate (including the right to buy land, to engage in wholesale trade, to own property in town and country, to be spared corporal punishment). Importantly, too, the preamble to the Declaration set out a view of *dvoryanstvo* that combined the meritocratic notion of reward for service with the notion of inherited rank: 'The right to the name of *dvoryanin* comes down from the quality and virtue of those men who took the lead in

[22] See N. Crowe's biographical article in N. Cornwell (ed.), *A Reference Guide to Russian Literature* (London, 1998). On the other hand, it is important to remember that Chulkov belonged to a minority: only 25 per cent of officials in classes 1–5 came from outside the nobility in 1755, and the proportion declined slightly over the next century. S. Dixon, *The Modernisation of Russia 1676–1825* (Cambridge, 1999), 99.

[23] Catherine II, *The Grand Instructions of the Commissioners Appointed to Frame a New Code of Laws for the Russian Empire, composed by her Imperial Majesty Catherine II, Empress of All the Russias [. . .]*, trans. M. Tatishcheff (London, 1768), section 380.

[24] Catherine II, *The Grand Instructions*, section 378. See also D. M. Griffiths, 'Eighteenth-Century Perceptions of Backwardness: Projects for the Creation of a Third Estate in Catherinian Russia', *Canadian-American Slavic Studies* 13 (1979), 452–72.

ancient times and distinguished themselves by particular service.'[25] In order to institutionalize this interpretation of *dvoryanstvo* as *hereditary* service, the law ordained that one duty of the 'assemblies of the *dvoryanstvo*' in regional centres should be to keep genealogical records (*rodoslovnye knigi*) of all the *dvoryane* in the locality. These books were intended 'to commemorate [the past] for future generations', and to 'to allow every well-born *dvoryanstvo* family the opportunity to carry its worth and its name into heredity, from generation to generation, unshaken and undamaged from father to son, to grandson, to great-grandson and to all legitimate offspring, for as long as God shall choose to continue that heritage'.[26] To underline the heritage principle, the books were to be divided into six sections, with those individuals who could trace *dvoryanstvo* status back to 1685 or earlier listed separately from those who could not. The legal emphasis on inherited rank was backed by dissemination of Western European signifiers of that rank: for example, the curriculum of Catherine's flagship Imperial Society for the Education of Well-Born Young Women, popularly known as 'Smol'nyi Institute', and founded in 1764, included both genealogy and heraldry.[27]

Catherine's reign, then, witnessed an ambiguity creeping in to the conception of upper-class status. Elevation to the *dvoryanstvo* on merito-cratic grounds continued, but those with long family histories were encouraged to take pride in lineage; service still conferred prestige, but elegant unemployment was now seen as an expression of refined identity too. A *dvoryanin* was no longer defined merely as a servant of the court: he was also someone who expressed his refinement through what he owned and the company he kept (not for nothing did Catherine's reign see the founding not only of 'assemblies of the nobility' (*dvoryanskie sobraniya*), but also of the prestigious 'English clubs' in St Petersburg and Moscow, and, more clandestinely, of Masonic lodges all over the Russian empire).[28]

---

[25] See statute 16187, 21 Apr. 1785, *PSZ* xxii. 347.

[26] Ibid., *PSZ* xxii. 351. The *dvoryanskie sobraniya* themselves dated from 1775.

[27] A British visitor to Russia in the 1780s recorded that the Smol'nyi girls were also given tuition in genealogy at the time when she visited the school. (Elizabeth Dimsdale, *An English Lady at the Court of Catherine the Great: the Journal of Baroness Elizabeth Dimsdale, 1781*, ed. A. G. Cross (Cambridge, 1989), 49. See also D. Schakhovskoy, 'Heuristique et généalogie de la noblesse russe', *Cahiers du monde russe* 34 (1993), 267–76, and S. O. Schmidt, 'Obshchestvennoe samosoznanie noblesse russe', ibid. 11–31. Heraldry had been part of the syllabus originally drafted for Smol'nyi (it was supposed to be taught to the third level, ages 12 to 15.) See Betskoi, *Ustav vospitaniya*, 13.

[28] The English Club in St Petersburg (limited to 300 members from 1780 to 1817, and 350 from 1817 to 1853) was founded in 1770, its Moscow counterpart in the 1790s (closed down by Paul I, it was refounded in 1801). On these, the *dvoryanskie sobraniya*, and other less prestigious associations, see BE xv. 426–8, headword *Klub*. Freemasonry was introduced to Russia well before Catherine's reign began (in the 1730s), but became widespread in the 1770s. By the end of the 18th cent., there were over 135 Masonic lodges with 3,000 members all over the Russian empire, in the teeth of growing official disapproval from the second half of the 1780s onwards.

The division between the 'official' and 'sociable' interpretations of the *dvoryanin* is amusingly evident in the architecture of N. A. Durasov's beautiful villa at Lyublino, a pavilion of pleasure on the banks of a tranquil small lake not far from Moscow. According to a plausible legend, the house was constructed on the plan of a Greek cross within a colonnade because the owner wanted to commemorate having been awarded the similarly shaped Cross of St Anne. Whatever the truth of this, a similar tension between *chinopochitanie* (rank consciousness) and striving for refinement was certainly evident in late eighteenth- and early nineteenth-century portraiture. On the one hand, portraits often represented ladies or gentlemen according to their rank in court or civil service, the men emblazoned with glittering decorations (*ordena*), the women with the diamond-encrusted *shifry* (monograms) awarded to distinguished ladies-in-waiting. But on the other, this recording of mechanical social advancement was countered by a new tradition of genteel genre-painting, 'conversation pieces', which showed well-off Russians whiling away their time in such refined pastimes as music or drawing, as well as conversation, in settings which were clearly meant to represent the domestic space that they inhabited.[29]

Notable in this new tradition of portraiture is the prominence of women, who are just as likely to be shown painting or reading as their male contemporaries. In order to spread the civilizing influence of women more effectively, Catherine became a powerful and effective advocate of education for upper-class girls. Smol'nyi Institute was radically new in its emphasis upon the need to combine tuition in the accomplishments considered necessary in polite society and intellectual education (*obrazovanie*) with moral education (*vospitanie*). Subjects studied included, besides dance, music, sewing, drawing, and household economy, law, mathematics, languages, geography, history, economy, architecture, science, and

On Freemasonry as a social phenomenon in the broader context of 18th-cent. sociability, see Douglas Smith, 'Freemasonry and the Public in Eighteenth-Century Russia', in J. Burbank and D. L. Ransel, *Imperial Russia: New Histories for the Empire* (Bloomington, Ind., 1998), 281–304; idem, *Freemasonry and Society in Eighteenth-Century Russia* (DeKalb, Ill., 1999).

[29] The importance of the 'conversation piece' should not be exaggerated: such works are relatively rare, and were often commissioned by expatriates from distinguished foreign painters (e.g. Pompeo Batoni). An early example, by Lüders, shows the ambassador Count Petr Grigor'evich Chernyshev (1712–73) and family (Grand Duke Nicholas Mikhailovich, *Russkie portrety*, 5 vols. (St Petersburg 1905–1907), v, pl. 102); for a later example, see Fig. 3). But there is a small but significant number of representations of gentility in terms of the ownership of cultural artefacts and/or engagement in refined activities: e.g. Borivikovsky's portrait of Derzhavin at his desk with books (*Russkie portrety*, i, pl. 39), or an anon. portrait of Countess Mariya Rodionovna Panina (*c*.1740–1775) painting her daughter Sofiya (ibid. ii, pl. 41), or an Angelica Kaufmann of Aleksei Vasil'evich Naryshkin (1742–1800) writing in his library with a bust (no doubt of the Muse, since he was a writer and scholar: ibid. v, pl. 9). But these are relatively rare among the countless portraits of decorated officials of both sexes.

Гр. Николай Александровичъ, 1765–1816,
и Гр. Анна Ивановна, 177.–1825,
Толстые

Le Comte Nicolas Alexandrowitch
Tolstoi, 1765–1816, et sa femme
Anna Ivanowna, 177.–1825

FIG. 3. A 'conversation piece' of Count Nikolai and Countess Anna Tolstoi, holding their son Aleksandr on silken reins (anonymous artist, French school, *c.*1795).

ethics. The female-dominated teaching staff included moral guides, the *klassnye damy* (*dames de classe*), who were supposed to supervise the pupils constantly and give attention to their moral education; and the syllabus envisaged hefty doses of theoretical tuition in morality as well.[30] By contrast, under the considerably less intensive plans drawn up by Fedor Saltykov at the instruction of Peter I, young women had been expected to go through courses in 'reading, writing, cyphering' (the last considered necessary 'for housekeeping'), French and German ('for elegance in languages'), literature and drawing 'for amusement', and music and dance 'for amusement in places where cheerful sociability is the rule'.[31] For all the limitations of the education offered by Smol'nyi, which were to be relentlessly dwelled on by Catherine's enemies, and which have been noted by historians since,[32] it was revolutionary by comparison with anything that had been offered in Russia before.

But whatever her hopes for Smol'nyi graduates as messengers of cultivation in the Russian aristocracy and gentry, Catherine was aware of the limits to the influence of the necessarily limited numbers of highly educated young women. Her didactic mission was also aimed at adults. These she sought to reach above all through 'amusement in places where cheerful sociability is the rule'. Like most allies of the Enlightenment, Catherine was convinced of the civilizing efficacy of the theatre, which could propagandize decorous behaviour both through what it represented on the stage, and through the studious demeanour that was required from spectators.[33] Catherine's own contributions to stage tradition included a number of lively satires, such as *Mrs Grumpy's Name Day*, which represented a matriarch who was everything that she should not have been in terms of the 'woman as moral educator' model: a foul-mouthed termagant rather than a dispenser of 'sweetness and reason'.[34]

Catherine was also a prolific composer of fiction, no doubt aware that this was the most popular genre of printed text in the Russia of her day. Moralists might despise novels and romances, but these enjoyed a huge

[30] On the *dames de classe*, see N. P. Cherepnin, *Imperatorskoe Vospitatel'noe obshchestvo blagorodnykh devits. Istoricheskii ocherk 1764–1914*, 3 vols. (St Petersburg, 1914–1915), i. 56–8. The syllabus is given in Betskoi, *Ustav vospitaniya*.

[31] Quoted in Cherepnin, *Imperatorskoe Vospitatel'noe obshchestvo*, i. 27.

[32] See particularly E. Likhacheva, *Materialy dlya istorii zhenskogo obrazovaniya v Rossii (1086–1796)* (St Petersburg, 1890); C. S. Nash, 'Educating New Mothers: Women and the Enlightenment in Russia', *History of Education Quarterly*, 21/3 (1981), 301–16.

[33] See the good discussion in O. E. Chayanova, *Teatr Maddoksa v Moskve, 1776–1805* (Moscow, 1927).

[34] Catherine II, *Imyaniny gospozhi Vorchalkinoi*, in *Sochineniya Imperatritsy Ekateriny II na osnovaniyakh podlinnykh rukopisei: Dramaticheskie sochineniya*, ed. A. P. Pypin, i (St Petersburg, 1901), 49–114: see e.g. 81–2. The opening line of the play, spoken by Vorchalkina's daughter Olimpiada to her maid, 'Leave off of me!' (*Otsepis' ot menya*) has a shock effect not too dissimilar to that produced by the first word of Alfred Jarry's infamous avant-garde farce, *Ubu Roi*.

success among literate Russians, who learned from sources such as Rousseau's *La Nouvelle Héloïse* and Richardson's *Pamela* a new repertoire of gestures and a new emotional vocabulary.[35] And works that strict guardians of virtue considered more edifying, such as Fénelon's narrative poem *Télémaque*, were routinely used as part of school education in order to place behaviour ideals before young readers.[36] Catherine's own moral tale, 'Prince Khlor', invoked in a famous poetic tribute to its author by Derzhavin, sought to tap literature's popularity to didactic ends. It showed a young man kept from the blandishments of idleness and self-indulgence by a Turkish princess, Felitsa, his guide on the path to pluck the 'thornless rose' of Virtue. In her journals *Allsorts* and *Fact and Fable*, Catherine inclined to homilies of a more light-hearted kind,[37] making fun of ignorant country squires, and also of fashionable young ladies who lounged in bed all morning before spending the afternoon on choosing new dresses, having their hair dressed, and mooning over young men:

Tuesday. Got up just after noon.

NB. The reason for rising so early was that I had got to bed betimes: at 3 in the morning, not a minute later.

NB. My husband in his half of the house. Here as in Paris we keep ourselves to ourselves.

The hairdresser did my hair far too tidily: it took me nearly an hour to get myself fit to be seen in public.

Lunched at 5 pm.

Dear me, Petersburg is tedious in the summer: it is light all the time, so I have to spend the entire day and night with the curtains drawn. It is not well-bred to let the sun in.

Went to the comedy in the hope of seeing K... (I suspect him to be making eyes at A.). No sign of him in the pleasure garden. Happened to overhear that that he had spent all day playing whist at Z's.

A. looked a real fright: like a shepherdess out of an opera. They tried to feed me meat-balls at supper. Revolting. Were they trying to poison me or something?[38]

---

[35] There is an extremely substantial literature on *belles-lettres* and the construction of behaviour before 1825: see e.g. L. Sazonova, '"Lyubovnyi leksikon" v Rossii XVIII veka—amoris documentum', *Novaya delovaya kniga* 37 (1997), 25–30; Yu. M. Lotman. '"Ezda v ostrov Lyubvi" Trediakovskogo i funktsiya perevodnoi literatury v russkoi kul'ture pervoi poloviny XVIII veka', *Problemy izucheniya kul'turnogo naslediya* (Moscow, 1985), 222–30.

[36] *Télémaque* was so familiar a schoolroom reader that a punishment for miscreants in one late 18th-cent. St Petersburg tavern was being made to recite from the text: see G. E. Munro, 'Food in Catherinian St Petersburg', in M. Glants and J. Toomre (eds.), *Food in Russian History and Culture* (Bloomington, Ind., 1997), 45.

[37] The fact that her participation in these (as opposed to her authorship of the moral tales) was not generally known (see Madariaga, *Catherine the Great: A Short History* (New Haven, 1990), 92) was perhaps disinhibitory.

[38] Catherine II, 'Zapisnaya knizhka sestry moei dvoyurodnoi, mesyatsa iyulya, 1 sed'mitsy, 1783 goda', from *Byli i nebylitsy: Sochineniya Imperatritsy Ekateriny II: Proizvedeniya literaturnye* (St Petersburg, 1893), 402.

But Catherine's influence on print culture went beyond authorship alone. By means not only of direct personal censorship, but by example, and by her sponsorship of translation as an enlightening force, she imposed the concept of 'polite letters' upon other writers.[39] This required the use of appropriately decorous language, and the dissemination of civilized values, in texts intended for public consumption. True, there was a not inconsiderable market for novels of sexual dalliance, but elite literature treated potentially scandalous subjects with delicacy.[40] And writers such as Aleksandr Sumarokov, Denis Fonvizin, Yakov Knyazhnin, Nikolai Novikov, and V. V. Kapnist joined the empress in lambasting false refinement and pouring scorn upon ignorance.[41]

Profoundly affecting the history of didactic *belles-lettres*, Catherine also presided over an upsurge of non-fictional publications that propagandized refined conduct. As in the case of literature, she could to some extent build on established tradition. Conduct literature had begun to circulate in the early eighteenth century, not only in Western languages (French and German) but also in Russian translation. Peter the Great's encouragement of publications on statecraft, military technique, and shipbuilding was accompanied by the sponsorship of a famous treatise on polite behaviour, *The Honourable Mirror of Youth, and the Crown of Maidenly Honour and Virtue* (1717).[42] Twenty years later came another landmark edition: the writer Vasily Trediakovsky's translation of Rémond Des Cours's 1692 manual of good manners, *The True Politeness of Important and Well-Born Persons* (1737); published in a print-run of 1,200 (large, by the standards of the day), it was to be reprinted in 1745,

---

[39] Soviet accounts of Catherine's reign emphasized the monarch's intolerance and despotism (see e.g. Georgy Makogonenko's introduction to N. Novikov, *Izbrannye sochineniya* (Moscow and Leningrad, 1954), pp. viii–xii, xxi–xxiii). Recent Western accounts of the monarch's activities have been more nuanced, stressing Catherine's sensitivity to dangerous dissent, rather than all dissent, and also the constructive character of her activities in allowing private presses in 1783, and in sponsoring translation. See Marker, *Publishing, Printing and the Origins of Intellectual Life*; K. A. Papmehl, *Freedom of Expression in Eighteenth-Century Russia* (The Hague, 1971); I. de Madariaga, *Russia in the Age of Catherine the Great* (London, 1981).

[40] On the market for erotic fiction, see Marker, *Publishing, Printing and the Origins of Intellectual Life*, 119. A comparison of Sumarokov's early farce *Ssora muzha s zhenoi* (1759), an extremely broad and indeed coarse depiction of a marital tiff, and his later comedy *Rogonosets po voobrazheniyu* (1772), a witty delineation of a needlessly jealous husband, gives a vivid sense of changing tastes.

[41] Fonvizin's plays *Brigadir* and *Nedorosl'* (The Minor) are only the most famous examples of a very widely developed satirical tradition that also embraced Knyazhnin's *The Boaster* (Khvastun), Kapnist's *The Tatler* (Yabednik), and also such now forgotten pieces as Dmitry Khvostov's *The Russian Parisian* (Ruskoi parizhanets), in which boorishness and pretentious Gallomania (e.g. absurd neologisms such as *ekshpektovat'*) are held equally absurd. (See *Rossiiskii featr: ili Polnoe sobranie vsekh rossiiskikh Featral'nykh sochinenii* 15 (1787), 151–260.)

[42] Anon., *Yunosti chestnoe zertsalo*. The book appears to have been based on a compilation of various Western books of manners, by Erasmus and others.

1765, and 1787.[43] At about the same date when Trediakovsky's book was first published, well-informed Russian nobles, such as A. F. Khrushchev, began buying another kind of book on manners, instructing them on how to educate their daughters (Khrushchev translated two famous treatises of this kind, Fénelon's *Traité de l'éducation des filles* and Chétardie's *L'Éducation d'une jeune princesse*, in 1738; the translations were never published, but almost certainly circulated in manuscript).[44] And in 1742, Sergei Volchkov published *The Courtier*, his translation of Baltasar Gracián y Morales' famous *Oráculo manual y arte de prudencia* (1647), a treatise counselling self-restraint and the ability to dissemble as techniques for surviving in court life. According to the preface, the translation (which was dedicated to Empress Elizabeth) had been completed in 1735;[45] like Khrushchev's Fénelon versions, it had no doubt had a pre-publication life in manuscript.

Between 1749 and 1760, books on 'morals and pedagogy' (*moral' i pedagogika*) made up the third most popular category of French-language material sold at the Academy of Sciences bookshop in Moscow. Books in demand included, besides Fénelon, *Véritables devoirs de l'homme d'épée*, *Les Devoirs d'un gentilhomme*, *Entretiens utiles et agréables sur le moyen de plaire*, and *Le Passe partout galant*.[46] In 1761 came a first edition in book form of Madame de Lambert's *Avis d'une mère à sa fille et à son fils*, published, like Trediakovsky's translation, in a print-run of 1,200.[47]

But if books on conduct had gained some currency before Catherine II's

[43] [De Kur], *Istinnaya politika*. On the size of the print-run, compare the sales for the first edition of *Yunosti chestnoe zertsalo*, 311 copies (see Marker, *Publishing, Printing and the Origins of Intellectual Life*, 35). Lifetime sales for this book in its different editions were around 1,500. The most popular books in Russia from the early 18th cent. right up to the Revolution were calendars and devotional booklets such as psalters, which, as early as the 1710s, were printed in tens of thousands (ibid.). But a run of 1,000 copies was well above average for secular books.

[44] See P. I. Khoteev, 'Frantsuzskaya kniga v Biblioteke Peterburgskoi Akademii nauk (1714–1742 gg.)', in S. P. Luppov (ed.), *Frantsuzskaya kniga v Rossii XVIII veka: ocherki istorii* (Leningrad, 1986), 38.

[45] Gratsian, *Pridvornyi chelovek*, iii.

[46] For the dissemination of books on *moral' i pedagogika* generally, see N. A. Kopanev, 'Rasprostranenie frantsuzskoi knigi v Moskve v seredine XVIII veka', in Luppov (ed.), *Frantsuzskaya kniga v Rossii XVIII veka: ocherki istorii*, 83, Table 6; on the numbers of specific titles, see 81, Table 5. Kopanev does not give publication details for the books concerned: the only ones listed in Alain Montandon, *Bibliographie des traités de savoir-vivre en Europe*, 2 vols. (Clermont-Ferrand, 1995) are *Les Devoirs d'un gentilhomme*, by William Chappell (Amsterdam, 1709), and *Véritables devoirs de l'homme d'épée*, by Rémond des Cours (Paris, 1697).

[47] [A. de Lamber], *Pis'ma gospozhi de Lambert*; another trans. had appeared as early as 1732, in the journal *Primechaniya k vedomostyam* (on the latter see R. Yu. Danilevsky, 'Klassitsizm' in Yu. D. Levin (ed.), *Schöne Literatur in Russischer Übersetzung: von den Anfängen bis zum 18. Jahrhundert*, 2 vols. (St Petersburg, 1995), i. 113). The text continued to be read well into the 19th cent.: another trans. (from the German!) appeared in 1814 as *Rassuzhdeniya o vospitanii devits*, and an adaptation by Professor K. G. Geidenreikh in 1838 (as *Pridanoe moei docheri, sochinenie [. . .] izvlechennoe iz tvorenii znamenitoi pisatel'nitsy markizy de Lambert*: see the card-index of translated works in RNB).

accession, the number of publications in this area increased out of all recognition thereafter. The subject index of eighteenth-century books available in the Muzei Knigi, Moscow (the rare books department of the Russian State Library) lists more than 300 publications in the category of 'ethics' between 1762 and 1800, as compared with fifteen between 1700 and 1762. Notable among these were the first Russian translation of Fénelon's *De l'éducation des filles* (1763, in a print-run of no less than 1,800 copies), and a version of one of the most famous etiquette manuals in European culture, Erasmus of Rotterdam's *De civilitate morum puerilium*, which appeared in two separate editions in 1788, one of them with parallel texts in Russian and Latin.[48] Of course, the most cultivated Russians often continued to read such materials in the French original, or—if the original were in German or English—in French translation. The library of Princess Ekaterina Dashkova, one of the most influential figures of Catherine's reign, included two conduct books in French, *Discours sur l'éducation des dames* and *Cour d'éducation des demoiselles*, as well as the anonymous *Duties of the Female Sex*, translated into Russian from German (but perhaps based on a French original, Jacques Desmothes' *Les Devoirs des filles chrétiennes*).[49]

Behaviour manuals were by no means the only source through which new concepts of politeness and polite language might be acquired. Others were letter-writing guides, such as P. I. Bogdanovich's *A New and Complete Letter-Writer, or a Detailed and Clear Guide to Writing Commercial and Official Letters, Letters of Petition and Complaint, Congratulation, Friendship, Greeting and all kinds of Business letters; also Advertisements, Contracts, Records, Witnesses, Deeds of Trust and Obligation, Wills and So On* (1791), a book as compendious as its title, with an appendix of letters by famous people such as Christina Queen of Sweden, Pope Clement XVII, Voltaire, and Chesterfield (an abridged edition of whose works, *Dukh lorda Chesterfil'da*, was to come out in Russia in 1815).[50] Here, new forms of address were communicated, and a novel kind of correspondence, based on exchange of compliments as much as on exchange of information, flowery rather than practical, was introduced to the Russian public. Perhaps the most

---

[48] Fénelon, *O vospitanii devits*; Erazm Roterdamskii, *Molodym detyam nauka kak dolzhno sebya vesti*....

[49] On Dashkova's library, see A. Woronzoff-Dashkoff, 'Princess E. R. Dashkova's Moscow Library', *Slavonic and East European Review*, 72/1 (Jan., 1994), 70. Anon., *Dolzhnosti zhenskogo polu*.

[50] See M. P. Alekseev, 'Chesterfil'd v russkikh perevodakh', in Chesterfil'd, *Pis'ma k synu* (1978), 314. Alekseev argues that early Russian translations were based on Chesterfield's *Miscellaneous Works* of 1779 (ibid., 312); another source seems likely to have been popularizing anthologies of *bon mots* such as *Lord Chesterfield's Maxims: Or a New Plan of Education, on the Principles of Virtue and Politeness, in which the exceptionable Parts of the Noble Lord's Letters to his Son are carefully rejected, and such only preferred as cannot fail to form the Man of Honour, the Man of Virtue, and the Accomplished Gentleman* ('New edn.'; London, 1786).

triumphantly non-utilitarian communication in Bogdanovich's collection was the following letter to a correspondent thanking him—for being a correspondent:

Your most delightful letter of the . . . th of this month, filled with expressions of Your especial favour towards me, has reached me here in its due time; it brought me new confirmation of Your kind attention, for which I am indebted to You in the very liveliest manner, so that I consider it my duty to communicate to You by this letter my most respectful gratitude, and my assurance that the correspondence that You are conducting with me gives me extreme pleasure, increasing the sense of candour and goodwill that I feel towards You, and with which I have the honour to remain,
    Your most humble servant . . .[51]

Further sources of implausibly refined social relations were collections of compliments, witticisms, and other gems for inserting into conversation, and also phrasebooks and other texts used for language learning, such as the trilingual *Conversations on Domestic Matters* published in 1749, which went into eight editions by the end of the century. Here Russians could read model dialogues in which unfailingly patient masters conversed with their always well-spoken and courteous servants.[52] And eighteenth-century dictionaries indicate the process by which the Russian language absorbed new concepts of politeness. The terms *blagochinnost'*, *blagorodnost'*, and *blagopriyatnost'* had existed in medieval Russian, but *vezhlivost'*, which had formerly signified 'knowledge' (as opposed to 'ignorance') now came to signify someone who was 'knowing' in the sense of socially skilled, courteous.[53] And new adjectives appeared, first of all the direct borrowing from Western languages *politichnyi* (current in the first half of the eighteenth century, after which it—ironically!—became a vulgarism). Longer-lasting were *uchtivyi* (polite, considerate), and *blagovospitannyi* or *vospitannyi*, calqued from the French *bien-élevé*, which introduced a novel sense of good

[51] Bogdanovich, *Novyi i polnyi pis'movnik*, 175. See also Anon., *Nastavlenie, kak sochinyat' i pisat' vsyakie pis'ma* (1765). The subject of letter-writing etiquette in the 18th cent. has been extensively explored in G. Scheidegger's excellent study, *Studien zu den russischen Briefstellern des 18. Jahrhunderts und zur "Europäisierung" des russischen Briefstils* (Bern, 1980).

[52] *Gespräche von Haussachen/Razgovory o domashnikh delakh/Dialogues domestiques*. It is not clear how widely known in Russia was *The Traveller's Companion for Conversation, being a Collection of Such Expressions as Occur Most Frequently in Travelling, and in the Different Situations of Life* [. . .] *in Six Languages, English, German, French, Italian, Spanish and Portuguese* (new edn.; Leipzig and London, 1817), Madame de Genlis's diverting compendium of refined intercourse, which instructed the reader on everything from demanding 'pomegranate peelings and almond milk' for the complexion to giving lessons on manners as a governess ('You must not loll on the table with your elbows'). On compliments books, see Marker, *Publishing, Printing, and the Origins of Intellectual Life*, 35.

[53] On these terms, see I. I. Sreznevsky, *Materialy dlya slovarya drevnerusskogo yazyka*, 3 vols. (St Petersburg, 1893–1903), and compare with *Slovar' russkogo yazyka XVIII veka* (Leningrad, 1984–).

behaviour as the culmination of a process of moral indoctrination and socialization. There was also an explosion of different terms for rudeness, with *naglyi* (which had signified 'sudden', 'angry', or 'impetuous' in medieval Russian), and *derzkii* (which had meant 'daring' or 'brave') now coming to render *insolence, effronterie, véhemence*. Other terms pointed to the expected lack of refinement in what was beginning to be known as the *prostonarod'e*, or 'common people': *prostolyudnyi, prostonarodnyi, podlyi*, and *niskii (sic)* were all used in Zhdanov's Russian dictionary of 1784 to render the English word 'vulgar' (later, in the 1830s, *poshlyi* and *vul'garnyi* came into use in this sense as well). Gradually, too, 'improper' and 'indecent' words (which could now be described as *nepristoinye* and *neprilichnye*) such as *blyad'* (whore), began to disappear from the printed page. And the opposition *grubyi pol/nezhnyi pol* (coarse sex/tender sex)[54] which came into use in the late eighteenth century, not only stressed the importance of distinctions between the sexes, but also emphasized the role that women were supposed to play in the new polite culture as civilizers of the barbarous male, a role stressed in behaviour literature too. The next part of the chapter looks more closely at this literature, taking women and men in turn, since the genders were invariably considered separately in treatises of the day.

'THIS CONSIDERATION FOR ONESELF IS TERMED "MODESTY"': MORAL EDUCATION FOR WOMEN AND THE REPRESENTATION OF MATERNITY

The influence of women on the morals of their country, on the inner well-being of their families, and on the education of children, is generally recognized. *It is they who mould their daughters into all the virtues of their sex; it is they who first engrave in the hearts of their sons the love of God, of their sovereign, and of honour.*

(Madame Campan, *De l'éducation* (1824); emphasis in original)

---

[54] This information is based on a study of polyglot and defining dictionaries of the late 18th cent.: P. Zhdanov, *A New Dictionary of English and Russian. Novoi slovar' angliiskoi i rossiiskoi* (St Petersburg, 1784); Ivan Geym (Jean Heym), *Novyi rossiisko-frantsuzsko-nemetskii slovar', sochinennyi po slovaryu Rossiiskoi Akademii* (Moscow, 1799–1801); *Slovar' Akademii Rossiiskoi po azbuchnomu poryadku raspolozhennyi*, 1st and 2nd edns. (St Petersburg 1794–6 and 1806–22). *Slovar' russkogo yazyka XVIII veka*, ii. 72, asserts that *blyad'* disappeared from print in the 1730s. However, it is still to be found in Zhdanov, *A New Dictionary*, and in Heym, *Novyi rossiisko-frantsuzsko-nemetskii slovar'*, along with such resonant derivatives as *blyadnya* (whoredom) and *blyadin syn* (whoreson), though it had disappeared by the time that F. Reif (Philippe Reif) published his *Russko-frantsuzskii slovar'* (Moscow, 1835). On *grubyi pol/nezhnyi pol*, see *Slovar' russkogo yazyka XVIII veka*, v. 249.

Guides to appropriate behaviour for women published in the late eighteenth and early nineteenth centuries were of two types. The first advised women, and particularly young women, on how they should themselves behave. The second, and equally important, type counselled women on the upbringing of their children, and particularly of their daughters.

Immediately striking, in the case of the first type of book, is the paucity of detailed advice on etiquette and gesture—how to hold one's fork, how to greet others, how to make conversation, and so on. *On the Duties of Man and of Citizen*, which was used for teaching in Smol'nyi, has a section on manners which includes instructions on posture, expression, and demeanour at table, but the only point specifically addressed to women is on greetings: 'Men should always greet people by taking off their hat and cap . . . and women merely by inclining their head.'[55] Generally, it was only in popular medical treatises such as booklets about how to stay healthy that young women were given special information about female conduct: here assumptions about the delicacy of the female constitution meant that especial restraint in the use of stimulating substances such as wine and tobacco was recommended, though the books also warned their readers not to be afraid of fresh air and of moderate exercise.[56]

One reason for the absence of meticulous instruction on etiquette was, no doubt, that the teaching of manners was assumed to be transmitted by face-to-face contact. If a girl were educated at home, her mother and governess would correct her manners; if she were sent to an institution, the *dames de classe* would supervise her observation of the proprieties. But another, and equally important reason was the books' determination that polite accomplishments should be only part of a girl's schooling. Typical was *The Pocket-Book, or Aide-Mémoire for Young Ladies* (1784), used, like *On the Duties of Man and Citizen*, for teaching at Smol'nyi, which informed readers of society's demand for amusement—'Society is a form of trading exchange: everyone who wants to be involved has to pay his or her dues so as not to be a burden'—but which also examined at length the contribution to virtuous living that was made by the arts.[57] Similarly, Pierre Boudier de

---

[55] *O dolzhnostyakh cheloveka i grazhdanina*, 67; quoted from Black, *Citizens for the Fatherland*, 233.

[56] See e.g. Dzh. Gulen, *Damskii vrach* (1793); Anon., *Kakim obrazom mozhno sokhranit' zdravo…* (1793). It was less menstruation as such than the loss of energizing juices it involved that caused anxiety. Goulin sees women's frailty as a result of their propensity for weeping (93), and A. G. Bakherakht, *O neumerennosti v lyubostrastii oboikh polov*, in *Sobranie raznykh poleznykh lekarstv* (1779), 16, warns that masturbation and excessive congress in men cause weakness and 'effeminacy'. Material on decorum is included in 'The Crown of Maidenly Honour and Virtue' (the supplement to *Yunosti chestnoe zertsalo*), but this points to the old-fashioned nature of the advice there (see below).

[57] Anon., *Karmannaya, ili Pamyatnaya knizhka*, 6.

Villemert's *The Friend of Women* (1765) sententiously observed, 'The mind is always delighted by works of painting, music, and versifying, and particularly if these are in harmony with accepted morality.'[58] A condemnation of leisure pursuits that were considered threatening to decorum was a standard element in behaviour books for women.[59] Though reading was warmly recommended as a method of mental improvement, the well-conducted young woman should avoid anything salacious. As the Russian translation of Sarah Pennington's *An Unfortunate Mother's Advice to Her Absent Daughters* put it, 'Never devote yourself to the reading of Fairy Tales and Novels; it is true that some of these do contain good instruction for the morals, but since this is confused with indecent matters, they should still not be read.'[60]

As the phrase 'indecent matters' makes clear, it was above all the novel's celebration of love that was considered dangerous, since it lent lustre to an emotion of which moralists were in any case suspicious. (Some authors of behaviour books were careful to make clear that improving novels were perfectly acceptable, even if romantic ones were not.) Readers of tracts on behaviour were urged to prefer friendship, a more dependable and dignified emotion than love: as Madame de Lambert wrote in her *Traité de l'amitié* (1736), translated in 1772: 'When women show a love of duty, and demonstrate themselves equal in dignity to men, can there be anything better than [for men] to unite with them in ties of friendship?'[61] And behaviourists dwelled with mind-numbing repetitiveness upon the need for 'modesty' (*skromnost'*) in their young women readers: the phrase used by one writer, 'Modesty is the most amiable virtue in a young woman, and one essential at any age',[62] was a relatively laconic statement of a view expounded at much greater length on the pages of behaviour books from the early eighteenth century to the early nineteenth.

The negative trait equivalent to modesty was coquetry, roundly assailed by the Chevalier de La Chetardie, one of the authors translated by Khrushchev in the late 1730s, as

judgeable by the bad qualities that accompany persons branded by this infamous mode of behaviour: you will find in them a self-willed, spoiled demeanour [*un esprit gâté*], a corrupt heart, a soul without fidelity or tenderness, a reason bare of

---

[58] Bud'e de Vil'mer, *Drug zhenshchin*, 23.

[59] See e.g. Bud'e de Vil'mer, 'A woman infected with the inclination for frivolous amusements can never be a mother, a wife, a friend, or a citizen' (*Drug zhenshchin*, 53).

[60] [S. Penington], *Sovety*, 51. On Pennington, see J. Todd (ed.), *A Dictionary of British and American Women Writers 1660–1800* (London, 1987), 245–6: *An Unfortunate Mother's Advice* was the author's most popular work, going through at least ten editions in English alone between 1761 and 1800.

[61] A. Lamber, *Rassuzhdeniya o druzhestve*, 34.

[62] Espinasi, *Opyt o vospitanii*, 15.

good sense, a petty, constricted judgement, a vanity directed at nothing whatever, desires not oriented to a better principle, a shameful conversation filled with trivialities and with nonsense, a constant dissimulation, a false goodness seeking nothing but treachery under the mask of banal compliments, compliments only rendered in order to receive the same in return. In short, they serve up a mish-mash of words, of which they make a jargon that they prostitute to all the world . . .[63]

As the books also made clear, however, modesty was not simply the end point of women's self-denial, the instrument of their subjugation; it was also the source of their power. The case was made particularly effectively in a free translation of Louise d'Épinay's collection of dialogues *Conversations d'Émilie*, in which a mother clarified for her daughter the meaning of the term 'modesty':

MOTHER: And when men speak to you, then answer politely and with dignity; this consideration for oneself is termed *modesty*. . . .
DAUGHTER: How should a well-bred young lady behave?
MOTHER: She must become used as early as possible to being the most effective guardian of her own self.[64]

Modesty, that is, was a form of self-assertion, a refusal to become unduly reliant upon the good opinion of others. Hence Lambert's suggestion that, while being modest, one should not be excessively docile:

So far as religion goes, you should submit to the authorities; on every other subject, you should heed no other authority than reason and evidence. If you give too much place to docility, you assault the rights of reason, and do not make use of your own lights, which will accordingly grow dimmer. To confine your ideas to those of others is to allow them too narrow a space.[65]

The sense that moral guardianship was the source of a woman's authority was also the starting point for the second type of behaviour book, the guide to women on bringing up their daughters. By far the most important of these was Fénelon's *Traité de l'éducation des filles*, which went through four editions in the eighteenth century, and maintained its influence until at least the 1850s.[66]

---

[63] J. J. Trotti de La Chetardie, *Instruction pour une jeune princesse* (Paris, 1771: facs. edn., Paris, 1983), 154. Chetardie's book, first published in 1684, was often bound, in later edns., with Fénelon's *De l'éducation des filles*; this is the case with the 1771 edn. cited here. Anon., *Dolzhnosti zhenskogo polu*, warns women not only against immodest talk with men, but also against scandalous conversation with women: an industrious woman 'does not listen to the chatter of her gossip, and does not drink tea in anger; diligence is the substance of her talk' (46).

[64] [Epine], *Uchilishche yunykh devits*, conversation 5. Emphasis original.

[65] Anne-Thérèse de Lambert, 'Avis d'une mère à sa fille' in her *Œuvres*, ed. R. Granderoute (Paris, 1990), 113.

[66] The 1763 edition of Fénelon, *O vospitanii devits* was reprinted in 1774 and 1788; a new edition in 1794 included a translation of 'Lettre à une dame de qualité' (*SK* no. 7705). Another

Fénelon assumed that, from the age of 3 until adulthood, a daughter's education would be, directly or indirectly, the responsibility of her mother. Between 3 and 7 (the 'age of reason' in traditional theology), the mother would be responsible for teaching the daughter, or seeing that she was taught, her letters and also the fundamentals of religion (these two aspects of education were in fact inseparable from each other, given that a child's first reading materials in a primer were, up to the late eighteenth century, invariably taken from scripture).[67] Thereafter, she was either to engage a governess (instructions on choosing a good one were provided), or to continue instructing her daughter herself. Fénelon was insistent that a girl's education should be of the highest possible quality and that supervising it was an entirely appropriate task for the aristocratic women to whom he addressed himself. Though convinced of the innate difference of men and women (he thought women more inclined to 'moral frailty', and in particular, to vices such as frivolity), he was an ardent supporter of women's education as a corrective to this, and not only for negative reasons (because it taught girls to avoid vice), but also for positive ones—because it provided women with interests other than pleasure and love, and gave them a sense of autonomy—a point that also applied to the mother (since spending time in the schoolroom was preferable to gallivanting in the *grand monde*).

This emphasis on the link between education, continence, and self-reliance was also found in the works of Fénelon's successors, such as Madame de Lambert, or Mademoiselle d'Espinassy, author of *An Essay on the Education of Young Noblewomen* (1778):

When giving your daughter instruction, you should attempt to stamp out in her those fantastical [*mechtatel'nye*] and laughable fancies to which so many women are subject. Here I am speaking not only about the fears and whims that come to them from childhood, but their opinions on dreams, portents of happiness, and all kinds of secret knowledge, which run directly contrary to sound reason [*zdravyi razum*] and which have no other foundation than the superstition of the common people; so too [should you try to stamp out] that

trans. appeared in 1794. He was much admired by Catherine II, who claimed to read him every day. In the 1850s, the famous male feminist M. L. Mikhailov was still citing Fénelon's *Traité de l'éducation des filles* quite seriously as a source on the purposes of women's education. (I owe this information to a paper on Mikhailov presented by Jennifer Lonergan to the seminar on Women in Russia and Eastern Europe at CREES, University of Birmingham, 28 Feb. 1996.) In Fonvizin's play *The Minor*, IV. i, the *raisonneur* Starodum ('Mr Oldthoughts') congratulates the virtuous heroine when he finds her reading Fénelon: 'I do not know your book, but the author of *Télémaque* will never corrupt anyone's morals with his pen.' *O vospitanii devits* is perhaps the likeliest candidate for Sof'ya's book, though other conduct guides by Fénelon translated into Russian include *Obshchiya pravila* (1779).

[67] See Max Okenfuss, *The Discovery of Childhood in Russia: the Evidence of the Slavic Primer* (Newtonville, Mass., 1980), for a brief account of a subject that badly needs a fuller treatment.

extreme instability of feelings [*mezhnost' chuvstv*] which so often causes them unhappiness.[68]

Independence of mind was the more important because all the writers assumed that the overriding purpose of women's education was to prepare them for dynastic marriages where affect would play little, if any, part. In this world where men impinged on women primarily as inseminators or as sexual predators, virtue was essential as a means to independence. And it was a mother's duty to prepare the way to autonomous adulthood for her daughter, inculcating wisdom that would in turn be transmitted to her daughter's own daughters, and so on in an endless tradition of *éducation maternelle*. It should not be supposed that the knowledge imparted was limited to domestic matters (though that impression is sometimes given in secondary discussions): the books advocated quite a wide syllabus, embracing not only household management but also accountancy (important so that a woman can manage her own inheritance), and not only modern languages, music, embroidery, and other such genteel accomplishments, but also history, literature, and sometimes even classical languages, mathematics, and science.[69] The Smol'nyi programme in the early years of the institute was similarly broad (as mentioned earlier, it included geography, economics, history, architecture, ethics, science, and household economy)—and the goals of the moral education given there were self-restraint, self-sufficiency, and cooperation with other women. Betskoi's plan for the school urged that girls who were shy and melancholy should be gently encouraged to come into society. There was to be no 'excessive sentimentality' (*izlishnyaya nega*) in their treatment, but also no needless authoritarianism. The organization of plays and concerts would give pupils who performed a chance to increase their social self-confidence, and pupils who directed an opportunity to get used to exercising authority politely.[70] The goals of the education were 'obedience to superiors, mutual politeness, gentleness, self-control, egalitarian morality, and a pure, just heart zealous for doing good'. Graduates of the school were awarded a certificate testifying to their absorption of these values as well as to their intellectual accomplishments:

The well-born young woman named .... who holds this certificate has completed a twelve-year course of education at this SOCIETY and, having worked with zeal and application, has attained excellent levels in the decorous

---

[68] [Espinasi], *Opyt o vospitanii*, 37.

[69] See e.g. Fénelon, *De l'éducation des filles*, chs. xi–xii; Anon., *Sovety ot vospitatel'nitsy k vospitannitse* (1787), 43–4: 'There are sciences far more useful than needlework [. . .] those demanding attentiveness and a good memory.. Those specified include history, geography, drawing, and the reading of worthy books.

[70] Betskoi, *Ustav vospitaniya*, *passim*. See also Black, *Citizens for the Fatherland*, ch. 7.

conduct appropriate to good breeding, as well as excellent levels in the intellectual disciplines, and in the sciences and handicrafts that are appropriate to her sex and requisite for the management of the household . . .'[71]

As interpreted by Enlightenment educational theorists, then, modesty was a prerequisite not only of female honour, but of women's role as elevated moral beings; as guardians of modesty, mothers were not merely preserving their daughters from social disaster, but also ensuring their own supremacy as the regulators of morality. The view of maternity as above all a pedagogical and moral condition, coupled with the rise of euphemism in print culture, meant that the biological aspects of the mother–child relationship were more or less elided in eighteenth-century guides for women. Books giving advice on women's health discuss sexual reproduction in a manner that is at times so abstract as to be nearly incomprehensible: take, for instance, this coy definition published in a guide translated from the German that appeared in Russia in 1793: 'Pregnancy is when a woman, a few days after her connexion with a man, finds herself in a condition other than the one in which she previously was.'[72]

This hierarchy of maternity dictated that impolite and messy tasks such as breast-feeding, nappy-washing, and other necessities of infant care, remained the concerns of lower-class women (*mamki* and *nyani*), while the upper-class lady busied herself with the spiritual and intellectual development of her child. Maternal love, a quality that began to be of considerable concern to theorists in the second half of the eighteenth century, was little discussed as such, and there was little emphasis on any biological bond between mother and child.[73]

This coherent, albeit rather restricted, view of the maternal role did not long hold unchallenged sway in Russia. The eccentric chronology so often evident in Russian importation of Western ideas meant that Fénelon and Lambert, with their emphasis on women's need for autonomy within marriage, on the primacy of moral education, and on a rational rather than emotional appreciation of family relations, arrived on Russian soil at much the same time as a very different view of the ideal family. This stressed that a woman's central duty was to her husband rather than to her children, and that the focal point of family relations was harmony rather than reason. Those expressing it included Marie Leprince de Beaumont, author of

---

[71] Quoted in Cherepnin, *Imperatorskoe vospitatel'noe obshchestvo*, i. 224. On the *klassnye damy* see ibid. i. 56.

[72] Gulen, *Damskoi vrach*, 168. Goulin is equally coy about the sexual act, describing it as 'the moment when two hearts that are strongly bonded and feel the impression of the tenderest love, surrender themselves to pleasure in its most vivid form' (158). On nurses' responsibility for infancy, see Espinasi, *Opyt o vospitanii*, 2–3.

[73] For a helpful, if rather schematic, survey of discussions of maternal love, see Y. Knibiehler and C. Fouquet, *L'Histoire des mères: du moyen-âge à nos jours* (Paris, 1980), 140–214.

massively popular sub-Socratic dialogues for the schoolroom in which a governess, 'Madame Morality', instructed her youthful pupils, 'Mademoiselle Impetuous' and others, on the rules of good conduct and rational behaviour. Especially popular was *Magasin des enfans*, translated as *Detskoe uchilishche* (1761–7), which had gone into twelve Russian editions, in print-runs as high as 2,000 copies, by 1800. The book also circulated in French.[74]

Leprince de Beaumont was, indeed, so well known in Russia that Louise d'Épinay's much livelier *Les Conversations d'Émilie* was attributed to Beaumont when first translated into Russian in 1784, and given a title, *Uchilishche yunykh devits*, that imitated the titles of the latter's works in Russian.[75] There was considerable irony in this, given that Épinay, a feminist known for her polemics with Diderot, very much conformed to the older 'Lambertian' model of autonomy within marriage, while Leprince de Beaumont went so far, in *Magasin des adolescentes*, as to suggest that even modest attire should be given up if the husband required it. Indeed, one of the moral tales inserted in Leprince de Beaumont's *Magasin des enfans* was her famous retelling of *La Belle et la bête*, in which a young woman (who, being motherless, has not been the object of *éducation maternelle*) learns to respect and love an apparently forbidding husband whom she has not chosen for herself.[76]

By the 1780s, Russians who could read French were also able to absorb the ideas of Madame de Genlis, another advocate of educating girls to suit their husbands. Her treatise-as-epistolary-novel *Adèle et Théodore* (1781), composed as a series of letters written by Adèle and Théodore's mother, set out quite a formidable syllabus of reading for Adèle, ranging from Aquinas to Cervantes, from Corneille to Thomson and Shakespeare, from Ariosto

[74] Leprins de Bomon, *Detskoe uchilishche, eadem, Yunosheskoe uchilishche* (1774); *eadem, Uchilishche devits* (1784); *eadem, Nastavlenie molodym gospozham* (1788); *Pravila dlya obshchezhitiya* (1800–1). Leprince de Beaumont's popularity may have had something to do with a Russian connection—see her *Magasin des Enfans* (London, 1792), 5, which has a dedication to Pavel Petrovich, 'grandson of Peter the Great', and a flattering tribute to Tsaritsa Elizabeth: 'she combined in the same degree the qualities that go to make great rulers and those that are proper to persons of her sex'.

[75] [Epine], *Uchilishche yunykh devits* (in the note to *SK* 3461, the editors state 'Frantsuzskii original ne ustanovlen'). Épinay's book appeared in Russian under its own name in 1798, but was not as popular as Leprince de Beaumont's works (though Karamzin had certainly read Épinay: see W. Mills Todd III, *The Familiar Letter*, 96).

[76] On Leprince de Beaumont's version, see Marina Warner's interesting comments in her *From the Beast to the Blonde: On Fairy Tales and their Tellers* (London, 1994), 292–7. Sergei Aksakov's *Detskie gody Bagrova-vnuka* contains a version of the Beauty and the Beast narrative, 'Alen'kii svetochek', which is told to the narrator by his Russian nanny, and described as 'an Oriental tale' (see *Semeinaya khronika*, 262). However, Aleksandr Ospovat is surely right to state that Leprince de Beaumont's version is the source here too (see 'Aksakov, S. T.', *Russkie pisateli: biograficheskii slovar'*, i (Moscow, 1987), 38). A telltale linguistic detail is that the Beast is transformed at the end of the tale not into a *knyaz'* but a *prints* (*Semeinaya khronika*, 363).

through Petrarch and Molière to Boileau, Pope, Locke, and even (after her marriage) Rousseau, and including women writers such as Mary Wortley Montagu and Madame de Lafayette. However, Adèle, as her mother made clear, had been prevented from consuming unduly imaginative works, not because these were likely to corrupt her, but because women were born for 'a dependent and monotonous life', and so 'genius is for them a useless and dangerous gift' (*le génie est pour eux un don inutile et dangereux*).[77] Rather than the key to resourcefulness after marriage, education that develops the mind (and does not simply furnish a woman with the means of entertaining her husband) is now seen as a threat to conjugal stability.

Éducation maternelle was not under assault only by conservative writers such as Genlis. Since the 1760s, attacks upon over-educated brides, and advocacy of education by the husband, had also been coming from the opposite political direction. The fifth part of Rousseau's *Émile*, for example, assaulted girls' boarding schools, poured scorn on female intellectuals ('I would a hundred times rather have a homely girl, simply and crudely brought up, than a learned lady and a wit who would make a literary circle of my house and instal herself as its president'), and presented Sophie as a properly empty vessel to be filled with Émile's ideas:

[Sophie's] education is neither showy nor neglected; she has taste without deep study, talent without art, judgement without learning. Her mind knows nothing, but it is trained to learn; it is well-tilled soil ready for the seed. She has read no book but *Barème* and *Telemachus* which happened to fall into her hands; but no girl who can feel so passionately towards Telemachus can have a heart without feeling or a mind without delicacy. What a charming ignoramus! Happy is he who is destined to instruct her. She will not be her husband's teacher but his scholar; far from seeking to subject him to her tastes, she will take on his. She will suit him far better than a learned woman [*savante*]; he will have the pleasure of teaching her everything.[78]

All this was hardly going to appeal to Smol'nyi's creator, who piqued herself on her intellectual independence; and indeed, Catherine had banned the import or sale of foreign editions of *Émile* in 1763, shortly after her accession, and a year before the foundation of the Russian St Cyr.

[77] Quotation from S. de Genlis, *Adèle et Théodore, ou lettres sur l'éducation, contenant tous les principes relatifs aux trois différens plans d'éducation, des princes, des jeunes personnes, et des hommes*, 3 vols. (Maastricht, 1781), i. 31. Russian translations (as *Adeliya i Teodor*) appeared in 1791, 1792, and 1794. Genlis's novel occupies a sort of intermediate genre between the educational treatise and didactic fiction, in which she also specialized. Her works and those of Sophie Cottin (author, *inter alia*, of *Élisabeth, ou les éxiles de Sibérie* (1806) and *Malvina* (1800)) were extremely popular in Russia. The fact that variants of the phrase 'useless gift' can be found in the work of Russian women writers of the early 19th cent., e.g. Elena Gan and Karolina Pavlova, may be in part a tribute to Genlis's influence.

[78] J. J. Rousseau, *Émile, ou de l'éducation*, ed. Charles Wirz and Pierre Burgelin (Paris, 1995), 604, 605–6. English trans. adapted from *Émile*, trans. Barbara Foxley (London, 1992), 445, 447.

A Russian translation of Part V that appeared in 1779 (as *Émile and Sophie, or the Well-Brought-Up (blagovospitannye) Lovers*) was heavily cut, omitting both the passages cited above, though it did still make clear Sophie's destiny as virtuous wife (indeed, the Russian text, by substituting *blagopoluchie* for *schast'e*, placed a greater emphasis on duty than the original):

No one can have a higher ideal of a virtuous woman, and she is not in the least daunted by this; but she would rather think of a virtuous man, a man of true worth; she knows that she is made for such a man, that she is worthy of him, that she can make him as happy as he will make her; she is sure she will know him when she sees him; the only difficulty is to find him.

Не можно иметь понятия о честной женщине, выше того каковое она себе зделала; и оно ее не ужасает. Но о честном мущине, о мущине с достойнствами, она снисходительнее помышляет. София чувствует, что она рождена для такового мущины; что его достойна, и что может наградить его взаимным благополучием, что она умеет его узнать, только бы встретиться с ним.[79]

But after Catherine's death, the embargo on Rousseau was lifted, and in 1813, the first full-length translation of the text into Russian appeared.[80]

To be sure, there were some limits on the absorption of 'natural motherhood' in Russia. Perhaps because of the famous prevalence of French in the Russian upper classes, and the near-universal use of nurses, the notion of mother as initiator of the child's first linguistic experiences impinged little on the Russian consciousness. Though the Swiss theorist Johann Heinrich Pestalozzi's treatise on maternal supervision of the early years of childhood, *Das Buch der Muetter*, was translated into Russian in 1806, it was not reprinted, and it was the earlier model, according to which the mother took charge of the child only once it was considered rational, that had more currency.[81] But the notion of an innate bond between child and mother, and of a biologically determined female destiny, did begin appearing in manuals during the early nineteenth century. For example, Ivan Bogdanovich, author of a pioneering Russian childcare manual published in 1807, informed his readers that it was 'the very first duty of every mother not to deprive her infant of that food which has been destined for him by nature'. The arguments that Bogdanovich employed involved social squeamishness (wet-nurses were likely to come from 'a situation in life that is still ill-equipped for such a high duty') and the puritanical notion that a mother who was kept

---

[79] Rousseau, *Émile*, 588 (trans. adapted from Foxley's, 431–2). Russian text from Zh. Zh. Russo, *Emil' i Sofiya*, 18.

[80] Russo, *Emil'* (1813).

[81] Pestalotstsi, *Kniga dlya materei*. The Russian State Library has only one copy of this book, kept in the Muzei Knigi, an indication of its rarity.

breast-feeding was unlikely to have time to spend in idle and frivolous coquetry.[82]

By the early nineteenth century, then, three different views of women's education were available to Russian readers. According to the first, it was supposed to prepare them for independence in a marriage that might very well offer them little emotional closeness. Hence the importance of *Éducation maternelle*, education of daughters by mothers, the intellectual and moral preparation for a life in which a woman's instruction of her own children was not only her highest duty, but her most reliable pleasure. According to the second view, marriage was above all important as a relationship between husband and wife; the moral education of daughters, while important, had as its end the production of a dutiful and companionable wife, whose accomplishments were such as were soothing, rather than challenging, to her spouse. According to the third view, which was an extreme version of the second, almost all education offered to a woman before marriage risked trespassing on a husband's rights to mould the wife that he required; it was also a foolish attempt to interfere with the inalienable biological difference between men and women. All three views concurred on the point that women should manifest 'modesty', but two alternative understandings of that term were available. For writers such as Rousseau and Genlis, 'modesty' signified intellectual passivity, self-control and self-denial in the cause of accommodation to a husband's interest; but for Fénelon, Lambert, and later Louise d'Épinay, it meant a heightened sense of self-awareness and self-respect; something not too dissimilar, in fact, from the sense of 'honour' that was demanded of young men.[83]

'MAN IS PREDETERMINED TO LIVE IN SOCIETY, AND DUTIES ARE THE TIES THAT BIND HIM TO THAT SOCIETY': MEN'S MORAL EDUCATION FROM 1760

It is pleasant to think that you will see my name among those of the young people indebted to you for the happiest days of their life, and be able to say: 'No one who studied in the Lyceum can be accused of ingratitude.'

(Pushkin, 1817)[84]

---

[82] See Bogdanovich, *O vospitanii yunoshestva*, 15, 21, 17–19. Cf. Levshin, *Polnaya khozyaistvennaya kniga* (1813), 198.

[83] In *Pis'ma Gospozhi Lambert*, the term used is *blagochestie*, or 'inner honour' (see e.g. p. 92).

[84] Note in the album of E. A. Engel'gardt, the first Director of the Tsarskoe Selo Lyceum. *PSS* xvii. 228.

One striking difference between materials on the moral education of men and of women is the lack of books under the title *Advice to Fathers on Bringing Up Their Sons*. This is not because normative guides took this to be the sole duty of the mother—though some writers, such as Fénelon, did assume that women would have care of their sons between the ages of 3 and 7, during which time they would be taught alongside their sisters—but because institutionalization always played a more considerable role in the education of boys than of girls. Once Peter I had enforced a connection between schooling and service by making adequate education a require-ment of post-holders in public service, boys' education necessarily acquired a vocational character. Preference for high-level posts in the civil or military service was given to those who had been prepared from the beginning for a life of duty and active citizenship by being educated in an elite institute such as the Corps des Pages, the School of Guards Sub-Ensigns and Cavalry Junkers, the Tsarskoe Selo Lyceum (founded 1811) and the College of Jurisprudence (founded 1835). Moreover, moral education at boys' schools was above all centred on the dissemination of social duty. Among the essay titles which Koshansky, teacher of rhetoric and literature at the Tsarskoe Selo Lyceum, set to his pupils was, for instance, the following *sententia*: 'The strict execution of one's duties is the source of the greatest possible pleasure'; a surviving attempt at the subject, by Pavel Illichevsky, began with the words, 'Man is pre-determined to live in society . . . and duties are the ties that bind him to that society.'[85]

The emphasis on 'citizenship' did not, however, mean that boys were not inducted in manners as well. On the contrary, their upbringing provided them, like girls, with tuition in the social graces. Indeed, behaviour books for boys provide much more concrete guidance on the details of etiquette than those for women. The pattern was set by *The Honourable Mirror of Youth* (1717): while the second part of this instructed young women in such abstract qualities as piety and humility, its first part, the *Mirror* proper, aimed at young men, was an eminently practical behaviour manual. Readers were told to stand up straight, rather than 'lolling in the sun like a peasant'; not to interrupt; to be obedient and respectful to their parents; to avoid drunkenness, gaming, spiteful gossip, and fornication. In company, the guide went on, one should not belch, cough, eat greedily; swearing and staring at women in church were both to be avoided. Though the reader was informed that a training in languages and eloquence might prove useful, the main education envisaged was in the restrained manners expected in a 'civilized', which is to say European, society.

[85] K. Ya. Grot, *Pushkinskii litsei: Bumagi pervogo kursa, sobrannye akademikom Ya. K. Grotom* (St Petersburg, 1911), 361. Citations henceforth in text, as Grot, 000 etc.

What is more, behaviour manuals aimed at young men preoccupied themselves at length with the question of how to behave with those further up the social scale than oneself. This is already evident in the *Mirror*'s emphasis on 'obedience' and 'respect'. Nearly sixty years later, another behaviour book aimed at men, *The Science of Being Polite* (1774), was a good deal more detailed in its injunctions. The tone to be adopted in conversation was a mixture between cheerfulness and solemnity (*veselie* and *vazhnost'*); impertinence and fawning self-abasement were alike to be avoided (the reader was told not to rush to praise someone's jewel, which might look like flattery, but to be certain to admire it when the opportunity arose). There was a need for especially scrupulous behaviour in the company of a *vazhnaya osoba* (important person). For example, it was important to cede precedence when entering a room, walking round a garden, or down a street, and one should wait patiently to be seen when paying a call.[86] Conversational refinements should also be observed: for example, one should not say, 'Ty sdelai' (You do that), but 'Pokorneishe proshu zdelat' siyu milost'' (I humbly beg of you to do me this favour); one should use 'Sir' and 'Madam' constantly in conversation, and one should avoid self-praise and boasting about one's wife and children (or indeed, talking of them at all).[87] As another advice book summed up: 'Courtesy is the polite and politic bewitching of persons of high rank' (*Uchtivstvo est' politicheskoe volkhvovanie vysokikh person*).[88]

In contrast, where a status ladder was alluded to in books for women, the reader was generally assumed to be at the top of it. Hence, there was considerable concern with the proper manner in which to treat servants and inferiors, rather than advice on how to be ingratiating with superiors. What is more, the relationship with servants that is suggested was of a different order: women were generally advised to be condescending but affable, but men to establish a clear social distance between themselves and their underlings. As phrased by *Friendly Advice to a Young Man Beginning to Live in the World* (1765), 'Do not have any social contact with your servants. Always remember, that you are their master; however, be forbearing and merciful in your dealings with them.'[89]

---

[86]   *Nauka byt' uchtivym*, passim. Cf. *Pravila uchtivosti* (1779), rules 8–27.

[87]   Ibid., rules 9, 8, 13. Besides this, the writer also advises that one should not use 'sir' ambiguously, as in the sentence 'Ya znayu, sudar', chto vy loshad' kupili' (approximately, 'Sir, I know you to be an ass's owner').

[88]   [Grabinsky], *Druzheskie sovety*, 29. This immensely popular book went through no less than eight editions between 1765 and 1794 (see *SK* 2034–2041).

[89]   For the advice to men, see [Grabinsky], *Druzheskie sovety*, 34. On women's treatment of servants, see e.g. Lambert, Genlis, *Adèle et Théodore*; and cf. Catherine II's note on manners, quoted above. Aksakov's fictional autobiography recounts how the narrator's mother struggled to overcome the traditional family hierarchy that was imposed on women as well as men. After the death of the Bagrov grandmother, she, as the wife of his eldest son, was considered the head of

The treatises also drew a distinction between the perceived role of men and women regarding the enforcement of society's moral regulations, with women seen as the quintessential arbiters of correct behaviour. Young men were often directed (as, for example, in *The Science of Being Polite*) to be particularly courteous in the company of women: ('be more careful to observe [in their company] than elsewhere, whether you can do something to please'); women, conversely, were counselled against an undue reliance on the good opinion of men.

It is possible that the authors of treatises on women's education and on men's behaviour expected their readers to be distinguished not only by sex, but by class. Certainly, the former seem to have anticipated as readers upper-class women concerned to safeguard their daughters from too early an initiation into the dubious morals of society, whose manners these daughters were, however, expected to osmose without being given special training. The latter, on the other hand, perhaps spoke primarily to young men from outside the upper classes eager to get on in the world, but with no idea about how to hold their forks or with what to blow their noses.[90] However, implied and actual readers are not necessarily the same, and there is some evidence that that etiquette manuals were used in the education of upper-class boys as well: Prince Dmitry Dashkov, for example, complained to a correspondent about being 'plagued' with a publication under the title *Manuel de civilité honnête et puerile* (no doubt a French adaptation of Erasmus) while at school.[91] The instructions to observe deferential manners had an eminently practical function in a social context where a young man would need patrons in order to advance himself, just as the advice that one should not assert one's own opinion too confidently was mere common sense in a society where abrasiveness was

the female side of the family, but repudiated this position, and tried to persuade her 'junior' female relatives (i.e. her husband's sisters) that their relationship should be on a footing of equality: 'Aleksei Stepanych, please advise your sister that she should not attempt to wait on me like a chambermaid' (*Detskie gody Bagrova-vnuka, Semeinaya khronika*, 332).

[90] The reluctance of nobles to become involved in drudgery meant that chancellery posts could be a route to social self-betterment on the part of literate boys from merchant and clergy families. Two cases in point were the writers Ivan Barkov and Mikhail Chulkov. On the *krapivoe semya* ('nettle-seeds'), see also M. Raeff, *Origins of the Russian Intelligentsia: The Eighteenth-Century Russian Nobility* (New York, 1966), 52–3.

[91] See W. Mills Todd III, *The Familiar Letter as a Literary Genre in the Age of Pushkin* (Princeton, 1976), 67. Erasmus was no less committed to deference than were the authors of other manuals: he advised his readers to repeat people's titles often, cede precedence when walking, and to adopt a modest and industrious posture: Erasmus Desiderius, *Declamation contenant la maniere de bien instruire les enfans, des leur commencement. Auec ung petit traicte de la ciuilite puerile. Le tout translate nouuellement de Latin en Francois, par Pierre Saliat* (Paris, 1537). *De civilitate* is 55–74. Similar advice was given also by the impeccably rational John Locke, who recommended in his *Some Thoughts Concerning Education* (1690), section 109, 'deference, complaisance and civility' rather than 'insolent domineering' (see section 111 of the Russian text, *O vospitanii detei gospodina Lokka*, 246).

unlikely to win powerful friends.[92] As a trilingual anthology of maxims from Fénelon summed up in ghastly doggerel:

> Совету следуйте разумному других;
> Не будьте в мнениях упорными своих —
> О чем вам говорят, прилежно то внимайте;
> Высокоумия всемерно избегайте.[93]

> List to the counsels that you hear, if these be wise,
> Do not be hard-necked in arguing your side;
> Be sure you listen carefully to whatever people say;
> Avoid being uppity in any way.

At the same time, the advice literature emphasized the fact that reticence on its own was not enough. Madame de Lambert, for example, advised against undue shyness in company: 'Nothing less suits a young man than modesty of a certain kind [*une certaine modestie*], which makes him believe that he is not capable of great things.'[94] Given that persuasiveness would be necessary in order to engage and please a patron, eloquence was seen as a key to social success: some books, such as Vasily Trediakovsky's version of *The True Politesse of Important and Noble Persons*, urged on readers the need to become skilled in formal rhetoric:

This most remarkable science [*siya preizryadnaya nauka*] is sometimes of great aid, and most particularly in those situations in which strength, bravery and courage are not effective. It provides an artful way of gaining favours from Princes and great persons, and also of ordering affairs and contracts with others, with enemies and also with foreign persons.[95]

The Russian version of Gracián went so far as to argue that constrained manners were fatal to true politeness: 'Not only does a bad manner spoil everything, but it also makes sincerity and reason ugly . . . But an unaffected manner that is naturally free [pleasantly] surprises other people, and makes the whole of human existence more beautiful.'[96] For its part, a treatise by the Abbé Bellegarde, *A Consideration of What Pleases*

---

[92]   On patronage, cf. G. Derzhavin, *Zapiski*, ed. P. Bartenev (Moscow, 1860), 25, 122; and see the excellent short discussion in Dixon, *The Modernisation of Russia*, 137–9.

[93]   *Obshchiya pravila zhizni*, 7. Cf. [Trotti de la Shetardi], *Nastavlenie znatnomu molodomu cheloveku* (1778), which advises young men they should prefer the rules of the Gospels to those of society when dealing with 'offences' (section 19), but also instructs them: 'If you are to succeed at court, you must know the value to yourself of the personages that you will encounter there' (section 38); and the emphasis upon 'address' in *Lord Chesterfield's Maxims*, 3–4, 22, 25.

[94]   Lambert, 'Avis d'une mère à son fils', *Œuvres*, 60–1; *Pis'ma Gospozhi de Lambert*, 7.

[95]   [De Kur], *Istinnaya politika*, 16. Cf. *Lord Chesterfield's Maxims*, 100–1. On rhetoric in men's education see Andrew Kahn's Introduction to M. N. Murav'ev, *Institutiones Rhetoricae: A Treatise of a Russian Sentimentalist* (Oxford, 1995), pp. xiii–lxix.

[96]   Gratsian, *Gratsian, Pridvornoi chelovek*, rule 14, p. 10.

and Does Not Please in Social Intercourse, which appeared in Russian translation in 1795, saw those who could not speak convincingly as bumpkins: 'The denizens of provincial towns and pedants are equally tiresome in their politeness; if they once begin paying compliments, then there is no end to the business.'[97] In the typically elegant formulation of Madame de Lambert, the distinction between morality for men and morality for women was that the former operated according to a vertical measure, the latter according to a horizontal measure: 'There are some great virtues which, taken to a certain degree, allow many faults to be pardoned: supreme bravery [*valeur*] in men, and extreme modesty [*pudeur*] in women. Agrippina, wife of Germanicus, was pardoned everything on account of her chastity.'[98] As *valeur* and *pudeur* are opposed, so too are 'supreme' and 'extreme', with their connotations of ascent and sideways movement. In the horizontally determined arena of honour in which women were seen to move, the danger of approaching another sort of 'extreme'—that beyond the bounds of decent society—was always present. Accordingly, modesty, self-deprecation, and restraint were absolute pre-requisites of female behaviour, and to be constantly reinforced by the vigilance of the maternal eye; however, men could gain everything if they would only dare to try. Yet there were also alternative voices: for example Nikolai Kurganov's much-reprinted *Letter-Writer* (which, despite its name, was actually a collection of grammatical rules and moral precepts), directed its readers: 'The world is no more than a spectacle [*pozorishche*], where everyone in turn comes out to play his part. . . . Neither high ranks [*imenitye chiny*] nor great riches make a person completely happy, but something else, pertaining to peace and quiet of the heart and spirit.'[99] The prevalence of such sentiments was reinforced not only by the Orthodox tradition of regarding *smirenie*, humility, as a positive trait in both sexes, but also by Masonic concepts of virtue, which emphasized inner stillness and external self-control.[100]

Something of a contradiction, then, emerged from advice literature for men. On the one hand, the ideal young man was self-restrained, modest, and malleable; on the other hand, he was eloquent, assertive through

---

[97] *Rassuzhdeniya o tom, chto mozhet nravit'sya*, 249.

[98] 'Avis d'une mère à sa fille', *Œuvres*, 100; *Pis'ma Gospozhi de Lambert*, 93. The dichotomy between valour and shame that Lambert sets up was wholly conventional, in terms of French culture—see I. Maclean, *Woman Triumphant: Feminism in French Literature, 1610–1652* (Oxford, 1977), 1–63—but apparently new in Russia: it is striking that the title of the 1761 translation of Lambert drew attention to it by inserting the words *chest'* and *dobrodetel'*.

[99] Kurganov, *Pismovnik [sic.], soderzhashchii v sebe nauku rossiiskogo yazyka*, i. 316. First printed in 1777, the *Pismovnik* was republished in 1777, 1788, and 1790, and remained in print (with interpolations by diverse hands) until well into the 19th cent.

[100] For a discussion of this, see Smith, 'Freemasonry and the Public', 291–5.

manipulation if nothing else, and not unduly modest. Clearly, with modesty seen as a necessary attribute of those low down in the social ranks, a young male of the upper classes was in something of a dilemma about whether and how to manifest it. The books were ambivalent, too, about how far freedom and ease of manner should go in another sense: the revelation of one's inner feelings. For Gracián, the 'perfect man' was restrained, firm-willed, and self-controlled, yet one of the three hundred rules of life was 'to be secretive and reserved at times, at others to be open and direct' (*vremenno skrytno, drugim otkrovenno postupat'*).[101]

All in all, the emphasis, in men's upbringing, on 'outward education' *vneshnee vospitanie* and on social duty, in no sense excluded the expectation that they would also acquire a private or personal sense of morality, however much this might be suggested by a superficial reading of Pushkin's playful description of Evgeny Onegin's education:

Судьба Евгения хранила:
Сперва *Madame* за ним ходила,
Потом *Monsieur* ее сменил.
Ребенок был резов, но мил.
Monsieur l'Abbé, француз убогой,
Чтоб не измучилось дитя,
Учил его всему шутя,
Не докучал моралью строгой,
Слегка за шалости бранил
И в Летний сад гулять водил.   (I. iii)

Fate took care of Evgeny;
First of all *Madame* looked after him,
Then *Monsieur* replaced her.
The child was playful, but sweet.
Monsieur l'Abbé, a nondescript Frenchman,
In order not to tax the child's strength,
Made a joke out of all his lessons,
Did not bore him with strict morality,
Scolded him a little when he was mischievous,
And took him for walks in the Summer Garden.

The irony of this passage, undermining Evgeny's later status as moralizer, would have lost its force had the young men of Pushkin's generation invariably been left to form their own views of right and wrong undirected. In fact, normative sources were as concerned with the moral education of men as of women. Catherine II, in one of her didactic tales, depicted the

---

[101] Gratsian, *Gratsiana, Pridvornoi chelovek*, maxims 6 and 11.

perfect modern upbringing that had been given to Tsarevich Fevei under the supervision of his father:

The Tsar applied himself zealously to the education of his son. He engaged a nanny for him, a sensible widow-woman who knew whether the child was crying because he was cold or sick, or merely out of caprice . . . His favourite toys were those which added to the store of his knowledge. The tsarevich had a kind heart; he was merciful, generous, obedient, grateful, respectful to his parents and tutors; he was polite, welcoming, and benevolent to everyone, not quarrelsome, not obstinate, not fearful; he was always obedient to the dictates of sincerity and good sense, he loved to speak and to hear the truth; but he had a disgust for lying so great that he eschewed it even in play.[102]

The results of the upbringing are also indicative: Fevei has become a nosegay of Enlightenment virtues: polite, sociable, and committed to the truth. For her part, Madame de Lambert had urged the pursuit of a similar code of virtue on her son: 'Amidst the tumult of the world, my son, have some reliable friend, who will allow the words of truth to flow in your heart . . . there is no certain and durable kingdom but that of virtue.'[103] And the characteristics of an 'ideal citizen', as set out in one of the few native Russian conduct manuals to be published in the early nineteenth century, Pavel Voloshinov's *A Father's Letters to His Son Upon the Nature of A Life Distinguished by Virtue and Free of Mischief* (1810), included not only such civic virtues as bravery, philanthropy, and mercy, but also piety and fear of the Lord. Voloshinov's final image of virtue was of a poor man who, 'having shut himself in his cave, in that humble dwelling, sitting among his devoted family, among his tiny mites, devotes himself to the pleasurable contemplation of nature'.[104]

The ambiguities of the code of male virtue were encapsulated in the term *chest'*, which embraced both external attributes of status ('honour') and the internal regulation of behaviour via the dictates of conscience ('honesty').[105] They were also intriguingly evident in the teaching of the most important boys' school of the early nineteenth century, the Tsarskoe Selo Lyceum. Founded in 1811 as an elite institution intended to train

---

[102] Catherine II, 'Tsarevich Fevei', *Sochineniya Imperatritsy Ekateriny II: proizvedeniya literaturnye*, ed. A. I. Vvedensky (St Petersburg, 1893), 375.

[103] Lambert, 'Avis d'une mère à son fils', *Œuvres*, 45.

[104] Voloshinov, *Otets pouchayushchii pis'menno syna svoego zhitiyu dobromu i ne zazornomu*, 98.

[105] In his article on the duel in Russian culture ('Duel'', in *Besedy o russkoi kul'ture: Byt i traditsii russkogo dvoryanstva XVIII-rannego XIX veka* (St Petersburg, 1994), 164–79), Yury Lotman points to a conflict between the 'inward' and 'outward' perceptions of *chest'* as a feature of the early 19th cent. But the 'distinction/probity' division had emerged much earlier in translations of foreign texts: see e.g. La Shetardi, *Nastavlenie znatnomu molodomu gospodinu*, which advises its readers to look after their 'spiritual gifts' (sect. 13 p. 11) but also not to despise 'qualities that are outwardly visible' (sect. 12 p. 11).

highly qualified entrants for the Russian Civil Service, the school was also one of the first boarding schools for boys whose pupils could compete with the alumnae of Smol'nyi on the grounds of cultivation and refinement. The conduct reports submitted by the schoolmasters at the Tsarskoe Selo Lyceum after the school's inaugural year lay bare the intensive process of moral classification that ran through the school's programme. Each boy was given a wide-ranging *kharakteristika* of a specificity that leaves far behind such modern pedagogical clichés as 'could do better' or 'needs to pay more attention in class'. The positive and negative qualities identified may be tabulated as follows:

POSITIVE	NEGATIVE
Intellectual	
(faculties)	
имеет счастливую память	ограничен (limited)
одарен живым воображением	
проницателен	
(has a good memory, vivid imagination, a penetrating mind)	
(effort expended)	
прилежен	вял, ленив, мешкотен
исполнителен	(dull, lazy, dreary)
начитан	
(zealous, efficient, well-read)	
Moral	
(sincerity, openness)	(furtiveness)
простосердечен, искренен	скрытен
добродушен, обходителен,	задумчив, угрюм
свободен в обращении	странен в обращении
(open-hearted, sincere, kind, sociable, free in his ways)	(secretive, thoughtful, gloomy, odd in his ways)
(modesty, obedience)	(arrogance, self-love)
скромен, услужлив, покорен,	самолюбив, властолюбив,
к старшим почтителен	честолюбив
(modest, helpful/servile, obedient, respectful to elders/seniors)	(self-loving, domineering, ambitious)
(politeness)	(rudeness)
любезен, вежлив, снисходителен,	груб, докучлив, насмешлив
со всеми одинаков	
(amiable, courteous, condescending, the same to everyone)	(coarse, tedious, mocking)
(sensitivity)	(insensitivity, over-sensitivity)
кроток, нежен,	груб, угрюм,

(в мере) чувствителен	(чересчур) чувствителен
(gentle, tender,	(coarse/rude, sullen,
(appropriately) sensitive)	(over-)sensitive)
(reflectiveness)	(frivolity, hastiness)
степенен, верен, терпелив,	пылок, вспыльчив, гневен,
рассудителен, равнодушен	неосмотрителен, ветрен,
	легкомыслен, резов,
	развлечен
(steady, faithful, patient,	(fiery, hot-tempered, cantankerous,
reasonable, equable)	slapdash, giddy,
	frivolous, mischievous, easily
	distracted).

[*Source*: 'Reports for Class One' (*Otzyvy nastavnikov o pervom kurse*), Grot, 357–62.]

Some of the positive qualities can be clearly associated with proper behaviour in terms of the hierarchy: these include *usluzhliv* (obliging), *pokoren* (obedient) and *k starshim pochtitelen* (respectful towards his seniors), as well as *sniskhoditelen* (condescending—a positive term in the early nineteenth century, as indicated by the comment of Jane Austen's Mr Collins on Lady Catherine de Burgh, 'all affability and condescension'). One pupil (V. Val'kovsky) was particularly commended for being 'friendly, complaisant, polite, and the same with everyone' (Grot, 357). On the other hand, overbearing boys were criticized as *samolyubiv* (vain), *vlastolyubiv* (overbearing), and *chestolyubiv* (arrogant). But the most important point was that boys were supposed to take a full part in society. Eccentricity and reserve were not at all welcome: Pushkin's friend, the young Kyukhel'beker, was described as 'having a curious manner' (Grot, 359), and (indicatively, for an age in which literature was associated with politeness), his want of refinement was also said to spill over into his compositions: 'His compositions particularly are strained and high-flown, often to the point where they part company with decorum' (*prilichie*). (Grot, 359). Of Pavel Yudin, the masters warned that his reserve bordered on the pathological ('we must make efforts that it does not turn . . . into pensiveness' (Grot, 362). Naturally, conversational powers were highly valued: of Dmitry Maslov, it was noted 'his speech is manly, entertaining, and witty' (Grot, 361). However, 'wit' (*ostroumie*) was seen as a double-edged quality, veering a little too closely towards 'arrogance'. So much is evident, for instance, in the detailed comments on Pushkin's conduct:

Self-love mixed with ambition causes him to be sometimes shy; sensitivity and cordiality, hot bursts of violent temper, frivolity and a peculiar garrulousness mingled with sharp-wittedness are his characteristics. At the same time, kind-heartedness is evident in him; recognizing his own weaknesses, he is ready to take advice and applies this with a certain degree of success. His garrulousness and sharp-wittedness have now taken on a new and better form, and the cast of his thoughts has altered for the better, but overall, his character still lacks stability and steadiness. (Grot, 361)

Finally, the school reports also pointed to an interesting tension between an Enlightenment emphasis on control of the passions above all, and an emphasis on the development of emotional expression that was traceable to a late eighteenth-century cult of sensibility. 'Hot bursts of violent temper' were criticized and curbed, yet the school syllabus laid considerable emphasis on the appreciation and cultivation of literary skills, and individual talents in, and contributions to, this were seen as relevant to the conduct reports, as well as to accounts of progress in that particular subject. (Just so, despite the understanding of the school as ideal collective, many aspects of school life emphasized privacy: the boys slept in separate cubicles in their dormitories and had their own reading desks in the libraries.)[106]

The Lyceum reports provide extremely interesting contemporary documentation of attempts to regulate male behaviour. Some of the material in the reports is very similar to the observations made in late eighteenth-century conduct reports from Smol'nyi Institute. Of the 4th Class in February 1785, for example, 'Mademoiselle Bogdanoff' was said to be polite and amiable ('elle se rend agréable par sa politesse et par son affabilité'), and 'Mademoiselle Balachoff' combined these qualities with sensitivity ('elle possède toutes les qualités, qui désignent un bon caractère, un cœur sensible, beaucoup de douceur, une humeur gaye s'égale et joint à elle des manières prévenantes, beaucoup de politesse et d'amabilité'). But the girls' behaviour, unlike the boys', was never judged in terms of rank in a hierarchy; 'the same with everyone' was always the underlying ideal.[107]

THE LEGACY OF MORAL TEACHING: ETIQUETTE AND 'ANTI-BEHAVIOUR' IN EARLY NINETEENTH-CENTURY RUSSIA

There is no doubt whatever that behaviour books, and most particularly pedagogical treatises, made their mark in Russia in one sense: their popularity with Russian readers. Not only the numbers of advice books

---

[106] See John O'Connor, Jr., *A History of the Imperial Lyceum of Alexander I* (Concord, Mass., 1977), 67.

[107] Cherepnin, *Imperatorskoe vospitatel'noe obshchestvo*, iii. 159, 161. This is not of course to suggest that institute girls were not status-conscious: memoirs of institute life (e.g. Sof'ya Khvoshchinskaya's) indicate that *chvanstvo* was quite prevalent—and its occurrence could only have been encouraged by the teaching of subjects such as genealogy (see above).

per se (see Appendix 1 Table 1), but the large number of re-editions for authors such as Fénelon and Lambert, were indications of steady demand in what was still an underdeveloped and primitive book market. According to a specialist on eighteenth-century print culture, the success of pedagogical texts was particularly marked.[108] But there was also a reasonable currency for letter-writing manuals, for etiquette books, and for health guides. How successful were these books in implanting the refined behaviour that they propagandized?

At the level of symbolic representations, there is no doubt that the level of success was high. The link between morality and motherhood was ubiquitous in literature and art: it was not only fostered, but exploited, by Catherine II herself. She refused the title 'mother of the nation' when offered it officially, but tolerated semi-official representations of herself in that role. *La Mère de ses peuples*, a late eighteenth-century French bronze after a portrait by Jean-Baptiste Deloye, shows the empress as the apotheosis of the 'pedagogical mother': not encumbered by anything so inelegant as a baby, but exercising benevolent tutelage over subject-children now that they have attained, or are approaching, the age of reason (Fig. 4). Where the empress as 'mother of the nation' led, others followed: the right of adult women to exercise a quasi-maternal civilizing role was celebrated in idyllic visions of the social institution whereby an upper-class woman took a ward (*vospitannitsa*), possibly but not necessarily a relation,[109] to whom she offered motherly guidance and social patronage (aid with the polishing of manners and the facilitation of introductions) to a younger woman. The *vospitannitsa* arrangement was enthusiastically depicted in Anna Labzina's memoirs (Labzina had been a *vospitannitsa* of the poet Elisaveta Kheraskova, herself one of the best-educated Russian women of the eighteenth century).[110] Later, in the 1830s, it was to be evoked in two fine bravura portraits by Karl Bryullov of his mistress Countess Samoilova, *The Countess Samoilova Returning from a Masquerade* (1839) and its pendant, *The Countess Samoilova and Her Ward* (1834). The latter, a magnificent and theatrical work, shows the countess posed at one end of an opulent interior, before a dramatically draped velvet curtain.

[108] 'The anomalous manifest openness to new and unfamiliar books aimed at parents and tutors was a striking indication of just how profound the focus on childhood and childbearing was among educated groups' (Marker, *Publishing, Printing, and the Origins of Intellectual Life* , 211).

[109] In some cases, a *vospitannitsa* may have been a woman's own, or her husband's, illegitimate child (on the practice in England of 'adopting' such children, see Amanda Foreman, *Georgiana, Duchess of Devonshire* (London, 1999), 73). But this was by no means always the case.

[110] See Anna Labzina, *Vospominaniya 1758–1828*, ed. B. L. Modzalevsky (Newtonville, Tenn., 1974), 47–8. Novels were carefully censored in favour of *lectures solides*, and moral issues assiduously propagandized by the Kheraskovs. She herself was later to take a *vospitannitsa*, S. A. Mudrova (1797–1870), and the pair were the subject of a touching portrait by Borivikovsky (*c.*1803). (It is reproduced in the fold of plates at the back of Lotman, *Besedy o russkoi kul'ture*.)

FIG. 4. After J. B. Deloye, *La Mère de ses peuples*
(bronze of Empress Catherine II).

Apparently in the midst of walking into the room from the balcony, she is
caught mid-step, suggesting energetic *perpetuum mobile*. To her right is a
small African page, to her left her ward, while a dog puts its paws on the
front of her heavy silk skirt. Among painters of a later generation (for
example, Fedotov), as among some of the writers of Bryullov's own, such a
composition might have been satirical in effect, suggesting that the
countess's ward and page occupied a similar place in her affections to the
dog. Here, however, the countess's reactions to each are carefully
distinguished: it is only the two humans whom she deigns to notice, and
of the two, it is the ward towards whom she gesticulates. The portrait is a

representation of idealized maternity in which the relationship between older and younger woman is no less 'natural' because there is no direct blood relationship.

The fact of a blood relationship did not of course preclude admission to the select ranks of refined maternity. Funerary architecture of the late eighteenth and early nineteenth centuries, as displayed in such fashionable cemeteries as the Lazar'evskoe Cemetery next to Aleksandr Nevsky Monastery in St Petersburg, or the cemetery in the Don Monastery in Moscow, abounded in tributes to virtuous mothers, both in the form of epitaphs and in the form of stone carvings. The monuments, comparable in terms of inspiration (if not in terms of execution) with those of Flaxman or Canova, were only the most durable tributes to a veritable cult of maternity that developed in Russia during the late eighteenth and early nineteenth centuries. Other idealizations of the mother–child theme included portraits, especially those executed by Élisabeth Vigée Le Brun during her stay in Russia in the 1790s.[111]

But ideals are not, of course, the same as practices, and the question of how visions of feminity were understood is complicated. Dmitry Levitsky's charming paintings of the first Smol'nyi alumnae, for instance, resemble allegories as much as naturalist portraits: as they demonstrate their accomplishments (singing, dancing, declamation), the young women have a slightly characterless grace that recalls representations of the Muses, symbols of the arts rather than pictures of artists. And the proliferation of female allegories in the eighteenth century (cartouches on maps and topographical views showing the Tsaritsas Elizabeth and Catherine attended by the virtues, funerary and garden sculptures, architectural motifs) did not necessarily broaden the possibilities available to real women; as Marina Warner has pointed out, allegorical representations have an ambiguous effect, gaining their authority by their distance from perceived reality.[112] In a culture where secular allegory was a new phenomenon,[113] it was likely to be seen as particularly remote from the lives of real women; and conversely, there was a danger that portraits (whether in words or paint) of women doing anything unusual would be interpreted as allegory.

[111] On funerary architecture, see my article, 'Educating Tatiana: Manners, Morals and Motherhood in Russia, 1760–1830', in Linda Edmondson (ed.), *Gender in Russian History and Culture* (London, 2001). The *maternités* of Vigée Le Brun, Angelica Kaufmann, and others can be found in Grand Duke Nikolai Mikhailovich, *Russkie portrety*.

[112] M. Warner, *Monuments and Maidens: The Allegory of the Female Form* (2nd edn., London, 1996), p. xx.

[113] Allegorical representations are relatively rare in Orthodox iconographical tradition (an important exception being the icon of Sophia, or Divine Wisdom). As late as 1698, Petr Tolstoi could still write in splendidly alienated fashion of 'a carved stone person of the female sex in the image of Justice' (*The Travel Diary of P. A. Tolstoi*, 92.)

Yet the established pedagogical tradition of using collections of biographies (Plutarch's *Lives* and later imitations of the genre)[114] in order to encourage children to measure up to heroic achievement may have acted as a counterweight, making the new models of female virtue seem 'remote but attainable through effort' rather than 'remote and unattainable'. By the late eighteenth century, even those who clung to the past often took as their starting point assumptions that would have seemed startlingly novel a century earlier. Now even the conservative historian M. M. Shcherbatov accepted without question the need for young women to be educated: 'Neither learned nor moral young ladies have come out of Smol'nyi, or only those who were provided with such qualities by nature, and the education consisted more in playacting than in correcting [the pupils'] hearts, manners or reason.'[115] Negating Smol'nyi's achievements, Shcherbatov at the same time accepted its aims: the education of 'learned and moral' young women, and the correction of 'hearts, manners and reason'. Even this opponent of modernity could accept the link between proper femininity, education, and morality.

The view of women's special capacity to act as tutors in *nravy*, manners and morals, resonated beyond the schoolroom. For late eighteenth-century Russian gentlemen such as Ivan Dolgorukov, the houses of well-bred women were seen as finishing schools where extra polish might be acquired. Dolgorukov recalls with gratitude his visits to the household of a French émigrée, Madame de la Ville: 'I was much obliged to this woman; she polished my manners [*ona menya vyterla*] and made it possible for me to appear in high society [*bol'shoi svet*]; without the layer of schoolroom dust and pedantry which crusts us over if we go there directly from the supervision of our tutors at home.' That this role could be exercised by Russian women as well is clear from a similar observation on 'the amiable' Katerina Petrovna Shuvalova: 'A house like theirs would be hard to find nowadays. This is a great pity for our young people, since such circles [*podobnye obshchestva*] are the very best practical school of social life [*obshchezhitie*] for them.'[116] By extension, mixed-sex assemblies were the place for literary culture as a polite pastime: the playing of flirtatious literary

---

[114] See e.g. Anon., *Zertsalo zhenskoi drevnei uchenosti, ili Opisanie zhizni drevnikh filosofok*, trans. F. Bakhteyanov (Moscow, 1800), which includes Anna Komnena, Diotima, and Aspasia, as well as a host of more unexpected and obscure figures (Hippartia, Hypatia, Amphicia, etc.); and Sergei Glinka, 'Istoricheskoe izobrazhenie dobrodeteli i slavy Rossiyanok drevnikh i novykh vremen', *Moskovskii al'manakh dlya prekrasnogo pola: izdanyi na 1826–i god Sergeem Glinkoyu* (Moscow, 1825), 5–87.

[115] M. M. Shcherbatov, *O povrezhdenii nravov v Rossii* (1787), ed. A. Lentin (Cambridge, 1969), 134, 252. Lentin's edition contains an English parallel text, but the translation here is my own.

[116] Dolgorukov, *Kapishche moego serdtsa*, 58–9, 221–3.

games, and the inscription of 'madrigals', flattering verses, in the hostess's album. Surviving examples of albums retain the sadly faded traces of once lively interchanges employing the form.[117]

Alongside this understanding of literature as flirtation, a very different and much more earnest view of women's place in literary culture was also developing in the late eighteenth century. This arose from the association of moral judgements with judgements of taste. Credited with a superior capacity for arbitration of morality, and with superior sensitivity, women were also assumed to be superior to men in their arbitration of questions of taste. In David Hume's words: 'Women, who have more delicate passions than men, have a more delicate taste of the ornaments of life, of dress, equipage, and the ordinary decencies of behaviour.'[118] With the rise of the 'cult of sensibility', the faint disapproval with which a rationalist such as Hume had regarded emotional delicacy was suspended; women's reputed delicacy of taste and passion now made them ideal consumers of works of art, and above all ideal readers. An exemplary text of 1796, Karamzin's 'Epistle to Women', eulogized women in their capacities as ideal readers of and sources of poetry, guides to the philosopher, and educators of the young:

С любовью матери он [младенец] мило расцветает,
Из глаз ее в себе луч кротости впивает,
    И зреет нежною душой.[119]

With the love of his mother he [the baby] sweetly blossoms,
From her eyes he drinks in the ray of gentleness,
And ripens with his tender soul.

Karamzin goes on to speak of his own motherless childhood, which has left only 'that sweet, sacred image | imprinted in my breast' (*obraz tvoi svyashchennyi, milyi | V grudi moei napechatlen*, 235). He recalls the important role played by women as companions to philosophers, mentioning Socrates' regard for Aspasia (Socrates' equally famous tussles with his irascible wife, Xantippe, are tactfully ignored!):

Любезность мудреца
Должна быть истины приправой;
Иначе скучен нам и самый разум здравый,
Любезность же сия есть ваш бесценный дар.   (ll. 248–9)

---

[117] See the excellent article by G. Hammarberg, 'Flirting with Words: Domestic Albums, 1770–1840' in H. Goscilo and B. Holmgren (eds.), *Russia: Women: Culture* (Bloomington, Ind., 1996), 297–31. In the early 19th cent., literary games sometimes appeared in journals: e.g. V. A. Zhukovsky's 'Otvety na voprosy, v igre, nazyvaemoi "sekretar"' came out in *Rossiiskii muzeum* 10 (1815). (See *Sochineniya v 3 tomakh* (Moscow, 1980), 360–1, 428.)

[118] D. Hume, 'Of the Delicacy of Taste and Passion', *Essays Moral, Political, and Literary*, part i (1752), in *The Philosophical Works of David Hume* (Boston and London, 1854), iii. 3.

[119] N. Karamzin, 'Poslanie k zhenshchinam', *Aonidy* i (1796), 234.

> The amiability of a wise man
> Must be the seasoning of his truth;
> Otherwise even good sense is dreary to us;
> That amiability is your priceless gift.

Karamzin ends by enthusiastically wishing, that upon his death, his grave might be inscribed with the words: 'He loved. | He was the tenderest friend of tender woman' (*On lyubil* | *On nezhnoi zhenshchiny nezhneishim drugom byl*, l. 248).

The idea that the ideal reader of polite literature was an 'amiable lady' resonated in a literary form of the album as an anthology of prized literary texts, rather than as a record of light-hearted games.[120] From the 1760s, it facilitated the entry into actual literary composition of some women. The poet Gavrila Derzhavin's first wife, Ekaterina, for instance, belonged to a circle that included Elisaveta Kheraskova, wife of the epicist Mikhail Kheraskov, and Ekaterina Urusova, the most ambitious woman poet of the eighteenth century.[121]

But it would be a mistake to take the world in which Princess Urusova welcomed her 'Parnassian sisters' to the composition of poetry as typical of Russian life, even in the landed gentry. Indeed, Derzhavin's own mother, Fekla Andreevna, remained barely literate all her life: her letters to her son were dictated, except for the signature, and were unpretentiously domestic in content (a catalogue of problems with errant serfs, the recruiting authorities, aggressive neighbours, and so forth).[122] To be sure, this was partly a function of generation. By the 1810s, a woman of Derzhavina's social standing would certainly not have had her letters transcribed for her, and the behaviour models and language of refinement had become familiar to the provincial gentry, as well as metropolitan aristocrats. Where Fekla Derzhavina had written touchingly and artlessly to her daughter-in-law of her 'warm maternal feelings' in 1778, the letters to her relations of Mar'ya Moier (née Protasova) in the 1810s espouse a much more complex emotional rhetoric.[123] It is a matter of fact that there were more women

[120] On albums of this kind, see M. P. Alekseev, 'Iz istorii rukopisnykh sobranii' in idem (ed.), *Neizdannye pis'ma inostrannykh pisatelei XVII–XIX vekov iz leningradskikh rukopisnykh sobranii* (Moscow, 1960), 11–24; V. E. Vatsuro, 'Literaturnye al'bomy v sobranii Pushkinskogo doma' (1750–1840 gg.)', *Ezhegodnik rukopisnogo otdela Pushkinskogo doma na 1977 god* (Leningrad, 1979), 3–56.

[121] See Urusova's letter to Derzhavina of July 1786, *Sochineniya Derzhavina*, ed. Ya. Grot, v (St Petersburg, 1876), 521–3 (no. 463). Derzhavina's tomb, in the Lazar'evskoe Cemetery, bears the following touching inscription by Derzhavin himself: 'Ah! virtue and beauty, whither fled? | – Who can find where her feet now tread? | Alas! heaven's doors have opened wide | And she slipped through, into the light!'

[122] See e.g. *Sochineniya Derzhavina*, v. 292 (letter no. 290).

[123] Moier's correspondence appears in *Utkinskii sbornik*, i (St Petersburg, 1904). See e.g. pp. 264–6, a letter to A. P. Elagina, 23 Oct. 1821, in which she describes an acquaintance,

subscribing to books, recording their reading in letters, and publishing, or aspiring to publish their works, in the 1820s than there were in the 1780s or even the 1800s, which in itself is a reliable indication of the spread of polite culture as understood at the time.[124]

Yet practices seem to have changed more haphazardly than the contemporary cliché of inexorably advancing civilization would have suggested. Generational change did not always go the same way: the memoirist Andrei Bolotov, for instance, found his mother-in-law a good deal more interested in his cultural innovations than his wife.[125] And, enriched by land grants and the proceeds of their mines and factories, many upper-class Russians behaved like the newly wealthy in any society—they regarded the spending of money as a worthwhile activity in its own right. In the 1720s, European visitors had commented with approval upon the sumptuous gowns and opulent coiffures, dripping with jewels, of ladies at the Russian court, but with less warmth about the gauche behaviour of those in the fine clothes.[126] The best part of a century later, as Catherine and Martha Wilmot recalled, mixing at a social gathering with the cream of Russian society still created rather a similar impression: the sisters ran the gauntlet of inquisitive stares as the cost of their attire was expertly assessed and found wanting by diamond-bedizened women.[127] Where improvidence (*motovstvo*) was a signifier of high status, fine crystal glasses were as likely to be smashed after a drinking-bout as to inhibit excessive consumption. Even the enthusiastic Vigée Le Brun wrinkled her nose at the awful manners and boring company of 'a Russian banker' and his friends: 'one might have thought them stuffed dummies if they had not eaten like ogres!'[128] The term 'tender sex' was not exactly suitable for many Russian women of the late eighteenth and early nineteenth centuries either. A Princess Golitsyna, glimpsed by F. F. Vigel' at an inopportune moment ('I had never seen such a frightful fit of rage') launched into a tirade that defied the rules of politeness: 'Forgetting that she had children and servants looking on, she rained curses down on the tsar and on everyone, on the people and on the army that served him, and quietened down only when she had exhausted herself.'[129] Even as late as the 1840s, an English visitor to

Margarita Tuchkova, as 'an amiable and very sentimental [*sentimental'naya*] woman, *parlant toujours de son malheur, de sa perte*'.

[124] For a detailed biography of such a woman, see W. Rosslyn, *Anna Bunina (1774–1829) and the Origins of Women's Poetry in Russia* (Studies in Slavic Languages and Literatures, 10: Lewiston, NY, 1997).

[125] *Zapiski*, 3 vols. (Leningrad 1931), ii. 306–7.

[126] See Hughes, *Russia in the Age of Peter the Great*, 189.

[127] See M. Wilmot and C. Wilmot, *The Russian Diaries* (London, 1934), 210, 36 (18 Feb. 1806 and 6 Aug. 1803).

[128] Vigée Le Brun, *Memoirs*, 219.

[129] F. F. Vigel', *Zapiski*, 2 vols. (Moscow, 1928), i. 72.

the Russian provinces recorded of her hostess: 'There was . . . but little kindly feeling in her nature. She was a perfect type of a certain class of Russian ladies: passionate, severe, tyrannical, capricious, and unsympathising . . . her servants and children never approached her without trembling.'[130]

The Russian upper-class man or woman whose aspirations to Western ways were limited to an obsession with fine clothes and fashionable pastimes remained a figure of fun in the early nineteenth century as he and she had in the eighteenth, and here the continuity of satirical tradition undoubtedly reflected the real-life persistence of such figures.[131] Given the emphasis on refinement as outward form, it was not uncommon for parents' contribution to the education of their children to stop at the hiring of a foreign governess or tutor, who in turn was as likely to be a *modiste* or *fille de joie* from Dijon, or a tailor from Toulouse, writing a half-literate French and speaking a formidable patois, as he or she was to be an exiled comte or marquise.[132] In its turn, the fact that many foreigners astutely took advantage of Russian credulousness fuelled a xenophobic mistrust of 'foreign fripperies' that was to acquire retrospective justification during the era of the Revolutionary Wars, which witnessed an eruption of scurrilous poems disparaging the masculinity of the French, and of cartoons showing shopkeepers confecting face-creams whose 'secret ingredient' was the contents of a commode.[133]

It was also perfectly possible for highly intelligent upper-class Russians to own the latest behaviour books, take an intellectual interest in these, yet behave, in reality, as if the behaviour books had never been written. Pushkin's library contained at least one very modern book on the family,

---

[130] See A. Lyons, *At Home with the Gentry: A Victorian English Lady's Diary of Russian Country Life* (Nottingham, 1998), 15.

[131] See e.g. Anon., 'Dnevnik molodoi zhenshchiny', *VE* 58 (1811), 20–4, a text closely similar to Catherine II's 'Dnevnik sestry moei dvoyurodnoi', in which a young lady describes a day that begins with drinking chocolate in bed in the early afternoon and continues with having a servant flogged for treading on her lapdog's paw.

[132] In the notes to his *Russkie narodnye kartinki*, 5 vols. (St Petersburg, 1881), iv. 429, D. Rovinsky quotes the acid comments of Count Rostopchin on the importation of such ignorant *madamy*. Moreover, priorities in education varied widely. Francesco de Miranda, who visited the country in 1787, for example, called on his acquaintance Prince Gorchakov to find the entire family learning to dance 'from their very petulant French dancing-master . . . These people think that their children are well educated if they know how to dance. Character and not learning is what I want, Madame Kamenskaya said to me. As if you could separate the one and the other.' (*Diario de Moscú y San Petersburgo* (Caracas, 1993), 39–40.)

[133] One such scurrilous poem is 'Vstrecha' (see A. Zorin and N. Sapov (eds.), *Devich'ya igrushka, ili Sochineniya gospodina Barkova* (Moscow, 1992), 170), which depicts a French soldier raped by a Russian shopkeeper: 'Frantsuzskaya dyra khila | Ne terpit russkogo stvola . . . Krichit mos'e, syskatel' mody novoi' (A Frenchman's hole is all too weak | A Russian screw is more than it can stand . . . The monsieur shrieks, that fan of foreign fashion). For a typical cartoon, see **Fig.** 5.

Французской Магазинъ помады и духовъ
1^я французское ли это? 2^я о мосіе самое свѣжее

Fig. 5. 'The Secret Ingredient of French Face-Creams'. This chauvinistic subject is typical of caricatures produced in Russia in the early nineteenth century.

The Education of a Mother, or on Women's Civilization of the Human Race (1833), as well as a copy of the complete works of Rousseau.[134] But as his sister, Ol'ga Pavlishcheva, observed: 'Aleksandr thrashes his little boy, who's only two, and he beats Masha as well; but however, he's a tender enough father.'[135] Only exceptional Russians would, when talking to native servants and waiters (as opposed to foreign ones), have used the polite second person, as was recommended by French advice literature of the late eighteenth and early nineteenth centuries.[136] Equally, it was not necessarily the case that the many upper-class Russian women who had read Fénelon, Lambert, Le Prince de Beaumont, and Genlis earnestly put into practice the principles that they had gleaned from there.

To be sure, the extent of impoliteness must also not be exaggerated. Few of the horror stories about Russian crudity or harshness (behaviour to serfs aside)[137] can compete with the reminiscences of Mrs Elizabeth Shackleton, a Yorkshire gentlewoman who in the 1780s was complaining of her husband, 'went snoring to clean bed, where he farted and stunk like a Pole cat', and worse, 'He shits in bed with drinking so constantly.'[138] It was not only in Russia, but also in France or Britain, that a Sèvres saucer might be used for feeding cream to a lapdog or as an offensive weapon in a domestic dispute, rather than to prevent a chocolate-cup from leaking on a veneered surface.[139] And just as in Britain or France, the laments about coarse and rude behaviour, on the part of Russian commentators such as Vigel', point

---

[134] Louis-Aimé Martin, *De l'éducation des mères de famille ou de la civilisation du genre humain par les femmes* (Brussels, 1833). The book is a long dissection of women's moral role, which, it is alleged, has been damaged by the frivolity of contemporary life; there are strong Catholic overtones. On Pushkin's ownership of it, see B. L. Modzalevsky, *Biblioteka A. S. Pushkina: Bibliograficheskoe opisanie* (St Petersburg, 1910), item 1141. For the Rousseau, see ibid., item 1332. (The pages of the *Émile* volumes are uncut, but this may signify that Pushkin had read the text before he acquired the edition, or else that he knew its contents so well by hearsay that he could not be bothered to read it.)

[135] O. S. Pavlishcheva, letter to N. I. Pavlishchev of 22 Nov. 1835: *Pis'ma O. S. Pavlishchevoi k muzhu i otsu 1831–1837: Famil'nye bumagi Pushkinykh-Gannibalov*, ii (St Petersburg, 1994), 129.

[136] See e.g. Genlis, *The Traveller's Companion*, 152: 'N'avez-vous pas des serviettes plus fines, moins grosses, plus belles?' (rendered in the English parallel text as 'Have you no finer napkins, not so coarse and more genteel?') Contrast Gogol''s imaginary conversation with a servant in his *Vybrannye mesta iz perepiski s druz'yami*, ch. xx: 'Heh, you, filthy mug! You're smeared with soot so you can hardly see your eyes, and you don't want to give credit where credit's due' (Akh, ty, nevymytoe rylo! Sam ves' zazhal v sazhe, tak chto i glaz ne vidat', da eshche i ne khochesh' okazat' i chest' chestnomu. (*Sochineniya* (St Petersburg, 1889), iv 120.)

[137] The elegant Prince Yusupov praised by Pushkin, for example, kept a harem and forced his serf actors to strip at a prearranged signal during performances. See Roosevelt, *Life on the Russian Country Estate: A Social and Cultural History*, 144, 304. For further discussion of this topic, see Ch. 2.

[138] See Amanda Vickery, *The Gentleman's Daughter: Women's Lives in Georgian England* (New Haven, 1998), 216.

[139] Cf. Sarah Richards's account of the diverse uses of china in *Eighteenth-Century Ceramics* (Manchester, 1999).

to the dissemination of new ideas about propriety and politeness. There was now a need to draw distinctions between civility and barbarism, politeness and vulgarity; by expressing shock at vulgar tirades before 'children and servants', for instance, memoirists not only indicated the presence of an appreciation according to which such behaviour was deemed intolerable, but also established their own credentials as civilized persons.

And just as there were Russian historical subjects who passionately espoused genteel values, so there were mothers who had thoroughly internalized the ethos of refined maternity. In 1820, Mar'ya Moier (brought up on didactic texts by Maria Edgeworth and Madame Genlis) was exercising 'maternal concern' on the care of orphaned wards (boys as well as girls) on her estate, and referring to her own experience of labour in impeccably euphemistic terms (adding a further layer of elegance by lapsing into French): 'Il est vrai, la douleur est terrible—mais quelle est la mère qui voudrait ne pas l'avoir éprouvé?'[140] The moralizing album that M. B. Dargomyzhskaya kept for her daughter in the 1810s sought to inculcate both 'character' and 'learning'; it was Dargomyzhskaya's wish 'that not fashion, but reason should govern you; therefore, you will not find any passionate or romantic materials here'.[141] A similar paragon of maternal concern was the mother of Lev Tolstoi, who, till her early death, kept elaborate notes on her children's education and moral development.[142] Cases of exemplary 'pedagogical mothers' recorded in Ivan Dolgorukov's fascinating memoir-dictionary *Temple of my Heart* include, among others, Katerina Nikolaevna Apochinina, Anis'ya Fedorovna Vel'yaminova, Katerina Ivanovna Voeikova, Elisaveta Sergeevna Golovina, Varvara Alekseevna Trubetskaya, Natal'ya Petrovna Kurakina, and Elisaveta Ivanovna Lanskaya. Prince Nikolai Borisovich Yusupov's wife, Tat'yana Ivanovna, Prince Potemkin's niece, devoted herself after their separation entirely to the upbringing of her son.[143]

But the very reverence with which these cases were cited suggested that such women were still, in the late eighteenth and early nineteenth centuries, considered unusually, even prodigiously, devoted. It is noticeable, too, that they tended to come from the most privileged and metropolitan layers of Russian society; in provincial towns, and among

[140] Letter to A. P. Elagina, 2 Nov. 1820, *Utkinskii sbornik*, i. 246. Exemplifying the diversity of maternal practices as well as models, though, Moier took pride in having breast-fed her child (ibid. 247). On her reading of Edgeworth and Genlis aged 13, see A. E. Gruzinsky's introduction, *Utkinskii sbornik*, i, p. iv. French grammar follows original.

[141] Quoted in Vatsuro, 'Literaturnye al'bomy', 14.

[142] See Tolstoi's own account in his late memoir 'Vospominaniya', *PSS* xxxiv. 349–51.

[143] I. M. Dolgorukov, 'Kapishche moego serdtsa, ili slovar' svekh tekh lits, s koimi ya byl v raznykh otnosheniyakh v techenii moei zhizni', *Russkii arkhiv* 1, 3, 6, 9 (1890). On Potemkina, see Grand Duke Nicholas Mikhailovich, *Russkie portrety*. Cf. E. N. Vodovozova's recollections of her grandmother in the 1790s (*Na zare zhizni* (Moscow, 1987), i. 56–7).

middle-ranking gentry, matters were rather different. In the town of Penza, for instance, quite a stir was caused, in the 1790s, by Madame Kek, a graduate of Smol'nyi who occupied herself with translating and educating her children.[144] Even in the 1820s and in Moscow, mothers such as Natal'ya Ivanovna Goncharova, who allowed her daughters to wear shabby clothes and was known to slap them on the face in public, were not by all accounts particularly unusual, though they might be considered 'coarse' and 'vulgar' by those from more refined circles.[145] One interesting detail that points to the formality of mother–child relations in Russia at this period is the fact that the 1784 Russian text of Louise d'Épinay's *Conversations d'Émilie* substituted 'Matushka sudarynya' for 'Maman', and the second-person singular for Épinay's honorific use of the second person plural to the child. And if dedications to books are anything to go by, upper-class Russian women were just as likely to feel that they owed their education to their fathers as to their mothers. For example, in her 1792 retranslation of Fénelon's *Traité sur l'éducation des filles*, Nadezhda Niki-forova, a young gentlewoman from Tambov province, appealed to her father as absolute intellectual authority, 'the originator of my intellectual efforts' and 'architect of my knowledge'.[146]

---

[144] 'Zapiski Filippa Filippovicha Vigelya', *Russkii arkhiv* 9 (1891), supplement p. 211 (this passage is cut from the 1929 edn.).

[145] Princess E. A. Dolgorukova, for instance, who recalled N. I. Goncharova as having 'bad, coarse manners and a degree of vulgarity in her ways'. (Quoted in V. Veresaev, *Pushkin v zhizni* (Moscow, 1984), 244). Pushkin's own mother, while a good deal better bred, according to contemporary standards, than this, inclined to humorous briskness rather than sentimentality in her relations with her children: her letters to her daughter are concerned above all with the latter's physical health. See *Famil'nye bumagi Pushkinykh-Gannibalov*, i (St Petersburg, 1993), e.g. 20 Aug. 1829 p. 51: 'If only you would agree to make up a decoction of oak-bark and use it to rinse your . . . every morning, it would do you a vast amount of good.' (The ellipsis indicates a word omitted by the editors on censorship grounds, perhaps 'cunt' or 'arse'.)

[146] Fénelon, *O vospitanii devits* (1794), [p. i, p. iii]. In her general study of the Russian upper-class family in the early 19th cent., Jessica Tovrov argues that the most important defining factor in cultural transmission was gender: values were transmitted from mother to daughter, from father to son. (J. Tovrov, *The Russian Noble Family: Structure and Change* (New York, 1987). See also J. Tovrov, 'Mother–Child Relationships Among the Russian Nobility', in David Ransel (ed.), *The Family in Imperial Russia: New Lines of Historical Research* (Urbana, Ill., 1978), 15–43.) However, conduct literature, memoirs, and letters suggest that the situation was more fluid: men could exercise didactic roles not only with regard to their wives, but also with regard to other women relatives. Another relationship into which a didactic note often crept was that of brother to sister; and once a father had died, a young man could often adopt a tutelary role vis-à-vis his mother (both these roles are inhabited by Nikolai Gogol' in his correspondence with his family from St Petersburg). (See e.g. Gogol''s letter to his mother, 9 Oct. 1831, recommending that his sisters should attend the 'Patriotic Institute' for their education (*PSS* x. no. 118). But if men could act as surrogate fathers, the reverse seldom held: few sisters found themselves in the role of mothers to orphaned brothers, even much younger ones, while the attempt by a mother to exercise control over her sons was less straightforward than that of a father to dominate his daughters (see e.g. the case of Ivan Turgenev: James L. Rice, 'Varvara Petrovna Turgeneva in Unpublished Letters to Her Son Ivan (1838–1844)', *SR* 56 (1997), 1–14).

Exposed to conflicting behaviour models and to a wide range of different imperatives, it is perfectly natural that Russians from the cultural elite were not always consistent in their gentility. Different values jostled in the same person as well as in separate individuals. According to Vigel', 'any low woman bazaar-trader, any peasant man was politer and more decent' than Madame Kek, the ex-Smolyanka and devoted pedagogical mother.[147] The sheer novelty of the ideology of politeness, its status as an exotic and intriguing importation from the West, undoubtedly played a role in fostering inconsistencies. Certainly, moral advice of a specifically religious kind had been disseminated to Russians since Christianization by texts such as sermons or didactic discourses (for example, *The Testament of Vladimir Monomakh*), while models of virtuous behaviour were set out in the Lives of the Saints. However, the etiquette treatise as such was an unknown genre before the publication of *The Honourable Mirror of Youth*. The outline rules for small boys contained in seventeenth-century materials such as primers concentrated on the need above all to 'kiss the rod, the whip, and the stick' (*tseluite rozgu, bich i zhezl lobzaite*), with only a very occasional author venturing into table-manners, counsels not to blow one's nose on one's hat or sleep naked, and above all to avoid splashing others when urinating.[148]

Still more unfamiliar was the notion of women as the arbiters of morality, politeness, and taste. In a Western context, as Amanda Vickery has argued, eighteenth-century views of motherhood constituted 'an overlaying of a range of secular celebrations on the ancient religious solemnizations'.[149] In Russia, with a quite different set of traditions, the 'secular celebrations' did not emerge so obviously from 'religious solemnizations'. There was, for instance, no iconographical tradition analogous to the late medieval Western representations of St Anne teaching the Virgin to read,[150] or of the Virgin gazing at the Angel Gabriel from behind her book-filled lectern; nor did the early modern Orthodox Church have anything resembling the powerful teaching orders of nuns, such as the Ursulines and the Sacred Heart, which emerged in the West during the seventeenth century. The 'pedagogical mother' was in signal respects something quite new.

To be sure, late medieval and early modern normative texts, such as hagiographies, had occasionally stressed the part that could be played by a mother, or mother-substitute, in bringing up her daughter to piety. In the *Life of St Yulianiya Lazarevskaya*, for example, we are informed that the

[147] 'Zapiski Filippa Filippovicha Vigelya', *Russkii arkhiv* 9 (1891), supplement p. 211.

[148] The first quotation is from Simeon Polotsky's *Uveshchanie* (1679), the second from an untitled text by Karion Istomin (1696). See E. O. Putilova (ed.), *Russkaya poeziya detyam* (2 vols.; St Petersburg, 1997), i. 82, 85.

[149] *The Gentleman's Daughter*, 93.

[150] On St Anne in the West, see Warner, *From the Beast to the Blonde*, 81–96.

saint's grandmother, who fostered her from the age of 6, 'raised her in piety and purity' (*vospitayushche vo vsyakom blagoverii i chistote*).[151] But there was no suggestion that this 'raising' went beyond the provision of an elementary religious education (the communication of basic literacy in order to read the scriptures, the teaching of prayers, and the passing-on of the precepts of the Orthodox faith). Anything more than this would have come close to endangering the authority of a husband, who was held, in late medieval Russian normative texts, to be absolute ruler in the kingdom of the household. As the most important domestic oracle of pre-Petrine Russia, the sixteenth-century *Domostroi*, had put it:

Подобаетъ поучити мужемъ женъ своихъ, с любовию и благоразсуднымъ наказаниемъ, жены мужеи своихъ вопрошаютъ о всякомъ благочинии како душа спасти Богу, и мужу угодити, и домъ свои добре строити и во всемъ ему покарятися, и что мужъ накажетъ то с любовью примати и творити по его наказанию, пърьвие имъти страх Божии и телесная чистота яко же впреди указано было.

Husbands should instruct their wives lovingly and with due consideration. A wife should ask her husband every day about matters of piety, so she will know how to save her soul, please her husband, and structure her house well. She must obey her husband in everything. Whatever her husband orders, she must accept with love; she must fulfill his every command. Above all, she must fear God and keep her chastity as decreed above.[152]

A wife who had already been given a complete education by her mother might well not 'accept whatever her husband ordered with love', and would scarcely have been considered a welcome match. In any case, this was a culture where learning for its own sake had little prestige in the elite; it was an exceptional woman (or man) who acquired more than the rudiments of literacy.[153] There was no reason, therefore, to make a link

---

[151]   See N. K. Gudzy (ed.), *Khrestomatiya po drevnei russkoi literature* (Moscow, 1973), 313. For an example of women's religious authority in practice, see the letters of an Old Believer noblewoman, *Die Briefe der Fürstin E. P. Urusova: Faksimile der Handschrift, Einleitung, Text, Glossar*, ed. M. Schmücker-Beloer (Hamburg, 1990). I am not intending to suggest here that Russian mothers felt little affection for their children in the pre-Petrine period: in her magisterial survey, *Die Russische Frau im 17 Jahrhundert*, N. Boškovska notes the stereotypicality of emotional rhetoric in letters (159), but argues that the mother–child bond was more important than the marital one (161).

[152]   *Domostroi*, Sil'vesterskaya redaktsiya, ch. 29: *Domostroi* ed. V. V. Kolesov and V. V. Rozhdestvenskaya (St Petersburg 1994), 104; English version from *Domostroi: Rules for Russian Households in the Time of Ivan the Terrible*, ed. and trans. C. J. Pouncy (Ithaca, NY, 1994), 124. The *Domostroi* continued to be held in provincial gentry libraries until some time into the 18th cent. (see ibid. 45–6).

[153]   In late medieval elite circles, where dynastic marriage was the norm (see Nancy Shields Kollmann, *Kinship and Politics: The Making of the Muscovite Political System, 1345–1547* (Stanford, Calif., 1987), ch. 4) the essential in a bride was powerful family connections. Though the education of Peter I's half-sister Sophia included theology, poetry, and possibly

between intellectual command and virtue. Indeed, in some respects, the period between 1550 and 1700 (like the sixteenth century in Western Europe) seems to have seen a rise in misogynist feelings among clerics (as manifested in texts such as *The Father's Word to His Son on the Wickedness of Women*), though the picture is complex, since the period also saw the expression of more balanced views of the sexes' propensity for good and evil (as in the sixteenth-century *Tale of Peter and Fevroniya*), and the emergence of an ethos of gallantry to women.[154] And, while pronouncing on practices is difficult because of a paucity of sources, the fact that bondswomen were used as wet-nurses and as supervisors for young children (*mamki, nyani*), would have limited contact between them and their mothers.[155]

In Peter I's reign, as Lindsey Hughes has pointed out, 'the ideals of womanhood propagated by the Orthodox Church and best known through . . . the *Domostroi* remained intact and were even reinforced in novel ways.'[156] As late as 1725, in his funeral eulogy for Peter I, Feofan Prokopovich made a significant choice of words to legitimate Peter's successor, his second wife Catherine (who reigned as Catherine I): he described her as combining 'the reason of a ruler and the nurture of a mother'.[157] The notion of 'reasonable maternity', it seems, was not a sustainable one at the time.

If 'reasonable maternity' was something that had partial support at best in Russian religious tradition, the ethos of modesty as autonomy could also not be extrapolated from there without problems. Though modesty had been an expected quality of the 'good woman' in medieval religious writings, it was more often seen in terms of the need to repress undesirable traits than as a quality worthy of admiration in its own right, an aspect of noble refinement and an expression of self-respect, even self-assertion.[158]

also Polish and verse composition, taught by the pioneering Baroque poet Simeon Polotsky, Lindsey Hughes points out that 'any one of these accomplishments would have distinguished [Sophia] from her Russian female contemporaries' (*Sophia: Regent of Russia 1657–1704* (New Haven, 1990), 34–5).

[154] See e.g. L. Sazonova, '"Lyubovnyi leksikon" v Rossii XVIII veka—amoris documentum', *Novaya delovaya kniga* 37 (1997), 25–30; N. Pushkareva, *Chastnaya zhizn' russkoi zhenshchiny: nevesta, zhena, lyubovnitsa (X–nachalo XIX veka)* (Moscow, 1997), esp.. 110–14. For a good short survey of 16th-cent. Western misogyny, see Hugh Cunningham, *Children and Childhood in Western Society since 1500* (London, 1995), 42–52.

[155] Pushkareva, *Chastnaya zhizn'*, 88–9.

[156] L. Hughes, '"The Crown of Maidenly Honour and Virtue": Redefining Femininity in Peter the Great's Russia' (paper presented at the Berkshire Women's Conference, 1999).

[157] Feofan Prokopovich, 'Slovo na pogrebenie vsepresvetleishego derzhavneishego Petra Velikogo . . .' (1725), in *Sochineniya* (Moscow and Leningrad, 1961), 128.

[158] 'Modesty' in the positive sense is found in Byzantine writings: Anna Comnena, for instance, refers approvingly to her mother's 'extraordinary modesty' (Book 12, ch. iii), and her grandmother's piety and virtue (Book 3, ch. viii), and refuses to give details of an act performed

The afterword to *The Honourable Mirror of Youth*, 'The Crown of Maidenly Honour and Virtue' required of young women sexual continence, a self-contained demeanour in public, respect for those in authority (parents, husband), and deference to the precepts of established religion, rather than a command of intellectual topics or moral authority.

Given this background, it is inevitable that Western ideas about maternity, and its link with the role of woman as cultural nurturer, were to prove particularly controversial. Even in eighteenth-century England, a country with some centuries of exposure to the ethos of civility, the 'women, urbanites and upright patriarchs' who espoused this ethos faced formidable opposition from 'unashamedly parochial sportsmen and irresponsible bachelors'.[159] In Russia, not all 'upright patriarchs' were as urbane as Nikolai Karamzin; some, such as M. M. Shcherbatov, directly associated cultural change with the encouragement of the 'propensity to authoritarianism' that they held to be particularly characteristic of women.[160] (A censor of the early nineteenth century, in similar vein, protested against the publication of an entirely decorous and conventional love poem on the grounds that it was 'sinful and humiliating for a Christian to sit at the feet of a woman'.)[161] 'Irresponsible bachelors' tended to express themselves differently, but they too often found the new cultural prominence of women ridiculous rather than admirable. A case in point was Ivan Krylov (1769–1844), impoverished member of the gentry, celebrated boor, card-sharper, and wit, whose satirical play *The Mischief-Makers* (1782), viciously lampooned the pioneering woman poet Elisaveta Sumarokova, and her husband Yakov Knyazhnin, under the masks of the ludicrous Rifmokrad (Mr Rhymestealer) and his wife Taratora (Mrs Gabbler).[162]

Krylov's play is intriguing because it demonstrates the existence, in late eighteenth-century Russia, of a mixed-gender literary gathering that was more than simply a space for flirtatious games. Behind the outrageous caricature of *The Mischief-Makers*, it is possible to see a resemblance between the gatherings of Knyazhnin and Sumarokova, and the salons of

by a pope on envoys sent by a king with whom he was in dispute: 'I would have given a name to the outrage, but as a woman and as a princess, modesty forbade me . . . if I had described it in detail, reed-pen and paper would have been defiled' (Book 1, ch. xiii). (See *The Alexiad of Anna Comnena*, trans. E. R. A. Sewter (Harmondsworth, 1969], 375, 120, 62.) But in the *Domostroi*, women are abjured to refrain from drunkenness etc. rather than urged to think of modesty as an achievement.

[159] See Vickery, *The Gentleman's Daughter*, 287.

[160] See Shcherbatov, *O povrezhdenii nravov*, 246; cf. Shcherbatov's denial of 'maternal instincts' in Catherine II, p. 254. This class of 'patriarch' will be considered at more length in Ch. 2.

[161] A. V. Blyum, *Za kulisami 'Ministerstva pravdy': tainaya istoriya sovetskoi tsenzury, 1917–1929* (St Petersburg, 1994), 249 (no source given).

[162] I. Krylov, *Prokazniki, Sochineniya* (Moscow, 1984), ii. 62–183.

seventeenth-century France.[163] At these mixed-sex gatherings, writing and reading were equal in status, both being seen as creative processes; and the authenticity of the salon text depended on its fidelity to the language of the group among which it was created and circulated, rather than on individual authorship.[164] In other words, women at such literary gatherings were precisely *not* facilitators or inspirers of literary work; they were themselves directly involved in literary production.[165]

The collaborative creativity in the Sumarokova-Knyazhnin ménage was represented uncomprehendingly by Krylov, who perceived this as plagiarism (in the case of Rifmokrad) and literary ineptitude (in the case of Taratora, who was shown pestering her hairdresser to supply her with rhymes, and bossily foisting her inane literary judgements upon the poetasters hanging about the house). Unconsciously indicating how peculiar Russian *littérateurs* found the authority vested in the salon hostess, Krylov represented Taratora as a stereotypical eighteenth-century termagant, a blood-curdling tyrant to her husband Rifmokrad and all around her. Equally inevitably, in terms of the standard plots of eighteenth-century comedy, Taratora's main concern was to foil the marriage of the young heroine to the man that she loved.[166] All the more absurd, then, from the point of view of Krylov's satire, was Rifmokrad's deference to his wife on literary points:

RIFMOKRAD: But incidentally: today Tyanislov [Driveller] wanted to read me some of his verses. Do you have any idea whether he can write?

TARATORA: My dear, I can never stop myself laughing!

[163] The term 'salon' is something of an anachronism, since assemblies could just as easily be held in a boudoir or bedroom as in a drawing-room, and 'salon' gained the fixed meaning of 'a room . . . where one may assemble' only in the 1760s (J. Whitehead, *The French Interior in the Eighteenth Century* (London, 1992), 84). Early Russian 'salons' seem to have had a similar fluidity of setting, but gradually the *zala* (salle) or *gostinaya* (guest room) became established as a meeting place. The letter-for-letter transliteration *salon* is recorded from the 1850s (see *Slovar' russkogo yazyka*, 4 vols. (Moscow, 1984), iv. 15), but earlier sources (e.g. Reif, *Russko-frantsuzskii slovar'*) give only *zala*. The gatherings themselves were generally known, throughout the 18th, 19th and early 20th cents., by the day on which they were held (Tuesdays, Wednesdays, Thursdays, etc.).

[164] 'True salon writing is without an internal authorial signature, somehow beyond personality, the collective style of a literary assembly—or of a politically disabused generation.' J. De Jean, *Tender Geographies: Women and the Origins of the Novel in France* (New York, 1991), 60; see also 83–4.

[165] D. Goodman, *The Republic of Letters: A Cultural History of the French Enlightenment* (Ithaca, NY, 1994), 102, argues that the French Enlightenment salon was itself based upon self-effacement on the part of the hostess: 'The *salonnière*'s art was thus based upon selflessness, which allowed her to manage the egos of others without imposing her own upon them. Her virtues were negative virtues, "female" virtues, such as modesty.' The memoirs of Vigée-Le Brun, which reproduce numerous examples of salon verse by women, though, suggest that there was more than one model of a literary salon in pre-revolutionary Paris.

[166] A sign of the haste with which Krylov scribbled his comedy is the fact that the girl is described at various points as Taratora's 'ward', her 'niece', and her 'daughter'.

RIFMOKRAD: He wanted to bring them so that I could pass judgement. But you know my way; I don't like damning anything, and I say everything is wonderful.
TARATORA: I see! So you want me to be scathing in your place.[167]

Emasculated in a critical sense, Rifmokrad was also sexually disadvantaged—Taratora might disport herself with all and sundry, but Rifmokrad's half-hearted efforts at adultery with a young woman in the pay of his enemies were soon exposed and routed. *The Mischief Makers*, then, at the same time as recording the existence of mixed-gender gatherings devoted to literary pursuits, also, by caricaturing the men attending such gatherings as unsexed boobies, and the women involved as harpies, indicated the limits of tolerance of women's novel cultural prominence. Krylov's suspicion of the salon was not a personal idiosyncracy (though he was notorious even in literary circles for his bad manners). In his poem 'To Parasha', Ivan Dolgorukov schematically contrasted the artificiality of the salon hostess Selimena, with her pretensions to literary taste, and the simplicity and directness of Parasha, an ordinary girl who, like Émile's Sophie, knew her place and her heart.[168]

Significantly, Krylov's scathing portrait of the Taratora-Rifmokrad ménage is almost the only substantial portrait of a late eighteenth-century 'salon' in the serious sense.[169] And in the early nineteenth century, the reservations of commentators of his kind were reinforced as the reaction against salon culture that had come about in revolutionary France began to make its way into Russian culture.[170] 'On Frenchwomen of the Nineteenth Century', an article translated from the French in 1805, observed with approval that now many Frenchwomen had wisely realized that they knew nothing about politics: family life had benefited from this, if also the prosperity of milliners and ribbon-sellers.[171] As serious literary dicussion became politicized, the result was a sterner attitude to the appropriate forms of discourse. Madame Genlis lamented in 1818 the decline of the old

---

[167] Krylov, *Prokazniki*, 94.

[168] See G. V. Ermakova-Bitner (ed.), *Poety-satiriki kontsa XVIII–nachala XIX veka* (Leningrad, 1959), 399–402.

[169] Vigel' recollects that the woman writer Aleksandra Khvostova held 'tasteful' salons in her house, but also records that she, as an unhappily married woman, was ostracized by much of society (*Zapiski*, i. 274).

[170] No doubt Rousseau had an influence here too: as Peter France points out, 'notably [in] the *Lettre à d'Alembert* and *La Nouvelle Héloïse*, Rousseau compares Parisian high society unfavourably with the cruder, more homely world of Switzerland, the Geneva *cercles* for instance. A particular bugbear of his is the place of women in the Paris salon world; he sees female preponderance as a danger to the "manly" virtues (frankness, courage, etc.) which a free society needs' (*Politeness and its Discontents: Problems in French Classical Culture* (Cambridge, 1992), 70). It is interesting that the term *cercle* was to find its way into early 19th-cent. Russian as *kruzhok*, a term for an intimate (and male-dominated) gathering.

[171] Anon., 'O frantsuzskikh zhenshchinakh 19–go stoletiya', *VE* 28 (1805), 16–31.

elegance—though never frivolity—of the salon, and of its peculiar 'feminine' language (prohibiting the use of nouns unqualified by adjectives and of the informal second-person singular to women), under pressure from the contemporary taste for politics:

Now all these customs have vanished. Every man can now say:
  De soins plus importants mon âme est agitée.
  [My soul is stirred by more important things.]

No one is remotely concerned by the social delicacy of the past, since even in salons, all the talk is of nothing but great political affairs.[172]

In Russia, reaction against the domination of the salon (which in any case had been only a potential domination) was exacerbated by a burgeoning irritation with the domination of polite conversation by the use of French. In 1802, even the gallant Karamzin had protested against linguistic Gallomania:

Let us leave it to our amiable ladies of polite society to maintain that the Russian language is coarse and unpleasant; that *charmant* and *seduisant*, *expression* and *vapeurs* cannot be expressed in it, and that, in a word, it is not worth the effort of knowing. Who would dare to show a lady that she is mistaken? But men do not have the amiable right to be mistaken. Our language can express not only high eloquence and resonant, picturesque poeticisms, but also tender simplicity, the sounds of the heart and of feeling. It is richer in harmony than the French; more capable of expressing shadings of the spirit, and it has a larger number of synonyms.[173]

The silly views held by ladies on serious subjects (and by implication these views were certain to be silly) might be patronizingly tolerated in mixed company, but earnest literary business was now not supposed to concern itself with such trivialities.

The rise of a new and more earnest masculine literary culture (expressed through the formation of literary societies, such as the Society of Lovers of the Russian Word) was further encouraged by open articulation of an 'ideology of separate spheres', according to which women's contribution to public life was held to be distinctive, limited, and indirect. To be sure, it would be both misleading and sentimental to represent Catherine II's reign as an era of free speech for women. The empress herself held some decidedly repressive ideas about the female place, as expressed, for instance, in her expostulation against gossip in her reading primer for schools:

---

[172] Madame Genlis, *Dictionnaire critique et raisonné des étiquettes de la cour, des usages du monde, des amusemens, des modes, des moeurs, etc.; depuis la mort de Louis XIII jusqu'à nos jours [. . .] ou l'esprit des étiquettes et des usages anciens, comparés aux modernes*, 2 vols. (Paris, 1818), ii. 347, headword *Ton des hommes avec les femmes*. See also Goodman, *The Republic of Letters*, 239–40.

[173] Karamzin, 'O lyubvi k otechestvu i narodnoi gordosti', *VE* 4 (1802): repr. in *Izbrannye sochineniya v 2 tomakh*, 2 vols. (Moscow and Leningrad, 1964), i. 286.

The duties of a good mistress of the house are to be quiet, modest, constant, careful; zealous in her duties to God, respectful to her parents-in-law, loving and orderly with her husband; to bring up her children to a love of justice and of their neighbour; to treat man- and maid-servants with mercy; to listen eagerly to virtuous talk, but shun lies and falsity; not to be idle, but industrious in all that she does and to be thrifty in her spending. What corrupts a home is when the mistress of the house loves to hear low tattle from men- and maid-servants and to pass this on, with embellishments of her own, to her husband, and when the husband believes it.[174]

But as a ruler who overtly exploited feminized imagery as legitimation, Catherine evoked in her own person female roles that went beyond that of the 'mistress of the house'; moreover, she was determined to enforce a civilizing role for elite women. By the early nineteenth century, the so-called 'ideology of separate spheres' was placing strict boundaries round the public issues that were on and off limits to female discourse. As a speech given by Nicholas Paqui de Savigny at the founding of Khar'kov University in 1811 put it, 'Men make laws and women morals.'[175] The shift in ideology was reflected in changes to the school syllabus at Smol'nyi. Instead of reading *On the Duties of Man and of Citizen* in classes, pupils in the lower levels were assigned *Fatherly Advice to My Daughter*, a publication by the prolific German advice-book author Joachim Heinrich Campe, which emphasized the virtues of housekeeping and obedient wifedom over intellectual accomplishment. Of a hundred 'composeresses, painteresses, embroideresses, ballerinas', hardly one was 'a sensible and good wife', complained Campe; and in a passage certainly more relevant to the graduates of Smol'nyi, he asserted that 'learned conversation at table' did not compensate for 'disorderliness in the household' and 'neglect of the laundry'.[176] Rather than being prepared for life as citizens, women were supposed to meditate upon their life of service in the family, and to grasp that this was subordinate to patriarchal authority.[177]

---

[174] Catherine II, *Rossiiskaya azbuka*, 37–8.

[175] See N. Paqui de Savigny (citing Ségur), 'Ob usovershenstvovanii, priobretennom chrez uprazhnenie v slovesnykh naukakh molodymi lyud'mi oboego pola', *VE* 61 (1812), 270.

[176] See J. H. Campe, *Väterlicher Rath für meine Tochter: ein Gegenstück zum Theophron der erwachsenem weiblichen Jugend gewidmet* (Frankfurt and Leipzig, 1790), 49–50. On the use of the Russian translation, *Otsovskie sovety docheri*, at Smol'nyi, see Cherepnin, *Imperatorskoe Vospitatel'noe obshchestvo*, i. 331. My thanks to Wendy Rosslyn for identifying Campe's book, the companion to the equally boring *Theophron, oder der erfahrne Rathgeber für die unerfahrne Jugend* (3rd edn.; Tübingen, 1786). Another text of this kind was Marshal Suvorov's advice to his daughter, published in Sergei Glinka, *Moskovskii al'manakh dlya prekrasnogo pola* (Moscow, 1825), 161–2, which advises his daughter to be modest both in the sense of decorous behaviour with men and of avoiding 'brilliant company', which usually manifests 'corrupt morals'.

[177] Cf. the arguments of Diana Greene, 'Mid-Nineteenth-Century Domestic Ideology in Russia', in R. Marsh (ed.), *Women and Russian Culture: Projections and Self-Perceptions* (New York, 1998), 78–90. Amanda Vickery argues forcefully in *The Gentleman's Daughter*, 7, that the ideology

Propagandization of the 'ideology of separate spheres' in turn had marked effects upon perceptions of women's roles as moral guides. To be sure, the new emphasis upon the centrality of family roles did not necessarily generate a view that women should no longer be educated. Savigny argued forcefully that laughing at women's education should be left to 'the rabble', and that women needed tuition in morals and in a wide range of subjects in order to strengthen their authority in the family, and make them worthy mothers to their children (male as well as female).[178] The same argument had been voiced by a woman writer in 1811, who had stressed that without education women could not be adequate wives or good guides to their daughters.[179] But this view of the importance of an *éducation maternelle* that combined intellectual and moral stimulation, familiar in Russia since the arrival of work by Fénelon and his sucessors, began to lose ground before more restrictive views of women's education. As a woman writer responding to 'K... R...a' put it in 1811, tuition in house management and morality was quite enough for women, since there was no need for them to be corrupted by the desire to 'shine' in society.[180] And a repressive view of morality as something that stopped women from asserting themselves was combined with emphasis upon the importance of male power in the family.

In principle there was no reason why the 'ideology of separate spheres' should not have been compatible with an emphasis upon 'pedagogical motherhood'. But although the education of children was now universally accepted, in discussions and in symbolism, as the task of women, the social power that this accorded women was played down. The image of the actively educating mother, usually in company with a girl-child, was challenged by the image of a virtuous but silent woman united in a mystical bond with a male infant. Exemplary was 'Epistle to the Grand Duchess Alexandra Feodorovna on the Birth of Grand Duke Alexander Nikolaevich' (1818), by Vasily Zhukovsky, who in the 1810s occupied a role approaching that of unofficial poet laureate to the royal house. Zhukovsky's poem identified royal maternity with nurture in the sense of loving watchfulness and protection against harm, rather than with active intellectual guidance:

---

of separate spheres was 'a cry from an embattled status quo, rather than the leading edge of change'. I would accept this interpretation for the Russian case too; however, the backlash against the female presence in public life was a more serious matter in a country where that female presence itself was a phenomenon of relatively recent date.

[178] Savigny, 'Ob usovershenstvovanii', 270–80.

[179] K...a R...a, 'Nuzhny li zhenshchinam nauki i poznaniya?', *VE* 57 (1811), 58–60.

[180] A...a D...a, 'O vospitanii zhenshchiny', *VE* 57 (1811), 146–51. The author cites *Vocquelin's *Reflexions sur l'éducation des demoiselles*.

Теперь, едва проснувшийся душой,
Пред матерью, как будто пред Судьбой,
Беспечно он играет в колыбели,
И Радости младые прилетели
Ее покой прекрасный оживлять;
Житейское от ней еще далеко...
Храни ее, заботливая мать;
Твоя любовь — всевидящее око;
В твоей любви — святая благодать.[181]

Now, scarcely awakened with his soul,
Before his mother, as it were before Fate,
He plays in his cradle, free of care,
And the young Joys have flown in
To enliven his beautiful rest.
Quotidian cares are still far away...
Guard the cradle, careful mother;
Your love is an all-seeing eye,
And in your love is sacred grace.

The phrase 'the all-seeing eye' attributes to mother-love the power of the masculine divinity. But the central image is that of the 'Protection' of the Mother of God: an iconic guarantee of familial, imperial, and national security that rests on benevolence rather than upon active intervention.

The decline of 'pedagogical motherhood' in the symbolism of the royal house was, of course, linked to the demise of the archetypal 'pedagogical mother', Catherine II, and to the concerns of Catherine's male successors to efface the spectre of her reign by stressing that maternity was a condition dependent upon patriarchal authority.[182] But it had wider social resonance as well. The Napoleonic Invasion in 1812, which naturally produced a surge of patriotism throughout Russian society, had also generated an emphasis upon military valour as the ultimate expression of heroism. Savigny's assertion, in 1811, that the education of boys should produce a 'softening of male manners' came just before the shift in values; in Zhukovsky's 'The Singer in the Encampment of Russian Warriors', 'softness' was the province only of the women and children left behind by their male defenders: 'There, our wives and tiny mites | Weep for us to the Creator; | And we are the joy of their life.'[183] The distinction between

---

[181] V. A. Zhukovsky, *Gosudaryne velikoi knyagine Aleksandre Feodorovne na rozhdenie v. kn. Aleksandra Nikolaevicha. Poslanie* (Moscow, 1818); quoted from *Sochineniya v 3–kh tomakh* (Moscow, 1980), i. 225.

[182] See R. Wortman, *Scenarios of Power: Myth and Ceremony in Russian Monarchy* (Princeton, 1995), i. 250–1.

[183] 'Tam nashi zheny, chada; | O nas ikh slezy pred tvortsom; | My zhizni ikh otrada' (Zhukovsky, 'Pevets vo stane russkikh voinov', *VE* 23–4 (1812): see *Stikhotvoreniya v trekh tomakh*, i. 129.

professional male detachment and commitment, and female emotion, was extremely important to the 'ideology of separate spheres'.[184] Important also was the force of the locution 'our wives', which rendered motherhood but one part of wifehood. For the doctrine of 'pedagogical motherhood', 'marital ties' had not been primary or even necessary (a virtuous woman could perfectly well exercise motherhood by proxy to a ward). It was the mother that ensured virtue in her daughter, a virtue whose dictates were to be observed even if this were unpleasing to a husband. The alternative doctrines of 'conjugal education', on the other hand (as voiced by Rousseau, Leprince de Beaumont, and Genlis) stressed the importance, above all, of accommodating a husband's tastes.

The belief in 'natural motherhood' that also began to gain a foothold in Russian society in the early nineteenth century might have seemed to threaten the authority of a husband just as much as belief in 'pedagogical motherhood' had done. But it was extremely rare for that possibility to be sensed. Tolstoi's representation of Natasha in *War and Peace*, which shows an obsessive and elemental maternal feeling that overturns any sense of propriety or moral boundary, and which makes Natasha's relationship with her husband peripheral at best, was exceptional even in its own day (the 1860s). In the 1810s and 1820s (the ostensible setting of *War and Peace*) the natural aspects of motherhood were not allowed to intrude as indecorously as in Natasha's case (it is one thing to breast-feed a child in decent solitude, and quite another to brandish that child's green nappies before visitors).[185] The bond between child and mother could be tolerated because it was susceptible to regulation, and because it could be invoked coercively in representations of women who asserted themselves as 'unnatural mothers' (a point evident not only in Nadezhda Smirnova's light-hearted reference to a 'disgraceful' dog of hers who 'was indifferent to motherly cares',[186] but

---

[184] Cf. (in a non-military context) Madame de Campan's description of a marriage: 'Every different position in life has its own language, and the language of the best husband is no longer that of the lover. Men, being committed to serious work (*livrés à forts travaux*), cannot have the sweetness and gentleness of a woman in their manners and in the sound of their voice.' (*De l'éducation, suivi des Conseils aux jeunes filles, de quelques essais de morale, et d'un théâtre pour les jeunes personnes* (2nd edn.; 4 vols.; Paris, 1832), iii. 88).

[185] The impropriety of Natasha's action would have been great indeed in a generation where Vigel' could deem eccentric the case of a woman who mended her husband's plush drawers and daughter's spencers while receiving guests in her drawing room (in relating the story, he also notes that this woman was an Armenian, as though her non-European origin explained her curious ways: *Zapiski*, ii. 303).

[186] A. O. Smirnova, *Vospominaniya. Pis'ma* (Moscow, 1990), 322. Cf. Madame de Ségur (née Countess Sofiya Rostopchina) in a letter of 5 Aug. 1824: 'The she-ass is very pretty and sweet, but she is an unnatural mother [une mère dénaturée]: she leaves her foal in the field while she climbs a bank that he cannot climb' (*Correspondance*, ed. M.-J. Strich (Paris, 1993), 2.1. Cf. E. A. Protasova's rebuke to her daughter A. P. Elagina for contemplating entering a convent upon

also in Mariya Zhukova's story *Baron Reikhman*, in which a wife who transgresses the proprieties by appearing to take a lover loses both her husband and her child).[187]

Another correlative of the new emphasis on 'natural' motherhood was that pedagogical motherhood came to seem 'unnatural'. Tolstoi's splitting of maternity into its 'natural' and 'pedagogical' aspects (embodied in the first case by Natasha, and represented in the second by Princess Mar'ya) captured a symbolic truth of the period he intended to represent. The 1820s and 1830s witnessed a decline in the lustre of what Vigel', an eminently characteristic figure of the late eighteenth century, had termed 'the touching custom' of taking a *vospitannitsa*.[188] In texts such as Pushkin's *The Queen of Spades* (1834), the relationship between sheltering adoptive mother and ward was now seen as one of institutionalized exploitation (having suffered herself as ward to the tyrannical countess, Liza goes on to take a ward herself, and, by implication, to perpetuate tyranny).[189] And young men of a democratic coloration, the real-life counterparts of Tolstoi's Pierre, took, like him, a fervent interest in the ideas of Rousseau, whose lustre could only be increased by the intolerance of Catherine, given that the empress had come to seem the epitome of tyrannical female misrule.[190] *Pace* Tolstoi's suggestion in *War and Peace*, though, in practice it seems to have been less Rousseau's sponsorship of 'natural motherhood' than his model of the 'conjugal marriage' that appealed. Certainly, biologistic definitions of femininity did have some currency in Russia in the 1820s and 1830s. For example, in a letter to his wife Natal'ya, Pushkin cited the phrase 'woman is a weak and sick creature [*un animal faible et*

widowhood: '[God] has given you the capacity to raise [*vospitat'*) your children; that is your *talent*, which you have been lent for a time, and it will do you no good to bury it in the ground' (letter of Spring 1814, *Utkinskii sbornik* i. 290).

[187]   Zhukova's *Baron Reikhman* is one of the stories from her cycle *Vechera na Karpovke* (1837–8: repr. Moscow, 1986). An English version of the story is available in Joe Andrew (ed.), *Russian Women's Shorter Fiction, 1837–1863* (Oxford, 1996), and contrasting interpretations of it are given in Andrew's 'Maria Zhukova and Patriarchal Power', in *Narrative and Desire: Masculine and Feminine in Russian Literature, 1822–1849* (London, 1993), and in ch. 2 of C. Kelly, *History of Russian Women's Writing 1820–1992* (Oxford, 1994).

[188]   *Zapiski*, i. 60.

[189]   Later instances of the exploited *vospitannitsa* include the heroine of Zhukova's story 'The Locket' (Medal'on) (see *Vechera na Karpovke* and Andrew, *Russian Women's Fiction*), and N. V. Nevrev's painting 'Vospitannitsa' (1867): see M. N. Shumova, *Russkaya zhivopis' serediny XIX veka* (Moscow, 1984) [this edn. has no page nos.]. In Tolstoi's *Anna Karenina*, the *vospitannitsa* relationship is treated satirically: while neglecting her own daughter by Vronsky, Annie, Anna adopts Hannah, the daughter of her English groom, as a ward.

[190]   On Rousseau's 'underground' popularity with young idealists even during Catherine's reign, see L. N. Kiseleva, 'S. N. Glinka i kadetskii korpus (iz istorii "sentimental'nogo vospitaniya" v Rossii)', *Uchenye zapiski Tartuskogo gosudarstvennogo universiteta* 604 (1982), 48–63—education at the Sukhoputnyi shlyakhetnyi kadetskii korpus, which Glinka attended from 1782 to 1794, was as close to Rousseau's model as possible.

malade]'. This was taken from an essay by the minor eighteenth-century writer, Abbé Galiani, who was very popular with Pushkin and his circle. In the essay, 'Croquis sur les femmes', Galiani had adduced biological reasons for woman's innate 'weakness', a weakness uncorrectable by education, since a female spent six days a month—in total a fifth of her life—indisposed (due to menstruation), even before pregnancies were taken into account.[191] Pushkin's reference to Galiani came as part of an exhortation to take care while pregnant, but elsewhere he offered advice on the other significant malady besetting Natal'ya: 'Above all, take care when you've got your periods—don't read filthy books [skvernye knigi] from grandfather's library, don't foul your imagination [ne marai], wifey.'[192] But far more noticeable than any biologistic emphasis in the letters are Pushkin's constant attempts to regulate Natal'ya's conduct in a moral sense, and to provide his bride with a moral education. Like Rousseau's *Émile*, he assumes his wife to be a moral *tabula rasa* upon which he inscribes the education that he feels she should have, rather than adapting himself to the one that she has received from her mother. At times, the letters speak in phrases straight out of a conduct book. 'Modesty is the greatest ornament of your sex', Pushkin opined on 6 May 1836 (*PSS* xvi. 112, no.1190), in a phrase that reads like an unconscious quotation from *Essay on the Education of Young Women* (1788)[193] His self-ironizing asides—'well, there's a moral for you' (*PSS* xv. 153, no. 947)—his affectionate use of the studiedly inappropriate endearment 'zhinka' ('wifey'), and his occasional warm sensuality only partly disguise the fact that he is earnestly attempting to provide Natal'ya with the education with which, according to some perceptions, she should have been provided by her mother.

A later and more vehement exponent of 'conjugal education' was the young Tolstoi, who treated his ward and almost-betrothed Valeriya Arsen'eva to a dauntingly pompous correspondence course in decent behaviour:

Everything is achieved by hard labour and self-sacrifice. The harder the labour, the harder the self-sacrifices, the greater the reward. The task requiring our labour is an enormous one—that of understanding each other and maintaining each other's love and respect . . . Please *do* go out for a walk every day, no matter what the weather is like. Any doctor will tell you that, and make sure to wear a corset and

[191] *Opere de Ferdinando Galiani*, in *Illuministi Italiani* vol. 6, ed. Furio Diaz and Luciano Guerci (Milan and Naples 1975), 635–42. Galiani's essay was written as part of a disputation with Louise D'Épinay: see Diaz and Guerci in *Illuminich Italiani*, 625.

[192] Letter of 20/22 May 1834, *PSS* xv. no. 919. The intellectual provenance of this advice is unclear.

[193] Cf. 'Modesty is the most amiable virtue in a young woman' (Espinasi, *Opyt o vospitanii*, 15).

put on your own stockings, and generally make improvements of that kind in yourself. Don't despair of becoming perfect. But that's all a lot of nonsense. The main thing is to live so that every night, when you go to bed, you can say to yourself: today I've (1) done a good deed for somebody and (2) become just a little better myself.[194]

Here, as in the case of Pushkin and Natal'ya Pushkina, the male correspondent's interest in the addressee is intimately connected with the idea that the wife who is badly brought up in a conventional sense may be the more easily moulded to a husband's feelings and desires.

The model of conjugal education maintained the association between women and morality that had been evident also in the model of maternal education, but subordinated the moral regulation executed by women to male control much more explicitly. The husband's authority was now absolute; thus—in ideology and symbolism—a coercive emphasis on maternal duties could be brought into harmony with a coercive emphasis on duties to the husband. When it came to a contest between the two, it was the latter that prevailed—as in the case of Princess Mar'ya Volkonskaya, wife of the Decembrist, who rose from giving birth to her child in order to follow her husband into exile, abandoning her small baby to the care of relatives.[195]

If the early decades of the nineteenth century saw an erosion of women's claim to authority within the family, it was only natural that their claim to superior ethical and aesthetic powers—which had always been relatively controversial—should excite suspicion. And this suspicion was enhanced, in the 1810s, by the impatience with moral governance per se that had now begun to be felt by many adult members of the Russian metropolitan and provincial *dvoryanstvo*. Tutored in Western manners in childhood and adolescence, they felt no need to consult manuals of etiquette in order to learn how to behave in polite society. Advice on conduct had become associated with the nursery and the schoolroom, and, outside these specific settings, was regarded as the ludicrous iteration of information of which all well-bred persons were only too well aware. The standard word for good behaviour remained *vospitannost'*, emphasizing that manners were the result of the *vospitanie* (upbringing, moral education) received during childhood; but comment on this process now seemed egregious.

One result of the expectation that the rules of etiquette would be known automatically was a shift in consumption patterns according to which guides on the internal regulation of behaviour (*vospitannost'*) became less

---

[194] Tolstoi, letter to V. Arsen'eva of 2 Nov. 1856: *PSS* lx. 97–8.

[195] See Mar'ya Volkonskaya, *Zapiski*, ed. M. S. Volkonsky (St Petersburg, 1904); and also Nekrasov's *Russkie zhenshchiny*, which mythologized this incident for later generations of Russians.

popular than guides on external behaviour (estate management, gardening, fashion), which had been a relatively insignificant genre in the late eighteenth century.[196] (Etiquette books published between 1800 and 1840 tended to be special cases, such as *The Rules of Worldly Behaviour and Politeness* (1829), a self-consciously zany publication emphasizing worldliness rather than politeness in its advice—readers were to flourish their watches to choke off boring guests, present their superiors with baskets of game, and absolutely never attend amateur concerts.)[197] Another was the rise of humorous behaviour literature offered in a spirit of ridicule or parody. In the mid-1820s, for example, Pushkin inscribed this rather charming little piece of rhyming mock-advice in the album of Vyazemsky's young son:

> Душа моя Павел
> Держись моих правил:
> Люби то-то, то-то,
> Не делай то-то.
> Кажись, это ясно.
> Прощай, мой прекрасный.   (*PSS* iii. 55)

> My dear friend Paul,
> Obey these rules, or none at all:
> Be sure do this and that,
> But don't do this and that.
> I think that's fairly clear.
> Good day to you, my dear.

And a poem written later, but fully in the same spirit, Aleksei Tolstoi's 'Wisdom of Life', was a *reductio ad absurdum* of such routine counsel on etiquette as the advice not to belch at table, subverting polite statements of the obvious by spelling out *faux pas* about which modest writers kept silent:

---

[196] See Appendix 1, Table 1, and compare figures for 'moral instruction' on the one hand, and 'recipes and handy hints' on the other. Most household manuals in the 18th cent. were translations of, or compilations taken from, foreign sources: see e.g. Kompan, *Tantsoval'nyi slovar'* (1790); Levshin, *Vseobshchee i polnoe domovodstvo* (trans. from *La nouvelle maison rustique*); Osipov, *Starinnaya ruskaya khozyaika* (1790) On the development of this branch of advice literature as a form of nationalist discourse from the late 1800s, see Ch. 2. Even the most original 18th-cent. household manual, Osipov's *Karmannaya kniga* (1791), which contains some splendidly opinionated comments about, for instance, pigs and cats ('they are only useful when killed' in the first case (p. xxv) and 'gelded male cats are much better, bigger, and more reliable than any others' (p. 275)), and the efficacy of making small children help with herding animals (pp. xvii–xx), is free of the nationalist tone of later work by Levshin.

[197] *Pravila svetskogo obkhozhdeniya*, 39–40, 71, 61. A special case of a different kind is a manual for young officers, *Put' chesti* (1837).

Если кто невольным звуком
Огласит твой кабинет,
Ты не вскакивай со стуком,
Восклицая: «Много лет!»

.   .   .   .

Всем девицам будь отрада,
Рви в саду для них плоды,
Не показывай им зада
Без особенной нужды.[198]

If someone sends a certain sound
Rolling and echoing around
Your study, don't jump brightly up
And shout: 'I say, old chap, bad luck!'

.   .   .   .

Make sure that you delight the ladies
By picking fruit for them, and berries,
But do not bare your nether regions
Unless you must; that's quite indecent.

The most brilliant exploitation of moralistic tradition came, however, in the fables written by Ivan Krylov in the 1810s, which wickedly reworked a genre associated with the presentation of leaden *sententiae* to schoolroom audiences. In some of his fables, Krylov subverted the notion of moral guidance directly. In 'Musicians', for example, he mocked a foolish landowner who defended the frightful caterwauling and bellowing of his serf chorus by pointing out that the conduct of the singers could not be faulted:

— То правда, отвечал хозяин с умиленьем,
    Они немножечко дерут;
Зато уж в рот хмельного не берут,
    И все с прекрасным поведеньем.

А я скажу: по мне уж лучше пей,
    Да дело разумей.[199]

---

[198] A. K. Tolstoi, 'Mudrost′ zhizni', *Sobranie sochinenii v 4 tomakh* (Moscow, 1963), i. 417, 419. (The editors of the vol. date the poem to the mid-1870s). My thanks to Vladimir Orel for drawing my attention to this piece. For parody advice literature of a different kind, cf. Voeikov's use of the official civil servants' list (*adres-kalendar′*) as a statement of group affiliation: 'Parnasskii adres-kalendar′' (G. V. Ermakova-Bitner (ed.), *Russkaya stikhotvornaya satira kontsa XVIII- nachala XIX veka* (Leningrad, 1959), 597–600). On the consumption of conduct literature in childhood by members of the *dvoryanstvo*, see e.g. Aksakov, *Detskie gody*, 73, 76–7, which states that Bagrov's nursery reading included a didactic publication under the title *Zerkalo dobrodetelei* and Bukhan's 'home medical guide'. as well as Novikov's children's journal *Detskoe chtenie dlya serdtsa i razuma*.

[199] I. A. Krylov, *Basni* (Moscow, 1944), 29. For a more moralistic employment of the genre of fable, see e.g. Shishkov's 'The Impudent Young She-Fly' (Derzkaya molodaya muka), in which the eponymous creature falls into boiling water after disobeying her mother: *Sobranie sochinenii i*

'Sure, sure!' the indulgent master cried,
  'Their singing is a little rough;
  But they *behave* so well! And then, besides
They never touch a drop of the hard stuff.'

  In my view: better *touch* a drop,
  And do a decent job.

Even where Krylov's point was more closely in harmony with conventional morality, the raciness of his language, and the eccentricity of his metaphorical vehicles, ensured that sententiousness was left far behind. An injunction against boasting was illustrated with the splendidly bizarre figure of a bluebird who boasted about setting the sea on fire, and a comment on knowing the value of things with a portrait of a monkey who irritably smashed a pair of eye-glasses to pieces.[200]

This robust tradition of etiquette-parody was of course at some level an indication of the success of conduct guidance (there are cases when rebellion is the sincerest form of recognition), but it also pointed to an important and wide-ranging impatience with finger-wagging morality of all kinds (an impatience that is understandable enough in those subjected to the often mind-numbingly tedious moral literature aimed at children in the late eighteenth and early nineteenth centuries).[201] Impatience with propaganda for virtue was surely one reason why the curious combination of deference and egalitarianism inculcated at the Lyceum did not, as the teachers there had perhaps hoped, produce a healthy balance between self-reliance and docility in the elite civil servants who graduated from the school. Among the unreflective pupils, as someone who had studied there in the 1820s recalled, 'Everyone counted the days till we would be able to graduate, thinking only of his future career and the rank which he would have upon leaving' (Grot, 418). Like most kinds of conduct literature, the Lyceum reports reflected real life rather haphazardly. As Yakov Grot, who

perevodov Admirala Shishkova, 17 vols. (St Petersburg 1818–39), i. 56–7. Closer to Krylov's in approach, though using the lighter conversational style of the Karamzinists, are the fables of Vasily Zhukovsky, e.g. 'Martyshki i lev' (first published *VE* 8 (1807), see *Sochineniya v trekh tomakh*, i. 331).

[200] Krylov, 'Sinitsa', *Basni*, 40; 'Martyshka i ochki', ibid. 41–2.

[201] Such as J. H. Campe's *Kleine Kinderbibliothek* (1779–84), which was staple fare in Russia too, being reprinted by magazines such as *Detskoe chtenie dlya serdtsa i razuma*: see V. D. Rak, 'Perevodnaya literatura v periodicheskikh izdaniyakh' in Levin (ed.), *Schöne Literatur*, i. 294–5. Cf. *Nravstvennye kartinki: sbornik 24 nravouchitel'nykh rasskazov dlya detei*, trans. M. and G. Ivanenko (Moscow, 1800). The translator's introduction inveighs, in a manner worthy of Krupskaya, against imaginative literature: 'Why fill children's heads with things that do not exist?' (p. I), and insists on the tales' exemplary function: 'I trust, amiable children! that you will read this book not in cold blood, but with the fervent wish to imitate the rare and noble examples that you will find here on every page' (p. II).

studied at the school in the 1820s, recalled, the Lyceum boys were
themselves a good deal more status-conscious than their masters:

The relationship between the two courses (as the two classes were known) was
purely patriarchal in character. The younger boys looked up to the older with
respect, indeed sometimes with reverence, modelled themselves on them in
everything and were, indeed, more inclined to take direction from them than
from their tutors. (Grot, 419)

A side-effect of this reverence was the development of 'passions' among
younger pupils for older ones. While this was a phenomemon of girls'
schools as well, as recorded in many institute memoirs, there was a stronger
edge of 'homosocial anxiety' in the case of the boys. The diary of Sergei
Komovsky, a contemporary of Pushkin's, written in 1815, records that
Komovsky was teased on account of his 'passion' for Modest Korf, and that
other boys, in particular Ivan Pushchin, tormented him by flirting with
Korf.[202] None of this was recorded by the benign surveillance of the
Lyceum masters, who considered Ivan Pushchin's conduct exemplary.

But whatever their incidental practical failures, the censorious descriptions to which pupils were subjected were unusually effective in constructing a network of moral terminology that was inviting in its very
indeterminacy and lack of precision, and which was to have profound
resonance in the later life of their most intelligent and sensitive pupils. For
these, it was the Enlightenment emphasis upon universal moral values that
was of consequence; commitment to egalitarianism was brandished
defiantly in the face of the established social hierarchy. So much is
indicated in Pushkin's moving commemoration of the school as the
locus of true friendship, a bulwark from the hostile world, in '19 October
1825':

> Друзья мои, прекрасен наш союз!
> Он как душа неразделим и вечен —
> Неколебим, свободен и беспечен
> Срастался он под сенью дружных муз.
> Куда бы нас не бросила судьбина,
> И счастие куда б ни повело,
> Всё те же мы: нам целый мир чужбина;
> Отечество нам Царское Село.　　　　(*PSS* iii. 375)

> My friends, our union is sublime!
> It is indivisible and immortal as the soul—
> Unshakeable, free and carefree

---

[202] See Grot, 4–22. The term 'homosocial anxiety' was coined by E. Kosoffsky Sedgwick: see
her *Between Men: English Literature and Male Homosocial Desire* (New York, 1985) and *The
Epistemology of the Closet* (London, 1994).

It grew up under the aegis of the friendly muses.
No matter where fate casts us,
No matter where fortune leads us,
We are always the same, the whole world is foreign to us,
For Tsarskoe Selo is our fatherland.

For the young Pushkin, the appropriate 'fatherland' was one where 'sons'
were not subjected to 'fathers'; the phrase 'the whole world is foreign to us'
posited that any conflict between the products of enlightened education
and society was the fault of that society.

The myth was as frail as it was enrapturing: the fact that Lyceum
graduates were 'always the same' was far from advantageous in a society
that was becoming not more egalitarian, but more hierarchical (see Chapter
2). Conflict was exacerbated by a tendency among the more rebellious
young graduates of the Lyceum to repudiate even the benign control that
had been exercised over them by their masters. For instance, Pushkin's
poetic autobiographies reflected not so much a mechanical reproduction of
the values in which he had been instructed, but a witty and subversive
transmutation of these. The image of Pushkin the boy that emerged from
the school reports—chattering, hasty, witty (a 'rattle')—was to be of
profound import in his construction of identity later on. Adjectives used
by his masters to criticize deviations from the ideal of self-control,
stepennost', such as *pylkii* (fiery) and *rezvyi* (hasty), acquired a positive and
incentive function. *Pylkii*, for example, became a key-word for the
transports of illicit love:

В мечтах надежды молодой,
В восторге пылкого желанья,
Творю поспешно заклинанья,
Зову духов...

In the fancies of young hope,
In the excitement of *fiery* longing,
I hastily compose incantations,
Summoning the spirits...

(*Ruslan and Lyudmila, PSS* i. 438)

Rezvyi, on the other hand, became an epithet associated with enthusiasm,
energy, and social charm (as in the affectionate reference to Evgeny
Onegin, 'The child was hasty, but sweet' (*Rebenok byl rezov, no mil*, ch.
1 verse 3); more importantly, though, it was associated with the process of
creation (as in the poem 'Rhyme' (*Rifma*, 1830), in which the addressee
was described as *rezvaya deva* (mischievous maiden).[203]

[203] For other usages of *pylkii* and *rezvyi*, see *Slovar' yazyka Pushkina*, 4 vols. (Moscow, 1956–
59), iii. 896, 1008.

More serious than such private linguistic quibbles were outbursts of rebelliousness in public. A telling real-life example of this was an episode in which Pushkin was involved on 20 December 1818. On the evening of that day, he visited the theatre, where he became embroiled in an altercation with a minor civil servant called Perevoshchikov, who had been annoyed by Pushkin's coming to stand next to the seats in the stalls where Perevoshchikov was sitting with his wife, and had requested him to move away. Pushkin responded 'by speaking to him rudely [*nadelal emu grubosti*] and in abusive and indecent language'. Perevoshchikov complained to the St Petersburg police, with the result that Pushkin received a formal reprimand from his immediate superior in the Foreign Ministry, Petr Yakovlevich Ubri.[204]

In order to grasp the full offensiveness of this encounter to Pushkin's contemporaries, it is necessary to reconstruct the proprieties that were disrupted. By no means the only, or even most important, misdemeanour committed by Pushkin lay in his use of offensive language. Far graver was his subversion of the social hierarchy by rudeness to a more senior official, against whom he had transgressed, long before an obscene word was uttered, by territorial trespass (what would now be called 'encroaching on personal space') and by his failure instantly to obey the request that he moved. Thus could sincerity and spontaneity, 'being the same to everyone', seem dangerous defiance once it was unleashed into a world where the observation of minute distinctions of rank was crucial, and where, in Catherine Wilmot's words, young men hopeful for patronage from grandees such as Princess Dashkova 'appear[ed] slinking at doors, still in powder and pomatum and new cloaths, with their french Tutors watching the effect of their first hopeful bow and scrape into the awful circles of their Superiors!'[205] By contrast, Griboedov's famous play *Woe from Wit* (1824) portrayed as disgusting and ungentlemanly the 'bowing and scraping' of Molchalin, secretary to the rich and well-born Famuzov. Speaking in words straight from a conduct book, Molchalin announced:

> В мои лета не должно сметь
> Свое суждение иметь.[206]

> At my tender age, the thought I should
> Express my opinions is not good.

The play's protagonist, Chatsky, on the other hand, determinedly expressed his opinions to all and sundry with a directness that his elders

---

[204] P. Shchegolev, 'Neprilichnyi postupok Pushkina', in his *Iz zhizni i tvorchestva Pushkina* (Leningrad, 1931), 279–80.

[205] Wilmot and Wilmot, *The Russian Diaries*, 219, letter of 18 Feb. 1806.

[206] *Sochineniya v stikhakh* (Leningrad, 1987), 107.

found astonishing and insolent, but which was likely to be interpreted by fiery youth as a gesture of doomed heroism in the face of repressive and unjust social convention.

The behaviour imperative among Romantics, then, was to disrupt or ridicule accepted proprieties by demonstratively doing the opposite of what was required. Since conventional codes of manners held impoliteness to women especially outrageous, it was an attractive way of demonstrating unconventionality. In the case of the 1818 incident, Pushkin's use of foul language in front of Perevoshchikov's wife was as significant as his offensiveness to a superior.[207] It was a manifestation of a rebellion against the traditional view of the *honnête homme* as emollient and deferential that had begun spreading from France in the late eighteenth century, of a behaviour type that was known in France as the *petit maître* and in England as the *dandy*.[208] Male superiors and grand ladies were alike in that both exercised authority, the former in chanceries and the latter in drawing-rooms and ballrooms. The connection between the two forms of regulation was explicitly made by Pushkin's friend Vyazemsky, who said of women, 'They are fastidious in matters of art; they have their own kind of exclusivity, their own kind of pedantry, and their own form of "kow-towing to rank" (*chin china pochitai*).'[209]

In a society where the authority of senior males could not be avoided, failure to exercise due deference was extremely dangerous. The Lycean tradition of behaving in 'the same way to everyone', very poor preparation for work in the Russian civil service, bore particularly bitter fruit in the participation of Pushkin's friend and class-mate Vil'gelm Kyukhel'beker in the abortive Decembrist Rebellion of 1825. Aside from outright rebellion or punishable offences, though, there were few ways of challenging the hauteur of senior officials with impunity, chafe though Lyceans such as Pushkin might at the brusqueness of their superiors.[210] Attempts by young

---

[207] A comparable, though more amusing and less scandalous, case is recorded by Vigel'; exiled to Odessa in 1823, Pushkin taught a lady's magpie to swear, whereat 'the unhappy bird was doomed to live immured' (*Zapiski*, i. 236).

[208] See J.-P. Saidah, 'Le dandysme: continuité et rupture', in A. Montandon (ed.), *L'honnête homme et le dandy* (Tübingen, 1993), 123–50. In the Russian context, early 19th-cent. 'dandyism' has been analysed by Yury Lotman ('Russkii dendizm', *Besedy o russkoi kul'ture*, 123–36) and Sam Driver (*Pushkin: Literature and Social Ideas* (New York, 1989), among others, but a thorough study of the subject, including French as well as English influences, has still to be attempted.

[209] P. Vyazemsky, *Staraya zapisnaya knizhka*, ed. L. Ginzburg (Leningrad, 1929), 159.

[210] A case in point was Pushkin's dealings with Count Mikhail Vorontsov, his overseer in Odessa in 1823–4. Pushkin's claim, in a letter to A. I. Kaznacheev of 2 June 1824, *PSS* xiii. 95 no. 85, 'I think too much of the man to abase myself before him' was a considerable understatement. After Pushkin had not only composed a rude epigram on Vorontsov describing him as 'half milord, half merchant | Half wise man, half ignoramus | Half scoundrel, though there is hope | He'll be a complete one soon' (*PSS* ii. 284), but also cuckolded him, he was banished to further exile on the family estate in Mikhailovskoe.

men to make their seniors subject to regulation by the practice of duelling, the standard method of response on the part of an early nineteenth-century Russian gentleman to a perceived insult that came from a social equal, were doomed to failure.[211] The revolt against the moral authority of upper-class women was rather easier. One way of contriving it was demonstratively to shun the excessively learned products of Smol'nyi, the 'she-seminarists in their yellow shawls', as Pushkin called them in chapter 1 of *Evgeny Onegin*, and to espouse the company of coquettes, those exponents, in Chetardie's words, of 'shameful conversation filled with trivialities and with nonsense', 'constant dissimulation', and 'treachery under the mask of banal compliments'. In his 1825 essay 'The History of Coquetry', Baratynsky played tribute to the degraded, but attractive, arts of such a woman, a degenerate Venus who, expelled from Rome with the dawn of Christianity, had been resurrected in eighteenth-century Italy and France.[212] Rather than haunt the houses of aristocratic women to polish their manners, Romantic poets preferred to engage in risqué literary parlour games with flirtatious married women. For example, in the household of Sof'ya Ponomareva, the wife of a civil servant, young poets would gather to engage in exchanges of parody and in role-playing through verse.[213]

If deference to women *qua* women seemed ridiculous under any circumstances, and calling a woman a moralist was the same as branding her a bore, it may be imagined how much more absurd appeared the notion that accommodating female taste was the best measure of literary achievement. To the new generation of Romantics, the pedagogical mother seemed neither more nor less than a censor in skirts, and an ineffectual one at that. In the dedication to his *Ruslan and Lyudmila* (1818), Pushkin parodied the notion of the 'ideal reader', and its associations with the moral elevation to which the poet was supposed to aspire:

> Для вас, души моей чарицы,
> Красавицы, для вас одних
> Времен минувших небылицы,
> В часы досугов золотых,

---

[211] Irina Reyfman, 'The Emergence of the Duel in Russia: Corporal Punishment and the Honor Code', *RR* 54 (1995), 26–43, traces both the evolution of the duel as a means of redress, and the limitations on its functioning: see particularly p. 42, on fruitless attempts in 1822 by young officers to challenge their commanding officer, Grand Duke Nicholas Pavlovich (later Nicholas I).

[212] Baratynsky, 'Istoriya koketstva', *Polnoe sobranie sochinenii Evgeniya Boratynskogo [sic]*, ed. M. Gofman, 2 vols. (Petrograd, 1915), ii. 204–7.

[213] V. E. Vatsuro, *SDP: iz istorii literaturnogo byta Pushkinskoi pory* (Moscow, 1989). Cf. Pushkin's letter to Natal'ya, 8 Oct. 1833: 'I don't forbid you coquetry, but I do demand coldness, decency, grandeur from you—not to speak of irreproachable behaviour, by which I don't mean *tone*, but something else, the most significant thing' (*PSS* xv. 85, no. 851).

Под шепот старины болтливой,
Рукою верной я писал;
Примите же вы мой труд игривый!
Ничьих не требуя похвал,
Счастлив уж я надеждой сладкой,
Что дева с трепетом любви
Посмотрит, может быть украдкой,
На песни грешные мои.   (*PSS* iv. 7.)[214]

For you, enchantresses of my soul,
For you, for you alone,
The fables of past times,
In the hours of my golden leisure,
With the whisper of chattering old age in the background,
I have written with a true hand;
Accept my playful work!
Not demanding praise from anyone,
I am happy with the sweet hope
That a maiden, wracked by love's trembling,
May gaze, perhaps secretly,
On my sinful songs.

Rather than using a claim to female approval as its guarantee of moral elevation, *Ruslan and Lyudmila* trumpets its subversive nature by suggesting that it appeals to the clandestine tastes of girls reading 'in secret' (i.e., away from the vigilant, but fortunately not 'all-seeing', eyes of their mamas, who undoubtedly—if they had read their Fénelon—would have forbidden the consumption of such a very naughty book).

The association between politeness and the language of women was also held up to ridicule. In Izmailov's poem 'Tsenzor i sochinitel'', for example, the censor's reluctance to help a real writer see his work into print contrasts with his enthuasiasm for the work of two popular women writers:

ЦЕНСОР
Есть новый у меня один роман французский —
Жанлис, не то Радклиф. Не худо бы на русский
Перевести его. Я вам сейчас сыщу.

СОЧИНИТЕЛЬ
[*кланяется и уходит*]
Не беспокойтеся.

---

[214] In his Preface to the second edition of the poem (1828), Pushkin touched on the same topic, sarcastically twisting Voeikov's suggestion (made in a review in *Syn otechestva* 43 (1820)) that *Ruslan* should bear the motto 'La mère en défendra le lecture à sa fille' into the distinctly indelicate Russian paraphrase, 'Mat' docheri velit na etu skazku plyunut'' (The mother orders her daughter to spit on this tale). (See *PSS* iv. 371, 436 n.)

ЦЕНСОР
[*вслед ему*]
Я все там пропущу.[215]

CENSOR
Hang on, I have a novel here in French—
By Radcliffe, or Genlis. I'd recommend
You might translate it. Just wait there a mo
And let me find it.

WRITER
[*bows and exits*]
      Thank you, no.

CENSOR
[*in his wake*]
I'll let it through uncut, you know.

At best, the 'feminine' language that Karamzin had once seen as the natural language of polite literature was seen as one among many sources of literary style (others included the excitingly coarse speech of 'the Russian people').[216]

One result of the assumption that polite culture stifled male identity was that the composition of works offensive to propriety acquired a new status. The underground pornographic tradition (known as 'Barkoviana' after its most notorious practitioner or alleged practitioner, Ivan Barkov), and subverting eighteenth-century convention by sprinkling taboo words among the clichés of neo-classical poetry, was now seen as a form of heroic protest.[217] Pushkin, for example, is reputed to have said to Baratynsky's son, 'The first book that will be published in a censorless Russia will be the complete collection of Barkov's poems'.[218] In conversa-

[215] A. Izmailov, 'Tsenzor i sochinitel'' (1811), Ermakova-Bitner (ed.), *Russkaya stikhotvornaya satira*, 362.

[216] On the earlier link between women and polite speech, see V. Alekseev, 'Yazyk svetskikh dam i razvitie yazykovoi normy v XVIII veke', in *Funktsional'nye i sotsial'nye raznovidnosti russkogo literaturnogo yazyka XVIII veka: sbornik nauchnykh trudov* (Leningrad, 1984), 82–95; B. A. Uspensky, *Iz istorii russkogo literaturnogo yazyka XVIII–nachala XIX veka: yazykovaya programma Karamzina i ee istoricheskie korni* (Moscow, 1985).

[217] See Zorin and Sapov (eds.), *Devich'ya igrushka* for an excellent selection of such material, and a survey of its history, reception, and the problems of attribution (much of the material patently post-dates Barkov's date of death). A short English introduction to Barkov, together with a translation of a section from a play attributed to him, *Ebikhud* (Nofuccus) is available in D. Jones (ed.), *The International Encyclopedia of Censorship* (London, 2001). Later collections of 'Barkoviana' included V. Ogarev, *Russkaya potaennaya muza* (London, 1865) and Anon., *Russkii erot ne dlya dam* (Geneva, 1879). Parodies of neo-classical texts are only one of the many genres of 'Barkoviana'; later, texts set for rote-learning in the schoolroom (such as Lermontov's *The Demon*) generated their own obscene Doppelgänger, and a quite different genre again is represented by the bawdy poems about randy priests and merchants' wives, which come from a 'carnival' tradition going back to medieval times.

[218] Quoted in A. Zorin's introduction to *idem* and N. Sapov (eds.), *Devich'ya igrushka, ili*

tion, plain speaking was also applauded. Pushkin and Baratynsky revelled in Fonvizin's doggerel epigram upon the heroine of Maikov's tediously proper neo-classical play, *Argiopa*, 'Argiopa is a shitty arse' (*Argiopa— zasranna zhopa*: see Pushkin, *PSS* xiv, 143, letter no. 562), and the avoidance of genteelisms such as *beremenna* ('expecting') in favour of unvarnished colloquialisms such as *bryukhata* ('big-bellied', i.e. 'great with child') was a point of honour in the correspondence of the Pushkin pleiad.

The circulation of material of this kind in all-male company (a practice underlined by the title of an anthology of 'Barkoviana' published outside Russia in the 1870s, *The Russian Eros: Not For Ladies*) was nothing new. Rather more shocking and subversive to polite convention was the citation of 'unseemly' material in texts explicitly intended for the eyes of lady readers. The beginning of Pushkin's *Ruslan and Lyudmila*, in which Lyudmila was snatched from her marriage bed at the moment of consummation, was shocking enough to delicate minds; far more so was a passage where *The Gabrieliad* (1822), an irreverent joke in which the Virgin Mary was penetrated in turn by God, Satan, and the Angel Gabriel, was offered for the erotic delectation of a female reader:

> О милый друг! кому я посвятил
> Мой первый сон надежды и желанья,
> Красавица, которой был я мил,
> Простишь ли мне мои воспоминанья,
> Мои грехи, забавы юных дней,
> Те вечера, когда в семье твоей,
> При матери докучливой и строгой
> Тебя томил я тайною тревогой
> И просветил невинные красы?   (*PSS* iv. 131)

> O sweet friend! to whom I dedicated
> My first dream of hope and desire,
> My beauty, to whom I was dear,
> Will you forgive me my memories,
> My sins, the amusements of my youth,
> Those evenings, when in your family,
> In the presence of your tedious and strict mama,
> I tormented you with secret emotion
> And enlightened your innocent charms?

To be sure, *The Gabrieliad*, unlike the priapic fantasies attributed to Barkov, was not characterized by the laborious naming of parts in obscene language, by throngs of personified pricks and cunts and characters with names like

Sochineniya gospodina Barkova (Moscow, 1992), 16. The introductory essays by Zorin and Sapov are invaluable for their resumé of the mythologization of Barkov.

Ebikhud (Nofuccus), but by delicate periphrasis, as at the climactic moment moment of Gabriel's battle with Satan:

> Уж ломит бес, уж ад в восторге плещет;
> Но, к счастию, проворный Гавриил
> Впился ему в то место роковое
> (Излишнее почти во всяком бое),
> В надменный член, которым бес грешил.   (*PSS* iv. 133)

> See Hell rejoice; Satan's the upper hand:
> But then! o joy! see Gabriel make his stand,
> Sinking his teeth—a brilliant deduction—
> Into the part with which Satan's seduction
> Itself was earlier achieved (an action,
> That, in most forms of wrestling, is banned).

But the suggestion that the female reader was a confederate in corruption, and perhaps also a sexual partner, offered a more explicit challenge to propriety than 'Barkoviana', which did not dwell on the implied reader in this manner.[219]

CONCLUSION

From 1762, when Catherine II ascended the Russian throne, Russians from the *dvoryanstvo* were exposed to a huge number of different influences on behaviour, among them legislation; alteration of the urban milieu and of domestic interiors; education; didactic literature and treatises on conduct. All of these influences took as their starting point conditions in the West, most particularly in France (especially before 1789), and Prussia. But in the area of behaviour (as in any other area of human activity), practices sometimes adapted to their new setting idiosyncratically. In the case of women's and men's education, developments were particularly haphazard. The prestigious educational institutions founded by Catherine II and by Alexander I, Smol'nyi and the Tsarskoe Selo Lyceum, offered teaching in the spirit of their best counterparts in Western Europe, but their graduates were often ill-suited to life in the society that greeted them once they had left the shelter of their Alma Mater. Women from Smol'nyi were likely to be better educated than their husbands, and to have new-fangled ideas about taking an active part in educating their children, which ideas did not

---

[219] To be sure, one well-known late 18th or early 19th-cent. collection of 'Barkoviana', *The Maiden's Plaything*, contained an introduction presenting the material for the delectation of the 'fair Belinda', and archly suggesting that only those of impure minds would find it offensive (see Zorin and Sapov, *Devich'ya igrushka*, 39–40). But this sophisticated combination of erotic and literary challenge is unlike anything in the poetic texts anthologized.

always go down well in traditional circles. The most intelligent graduates of the Lyceum, those who had learned most from the education offered there, were also those who fitted least well into the status-conscious and increasingly static world of the Russian civil service (aside from the very few of them who ended up in its least 'official' branches, such as a university). Also confusing was the sheer range of different cultural information that was available. Material about women's education and conduct offered the competing models of *éducation maternelle* and conjugal education, as well as the incompatible ideas of 'natural' and 'pedagogical' motherhood. Men's education emphasized self-reliance and independence, but also self-abasement before those in authority. Among the results was the haphazard evolution of family relations. Intelligent Russians, such as Pushkin and later Tolstoi, espoused at one and the same time the notion of a wife's subordination to her husband, and of her right to autonomy, a situation aphoristically encapsulated in Mariya Zhukova's story *Baron Reikhman*, in which husband addresses to wife the ethical impossibility: 'I want you to be free.'[220] Pushkin's letters indirectly articulate something of the same contradiction in terms, as he struggles to make Natal'ya freely accept a view of her behaviour that he has imposed on her. And the consequences of men's education included not only manifestations of dandified 'anti-behaviour' among Romantic poets, but also a deep-rooted social disaffection that was expressed in the abortive Decembrist uprising of 1825.

Even in the area of symbolism, the spread of ideals of refinement was uneven. Certainly, representations of women exercising a new role as arbiters of taste and morality began to proliferate in the late eighteenth century; but there was considerable resistance to their dissemination. The salon never played as large a role as it had in the French literary world whose influence was so palpable in Russian culture: the association between women and the arbitration of morality and taste was generally perceived as repressive rather than inspirational, provoking bursts of anti-feminine feeling among younger writers after 1810, and at the same time creating an atmosphere in which women's voices seemed either tediously moralistic, or else charmingly trivial. The newness and strangeness of imported behaviour patterns, the fact that 'the politeness and refinement [of educated Russians] [had] the appearance of being placed upon them . . . rather than proceeding from any internal feeling'[221] made these behaviour

[220] Mariya Zhukova, 'Baron Reikhman', *Vechera na Karpovke* (1837–8) (Moscow, 1986), 40–75. Compare Carlyle's comments on the black man's 'right to be compelled' (see his *The Nigger Question*, quoted in R. West, *Black Lamb and Grey Falcon* (Edinburgh, 1993), 1091).

[221] Lyons, *At Home with the Gentry*, 23. The 'theatricality' of early 19th-cent. Russian culture is a prominent theme in much recent historiography: apart from Yury Lotman's extremely influential 'Iskusstvo zhizni' (*Besedy o russkoi kul'ture* (St Petersburg, 1994), 180–209, see

patterns increasingly uncongenial to a culture that had been infused by the Sentimentalist movement with a vivid enthusiasm for 'internal feeling'. This was to be expressed particularly fiercely in the genre of 'society tale' (*svetskaya povest'*), which depended upon a schematic division between external propriety and inner emotion, manners, and feeling.

Yet the radical nature of early Romanticism's assault on refinement should not be exaggerated. To some extent, it constituted a novel form of what Boris Uspensky has termed 'anti-behaviour',[222] parasitic upon the norms of the behaviour system out of which it grew, reinforcing rather than undermining these. The imagined female reader retained her importance, though split now in two (with the irate mama used as a measure of the transgressive nature of material that was supposed to delight her daughter). And the revolt against propriety had strict boundaries. Pushkin's comment about the publication of Barkov was meant as an excellent joke: a society in which he might be published was absolutely unimaginable. Outbursts of impertinence remained isolated incidents, not signifying a society in deep crisis. Pushkin is reputed to have responded to Princess Zinaida Volkonskaya's request to recite one of his poems in her salon with a performance of 'The Poet and the Mob', a denunciation of society's claims to regulate a writer's conduct, but it is inconceivable that young men of the Russian court would have unceremoniously spurned the empress's invitation to take part in the dance, as happened at Versailles in the 1780s.[223] And, in time both political circumstances—in particular, the catastrophic failure of the Decembrist Rebellion—and personal circumstances—notably, the decreased appeal of fantasies about adulterous wives once rebellious young men had themselves married—inclined the former transgressors to seriousness.[224]

With a resurrection of moral commitment, too, came a renewed respect

---

W. Mills Todd III, *Fiction and Society in the Age of Pushkin* (Cambridge, Mass., 1986), ch. 1; Roosevelt, *Life on the Russian Country Estate*, ch. 5. However, this theatricality was not purely ludic; it was also the result, and source, of alienation and cultural conflict.

[222] See B. A. Uspensky, 'Antipovedenie v kul'ture Drevnei Rusi', *Problemy izucheniya kul'turnogo naslediya*, ed. G. V. Stepanov (Moscow, 1985), 326–36. In contradistinction to medieval 'anti-behaviour', though, Romantic social rebellion was not perceived as harmless by members of the establishment: for a general discussion of this dynamic, see my Introduction.

[223] The Pushkin story comes from S. P. Shevyrev (see V. Veresaev, *Pushkin v zhizni* (Moscow, 1984), 131); on Versailles, see E. Vigée-Le Brun, *The Memoirs of Elisabeth Vigée-Le Brun, Member of the Royal Academy of Paris, Rouen, Saint-Luke of Rome, Parma, Bologna, Saint Petersburg, Berlin, Geneva and Avignon*, trans. S. Evans (London, 1989), 35 (ch. 5).

[224] In his later years, Pushkin was to deny his authorship of *The Gabrieliad*, a gesture probably based as much on aesthetic distaste (and religious remorse) as on a desire to subdue the scandal caused when a manuscript of the poem came to light in 1828. In his deposition to the police of 19 Aug. 1828 he refers to his distress in being credited with the authorship of 'such a miserable and shameful work', and claims that nothing so blasphemous would be found in any of his writings (*PSS* xvii. 621).

for women's language and women's taste. By 1830, 'At the beginning of life I remember a school', a poem by Pushkin in Dantean terzinas (a form associated in his work with confessional autobiography) was to see the writer's creative impulses as emanating not only from the congenial, if morally questionable, company of 'two demons': statues in a garden grotto representing Apollo and 'a woman-shaped [*zhenoobraznyi*] idol | Dubious and false | A magic demon—lying, yet sublime', but also the tutorship of a 'humble, badly-dressed | But majestic' schoolmistress (*PSS* iii. 354).[225] And, while Pushkin himself maintained absolute intellectual and moral authority in his marriage, and definitely did not want what Rousseau called 'a learned lady, a wit, and the president of a literary tribunal' as his spouse, several of his literary texts (notably *Evgeny Onegin* and *Dubrovsky*) show a woman resisting 'conjugal education' on the part of an aspiring spouse in order to find autonomy within a loveless dynastic marriage that more closely resembles the pattern of equality in separateness evoked by Fénelon and by Lambert than it does Rousseau's fantasies of conjugal partnership and natural motherhood.[226] For their part, the wives of some of Pushkin's contemporaries, notably Sof'ya Del'vig and Anastas'ya Baratynskaya, took a much fuller part in the literary lives of their husbands than Natal'ya Pushkina.[227] And eventually, under threat from a new hard-nosed literary professionalism represented by plebeian writers such as Faddei Bulgarin, who did not flinch from inaccurate but painful *ad hominem* attacks on Pushkin and his circle as 'aristocrats' out of touch with the tsarist regime's new ideology of *narodnost'*, 'national populism', those who had formerly mocked refinement started to retreat into a defence of its virtues, to see the salon no longer as a tiresome way of imposing petticoat censorship upon literary activity, but as 'an international journal of conversation produced and edited by charming women'.[228] It is notable also that the incursion into

[225] For a fuller reading of this poem, see P. Davidson, 'The Muse and the Demon in the Poetry of Pushkin, Lermontov, and Blok', in *eadem* (ed.), *Russian Literature and its Demons* (New York, 2000), 148–54; Catriona Kelly, 'Pushkin and *vospitanie* (moral education): A Reading of "At the beginning of life I remember a school"', forthcoming in *Alexander Pushkin and European Spiritual and Cultural Life* (Vienna, 2001).

[226] See Catriona Kelly, 'Educating Tatiana: Manners, Morals and Motherhood in Russia, 1760–1830', in Linda Edmondson (ed.), *Gender in Russian History and Culture, 1800–1990* (London, 2001).

[227] On Del'vig, see Sof'ya Del'vig's note on a letter to Anna Kern negotiating terms for the latter's translation of Sand: A. A. Del'vig, *Sochineniya* (Leningrad, 1986), no. 101 (p. 340). Sof'ya Del'vig is better-known as the promiscuous harridan who drove her wretched husband to an early grave; as in the case of Sumarokova-Knyazhnina, all that remains of her presence in history is a caricature. On Anastas'ya Baratynskaya, see Benjamin Dees, *Evgeny Baryatynsky* (New York, 1972), 19; G. Khetso (Kjetsaa), *Evgeny Baratynsky: Zhizn' i tvorchestva* (Oslo, 1973), 124–9, is a more hostile portrait.

[228] Vyazemsky, *Staraya zapisnaya knizhka*, 286. This observation is particularly striking because it takes the form of a diary entry: during the 1820s, such private or semi-private remarks had often

Russia of 'the ideology of separate spheres' in militant form from the late 1790s did not express itself in the form of a limitation of married women's property rights; the generous powers of agency accorded to women by a decree of 1753 withstood encroaching gender conservatism.[229] Indeed, women's property rights were sometimes enhanced during the early decades of the nineteenth century, when '[the] new accent on virtue served to undermine some of the existing gender inequities in the implementation of property law'.[230] By 1830, the figure of the female arbiter of morality and taste had a securer place in Russian culture than ever before, despite the widely held view that manners were constrictive and artificial. And this contradiction was to become still more important in the middle decades of the nineteenth century, which witnessed the rise of a nationalist conservatism marrying full-scale nationalist reaction against the 'emptiness' of 'Western civilization' to the conviction that moral rectitude and family solidarity were defining features of 'Russian', as opposed to 'Western', culture.

been the vehicles of a light-hearted or not so light-hearted misogyny. Equally, Pushkin's response to official disapproval of the original Lyceum (as manifested in Bulgarin's 1826 denunciation to the Third Section of the 'Lyceum spirit'—'when a young man does not respect his elders and treats his superiors in a familiar way, his equals in an arrogant one, and his inferiors in a contemptuous one' (A. Reitblat (ed.), *Vidok Figlyarin: Pis'ma i agenturnye zapiski F. V. Bulgarina v III otdelenie* (Moscow, 1998), 105), was to represent the school in the context of patriotic feeling: see e.g. 'Vospominaniya v Tsarskom Sele' (1829), where the 'holy memories' of childhood take place against a background of the 'national battles' of 1825 (*PSS* iii.189–90).

[229] For a discussion of the background and consequences of the decree, against the background of renewed emphasis upon 'gender tutelage' in Western Europe (in 1804, French married women were deprived of the control over property they had won during the French Revolution), see Michelle L. Marrese, 'The Enigma of Married Women's Control of Property in Eighteenth-Century Russia', in *RR* 58 (1999), 380–95.

[230] See Marrese, 'Gender, Morality', 2.

CHAPTER TWO

The Beauties of Byt: *Household Manuals, Social Status, and National Identity, 1830–1880*

Полезно ль просвещенье?
Полезно, слова нет о том.
Но просвещением зовем
Мы часто роскоши прельщенье
И даже, нравов развращенье:
Так надобно гораздо разбирать,
Как станешь грубость кору с людей содрать,
Чтоб с ней и добрых свойств у них не растерять,
Чтоб не ослабить дух их, не испортить нравы,
Не разлучить их с простотой,
И, давши только блеск пустой,
Бесславья не навлечь им вместо славы.
Об этой истине святой
Преважных бы речей на целу книгу стало.

(Krylov, 'The Gold Rouble')[1]

Pushkin's paean to Prince Yusupov as the perfect Westernized Russian aristocrat, with which the the previous chapter began, was also a hymn to social harmony. Associating with members of the Third Estate, such as Voltaire, Diderot, or Beaumarchais, as effortlessly as he did with Marie Antoinette and her court, Yusupov exemplified the Enlightenment virtue of *lyubeznost'*, amiability, a quality that, like self-restraint, wide reading, and sparkling conversation, was considered essential to civilized behaviour. Undue pride in rank, or *chvanstvo*, had begun to fall out of favour in the age of Catherine II, who herself, as one foreign visitor remarked admiringly,

---

[1] 'Is enlightenment useful? | Yes, there is no question of it. | But often what we call 'enlightenment' | Is the seduction of luxury | Or even the corruption of morals: | And so, one should consider carefully | That, if you tear the husk of crudity from people | Whether their good qualities might not also be lost; | Whether their spirit may be weakened, their morals and manners spoiled, | And they be sundered from simplicity; | Whether, acquiring a false glitter, | They might not achieve infamy rather than fame. | This sacred truth | Would provide enough solemn discussions to fill a whole book' (I. A. Krylov, 'Chervonets', *Basni* (Moscow, 1944), 44–5).

behaved with charming directness and simplicity: 'The complete freedom [of her manners], her cheerful conversation and the entire absence of any dreary stiffness meant that only the magnificent palace reminded me that I was not simply at the country house of the most amiable woman of the world.'[2] Since the sovereign—as in any traditional monarchy—set the tone, such 'amiability' spread outwards. And by the early nineteenth century, *chvanstvo* seemed amusing or bizarre, as is clear from Elizaveta Yan'kova's recollections of her grandmother, a hospitable but haughty woman who took care to impress herself on all her country neighbours:

> My grandmother Evpraksiya Vasil'evna [Shepeleva, née Tatishcheva] had, they say, rather an overbearing disposition. High-born, grand, and used to being paid court to in society, she made little effort to condescend to her less important neighbours, so that many women living round about did not even dare to enter her front door, but would use the side-door kept for the maids.[3]

This may have been the norm in the mid-eighteenth century, but by the time that Yan'kova, born in 1768, set down her reminiscences (which were recorded by her grandson in the 1850s), condescension was so generally expected that Shepeleva's behaviour seemed an entertaining eccentricity: such stiffness could by then have been expected only in provincials, such as Ivan Belkin, the fusty narrator of Pushkin's story 'The Shot' (1829). His rustic shyness and over-anxious use of 'your Highness' grate against the easy metropolitan charm of Count and Countess B★★★, who 'were delighted that [Belkin] had relaxed and begun talking', and refer to each other by their first names in the presence of strangers.[4]

Russian manners were relaxed enough to come as a pleasant surprise to visiting foreigners. Vigée Le Brun, for example, commented that grand Russian ladies were 'totally free of the haughtiness so prevalent in our own French ladies'.[5] It is amusing to consider the way in which brusque Bazarov, the nihilist hero of Turgenev's *Fathers and Children*, might have been received at Barchester Towers, and it is instructive that when conflict

---

[2] L. F. Segur, 'Zapiski o prebyvanii v Rossiii v tsarstvovanie Ekateriny II', in *Rossiya XVIII v. glazami inostrantsev* (Leningrad, 1989), 362.

[3] D. Blagovo, *Rasskazy moei babushki: iz vospominanii pyati pokolenii* (Leningrad, 1989), 11.

[4] A more informal way of referring to nobles at this date would have been by title ('graf', 'grafinya'). By the late 19th cent., democratic titled persons (such as Tolstoi) uniformly preferred the address by name and patronymic—even from servants—to the use of a title, let alone of official formulae of address ('your grace').

[5] *The Memoirs of Elisabeth Vigée Le Brun, Member of the Royal Academy of Paris, Rouen, Saint-Luke of Rome, Parma, Bologna, Saint Petersburg, Berlin, Geneva and Avignon*, trans. S. Evans (London, 1989), 173. Cf. the Marquis de Custine: 'The *ton* of high society in Russia is an easy politeness whose secret has been almost lost in France' (*La Russie en 1839*, 2 vols. (Brussels, 1843), i. 83; or a later visitor, Donald Mackenzie Wallace, remarking the absence of 'a haughty consciousness of innate superiority over the lower orders' in his Russian acquaintances (quoted in J. Tovrov, *The Russian Noble Family: Structure and Change* (New York, 1987), 33).

does break out, it is in the gentlemanly form of the duel (in Prussia, the plebeian Bazarov would have been considered 'not challengeable', *nicht satisfaktionsfähig*).[6]

The spread of *lyubeznost'* put an end to the old pre-Petrine arrogance of rank (which meant, for instance, that Prince Grigory Kozlovsky had to be forcibly transported against his will, 'in a simple cart', to a dinner at the patriarch's residence in 1691, and then lay on the floor, refusing to sit at the table, because he considered his fellow guests inferior to him in rank).[7] But it should not be confused with a 'democratic' attitude to family origins. On the contrary: the reigns of Catherine's successors saw a consolidation of the emphasis upon hereditary rank that had been reintroduced by the Charter of the Nobility in 1785. In 1797, Paul I ordained the composition of a unified heraldic register (*obshchii gerbovik*), and in the same year, his empress, Maria Feodorovna, who had succeeded Catherine as patron of Smol'nyi, composed a rule that the 'well-born young women' admitted there should be 'from the ranks of the *dvoryanstvo* in its essence', which is to say, should be the daughters of hereditary and not personal nobles.[8] Maria Feodorovna's curatorage also saw the syllabus of the *meshchanskoe otdelenie* ('bourgeois section') of Smol'nyi more carefully differentiated than previously from that of the section for 'well-born young women'.[9] During the reign of Nicholas I (very much his mother's son), social differentiations were still further reinforced. From 1845, Smol'nyi entrants might only come from Books 5 and 6 of the genealogical textbooks.[10] The new elite schools for men founded after 1800—the Tsarskoe Selo Lyceum, and the College of Jurisprudence in St Petersburg—were equally punctilious in their attitude to ancestry.[11] And under Alexander II, in 1856, 'hereditary *dvoryanstvo*' began to be conferred only upon holders of the top four ranks of the civil service (and the top six of the military service), and 'personal *dvoryanstvo*' only on holders of the top nine.[12]

Gradations of this kind both reflected and constructed attitudes among

---

[6] For Turgenev as author, to be sure, Pavel Kirsanov's challenge is an indication of the degeneration of duelling rules; however, the point here is that Pavel Kirsanov himself considers Bazarov a possible antagonist. On *Satisfaktionsfähigkeit* in Germany, see M. Kitchen, *The German Officer Corps 1890–1914* (Oxford, 1968), 54.

[7] See L. Hughes, *Russia in the Age of Peter the Great* (London, 1998), 179.

[8] See N. P. Cherepnin, *Imperatorskoe vospitatel'noe obshchestvo blagorodnykh devits: Istoricheskii ocherk 1764–1914*, 3 vols. (St Petersburg, 1914–15), iii. 210.

[9] Ibid. i. 331.

[10] See Brockhaus-Efron, *Entsiklopedicheskii slovar'*, lii. 920, headword *Rodoslovie i rodoslovnye knigi*; Cherepnin, *Imperatorskoe vospitatel'noe obshchestvo*, ii. 135–7.

[11] On the Uchilishche pravovedeniya, see statute no. 8185 (1835), *PSZ* xii.

[12] On the basis of different evidence (the vocabulary used in abstract discussions of Russian society), Gregory Freeze argues in 'The Soslovie (Estate) Paradigm and Russian Social History', *American Historical Review* 91 (1986), 11–36, that 'the modern notion of *soslovie* arose only in the nineteenth century' (14).

dvoryane, whose *lyubeznost'* often had well-marked limits so far as those from outside the *dvoryanstvo* were concerned. Aleksandr Nikitenko, a young man from humble origins who arrived in St Petersburg in the mid-1820s (and later a famous censor and diarist), recorded in his diary for 1826 that it had been a relief to meet the mother of his friend Mikhailov. She was 'highly intelligent, well read, showed great delicacy and amiability, and was only slightly infected with that stuffiness and woodenness (*chopornost' i prinuzhdennost'*) which persons of the so-called bon ton cannot seem to do without'.[13] Anxiety about social mobility is evident (here from the point of view of those seeking to exclude rather than the excluded) in Krylov's fable 'The Toad and the Ox', in which the eponymous amphibian 'bursts and dies' when he tries to puff himself up to the size of the larger animal:

> Пример такой на свете не один:
> И диво ли, когда жить хочет мещанин,
>   Как именитый гражданин,
> А сошка мелкая, как знатный господин.

> This is not the one such case we'd find;
> No wonder too, when any *meshchanin*
> Wants to live an 'honoured citizen',
> And any minnow like a mighty *dvoryanin*.[14]

Krylov's moralizing was as direct as his metaphor was (by his standards) uninspired. A more passionate and creative denunciation of social climbing was made in Gogol''s great play *The Government Inspector* (1836), and in his equally important novel *Dead Souls* (1842). Both depict the social upheavals caused when a plausible imposter exploits to his own selfish ends the confusion, in the minds of provincials, between metropolitan sophistication and genuine social prestige.

But the concern among *dvoryane* of middling or small means to keep outsiders in their place could not disguise the widening gap between these *dvoryane* and the 'aristocracy' in a narrow sense, a gap to which Pushkin— the celebrator of disinterested 'amiability'—himself drew attention in 'My Family Tree' (written, like 'To a Grandee', in 1830). Here the poet

---

[13] *Dnevnik*, 3 vols. (Leningrad 1955–1956), i. 32. A striking literary example of rank-pulling is 'Maksim Maksimych', one of the stories in Lermontov's *A Hero of Our Time*, in which Pechorin deliberately snubs the low-ranking army officer with whom he has formerly been friendly.

[14] *Basni* (Moscow, 1944), 31. 'Honoured citizen' (*imenityi grazhdanin*) was a title conferred on prominent townsfolk who did not come from the nobility or gentry, such as bankers and university professors. Cf. V. A. Levshin in his anti-Gallomaniac rant *Poslanie ruskago k frantsuzolyubtsam: Vmesto podarka v novyi 1807 god* (St Petersburg, 1807), 38, citing, as an indication of how society has gone downhill, the fact that merchants 'now want to be *dvoryane*, and extort official positions [*chiny*] for themselves', and how even the lowly *meshchane* have now lost all respect 'and doff their hats to no one'.

questioned the very basis of the association between refinement and aristocratic status that he had taken as a given in 'To a Grandee', assaulting both the aristocracy's claim to hereditary legitimacy and its claims to cultivation. In a series of pungent caricatures very much in the manner of Rowlandson, aristocratic courtiers are lambasted as catamites, creeps, and upstarts who have risen from lowly origins to social prominence:

Родов дряхлеющих обломок
(И, по несчастью, не один),
Бояр старинных я потомок:
Я, братцы, мелкий мещанин.

Не торговал мой дед блинами,
Не ваксил царских сапогов,
Не пел с придворными дьячками,
В князья не прыгал из хохлов,
И не был беглым он солдатом
Австрийских пудреных дружин;
Так мне ли быть аристократом?
Я, слава Богу, мещанин.   (*PSS* iii. 262–3).

A last tatter of two worn-out family lines
(But unfortunately, not *the* last)
I am the descendant of old-time boyars:
That is, chaps: I'm a petty *meshchanin*.

My grandfather didn't sell pancakes on the street,
Nor did he polish a tsar's boots,
He wasn't one of the court choirboys,
He wasn't a jumped-up Polack[15] turned prince,
He wasn't a runaway private
From an Austrian regiment, in a powdered perruque,
So how can I be an aristocrat?
I'm a *meshchanin*, and thank God for it.

The especially problematic point here is that Yusupov, for all his wealth, education, distinguished career, and glitter, was (when compared with a Dolgorukov, Obolensky, or Golitsyn, for example), relatively speaking a parvenu, descended from a Tatar prince who had entered Muscovite service only in the seventeenth century. The fact that this mattered can be sensed in Vyazemsky's reference, in *Old Notebook*, to Yusupov's intelligent but 'somewhat Genghis-Khanite' wit.[16] To be sure, Yusupov

[15] Literally, 'Ukrainian'.

[16] *Stikhotvoreniya. Vospominaniya. Zapisnye knizhki* (Moscow, 1988), 274. Cf. the comments of Grand Duke Nikolai Mikhailovich: 'Endowed with great native wit, he had enjoyed a brilliant education; the *descendant of a seventeenth-century Tatar*, he was, in terms of his tastes and manners, an eighteenth-century European' (see *Russkie portrety/Les portrets russes*, 5 vols. (St Petersburg, 1905–08), i, pl. 62: my emphasis).

is not included in the list of those explicitly satirized in 'My Family Tree' (the founders of the Men'shikov, Kutaisov, Razumovsky, Bezborodko, and Kleinmikhel' lines), but he could (given Pushkin's frame of reference) perfectly well have been described as a 'jumped-up Tatar' (*prygal iz tatar*). Named in line 9 of 'To a Grandee' as *schastlivyi chelovek* (a happy/fortunate man), Yusupov is shown to be so in a quite different sense from the rebellious Prince Yakov Dolgoruky, called 'schastliv' in 'My Family Tree' ('Schastliv knyaz' Yakov Dolgoruky | Umen pokornyi meshchanin, lines 47–8). In 'To a Grandee', 'happiness' signifies the serene accommodation of historical circumstance; in 'My Family Tree' it means the valorous and principled refusal to serve one's ruler or one's times.

The contradiction is made still sharper by Pushkin's delicate suggestion, in 'To a Grandee', that the Yusupovs had described just such a trajectory as the Bezborodkos or the Razumovskys—that is, advanced themselves by a very particular kind of service to their rulers. In line 14 of the poem, Pushkin describes Yusupov as 'the envoy of the young crowned wife [*poslannik molodoi uvenchannoi zheny*]' (*PSS* iii. 217). Like all the instances of periphrasis in the poem, this is no idle figure of decorative convention: by emphasizing Catherine's gender, her youth, and her marital status (*uvenchannaya* suggests the marital as well as the Imperial crown), he alludes obliquely to the institution of favouritism.

Placed together, 'My Family Tree' and 'To a Grandee' make clear Pushkin's conflicting attitudes to the aristocracy: a group of coarse-mannered parvenus quite unlike genuine *dvoryane* on the one hand, the epitome of cultivation and of *dvoryanstvo* identity on the other. This conflict is evident also in his draft essay 'Journey from Moscow to St Petersburg', begun at the end of 1833, and intended as a riposte to Radishchev's radical assault on autocratic rule, where the writer expressed nostalgia for the vanishing traditions of aristocratic patronage. Crabbe, the early nineteenth-century British author who addressed his poems to 'his Grace the Duke' was no less (indeed, Pushkin implies, he was more) honourable than those modern writers who curried favour with journalists to ensure themselves good reviews. At the same time, Pushkin drew a sharp distinction between 'the aristocracy of birth and money' and 'the aristocracy of writing talents', to the evident detriment of the former.[17] The broader argument into which this division was integrated was significant: 'Journey from Moscow to St Petersburg' defended serfdom as no more unjust than the exploitation of factory workers by entrepreneurs in

---

[17] 'Chto znachit aristokratsiya porody i bogatstva v sravnenie s aristokratsiei pishushchikh talantov?' (*PSS* xi. 264). The use of the alternative spelling *aristokratsiya* may be taken from the Polish *aristokracja*, but it is equally possible that it is a Russification of the English term 'aristocracy' in the sense of 'any elite group' (not necessarily social).

England, insisted on the beneficence of censorship, and pointed to the progressive role of the Russian autocracy in civilizing the Russian people— 'Since the house of Romanov ascended the throne, the government has always been at the forefront of education and enlightenment' (*PSS* xi. 244). A pioneering text in what I will term here Russian 'nationalist conservatism' (see below), 'Journey from Moscow to St Petersburg' not only expressed Pushkin's move away from Romantic rebelliousness, but raised pressing questions of personal, social, and national identity which preoccupied most reflective members of the cultural elite in his day, and for decades afterwards.

ARISTOCRATS AND GENTLEMEN: CONFLICTS IN THE *DVORYANSTVO*

The divide between the 'aristokratiya' and the rest of the *dvoryanstvo* was not a question merely of imaginative reality. By the second third of the nineteenth century, a separation of the *dvoryanstvo* into layers enjoying different prestige and monetary resources, had become painfully obvious. The official order of precedence within the estate was, right up to the Revolution, according to service rank, modulated (after 1785) by the drawing of divisions between families according to the length of time that they had belonged to the *dvoryanstvo*.[18] But in practice, the distinctions seem to have been far more complex than this. The first exhaustive Russian peerage, published in the mid-1850s, divides the families listed into a large number of different groups, depending on their supposed distinction or antiquity. Chapters 1, 2, 3 list 'Russian princes, counts, and barons' (in that order); Chapter 4 has 'foreign princes, counts and barons'; Chapter 5 families reputedly tracing descent from Ryurik; Chapter 6 families named in the *Velvet Book* (*Barkhatnaya kniga*, a genealogical record compiled in 1682–86); Chapter 7 families established before 1600; Chapter 8 Baltic families established at the time of the Livonian Order; Chapter 9 Lithuanian and Polish families established before 1600; Chapter 10 foreign families established before 1600 and now holding Russian nationality; Chapter 11 families whose ancestors had held boyar and other court titles during the seventeenth century; Chapter 12 Ukrainian families holding pre-1764 military titles; and Chapter 13 families who had held the top two ranks in the civil service from the time of Peter I onwards.[19] While this

---

[18] See Ch. 1.

[19] P. V. Dolgorukov, *Rossiiskaya rodoslovnaya kniga*, 4 vols. (St Petersburg, 1854–57). Dolgorukov's book was a landmark publication in terms of breadth, though less exhaustive lists of *dvoryanstvo* members, e.g. Knyazev's *Vybor iz zakonov o dvoryanstve* and Miller's *Izvestiya o dvoryanakh rossiiskikh*, had begun being produced in Catherine II's reign.

categorization was informal—in contrast to the situation in Britain, there were no 'premier dukes' etc.—there is no doubt that differentiations of this kind were a matter of passionate interest to many *dvoryane* themselves.[20]

Matters were further complicated by the importance of wealth, whose lustre is conveyed by the formula 'chiny i den'gi', 'rank and money', ubiquitous in 'society tales' of the 1830s.[21] The gap between a landowner permanently resident on his country estate and owning no more than fifty souls, and a landowner with 3,000 serfs living in Moscow or St Petersburg, was no less than enormous.[22] But a refined existence required such a very substantial income that even landowners in the second of these two groups might be hard put to remain solvent. Arcadius Kahan has hypothesized that the decline, between 1762 and 1834, in the percentage of the entire serf population owned by landowners with holdings of 1,000 or more serfs was brought about by spending on luxury goods (imported foodstuffs, fabrics, books), education, and travel.[23] Even in the upper echelons of the *dvoryanstvo*, a case like Yusupov, with 31,000 serfs, and an income of over a million and a half roubles in 1827, was the exception rather than the rule: only 127 individuals owned more than 3,000 serfs in 1859.[24] And middling landowners, with between 1,000 and 5,000 souls, say, who attempted to ape the taste, and match the expenditure, of their wealthy neighbours, maintaining an establishment in town as well as in the country, educating their children in the accomplishments proper to educated society, and spending time in Paris or at fashionable spas, were at very serious risk of insolvency: in the words of August Haxthausen, who visited

[20] Dolgorukov himself, as a member of a distinguished but decayed family, was certainly no independent witness (on this see below, p. 103). But that these distinctions were not personal to him is indicated by annotations to the copy in the Bodleian Library, shelfmark 218855 d.5; a 19th-cent. Russian owner of the book has pencilled in families omitted by Dolgorukov, in some cases because they were elevated to the *dvoryanstvo* after the book was published.

[21] See e.g. Evdokiya Rostopchina, 'Chiny i den'gi' (1839).

[22] Statistics from 1837 indicate that around half of all Russian *dvoryane* had twenty or fewer serfs, that is, lived below the poverty line (estimated at twenty-five or more serfs). Those possessing 1,000 or more serfs made up less than 2 per cent of the *dvoryanstvo*. (T. Emmons, *The Russian Landed Gentry and the Peasant Emancipation of 1861* (Cambridge, 1968), 4–5.)

[23] A. Kahan, 'The Costs of Westernization in Russia: The Gentry and the Economy in the Eighteenth Century', *SR* 25 (1966), 61–2. Anecdotal evidence to support this case comes from F. Vigel', *Zapiski*, 2 vols. (Moscow, 1928), written in the 1840s, which recall—as a curiosity—the fact that in late 18th-cent. Penza, only the largest serf-owners (those with 1,000 or more souls) owned silver ('six teaspoons or so') and that china (as opposed to pottery) was not in common use (i. 60). The clear implication is that these luxuries had become far commoner fifty years later.

[24] See D. Lieven, *The Aristocracy in Europe, 1815–1914* (London, 1992), 41, quoting *Predlozhenie k trudam revizionnoi kommissii* (St Petersburg, 1859). To be sure, many of the richest landowners had enormous debts (Yusupov died leaving debts of over 2 million roubles), but their assets were such that debts could be cleared more easily than they could by smaller landowners.

Russia in 1843, 'money is made and spent almost immediately'.[25] Unless a son of a financially unstable household was able to marry a rich heiress or make a success of his service career, he was forced to make ends meet by mortgaging the estates, by arranging informal loans with friends and relations, and by pawning high-status items such as jewellery. Individuals in this category could aptly be described, in George Orwell's phrase, as 'shabby genteel', since 'practically the whole family income [went] on keeping up appearances'.[26]

The financial straits into which attempted elegance could push middling landowners make themselves felt in a representative household budget that has survived because of the head of that household's fame. In 1834–35, the outgoings of Pushkin and his family (the poet and his wife and children, plus Pushkin's wastrel younger brother Lev, for whom the poet was financially responsible) amounted to roughly 30,000 roubles. This included 6,000 roubles for the rent of a twelve-roomed apartment in the centre of St Petersburg close to the Winter Palace, and located on the first floor (the 'best' part of the block), 678 roubles to a coach-maker's, 200 roubles for wallpaper, 1,000 roubles to a cabinet-maker, 1,000 roubles to Sichler for Natal'ya Pushkina's dresses, and some few hundred roubles on Pushkin's gambling debts. At the same time, Pushkin's official salary stood at about 10,000 roubles. The entire sum cleared on *The Captain's Daughter* during its author's lifetime was about 20,000 roubles, of which he received about 4,000 in the months after the book was published in December 1834.[27] The shortfall between income and expenditure was made up by capital from the family's mortgaged serfs, by loans from more solvent acquaintances and by regular visits to the pawnbroker with items such as shawls, pearls, and silver. (*PSS* xvii. 355).

In the 1800s, as Martha Wilmot, a foreign observer of Moscow *dvoryanstvo* society, recorded, Russia was polarized between 'Noble' and 'Plebeian', and 'a middle state such as happy England boasts [was] not understood'.[28] The costs of keeping up appearances, and the spread of

[25] August Haxthausen, *The Russian Empire: Its People, Institutions, and Resources*, trans. R. Faire (London, 1856), 85.

[26] See G. Orwell, *The Road to Wigan Pier* (London, 1989), 115.

[27] *PSS* xvii. 334–52 (documents 40–7). Document 46, Pushkin's anticipated budget for 1835–36, anticipates an outlay of 4,000 roubles on clothes, 4,800 for culinary expenses, 4,000 for keeping a carriage. For a detailed discussion of the Pushkin family's financial affairs, see P. E. Shchegolev, *Pushkin i muzhiki: Po neizdannym materialam* (Moscow, 1928). Pushkin's parents owned 1,500 serfs between them, so the case of this family illustrates how fragmentation through inheritance (division between children reduces all descendants to middling landowners) and extravagance bedevilled even those who, statistically speaking, formed part of a socio-economic elite.

[28] See M. Wilmot and C. Wilmot, *The Russian Diaries* (London, 1934), 54, entry for 1 Oct. 1803.

Western ways, meant that, in the following decades, this simple polarization began breaking down. Among *dvoryane* in the country, assimilation to refined standards often meant no more than the possession of a few symbolic items. The Sapunov family of Ryazan' province, for instance, inhabited, from the late eighteenth century until the mid-twentieth, what was essentially a large log cabin, converted to hand-me-down Palladian with plank cladding and what passed for a belvedere (a half-moon shaped top window). The furnishings of the house were extremely simple: a large leather divan in the salon, and oak and wicker chairs round the walls; an oak sideboard, table and chairs in the dining-room; and one solitary bed (used by the senior female) in the entire house. Gentility was suggested by a few treasured items: the seventeenth-century document granting the family *dvoryanstvo* identity and a parcel of land; a fly-blown engraving in a mahogany frame; some porcelain ornaments; one good French clock; a grand piano; and a small library of books.[29]

If *dvoryane* were, by the standards of a St Petersburg magnate, sometimes barely members of refined society, it was also the case that, as Enlightenment concepts of 'refinement' and 'polite society' spread, to be a *dvoryanin* was neither a sufficient nor a necessary criterion for acceptance as a 'polite person'. As early as 1760, Lomonosov was to assail the snobbery of Count Stroganov, who had disparaged Lomonosov's own lowly origins, by pointing out, 'In rebuking [my] lack of *dvoryanstvo*, he himself is behaving in a manner unsuitable to a *dvoryanin*.'[30] The fact that the Russian term *dvoryanin*, and its popular equivalent *barin*, 'lord', never acquired the social fluidity of the English term 'gentleman' (which was applied from the mid-sixteenth century to professionals such as lawyers, and from the late fourteenth to persons of 'chivalrous feelings'), points to the persisting and very real privileges of the *dvoryanstvo*, but also indicates that 'gentlemanliness' in the sense of politeness was not necessarily understood as determined by estate affiliations.[31]

[29] See B. V. Sapunov, 'Grezy o proshlom', *Russkaya usad'ba* 5 (1999), 327–37. The family possessed 300 books in the early 20th cent., though the majority of these had been published between 1880 and 1910, judging by Sapunov's description (see p. 336). The circumstances are much those of Pushkin's fictional Larin family (*pace* Martha Fiennes's absurd cinematic version of *Evgeny Onegin*, which shows them living in a substantial stone mansion lavishly furnished in Karelian birch). The Sapunovs' circumstances were so modest, indeed, that the family managed to retain the house for private use until well into the Soviet period. See also Fig. 6.

[30] 'On, poprekaya [moe] nedvoryanstvo, sam postupil ne po-dvoryanski'. M. Lomonosov, letter to I. I. Shuvalov, 17 May 1760, *PSS* x (Moscow and Leningrad, 1957), 539.

[31] On *dvoryanin*, see *Slovar' russkogo yazyka XVIII veka*, vi. 27; on gentleman *OED* (2nd edn.) vi. 451–3. The word *gospodin*, which came into use during the late 18th cent. to signify anyone belonging to the social elite, perhaps as a translation of the German 'Herr', retained—at least until the abolition of serfdom—something of its original sense of 'master', becoming a genteelism in common use only in the late 19th cent. (On *gospodin*, see *Slovar' russkogo yazyka XVIII veka*, v. 190–1 (citing Karamzin's *Pis'ma russkogo puteshestvennika*: but when Karamzin introduced himself

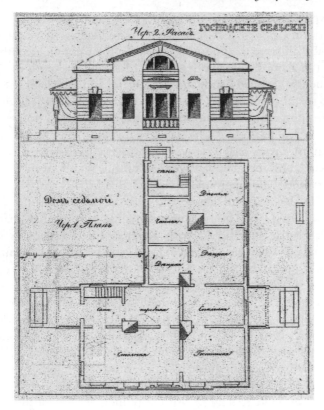

FIG. 6. A model gentleman's residence, from P. Mukhanov, *A Landowner's Portfolio* (1840). This house—which would normally have been built in wood, rather than the stone that Mukhanov's sketch suggests—is typical of the kind of dwelling built by all but the richest Russian landowners, and also by the wealthier merchants, both in the country and in cities.

to Kant, he used the word *dvoryanin*). Dal′'s dictionary suggests that *gospodin*, when not meaning simply 'master', was used according to rank: '*Gospodinom* chestvuyut lyudei po zvaniyu, dolzhnosti ikh' (*Tolkovyi slovar′ zhivogo velikorusskogo yazyka* (2nd edn.; 4 vols.; Moscow, 1880–2), i. 385). An example of later usage is Bunin's story 'Gospodin iz San-Frantsisko' (The Gentleman from San-Francisco, 1916). By contrast, the word *dama* not only entered the Russian language earlier than any foreign-influenced term for 'gentleman'—it is recorded from the early 18th cent.—but also seems to have become established in the meaning 'a member of polite society [irrespective of precise rank]' more quickly. See *Slovar′ yazyka XVIII veka*, vi. 31–2. In *Selected Passages from Correspondence with Friends*, for example, Gogol′ routinely uses the locution 'damy i muzhchiny' (ladies and men). The word *dzhentel′men* was borrowed into Russian in the 19th cent. (it does not appear in *Slovar′ russkogo yazyka XVIII veka* or in Dal′), but had a somewhat recherché and occasionally facetious intonation: cf. the example from Pogodin's *Tsvety zhivye* (1960): 'Kolya, bud′te dzhentel′menom, provodite do tramvainoi ostanovki' (*Slovar′ russkogo yazyka*, i. 396).

The expenditure required by genteel existence was also a levelling feature, since the richest merchants were more likely to have the resources to sustain it than were the poorer *dvoryane*. In the early nineteenth century, houses in the Zamoskvorech'e region of Moscow just south of the centre quite frequently changed hands and back again, and merchant owners were as likely as members of the *dvoryanstvo* to commission a plaster ceiling, or to have the front of a formerly modest, flat-fronted wooden house decorated with neo-classical pilasters.[32] The standard dwelling for well-off inhabitants of towns in most parts of Russia was a *gorodskaya usad'ba*, literally an 'urban manor house', and the merchant version of this, set about by outbuildings (stables, servants' and apprentices' quarters) and perhaps even a formal garden, had the self-sufficiency and the feudal air of its *dvoryanstvo* equivalent.[33] Inside the house, furniture might be plainer than that in the richest gentry households, with Karelian birch veneer or solid oak replacing inlaid tulip-wood, mahogany, rosewood, and ormolu, and locally-made porcelain Sèvres, but it was still thoroughly Westernized, and—by the 1820s—so too, might the clothing of the household's inhabitants be. The portraits executed by successful painters, such as Vasily Tropinin (1776–1857), in the second third of the nineteenth century provide an excellent record of cultural assimilation. The occasional male merchant still sits proudly in his traditional caftan and medals, but many from this estate are indistinguishable, in terms of the clothes that they are wearing and of the conventions according to which they are represented, from the rest of polite society.[34] Nor did refinement stop at the acquisition

[32] See *Pamyatniki arkhitektury Moskvy: Zamoskvorech'e* (Moscow, 1994): e.g. a house in Malyi Tolmachevskii pereulok with neo-classical pavilion (p. 150 pls. 137–9), or the building at 4 Lavrushinskii pereulok (p. 170 no. 378), or the grand mansion in Srednii Ovchinnikovskii pereulok (p. 286 no. 413). For a similar case in Kursk, see V. Polunin, *Three Generations: Family Life in Russia, 1845–1902*, trans. A. F. Birch-Jones (London, 1957). Polunin's maternal grandfather, a merchant named Okorokov, bought a bankrupt *dvoryanin*'s grand town house in the 1840s, and made few changes, apart from 'hang[ing] a few indifferent family portraits in the hall, and replac[ing] a partially nude Psyche by a portrait of a bishop of his acquaintance' (p. 71). D. L. Ransel, 'An Eighteenth-Century Merchant Family in Prosperity and Decline', in J. Burbank and D. L. Ransel (eds.), *Imperial Russia: New Histories for the Empire* (Bloomington, Ind., 1998), 267–8, describes the construction of a three-storey cut-stone house in Dmitrov by Ivan Tolchenov, which had a substantial orangery, 'at a time when few nobles could boast' such a structure.

[33] See e.g. Ivan Goncharov's description of the house in Simbirsk where he was brought up: 'Our house was what is known as "a cup that runneth over"—something that was true, incidentally, of all families living in the provinces but without their own village nearby to rely on. It had a big courtyard, indeed two courtyards, set about with numerous buildings: various quarters for servants, stables, cattle-sheds, barns, haylofts, a hen-house and a bathhouse. We had our own horses, cows, even our own goats and sheep, hens and ducks—that took up the two yards. The barns and cellars and ice-houses were crammed with provisions: flour, various kinds of grain, everything imaginable, to feed us and the huge staff. In a word, it was a whole estate, a country village' ('Na rodine', *Sobranie sochinenii v 8 tomakh*, vii (Moscow, 1954), 233).

[34] Fig. 7. For further examples, see E. F. Petinova, *Vasily Andreevich Tropinin* (2nd edn., Leningrad, 1990). Tropinin's paintings, like those of his Scottish contemporary Raeburn (on

FIG. 7. Vasily Tropinin, *Portrait of the Shuya Merchant I. I. Kiselev* (1842). Kiselev, a denizen of a small town in the Moscow region, is in no sense immediately identifiable as a merchant through his clothes.

whom see D. Thomson, *The Art of Sir Henry Raeburn, 1756–1823*, Scottish National Portrait Gallery, Edinburgh, 1997), depict an interestingly varied cultural elite, ranging from distinguished members of the landed gentry to 'trade', with medal-hung civil servants, such as D. P. Tatishchev (pl. 24) alongside writers such as Voeikov, Karamzin, and Zhukovsky. In the context of my discussion later in the chapter, it is not without interest that he seems to have been close to Slavophile circles: his subjects include members of the Kireevsky and Protas′ev families, and also Ivan Samarin. (Cf. Petinova's remarks on p. 89 and p. 92 of the above vol.) Though Tropinin is known to have portrayed at least some of his subjects using studio props, he provides an accurate record of changing patterns: Haxthausen, for instance, remembers meeting two generations of a Rybinsk merchant family in 1843, the father wearing traditional clothes (but with a totally Westernized house), and the son in completely Western attire. (See Haxthausen, *The Russian Empire*, 143.)

of objects. A typical Muscovite merchant library of the early eighteenth century was dominated by devotional books; by the 1830s, a young man from a merchant family in Moscow was revealing in his diary a fashionable taste for melancholic introspection and sentimental poetry.[35] Ivan Goncharov, later a writer and literary censor, noted the levelling effects of education in his recollections of Moscow University, describing his *alma mater* as 'a real republic'.[36] The spread of education meant even some women from classes beyond the *dvoryanstvo* had acquired a taste for literature: in the 1820s and 1830s, for instance, the Teryukhina sisters, Nadezhda (1814–48, married name Teplova) and Serafima, became quite celebrated for their polished verses.[37] And in the 1840s, members of the classes new to gentility were to acquire their own etiquette books, such as D. S. Sokolov's *A Man of the World* (1847), which promised to replace the tuition given in the nursery to more fortunate members of society, and to give those not fortunate enough to be inducted in good manners from birth a grasp of 'all the subtleties of life in society and that varied etiquette which is the essential characteristic of persons of *bon ton*'.[38] The 'subtleties' in which the book instructed novice socialites included the need for restrained behaviour in married couples (no squabbling or displays of jealousy in public); the inadvisability of wearing dressing-gowns (*khalaty*) in company; and the importance of self-control while visiting (no sprawling in one's chair, purloining of others' snuff, rocking of chairs, or 'would-be elegant raising and lowering of the eyes').[39] At the same time, the satirical plays of Ostrovsky, mocking the ignorance and coarseness of Moscow and provincial merchants, began to act as a 'school of manners' for the aspirant members of the group at which they poked fun, performing as pivotal a role as the didactic plays of Catherine II and Fonvizin had for the *dvoryanstvo* more than sixty years earlier.[40] And the merchants also had their own clubs, including the Schuster Club (founded 1772) and the Commercial Society (founded 1784) of St Petersburg.[41]

[35] Compare N. A. Baklanova, 'O sostave bibliotek moskovskikh kuptsov vo vtoroi chetverti XVIII veka', *Trudy otdela drevnerusskoi literatury* 14 (1958), 644–9, and A. E. Polilov, 'Iz dnevnika yunoshi "tridtsatykh godov"', *VE* 7 (1908), 97–120. In the Tolchenov family in the 1780s, 'an attraction to Europeanized culture . . . combined easily with an abiding and deeply rooted commitment to Orthodox practice and spirituality'. See Ransel, 'An Eighteenth-Century Merchant Family', 271.

[36] 'V universitete', *Sobranie sochinenii v 8 tomakh* (Moscow, 1954), vii. 203.

[37] R. Bowman, 'Teplova, Nadezhda Sergeevna', in M. Ledkovsky, C. Rosenthal, and M. Zirin (eds.), *Dictionary of Russian Women Writers* (Westport, Conne., 1994), 645–7.

[38] D. S. Sokolov, *Svetskii chelovek*, [p. iii].

[39] Ibid. 17–18, 29, 40.

[40] On the social function of Ostrovsky's plays, see esp. Louise McReynolds and Cathy Popkin, 'The Objective Eye and the Common Good', in C. Kelly and D. Shepherd (eds.), *Constructing Russian Culture in the Age of Revolution* (Oxford, 1998), 121–2.

[41] See *BSE* xv. 427, headword *Klub*.

The growing convergence of taste between *dvoryanstvo* and merchants, and even occasionally members of other social groups (the clergy, the *meshchanstvo*, or plebeian town-dwellers), the emergence of what Amanda Vickery has termed, in the context of eighteenth-century England, a 'genteel culture',[42] was in part a result of 'civilization' in the fundamental sense—the fact of living in a city, on a street where neighbours were (by country standards) close at hand, and could not be chosen. This kind of homogenization was particularly evident in Moscow, which had been reduced by political change to not-quite-capital, and whose status had declined still further in the wake of the Great Fire of 1812. As Pushkin sadly observed in 1833, 'Today Moscow is humbled: the great lordly houses stand drear, with grass growing in their big courtyards and with their gardens overgrown and running wild. Below a gilded coat-of-arms hangs a sign put up by a tailor who is paying the owner 30 roubles a month for his quarters; the magnificent bel-étage has been rented by a madame for her young ladies' pension (and let's be thankful no worse fate has overtaken it!)'[43] As the middling *dvoryanstvo* decayed into poverty, and the other free classes became richer and more 'Europeanized', serf ownership became one of the most important distinguishing characteristics of *dvoryanstvo* status. Yet even this was more notable in the country than in the city. By the early nineteenth century, over half of servant employers in St Petersburg used wage labourers, rather than bonded labour, and by the middle of the nineteenth century, this figure had risen to 70 per cent.[44]

What is more, serf ownership also generated a painful paradox within gentry culture. The open-handed hospitality and high staffing levels that foreign visitors saw as a nationally distinctive feature[45] depended upon the availability of serf labour, as did the exploitation of agricultural and economic resources that kept wealth flowing into the coffers of the aristocracy (and the imperial family, whose lavish resources stand in significant contrast to the money problems of the Hanoverian dynasty in

---

[42] *The Gentleman's Daughter: Women's Lives in Georgian England* (New Haven, 1998).

[43] Pushkin, 'Puteshestvie iz Moskvy v Peterburg', *PSS* xi. 246. Cf. the laments of Elizaveta Yan'kova: 'Now not even a shadow of the past remains: all the most important and richest people have removed to Petersburg, and everyone in Moscow is either old or poor. They sit quietly at home and live like paupers, not like noble lords [*ne po-barski*] in the old way, but like bourgeois [*meshchane*], keeping themselves to themselves. . . . Have you ever heard of such a thing, people of noble birth [*blagorodnye lyudi*] living in inns or furnished rooms, with God knows who living the far side of the wall?' (*Rasskazy moei babushki*, 114.)

[44] See M. Hildemeier, *Bürgertum und Stadt in Russland, 1760–1870. Rechtliche Lage und Soziale Struktur* (Vienna, 1986), 449, 457. A. Rustemeyer, *Dienstboten in Petersburg und Moskau, 1861–1917* (Stuttgart, 1996), 53–60, is a useful survey of employment of servants by non-*dvoryanstvo* owners before 1861.

[45] See e.g. *The Russian Journals of Lady Londonderry*, ed. W. A. L. Seaman and J. R. Sewell (London, 1973), 74, on Prince Golitsyn's *déjeuner dinatoire*, a banquet served in a garden pavilion.

Britain during most of the eighteenth century). Aristocratic civilization of the kind represented in Pushkin's 'To a Grandee' was doubly dependent upon serf labour—the work of cooks, kitchen scullions, and maids, and the toil of labourers on the farms and in the factories that brought Yusupov his income.[46] While supporting refined existence, though, serfdom at the same time increasingly undermined the Russian elite's pretensions to civilized status. Once other European countries had abolished serfdom or significantly enhanced the rights of serfs,[47] the existence of the institution in unmodified form began to strike foreign visitors, and many Westernized Russians, as an embarrassing anachronism, the single most important proof that Russia was backward and barbaric. If Vigée Le Brun, visiting in the late eighteenth century, had marvelled at how kindly Russians treated their serfs, for later visitors, such as the Marquis de Custine, their very existence seemed a disgrace.[48] Distaste was exacerbated if one witnessed, as Amelia Lyons did, such behaviour as that of a Russian lady who 'took off one of her slippers, and beat it until it was torn to pieces, about the head and face of [a manservant] who made no resistance', because he had allowed her lapdog to stray.[49] Increasingly, too, as aristocratic Westerners themselves began to lead plainer and more withdrawn lives, and the country house began to be seen as a moral kingdom

[46] The enterprises in Arkhangel'skoe village included a manufactory of shawls and silks, a yarn-spinning works, a sheepskin factory, and a cloth factory, all of which employed serfs (over half of whom, in the last case, were children). See Bessonov, *Arkhangel'skoe*, 164.

[47] In France, serfdom had disappeared at an early stage of the Revolution (in 1789 the *régime féodal* was declared 'destroyed' and in 1793 feudal rights to land and dues were abolished). In the Holy Roman Empire, a measure instituted by Joseph II in 1781 had permitted serfs freedom of movement and freedom of occupation, as well as the right to educate their children as craftsmen. In Prussia, a similar measure had been instituted in 1807. In both the Holy Roman Empire and Prussia, wrangles over the resolution of feudal dues dragged on—in the Prussian case until 1850—but in both places peasants enjoyed significantly broader rights than their counterparts in the Russian empire.

[48] 'There is one country for the serf and one for the master . . . those of high society have as cultivated natures as though they lived in some other country, and the peasant is ignorant and savage as though he were the subordinate of masters as ignorant and savage as himself. . . . For Russian lords are indeed masters, and masters whose power is all too absolute in their domains; hence the excesses which cowardice and hypocrisy conceal in softly spoken words of humanity, words that deceive not only travellers, but often even members of the government.' *La Russie en 1839, par le marquis de Custine*, 2 vols. (Brussels, 1843), ii. 25, letter 32. According to Haxthausen, 'every day shows more clearly that it will be impossible much longer to retain [serfdom]. No intelligent Russian disguises this fact from himself' (*The Russian Empire*, 112). There were of course exceptions among 'intelligent Russians', for example Gogol' in his notorious *Selected Passages from Correspondence with Friends* (see below). But the controversy that greeted this book—among conservatives as well as radicals—is an indication of the marginality of Gogol''s position. (See R. Sobel, *Gogol's Forgotten Book: Selected Passages and its Contemporary Readers* (Washington, 1981): Sobel points out, for example, that Ivan Aksakov was the sole member of his family to admire Gogol''s book: p. 239).

[49] A. Lyons, *At Home with the Gentry: A Victorian English Lady's Diary of Russian Country Life*, ed. J. McNair (Nottingham, 1998), 16.

rather than a haven of luxury,[50] serf ownership seemed a distasteful fusion of exploitation and self-indulgence; aristocratic waste and peasant wretchedness appeared part of the same monstrous pattern.

All of these various factors—the costs of buying the prerequisites of refinement (education, travel, and luxury goods), the impoverishment of the lower gentry, the progressive refinement of those outside the gentry, the growing exclusivity of an aristocratic elite—contributed to the increasing displacement of the *dvoryanstvo*'s unquestioning caste pride and solidarity by a sense of division between 'true *dvoryane*' and *aristokraty*.

It has been calculated that 'high society' in England consisted of no more than 400 families.[51] The equivalent elite in Russia was even smaller, consisting of a few dozen clans, among them the Stroganovs, Sheremet′evs, Vorontsov-Dashkovs, Trubetskois, Belosel′sky-Belozerskys, Lobanov-Rostovskys, and Yusupovs.[52] The majority of families belonging to it were rich, held a title of 'prince' or 'count' going back to, at the latest, the end of the eighteenth century, and had members with prominent positions at court, or in the civil or military service. Lesser circles of the *dvoryanstvo* included relatively impoverished princely families, such as the Obolenskys, Dolgorukys, or Vyazemskys; untitled but rich members of the nobility, such as the Chertkovs (a member of which clan was the fourteenth largest serf-owner in 1859); and recent elevations to titled rank, such as the Bludovs (created count in 1842) or the Ignatievs (who bore the title of count from 1877).[53] Below these again came untitled and less wealthy members of the nobility, and below them, those elevated to the hereditary nobility through service. In the Anglophone world, the most nearly analogous social group to the *dvoryanstvo* was the Anglo-Irish ascendancy, whose members enjoyed a collective sense of superiority over Irish

[50] See L. Davidoff, *The Best Circles: Society Etiquette, and the Season* (London, 1986), 35–6. In 18th-cent. England, on the other hand, aristocrats entertained as expansively as Golitsyns or Yusupovs in the early 19th cent.: on the Public Days at Chatsworth in the middle of the century, see A. Foreman, *Georgiana, Duchess of Devonshire* (London, 1999), 28–9. A. Schönle plausibly argues, in 'The Scare of the Self: Sentimentalism, Privacy, and Private Life in Russian Culture, 1780–1820', *SR* 57 (1998), 723–46, that withdrawal from public life was at first perceived by Russian observers with alarm (Karamzin in London, for example, was disconcerted by the habit of admitting visitors only to certain rooms, and found the 'cold politeness' of the inhabitants alienating). But among conservative Russians writing in the middle and second half of the 19th cent., practices of this kind had become well established: see e.g. Konstantin Leontiev's reminiscences of his mother's private sitting-room below.

[51] See Davidoff, *The Best Circles*, 20.

[52] These families all appear on the list of major serf-owners in 1859, in a list of premier St Petersburg households compiled by a society memoirist in 1890, and on a list of major landowners around 1900. (See Lieven, *The Aristocracy in Europe*, 44–7.)

[53] See Count Aleksandr Bobrinskoi, *Dvoryanskie rody, vnesennye v Obshchii Gerbovik Vserossiiskoi Imperii*, 2 vols. (St Petersburg, 1890), i. 154, 356. Both these families had a long record of *dvoryanstvo* status, unlike the Kutaisovs (ii. 576–7), ennobled and created counts in 1798; however, of the three it was the Kutaisovs who were the wealthiest and most prominent.

Catholics, from whom they were separated by education, language, and, in the Penal era, enhanced property rights (the right to primogeniture) and sumptuary rights (the ownership of riding-horses and weapons), as well as religion (Protestant), but who had a very nice sense of relative status among themselves. One Anglo-Irish nobleman summed this up in terms of 'rows'. 'Row A. Peers who were Lord or Deputy Lieutenants, High Sheriffs and Knights of St Patrick . . . Row B. Other peers with smaller seats, ditto baronets, solvent country gentry and young sons of Row A . . . Row C. Less solvent country gentry . . . Row D. Loyal professional people, gentlemen, professional farmers, trade.'[54] This model—adapted for local conditions, with titles such as Privy Councillor replacing the Irish Lord Lieutenant—fits the Russian situation rather well. Though the 'rows' naturally intermingled socially, the barriers between them were real—for example, a Row B or C gentleman would not have been received with warmth as a suitor for the daughter of a Row A household.[55] And while members of Rows B and C might not be openly snubbed in the *vysshii svet* (*grand monde*) of St Petersburg, they would not necessarily be welcomed (one has only to recall the tribulations of the socially marginal Liza and Hermann in Pushkin's 1834 story 'The Queen of Spades'). The 'democratic' friendships treasured by young male and female graduates of elite boarding schools seldom resulted in marriages between the aristocracy in a strict sense and plain *dvoryane*, or indeed in close relations outside the walls of the school.[56] To manifest status-consciousness too overtly might now be considered vulgar, but status-consciousness was (for all that) extremely

---

[54] Lord Rossmore, *Things I Can Tell* (London, 1912), and Norah Robertson, *Crowned Harp* (Galway, 1960): quoted in Peter Somerville-Large, *The Irish Country House: A Social History* (London, 1995), 340.

[55] Pushkin, for instance, from a Row B family that poverty had pushed into Row C, associated with both Row B (the Raevskys, the Vyazemskys, the Karamzins) and with Row A (Yusupov), but married into the Goncharov family, which was a rung down the social scale from the Pushkins and was certainly by no stretch of the imagination part of the aristocracy: cf. Vyazemsky's comment on how Natal'ya felt no shame in Pushkin's occupation as writer: 'She had no trace of stuffiness [*chvanstvo*], and in any case she did not belong by birth to the upper echelons of aristocratic society' [*vysshii aristokraticheskii krug*]. (Quoted in Veresaev, *Pushkin v zhizni*, 478). Where aristocrats 'married out' in the late 18th and early 19th cents., they often married money: to quote Martha Wilmot, 21 Oct. 1806, 'the Princes of the country are breaking down all ideal barriers and marrying the daughters of the merchants as fast as they can!' (Wilmot and Wilmot, *The Russian Diaries*, 235).

[56] See the anon. tale about graduation from a boarding school published in Pushkin's *Sovremennik*: S. Zakrevskaya, 'Pis'ma sovospitannits', *Sovremennik* 8 (1837), 273–312. A fascinating literary example which depicts the tensions between 'Row A' and 'Row B' is Tolstoi's *Anna Karenina*. Anna, herself born Princess Oblonskaya (for which read, Obolenskaya) does not fit particularly well into the 'fast set' surrounding Betsy Drubetskaya (for which read, Trubetskaya)—wealthy, pleasure-loving, urbane, and self-indulgent. On status-consciousness as a source of social divisions among officers serving in different regiments, see W. C. Fuller, *Civil-Military Conflict in Imperial Russia, 1881–1914* (Princeton, 1985), 22.

prevalent. An impoverished Prince Obolensky might secretly despise a newly rich Count Kushelev-Bezborodko, and just so might a rich though untitled Chertkov look down upon a recently titled Kutaisov; however, the Kutaisovs and Kushelevs were every bit as likely to hold themselves aloof from a raggle-taggle Golitsyn or an untitled Aksakov.[57]

A concrete illustration of this point came in the disedifying scandal that broke out in the 1850s, when the genealogist Prince Petr Dolgorukov was accused of trying to extort the enormous sum of 50,000 roubles from Count Mikhail Vorontsov. Dolgorukov had allegedly sent a letter in a feigned hand insinuating that this payment would be necessary if Vorontsov wished to have his lineage traced to a boyar clan in his forthcoming peerage, rather than have the family exposed as eighteenth-century newcomers. Dolgorukov himself countered by accusing Vorontsov of trying to browbeat *him* into a false statement of the family's boyar lineage, the absence of which would have been evident, he felinely hinted, to anyone studying the *Velvet Book*. Vorontsov's son was later to sue for defamation of his father's memory.[58] Whatever the detailed facts behind this murky episode, it well illustrates the detestation in the lower ranges of the *dvoryanstvo* for the aristocratic magnates (and vice versa). In his tract *The Truth About Russia*, published abroad in 1860, Dolgorukov poured scorn on the principles of advancement in the civil service, thundered that there had never been a true 'political aristocracy' to 'act as a brake to anarchy and to despotism' in Russia, and described the court grandees as a 'camarilla'.[59] This last term well illustrates the widespread sense among the less powerful *dvoryane* of the *aristokratiya* as alien, united by kinship and behaviour with its counterparts in other despotic societies, and cut off from the educated population for which it should have acted as exemplum.

[57] Ariadna Tyrkova, *To, chego bol'she ne budet* (Paris, 1954), 151, recalling her childhood in the 1870s, argues that the free-and-easy Chertkovs were part of the 'genuine pinnacle' of St Petersburg society, while the stuffy Ignat'evs were 'new people, service people'. As a member of an old, untitled *dvoryanstvo* family, Tyrkova herself had an axe to grind, but the example illustrates how prevalent boundary-drawing was in the reaches of the *dvoryanstvo* just below the aristocracy.

[58] For Dolgorukov's side of the story, see *La Verité sur la Russie* (Paris, 1860), afterword, 3–7. A more rounded discussion of the case can be found in V. I. Mil'don's biographical article in *Russkie pisateli 1800–1917: biograficheskii slovar'* (Moscow, 1992), 151–3.

[59] *La Verité*, 85, 153, 374.

IDEOLOGIES OF THE 'MIDDLE STATE': RADICALS, LIBERALS, CONSERVATIVES

One effect of this resentment of the aristocracy was that, by the second third of the nineteenth century, the old boundaries of estate began to dissolve as political and intellectual affiliations were formed across them (indicative was the case of the radicals grouped around the journal *Sovremennik* in the 1840s and 1850s, who included the *dvoryane* Nekrasov and Panaev, but also Avdot'ya Panaeva, daughter of actors at the Imperial Theatre, Chernyshevsky, son of a priest and ex-seminarian, and Belinsky, son of a naval doctor and grandson of a priest).[60] Circles of this kind were *raznochinnye*, 'without social rank', not only because many of their members were *raznochintsy*, drawn from social groups outside the official classification, and not just because rank (*chin*) was immaterial to their members, but because these members sought to defy *chin* in the older sense of propriety and order. For Russian radicals, rebellion against the established order might be difficult and even dangerous in practical terms, leading to the repression of a person and the suppression of his or her written work, but it was straightforward in conceptual terms, depending upon recreation of self through severance from the past. Attitudes to identity were individualistic and existential, rather than retrospective: pride in one's descent was considered absurd, and even familial piety was suspect, relationships of affect being regarded much more highly than ties of blood. Private behaviour was explicitly ideologized, and violation of propriety raised to the level of a manifestation of political engagement. In this sense, radicalism had kinship to the 'dandyism' discussed in Chapter 1. However, where 'dandyism' was a form of 'didactic anti-behaviour' that emanated from within *dvoryanstvo* culture, in which the younger male members of that society marked their dissatisfaction at the ordinary requirement that they redeem their low status by ingratiating behaviour and politeness to ladies, the radicals sought to create an autonomous alternative society. Refinement and politeness were rejected entirely, rather than rebelled against, and plain living and sincerity cultivated with assiduity.[61] Indica-

---

[60] Even before this, democrats such as those involved in the Decembrist revolt had regarded social distinctions as ridiculous. Reproving Pushkin for his rancour over the hauteur of his Odessa superior Count Vorontsov on 20 November 1825, Ryleev observed: 'the existence of civil distinctions [*grazhdanskie preimushchestva*] is absurd' (*PSS* xiii. 241, no. 225).

[61] There is a substantial historiography dealing with the construction of identity among the radicals. See in particular L. Ginzburg, *O psikhologicheskoi proze* (Leningrad, 1977); I. Paperno, *Chernyshevsky and the Age of Realism: A Study in the Semiotics of Behavior* (Stanford, Calif., 1988); R. Stites, *The Women's Liberation Movement in Russia: Feminism, Nihilism and Bolshevism* (Princeton, 1978), esp. 103–5; H. Hoogenboom, 'Vera Figner and Revolutionary Autobiographies: The Influence of Gender on Genre', in Rosalind Marsh (ed.), *Women in Russia*

tively, the moral literature of earlier generations was the subject of scorn: Dmitry Pisarev, for example, poured contempt on Pushkin's poem '18 October 1824' as 'exactly in the tone of those impeccably official speeches pronounced—after the roast, of course—in honour of beneficent authority . . . One must be a completely crippled person, a double of Onegin, to utter such bogus, such totally false compliments to school-friends and pals from one's youth.'[62] If this was the reaction to sophisticated literary texts, it is not surprising that humble advice literature seeking to inculcate the proprieties should have been a source of sardonic mockery, as it was, for instance, in Belinsky's 1849 review of Sarah Ellis's *Advice to Young Ladies and Girls Concerning the Conservation of Beauty, the Preservation of Health, How to Dress, and Education*, which had just appeared in a Russian translation.[63]

The search for simplicity and candour led, in some cases, to the formation of radical 'anti-salons', whose hostesses acted as arbiters of rudeness rather than of courtesy, as is indicated by a fascinating account in Il'ya Repin's memoirs of a reception held in the house of Valentina Serova, composer and mother of the famous painter Valentin Serov. Many of the guests were in provocatively unconventional clothing (Irène Viardot, daughter of Turgenev's mistress Pauline had, according to Repin, donned a short black dress and heavy knee-boots). Valentina Serova herself was anything but the gracious hostess, 'having a great deal of impudence and sarcasm in her gaze and manners'. The disregard of these 'nihilists' for etiquette was such that many of them talked the entire way through a piano recital that was being provided as entertainment. Rather obtusely, in the circumstances, Repin, seeing his hostess without a seat, decided to offer her his chair, only to be brusquely rebuffed. His companion and fellow artist Mark Antokol'sky had to set him right: ' "You see, young people with the new views see society manners as vulgar. Young women and men are equal; and paying court offends them... Students long ago dropped all those medieval Chinese ways." '[64]

The ritualistic character of the radical rebellion against polite behaviour, where the 'medieval Chinese ways' of polite society were inverted, is well conveyed in a joke about the nihilists that, as Repin records, was doing the rounds at the time when he visited Serova's anti-salon:

and *Ukraine* (Cambridge, 1996), 78–93; and S. K. Morrissey, *Heralds of Revolution: Russian Students and the Mythologies of Radicalism* (New York, 1998).

    [62] 'Lirika Pushkina' (1865), *Sochineniya*, 4 vols. (Moscow, 1955–6), iii. 381.

    [63] See *Sovremennik* 2 (1849), 143. On this episode, and Ellis's book in general, see Diana Greene, 'Mid-Nineteenth-Century Domestic Ideology in Russia', in R. Marsh (ed.), *Women and Russian Culture: Projections and Self-Perceptions* (New York, 1998), 79–80.

    [64] I. Repin, 'Valentin Aleksandrovich Serov': *Dalekoe blizkoe* (Leningrad, 1982), Section 1, 352.

There was one specially amusing story about some young priest's daughter or aristocratic young lady going through the rite of initiation into a nihilist women's group of some kind.

The strapping young woman with thick luxuriant hair (in most versions of the story she was a provincial girl and a priest's daughter) crossed the threshold of the organizing committee's room shyly and reverently. Here she had to answer three questions with due solemnity, in the presence of certain mysterious, stony-faced witnesses.

The woman carrying out the finale of the ritual, the cutting of the participant's hair, stood close by with her sharp scissors.

The rite was very brief: the three questions that had to be answered were the following:

First question: Do you renounce the old order?
Answer: I do renounce it.
Second question: Do you consign Katkov to damnation?
Answer: I do consign him to damnation.
Third question: Do you believe in Vera Pavlovna's third dream?
Answer: I do believe in it.
With that, the sharp scissors gave a single, loud, energetic click.[65]

Though facetious, the story suggests the monastic character of some radical groups—the hair-cutting ritual imitates the shearing of the novice's locks to mark his or her entry into full monastic vows. It also indicates these groups' broad social base (one point of Repin's recollection being that *it does not matter* whether the participant is a priest's daughter or an aristocratic young lady).

If Repin's story caricatures the quasi-religious fervour of radical life, and the devotion of oppositional groups to certain sacred texts (here, Cherny-shevsky's *What is to be Done?* of 1863), a more sober and plausible account of radical life is given in Nadezhda Khvoshchinskaya's story *The Boarding-School Girl* (1859), whose heroine, Lelen'ka, escapes from life in the provinces to become a member of her intellectual aunt's circle in the capital. Here men and women meet on equal terms to discuss the crucial questions of the day in a utopian atmosphere of comradeliness and dedication to the cause of art, and in a domestic setting that encapsulates Wordsworth's ideal of 'plain living and high thinking'. Rather than elegance, modesty is the key:

While they were having dinner, [Lelen'ka] took a newspaper from a table next to the dining-table and began reading extracts aloud; a very lively discussion about the Italian war and the Italian campaign of liberation began. Lelen'ka knew a great deal and had been very thorough in her reading. . . . Next to the reception room

<hr />

[65] Repin, *Dalekoe blizkoe*, 354.

was [Lelen'ka's] own room, a drawing-room, studio, study all in one. On the walls were a few paintings in frames, on the floor, unfinished studies and canvasses turned upside-down; on the easel was an unfinished portrait (probably of her aunt); a palette hung coquettishly on the fretwork frame of the mirror, plaster busts and statuettes, casts of antique heads were standing on shelves and night-tables. A big desk and two bookcases were full of books; a couch and some soft armchairs were pulled up cosily round the fireplace. It was only that one corner that spoke of rest; the remaining features of the room asserted intensive, unceasing work, work in which every hour counted. And Lelen'ka was in fact looking at her watch at this very moment.[66]

Khvoshchinskaya sets out a detailed model of the inverse relation between intelligentsia existence and ordinary *vospitannost'*, an inversion doubly evident in the central metonym of the 'unfinished sketches and canvasses, *turned upside-down on the floor*' (the paintings not only have their innards up, but are placed on the floor rather than the walls). Everywhere there is emphasis on creative disorder, not only in the tangle of materials in Lelen'ka's room, but in the fact that her quarters flout the customary division of domestic space into 'drawing-room, studio, and study'. Lelen'ka's manners are as disorderly as her possessions: the impulsive decision to read from the paper at table violates ordinary etiquette (according to which nothing must disturb the smooth conduct of *zastol'naya beseda*, or dinner conversation—it was only in monasteries where reading aloud during meals was an ordinary practice, though the Lives of the Saints, rather than a newspaper, would be the appropriate sacred text there). And when the talk does flow, it becomes a demonstration of Lelen'ka's erudition (an absolutely improper purpose of social exchange, by the rules of etiquette). Her gesture in looking at the clock when her work has been interrupted too long was also, by the ordinary standards of etiquette, exceedingly rude.[67] At only two points is there a suggestion that this world, and the ordinary world of the drawing-room, might be connected: the first is in the sardonic reference to Lelen'ka's palette, which hangs 'coquettishly' on the mirror-frame (a reference that only serves to heighten the distinction between Lelen'ka and the ordinary coquette), and the second is in the comfortable chairs, which are, however, placed in order to facilitate rest rather than leisure: these will be the site of relaxation rather than of recreation. If all the objects in the room speak of utility, rather than acquisition for its own sake, it is also highly significant in terms of the theme of renouncing materialism that Lelen'ka finds herself

[66] N. D. Khvoshchinskaya (V. Krestovsky-psevdonim), *Povesti i rasskazy* (Moscow, 1963), 182.

[67] Sokolov, *Svetskii chelovek*, 67, for instance, advises readers that it is impolite to 'glance at the clock or one's watch every moment' (*pominutno smotret' na chasy*).

work as a copyist and translator, professions which mean that she can show appreciation for the arts without entering the dangerous area of commodification (she does not have to negotiate the issue of how much an original artistic work is 'worth'). In this world of anti-connoisseurship, a copy was as valuable as the original, since it generated an equal amount of intellectual stimulation (the sensual difference between real marble and plaster, or between different languages, was not a consideration of moment).

The Russian radicals' hostility to quotidian existence was to shape the dominant tradition of Russian letters in the nineteenth and twentieth centuries. Fundamental here was not only the legacy of the Russian Revolution, which placed a later generation of radicals at the summit of political and cultural authority, but also the effects of the modernist movement, which—as all over Europe—articulated a deeply-felt disgust against the commodification and trivialization of culture, and more broadly, against materialism.[68] Often, in cultural histories of Russia, this revolt against 'ordinary objects' has been taken to typify Russian intellectual culture as a whole, with the aesthetic distaste for *byt* and for the constraints of custom seen as an identifying particularity of the intelligentsia.[69]

As I argued in the Introduction, such arguments back-project Soviet perceptions of the intelligentsia onto the very different social relationships of the nineteenth century. In the Soviet period, the intelligentsia unquestionably did see its role as being to lambast every manifestation of materialism as a form of *meshchanstvo*, 'petit-bourgeois vulgarity': it was an axiom of intelligentsia existence that an *intelligent* was not a bourgeois.[70] In the late eighteenth and early nineteenth centuries, though, the term *meshchanstvo*, when not used neutrally, in its legal meaning 'the estate of free plebeian town-dwellers', evoked a positive vision of a cultivated, forward-looking, entrepreneurial class of the kind supposedly to be found in Western Europe. This was the meaning in which it was used in Catherine II's *Grand Instructions*, and the drafts of Pushkin's 'My Family Tree' suggest that he was aware of this connotation. One of the refrains used at the end of the stanzas was originally to have read, 'Happy is the man

---

[68] On modernism, cf. Federico García Lorca's talk 'Paraíso cerrado para muchos, jardines abiertes para pocos', *Obras completas*, iii (Barcelona, 1997), which describes Granada as the home of 'an aesthetic of the diminutive, an aesthetic of small things' (80)—that is, a place of small-mindedness and claustrophobic self-obsession: as the Russian modernists would have put it, of *byt*.

[69] See e.g. Svetlana Boym, *Common Places: Mythologies of Everyday Life in Russia* (Cambridge, Mass., 1994), which—following Roman Jakobson—argues that 'Russian, and later Soviet, cultural identity depended on heroic opposition to everyday life' (3), and insists on 'the Russian hatred of daily routine and stagnation' (26), and on the centrality of the distinction *byt/bytie* to Russian intellectual culture (29).

[70] See further in Chs. 4 and 5.

who definitely is a bourgeois' (*schastliv besspornyi meshchanin*: *PSS* iii. 874). Used interchangeably was the term 'middle state', as in *lyudi srednego sostoyaniya*. In a riposte to his critics written in 1830, Pushkin asserted that 'the old *dvoryanstvo*' attacked by them had in fact come to form, because of 'the fragmentation of estates', 'more of a middle state [*srednee sostoyanie*], a respectable, diligent, and enlightened state' (*PSS* xi. 173). *Srednee sostoyanie* was employed in this approbatory sense as well by Nikolai Polevoi, and by his sister Ekaterina Avdeeva in the foreword to her *Handbook of the Experienced Russian Housewife* (whose title appears to been modelled on the indubitably middle-class Elizabeth Raffald's *The Experienced English Housekeeper* (1769).[71] It was not until the end of the nineteenth century that *meshchanskoe* began to be widely used to signify 'bourgeois' in a negative sense (i.e. vulgar), a development that was associated with the growth of a belief among *intelligenty* that they belonged to a group outside class.[72]

The concept 'bourgeois', then, was not always one with which Russian intellectuals felt uncomfortable; indeed, some of them seem to have felt happier with it than their contemporaries in the West, no doubt as a result of social security. In Western Europe (or so, at least, it is usually argued), the late eighteenth and early nineteenth centuries saw what had once been despised as 'bourgeois' values, such as piety, thrift, and the sancrosanct character of domestic space, spread into the gentry and indeed the aristocracy.[73] But in Russia, the *dvoryanstvo* set the tone until well after Emancipation. Merchants who married into the *dvoryanstvo* (a not

[71] 'In describing our Russian domestic economy, I do not address myself to the highest ranks, but to the domestic existence [*byt*] of people of the middle standing' (Ekaterina Avdeeva, *Ruchnaya kniga russkoi opytnoi khozyaiki, sostavlennaya iz sorokoletnikh opytov i nablyudenii dobroi khozyaiki russkoi, Kateriny Avdeevoi* (8th edn., Moscow, 1854), i. Cf. Sokolov, *Svetskii chelovek*: 'The present book is intended to . . . act as a guide for young people entering *the middle circles* of society. An aristocrat who has grown up in circles distinguished by polished refinement will not have any use of it.' (p. iv, my emphasis). In a note on the Russian censorship written for the Third Section (the tsarist secret police) in 1826, the conservative journalist Faddei Bulgarin divided Russian society into three *sostoyaniya*, of which the 'middle state' included 'well-off gentlemen in service, estate-owners living in the country, poor gentlemen educated in government institutions, rich merchants and factory-owners, and even some *meshchane*'. See A. Reitblat (ed.), *Vidok Figlyarin: Pis'ma i agenturnye zapiski F. V. Bulgarina v III otdelenie* (Moscow, 1998), 46–7.

[72] See Ch. 3 for a further discussion of this topic. An early 19th-cent. instance of *meshchanskoe* used derogatorily can be found in Gogol''s story 'Diary of a Madman'. However, it is used by one of the lapdogs that the madman imagines to be conducting a correspondence with each other ('Dear Fidèle—ugh, I am really appalled that you have such a bourgeois [*meshchanskoe*] name!'). This suggests that it began life as a usage among the official classes, and was first perceived by intellectuals satirically. But an important contribution to the dissemination of the term was made by the writings of the Russian radicals, where the bourgeois philistinism of Western societies was sharply criticized (see e.g. Herzen's essay 'Kontsy i nachala' (1862): *Sobranie sochinenii v 30 tomakh*, xvi (Moscow, 1959), esp. 136–40, 196–7).

[73] See e.g. N. Elias, *The Civilizing Process*, trans. E. Jephcott (Oxford, 1978), or Davidoff, *The Best Circles*.

uncommon phenomenon in the nineteenth and even eighteenth centuries)[74] absorbed its appreciations of refinement. When the elite developed a culture analogous to Western bourgeois culture (emphasizing simplicity, informality, and privacy), this happened under the direct influence of the Western example, rather than rising up from the practices of a native middle class.[75] One may hypothesize that the absence of a socially abject indigenous source for the new values *decreased* resistance to these in the upper reaches of Russian society, just as the relative political impotence of merchants and tradespeople (until the late nineteenth century) reduced the sense of threat emanating from these.

What is more, intellectual culture in mid-nineteenth-century Russia was a good deal more diverse than analogy with the Soviet intelligentsia (as mythologized by members of that intelligentsia) would suggest. It included not only the Russian radicals (who themselves had analogues in other cultures), but educated people who were similar to the Western bourgeoisie in its more conventional manifestations: liberal, meritocratically inclined civil servants who took a thoroughly professional and diligent attitude to their work, and who were to acquire enhanced social weight after the reforms of the 1860s and 1870s reshaped legal institutions and the institutions of local government, and when civil servants with application, administrative skills, and legal expertise were required to run them.[76] There was also another large and significant group in the 'middle state': the group of conservative nationalists known as the 'Slavophiles', for whom *byt* (everyday life) was a source of reverence rather than distaste, and propriety something sacred rather than absurd; far from welcoming the dissolution of

[74] See Hildemeier, *Bürgertum und Stadt in Russland*, 117.

[75] Take, for instance, the *cottage orné* built by Nicholas I for Empress Alexandra at Peterhof in the late 1820s, whose dimensions and neo-Gothic architecture recall the villas that prosperous *bourgeois* in Europe were constructing for themselves at the time. Photographs of the building appear in E. Gaynor and K. Haavisto, *Russian Houses* (New York, 1991), 79–81. See R. Wortman, *Scenarios of Power: Myth and Ceremony in Russian Monarchy*, i (Princeton, 1995), 338–9, for a full discussion of the *Kottedzh* and its context. A similar case was the taste for Dutch genre painting, itself a thoroughly bourgeois genre, which in Russia was initiated by the royal household (see R. P. Gray, 'The Golitsyn and Kushelev-Bezborodko Collections and their Role in the Evolution of Public Art Galleries in Russia', *Oxford Slavonic Papers* 31 (1998), 65).

[76] An example is Ivan Goncharov, whose memoirs are a fascinating guide to the mentality of this sector of Russian society. In 'Slugi starogo veka' (1888), *Sobranie sochinenii v 8 tomakh*, vii, Goncharov gently questioned the claims of the radical populists to be in touch with the Russian people ('Most of them preferred to fuse with the People from a distance, sitting in their study in the country', p. 317). He admitted himself knowing the *narod* mainly through contact with servants (ibid.). The remainder of the essay is an account of his attempts to find servants who would ensure the clockwork-smooth running of the household that was essential to a life entirely dedicated to administration and writing. A fictional example (presented from a hostile viewpoint) is Tolstoi's Aleksei Karenin. For later instances, see D. Lieven, *Russia's Rulers under the Old Regime* (New Haven, 1989), esp. 179–83.

estate boundaries, such people saw the maintenance of these as essential to tradition.[77]

SANCTIFYING DOMESTIC EXISTENCE:
THE SLAVOPHILES AND *BYT*

Drawn from as many different social groups as the radicals whom they so feared and despised—not only the old-established gentry (the Aksakovs, Tyutchev, Khomyakov, Gogol', Tolstoi, Sokhanskaya), but also the service gentry (Dostoevsky, Katkov) and the merchant elite (Polevoi, Avdeeva) – Russian conservatives were a diverse group both sociologically and ideologically. Some, such as Khomyakov, were vehemently opposed to serfdom; others, such as Gogol' in his *Selected Passages from Correspondence with Friends* (1847), just as vehemently defended its existence, even suggesting that Europe was on the point of coming back to the practice: 'Now many in Europe have begun giving serious consideration to that ancient patriarchal way of life [*drevnii patriarkhal'nyi byt*], whose elements have vanished everywhere, except in Russia, and have started speaking openly about the advantages of our peasant way of life [*nash krest'yanskii byt*].'[78] From the early 1870s, Panslavism was to be another dividing factor, as some (notably the vehement patriot, anti-Pole, and anti-Semite, Ivan Aksakov) lent their authority to the Russian empire's policy of 'Slavonic protectionism' to the West of the empire's borders, while others, notably

---

[77] The Soviet history of using the terms 'conservative' and 'reactionary' as terms of abuse has led the term 'liberal' to be employed even in cases where it is clearly inappropriate: e.g. A. Reitblat, in a generally excellent introduction to the career of Bulgarin, describes him as a 'moderate liberal monarchist' (*Vidok Figlyarin*, 21), though the documents in this edn. make it clear that Bulgarin himself only ever used the term 'liberal' pejoratively (see e.g. p. 105). I follow A. Walicki (*The Slavophile Controversy: History of A Conservative Utopia in Nineteenth-Century Russian Thought* (Oxford, 1975), 8–9), though, in emphasizing the Slavophiles' conservative credentials (in the 19th-cent. European sense). Both these writers' anti-aristocratic standpoint, and their strong reservations about foreign influences, gave them quite a resemblance to English Tories in their conflict with Whig grandees, a resemblance recognized by Khomyakov in his writings on England (Khomyakov, *Sobranie sochinenii*, i. 129–32: cf. the complaint of John Nicholls, editor of the *Gentleman's Magazine*, in 1798: 'These great families, this oligarchy, destroy us' (quoted in Foreman, *Georgiana, Duchess of Devonshire*, 309). That said, the Slavophiles' critical attitude to autocratic rule made them seem radical in terms of the culture in which they were located, despite the conservatives' sincere protestations of loyalty to the tsarist regime. They formed a markedly different ideological stratum to official conservatives such as Bulgarin, editor of *Severnaya pchela*, or Sergei Uvarov (among whom the *reconcilability* of 'Russian' and 'Western' traditions, as embodied in the official Nicholaevan ideology of *narodnost'*, was a central dogmatic tenet).

[78] On Khomyakov, see Walicki, *The Slavophile Controversy*, 230. Gogol', *Vybrannye mesta iz perepiski s druz'yami*, letter 28, *Sochineniya* (10th edn., Moscow, 1889), iv. 162.

Tolstoi, turned into critics of this policy.[79] But conservative interests were held together less by consistency of specific ideas and policy than by a number of broad and rather abstract beliefs. These included Orthodox piety, respect for family values, and most particularly hostility to the West, and to the aristocracy as a glaring example of the social corruption brought by Westernization.[80] Important too was their rootedness in a Russia beyond the 'Western' capital of St Petersburg (Avdeeva was born in Kursk and later settled in Siberia, Sokhanskaya and Gogol' were from 'Little Russia' (Ukraine), Tolstoi—in the period in question—was permanently resident on his estate in Tula province, and Moscow was the home of the Aksakov family, Yury Samarin, and the Polevoi brothers, as well as being the birthplace of Dostoevsky).[81]

Arcadius Kahan has argued that a major result of the 'costs of Westernization' in Russia was the resort to enterprise: landowners put increasing pressure on the government to allow them to boost their income by turning to activities such as sugar manufacture and vodka-distilling.[82] But smaller landowners who lacked the income needed to back enterprise, and who also felt more keenly the desirability (for status reasons) of keeping a distance from trade,[83] were more likely (if they did not simply decline into utter indigence) to retreat from expenditure: to emphasize the virtues of self-sufficiency over excessive spending. Equally, even those merchants who had the resources to buy Western commodities

---

[79] Cf. Tolstoi's famous quarrel with Mikhail Katkov over the fate of Part 8 of *Anna Karenina*, which the latter was reluctant to publish in his journal *Russkii vestnik*: 'It turns out that Katkov *does not share my views*, and nor could he, considering that it's people exactly like him that I'm attacking' (*PSS* lxii. 326: emphasis original). The cause of the quarrel was Tolstoi's sardonic depiction of the Russian response to the Balkan crisis of 1876–7. Aksakov's anti-Jewish and anti-Polish writings are discussed at length in S. Lukashevich, *Ivan Aksakov 1823–1886: A Study in Russian Thought and Politics* (Cambridge, Mass., 1965).

[80] While not all conservatives were Slavophiles (and relations between the tsarist government and Slavophile groups were often vexed), the fact that conservatives were all avid patriots, and that most of them were devout members of the Orthodox Church, mean that they could be described as 'tending to a Slavophile direction', if nothing else.

[81] Unfortunately, I do not have space here to discuss the very interesting question of provincialism per se in the mid-19th cent.: the writings of regional authors such as Nikolai Leskov (see especially his novel *Soboryane*, 1872) are deeply concerned with the issue of how elite behaviour models were diffused in the Russian provinces. See also K. Grimstad, *Styling Russia: Structuring Mechanisms in the Prose Fiction of Nikolai Leskov* (Trondheim, 2001).

[82] See Kahan, 'The Costs of Westernization in Russia', 61–2.

[83] Cf. the comments of a well-informed English memoirist who spent three years on a country estate in Tambov: 'The poor man of noble birth is excluded by his rank from the right of adopting those employments and means of existence to which persons in the same position in other countries have recourse . . . They are prevented by their noble birth from taking any part in mercantile enterprises.' (Lyons, *At Home with the Gentry*, 82). That said, squeamishness about trade was not uniform: as Abbott Gleason has pointed out, Ivan Kireevsky's unworldliness was countered by Khomyakov's interest in technology and financial acumen (see *European and Muscovite: Ivan Kireevsky and the Origins of Slavophilism* (Cambridge, Mass., 1972), 145).

were sometimes hostile to a trade that was more beneficial to major entrepreneurs (those merchants who could afford the high taxes that gave access to the first guild, and hence to the right to conduct foreign business) than to medium and small businesses. Economic and moral impulses went hand in hand, as is shown by a move made in 1793 by two merchants, Nikolai Rezvoi and Mikhail Samoilov, to ban a number of imports that they saw as particularly costly and unnecessary. Their lists included fine fabrics (English muslin, lisle stockings), riding-horses, pet birds (canaries and larks), crystal and glass, cosmetics, foodstuffs (chocolate, cured products, gingerbread, oysters and coconuts 'except for [use by] apothecaries'), tobacco and fine wines. Samoilov's list is especially interesting because it includes sententious comments: macaroni and noodles are 'delicacies', while foreign tobacco is bought 'not for its merits and suitability, but out of fashion'; raki and rum are bought 'on a whim'. The phrase 'we have our own' is used time and again: of cheese, Samoilov comments 'those who want it can make their own at home, it takes but small skill'. Of fresh apples he says, 'of these, we have plenty', and of dried ones, 'of these we have still more'.[84]

Obviously, aristocratic magnates were just as capable as smaller landowners and merchants of generating and using their own produce. But smaller landowners and merchants were more susceptible to local as well as national patriotism. A grandee such as a Sheremet'ev or Stroganov who owned land in twenty different regions was unlikely to feel so protective about the produce of any one of his estates as a gentleman permanently resident on one estate in Tula or Ryazan' *guberniya* did about his, or as a wealthy merchant family in their well-built stone Moscow mansion did about the contents of their vegetable gardens, orchards, barns, and larders.[85] Certainly, the absenteeism and distance from real country life of the larger landowners was as constant a gripe among the middle-ranking *dvoryane* as it was among their Anglo-Irish equivalents.[86]

[84] See N. N. Firsov, *Pravitel'stvo i obshchestvo v ikh otnosheniyakh k vneshnei torgovle Rossii v tsarstvovanie Ekateriny Vtoroi* (Moscow, 1901–2), appendix, 343–53. The primary motive for the list, as Arkady Blyumbaum has pointed out to me, may well have been self-interest (it is a kind of primitive advertising for Samoilov and Rezvoi's own wares), but the patriotic rhetoric is still striking.

[85] An intermediate case was Princess Dashkova, whose wealth and social prominence made her a member of the *dvoryanstvo* elite, but who prided herself on using her own produce and on having helped to create her beautiful English park with her own hands (see Wilmot and Wilmot, *The Russian Diaries*, 191, entry for 24 Sept. 1805; 221, entry for 21 Mar. 1806). It is interesting that Karazin's nationalist speech *Rech' o neobkhodimosti* makes a spirited case for the economic importance of local patriotism (see esp. 16, n. 7).

[86] Compare Maria Edgeworth's satirical portraits of Anglo-Irish grandees in *The Absentee* (1812) and *Ormond* (1817) with Konstantin Aksakov's *Prince Lupovitsky* (Knyaz' Lupovitsky, *Sobranie sochinenii*, i (Moscow, 1915), 499–555: the hero of this splendidly obvious didactic play is cured of his silly attempts to introduce European ways by the strictures of a peasant raisonneur,

By the time that Pushkin's 'To a Grandee' was written, its nostalgic lament for aristocratic cultivation put Pushkin in rather a marginal position even among conservatives. This became painfully evident when the critic Nikolai Polevoi, in a satirical sketch under the title 'A Morning with a Grand Gentleman', represented the poet under the mask of an obsequious Italian abbé who was rewarded for his flattery for being invited to dine on Thursdays at his patron's table.[87] Indeed, Pushkin's representation flew in the face of an established tradition of work by gentry writers associating aristocracy and prodigality. The figure of Yusupov, with his cultivated and intelligent application of wealth, is the polar opposite of the portraits of aristocrats in two famous poems by Derzhavin written in the 1780s, 'Felitsa' and 'The Grandee'. Where Yusupov conducts decorous symposiums with his philosopher guests, Derzhavin's aristocrats lounge with nubile young females on soft, velvet-covered divans, over-indulge themselves on banquets of imported delicacies, and savour low entertainments such as Shrovetide fairs and performances by horn orchestras. Derzhavin's senten-tious edge is always evident as he contrasts the primrose path of dalliance with the stony way of duty and virtue (this latter hoary metaphor actually appears in 'Felitsa'). In 'The Grandee', whose very title makes clear its probable significance as an antagonistic inspiration of Pushkin's poem, Derzhavin begins with a statement of determination to praise not decora-tion (*ukrashen'e odezhd*) but dignity, worthy qualities (*dostoinstvy*). He sardonically apostrophizes those 'Sardanapals' (from a legendary Assyrian king whose supposed delights included dressing in women's clothes and working at the loom) who understand refined behaviour to be no more than sensual pleasure:

> А ты, вторый Сарданапал!
> К чему стремишь всех мыслей беги?
> На том, чтоб век твой протекал
> Средь игр, средь праздности и неги?
> Чтоб пурпур, злато всюду взор
> В твоих чертогах восхищали,
> Картины в зеркалах дышали
> Мусия, мрамор, и фарфор?

who suggests it will be 'harmful' (*obidno*) to 'throw off what we wear and put on other people's clothes' (p. 336) and that it would be better to 'pay the sexton to teach us our letters' than to open a school (p. 334).

[87] N. Polevoi, 'Utro znatnogo barina, knyazya Bezzubova', *Novyi zhivopisets obshchestva i literatury*, supp. to *Moskovskii telegraf* no. 10 (1830). Not surprisingly, it excited Pushkin's fury: see his riposte in *PSS* xi. 153. The divisions among those of conservative views are also indicated by the fact that the sketch's publication led to the dismissal of Sergei Glinka, the censor responsible for letting the piece through, from his post. (See S. Glinka, *Zapiski* (St Petersburg, 1895), 356–8.)

And you, a second Sardanapal!
Where do you direct the thrust of your thoughts?
Is it not to the desire that your life should flow on
Amidst games, amidst sloth and dalliance?
That porphyry and gold should everywhere
Delight the gaze in your apartments,
That pictures should be breathed in your mirrors
By mosaic, marble, and porcelain?

To the disapproving puritan gaze, a picture has the same value as a Meissen bowl or a marble-clad wall; all are expressions of self-indulgent consumption that preclude attention to the line of petitioners waiting for paternalistic largesse, the widow, the wounded officer, the hungry soldier. The duty of a grandee is not to set standards of taste, but to live according to the dictates of morality:

Блажен народ! где царь главой,
Вельможи—здравы члены тела,
Прилежно долг все правят свой,
Чужого не касаясь дела.[88]

Blessed is the people where the tsar is head,
Where grandees are healthy limbs of the body [of state],
Where zealously all execute their duties,
Not meddling in things that do not concern them.

The parable of the rich man and Lazarus sets the tone of Derzhavin's 'Grandee' (wealth is always possessed at the expense of someone else). By contrast, in Pushkin's representation, luxury, rather than inspiring disapproval, comes to seem more virtuous, as well as more resilient, than narrow-minded industriousness. Pushkin had used the famous tag from Horace's *Odes* i, 7, 'Carpe diem', as the epigraph for 'To a Grandee' in an early draft (*PSS* iii. 823), and the final version of the poem is very much in the spirit of Horace's counsel to use time gracefully because life will soon be over. Derzhavin's poem is a Christian and moralistic interpretation of the instruction to 'seize the hour', a *memento mori*: time should be spent in the pursuit of good because there may come a day when we are forced to account for our lives.

To be sure, not all Derzhavin's wastrels were grandees. The lazy and self-indulgent characters in 'Felitsa' included the obligatory country squire

---

[88] G. Derzhavin, *Stikhotvoreniya* (Leningrad, 1981), 105, 107. On the contrasting attitudes to 'duty' in Pushkin, cf. the fact that an early version of 'To a Grandee' made reference to Peter the Great as a 'carpenter' (*PSS* iii. 809): the tsar is evoked in the seventh stanza of Derzhavin's poem as a 'traveller covered in dust and sweat' (*Stikhotvoreniya*, 105). However, in Pushkin's poem Peter is a *parallel* to Yusupov the grandee, where in Derzhavin's he represents precisely the *opposite* life-pattern to that of aristocratic self-indulgence.

with a library consisting of the popular romances *Polkan* and *Bova the King's Son*, and a copy of the Bible (over which he dozed after games of blind-man's buff and louse-picking with his wife). But Derzhavin's poetry generally associated life in the country with a rational economy of moral and financial self-sufficiency. The most famous, and lengthy, exposition of this view was the verse epistle 'To Evgeny: On Life at Zvansk' (1807). As idyllic as 'To a Grandee', the piece is utterly different in its construction of an ideal world. Rather than roaming Europe, Derzhavin remains at home, taking delight not in sculpture by Canova and paintings by Correggio, but in a magic lantern and the sight of his well-tended park through the drawing-room windows. Work figures as well as play; the landowner spends an industrious morning consulting with his factors and viewing the property to check that all is in order. (This aspect of the portrayal was as flexible with the truth as Pushkin's delineation of Yusupov, since it was Derzhavin's energetic second wife, Dar'ya, who actually took responsibility for the practical organization of the estate.)[89] The poem represents an orderly and virtuous existence, a daily round ordered according to the rules of time-honoured custom. 'In Praise of Country Life' (1798) and 'Life in the Country' (1802) portray in equally loving detail existence on a middle-sized country estate, with its round of gardening, coppicing, putting food by, harvesting fruit, snaring game, relaxation in the fields, and family dinners:

> Бутылка доброго вина,
> Впрок пива русского варена,
> С гренками коновка полна,
> Из коей клубом лезет пена,
> И стол обеденный готов.
>
> Горшок горячих, добрых щей,
> Копченый окорок под дымом;
> Обсаженный семьей моей,
> Средь коей сам я господином,
> И тут-то вкусен мне обед.[90]

> A bottle of good wine,
> And a barrel of good Russian beer—
> The tankard is full right to the brim,
> And a cloud of froth spills over the top—
> And the dinner table is ready.

[89] See Grand Duke Nicholas Mikhailovich, *Russkie portrety*, i, note to pl. 40. For a general assessment of women's involvement in running estates, see Michelle L. Marrese, 'The *Pomeshchitsa*, Absent and Present: Noblewomen and Estate Management in Imperial Russia', paper presented at the 11th Berkshire Conference on the History of Women, June 1999.
[90] Derzhavin, *Stikhotvoreniya*, 139.

A bowl of good hot cabbage soup,
A knuckle of smoked ham, all steaming,
With my family sitting round,
And me as the lord of all:
That is the dinner I enjoy!

And the idyll of life on the country estate still held force in the 1810s, when Anna Bunina, in her defensive autobiography, 'Though Poverty's No Stain', eulogized the gentry life of which she had been deprived by her mother's death:

Палаты с флигельми в наследственном селе;
Вкруг сада каменна ограда;
    В одном угле
    Качели—детская привада,
  В другом различны теремки,
    Из дерева грибки,
    И многие затеи;
Лимоны, персики, тюльпаны и лилеи
    В горшочках и в грунту,
    С плодом и на цвету,
У батюшки мово считали как крапиву!
Орехи кедровы, миндаль,—
Ну, словом, все свое! Ни даже черносливу
    Купить не посылали вдаль
    На зимню трату!
Все в садике росло, хотя не по климату.
(Губерния Рязань, Ряжск город был уезд.)
    Груш, яблок... точно в небе звезд!

Houses with wings stood on the entailed estate;
    The demesne was ringed by walls of stone;
    One corner held our bait—
    Swings, the children's own—
The other held all sorts of little towers,
    And toadstools built of wood;
    And other decorations no less good;
Lemon and peach trees, tulips, lily flowers
    In flowerbeds or in pots,
    Blooming and bearing fruits,
At my papa's were common as the weeds!
    Pine nuts and almonds too,
Everything was our own! We never even needed
    To send away for prunes
    In winter time!
It all grew round about, despite the hostile clime.

(The Province of Ryazan, Ryazhsk city was nearby.)
Pears, apples... thick as stars up in the sky![91]

Where the appointments of Pushkin's Arkhangel'skoe are those of the idealized, 'Palladian' estate anywhere in the refined world,[92] Derzhavin and Bunina demonstrate the idiosyncracy and authenticity of their portrayed world with inventories of realia, testaments of material possessions—jars of honey, garden ornaments, magic lanterns—that weigh more in the balance than the furniture of the mind. The perception of the country estate as pleasing both to virtue and to *vertù* draws on eighteenth-century pastoral convention, but these texts are not routine rehearsals of genre: their light-hearted tone does not mask the cogent conviction of righteousness that they express. They are tributes to the rise of a conservative nationalism that had as its leitmotifs a construct of the country estate as utopia of social and aesthetic order, governed by a patriarch whose complement of appropriate possessions indicated his ability to balance gentility with morality.

The sense of common interests rooted in a defence of national tradition against the powerful advocates of novelty, luxury, and 'whim' meant that it was possible at once to believe that (in Gogol''s words) 'everyone should serve God in his own place and in no other'[93]—that social differences were God-given and inalienable—and that there were certain values common to all Russians who had not been seduced by Westernization. But if anti-Western feeling—the repudiation of 'the luxury and degradation that took root in Russia' in and after the reign of Peter I[94]—gave negative strength to

---

[91] A. Bunina, 'Khot' bednost' ne porok': in C. Kelly, *An Anthology of Russian Women's Writing*, 399–400; trans. S. Forrester, ibid, p. 4. Bunina's poem is a precursor of the later tradition of memoirs about idyllic country childhoods: on this, see A. Wachtel, *The Battle for Childhood: Creation of a Russian Myth* (Stanford, Calif., 1991).

[92] This general attachment to 'civilized values' and social rootlessness are one explanation for the fact that, as Richard Gregg has recently argued, 'nowhere does Pushkin show more than a perfunctory interest in doing what, according to Joseph Conrad, is the primary task of any novelist, namely, "to make you *see!*"' ('Pushkin's Novelistic Prose: A Dead End?', *SR* 57/1 (1998), 12).

[93] See Letter 22 of *Vybrannye mesta iz perepiski s druz'yami*, *Sochineniya*, iv. 118. This instruction was perhaps less offensive to non-*dvoryane* conservatives than modern readers might suppose, given that pride in family origin was by no means limited to the *dvoryanstvo*: see, for instance, the introduction by Ivan Vavilov to his *Besedy russkogo kuptsa o torgovle . . .* (St Petersburg, 1844), [p. iii]: 'I shall confine myself to giving simple talks [rather than lectures], since this is suitable to the social estate of which I am proud to call myself a member'. Cf. the comments of Praskov'ya Tatlina, a memoirist from the *meshchanstvo*, on her family: 'Vospominaniya', *Russkii arkhiv* 10 (1899), 190–1. (An English translation of this text appears in T. Clyman and J. Vowles, *Russia Through Women's Eyes* (New Haven, 1996).) Such attitudes had some official support: in 1807, Alexander I had introduced an equivalent of the 17th-cent. 'Velvet Book' for merchants. (See BE iii. 118).

[94] M. M. Shcherbatov, *O povrezhdenii nravov v Rossii*, ed. A. Lentin (Cambridge, 1969), 143. (My translation: the original Russian is 'roskosh' i unizhenie utverzhdali svoi korni'). For later examples of this theme-tune among conservatives, cf. the writings of Sergei Glinka. In his *Ruskoi*

conservatism, positive force was lent by the dream of creating alternative behaviour models that would be rooted in the Russian past and derived from local tradition. Private behaviour, and private life in general, were ideologized, just as the radicals had ideologized these, but in a diametrically opposed way. Rather than being inverted or subverted, the mores belonging to what was perceived to be the traditional culture of the middle ranks of society were lovingly and fervently asserted. *Samobytnost'*, the uniqueness of Russian life, was to be assured by appropriate *byt*, daily life, as manifested particularly in the lives of self-sufficient landowners on their country estates, merchants, and the most upright and solvent peasants.

The relationship between *byt* and *samobytnost'* is implicit in the poems of Derzhavin, who wrote at a period when the horrors of the French Revolution had already caused genteel Russians to be more circumspect about their love of things foreign. Indeed, his 'In Praise of Country Life' comes close to a direct articulation of a connection between domesticity and patriotism in two stanzas praising the activities of 'virtuous Russian wives' in ensuring decorous *byt*:

> Но будет ли любовь при том
> Со прелестьми ее забыта,
> Когда прекрасная лицом
> Хозяйка мила, домовита,
> Печется о его детях?
>
> Как ею—русских честных жен
> По древнему обыкновенью —
> Весь *быт хозяйский* снаряжен:
> Дом тепл, чист, светл, и к возвращенью
> С охоты мужа стол накрыт.[95]

> But is love, and all its delights
> To be forgotten?
> When the dear, industrious,
> And sweet-faced woman of the house
> Busies herself with the children?
>
> Consider how—according to the ancient custom
> Of virtuous Russian wives—
> She arranges *all domestic life*:
> The house is warm, clean, light, and when her husband
> Returns from hunting, he finds the table set.

vestnik, Glinka never ceased expostulating xenophobically against the hold of 'fashion' on the Russian mind. For a discussion of this, see Alexander M. Martin, 'The Family Model of Society and Russian National Identity in Sergei N. Glinka's *Russian Messenger* (1808–1812)', *SR* 57 (1998): 28–49, esp. 33, 37; and L. N. Kiseleva, 'Sistema vzgliadov S. N. Glinki (1807–1812 gg.), *Uchenye zapiski Tartuskogo gosudarstvennogo universiteta* 513 (1981), 52–72.

[95] Derzhavin, *Stikhotvoreniya*, 138. My emphasis.

As 'Viking Russian' feeling rose in the 1800s, so did appreciation of *byt*, maintaining its strength also through the following decades.[96] The term *byt* resurfaced in Khomyakov's essays 'The Old and the New' (1839) and 'On Rural Conditions' (1842),[97] as well as in Gogol''s *Selected Passages from Correspondence with Friends*, where it was used to eulogize serfdom (see above). It was approvingly applied also in a fragmentary note by Petr Chaadaev dating from the early 1840s, in which the philosopher, speaking from a standpoint diametrically opposed to that adopted in his famous *Philosophical Letters* of 1836–7, saw Russia's 'solitude', the peculiarities of her *byt*, as a source of strength rather than of tragic weakness.[98] But the first systematic statement of the connection between domestic life and the maintenance of national values was apparently made in Ivan Kireevsky's important essay of 1852, 'On the Character of Enlightenment in Europe and its Relation to Enlightenment in Russia'. Here, the terms *byt* and *samobytnyi* are used eighteen times in the space of forty-eight pages, overwhelmingly often (fifteen out of eighteen times) in contexts linked to a celebration of the unique virtues of traditional Russian life (*russkii byt*), which is said to be characterized by its true religiosity and its respect for custom. It was the Russian peasantry, Kireevsky argued, who had best preserved traditional *byt*. The objective of the essay, however, was to persuade readers from the educated elite to reabsorb traditional values, to turn from the falsity and frivolity of Western Europe to the solidity of the Russian past. Kireevsky's argument was linked to his concept of land-owning legitimacy. He asserted that part of the *samobytnost'* of Russia was that the ruling classes had historically enjoyed privilege because of their observation of collective morality, their fidelity to the dictates of *byt*: 'There [in Europe] the legal system is formal and logical; here it is derived from *byt* [. . .] There the laws are derived artificially, from general public opinion, here they were born naturally, out of *byt*.' The implication was that if the upper classes did not mend their ways, and turn back to traditional Russian culture, they would lose their moral right to enjoy the privileges and the cultural prominence that they had been inclined to take for granted.[99]

[96]   The term *varyagorussy* is used by Vigel', *Zapiski*, ii. 356–8: he dates their appearance to 1806. An example of a publication celebrating 'Russian customs' is V. N. Karazin, *Rech' o neobkhodimosti v nastoyashchikh obstoyatel'stvakh usilit' domovodstvo, proiznesennaya v Khar'kove 13 genvarya 1813 v torzhestvennom sobranii Filotekhnicheskogo Obshchestva* (Khar'kov, 1813), see esp. 11, 18 n. 10.

[97]   A. Khomyakov, *PSS* iii (Moscow, 1905), 11–29, 63–85.

[98]   See '[Otryvok is istoricheskogo rassuzhdeniya o Rossii]' (*c.*1842–3), in *Stat'i i pis'ma* (Moscow, 1987), 311–16; and contrast *Filosofskie pis'ma*, ibid., esp. 42–3, 107–9.

[99]   I. V. Kireevsky, 'O kharaktere prosveshcheniya Evropy i o ego otnoshenii k prosveshche-niyu Rossii', *Polnoe sobranie sochinenii v 2 tomakh* (Moscow, 1911), i. 174–222 (quotation here from p. 217). The terms *byt* and *samobytnost'* were used in a very similar manner in Konstantin

Apart from emphasizing the need to integrate religious practice into daily life, Kireevsky gave little guidance on what the broad term *russkii byt* was to be understood.[100] However, the writings of other writers inclined to Slavophile views make this clearer. The rise of conservative nationalism after 1840, and the growth of the sense that radical behaviour models must be combatted, were accompanied by the recontextualization of advice literature, and particularly by the emergence of the manual of domestic life as a serious contribution to public discourse.

As with celebrations of *byt* in general, there was a pre-history. In the early nineteenth century, occasional advice texts had already begun to present themselves as contributions to the construction of an autonomous national tradition of private life. In his introduction to *On the Education of the Young* (1807), Ivan Bogdanovich, for example, stated that he had been prompted to the composition of the book because 'having scrutinized the rules laid down by foreign writers, I found that these were frequently not in accordance with our situation, whether from a physical or from a moral point of view'. Bogdanovich argued that foreigners' contribution to the moral education of Russians must be at best imperfect because of their insensitivity to religious traditions and customs (*obychai, bogosluzhenie*), and his book was presented as an attempt to unite the universal ('the rules of morality are everywhere and always the same') and the local (the traits of 'national character').[101] Nine years later, Vasily Levshin, the author of many compilations of hints for householders on subjects from the keeping of vegetable gardens to the supervision of packs of hounds, and also the composer of a vehemently anti-French pamphlet, *The Russian's Epistle to Lovers of Things French* (1807), on the side, had presented his *The Russian Cookbook* as a counterblast to 'the acquaintance with things foreign, which, since the time it began, has acted in the same [pernicious] manner upon the purity of Russian manners and morals [*nravy*] and on the taste of the food set before us'.[102]

Aksakov's 'Ob osnovnykh nachalakh russkoi istorii' and 'O tom zhe' (*PSS* i (Moscow, 1861), 7–17), which argued for Russia's difference from the West ('Russia is a totally particular land' [*zemlya sovershenno samobytnaya*], 7), one reason for this being its 'idiosyncratic everyday life' (*svoeobraznyi byt*) (2).

[100] This was in line with his vagueness about the history of the *dvoryanstvo* generally: 'One never hears from Kireevsky, for instance, what role members of his own class played in the communal society of the past, with its sacred, inviolate traditions.' (Gleason, *European and Muscovite*, 170).

[101] I. Bogdanovich, *O vospitanii yunoshestva* (Moscow, 1807), 5, 6–7.

[102] V. A. Levshin, *Russkaya povarnya*, 'Izvestie' to pt. 4; *Poslanie ruskago k frantsuzolyubtsam*; his other works include *Vseobshchee i polnoe domovodstvo* (1795). As a small landowner (his family had around 200 serfs) who felt a fierce pride in his *dvoryanstvo* descent (his many publications included *Rodoslovnaya kniga blagorodnykh dvoryan Levshinykh, soderzhashchaya v sebe Dokazatel'stva o proiskhozhdenii ikh familii . . .* (Moscow, 1791), Levshin was a highly typical member of the *srednee sostoyanie* from whom patriotic works on *byt* tended to derive.

Levshin was also a pioneer in another tradition that was to be very important for later national conservatives: the manual of appropriate behaviour for the landowner. His *Complete Household Book* (1813) was prefaced with stern warnings about the duties of the landowner and his wife to maintain order among their family and underlings: 'If the master does not reflect upon his duties in relation to his household officials and his servants, and does not organize theirs;—if the mistress does not concern herself in the same way with the female officials in the household and with the womenservants, then what kind of order is to be expected in the house?'[103] The book provided detailed advice on every aspect of estate management, from the supervision of farms to the management of the vegetable garden, from the salaries payable to servants to the need for moral education of the children of house serfs, a subject which, Levshin alleged, often received less attention than the training of *borzois* for the chase: '[These children] grow up willy-nilly, running hither and thither at will; they become accustomed to do as they like [*svoevol'stvovat'*], to resist orders, to fight and to use foul language.'[104] For her part, the mistress of the house was advised on how to run the cellar and the kitchen, and lectured upon the importance of her own involvement in childcare: she was not to rely upon nurses, still less upon 'Frenchwomen, Englishwomen, and other foreigners', 'whose religion, manners and customs are quite dissimilar from ours'.[105]

For all the interest of Levshin and Bogdanovich as pioneers, though, their works did not capture the public imagination in the way that successor texts, such as Gogol''s *Selected Passages from Correspondence with Friends*, Akim Charukovsky's *National-Popular Medicine, Adapted for Russian Daily Life [Byt] and to the Climate of Russia* (1844), or the works of Ekaterina Avdeeva (1789–1865), were to do. This was partly a question of public mood. In the 1840s, advice literature texts were accorded reviews by intellectually heavyweight and influential 'thick journals' such as *Sovremennik* and *Otechestvennye zapiski*, which treated them as serious contributions to social debates and to historical investigation. Avdeeva's *Pocket Cookbook*, for example, was the subject of a rapturous anonymous review in *Otechestvennye zapiski*, which favourably contrasted the 'modest wisdom' of such books, 'in which simple recipes for creating the modest menus of happy family life are transcribed from the words of busy housewives', to books that described 'how to make paper lace for decorating vast trenchers of fish'.[106] But it was also because of the more purposive tone of the books

---

[103] Levshin, *Polnaya khozyaistvennaya kniga*, esp. vol. i, pp. ix–x.   [104] Ibid. i. 173.
[105] Ibid. i. 199.
[106] Anon, 'K— A——. *Karmannaya povarennaya knizhka* (St Petersburg, 1846)', *Otechestvennye zapiski* 10 (1846), sect. 6, 83–4.

themselves, which depended less heavily on borrowings from foreign texts,[107] and more successfully harmonized the themes of 'patriotism', 'family life', and 'the moral economy of the estate' than their predecessors had. Charukovsky's *National-Popular Medicine*, for instance, gave a patriotic twist to its hygienic guidance, declaring that 'In the cold and temperate parts [of the Russian empire], clothing the entire body in Russian dress (and in the warm and hot belts, in Cossack or Circassian dress) is the most decent and appropriate [mode of behaviour]. But, in despite of experience and of common sense, we serve a single idol—fashion, sacrificing to him the innocence and shame of our wives and daughters and even our own health.'[108] And it specifically addressed itself to landowners as disseminators of culture, asserting, for instance, that they should 'instruct the rustic [*poselyanin*] that in the springtime it is easy to catch cold'.[109] Similarly, Avdeeva's *The Experienced Russian Housewife's Handbook, Composed on the Basis of Forty Years' Practice and Observation by a Good Russian Housewife* (1842) (a book which went through eleven editions and remained in print till the late 1870s), began with a litanaic expostulation to 'Russian tradition':

Domestic economy is the means of securing the comfort of everyday, domestic existence (*udobstva byta v domashnei zhizni*) . . . it provides the means of poeticizing, so to speak, the most prosaic objects, such as the kitchen and household tasks. . . . Just as the mother of the household's supervision is essential when one employs tutors and governesses for the children, so even in a household with cooks and housekeepers, the mistress of the house must remain the mistress of the house. . . . I should add a few words on the adjective *Russian*. My book is intended specifically for the *Russian* household, and I speak in it about the Russian national table, Russian food, the Russian kitchen. While not repudiating either the German or the French kitchen, I think that Russian food, our native food, the food to which we have become used, the food that we have grown to love, which is derived from the experience of the centuries, which is handed down from fathers to children and is justified in terms of the location and climate of life, is healthier and more nutritious to us in every way.[110]

---

[107] The anonymous B. V—n, author of *Entsiklopediya molodoi russkoi khozyaiki* (1839), i. I, remarks on Levshin's dependence on early 18th-cent. German sources. Among these may have been *Der sorgfaltige Haus-Wirtschafts-Verwalter* (Breslau and Leipzig, 1752), *Des galanten Frauenzimmers bequemes und nützliches Handbuch* (Esslingen, 1756), and *Adlige Hauswirtschaftskunst* (Erfurt, 1757), copies of all of which are held in RNB.

[108] Charukovsky, *Narodnaya meditsyna*, 329. The book had gone into a 4th edn. by 1848.

[109] Ibid., p. xxii.

[110] Avdeeva, *Ruchnaya kniga*, pp. i, iii, iv. Emphasis in original. The last edition (as *Novaya ruchnaya kniga*) was in 1877. See the biographical articles by M. Zirin, in M. Ledkovsky, C. Rosenthal, and M. Zirin (eds.), *Dictionary of Russian Women Writers* (Westport, Conn., 1994), 44; and S. N. Kaidash, in *Russkie pisateli 1800–1917: biograficheskii slovar'*, i (Moscow, 1987), 15–16.

Avdeeva's emphasis on 'poeticizing the prosaic' through wise spending distinguished the absorption in domestic matters which she advocated from the sort of pernicious concentration upon inessentials of which nationalist conservatives disapproved.[111] But it was above all the emphasis on religion which was used to sanctify the concentration on affairs domestic. The ideal landowner of conservative advice books dispensed religious instruction to his peasants along with practical advice. N. Pakhirev's *Guide for the Experienced Landowner* (1844) urged the reader on the one hand to take measures to ensure that the peasants were able to provide for themselves, rather than depending on the community or upon the landowner himself, and on the other stated that the space between the airy, south-facing estate house, with its gardens and river or pond, and the village should be occupied by 'a church with a priest's house alongside'.[112] The landowner in Gogol''s *Selected Passages*, incinerating a pile of banknotes before his peasants in order to illustrate that work mattered more than money, and kissing the Bible to show his respect for true religion, was but an extreme and eccentric version of a standard stereotype.[113] And in 'What a Wife May Be to Her Husband in Simple Domestic Life [*prostoi domashnii byt*]', Gogol' gave a religious tinge to the prudent management of expenses by propagandizing financial restraint not as mere thrift, but as a truly Russian and Orthodox form of self-restraint: 'Do not burn with shame if it gets about the town that your household is not *comme il faut*, but laugh inwardly to yourself, recollecting that what is truly *comme il faut* is what is demanded by the One Who made you.'[114] He suggested that household income should be divided into seven piles to cover various outgoings (the use of the mystic number lending ritual dignity to kopeck-pinching) and that these outgoings, alongside rent, food, the cost of a carriage, the wardrobe, pocket money, and unexpected expenses, should include regular donations of alms.[115]

On the whole, though, 'charity began at home' for conservative writers in another sense. The external effects of economical housekeeping in terms

[111] Contrast the purely matter-of-fact attitude to spending in Radetsky, *Al'manakh gastronomov* (2nd edn., pp. v–vi), which suggests that the less well-off might like to use the rich meals in the books for special occasions, while aristocrats can consume them all the time; or the introduction to the same author's *Khozyaika*, which offers the book to 'the less well-off' (*menee zazhitochnye*) as well as the rich.

[112] I. Pakhirev, *Rukovodstvo opytnogo pomeshchika* . . . (St Petersburg, 1844), 51–2, 63–7. Elena Molokhovets's *Podarok molodym khozyaikam. Domashnee, gorodskoe i sel'skoe khozyaistvo*, iii (1881), the 'home hints' supplement to the same author's famous cookbook *Podarok molodym khozyaikam* (1861), reproduces this model on a small scale, dictating that the house or apartment should contain a 'room for prayer' as well as bedrooms, a dining-room, etc.

[113] Letter 22, *Sochineniya*, iv. 119.

[114] Letter 24, ibid. iv. 138. The phrase 'comme il faut' is used in French in the original.

[115] Ibid. 136–7.

of liberating money for philanthropy were of less concern than the contribution made by good housekeeping to the stability of the patriarchal family, an institution which conservatives (not incorrectly) understood to be threatened by the radicals' campaign for the legal and emotional autonomy of women. In their campaign against 'the freedom of bandits and murderers, which considers slaughter to be honourable and theft virtuous',[116] conservative authors also emphasized that the maintenance of patriarchal tradition within the family depended upon the performance by women and girls of the domestic duties that were their peculiar respon- sibility. Avdeeva argued vehemently against the rarified upbringing given to girls of a class that could not afford the consequences: 'Often the daughters [of the middle rank] become genteelly idle [*beloruchki*], when neither the way of life they lead, nor their family relations, nor indeed the condition of their parents will allow this.' The neglect of training in housekeeping was catastrophic, given that 'A virtuous mother of a family and a good housekeeper is a guarantee of the serenity of her family'.[117] Another writer, Raida Varlamova, invoked the Victorian image of the 'angel in the house' to celebate the role of the housewife: 'The wife and mother is the honour of the home, a peaceful angel in the house, the visible spirit of domestic order and of prosperity.'[118] As these examples show, 'domestic order' and 'prosperity' were not merely ends in themselves, but contributions to the maintenance of social order. As Elena Molokhovets put it in the introduction to the third volume of her extremely popular, and much-reprinted, cookbook *A Gift for Young Housewives*, 'The young housewife must concern herself not only with her own family, servants, and peasants, but also with the welfare of her neighbour in the broadest sense, being both a mother to her household [*sem'yaninka svoego doma*] and a citizeness in the great family of humanity.'[119] Social participation, then, was but an extended form of membership in a family, while within the family the husband maintained the role of benevolent autocrat, busying himself with 'the preservation and defence of the family and with family

[116] See Dymman, *Nauka zhizni* (1859), 21–2.

[117] Avdeeva, *Ruchnaya kniga*, p. iii.

[118] Ibid. p. iii; Varlamova, *Semeinyi magazin*, p. i.

[119] Molokhovets, *Podarok molodym khozyaikam*, vol. iii. p. i. The reference to 'the welfare of her own peasants' in a book published twenty years after the Emancipation of the Serfs is a telling demonstration of the stability of the conservative vision of ideal *byt*. Despite her fame, very little is known about Molokhovets's biography, bar her date of birth (Arkhangel'sk in 1831), the fact that she was married to a provincial civil servant, and the titles of her many books (she is not included in standard biographical dictionaries such as *Russkie pisateli 1800–1917: biograficheskii slovar'* (Moscow, 1987, and continuing). For a brief biographical sketch, see Joyce Toomre (ed. and trans.), *Classic Russian Cooking: Elena Molokhovets' A Gift to Young Housewives* (Bloomington, Ind., 1992), 11–13; the remainder of Toomre's introduction provides an excellent discussion of the context and significance of Molokhovets's work.

happiness'.[120] From the point of view of conservatives, it was perfectly logical to reverse the equation and see family breakdown as a cause of social decay.[121] Alexander II's murder by terrorists in 1881 seemed to present overwhelming evidence to back up this conservative causality, being seen by the novelist Nadezhda Sokhanskaya, for instance, as a direct result of declining strictness in family relations:

Here is the burning fruit of the trust which the Tsar-Liberator himself placed in them and which you yourself welcomed not long ago. Who should be the first to repent? We are all 'guilty in all things', but guiltiest of all are the parents. . . . It is not father and mother who now command and regulate the family; on the contrary, children have now become the alpha and omega of everything. 'Everything for them, everything in the way they want!' So some ten-year-old pipsqueak Sashka can stand there in his school uniform and dare to tell his father and mother: 'You just don't know anything, you don't understand!' And his parents, instead of giving the little know-all to realize (by means of a good thrashing if nothing else) that father and mother have rights and dignity as well, that he is supposed to obey and respect them, and never mind what they do and don't know—father and mother fall into embarrassed silence! And if this Sashka doesn't have any sense of the authority within the family, of respect for his father and mother as his father and mother, what authority and what governing order in society at large is this fledging of a corrupt [*rastlennyi*] nest going to be pleased to bow down before?[122]

In similar vein, Natal'ya Grot, wife of the historian Yakov Grot, asserted that 'the literature, publicistics, and pedagogical writings of the 1860s and 1870s bore a terrible blame for the corruption [*rastlenie*] of Russian youth, for weakening religious faith, family bonds and familial affection'.[123]

While there was an element of self-lacerating masochism in conservative women's assertion of patriarchal values, a kind of triumphant 'kissing of the rod', the paradox was that Sokhanskaya and Grot's insistence upon traditional family roles allowed them access to one of the most fundamental discussion topics of the day. That is, by sermonizing about the need for women to confine themselves to a domestic existence, they were able to

[120] Varlamova, *Semeinyi magazin*, p. i. The association between patriarchal authority in the family and autocratic institutions was also made in tsarist legal codes, which represented the husband as 'tsar' within his family. (See W. Wagner, *Marriage, Property, and Law in Late Imperial Russia* (Oxford, 1994); Laura Engelstein, *The Keys to Happiness: Sex and the Search for Modernity in Fin de Siècle Russia* (Ithaca, NY, 1992), ch. 1; Gregory Freeze, 'Bringing Order to the Russian Family: Marriage and Divorce in Imperial Russia, 1760–1860', *Journal of Modern History* 62:4 (1990), 709–46.)

[121] See e.g. Kireevsky's diatribe against the emancipation of women in 'O kharaktere', i. 213.

[122] N. S. Sokhanskaya—letter to I. S. Aksakov, 10 Mar. 1881: O. G. Aksakova, 'Perepiska Aksakovykh s N. S. Sokhanskoi (Kokhanovskoi)', *Russkoe obozrenie* 12 (1896), 470.

[123] Natal'ya Grot, *Iz semeinoi khroniki: Vospominaniya dlya detei i vnukov* (St Petersburg, 1900), 27.

enter the public domain.[124] To be sure, Sokhanskaya's statement was made in a letter, and Grot's in her memoirs, which were privately printed. But the cases of Avdeeva (whose works flexibly interpreted 'house management' to include farming and estate management as well),[125] Varlamova, and Molokhovets illustrate that pronouncements on family life could take women directly into public discourse. And even if they were not always made 'in public' in the ordinary sense, by the mid-nineteenth century, pronouncements upon family morality, and morality more generally, were a means for women to achieve some sort of authority within circles of relatives and friends, hence influencing public discourse at one remove. Significantly, where Romantics and radicals on the whole preferred to keep serious talk for all-male, or male-dominated, groups, conservatives cultivated the 'salon' in a new, politicized sense: the drawing-rooms of women such as Avdot'ya Elagina, mother of the Kireevsky brothers, Karolina Pavlova, and later Anna Tyutcheva-Aksakova, provided a congenial environment for discussions about the future of the Russian nation and for the reading aloud of literary works.[126] In emphasizing the seriousness of the gatherings in their drawing-rooms, conservative women sometimes contrasted these with the supposedly more frivolous and worldly occasions in aristocratic households. The inanities of the aristocratic salon were satirized, for example, in Karolina Pavlova's 1846

[124] This manoeuvre was evident in the case of women conservatives in other countries as well (e.g. Madame de Genlis, whose *La Femme auteur* (published in Russian as 'Zhenshchina-avtor' in Karamzin's journal *Vestnik Evropy* 5 (1802), 245–85) was a text by an unstoppably prolific woman writer warning that creative writing might lead women into dangerous and foolish self-display).

[125] See e.g. Avdeeva, *Zapiski dlya gorodskikh i sel'skikh khozyaev* (1842), and eadem, *Rukovodstvo k ustroistvu ferm* (1863), which urge the adoption of English agricultural methods in order to make Russian estates more profitable.

[126] On Elagina, see Lina Bernshtein, 'Women on the Verge of a New Language: Russian Salon Hostesses in the First Half of the Nineteenth Century', in H. Goscilo and B. Holmgren (eds.), *Russia—Women—Culture* (Bloomington, Ind., 1997), 215–220; on Karolina Pavlova, Munir Sendich, 'Moscow Literary Salons: Evenings at Karolina Pavlova's', *Die Welt der Slaven* 17 (1972), 341–57. Even before the 1830s, conservative circles had provided a forum for some educated women. During the Napoleonic Invasion, the Women's Patriotic Society had encouraged women to make their contribution to defence of the motherland (see S. Glinka, 'Istoricheskoe izobrazhenie dobrodeteli i slavy Rossiyanok drevnikh i novykh vremen', *Moskovskii al'manakh dlya prekrasnogo pola*, 71). And Karamzin's daughter Sof'ya had been a formidable force in the 1810s and 1820s (see Aronson and Reiser, *Literaturnye kruzhki i salony*, 162–70). Cases such as this make problematic Diana Greene's assertion that 'the few upper-class women affected by [domestic ideology] generally remained isolated from each other' (see 'Mid-Nineteenth-Century Domestic Ideology in Russia', 90), given that the cult of domesticity seems to have been pervasive in the circles to which the Slavophile women belonged. At the same time, the salon continued its existence in another role—the 'court of final instance on manners, deportment, and marriages'. Princess Mariya Meshcherskaya, 'together with Countess Sheremetieff and a Miss Tuitcheff [*sic*: perhaps Dar'ya Tyutcheva, sister of Anna Tyutcheva-Aksakova, on whom see below], 'made up a trio known as the *conseil des infaillibles* in the Moscow society of the 1880s', pronouncing on such matters. (See Michael Ignatieff, *The Russian Album* (London, 1987), 23.)

novella *A Double Life*, in which Moscow hostesses use performances by fashionable poets in order to add lustre to occasions primarily intended for marketing nubile daughters, and in a poem of 1847 Pavlova contrasted her own 'life . . . in an intimate, family environment' (*byt . . . v predele tesnom i rodnom*) with the European travels and Petersburg glitter of another woman poet, Evdokiya Rostopchina.[127]

The prominence of women as moral commentators in conservative circles was aided by the fact that, as the Russian radicals asserted women's rights to a more intellectually ambitious education than hitherto offered, the formerly controversial notion of *éducation maternelle* began to be accepted even by those committed to patriarchy.[128] In memoirs by conservative writers, mothers, who in accounts by radicals tend to figure as the instruments of authoritarianism, embody the civilizing force in its most positive sense. The reverent portrayal of *mamin'ka* to be found in Tolstoi's *Childhood*, or Sergei Aksakov's *Family Chronicle*, began a tradition continued in, for example, Konstantin Leontiev's recollections, published in 1891, but referring to the 1830s and 1840s. Leontieva's sitting-room, embellished by her skill in decoration with fabric and paint, encapsulated the conservative ideal of *byt*, 'beauty and cosiness', but also economy ('none of this cost much money'). Her ability to secure places for her sons at the extremely exclusive Corps des Pages in St Petersburg by means of a petition to Empress Maria Feodorovna ('what right did the wife of a retired ensign have to this? . . . None at all, of course'), demonstrated both her commitment to the family and her loyalty to the royal house, portraits of whose members decorated the walls of her room. She was not only pious, but also 'loved silence, reading, and strict order in the disposal of her time and resources'. In other words, she epitomized a domestic ideal that it would not be inappropriate to term 'Victorian', one in which things of the mind and material conditions were in perfect harmony.[129]

If mothers had now become far more significant figures in the writings of male conservatives, it had also come to be expected that they would wield influence upon their daughters, providing them with a degree of intellectual and moral independence. This independence on the part of a wife, so Ivan Aksakov argued in 1865, was essential if her husband's authority were to be genuine:

[127] See *Polnoe sobranie stikhotvorenii* (Moscow and Leningrad, 1964), 134.

[128] See e.g. Avdeeva's statement that 'every mother of a family should set herself the duty of teaching her daughters 'the science of home economy', *Ruchnaya kniga*, p. iii; or the anonymous educational treatise *Sovety materi* (1853), which offers a rehash of Lambert's arguments from the late 18th cent. (see Ch. 1 above).

[129] K. Leont'ev, 'Rasskaz moei materi', *Sobranie sochinenii*, ix (Moscow and St Petersburg, 1913), 37, 38, 36, 37.

It is worthy of respect that I have to do [in you] with a being who is morally developed, that the woman whom I 'give the orders to' is not a cowardly slave, and not a child, but a free, intelligent and independent being. That is much harder and demands far more moral responsibility: you are not an impersonal personality [*bezlichnaya lichnost'*], not a *table rase*, on which I can write whatever I wish. And for this reason, your submission is utterly dear and joyful to me.[130]

The requirement that a wife be educated did not derive merely from a desire to be kept entertained in the long winter evenings, or from the piquancy that was brought by dominating an object worthy of domination. It was intimately related to the emphasis that Aksakov, like other conservatives, placed on the maintenance of appropriate *byt*, domestic existence. In another letter he encouraged Tyutcheva to obtain tuition in traditional ways from his mother:

I would wish that [Mama] should communicate to you all the traditions of the Aksakov clan [*rod*], all our family beliefs and customs, a sort of oral Family Chronicle, and, finally, tales of the life of days gone by that is in the process of being destroyed for ever and the daily life of Orthodoxy [*skazaniya o prezhnem, unichtozhayushchem byte, o bytovoi zhizni pravoslaviya*], about the phenomena of that ancient, organic life that is in the process of dying out. And you could communicate all this in turn to our own children, if God should grant us children.[131]

The act of commemoration was not to be one merely of passive family piety. Aksakov's dialogue with Tyutcheva about the future disposal of his ancestral property at Abramtsevo underlined the need actively to cherish the inheritance of the past, to live according to the rules of unostentatious gentry tradition. It was pointless for Tyutcheva to persist with her music, but homeopathy was a useful skill for a landowner's wife: she might have to care for peasant women who were reluctant to consult an ordinary doctor. A modest style of life was, however, not incompatible with comfort: Tyutcheva's room was to have a separate lavatory (*chernovoi kabinet lavatorio*); the furnishings for the 'small drawing-room' included a 'round soft divan'; and accommodation for two lady's maids was anticipated.[132]

---

[130] I. Aksakov, letter to A. F. Tyutcheva, 1 Nov. 1865: RGALI f. 10 op. 1. ed. khr. 236, ll. 128–9.

[131] Aksakov, letter to A. F. Tyutcheva, 19 Aug. 1865: RGALI f. 10 op. 1. ed. khr. 236, l. 25.

[132] Aksakov, letter to A. F. Tyutcheva, 5 Oct. 1865, RGALI f. 10 op. 1 ed. khr. 236, ll. 107–8. Cf. letters of 13 Dec. 1865 complimenting Tyutcheva as an *ispravnaya provornaya khozyaika* (l. 289) and 27 Dec. 1865 (l. 291) complaining about the lumpy stuffing in the mattresses her aunt had bought. In a published letter to A. D. Bludova of 7 Feb. 1861, Aksakov observes that his 'external life' (*vneshnyaya zhizn'*) was in good order, as 'the house in which we are living is comfortable, spacious and warm'. (See *Ivan Sergeevich Aksakov v ego pis'makh*, iv (St Petersburg, 1896), 181.) The 'lavatory' to which Aksakov refers was quite a modern comfort in the 1860s: in *Narodnaya meditsyna*, Charukovsky referred to 'English commodes and water-closets' as a means by which

Valuing domestic space as the precious vessel in which the essence of ideal patriarchy might be preserved, the Slavophiles did not see it as demeaning for a man of letters to worry about upholstery and sanitary facilities.[133] And in circles where house*work* in the sense of domestic labour (laundry, cleaning, fetching of water, day-to-day cooking) was performed by servants, house *management* in the sense of giving directions to servants, choosing menus, supervising cooking, controlling the household budget, arranging decoration, and choosing furnishings was something in which men could become involved without necessarily losing class status and the prestige of sex, once it had been accepted that it was a fit concern for cultivated persons of any kind.[134] The same was true of childcare: striking, for example, is late parent Vasily Zhukovsky's lyrical expostulation upon the joys of caring for small children, enclosed in a letter to V. I. Pletnev written in 1850:

Early moral education and children's early attempts to form thoughts belong to father and mother alone: they are something sacred, not to be shared with anyone. To whom can we surrender that delight of the first acquaintance with the first signs of spiritual and intellectual life of our infancy? What can more strongly

'rich people' might replace the earth closet and the chamber pot, and gave detailed instructions on the hygienic management of the last two devices only. By 1881, though, Molokhovets's model flats included a 'heated WC' as a standard feature (*Podarok molodym khozyaikam. Domashnee, gorodskoe i sel''koe khozyaistvo*, 3, e.g. plan ii). Cf. the account given by Prince Evgeny Trubetskoi, who grew up in the 1870s, of his parents' modifications to the immensely grand family house at Akhtyrka, a place originally built for 'show' rather than for 'comfort' so that the place became child-centred: they even added to the rather small number of usable rooms by blocking in the house's beautiful neo-classical colonnades with plywood. (E. N. Trubetskoi, *Iz proshlogo: Vospominaniya: Iz putevykh zametok bezhentsa: Umozrenie v kraskakh (Sofia-V'ena-Berlin, 1921–1926* (Newtonville, Tenn., 1976), 8, 37.)

[133]   Contrast, though, the views of Gogol', in 'What a Wife May Be for a Husband in Simple Domestic Existence' (Chem mozhet byt' zhena dlya muzha v prostom domashnem bytu), which rigidly enforces an ideology of separate spheres: 'Do not loiter about with your husband of a morning; urge him off to do his duties in his office, reminding him every minute that he should devote himself wholeheartedly to the common good and to the efficient running of affairs of state (the efficient running of his household is not his business; that should be your responsibility and not his).' (*Selected Passages from Correspondence with Friends* letter 24, *Sochineniya*, iv. 138.)

[134]   The distinction between housework and house management was suggested to me by Caroline Davidson's excellent survey of domestic labour in England, *A Woman's Work is Never Done: A History of Housework in the British Isles 1650–1950* (London, 1986): see especially p. 2. The reluctance of upper-class Russian *women* to involve themselves even in the latter should not be underestimated. According to Mariamna Davydoff (*On the Estate: Memoirs of Russia before the Revolution* (London, 1986), 139), even in the early 20th cent. '[the wives of wealthy landowners] never took any interest in household details; it was even considered improper for them to go into the kitchen or look into the matter of provisions. Their housekeepers were there for that purpose, and were given a free hand.' It was only in the 1910s that 'it became a matter of shame to ignore one's household' (ibid.). So far as Smol'nyi Institute was concerned, domestic instruction in the mid-19th cent. went no further than playing at cooking (the girls ground the sugar and pepper and stirred the pans on the stove, the cooks did everything else). (See E. N. Vodovozova, *Na zare zhizni* (Moscow, 1987), i. 403.)

enforce the union of hearts between parents and children than the *joint journey of the former back* into the years of their childhood which they now see resurrected in the infancy of their children, *and of the latter forward* into the first, fresh time of their best years, a meadow just beginning to blossom? Hand in hand they go with their mother and father, who alone can play with them in that meadow, forgetting their mature or perhaps even elderly years.[135]

The new importance of appropriate living also had its effects on realist literature, where the representation of domestic setting was intended not only to 'place' characters in social terms, but also to construct models of appropriate existence. From the 1840s, conservative writers began to make contributions to a genre that Toni Bowers has named (in the context of English literature) 'the novelized conduct book', a 'generically ambidextrous' form that both 'prescribes and fantasizes', and 'does not conform to traditional critical standards' (Richardson's *Pamela*, Part II, is the example of the genre that she herself analyses).[136] A text whose surviving fragments indicate that it has some relation to this genre is Gogol's *Dead Souls*, Part II.

Gogol's post-1842 writings have (at least until recently) proved a notorious embarrassment to critics, whether they value the writer as a realist hostile to autocracy (as in the official Soviet interpretation), an anarchic fantasist, or even a religious moralist (given that the preferred terms of discussion in the last case are normally abstract and metaphysical, rather than related to the *bytovaya zhizn' pravoslaviya* celebrated by Aksakov).[137] *Dead Souls* Part II is satisfactory in terms of none of these interpretations. Its world is not the nightmarish one of Part I: instead, the estates portrayed are recognizably those of a society close to Gogol''s own, in which the landowners discourse loquaciously on land management and the duties of a proprietor. What connection is there, one might think, between the splendidly whimsical description of Korobochka's church choir of guard-dogs, and Kostandzhglo's unbearably tedious disquisitions on the four-field system? Yet clear traces of the 'novelized conduct book' can be found in Part I as well. They are most particularly evident in the chapter on the Manilov family, the description of whose conduct, by Gogol''s standards a remarkably conventional piece of writing, comprises a

[135] V. Zhukovsky, letter to P. A. Pletnev, 6 Mar. 1850: see *Sochineniya v 3 tomakh* (Moscow, 1980), iii. 545–6. Emphasis original. A selection of Zhukovsky's delightful poems for children appears in E. O. Putilova (ed.), *Russkaya poeziya detyam*, 2 vols. (St Petersburg, 1997), i. 134–5.

[136] T. Bowers, *The Politics of Motherhood: British Writing and Culture, 1680–1760* (Cambridge, 1996), 153–4.

[137] An example of a metaphysical-Christian reading of Gogol' would be Merezhkovsky's famous essay *Gogol'*, *PSS* xv (Moscow, 1914), 187–312. For an interesting if not wholly coherent attempt to recuperate the post-1842 Gogol' in terms of a sustained case that Gogol' was an 'Orthodox writer' throughout his career, see S. A. Goncharov, *Tvorchestvo Gogolya v religiozno-misticheskom kontekste* (St Petersburg, 1997).

detailed induction into 'how not to behave' as a proper Russian land-owner. Do not give your children pretentious names, and most particularly if you do not know how to pronounce them ('Femistoklyuz' for 'Themistocles'); eat wholesome Russian food, rather than bad imitations of French messes; pay more attention to plain table manners than elegance in your dining habits (it is patently absurd to boast about your boy's future as a diplomat while his nose drips in his soup). Though the oddity of the Manilov chapter has been explained away as a satire on the St Petersburg court elite,[138] a more compelling reason for Manilov's palpable difference from the other figures in Part I is surely that he, like the miser Plyushkin, is a stock literary figure. A landowner who has decorated his garden with a lawn and flowerbeds 'in the English style' and a gimcrack pavilion masquerading as 'The Temple of Restful Contemplation', while his serfs inhabit hovels of crude logs, Manilov is a direct descendant of Pope's country squires with their botched imitations of Lord Burlington's ideal Palladianism, who will:

> load some vain Church with old Theatric state,
> Turn Arcs of triumph to a Garden-gate;
> Reverse your Ornaments, and hang them all
> On some patch'd dog-hole ek'd with ends of wall,
> Then clap four slices of Pilaster on't,
> That, lac'd with bits of rustic, makes a Front.[139]

Entirely conventional also is Gogol''s attribution of much of the nonsense to Manilov's wife, whose so-called education at a pension has provided her with no housekeeping skills, but many fanciful notions about conjugal bliss and genteel furnishings:

Of course, it would have been possible to observe that there are many other occupations about the house apart from indulging in lengthy embraces and preparing little surprises for one's husband, and there would also have been many questions that could have been asked. Why, for example, were affairs in the kitchen organized so senselessly and so inadequately? Why was there so little in the larder? Why was the housekeeper a thief? Why were the servants filthy drunkards? Why did all the house serfs sleep unremittingly and spend the rest of their time up to mischief? But all of these are low subjects of discussion, and Manilova had received an elevated education.(Part 1, ch. 2)

---

[138] D. S. Likhachev, 'Sotsial'nye korni tipa Manilova', *Izbrannye trudy* (Leningrad, 1987), iii. 245–56.

[139] *The Poems of Alexander Pope*, ed. J. Butt (London, 1963), 589. Among other examples of parallels to the Manilov family are some of the characters in Maria Edgeworth's books, e.g. Lady Clonbrony in *The Absentee*, who spent her life 'in continual apprehension every time she opened her lips, lest some treacherous *o* or *e*, some strong *r*, some puzzling aspirate or non-aspirate, some unguarded note, interrogative, or expostulatory, should betray her to be an Irishwoman.' (Edgeworth, *Tales of Fashionable Life* (London, 1833), iv. 7.)

The only specifically 'Gogolian' touch here is the impossible hyperbole of 'sleep unremittingly and spend the rest of the time up to mischief' (*zachem vsya dvornya spit nemiloserdnym obrazom i povesnichaet ostal'noe vremya*). The contrast between the useless 'lady' and the *bonne femme* is adumbrated not only in European literature, but in Russian literature, an earlier example being Dolgorukov's 'Parasha'.[140]

Intriguing traces of the 'novelized conduct book' are also to be found in Tolstoi's *Anna Karenina*. The intergeneric nature of Tolstoi's writing has been the subject of some of the most interesting critical studies of the author in recent years, with particular attention being attracted by the interrelationship between 'historical' and 'fictional' truth in *War and Peace*.[141] But *Anna Karenina*, so often taken for a more conventional novel than *War and Peace*, is no less a 'generically ambidextrous' text than its predecessor. Here, as in *Dead Souls* Part II, the 'novelized conduct book' has a meditation on the appropriate life of the country gentry at its heart. However, Tolstoi, unlike Gogol', contrived his *exempla* so seductively as to beguile rather than to repel. That *Anna Karenina* is intended not only as *bytopisanie*, or 'description of daily life', but as a demonstration of the right way to live, and a demonstration intended for active emulation, is perhaps most impellingly conveyed in the scene where Dolly Oblonskaya and Kitty Levina make *varen'e* (syrupy jam) with their mother Princess Shcherbatskaya:

The whole of the female company had gathered on the terrace. This was where they liked sitting after dinner anyway, but today there was work to be done as well. Along with sewing baby-jackets and knitting shawls, they were busy cooking jam by a method Agaf'ya Mikhailovna [the housekeeper] hadn't come across before: you didn't add water. Kitty had introduced the new method: they used it at her home. Agaf'ya Mikhailovna, who'd always been responsible for making the jam before, and thought that the way things got done in the Levin household couldn't possibly have anything wrong with it, had sneaked a bit of water into the strawberries and garden strawberries, but she'd been caught doing it, and so now the raspberry jam was being made with everybody there, so as to convince Agaf'ya Mikhailovna you really could make perfectly good jam with no water in it at all.

Her face flushed and sulky, her hair tangled, and her arms bare to the elbows, Agaf'ya Mikhailovna was stirring the jam in a basin over the outdoor stove, glaring at the raspberries and willing them with all her heart not to reach setting point. Princess Shcherbatskaya, who knew that Agaf'ya Mikhailovna's rage was going to

---

[140] On 'Parasha', see Ch. 1. The nationalist tenor of Gogol''s depiction of manners supplies a context for the material examined in a recent article by R. S. Valentino, 'A Catalogue of Commercialism in Nikolai Gogol's *Dead Souls*', SR 57 (1998), 542–62.

[141] See e.g. G. S. Morson, *Hidden in Plain View: Narrative and Creative Potentials in War and Peace* (Berkeley, 1987); A. Wachtel, *An Obsession with History: Russian Writers Confront the Past* (Stanford, Calif., 1994), ch. 5.

be directed first and foremost at her, since she'd been chief adviser on how to make the raspberry jam in the first place, was trying to pretend she had her mind on something else altogether, and had no interest at all in the jam; but, while talking about a quite different subject, she all the same darted the odd sideways glance at the stove.

'I always buy the maids dresses myself, somewhere not too expensive,' she went on, picking up a conversational thread from earlier. 'Shouldn't you skim it now, my dear?' she added, turning to Agaf′ya Mikhailovna. 'No, Kitty, don't you do it, it's boiling hot.'

'I'll do it,' said Dolly. She got up and started carefully running a spoon over the foaming sugar syrup, then tapping it every so often on a plate—the plate was already covered in a multi-coloured, yellow and pink sugar crust, with the crimson syrup welling up underneath. 'How they'll love being able to nibble on that with their tea!' she said to herself, thinking of her children, and remembering how amazed she'd been, in her own childhood, that grown-ups didn't eat the scum: it was the best bit.

'Stiva said it makes more sense to give them money,' said Dolly, going on with the fascinating conversation about what kinds of presents it was best to give the servants, 'but...'

At this point the 'jam' theme becomes subsidiary, though floating up every now and again in asides—'it forms figure-eight shapes when it's ready'. It is restored to the centre of attention at the end of the chapter:

'Well, Agaf′ya Mikhailovna, is the jam ready?' asked Levin, smiling at Agaf′ya Mikhailovna, and trying to cheer her up. Did it work out well the new way?'

'I daresay. Mind you, it's what we'd call overcooked.'

'But that's better, Agaf′ya Mikhailovna, then it won't spoil. We've nowhere to keep it fresh, you know, with the ice all melted,' said Kitty, who'd picked up on her husband's idea straight away and was addressing the old woman in the same spirit as he had. 'But your pickles are so good, mama says she's never eaten anything like them,' she added, smiling and patting Agaf′ya Mikhailovna's scarf straight.

Agaf′ya Mikhailovna looked crossly at Kitty.

'Don't try comforting me, madam. It's enough for me just looking at the pair of you,' she said, and Kitty was oddly touched by the coarse-grained phrase 'the pair of you', rather than 'the master and you'.

'Why don't you come mushrooming with us, you know all the right places?' Agaf′ya Mikhailovna smiled and shook her head, as if to say, 'I'd really like to be angry with you, but somehow I can't manage it.'

'Follow my advice,' said Princess Shcherbatskaya, 'and put a paper soaked with rum at the top of each jar, then even if you can't keep it on ice you'll have no trouble with mould.'

All of this, in the work of another writer, might be no more than a mere country *divertissement* or marking of narratorial time before Tolstoi moves forward to his two denouements: the death of Anna and the birth of Kitty and Levin's child. (The raspberry-picking scene in *Evgeny Onegin*, for instance, functions primarily in these two ways, even if it also serves to puncture the country idyll with irony, as readers are told that the serf girls have been ordered to sing so they cannot steal and eat the fruit.) Yet the relative length of Tolstoi's chapter (five pages in a novel where chapters of three or even two pages are not uncommon), and its location in Part VI, a section of the novel where the family theme is particularly close to the surface, point to a greater weight in the overall design. The scene in fact evokes a number of cherished and interlocking concerns: domestic economy; the handing down of cultural patterns; the role of female oral tradition in preserving these; the contribution of collective memory to the maintenance of harmony. It shows how apparently unimportant detail can be the source of potential conflict. Kitty and Princess Shcherbatskaya's new-fangled way of making jam irks Agaf'ya Mikhailovna, and when Levin walks in, at an intermediate stage between the passages quoted, he feels annoyed at the 'Shcherbatsky influence' (*shcherbatskoe vliyanie*) as manifested in the new recipe. But a potential flashpoint is averted by understanding and cooperation on all sides—and, significantly, an under-standing and cooperation that spans the genders. Making jam is an activity that is quintessentially virtuous, both from Tolstoi's point of view and from that of conservative thinkers more generally. It exemplifies culinary prudence, both because it makes use of local resources, rather than expensive imported produce, and because it requires foresight and a due determination to escape waste (hence the concern about stopping the jam from spoiling). A demonstration of food preparation as a craft, as a collective activity, and as a quintessential instance of good house manage-ment, the jam-making scene is totally different in effect from other food-related scenes in the novel, which revolve around consumption, as opposed to production. These include not only the 'characterless' if opulent dinner at Vronsky's estate, but Stiva Oblonsky eating oysters in the opening section of the novel,[142] or indeed Stiva organizing dinner for Karenin and Levin in Part IV, to a menu of 'live perch, asparagus, and *la pièce de résistance*: a wonderful, absolutely simple, piece of roast beef, with wines to suit'. Though Stiva has picked out the asparagus and fish himself (on the way to an adulterous liaison with a dancer), the whole occasion breathes expensive elegance, rather than 'simplicity'. Tolstoi's difference from Gogol', and similarity to Derzhavin, lies in the fact that he does not

---

[142] This latter scene is mentioned in L. Visson, 'Kasha vs. Cachet Blanc: The Gastronomic Dialectics of Russian Literature', in R. Belknap (ed.), *Russianness: Studies on a Nation's Identity* (Ann Arbor, 1990), 166, but without extensive discussion of the food ideology in *Anna Karenina* as a whole.

simply mock pretension in customs and manners (Stiva's concern to equip his manor house with a Chinese bridge and cretonne curtains, rather than an ironing board and wardrobes, is pure Manilov), but that he provides a positive counter-image of *russkii byt*.

Important, too, is the evocation of advice literature in the jam-making scene. To be sure, even by the standards of nineteenth-century recipe, the information given on jam preparation is incomplete in terms of quantities, proportions, and methodology. For example, Avdeeva's *Handbook of the Experienced Russian Housewife* tells her readers they should first make a syrup from five pounds of sugar and ten cups of water, boiled and skimmed, and then add to this ten cups of berries, picked in dry weather, and boil these in the syrup for about half an hour.[143] But the vestigial resemblance to a recipe text is none the less there, most particularly in Princess Shcherbatskaya's final sally about rum-soaked papers for the tops of jam-jars. The recipe is a type of text that encodes family practice, and hence the instrument of dominion over the household. Moreover, since the jam recipe actually works (it is perfectly possible to make satisfactory jam without water), it provides a model for advisory or didactic recipes of a larger and more complex kind: solutions to questions such as 'how to be happy'. In the jam-making scene, amiable squabbles about how to make jam are interleaved with discussions of two further issues: what sort of presents to give the servants (also an absolutely staple subject in household manuals), and how proposals are made. In the central section of the scene, too, Kitty, Princess Shcherbatskaya and Dolly contrive a 'recipe' for the happiness of Kitty's spinster friend Varen'ka: they will manoeuvre her and Sergei Koznyshev into a position where marriage becomes inevitable. By extension, one could understand the jam-making scene as offering the reader a simple recipe for family happiness: assemble one extended family, place at attractive country estate, arrange group activities which are both pleasurable and useful, rather than letting the day go past in atomized and self-indulgent pursuits, and setting point will be reached, rather than the mixture boiling over.

Like Gogol' (but again, more vividly), Tolstoi also provides readers with a guide to how *not* to do it, in the form of Dolly's visit to Vronsky's estate, with its English sanitary facilities, Petit Trianon-style model farm, and hospital, and hostess who is alienated from home management (this trait in Anna is used to symbolize her rootlessness throughout the novel). The theatrical artificiality of Anna's existence is underlined by the extraordinary number of times that she manages to change her clothes. The dramatism of Tolstoi's version derives from the fact that events are witnessed through

---

[143] Avdeeva, *Ruchnaya kniga*, 35.

Dolly's eyes, and she herself has an ambiguous response, at once identifying with Anna's transgression, smiling a 'rascally smile', and glad to leave when the sensationalism has worn off. However, Anna and Vronsky are heirs to Manilov in the sense that their slavish imitation of Western codes of refinement appears at once disgusting and absurd. From this point of view, *Anna Karenina* demonstrates less that 'all happy families are happy in the same way', than the fact that unhappiness has a dreadful and desperate predictability, and happiness a constantly renewable novelty, an endless *samobytnost'* through *byt*.[144]

REFINEMENT VERSUS NATIONAL IDENTITY: THE STRESSES OF CONSERVATIVE GENTILITY

Why was Rome strong? Because Romans loved their fatherland. Pourquoi un état est-il puissant? Pour la même raison.

(K. Aksakov, *Prince Lupovitsky*)

One of the more pernicious inheritances of the 'New Criticism', its popularization of the modernist creed of art's independence of life, has been a sweeping repudiation of 'didacticism' in art. This is partly because of a simple-minded understanding of 'didacticism' as the use of schematic plots and stereotypical characters, in order that moral *sententiae* may be rendered unarguable. Neither *Dead Souls* nor *Anna Karenina* will tolerate the extraction of a 'moral' in this straightforward sense ('corruption is certain to be found out', 'adultery leads to misery and social ostracism'). The novels are, however, didactic in another, more sophisticated way: they are concerned to set out the right mode of existence for the Russian gentry. That is, they offer prescriptive, rather than proscriptive, models for real behaviour, where—as in a seventeenth-century Dutch genre-painting—*byt* functions not simply as a setting, but as the morally resonant representation of appropriate (or inappropriate) domestic conduct. Behaviour is not observed objectively, as it was by the participant observer of the new science of ethnography (the model for the narrator in late nineteenth-century critical realism), but from the point of view of an ethically engaged polemicist who understands virtue above all as the proper observation of tradition. What is offered is not the faithful imitation of reality, but a representation of an ideal world, a world

---

[144] Interestingly, Anna Karenina also contains an example of a conservative salon at work, in the shape of Princess Shcherbatskaya's drawing-room, where conversation about high politics was avoided but the topic of classical versus scientific education was kept in reserve as 'heavy artillery' to be rolled out in a conversational crisis.

which—in Tolstoi's case—was intended as a provocative riposte to libertarian visions of affective relations freed from 'family' and 'domesticity', such as those offered in Chernyshevsky's *What is to be Done?*[145] And in this world, just as in Aksakov's letters, it is perfectly respectable for men, as well as women, to be involved in domesticity—witness the fact that, in the jam-making scene, Levin is as well aware as are any of the women that the question of whether water is added is every bit as important as the issue of how best to scythe a field.

'The family' that is championed in *Anna Karenina*, as generally in Slavophile conservatism, is the extended family, *rod* (clan). One of the reasons for the success of Levin and Kitty's relationship is that the two are supported by a network of congenial and sympathetic blood relatives and family connections who mitigate the tension that (in Tolstoi's view) inevitably accompanied sexual connections. The extended family in this sense had been celebrated in Sergei Aksakov's important Slavophile text *Family Chronicle*, a memoir that was also concerned with blood ties in the broader sense of family tradition (*War and Peace* can be seen as a generic descendant of the 'family chronicle' in this respect). If the radicals' view of identity was existential, Slavophile conservatives saw each person as predetermined by inheritance. In 'Though Poverty's No Stain', Bunina underlines the importance of family tradition by referring to the place inhabited by her family as *nasledstvennoe selo*, literally 'an inherited village';[146] but *nasledstvo* could equally mean solidarity across the extended family or clan, familial piety, the proper management of his patrimony by a landowner, fidelity to the established political order, or respect for time-honoured custom.

Yet whatever their fervent commitment to traditional ways, and their enthusiasm for Orthodoxy, conservatives were members of a cultural elite that had undergone a process of 'Westernization' too deep to be easily reversed. The conundrum was how to combine refinement and Russian-ness; how to imagine an autonomous national identity, and at the same time express fidelity to existing ideals of genteel behaviour.

It has been argued that Slavophile and proto-Slavophile commentators were distinguished from the 'Westernizing' radicals by their attachment to 'enlightenment' (*prosveshchenie*) rather than 'educatedness' (*obrazovannost'*), a distinction which drew on German discussions of 'culture' (*culture, Kultur*) versus 'civilization' (*civilisation, Zivilisation*).[147] This is an oversimplification,

---

[145] B. Eikhenbaum's *Lev Tolstoi: 70–e gody* (2nd edn., Leningrad, 1974), pt. 2, ch. 4 has a preliminary discussion of this.

[146] Kelly, *Anthology*, 35, 400.

[147] See C. Kelly, H. Pilkington, D. Shepherd, and V. Volkov, 'Introduction' to *An Introduction to Russian Cultural Studies* (Oxford, 1998), 8. On the *Kultur/Zivilisation* divide in German culture, see Elias, *The Civilizing Process*, esp. 7–8. Elias wrongly supposed this divide to be peculiar to

however. For one thing, the interest of many Slavophiles in 'Germany' was traceable not only to their absorption of German philosophy, but also to their adherence to a cultural model that privileged 'North' (clean, honest, frank) over 'South' (devious, dirty, unreliable), and which posited an aboriginal unity between Russians and other 'Northern races'. Khomyakov's account of his visit to Britain in the 1840s, for example, enthuses over the supposed links between Russian culture and 'the Celts'.[148] The anti-French writings of the Slavophiles have much in common with, say, Samuel Johnson's poem *London*, which satirizes the affection for pretentious Gallic culture among eighteenth-century British social upstarts, just as their reverence for medieval tradition closely parallels that in their British contemporary A. W. Pugin.[149] Similarly, the stereotype of the affected young male or female socialite mad for foreign luxuries, the *shchegol'* and *shchegolikha*, which had come into Russian literature in the eighteenth century, drew heavily on precedents in French and German literatures.[150]

More importantly, far from rejecting the concept of *tsivilizatsiya*, conservative thinkers, rather, attempted to recover this concept from what they saw as its undesirable (i.e 'French') connotations and to adapt it to their own purposes. In a letter to Nadezhda Sokhanskaya of 27 January 1871, for example, Ivan Aksakov wrote:

The fall of France was inevitable, since France is a country devoid of any political and religious ideal, a country that has broken with the traditions of the state and the Church and which has not found itself either a stable form of secular existence [*grazhdanskoe bytie*], nor a genuine religious foundation,—a country which has replaced proper organic growth by a revolutionary balancing act. There is no country more poor in spiritual content, in which materialism has taken so great a hold on the spirit. . . . Thus, in France words have become empty phrases, the dynamics of the spirit a mere pose, and one adopted even in private [*poza, v*

Germany: on similar debates in late 17th-cent. France, see Joan DeJean, 'Culture or Civilization?' in *eadem*, *Ancients Against Moderns: Culture Wars and the Making of a Fin de Siècle* (Chicago, 1997), ch. 4.

[148] A. S. Khomyakov, 'Pis'mo ob Anglii', *PSS* i (Moscow, 1911), 105–42. See also 'Zapiski o vsemirnoi istorii', *PSS* vii (Moscow, 1906), 17–24. Cf. Aksakov in a letter to A. D. Bludova of 20 Oct. 1861 lambasting Chicherin: 'His teachings are associated with an unthinking reverence for French centralization and mechanical forms of government and a hatred for England, or rather, for everything that is living and creative in England. Hence his detestation of the Russian commune [obshchina], for Old Russia, for Slavophile beliefs, for the principle of daily life (*bytovoe nachalo*), and so on' (*Ivan Sergeevich Aksakov v ego pis'makh*, iv. 203). For the background to these beliefs, see Julie A. Cassiday, 'Northern Poetry for a Northern People: Text and Context in Ozerov's *Fingal*', *SEER* 78 (2000), esp. 248–52.

[149] See e.g. *Contrasts* (2nd edn., London, 1841).

[150] On the *shchegol'/shchegolikha* stereotype, see E. E. Birzhakova, 'Shchegoli i shchegol'skoi zhargon v russkoi komedii XVIII veka', *Yazyk russkikh pisatelei XVIII veka* (Leningrad, 1981), 96–129.

kotoruyu stanovitsya chelovek sam pred soboyu]; moral imperatives have been replaced by the dictates of propriety; even elegance [*izyashchestvo*] has ceased to exist in and for itself, and has become mere *élégance* [*elegantnost'*], a show put on to impress others; the idea of beauty has been torn from its immutable eternal laws, and has become a conventional concept, an empty idea expressed in fashion. . . I think the Western world should do as Brutus did, when the Ancient World fell into decay; as he spoke of virtue then, so should we speak of our idol, civilization, now: 'Civilization—you are an empty word!' As a matter of fact, European civilization has logically reached the point of self-denial, or to put it another way: it has begun to permit those things of which it should be the negation. Opposing itself to the concept of savagery and coarseness, it is now crowned by the ultimate manifestations of savagery and coarseness. Science and learning, reason, conscience, all the gifts of the spirit have gone and paid tribute to crude force and to external truth.[151]

Aksakov's discussion depends not on a contrast between 'civilization' and 'culture', but upon an opposition between 'false' or 'barbarous' civilization, as evident in France under Napoleon III, and 'true civilization'—a mode of social organization in which the 'organic development' of a country is manifest, which has 'spiritual content', and which manifests *nauka* (learning), *znanie* (knowledge), *razum* (reason), *sovest'* (conscience), *izyashchestvo* (beauty/true elegance)—which is to say, the panoply of Enlightenment values—rather than mere *elegantnost'*.[152]

Very similar are the arguments voiced by Dostoevsky in his *Writer's Diary*. On the one hand, he sees the affectation of European ways as a degrading and ridiculous masquerade, something that makes 'monkeys' of educated Russians: 'We have forced European tastes upon ourselves, even eating all kinds of filth while trying not to wrinkle our noses. "Look at me, what a fine Englishman I am: cayenne pepper with everything."' On the other, he sees European identity as an essential part of Russianness: 'We simply cannot reject Europe: Europe is our second fatherland. . .the more powerfully and the more independently we were to develop according to our national spirit, the more we would respond to the European soul and, by becoming akin to that soul, would immediately be more comprehensible to it.'[153] Similarly, any reader aware of Tolstoi's preoccupation with the irreducible complexity of human existence is likely to be wary of seeing *Anna Karenina* simply as a tribute to the unproblematic serenity of the true Russian home. Even the jam-making scene has unresolved tensions—not just because Agaf'ya Mikhailovna's recipe for jam might have worked too,

---

[151] O. Aksakova, 'Perepiska Aksakovykh s N. Sokhanskoi', *Russkoe obozrenie* 11 (1896), 6–7.

[152] This distinction is certainly related to the division between 'false' and 'true' politeness in 18th-cent. French discussions (sometimes false politeness was named as *civilité* and true politeness as *politesse*, and sometimes vice versa). On this, see R. Chartier, 'Distinction et divulgation: la civilité et ses livres', *Lectures et lecteurs dans la France d'Ancien Régime* (Paris, 1987), esp. 69–72.

[153] Dostoevsky, *A Writer's Diary*, Jan. 1877, part 2: *PSS* xxv. 21, 23.

but because the recipe for Varen'ka and Sergei's happiness does not. There is a particular irony in the way that this latter recipe fails, as well. An exchange of voluble *advice* on the part of both participants allows no space for the wordless dialogue of 'looks and smiles' that has expressed agreement to marry in the case of Dolly and Oblonsky, and of the older Shcherbatskys, or of Levin and Kitty's secret code. There are also ironies of a broader cultural resonance. Despite the jam-makers' status as symbols of cultural virtue, and their relish of this countrified world in which a mistress can be 'touched' rather than 'outraged' by a servant's 'coarse-grained' address, they are themselves inextricably part of a world of Westernized refinement. In the middle of the scene comes a jarring reminder of cultural bilingualism: '"A propos de Varen'ka," said Kitty in French—indeed, they had all been talking French the whole time, so that Agaf'ya Mikhailovna wouldn't be able to understand them.' Tolstoi here points to a central difficulty—one of which all intelligent conservative nationalists were well aware—that of combining *samobytnost'* with refinement.

It was one thing, then, to celebrate national tradition in the abstract—to lambast 'foreign luxuries' such as cayenne pepper, to denounce fatuous slavery to Parisian furbeloes or the pretentious use of French words where Russian ones would do—and quite another to arbitrate the distinction between 'Western' and 'Russian' ways in practice. Conservatives' idealization of the 'harmony' and 'morality' of pre-Petrine culture in the abstract was accompanied, at least until mid-century, by fairly extensive ignorance of that culture's practices in the concrete.[154] Sometimes, too, the problem was that medieval texts themselves provided a view of the pre-Petrine world that was not entirely congenial to the Slavophiles' Victorian sensibilities. The *Domostroi*, rediscovered by educated society in 1841, was an embarrassment to many national conservatives rather than a way out of the impasse.[155]

In any case, the fact was that, by even the early nineteenth century, the identity of a cultivated Russian depended to such a large extent upon the possession of goods and clothing that imitated Western patterns, if they were not actually of Western origin, that it was almost impossible to distinguish between 'Western' and 'Russian' ways of life. The result was

[154] The work of I. E. Zabelin on the *byt* of pre-Petrine royalty (*Domashnii byt russkikh tsarei* (1862), and *Domashnii byt russkikh tsarits*, 1869) was revolutionary in this respect. A typical instance of the vagueness with which *byt* was described in the first part of the century is Sergei Glinka's attack on Western fashion, 'Kuznetskii most, ili Vladychestvo mody i roskoshi', *Ruskoi vestnik* 3 (1808), 331–60, which set up Tsaritsa Nataliya Kirillovna, Peter the Great's mother, as a model for modern Russian women, but stated of her behaviour only that she was philanthropic, concerned with the education of her son, modest and retiring, knew her native language properly, did not discourse on sentiment, and above all, never read novels.

[155] See V. V. Kolesov, 'Domostroi kak pamyatnik srednevekovoi kul'tury', in *Domostroi*, ed. *idem* and V. V. Rozhdestvenskaya (St Petersburg, 1994), 301–2.

that fervently anti-Western views were often found in an uneasy combination with completely or almost completely Westernized modes of behaviour. For example, Admiral Shishkov, leading Archaist and patriot of the early nineteenth century, assailed French culture in his essays, but had Western furniture, wore Western clothes, and employed French tutors to teach his children.[156] This schizoid pattern of existence can be perceived also in the behaviour of Griboedov's hero Chatsky, who produced a ringing denunciation of Western formal dress—

> Хвост сзади, впереди какой-то чудный выем,
> Рассудку вопреки, наперекор стихиям,

> A tail behind, a funny cut-out bit across your chest—
> It doesn't suit the cold, it flies in reason's face,

—while standing in a Moscow ballroom and dressed in the garments in question himself.[157]

Advice authors were subject to equally painful contradictions in the dispensations that they offered. 'Western education' (*prosveshchenie*) might be more or less uniformly treated with suspicion, but Western medicine was accepted with surprising readiness. Where Gogol''s *Selected Passages* questioned the value of education for the common people—'Teaching the *muzhik* his letters in order that he may read the vacuous books published by European philanthropists for the common people is utterly futile'— nationalist manuals on house management emphasized that 'cooking is a kind of science', and dispensed medical advice that was generally perfectly in accordance with contemporary practices in Western Europe.[158] And

---

[156] L. [N.] Kiseleva, 'The Archaistic Model of Behaviour as a Semiotic Object', in J. Andrew (ed.), *Poetics of the Text: Essays to Celebrate Twenty Years of the Neo-Formalist Circle* (Amsterdam, 1992), 28–34. For their part, Ivan Aksakov and his siblings were so patriotically anti-French in their childhood 'that when they came across a piece of French correspondence they confiscated it, took it to the attic, stabbed it with knives borrowed from the family pantry, and burned it triumphantly in an auto-da-fé.' (See Lukashevich, *Ivan Aksakov 1823–1886*, 17.) Yet all the children also grew up fluent in French.

[157] *Sochineniya v stikhakh* (Leningrad, 1987), 132. The notion of Western dress as 'unsuitable for the elements' was a cliché of conservative writing (see below). On cultural ambivalence, cf. also Custine's description, in Letter 20, of a visit to the household of an engineer at Schlüsselberg Fortress. Though vehemently patriotic, the women he met all spoke to him in French, and when he expressed surprise that Genlis's *Souvenirs de Félicie* should have been known to them, his hostess snapped angrily, 'I suppose you take us for Lapps'. (*La Russie en 1839*, ii. 190); and Stephanie Sandler and Judith Vowles, 'Beginning to be a Poet: Baratynsky and Pavlova', in M. Greenleaf and S. Moeller-Sally (eds.), *Russian Subjects: Empire, Nation, and the Culture of the Golden Age* (Evanston, Ill., 1998), 156–9 (on Karolina Pavlova's mixed attitude to civilization).

[158] Gogol', *Sochineniya*, iv. 121; contrast Avdeeva, *Polnaya khozyaistvennaya kniga*, I, and Charukovsky, *Narodnaya meditsyna*, 320, which warns, for instance, that an inadequately cleaned earth closet may poison the inhabitants of the house. Cf. the various pattern-books of buildings for the model estate, many of them heavily influenced by English example: see e.g. Rudol'sky, *Arkhitekturnyi al'bom dlya khozyaev* (1839); Mukhanov, *Portfel' dlya khozyaev* (1840). A piquant

Konstantin Grum's deceptively wide-ranging *Handbook on Upbringing* of 1843 integrated into its pronouncements on the ideal patriarchal family (with a father who was 'to draw attention to lapses made not only by his servants, but also by his wife') disquisitions upon the healthiness of the countryside for small children and upon the need to keep the dwelling dry, airy and clean. All this was perfectly in accordance with up-to-date European practice.[159]

Not surprisingly, confusion was still more evident at the level of detailed advice. For all their principled pronouncements upon the importance of 'Russian' diet to the well-being of the Russian stomach, the authors of cookbooks often took a rather elastic view, in practice, as to what might be considered 'Russian' food. The delights to be found in Levshin's *The Russian Cookbook* included a recipe for turkey with pickled lemons, for example.[160] And the cookery section of Avdeeva's *Ruchnaya kniga*, despite her hymn to 'the Russian table', actually included a fairly small selection of Russian recipes—about one-fifth of those in the book, which contains thirty-two pages devoted to 'The Russian Table' (by no means exclusively Russian, as it happens) as opposed to fifty devoted to 'The International Table' [*Vseobshchii stol*]. Avdeeva was no doubt sensitive to the foreign origins of salads, patés, cakes, and ice-cream, but even a conservative committed to traditional ways could not have lived upon the 'soup and kasha' that was the proverbial food of the Russian poor, or indeed upon the sheep's head, pancakes, noodles, and cabbage soup that was the diet that *The Experienced Russian Housewife* suggested should be set before the servants.[161] Equally, a 'woman of the middle standing' was supposed, in

case that illustrates the 'value neutral' status of Western medicine is Avdeeva's *Zapiski o starom i novom russkom byte* (St Petersburg, 1842), which argues for the efficacy of traditional folk practices by stating that hydropathy was known to the Russian peasantry before it was 'discovered' by Western medicine (114), but at the same time dismisses as 'charlatanism' the use of spells which accompanied the practice in its traditional form (133).

[159] Grum, *Rukovodstvo po vospitaniyu*, vols. i and ii, *passim*.

[160] Levshin, *Russkaya povarnya*, 5.

[161] See the section under the title 'Kushan'ya dlya sluzhitelei'. All the recipes here are included in other sections, but the point was that the servants got nothing but plain food (and were offered no sweet course). For other meals Avdeeva, despite her emphasis on economy, propounds a simple but discreetly opulent diet—roasts, soups with small pies, patés, cakes, ice-cream—close to that served in well-off *dvoryanstvo* households, such as the Durnovo household in St Petersburg during the 1850s: Yu. M. Lotman and E. A. Pogosyan, *Velikosvetskie obedy* (St Petersburg, 1996). On 6 November 1857, for example, the company (Petr Pavlovich Durnovo, Petr Vasil'evich Marchenok, Petr Ivanovich Rodashkovsky, Grigory Danilovich Bochatsky, and the 'English' (Scottish?) companion Eugenia Dick were served a soup of puréed celery, braised whitefish (*sig* in Russian), Pojarski cutlets with potatoes, brussel sprouts, and spinach, roast chicken and hazel hen, cardoons with brain sauce, and rice pudding with stewed pears. Cf. Radetsky, *Al'manakh gastronomov*, which announces in the introduction, 'At last the preparation of foreign victuals has begun to tire people', but which specifies menus including e.g. smoked goose, lettuce à la provençale, stuffed olives, and 'gelée printanière de violettes' (menu no. 1, 127–216).

Avdeeva's view, to have a modest, but impeccably Western, wardrobe, without a tight corset or high heels, but containing 'two or three silk dresses and several wool and muslin ones'.[162]

In his letters to Tyutcheva, Ivan Aksakov was to articulate a description of the predicament of 'ordinary' Russian people, stranded between the new culture and the old: 'One thing is clear: in Russia, modern education is open to the ordinary man only at the cost of his moral decline, i.e. he has to deny in his heart all his spiritual traditions and make his acquiescence in advance with everything that runs contrary to those traditions.'[163] But it was no easier for those who came from less 'ordinary' backgrounds to combine entry into 'civilization' with a sense of moral adequacy, and 'contradictions' between heritage and Western manners were just as vexed. As Aksakov himself piquantly put it in a passage immediately preceding that quoted above, 'We do not know how to deal with our heritage, we reject it, and now we appear *comme des bâtards* among civilized humanity.' The sentence is indicative not only on account of its melodramatic phrasing, but on account of the slippage between French and Russian, a slippage characteristic of Aksakov's letters to Tyutcheva in general. The Slavophiles resembled the hero of Konstantin Aksakov's didactic play *Prince Lupovitsky* after his conversion to native ways—convinced that sarafans and Slavonic psalters were best, but unable to keep French tags out of his conversation.

An area where conflict between nationalism and allegiance to Western perceptions of refinement was particularly evident was discussions of etiquette. Since the late eighteenth century, patriots had disapprovingly compared the polished insincerity of foreign manners, and most particularly French manners, with the straightforward, open-hearted directness of Russian behaviour. In his letters from Paris, written in the late 1770s, the playwright Fonvizin had bemoaned the Gallic propensity for mechanical chatter, and the frivolity, charlatanism, and avarice that he held to be the most important traits in the national character. He noted an obsession with outward appearances (especially fine dress) and an absence of spontaneity in hospitality: meals were served without anyone's bothering to circulate the plates, so the short-sighted Fonvizin, who could not see what was on offer at the far side of the table, was deprived of delicacies;

---

[162] Avdeeva, *Polnaya khozyaistvennaya kniga*, 80. An exception to the trend, though, was Lyubov' Yartseva's didactic children's book *Poleznoe chtenie dlya detei*, 6 vols. (St Petersburg, 1836–1838); also published as *Schastlivoe semeistvo, ili poleznoe chtenie dlya detei*, 6 vols. (St Petersburg, 1854), described by Mary Zirin as 'the first children's book in which young members of the gentry were described as dressing in Russian clothing, playing Russian games, and reading Russian history'. (See M. Ledkovsky, C. Rosenthal, and M. Zirin (eds.), *Dictionary of Russian Women Writers* (Greenwood, Conn., 1994), 250.)

[163] *Ivan Sergeevich Aksakov v ego pis'makh*, iv. 107.

wine bottles were not placed on the table in order to induce guests to drink less (though wine was cheap).[164]

Already a topos by Fonvizin's day (as Pushkin noted),[165] the subject of 'Gallic insincerity' was one upon which Russian conservatives loved to harp during the next century and more. Nikolai Strakhov's *A Pocket Guide to Moscow for Little Old Gentlemen and Ladies, Brides and Bridegrooms, Young Ladies and Old Maids, Dandies, Rattles, Young Puppies, and Gamblers, and So On and So On* (1795) was a tartly humourous anti-advice book aimed at socially pretentious visitors to the second capital. It suggested that gentlemen and ladies departing from their estates should stuff their carriages with 'waiting-maids, dresses, hoop petticoats, ribbons, hat boxes, crates, chests, packages, trunks large and small, bundles and cases'. Once arrived, they should purchase an eye-catching carriage rather than a durable one, be sure to bow to passing vehicles rather than their owners, and, above all, hire a 'crafty monkey' of a French footman as tutor to their children so that they could enjoy his impertinence at regular intervals.[166] Seven decades later, the emptiness of manners in the foreign style was still a constant theme. For example, one of the accusations made by Ivan Aksakov to support his attack on 'false civilization' in the letter quoted earlier was that French behaviour was bogus: 'in France words have become empty phrases, the dynamics of the spirit a mere pose, and one adopted even in private [*poza, v kotoruyu stanovitsya chelovek sam pred soboyu*]; moral imperatives have been replaced by the dictates of propriety'.[167] The narcissistic contortions of the Frenchman, parading before himself (this is the literal meaning of the Russian phrase used by Aksakov) as if in front of a mirror, suggest a counter-model of 'moral behaviour' in which sincerity would be indicated by plain-speaking and the eschewal of affectation. By the 1860s, the sincerity/falsity opposition had become such a cliché that it could be parodied by the conservative

[164] D. Fonvizine, *Lettres de la France, traduites de russe et commentées par Henri Grosse, Jacques Proust et Piotr Zaborov. Préface de Wladimir Berelowitch* (Paris and Oxford, 1995), 95, 154, 85. In the last case, Fonvizin's belief in French stinginess caused him to misinterpret a practice that was in fact a social nicety rather than a contribution to economy: both in France and in England at this date, it was considered vulgar, in refined private houses during the early 18th cent., to keep bottles on the table (as might have been done in a tavern); instead, glasses and wine were kept on side-tables, next to a fountain for rinsing the glasses, and each portion of wine poured into a fresh glass before being handed to a dinner-guest by a footman. (In 1760, King Louis XV caused a considerable stir by pouring wine for himself: see John Whitehead, *The French Interior in the Eighteenth Century* (London, 1992), 88.)

[165] See the marginalium to this effect in *Novonaidennyi avtograf Pushkina: Zametki na rukopisi knigi P. A. Vyazemskogo 'Biografiya i literaturnye zapiski o Denise Ivanoviche Fonvizine'* (Moscow and Leningrad, 1968), 37.

[166] See Strakhov, *Karmannaya kniga*, i. 9, 45–6, 50, 71.

[167] Aksakov, letter to N. Sokhanskaya: O. Aksakova, 'Perepiska Aksakovykh s N. Sokhanskoi', *Russkoe obozrenie*, 11 (1896), 6–7.

writer Sof'ya Soboleva in her story 'Pros and Cons' (1863). The narrator of the story, Madame Lisitsyna, a confident if also rather incoherent mixture of anti-radical views and conservative-feminist contempt for a female education based on accomplishments alone, recalls her dislike for the French: 'There is a brittleness in the French character which I find uncongenial, and I cannot bear associating with people to whom I can extend no real sympathy. Most of the French are empty phrase-mongers'—and her liking for 'the good honest Germans', while also recording that her vacuous husband soon began behaving like a native Parisian, but 'found Germany less enjoyable than France'.[168]

The condemnation of Frenchified insincerity, vehement enough when this was observed in foreigners, became particularly bitter when conservatives turned their attention to Russian society, and especially to the circles around the Russian court, which they held to combine a mania for things foreign, a taste for expensive luxuries, and pretentious heartlessness.[169] Yet whatever their doubts about the possible falsity of polite behaviour, and the incipient opposition in their writings between 'morality' and 'propriety', patriotic conservatives were not at all inclined to dismiss behaviour conventions as 'medieval Chinese ways' (to use the phrase attributed by Repin to his radical acquaintances). Rather, they saw the observation of these as essential to the maintenance of order and social harmony.[170] Conservative etiquette books, such as Efim Dymman's *The Science of Life*, criticized affectation (one should not treat one's children like 'an international exhibition of rare objects', Dymman observed, and 'self-importance' (*pretenziya na znatnost'*), a characteristic of 'social upstarts', was

---

[168] S. Soboleva, 'Pros and Cons' in C. Kelly (ed.), *An Anthology of Russian Women's Writing* (Oxford, 1994), 87–8. (For the Russian original of the story, see *Otechestvennye zapiski* 358 (1863), 395–448.) There is reason to believe that Lisitsyna's distaste for the French was shared by Soboleva herself: it was almost certainly Soboleva's parents who hosted the disastrous party attended by Custine at Schlüsselberg (the writer's father is known to have been engaged there as an engineer when she was born there in 1840). (See n. 157 above.)

[169] Typical here is Vera Aksakova (*Dnevnik Very Sergeevnoi Aksakovoi 1854–1855*, ed. N. V. Golitsyn and P. E. Shchegolev (St Petersburg, 1913), 33). Commenting on a letter sent by her brother to Countess Bludova refusing her offer of patronage to secure a place at court (in terms that even to a modern reader seem rather insulting), Aksakova expresses surprise that Bludova had taken umbrage: 'but court people always remain court people', that is, subject to the prevailing mood around them.

[170] An analogous phrase to Repin's is used in the memoirs of Antonina Bludova, who, writing in 1871, contrasts the contemporary view of politeness as 'hypocrisy' with her mother's idea of manners as benevolence to all: 'That was her attitude to what is now often known as *la politesse chinoise*, but what ought really to be referred to, following the current fashion, as "an expression of human feelings" [*vyrazhenie gumannosti*]' ('Zapiski grafini Antoniny Dmitrievny Bludovoi', *Russkii arkhiv* 7/8 (1872), 1230). Cf. Custine's reaction to the manners that he encountered at Schlüsselburg: 'The frank-speaking of these bourgeois ladies thoroughly reconciled me to the affectations of certain ladies of high society' (*La franchise de ces bourgeoises m'avait raccomodé avec les minauderies de certaines grandes dames*) (*La Russie en 1839*, ii. 191).

the subject of a special advisory chapter).[171] But they also emphasized the importance of tacit subordination to authority and of reconciliation with the social order. Taking the ticklish case of two school comrades who found themselves occupying different ranks in the civil service, Dymman observed, 'Everyone is obliged to behave, to make decisions and to act, according to his position, and to treat even a former comrade as a superior does an inferior, or an inferior a superior, and not as a comrade does an equal.'[172]

There was a potentially unresolvable contradiction, then, between two views of etiquette: on the one hand it was the ultimate expression of false civilization's insincerity and triviality, on the other a vital buttress of the social order.[173] The contradiction was especially bitterly felt by intelligent conservatives in court circles. Here, Slavophile sympathies were not uncommon, especially among women courtiers (examples were Pushkin's one-time friend and confidante, Aleksandra Smirnova-Rosset, and Countess Bludova, both of whom were contacts of the Aksakov circle). The particular problem for such observers was that the royal house's symbolism of authority, including the protocols observed at court, had been explicitly Western in character since the early eighteenth century.[174] As Pushkin put it in his 'Journey from Moscow to St Petersburg', it was precisely *Westernized* manners upon which social stability rested:

The court customs that were once observed at the court of our tsars were destroyed by Peter the Great during his general reworking [*perevorot*] of Russian society. Catherine II addressed herself to this area as well and set up a new kind of etiquette. It had the advantage over the etiquette that characterizes other countries of being founded on the principles of good sense and of politeness as universally understood, not on forgotten traditions and customs that have long altered. The late tsar [Alexander I] loved simplicity and directness. He weakened the force of etiquette—which, as a matter of fact, it would be no bad thing to renew. Of course, sovereigns have no use for ceremonies that they often find tiring; but etiquette is a kind of legal regulation and legitimation [*zakon*]; what is more, it is

---

[171] Dymman, *Nauka zhizni*, 323, 334–8.   [172] Ibid. 260.

[173] For a late example of this contradiction, see the memoirs of the most powerful conservative politician of the late 19th century: Konstantin Pobedonostsev, *Reflections of a Russian Statesman*, trans. R. C. Long (London, 1898). On the one hand, Pobedonostsev mourns: 'How seldom we find simplicity and directness in social intercourse . . . Relationship must at once be established, etiquette demands that this relationship appear natural. Conversation must begin, and once begun upon the barren soil of trivialities, it becomes a mere exchange of phrases on subjects touching upon ordinary life' (p. 111), and asserts that those 'who in the name of civilization arm themselves against the mass of improvised reformers . . . would do well to remember that they themselves have been the first to raise a daring hand against existing things' (p. 117). But on the other he criticizes the relaxation of 'rigorous discipline' on the part of head teachers in schools (p. 127).

[174] See R. Wortman, *Scenarios of Power: Myth and Ceremony in Russian Monarchy*, i (Princeton, 1995), *passim*.

essential at the court, since everyone who comes into contact with persons of the royal house must be aware of his or her duties and the boundaries of their service. Where there is no etiquette, courtiers are in constant danger of doing something improper. It is unfortunate to be branded an ignoramus; it is unpleasant to seem an upstart even to your subordinates. (*PSS* xi. 265)

Loyal servants of the autocracy whose nationalist views made them conscious of the artificiality of court life, and who were sensitive to the large gap that sometimes existed between 'ceremony' and 'courtesy',[175] could be precipitated, by the conflict between the legitimating role of court etiquette and its insincerity, into very serious crises of identity. One such courtier was Anna Tyutcheva, daughter of the poet, diplomat, and conservative thinker Fedor Tyutchev, and, from 1866, the wife of Ivan Aksakov, who spent more than ten years serving as a lady-in-waiting, and later royal governess, at the courts of Nicholas I and his successor Alexander II. The diaries which Tyutcheva kept during her period of service glorified the legitimating role of etiquette, pronouncing that 'The prestige of authority is to a high extent ensured by the etiquette and ceremonial that surround it, and which have a strong influence on the imagination of the masses. It is dangerous to strip authority of this mystique.' Even with the wisdom of hindsight, Tyutcheva condemned the relaxation of ceremonial that she believed to have ensued under Alexander II:

I cannot say that this laxity caused life at court to become more relaxed or pleasant. Court life is in its essence a conventional form of life and etiquette is essential in order to maintain its prestige. It is not only a barrier dividing the sovereign from his subjects but also a defence of those subjects from the caprice of the sovereign. Etiquette creates an atmosphere of general respect, in which each person purchases dignity at the cost of freedom and comfort. Where etiquette reigns, courtiers are grandees and ladies of society, where it is absent, they are reduced to the level of lackeys and maids, for intimacy without closeness and without equality is always humiliating, both for those who impose it on others and for those who have it imposed upon them. Diderot put it very wittily when speaking of the duc d'Orléans: 'That grandee plays the coquette with me by pretending we are equals, but I distance myself from him with politeness.'[176]

Here Tyutcheva followed a tradition of court memoirists' apologetics that had been established by Madame de Genlis's studies of *ancien régime*

---

[175] For a signal instance of this distinction, see Vigel', *Zapiski*, i. 146: 'Penza, like China, was a place of scant politeness and great ceremony.'

[176] A. F. Tyutcheva, *Pri dvore dvukh imperatorov: vospominaniya, dnevnik 1853–1855*, ed. S. Bakhrushin and M. Tsyavlovsky, 2 vols. (Moscow 1928–9), i. 188 (entry of 10 Jan. 1854), i. 101. For a fuller account of this memoir, see my 'The Uses of Refinement: The Memoirs of Anna Fedorovna Tyutcheva', in Astrid Brokke (ed.), *Aspects of Gender in Russian Literature*, *Nordlit: Arbeidstidskrift i literatur* 4 (1998), 61–98.

Versailles, and whose practitioners in Russia included Baroness Frederiks, lady-in-waiting to Empress Aleksandra Feodorovna.[177] Indeed, in some respects Tyutcheva's attitude to etiquette was still more fervent than that of other conservative memoirists. Nicholas I's brusque and sergeant-majorish correction of lapses in propriety, which struck some observers rather forcefully, was not remarked by her.[178] Nor did she, as some memoirists did, welcome the occasional suspension of protocol as a humanizing feature.[179] Yet at the same time as emphasizing the importance of etiquette, Tyutcheva also lamented its artificiality and its adverse impact upon human relations. Her diaries record loneliness, bitterness, and above all frustration of a desire to establish an emotional relationship with her immediate employer, Grand Duchess (later Empress) Maria Aleksandrovna. The condition of intimacy between them is constantly examined and found wanting:

> Truly, had she not been the Grand Duchess, I would have loved her sincerely, but at present I try to preserve the requisite polite indifference in myself. That is the reason for the falsity in our relations. We live in unnatural intimacy with people far superior to us, we see them constantly and see only them, and quite involuntarily associate our interests with theirs, while they, on the other hand, can only be interested in us so far as we come into contact with them, and they remain, and ought to remain, indifferent towards us and more or less alien to us. This is what makes life at court so empty for anyone who is not plunged completely into frivolity: one searches out emotional or intellectual interest, and finds nothing to satisfy one. (i. 120)

Rather than tracing her unhappiness to Maria Aleksandrovna's personal character, Tyutcheva explained it by the division between external

---

[177] Frederiks uses the identical term, *raspushchennost'* (laxity) in her critique of court manners under Alexander II: 'When, after the death of our wise tsar [Nicholas I],. an atmosphere of spinelessness and laxity crept into court life, everyone heaved a sigh of relief and pleasure . . . but what came of all this? The pride of morally crippled degenerates, who set themselves the task of betraying Russia's whole political structure under the mask of fidelity to the fatherland' (Frederiks, 'Vospominaniya', *IV* 71 (1898), 55). Genlis's dicta on the subject appear in e.g. *De l'esprit des étiquettes de l'ancienne cour et des usages du monde de ce temps*, ed. E. Quesnet (Rennes, 1885).

[178] For example, Custine: *La Russie en 1839*, i. 184, letter 11: 'The Emperor, before prostrating himself as the others had, cast at the congregation a rather ungracious glare of surveillance.'

[179] See e.g. Frederiks, 'Iz vospominanii', *IV* 71 (1898), 463–4. Lady Dufferin and Ava, who was presented at the Russian court when her husband was British ambassador to the Russian empire in the 1870s, found her first encounter something of an anticlimax: having anxiously prepared herself for a thoroughly correct occasion, she was introduced to a scene of muddle and confusion, as courtiers forgot to present her formally to the empress, and she failed to recognize that the drably dressed woman in black sitting in the room in fact was the protagonist of the ritual. She concluded: 'I always imagined the Russian court to be stiff, but there appear to me to be fewer formalities than at our own' (Harriot Dufferin and Ava, *My Russian and Turkish Journals* (London, 1916), 15–16, 26).

observances and internal feelings experienced by women of the royal house. She advocated rigid etiquette as an ideal, but also viewed it as an impediment to 'sincere love'; while insistent upon the importance of social barriers as a support to personal dignity, she yet nurtured a desire for a relationship with the grand duchess that was, in terms of her own perceptions, improper. Her memoirs—written, like many another Slavophile text, in French!—are an eloquent statement of the dilemmas of an unusually intelligent patriot confronted with a protocol that was, from a nationalist point of view, legitimate and illegitimate at the same time.[180]

It might seem a long way from Tyutcheva's memoirs, with their careful documentation of day-to-day misery and mundane events, to Dostoevsky's *The Idiot*, given that the latter is an expression of how 'in Russia the truth always has a totally fantastical character'[181] rather than—at any level—a chronicle of everyday life. Yet the novel is at the same time a profound and wide-ranging examination of social identity, and of the relationship between manners and morality. The hero of the novel, Prince Lev Myshkin, is not only an ardent Slavophile, but a living illustration of the oddities of *dvoryanstvo* status. Though coming from what ought to be a grand and ancient family, and raised eventually by an inheritance to the circles an eighteenth-century Myshkin might have inhabited, he is, at the beginning of the novel, reduced to a poverty so abject that he can be snubbed by the servants of his distant connections the Epanchins, though General Epanchin himself is a man of the people who has climbed into the nobility by service. The fact that Dostoevsky's 'reincarnated Christ' is no carpenter's son, but the scion of an ancient princely family (albeit one with an absurd name: Prince Leo Mousekin) is of relevance to the novel's moral project in various ways. It underlines the venality of St Petersburg high society (even someone who is 'one of them' cannot safely express dissonant views), while at the same time raising the question of whether this 'last tatter of worn-out family lines' really can be the saviour of Russia.[182]

[180] In time, scruples such as Tyutcheva's were reflected in court practice itself, which took a nationalist turn in the reign of Alexander III and Nicholas II. See R. Wortman, *Scenarios of Power: Myth and Ceremony in Russian Monarchy*, ii (Princeton, 2000). Tyutcheva's attitude to the empress is interestingly different from that of an intelligent woman from the court elite, Grand Duchess Elena Pavlovna, who found Maria Aleksandrovna 'intellectually mediocre' and 'inconsistent' (see note by Bakhrushin in Tyutcheva, *Pri dvore dvukh imperatorov*, ii. 108–9). The difference is explained not only by Elena Pavlovna's social status, but also by her liberal views (on which see e.g. A. F. Koni, *Ocherki i vospominaniya* (St Petersburg, 1906), 477–94).

[181] See F. M. Dostoevsky, *A Writer's Diary* (1873) pt. 15, *PSS* xxi. 119.

[182] Certainly, Myshkin's class does not disqualify him: both Zosima and Alesha, the spiritual leaders depicted in *Brothers Karamazov*, come from the *dvoryanstvo*. As for Slavophiles of the Aksakov mould, so for Dostoevsky, a humbled *dvoryanin* sympathetic to 'the People' was the ideal type of social activist.

Still more significant than the bald sociological facts represented in *The Idiot* is the novel's ambiguous employment of the terminology of manners and morals, which reveals an uncertainty about the moral significance of propriety typical of the patriotic conservatism that Dostoevsky had begun to espouse in the 1860s. At one level it is possible to see *The Idiot* as an exposition of the frailty of civilized values, an indication of how apparently 'well-bred' (*vospitannye*) persons are, when it comes to the point, rather less able to control their unworthy feelings than anyone else. Nastas'ya Filippovna and Myshkin offend constantly against the dictates of polite society, he unconsciously, she consciously, their outrageous actions creating some of the most dramatic (and funniest) scenes in the novel, as a supercilious young officer is provoked into suggesting that Nastas'ya needs to be 'horsewhipped', or Myshkin treats a drawing-room to a Slavophile tirade before inadvertently smashing a precious vase.

But the book is not simply a dismissal of conventional manners. Dostoevsky's moral universe is less straightforward than that of the 1830s Gogol'. In *Dead Souls*, the attempts of the would-be refined 'lady charming in all respects' and the 'simply charming lady' to arbitrate behaviour are doomed to failure, leading to such aberrations as the substitution of the phrase 'I relieved myself by means of my handkerchief' for the ordinary 'I blew my nose'. And in *The Nose*, the phrase 'respectable' invariably has an ironic ring, attaching itself like a discarded sweet-wrapper to the rear of the nonentious and noseless Major Kovalev. In *The Idiot*, on the other hand, terms such as *prilichnyi* (decent) or *chest'* (honour) may not be so unambiguously interpreted: they may be bogus or genuine depending upon context, or indeed both at the same time. The application of the term *poryadochnyi* (proper) to Nastas'ya Filippovna's protector (and, according to one interpretation, seducer), the elderly roué Totsky (part 1 ch. 4), or the description of the tiresome drunk General Ivolgin as having an 'imposing manner' (part 1 ch. 8) can only be ironic; and Dostoevsky's humorous intent is obvious when Totsky is quoted as having hypocritically condemned squalid Ferdyshchenko's '"lapses" into *mauvais ton* and "boastfulness of a particular kind"' (part 1 ch. 14). But on the other hand, the departures from propriety on the part of Ganya Ivolgin and his sister (most particularly in the scene in which Ganya lambasts Varvara, who then spits in his face, part 1 ch. 10) suggest that there is such a thing as true *poryadochnost'*, a set of absolute values offended by such behaviour. The existence of such values is also implied (from the opposite point of view) by Myshkin's capacity to win himself into the hearts of the members of the Epanchin household, from servants to mistress, through his 'polite and courteous conversation' (part 1 ch. 3) and his 'wonderful manners' (part 1 ch. 4). The point is that commitment to true courtesy may be at once ludicrous and admirable. The crucial case here is Kostya Ivolgin, who has swallowed his values whole from conduct literature, and who turns himself into a callow arbiter of the social graces, advising Myshkin and Evgeny, for instance, 'It is not decent for persons in high society to concern themselves unduly with literature' (part 2 ch. 7)—a sentiment that sounds as if it had come straight out of the silliest sort of advice book. Yet for all his laughable pomposity, Kostya eventually becomes the impressive and touching embodiment of the apparently ridiculous ideal of 'worldly honour' (*svetskaya chest'*) to which he aspires, squiring his elderly father through the streets of Petersburg when the latter has been stricken by apoplexy and deserted by his remaining relations and connections.

The destabilization of moral terminology has in turn a profound impact upon the representation of Myshkin and Nastas'ya Filippovna, the two central characters. There is no sense in which either character can easily be seen as 'a righteous being' (*pravednik/pravednitsa*) destroyed by society. Nastas'ya Filippovna, who allows herself to be bought off by Totsky in compensation for her 'maidenly disgrace, for which she was not responsible' (part 1 ch. 4) is certainly not an unproblematic vision of corrupted innocence, while Myshkin's 'wonderful manners' make him ill-placed to set to right a world which can be changed only by offending convention (and in which some of the most sympathetic characters, such as Mrs Epanchina, are those who stake least on the dictates of etiquette). Moral choices are still more difficult than matters of self-presentation. Left to herself, Nastas'ya Filippovna seems doomed to destruction; but Myshkin's attempt to save her precipitates the destruction of Aglaya (doomed to the farcical fate of marrying a Pole), and (in a much deeper sense) of Rogozhin and of himself. Thus, none of the characters can be finally exonerated or wholly blamed; equally, condemning Petersburg society wholesale is made problematic by the insistence that genuine 'decency' can exist there, and that 'propriety' is not simply a glossy screen set before grotesque and vicious reality. If 'civilization' seems hollow in the world of *The Idiot*, at the same time its association with genuine values makes difficult the perception of a 'real Russia' beyond civilization. Conversely, as so often in the history of patriotic reactions against 'false civilization', the attack on the illusory character of Europe calls into question the authenticity of a Russia now culturally assimilated to Europe. The final sentence in the book is Epanchina's blistering attack upon Europe as 'fantasy': ' "All this—all this abroad, all this Europe of yours, all of it is nothing but fantasy, and all of us living abroad are nothing but fantasy... Mark my words, you'll see it yourself!"—she concluded almost angrily, as she took her leave of Evgeny Pavlovich.' But since *The Idiot* itself conveys above all the sensation of all-embracing unreality endured from within that unreality, this last sentence has the function less of an authoritative comment upon 'Europe' than of a lamentation upon the perpetually elusive character of the 'motherland'. It is a fitting retrospective epigraph to a novel examining national identity, but composed in Baden-Baden; to a text where the Slavophile beliefs of Myshkin carry no more weight than the 'Western' atheistic rationalism of his intellectual 'double' Ippolit, and where the most authentically 'Russian' figure, the Old Believer Rogozhin, is the closest to embodying the forces of evil.

CONCLUSION

The classification of Russian society in terms of *sosloviya*, estates, lost one of its props with the Emancipation of the Serfs in 1861: the abolition of human bondage removed a salient distinguishing characteristic of the *dvoryanstvo*, which also lost its preferential right to the ownership of land. But even before the Emancipation, the *dvoryanstvo* was amorphous, including not only aristocrats in the strict sense, those distinguished by wealth (both in terms of capital and in terms of serf ownership), rank, and closeness to the Russian court through service, shared tastes, and occupation, but also a wide range of humbler figures whose modes of existence were not always easily distinguishable from those of educated members of the merchant classes. By the 1830s, with encroaching Westernization, the lower gentry, merchant classes, and some offspring of clergy families had begun jointly to form a sort of 'middling state', with some resemblances to the 'middle class' in eighteenth-century Britain. But members of the Russian 'middling state' resented their lack of political authority particularly fiercely, since this had come to seem 'backward' after the French Revolution of 1830 and the British Great Reform Act of 1832 had given their counterparts in other countries enhanced political authority. Their economic status was also more unstable, since the high costs of acquiring the appurtenances of Westernization, and the atomization of family lands, made reduction to pauper status a very real possibility. The result was not only that refinement became extremely important (as in the provincial landowners observed by Amelia Lyons, 'very poor, but well informed and of polite manners and cultivated delicate tastes')[183] but that self-restraint began to be seen as a vital part of cultivation.

Yet the 'middling state' was itself divided: Slavophile members of it had a concern with appropriate daily life, with areas such as furnishing, etiquette, and food that the Russian radicals considered beneath their

---

[183] Lyons, *At Home with the Gentry*, 82.

notice. Unlike the radicals, too, they were preoccupied with questions of status: with family history, with maintaining hierarchical divisions within the family, with safeguarding a mode of life that seemed to be under threat. In the event (as the next chapter will show), this way of life proved more resilient than the most pessimistic had feared: while the Emancipation of the Serfs brought increased poverty to those landowners who had relied upon estate income as their only source of support, those who maintained a profession survived the transition more comfortably.

The writers with whom this chapter has been concerned were responsible for the most considered and sustained repudiation of the Western code of refinement to take place at any stage of Russian history. Yet Western conventions of gentility remained vital to them, not only because they, like any polemicists, had willy-nilly to recognize antagonistic viewpoints, but also because concepts of status had been transformed by contact with Western perceptions and practices. Hence, while conservative nationalists were committed above all to the preservation of traditional values, they necessarily ended up by inventing new ones. And their beliefs were dynamic in other ways too. They introduced into Russian culture a debate on appropriate *byt* that resonated in literary texts from the 1840s to the 1880s. Their idealization of the patriarchal family allowed women entry into some areas of public discussion, if only to express their subordination within the family, and gave a new impetus to salon culture. Their hostility to 'false civilization' provoked an agonized contemplation of the nature of true politeness that was as novel, in terms of Russian culture, as the radicals' repudiation of etiquette.

By the late 1880s, the Slavophile dilemma had lost much of its sharpness. The accession of Alexander III, a tsar who congratulated himself for demonstrating to 'a surprised and morally corrupt Europe that Russia is still the same holy, Orthodox Russia as it was under the Muscovite tsars' marked the onset of an explicitly Russophile official nationalism, embodied in building programmes, state ceremonial, and foreign policy.[184] The search for alternatives to Western etiquette among writers was now far more confident and forceful, as can be seen, for example, in the rich, eccentric tradition of *bytopisanie*, 'writing of *byt*' espoused by the neo-Slavophile Vasily Rozanov in the early twentieth century, in the historian Vasily Klyuchevsky's 1892 eulogization of pre-Petrine education as a humane and loving alternative to the sterile institutionalization wrought by Catherine II, or in the radical populism

---

[184] Alexander III, letter to Empress Maria Feodorovna, 16 May 1884, quoted in R. Wortman, *Scenarios of Power: Myth and Ceremony in Russian Monarchy* (Princeton, 2000), ii. 235. See chs. 7–15 of Wortman's book for a magisterial survey of official nationalism during the reigns of Alexander and of Nicholas II.

of the late Tolstoi.[185] For all the ephemerality of the Slavophile debate over *byt*, though, and for all the ludicrous, and at times downright pernicious, character of the conservatives' protestations against foreign domination—from the anti-French rant of the 1800s to the downright malign tirades against Poles and Jews in the 1860s—the crusade against Western influence had some lasting effects. These included not only the relatively trivial benefit of a home-produced advice literature, but the composition of some of the most important novels of the nineteenth century, from 'novelized conduct books' such as *Anna Karenina* and *Dead Souls*, to the entirely unclassifiable *Idiot*, a work of imaginative genius, but also a profound examination of the difficulties of pronouncing upon morality and sincerity in a world where not only language, but also attitudes, cannot be other than permeated by falsity. There is a link, too, between the curious cultural situation of Tolstoi and Dostoevsky, permeated by uncertainty, and the artistic innovativeness of their work. Where a Western 'novelized conduct book' such as *Pamela* depended upon devices establishing the novelist's moral authority—prefaces advertising serious purpose, admonitory expostulations to the reader—Tolstoi and Dostoevsky's novels both invoke and undermine the authority of the moralist. In each case, moral commentary is only one of the narrator's functions, with aphoristic or 'straight' interpretation and expostulation sitting alongside dubious gossip (in the case of *The Idiot*), or lyrical evocation of life's fabric (in *Anna Karenina*)—to name only some of the modes upon view.

[185] On Rozanov and *byt*, see the discussion in Stephen Hutchings, *Russian Modernism: The Transfiguration of the Everyday* (Cambridge, 1997), ch. 6; V. Klyuchevsky, 'Dva vospitaniya', *Ocherki i rechi: Vtoroi sbornik stat'ei* (Moscow, 1913), 223–6. On Tolstoi, see the discussion in Ch. 3 below.

CHAPTER THREE

Self-Help and Spending Power: Advice Literature in Late Imperial Russia

Tact informs us how we should dress in different situations: diamonds are perfectly appropriate for visiting a friend who takes pride in us, but a modest toilette is essential when calling upon someone who likes to feel superior.

(K. Svetozarskaya, *Life in Society, at Home, and at Court*, 1890)

Every holiday, funeral, wedding—people stuff themselves stupid.

(Tolstoi, *The First Step*, 1890)

In the first century of its presence in Russia, the literature of conduct regulation had generally imagined a reader who was, while not necessarily an aristocrat, certainly a member of the privileged classes.[1] A well-bred person was assumed to have an education that had progressed beyond the rudiments of literacy and numeracy to include the appreciation of art and literature, a command of foreign languages, and at least a second-hand acquaintance with Western political and ethical writings; to have refined manners; and to adopt a discriminating attitude to personal possessions, so that objects were not acquired for their own sake, but for their symbolic associations as expressions of cultural values (whether those of connoisseurship, of intellectual asceticism, or of nationally coloured *russkii byt*).

The industrialization of Russia after 1861 placed this ideal of refined behaviour under assault from every side. The emergence of a new entrepreneurial plutocracy, many of whose members had risen from

---

[1] Until the 1830s, merchants were the lowest category of reader customarily acknowledged by advice-book authors. An exceptional book aimed at members of the lower classes was Vitzmann, *Nastavlenie poleznoe dlya slug* (1799), and even this, as the last page makes clear, was supposed to be read aloud to its targets (readers were informed that servants 'will serve far more zealously a master or mistress who reads them these instructions once a month', a less than convincing boast). In 1834–5, the Society for the Dissemination of Moral Brochures to the Common People (Obshchestvo, rasprostranyayushchee nravstvennye listki dlya chteniya prostolyudinov) put out a series of improving publications for the lower orders, including a booklet for female servants, *Podarok sluzhankam*, a temperance pamphlet (*Beregis' pervoi charki!*) and two others (*Pravila semeinye* and *Postaraisya eshche raz!*). However, the explicit religiosity of these books and their verbose style made them quite unlike the material that appeared in the late 19th and early 20th cents.

lowly origins as peasant craftsmen or street traders, not to speak of a new class of white-collar workers such as secretaries, accountants, and clerks, employed in industrial and financial enterprises, called into question the traditional association between spending power and education. There was now a public that craved refinement, but lacked the immersion in literature, fine art, history, and ethics that had traditionally been held to take the acquisition of objects, and the cultivation of leisure pursuits, beyond mere materialism and self-indulgence. The sight of entrepreneurs a generation or two from the enserfed peasantry dressing in Paris fashions and building themselves vast mansions, or shop-assistants in ready-made suits reading best-selling novels, sent shock waves through educated Russian society. The derogatory connotation that the term *meshchanstvo* had acquired in radical circles in the mid-nineteenth century was now ubiquitous in the Russian intelligentsia: the term encapsulated a combination of mindless consumption of cultural goods and insentivity to culture in the true sense.[2] No serious writer of the late nineteenth century would have referred to him or herself as a *meshchanin* even in jest, as Pushkin had in the early nineteenth century, nor would the term 'middle state' (*srednee sostoyanie*) have suggested anything other than 'the golden mean' of mediocrity. Sensibilities about the vulgarity (*poshlost'*: another catch word)[3] of the *meshchanstvo* were further inflamed by the emergence of a new kind of advice literature which, as we shall see, was directly aimed at those with money to spend and little idea of how to spend it, and which advocated an elaboration of existence that was anathema to intelligentsia tastes.

The well-heeled, but brutish, *meshchanin* who was the bugbear of writerly imaginations had a much more positive counter-stereotype: the decayed landowner ruined because he or she lacked the entrepreneurial skills necessary to make money out of farming in the post-Emancipation world. The gentle incompetence of the struggling small- to middle-sized proprietor, which had often been represented as a dereliction of duty before and during the years of Emancipation, was now seen through a mist of nostalgia, and held to signify an admirable, and characteristically Russian, distaste for trade (Chekhov drew on, and parodied, such attitudes in his play *The Cherry Orchard*, 1904). As a result, the established notion of *vospitannost'* was sometimes replaced by a term that laid more stress on the *innate* character of refinement: it was said that *meshchane*, unlike decayed

---

[2] See esp. D. S. Merezhkovsky, 'Gryadushchii kham', *Polnoe sobranie sochinenii*, xiv (Moscow, 1914), 5–39, in which *meshchanstvo* is assimilated to *khamstvo* (thrusting boorishness) and seen to emanate from the pernicious materialism of Western life.

[3] On *poshlost'* in the early 20th cent., see Svetlana Boym, *Common Places: Mythologies of Everyday Life in Russia* (Cambridge, Mass., 1994), 59–64.

dvoryane, lacked 'breeding' in the sense of favourable heredity, were not *porodisty* (a term used for animals, and people, with pedigrees). In Chekhov's story 'A Doctor's Case-Notes', for example, Doctor Korolev, called out to attend the daughter of a factory-owner near Moscow, gloomily studies the portraits in the drawing-room, observing the 'clumsy, low-bred body' of one of the subjects.[4] *Blagorodnyi*, or 'well-born', was often employed as a synonym for 'honourable' (cf. the English word 'noble'), and the term *intelligentnyi*, 'proper to a member of the intelligentsia', began coming into use as a synonym for 'refined' or 'cultivated'.[5]

But not everything in turn-of-the-century culture fostered pessimism. The intelligentsia's anxiety about the 'degeneration' of refined society through an influx of coarse 'new blood' was tempered by excitement over increasing opportunities for education, which promised to those of a populist turn of mind the almost infinite expansion of the potential audience for intelligentsia constructs of appropriate behaviour. The most important sites of contact between 'intelligentsia' and 'people'—the 'Sunday schools' and the underground organizations for political agitation in villages and factories—were not at all concerned with shaping the consumption patterns of the Russian lower classes, or giving them tutorials in correct behaviour: that is, with *vospitanie* as conventionally understood. Rather, they propagandized self-education and training in the pursuit of civic virtue (industriousness, political participation, collaboration in moral and intellectual debates). The project was lent urgency by an impelling sense of the need to compete for the affections of new readers with commercial publications. If didactic fiction for the lower classes had, as Jeffrey Brooks has shown, to vie for a readership with potboiling adventure novels about robbers and bandits, treatises on the co-operative movement, rational childcare, and self-improvement shared a market niche with such racier and less worthy contributions to the advice literature genre as brochures on the avoidance of sexually transmitted diseases, hairdressing manuals, and anthologies of model love-letters, whose authors (or more likely compilers) hid their identities under pseudonyms such as 'Uncle Serge' or 'Ivan Aleksandrovich Aleksandrov, retired staff-captain'.[6] In

---

[4] Contrast, though, Tolstoi's use of *porodistyi* for his plebeian heroine Katerina Maslova in *Voskresenie*.

[5] On *blagorodnyi*, see e.g. the remarks of B. Pares, *My Russian Memoirs* (London, 1931), 41. For a use of *intelligentnyi*, see Nataliya Nordman's address to Russian servant employers below. Contrast, though, the heroine's outraged remarks on the 'vulgarity' of the term (warmly supported by the autobiographical narrator) in M. Tsvetaeva, *Povest' o Sonechke, Sobranie sochinenii v 7 tomakh* (Moscow 1993–4), iv. 361.

[6] S. A. Vengerov, *Russkie knigi*, i (St Petersburg, 1895), 147–8, records the latter as the author of a book on avoiding 'nasty illnesses', *Pamyatnaya knizhka, kak izbezhat' zarazheniya sekretnymi*

contrast to such shadowy figures, the average author of the second, educative type of literature was a readily identifiable member of the educated elite who burned to share his or her expertise—practical, moral, or social—with those who required it. Often (though by no means always) he or she stood on the political left;[7] frequently, too, professional credentials ('Dr Ivanov', 'Professor Petrov', 'I. Nikolaev, agronomist') were brandished in order to underline the reliability of the advice given. Like the authors of improving tales, the authors of conduct manuals could feel that they were performing two useful functions at once: providing the lower-class public with enlightenment, and stopping them from reading trash.[8] Not that didactic material for lower-class readers was the only material composed by advice-book authors of ascetic inclinations: an entire literature addressed itself to the better-off, attempting to persuade those who could afford to indulge themselves that self-restraint was essential to personal health, and a contribution to the well-being of society at large.

Like the late imperial Russian publishing industry in general, then, advice-literature production stratified to cater for stratified demands: different types of text assumed more or less financially secure, educated, and socially self-confident readers. Accordingly, this chapter takes the different sub-genres of advice literature in turn, beginning with material that catered for what Pierre Bourdieu has termed 'the taste of luxury'[9] and

boleznyami. Sredstvo dlya istrebleniya parazitov, bespokoyashchikh cheloveka (St Petersburg, 1889), and seven other books on killing bugs, making bread, etc. Of course, it is possible that the good staff-captain really existed, but his name has a bogus ring (cf. 'John Smith' or 'Peter Jones').

[7] A contrasting example was Elena Molokhovets, whose *Simple Easy Food* (Prostaya obshchedostupnaya kukhnya) came out in 1884 (though in fact the book rather belied its title, as many of the recipes included were neither particularly simple nor particularly cheap, and its target was probably *meshchane* or even decayed gentry rather than peasants or workers).

[8] On commercial and improving fiction, see J. Brooks, *When Russia Learned to Read* (Princeton, 1985). The idea that the mass reader was ripe for didactic projects was such a commonplace that it attracted the attention of Vasily Rozanov, a notorious critic of *idées reçues*. 'Cheap books are lack of culture [*nekul'turnost'*]', he declared: accessibility lowered reading material to the level of vodka. (See *Opavshie list'ya* (St Petersburg, 1913), 329–30.) Commercial publishers, such as Ivan Sytin, were happier about bridging the 'trash/enlightenment' divide, and their publications fell into both categories. Sytin was involved with the Posrednik venture (see below), and his firm's publications between 1901 and 1910 included not only *lubki*, i.e. 'penny dreadful' popular fiction (598 titles, 33,959,833 copies), but also 'books against drunkenness and other evils' (33 titles, 705,620 copies), medicine and hygiene, veterinary (77 titles, 400,125 copies), self-education (94 titles, 388,000 copies), home management (32 titles, 117,280 copies), spiritual and moral topics (192 copies, 13,950,640 copies), and pedagogy and didactics (92 titles, 1,080,475 copies). (Figures cited in C. A. Ruud, *Russian Entrepreneur: Publisher Ivan Sytin of Moscow, 1851–1934* (Montreal, 1990), 201.)

[9] P. Bourdieu, *Distinction: A Social Critique of the Judgement of Taste*, trans. R. Nice (London, 1984), 6: 'The antithesis between quantity and quality, between substance and form, corresponds to the opposition—linked to different distances from necessity—between the taste of necessity, which favours the most "filling" and most economical foods, and the taste of liberty—or

then moving on to propaganda for 'rational living' and finally to literature 'for the people', before considering the question of how these attempts to regulate consumption were themselves consumed—a less straightforward question than might at first appear.

A PROLIFERATION OF GOODS: ADVICE LITERATURE AND THE 'TASTE OF LUXURY'

Industrialization not only created new classes of consumer: it also facilitated the dissemination of factory-made goods on a scale not previously seen in Russia, and wrought fundamental changes in the nature of shopping patterns. Especially in Moscow and St Petersburg, specialist shops and department stores, some with mail-order departments, expanded opportunities for retail and turned shopping into a leisure activity.[10] Books such as domestic manuals enthusiastically fastened on the new possibilities, setting out whole inventories of items essential to the well-regulated household. For example, Mariya Redelin's *The House and Housekeeping: A Guide to Rational House Management* (edition of 1900) belied its subtitle by suggesting a vast proliferation of objects that was required in the well-regulated household. Certainly, the kitchen was a room where function counted: it should be warm and free of draughts, as should the corridor along which the mistress progressed to the kitchen to give her orders to the waiting servants (nothing was said about draught-proofing their quarters). Practicality was also a matter of some moment in the living-room, which was to be airy and have a linoleum floor, though also requiring colour-coordinated wallpaper, a divan, a table, a piano, plants, besides 'a bird in a cage, a goldfish bowl, or, if possible, an aquarium'.[11] But by the time that the drawing-room was reached, all moderation had been flung to the winds. This room, a theatre for receiving guests (as is suggested by the Russian word *gostinaya*, literally 'guest room') was the obvious place for the display of wealth. In the words used by John Kasson about parlours in late nineteenth-century America, the *gostinaya* was a room for 'the artful displays of objects of cultural association'. And the objects themselves were similar to those in the West: books, *étagères*, side-tables, chimney-

luxury—which shifts the emphasis to the manner (of presenting, serving, eating etc.) and tends to use stylized forms to deny functions.'

[10] See Catriona Kelly and Steve Smith, 'Commercial Culture and Consumerism', in C. Kelly and D. Shepherd (eds.), *Constructing Russian Culture in the Age of Revolution* (Oxford, 1998), 106–64.

[11] Redelin, *Dom i khozyaistvo*, i. 19. My thanks to Barbara Heldt for presenting me with a copy of this publication. On pot plants and pets, see also Voskresenskaya, *Drug khozyaiki* (1909), 599–609, 619–28.

pieces, with the pièce de résistance the piano or the harmonium.[12] Redelin's stipulations for this temple of cultivated living included elaborate light-fittings (a central chandelier and candelabras or shaded lamps in corners), a parquet floor perhaps covered by a carpet, this to tone with the obligatory curtains, upholstered armchairs, pouffes, chaise longues, sofas, cushions, and portières. There should be a marble fireplace with a fire-screen before it and a clock and pair of vases on top, plus if possible 'Meissen statuettes, bronzes, and other pretty knick-knacks'; these last could also be placed on small side-tables and on *étagères* (open display cabinets). The ownership of a piano (and a grand piano at that: no measly upright) was taken for granted, the only anxiety being about where it should be placed:

If music has equal rights with other social entertainments, the grand piano is placed against a wall; if it plays a central role, then the instrument is given pride of place in the middle of the drawing-room. However, in the second case it is necessary to sacrifice a carpet, portières and heavy curtains, since they mute the sound of the piano.

When guests are not present, the piano may be covered by a cloth. Lately beautiful cloths with rich and colourful embroidery have started to be manufactured; usually they are decorated with flowers and arabesques.[13]

Primarily, as Redelin implies by her regretful reference to 'sacrificing' portière and curtains, the piano should be an extension of the room's decoration. Just so were books valued above all because they contributed to the festive display and might be of use during embarrassing breaks in conversation:

On elegant small tables should be placed illustrated books, albums, and publications of general interest in elegant bindings; these may be of use to visitors awaiting the arrival of the hostess if she should be held up, allowing them to spend time pleasantly; they may also be studied by guests when the company has assembled. The presence of books is also of use should a lapse in conversation occur, as sometimes happens, since it is then possible to introduce a new and interesting topic of discussion.[14]

The luxurious surroundings were not intended to stun the guests into baffled and perhaps mutinous silence; they were intended to be actively admired. The marble chimney-piece, for instance, was not only 'a real

---

[12] See J. F. Kasson, *Rudeness and Civility: Manners in Nineteenth-Century Urban America* (New York, 1990), 175–6.

[13] Redelin, *Dom i khozyaistvo*, 20.

[14] Ibid. Contrast the advice in B. V–n, *Entsiklopediya molodoi khozyaiki* (1839), i. 25, which advises readers: 'It is not a solid silver samovar, or grandiose candelabras, or the luxurious appointment of your rooms which will attract guests to visit you, but a friendly and affectionate address to them.'

Машинка для метенія ковровъ.

FIG. 8. An automatic carpet-sweeper, from
M. Redelin, *The Home and House*
Management (1900).

symbol of cosiness [*uyut*]', but also a sort of household god, the patron of
the necessary kind of social intercourse: 'They say that from its flickering
and crackling flames fly up the sparks that set alight a lively and animated
discussion.'[15]

For all that, however, the luxury imperative was most striking not in the
setting of the drawing-room, whose sole function was, after all, to receive
and to impress visitors, but in the inventories of supposedly functional
objects required to perform the formidable amounts of housework needed
to keep the house clean and the table covered with delicacies. Among the
various gadgets and gizmos recommended by Redelin were a carpet-
sweeper (then a relative novelty even in the West) (Fig. 8),[16] a patent door-
stop, and a curved tubular brush for sweeping under fixed furnishings. But
it was in the kitchen where acquisitive fancy took fullest flight. Household
manuals published in the mid-nineteenth century had either paid no
attention to equipment at all (the case with Avdeeva), or had implied
the need for flexibility and improvisation (the case with Molokhovets, who
alongside 'specialized items' had 'called into service anything that was

[15] Redelin, *Dom i khozyaistvo*, 20.

[16] See Caroline Davidson, *A Woman's Work is Never Done: A History of Housework in the British*
Isles, 1650–1950 (London, 1986), 123–7; according to Davidson, the technologization of housework began only in the 1860s, and a carpet-sweeper was such a novelty in one British household
of the late 19th cent. that it went unused until a housemaid, slamming it down in frustration,
caused the brushes to emerge so that the staff realized how it worked.

handy in the house or just inside the door').[17] Redelin, on the other hand, supplied a phenomenally detailed list of utensils. She demanded that almost every imaginable culinary task have its own piece—in some cases several pieces—of equipment. Leaving aside furniture and ovens, the inventory runs to over 100 objects. It is worth citing in detail because it is so characteristic of the punctilious and prosperous age in which Redelin lived:

1 enamel and 2 black iron frying pans
3 enamelled pots for boiling water
1 enamel and 2 iron stock pots
1 enamel and 3 copper saucepans
1 mincer
1 omelette pan
1 waffle iron
1 novelty baking sheet for aniseed biscuits
1 doughnut pan
2 flat baking sheets and 3 baking sheets with raised edges
1 preserving pan
1 kettle
1 fish-kettle
1 pudding steamer
1 pudding basin
2 English meat loaf tins
1 cake tin
2 jelly moulds
1 ring mould for jellied garnishes
6 small jelly moulds for garnishes
3 novelty vegetable cutters
1 rolling pin
1 cake knife
1 bread trough
1 board for making rissoles
6 pan lids
1 pair scales
3 graters
1 steel sieve
1 china sieve
1 bast sieve
1 soup strainer
2 hair sieves
1 salad shaker
2 water funnels
1 coffee funnel

[17] J. Toomre (trans. and ed.), *Classic Russian Cooking: Elena Molokhovets' A Gift to Young Housewives* (Bloomington, Ind., 1992), 45.

1 spatula for turning *bliny*
1 coffee mill
1 coffee roaster
1 brass pestle and mortar
1 egg-rack
1 ice-cream maker
2 pastry brushes
1 chopping knife
1 vegetable parer
3 kitchen knives
1 meat hammer
1 fish knife
1 carving fork
1 apple and potato peeler
1 cherry stoner
1 sugar grinder
1 knife grinder
3 sets of knives and forks for the servants
3 Britannia metal or silver plate serving spoons
3 larding needles
1 corkscrew
1 vegetable chopper
1 cabbage chopper
2 wooden forks or whisks
1 egg beater
3 trays
4 chopping boards
2 small round boards
1 spoon tray
1 china chopping board
2 enamel coffee trays[18]

And this does not include the items for cleaning the *batterie de cuisine*—among them 2 zinc and 1 enamel buckets, 1 bowl for washing up, 1 enamel bowl for washing tea-cups—or the laundry equipment (1 flat-iron, 2 gauffering irons, 2 iron-rests), or the necessaries for lamp-cleaning and heating (1 coal shovel, 1 pair of coal tongs, 1 poker, 1 kitchen axe), or the materials and tools used for heavy house-cleaning.

   Striking, apart from the sheer quantity of apparently essential objects, is the total lack of any attempt to hierarchize them. For a working cook, a rolling-pin and a novelty baking-sheet for aniseed biscuits, or a vegetable parer and a novelty vegetable-cutter, are not at all equivalent in value: the pin and the parer are likely to be used, during the average week, at least a

---

[18] Redelin, *Dom i khozyaistvo*, 74–5.

dozen times more often than the baking-sheet and vegetable-cutter. But in a society where the contamination of purpose was seen as improper per se, a novelty baking-sheet for aniseed biscuits could be considered as important as, or indeed more important than, a vegetable-parer: a few badly peeled vegetables in the stock-pot were a lot less likely to go amiss than eccentrically shaped pastries at Madame Gorchakova's *faiv o'klok ti*. The incursion of showiness into even the recesses of domestic space was gloriously satirized in Gor'ky's story 'How to Organize Your Home' (1899–1900), the first-person narrative of a rather irresolute young man whose wife's enthusiasm for treatises on domestic management is only matched by her entire inexperience in actually running a house. From her reading, the wife produces a list of essentials that is still more arbitrary than Redelin's:

'And so,' I said, 'I agree. Let's start with the kitchen. But what exactly do you need to set up a kitchen?'

My wife pulled a face like the Pythian oracle and began explaining to me in detail:

'First of all one buys some coarse linen cloth to make dish-cloths. Then you buy a wash-tub to launder the dish-cloths in and some soap. Then you need a slop-bucket, a water-bucket, tubs for boiling whites and for making kvas, a yoke for the buckets, baskets, a rolling-pin, a grater and a whisk—that's for making cakes. You need a coal-shovel, a pair of coal-tongs, a chimney for the samovar, a few earthenware pots and casseroles; then you need lots of vats: a vat for water, a vat for pickled cucumber, a vat for sour cabbage, a vat for pickled apples, for pickled cranberries, for salted watermelons, for the coals...'

I asked which method was best for preserving coals: pickling or salting?

'Neither, of course! You just put them in the vat in their natural state. It's more economical that way... if you keep them in a vat the oxygen in them lasts longer...'[19]

Treated to lectures on 'exactly why a fan is no use for beating egg-whites and why you must not push your cigarette-end into plant-pots' (p. 549), the husband proclaims, with an irony evident to all but himself, the values of higher education for women. The denouement is exactly as might be expected: having exhausted their limited resources, the couple find themselves not only without vital utensils, most particularly a samovar (though the pipe for its top has not been forgotten), but even without food, and are reduced to the kind of improvisation Redelin and her colleagues had sought to make redundant:

'Well, let's turn [the vats] into chairs and tables. The tall ones can be chairs and the low ones tables. We have only to drape them with some of my skirts! And if we put a basket on top of two tubs, put two cushions inside and drape it in my

---

[19] M. Gor'ky, 'Kak nuzhno ustraivat' domashnee khoziaistvo', *PSS* ii (Moscow, 1969), 548.

pale-blue house-coat, it'll make a wonderful sofa. Once we've got the kitchen sorted out, everything else falls into place! (552)

Gor'ky's satire on an upbringing that had precisely not fitted women for what he apparently supposed to be their main purpose in life, the efficient management of the house, was predictable enough, but his grasp of the new domestic ideology of 'form over function' was sure, and his assault on it well timed.

Not content with encouraging prosperous householders to expand their patterns of consumption of domestic objects, the authors of late imperial advice literature were also keen to foster an elaboration of ritual. Weddings were (then as now) considered a particularly opportune moment for the display of wealth. The bride's dress, one publication informed its readers, could properly be made of only two fabrics: heavy silk or cashmere.[20] Another book, a manual under the title *The Rules of Society Life and Etiquette, or Bon-Ton*, published in St Petersburg in 1889, advised its readers in obsequiously hushed tones upon how to choose suitably expensive gifts:

At the present time, instead of the classic 'wedding basket', it is customary [for the groom] to give the bride an elegant small worktable or work-box of costly materials and exquisite workmanship. In the drawer of this table, which should be closed by an elegant little key, or inside the box, if it is a box that is selected, should be placed a purse with gold coins inside; these are to be used for the purchase of gold jewellery . . . As well as giving presents to the bride, the groom should also give presents to the parents of the bride, and to her brothers and sisters.

For her part, the bride should also give a present to the groom: some small piece of gold jewellery such as is worn by gentlemen.

The bride's parents also give the bridegroom a valuable present of some kind.[21]

Pity the bridegroom who had reluctantly to settle for the obviously inferior variant of the work-basket rather than the work-table, or the bride whose collar-studs had to be of insignificant size and manufactured from low-carat gold or even (heaven preserve!) gilt.

Also central to the more expansive kind of advice literature for the prosperous was a faintly disapproving attitude to traditional custom. 'In so-called "respectable homes", the *devichnik*', observed *The Rules of Society Life*, referring to the party for the bride and her friends once customary in Russia, 'either does not take place at all, or is confined to a gathering for close friends of the bride on the eve of the wedding'.[22] For all that, advice on weddings did show some residual respect for local tradition (the 'Honiton lace' recommended for British brides was not mentioned as an option for a

[20] Svetozarskaya, *Zhizn' v svete* (St Petersburg, 1890), 99.
[21] Anon., *Pravila svetskoi zhizni*, 105.   [22] Ibid. 106.

Russian bride's toilette, and bridesmaids, if they figured at all, were said to take part alongside the traditional *shafery*, or male attendants for bride and groom).[23] The model christening, too, still observed a few established customs—for example, the godmother was expected to present the priest with a handkerchief—though readers were sternly warned against others. The practice according to which the godparents gave their godchild's mother cloth for a dress had 'already gone out of use in educated society [*intelligentnoe obshchestvo*]', one manual stated.[24] It was funerals where the convergence between Russian and Western practices, at least in the ideal, seems to have been greatest: at any rate, Russian and British sources are strikingly alike in the lengthy terms of mourning that they recommend (two years for a husband, a year for a wife or parent, six months for a grandparent, four months for a sibling, and so on) and in the elaborateness of the costumes that they specify (full mourning of deepest black with crape veils and ribbons, followed by a mixture of black and grey).[25]

When such demanding occasions were not in the offing, books and magazines also offered advice to the lady of the house herself on how to while away time, not only by organizing the decoration of her house, but also by engaging in such genteel occupations as painting on china. This was also the period at which activities that had formerly been the preserve of the upper classes, such as the composition of 'albums' of literary excerpts and watercolours, began to move down the social scale. The rules for romantic games dependent upon a knowledge of 'the language of flowers' and the symbolism of colours ('the ruby is the symbol of bravery and nobility', 'the wild pink signifies a refusal given of one's own free will') were set out in some mass-market conduct guides, while others provided models according to which aspirant young men might compose a poem to the young woman of their fancy:

> Для тебя, моя Мария,
> Хоть пойти в пономари я
> С радостью готов.
> Вместо дров согреть в камине,
> С головой увянуть в тине
> Без дальнейших слов...[26]

---

[23] On 'Honiton lace' for British brides, see Anon., *The Habits of Good Society* (London, 1860), 368.

[24] Svetozarskaya, *Zhizn' v svete*, 97.

[25] See ibid. 100–1; *Pravila svetskoi zhizni*, 130; and compare with *Modern Etiquette in Private and Public, Including Society at Large: The Etiquette of Weddings, the Ball-Room, the Dinner-Table, the Toilet Etc* (London, 1888), 61–2. However, the hearse and horses in Russia were white, rather than black: see C. Merridale, *Night of Stone: Death and Memory in Russia* (London, 2000), 107.

[26] For instructions on painting on china, see e.g. *Damskii kalendar' na 1917 god*, 141–50. 'The language of flowers' and symbolism of precious stones is set out e.g. in Svetozarskaya, *Zhizn' v*

> For you, for you, my Mariya,
> I'll go and work as a sexton, dear,
> Because I am so fond.
> I'll burn like a log upon your fire,
> And plunge head-first if you require
> Into the nearest pond.

The cultivation of refined pastimes on the one hand, and the preoccupation with 'elegance' and 'comfort' on the other, were of course possible only with domestic servants to keep the house running smoothly. In manuals, however, advice on dealing with servants is quite scanty (there is little material on their practical duties), and generally limited to their role in establishing social differentials (that is, in enhancing their employers' status). Redelin's manual, for example, contains elaborate advice on waiting at table, which makes it clear that maximum invisibility was required:

Any careless jostling of the guests sitting at table in whatsoever manner by the servant (for example, with her elbow as she puts down a bowl of soup), any noise from clattering plates, or from the sound of her feet as she walks (most particularly if she has squeaky shoes), or dropping of knives and forks, absolutely cannot be tolerated.[27]

The mistress of the house might not be able to treat servants as though they were invisible all of the time (after all, it was occasionally necessary to instruct them on their duties), but she was carefully cautioned against developing too close a relationship with them; respect was to be exacted in the first instance.[28] It is entirely in keeping with the maintenance of distance between employers and servants that tipping is generally advocated, and that little is said about servants' working conditions, a greater emphasis being placed on the need to regulate servants' moral tone and devotional habits.[29] And, at an era when cookery advice for the

---

svete, 51–64. The poem to Mariya is quoted from Anon., *Damskii ugodnik: Sbornik al'bomnykh stikhotvorenii na vsyakoe zhenskoe imya* (St Petersburg, 1898), 15.

[27] Redelin, *Dom i khozyaistvo*, i. 354.

[28] Brodersen, *Khoroshii ton*, 84. Even the material on 'bon ton' published by Rodina (Motherland) popular library, which advocates that employers should treat their servants well and help them improve their minds, maintains that servants should be gratefully aware of their dependence upon their employers: 'modest, anticipating their employers' needs [predupredi-tel'na], always remembering that their employers are their superiors and that they get food and clothes from them.' (Anon., *Khoroshii ton* (1907), 40.)

[29] For example, Brodersen, *Khoroshii ton*, 62, advises that servants should be tipped even if one doesn't have much money. In the nineteenth edition of her famous household manual *Podarok molodym khozyaikam* (Moscow, 1917), ii. 216, Elena Molokhovets advises, 'it is essential that every head of house . . . should try to instil and implant in his family and servants a boundless love of God.' Voskresenskaya, *Drug khoziaiki*, who does emphasize the need for adequate quarters and good food, and the importance of visits to the theatre and 'accessible entertainments' as well as church, also underlines that 'it is a mistress's sacred duty to protect the morality of her servants'.

privileged was advocating increasingly complicated and elaborate dishes, most domestic manuals still carried sections of suitable servant food, consisting of cheap, monotonous, and starchy dishes such as kasha, broths with pearl barley and noodles, rice and kasha pies, and kisel' or apple pie to follow.[30]

The emphasis on the asymmetrical nature of employer–servant relations was part of an anything but democratic representation of manners in a broader sense. Authors uniformly advised their readers to maintain great sensitivity to rank. S. Izvol'sky, author of *Interesting Notes for Young Men who Wish to Become Socially Adept, Dexterous, Well-Educated, and Amiable Cavaliers*, for example, recommended to his readers that they should treat their superiors with 'attentiveness and respectfulness', and their inferiors with 'amiability', while Kleopatra Svetozarskaya, the author of *Life in Society, at Home, and at Court* opened her section on 'society' with the assertion that 'knowledge of the world prescribes various laws to those of different social positions, ages, and sexes; these laws are not the same for an aristocratic lady and a bourgeoise, for a youth and an old man, for a young man and a young girl'.[31]

A command of linguistic etiquette was essential, authors insisted, in order to get on in the touchy world of late imperial social relations. It is increasingly common for advice on the use of titles to be provided, and deferential formulae were considered *de rigueur*. Izvol'sky, for example, provided examples of oleaginous compliments to persons that one wished to impress. On leaving the house, one should say:

I am profoundly grateful for your cordiality and amiability, which have exceeded all my expectations. [That this compliment could have been interpreted as bordering on the insulting seems not to have occurred to Izvol'sky!] I do hope that you will favour me with a visit in your turn.

It seems to me that never have I encountered such hospitality as upon the occasions when I have visited your house. That truly generous hospitality and the friendly conversation which you have done so much to facilitate have afforded us all many pleasant moments.[32]

The full flower of obsequiousness, however, was to blossom in letter-writing manuals' suggestions of how low-ranking employees might congratulate their superiors on occasions such as a name-day:

---

[30] See e.g. Dragomirova, *V pomoshch' khozyaikam*, sect. 18.

[31] Izvol'sky, *Interesnye zapiski*, 12; Svetozarskaya, *Zhizn' v svete*, 3. Cf. the last-named writer on the choice of godparents for a christening: 'It is not suitable to ask your superior at work or persons of high rank in general, firstly because it looks pushy [*eto pokhozhe na zaiskivan'e*], and secondly because it is unpleasant to receive a refusal, as is extremely likely' (p. 97).

[32] Izvol'sky, *Interesnye zapiski*, 60.

Your Excellency

A... A...

Be pleased to accept my sincere and heartfelt felicitations upon The Feastday of Your Saint, and also my humble and heartfelt wish that Your Excellency should enjoy a lengthy life, the best of health, and success in all Your affairs and enterprises.

With sincere respect and utter devotion I have the honour to remain

Your Excellency's most obedient servant

S.... K...[33]

To be sure, 'knowing one's place' was not the only behaviour pattern recommended. The enticingly named *Self-Education as a Path to Wealth* (1908) offers much advice on self-serving ingratiation, including the importance of listening carefully, of making sure that you do not argue with other people, of being amusing, and of paying compliments in order to manipulate those who may be useful to you. 'Playing skilfully upon the strings of his vanity, we can draw from him whatever sounds we wish, attuning him thus to our own purposes.'[34] The advice is very like that given in such late eighteenth-century books as *The Science of Being Polite*, and, as in the eighteenth-century tradition, it was suggested that every imaginable action (as well as some actions that are not so easily imaginable) had to be premeditated in terms of its relations to the observation of social nicety. An article on manners in *The Lady's World Calendar* for 1915 warned that it was inappropriate to use the telephone in order to invite those higher up the social ladder than oneself to pay a visit.[35] And, as in Western Europe, the exchange of visiting cards—the turning down of this or that corner, the leaving of specific numbers of cards, the inscription of 'P.P.C' (*pour prendre congé*) on cards left before departure—brought with it nightmarish negotiations of one's precise social position vis-à-vis those of the recipient, and the frightful possibility of committing some gaffe such as leaving one's card for a person of the highest rank (rather than inscribing one's name in their visitor's book) or failing to deliver a card for a social superior by hand.[36]

Women as well as men were part of the visiting-card exchange network; and they, like men, were now seen as part of a world defined by vertical

[33] See *Russkii pis'movnik* . . . (1890), 24. An even more unctuous model letter, upon a superior's promotion, appears ibid. 33–4. For an English translation, see my '*Kul'turnost'*' in the Soviet Union: Ideal and Reality', in G. Hosking and B. Service (eds.), *Reinterpreting Russia* (London, 1999), 204.

[34] *Samoobrazovanie kak put' k bogatstvu*, 32.

[35] *Kalendar' 'Damskii mir' na 1915 god*, 32.

[36] See Svetozarskaya, *Zhizn' v svete*, 45. On visiting cards in the West, see especially the amusingly tart observations of Leonore Davidoff in *The Best Circles: Society, Etiquette and the Seasons* (London, 1986), 42–3; and Andrew St George, *The Descent of Manners: Etiquette, Rules and the Victorians* (London, 1993), 114.

differentiation. In one manual, they were instructed to save cordiality (*serdechnost'*) for their friends, and to be the souls of tact when paying official visits, such as to the colleagues of their husbands. In this new interpretation of 'the ideology of separate spheres', the public world of work had begun to dominate permissible behaviour in private, and the hierarchy of office (or the office hierarchy) was carried into the drawing room.[37]

But the absorption of women into the vertically layered 'male' world in no sense signified that advice books for the better-off were egalitarian in their attitudes to gender. On the contrary: the need to be 'ladylike' was now emphasized with an insistence greater than ever before. Baroness Staffe's *Indications pour obtenir un brevet de femme chic* (1907: translated into Russian in 1912), underlined that a lady should move in a special way (slowly and deliberately), most particularly when descending from a carriage, and implied that she would be most unlikely to adopt the current 'boyish' fashions.[38] And, though the most egregious instances of self-abasement for men cropped up in the context of relations between employers and their underlings, and assumed masculine participants, male readers were constantly reminded of the need for polite behaviour to women, even when those women were strangers. Izvol'sky's *Interesting Notes* warned its readers against making 'Don Juan-like comments' to unaccompanied women in the streets, and recommended the company of ladies as a softening force for male behaviour: 'The best impressions are made, in the main, by that society which is frequented by well-bred ladies and young women. In their company, a young man involuntarily abandons the brash tone and coarse manners of male society and learns delicacy and the art of social intercourse.'[39]

If 'polite society' was firmly under the regulation of women, so was the domestic world in general. The 'ideology of separate spheres' was propounded with much greater fervour than in the mid-nineteenth century, and men now had no place in regulation of the household whatever. In the words of Mariya Redelin: 'If the master of the house is successful in his intellectual work, then this is usually because of the quiet

---

[37] That said, advice on precedence was never as elaborate as that given in British etiquette books, with their obsession about the relative status of a bishop's second wife's cousin as opposed to a baronet's third daughter. (See, for instance, the remarkably terse comments of Svetozarskaya, *Zhizn' v svete*, 130). However, this was not necessarily a sign of greater simplicity and directness in Russia: it perhaps stemmed in part from the familiarity of the official Table of Ranks to most educated Russians. Certainly, confronted with the case of where to seat a young man of high rank and an older one of inferior rank, Svetozarskaya suggests that it is foolish to invite two such people at once, and get oneself into such a 'ticklish situation' at all.

[38] See Staff, *Chto dolzhna znat' kazhdoi zhenshchine*, 89–90, 296.

[39] Izvol'sky, *Interesnye zapiski*, 31–2.

and unnoticeable contribution of his wife, the manager of the household, since it is her sphere, the household, which creates the right mood for his work, giving him spiritual and intellectual energy.'[40] Accordingly, almost the only domestic manuals addressed to the unnoticing male, rather than his ever-industrious wife, were those dealing with activities that could be classed as hobbies. In *How to Do It Yourself*, a pioneering guide to the world of pottering about in tool sheds, readers were advised on making such far from indispensable items as a punt, a dried-flower bouquet, a self-closing gate, and a rainproof tent.[41]

The division between professional success on the husband's part and the contribution made to this by the wife was underpinned by advice literature of a more intimate kind: that on personal appearance. A plethora of brochures and magazines offered guidance for women on the elaboration of attire. *What Suits Me?*, a guide to 'how to dress with taste' published in 1891, called for a vast array of different outfits suited to various occasions, from visiting a spa to going shopping, to travelling, to attending church, plus, of course, such special purposes as getting married or going into mourning. Readers were instructed that they should choose colours to suit the shades of their hair and eyes, and elaborate guidance was provided on coordinating colours and on which shades did *not* go together (clearly, the book should have been recommended to Natasha, the anti-heroine of Chekhov's *Three Sisters*, 1901).[42] Fashion advice was also the province of magazines: the fashion glossy was a new phenomenon of the era, and copiously illustrated and luxurious publications such as *The Ladies' World* (*Damskii mir*) and *The Housewife's Journal* (*Zhurnal khozyaiki*) offered spreads of glamorous and complicated outfits, the changing of which could well have been allowed to take up most of the day.

Literature for men, on the other hand, was mostly not concerned with telling men how to make themselves attractive to women. To be sure, there was a rather regretful note to the statement made in one compendium of advice 'for the elegant male', *The Gentleman*: 'The gentleman does not have the opportunity to scan dozens of fashion magazines, as ladies do, and to concern himself with the changing styles of sleeves or of skirts.' And the book stipulated quite a wide range of different outfits for various

---

[40] Redelin, *Dom i khozyaistvo*, i. 1. Cf. the observations of Sharon Marcus on late 19th-cent. French domestic manuals, which 'counseled women not only how to create . . . privacy but how then to keep their families, and particularly their husbands, within the confines of that delimited residential space' (*Apartment Stories: City and Home in Nineteenth-Century Paris and London* (Berkeley, 1999), 149).

[41] Shteinberg, *Kak eto samomu sdelat'?* (c.1910). However Anon., *Khozyain-domovod*, an unassuming brochure published by the Sytin company, provided advice on more practical matters such as painting, carpentry, and getting spots out of clothes.

[42] Anon., *Chto mne k litsu?*.

occasions, from hunting to tennis, from mountain-climbing to days at the races, as well as a dressing-table equipped with eau de toilette and hair lotions alongside the toothbrush, comb, and hairbrush. But at the same time, it emphasized the need for 'simplicity' above all: walking-sticks must not bear monograms, jewels, or initials, and a gentleman was distinguished by his 'impeccable linen' and hand-made shoes rather than by eye-catching garments of any kind.[43]

Counsel against ostentation was underpinned by the fact that the male reader was assumed to be in employment of some kind—as *The Gentleman* put it, 'Even if he has a fortune of millions, the gentleman is never idle.'[44] It was therefore essential for him to blend into his surroundings.[45] Psychologically, too, he was supposed to conform, applying himself diligently and disinterestedly to his professional career. In the late 1880s, the Victorian code of 'backbone' and 'manliness' began reaching Russia from Britain and France, and a plethora of books advised on 'the inculcation of character', sternly warning that 'weakness more quickly becomes habitual than energetic behaviour', underlining the insidious effects of pleasure, inveighing against introspection (shyness was seen as 'a defect' that 'degrades the character'), and advising on 'the education of the will'.[46] From childhood, males were to be indoctrinated in the new code of unbending diligence: to quote *The Gentleman* again: 'If we really want the best for our child, we will try to implant in him, as early as possible, the idea that there is nothing magical or fortuitous in life, that we ourselves forge our own happiness and success, a success which in its turn is the result of steady effort often extending over many years.'[47] The housewife might fill her empty hours by painting on china, but the man of the world was purposive even in his leisure, modelling himself on 'Englishmen', who had time for 'productive work, and insouciant cheerfulness, and for sport'.[48]

The division between the sexes was manifested also in a booming area of early twentieth-century advice literature: health literature. To be sure,

[43] Metuzala, *Dzhentl'men*, 67, 88–95, 42–6, 82, 75–6, 79.

[44] Ibid. 71.

[45] This advice would not have been necessary for Russian civil servants, who were required to wear a uniform—*mundir*—but no doubt came in handy for the new class of white-collar workers who, precisely because of Russia's militaristic traditions, lacked models of acceptable professional dress.

[46] See Marten, *O vospitanii kharaktera* (1888), 375, 400; cf. Dyuga, *Zastenchivost' i ee lechenie* (1899); Levi, *Ratsional'noe vospitanie voli* (St Petersburg, 1912); and the most popular of them all, Peio, *Vospitanie voli*, which had reached its 7th edn. by 1913. Catriona Kelly, 'The Education of the Will: Masculinity and "Backbone" in Early Twentieth-Century Russia', in B. Clements, R. Friedman, and D. Healey (eds.), *Russian Masculinities in History and Culture* (Basingstoke, 2001), explores this topic at greater length.

[47] Metuzala, *Dzhentel'men*, 100. Cf. Stolitsa, *Razvitie v detyakh zhizneradostnosti* (1912).

[48] Metuzala, *Dzhentel'men*, 3.

interest in medical literature aimed at the general reader was nothing new in turn-of-the-century Russia. Even in the late eighteenth century, the various types of advice literature available had included material on health and fitness. For example, Jean Goulin's *The Lady's Doctor* (1793) had provided information on the need to wear warm clothing to avoid catching cold, the importance of not over-eating, and the dangers of tobacco.[49] However, at this date the emphasis was as much on the avoidance of over-exertion as on the need to take regular exercise. By the second half of the nineteenth century, the view had reached Russia (in the first place, it seems, from Britain, Germany, and Scandinavia) that more strenuous activity was beneficial to the system. Anna Tyutcheva's plan for the education of Grand Duchess Maria Aleksandrovna (1858) included gymnastics; a year earlier a doctor attached to Smol'nyi Institute, after a fact-finding visit to England, had recommended that the young noble ladies be instructed in 'medical gymnastics' (teaching in the subject was in fact introduced a decade later).[50] In 1870, the Ministry of Popular Enlightenment issued a circular decreeing that gymnastics be introduced to educational institutions in Russia, and two years later, V. Ukhov's *Handbook of Pedagogical and Hygienic Gymnastics* was issued. Girls as well as boys were included in the new tuition, though certain exercises (notably, those that involved spreading the legs) were labelled as 'unsuitable'.[51] Nor was the preoccupation with fitness limited to the conservative upper classes: Chernyshevsky's Rakhmet'ev, the revolutionary hero of *What is to be Done* (1863), had nurtured his steely constitution and will on a combination of gymnastics, rational labour, and minced beef consumed raw.

Naturally, the preoccupation with physical training also influenced the advice-books market, with P. A. Litvinsky's *Strength and Dexterity* (1879) (aimed at children) one of the earliest publications. By the early twentieth century, exercise manuals were a boom area, with editions including 'Willi the Olympian's' *The Cult of the Body: Beauty and Strength*, D. Edwards's *The Ideal Culture of the Body*, and the English doctor Boyd Laynard's *The Secrets of Beauty, Health and Long Life*.[52] But the most popular of all was Jorger Møller's *My System: 15 Minutes of Daily Work for the Health*, which went

---

[49] Gulen, *Damskii vrach*, 84, 103. Medical literature was a subdivision of 'utilitarian books', and these, according to G. Marker, *Publishing, Printing and the Origins of Intellectual Life in Russia* (Princeton, 1985), 234, were, with 'devotional books', the most popular categories of printed material in 18th-cent. Russia.

[50] A. Tyutcheva, '[Zametki o vospitanii]', RGALI f. 10 , op. 1, ed. khr. 218, sheet 35 verso; N. P. Cherepnin, *Imperatorskoe vospitatel'noe obshchestvo blagorodnykh devits: Istoricheskii ocherk 1764–1914* (St Petersburg, 1914–15), ii, ch. 8.

[51] Ukhov, *Rukovodstvo k pedagogicheskoi i gigienicheskoi gimnastike* (1872).

[52] 'Villi Olimpiets', *Kul't tela* (*c*.1910); Edvards, *Ideal'naya kul'tura tela* (*c*.1910); Leinard, *Sekrety krasoty, zdorov'ya i dolgovechnosti* (1909).

FIG. 9. Front cover of D. Edwards, *The Culture of the Body* (*c.*1910).

into many editions, and enjoyed a colossal popularity among Russians in the 1900s.[53]

While exercise books sometimes varied in the programmes that they prescribed for men and for women (for example, Møller's *My System* had a companion edition of women's exercises), the most important distinction was in the purpose that they saw as lying behind exercise. Books for men encouraged them to take exercise in order that they might become energetic, efficient, and ready to manifest initiative. Boyd Laynard, for example, propagandized the need for healthy living by pointing to the Social Darwinist ideology of 'survival of the fittest':

[53] See e.g. Miller [*sic*], *Moya sistema* (1909).

Just as a steam engine whose furnace has been supplied with bad or insufficient fuel can never drive an express train, so men and women with debilitated constitutions are generally slow and have what is called 'no go' in them. In these days of keen competition such persons stand little chance in the great battle of life. They are pushed aside and others take their place. It is the great law of 'survival of the fittest'.[54]

Exercise books presented as the ideal a man with both backbone and muscles, bursting with health and ready for anything that the world could throw at him. Occasionally too (and most particularly in the publications of the 'Sokol' organization for young men), there was a militaristic tone to the guidance offered: fitness and muscularity were seen as preparation for the defence of the nation.[55]

Sources on hygiene for women, on the other hand, were not at all concerned with fitness. It was, rather, personal attractiveness that was seen in Social Darwinist terms. As articulated by a 1909 brochure, *A Woman and Her Duty*: 'Beauty is essential to a woman as a weapon in the struggle for her survival. Woe betide the woman who does not take care of herself and pay attention to her appearance, and who is therefore unable to appeal to men!'[56] In the pursuit of a man, physical health in the strict sense often came a poor second to the maintainence of an attractive appearance. A pamphlet on *How to Increase and Strengthen the Female Bust*, for example, suggested to its readers that they should eat plenty of greasy foods, drink beer, and avoid exercise in pursuit of the perfect female silhouette.[57] The body was treated here not as an obstreperous organism which required stern regulation for its proper functioning, but as a possession to be pampered—a variety of advice sources advised women on such frankly sybaritic forms of physical culture as massage, bathing, and the use of every possible form of skin potion.[58] And it was seen not as an intrinsic part of the

---

[54] Laynard, *Secrets of Beauty, Health and Long Life*, 5; the passage also appears in Leinard, *Sekrety krasoty, zdorov'ya, i dolgovechnosti* (1909), p. iv, with 'battle for life' rendered as 'bor'ba za sushchestvovanie'. On the link between the 'cult of the body' and the rise of capitalism, see L. McReynolds and C. Popkin, 'The Objective Eye and the Common Good' in C. Kelly and D. Shepherd (eds.), *Constructing Russian Culture in the Age of Revolution, 1881–1940* (Oxford, 1998), 75–8.

[55] See *Kurs sokol'skoi gimnazii* (1911); and *Boi-skauty: rukovodstvo samovospitaniya molodezhi po sisteme 'skauting'* (1917, which emphasizes the 'patriotic duty' for which the scout is to prepare himself. (The bellicose resonance of this can only have been helped by the fact that the transliteration 'boi-skaut' could be understood as a pun on the Russian word *boi*, 'combat'.)

[56] *Zhenshchina i ee obyazannost': Kak sokhranit' zdorov'e, molodost', krasotu i byt' lyubimoi* (Moscow, 1909), front cover.

[57] Lori, *Kak uvelichit' i ukrepit' zhenskii byust* (1909), 41. The author also claims, somewhat mysteriously, that reading 'sensual novels' can reduce the size of the bust (ibid.).

[58] See e.g. 'Krasota i gigiena', *Kalendar' 'Damskii mir' na 1915 god*, 37–45. This calendar also published an annual gazeteer of spas and resorts for 'taking the cure'.

self, but as an object which might be reshaped at need, an extension of the wardrobe.

Even washing was often treated less as a prerequisite of hygiene in a neutral sense than as a contribution to sexual appeal and social acceptability. For example, *The Woman Doctor*, a pamphlet on female hygiene published in 1909, sternly warned readers that careful washing was necessary to combat the 'bad smell' that emanated from any woman not scrupulous in her *toilette*:

It is a crime for a woman to smell bad. That is why we recommend that twice a day (morning and evening) you carry out an intimate toilette—wash your underarms and loins (the lower part of your stomach) in warm water. . . . If the slightest carelessness, the slightest negligence creeps into her intimate toilette, a woman begins to smell bad.[59]

Such advice, predictably enough, concentrated above all on the dangers to hygiene supposedly inherent in the process of menstruation. They dwelt on the need to wash especially frequently while menstruating, to change the underwear regularly, and to use sanitary protection (*binty*, or towels, held in place by a belt).[60] Since the female body was a potential engine of pollution, the truly hygienic woman was advised to have her own dressing-room equipped with a formidable array of equipment, including not only a basin, but also a bidet and an implement for arranging home enemas (women were assumed to be subject not only to the build-up of noxious substances in their reproductive organs, but also in their digestive system).[61]

A secondary strand in these books was women's role as 'future mothers'. Guides to gymnastics written for women emphasized the biologistic imperatives behind the taking of exercise. E. A. Mikhailova, in her *The Physical Education of Young Women* (1905), roundly proclaimed: 'All women's specialized professions, however elevated they may be, are too narrow compared with the infinitely broad occupation of being a mother. The preparation for this occupation should be as extensive and broad as possible.'[62] Sexual release for women was sometimes now seen as licit: Mikhailova approvingly quoted a doctor who had asserted at the 8th Congress of the Pirogov Society, 'Gentlemen, the act of coitus is as

---

[59] Anon., *Zhenshchina-vrach* (1909), 8–9

[60] See *Gigiena krasoty: Neobkhodimaya kniga dlya zhenshchiny* (1909), 34; Fisher-Dyukel'man, *Zhenshchina—domashnii vrach* (1909), 331.

[61] On the contents of the *cabinet de toilette*, see e.g. *Zhenshchina-vrach*, 9–15. Though the imagined reader must have been well-off to afford such items, the rather punitive character of some of this equipment makes it difficult to accept Georges Vigarello's distinction between bathing for pleasure (as practised by the bourgeoisie) and washing for hygienic reasons (as imposed upon the proletariat). (See *Concepts of Cleanliness: Changing Attitudes in France since the Middle Ages*, trans. J. Birrell (Cambridge University Press, 1988), 220.)

[62] Mikhailova, *Fizicheskoe vospitanie zhenskoi molodezhi*, 100.

essential for women as the act of defecation!' (94) But the sexual activities of women were generally seen as having a single legitimate aim: to further conception. Anna Fischer-Dueckelmann's *Die Frau als Hausärztin* (The Woman Doctor), a Russian edition of which appeared in 1909, for example, emphasized the importance of vulval tumescence because it was supposedly vital to conception.[63] Rather than being seen as a pleasurable activity, sex emerged as a stern duty engaged upon by the heroic female partner in full awareness of its dangers, particularly the fact that men, given their pernicious failure to control the sex instinct, were likely to have had access to 'commercial love' before marriage, and to have become infected with a sexually transmitted disease.[64] To be sure, such advice stemmed from an acknowledgement of the sober realities of the average conjugal relationship at the turn of the century, and in a sense represented a reconfiguration of the old feminist tradition of Fénelon or Lambert, with awareness of health issues now added to intellectual independence as a weapon for the wife seeking to defend herself against the dangers of a debauched husband. But in a context where advice on male personal hygiene (washing under the prepuce, for example) was never given, the emphasis on the cleanliness of women had overtones of coercion, enforcing a tendency to see women's sexual relationships as the exercise of obligation, and men's as the search for pleasure.

Some turn-of-the-century advice literature, then, explicitly stressed the necessity of maintaining and reinforcing divisions between different social classes, and between the sexes, and it emphasized acquisition as a prerequisite for refinement. If the former element was nothing novel in terms of Russian advice-literature tradition (though taken to extremes not previously witnessed),[65] the latter was something that was not only new, but also inflammatory, given the tradition of associating economy and morality. Not surprisingly, then, the early twentieth century saw an upsurge of books and articles propagandizing a quite different attitude to personal possessions, in which readers were encouraged to curb, rather than expand, consumption, to practise 'rational living' rather than exercising 'the taste of luxury'.

---

[63] Fisher-Dyukel'man, *Zhenshchina—domashnii vrach*, 305.　　[64] Ibid. 314–18.

[65] As argued in Ch. 2, mid-19th-cent. conservative advice literature generally accorded men, as well as women, a role in the home; in early 20th-cent. texts, this role, where mentioned at all, was limited to the social conditioning of sons (see Marten, *O vospitanii kharaktera*, chs. 11–14). And the assymmetry of turn-of-the-century hygiene advice was a novel feature. The sanitary guidance given in early conduct books is much the same whether for men or for women: compare the instructions about cleanliness in *Pravila uchtivosti* with those in *Kakim obrazom mozhno sokhranit' zdravo i krasotu molodykh zhenshchin* (1793), and in *O dolzhnostyakh cheloveka i grazhdanina* (1783) (for both sexes), or the instructions for the different sexes in Charukovsky, *Narodnaya meditsyna* (1844).

RATIONAL LIVING

A pivotal figure in the movement for 'rational living' was, of course, Tolstoi, whose tracts against intoxicating substances (alcohol, tobacco, tea, coffee, and later meat and rich foods) had begun appearing in the 1880s.[66] But Tolstoi, inspiring as his writings were to members of the Russian intelligentsia, was but a pioneer in a movement for 'rational living' which had, by the early twentieth century, thousands of followers, a wide range of concerns, and an emphasis on practical counsel that was rather different from Tolstoi's own rather abstract disquisitions upon the need to renounce high living. Though Tolstoi discoursed, in *The First Step* (1890), upon the evils of meat-eating (which was cruel to animals as well as an unsavoury indulgence of the flesh), it was left to other writers to expand upon the details of a vegetarian diet; and though he pronounced, in *What, Then, is to be Done?* (1887) upon the virtues of physical labour, the master did not condescend to contribute to the stream of books on 'rational exercise' that began appearing in the 1900s. What is more—and contrary to the standard argument according to which the contradictions of an era are most clearly traceable in the lives of its 'great men'—the very coherence of his puritanism made him reflect the preoccupations and uncertainties of his day partially and inadequately. At a time when 'care of the self' became an obsession with advice-book writers, and when self-improvement of different kinds was a near-universal preoccupation, the message of 'What People Live By'—'A person lives not by care about himself, but by love'—was, to put it mildly, unusual. But if Tolstoi was an uncharacteristic major figure, a minor figure whose life can be seen as an atlas of her age, mapping its desires, its fears, its uncertainties, was Nataliya Nordman (1863–1914), the partner of the famous realist painter Il'ya Repin, who also wrote under the pen-name 'Severova'.

At first sight, Nordman seems no more than a colourful eccentric, fit, perhaps, for inclusion in a second volume of Pylyaev's history of upper-class oddballs, *Zamechatel'nye chudaki i originaly* (1898). This is partly because she eschewed the blandly commonsensical tone that has traditionally characterized advice literature: the style of her works blended melodramatic over-statement (leather briefcases, she asserted, 'stank of death') and histrionic sarcasm (in one of her novels, *The Cross of Motherhood*, modern

---

[66] On Tolstoi's vegetarian views (from the point of view of intellectual history rather than sociology), see R. D. LeBlanc, 'Tolstoi's Way of No Flesh: Abstinence, Vegetarianism, and Christian Physiology', D. Goldstein, 'Is Hay Only for Horses? Highlights of Russian Vegetarianism at the Turn of the Century', in M. Glants and J. Toomre (eds.), *Food in Russian History and Culture* (Bloomington, Ind., 1997), 81–90, 91–102. The crucial Tolstoi text on vegetarianism is *The First Step* (Pervaya stupen') (see *PSS* xxix), a denunciation of the cruelty and self-indulgence of meat-eating.

young women are branded as 'frizz-haired flibbertigibbets eager to get their hooks into the first tail-coat that comes their way').[67] Yet her short but energetic existence brought her into contact with many of the most prominent ideologies and debates of the day, from feminism to animal welfare, from 'the servant problem' to the drive for hygiene and self-improvement. And her writings on conduct embrace many of the most important strands in the advice literature of the late imperial era. Fanatical about diet and healthy living, she fits neatly into an era when the cult of the body was beginning to take hold of the Russian upper and middle classes. Since much of her advice was also directed at the privileged, those who could afford to overeat, and who employed servants, she was a figure exemplary of an era when self-restraint, and the treatment of social inferiors, were beginning to be seen as indicators of what Nordman herself called 'the cultured life' (*kul'turnaya zhizn'*). While the *sum* of Nordman's concerns was decidedly bizarre, each individual element in her world-view had considerable currency with many far less colourful characters.

A vegetarian who eschewed not only meat, but eventually also milk products and clothing made of animal products,[68] Nordman propagandized the virtues of a healthy diet to anyone who would listen, and a fair number of people who would rather not have. Asserting that the eating of vegetables would allow the well-off to 'flush out the diet of corpses which has built up in their organisms', she set out recipes for meals including cooked dishes, raw salads, or pickled vegetables, depending on the season. Berries and mushrooms were other important constituents. And a tisane of stewed grass and herbs was warmly and repeatedly recommended by Nordman to both rich and poor as a panacea for all ills and an important constituent of every cooked vegetarian dish.[69]

Nordman's belief in the 'grass diet' may have verged on crankiness,[70] but

[67] Severova[-Nordman], *Raiskie zavety: stat'i i zametki* (1913), 51; *eadem*, *Krest materinstva: tainyi dnevnik* (St Petersburg, 1904), 127–8. The letter words are spoken by a sardonic 1860s radical, Ardanova, but the character is very obviously a mouthpiece for Nordman's own views.

[68] The precise time at which Nordman became a vegan, to use the late 20th-cent. term, is unclear, but it appears to have been in late 1910 or early 1911 (judging by the fact that the menu from 1910 quoted below includes ice-cream, while Nordman's later tracts are strictly vegetarian).

[69] Severova[-Nordman], *Povarennaya kniga dlya golodayushchikh* (1911), front cover; *eadem*, *Raiskie zavety*, 2–42, 65–7. Morozova (in Grabar' and Zil'bershtein, *Repin*, ii. 250) refers to a second and stricter period of Nordman's vegetarianism, allowing only raw food, but this can have set in only in late 1913, after the publication of her treatises. An account of Nordman's vegetarian beliefs, based on *Povarennaya kniga*, *Raiskie zavety*, and memoir sources, and a brief contextualization of these in terms of the history of vegetarianism in Russia, is given in Goldstein, 'Is Hay Only for Horses'.

[70] Goldstein, 'Is Hay Only for Horses', points out that hay had been used as a flavouring ingredient in traditional Russian recipes (for cooking ham, etc.); this defence does not seem wholly convincing; a diet based on a broth of salt and black pepper would seem curious, even though both are regularly used for spicing.

her concern for vegetarianism was in itself nothing curious at the time when she wrote. Though vegetarian practices had been relatively late in reaching Russia (they began to attract serious attention in the 1890s, rather than the 1860s), their advocates were well organized and vociferous. Two separate magazines, *Vegetarian Review* and *The Vegetarian Herald*, began being issued around 1910, while a vegetarian dining-room (*stolovaya*) in Kiev opened in 1910, served no less than 118,787 meals during its first year of operation.[71] The journals regularly carried articles by Nordman, and reports about her activities, and obituaries in both emphasized her importance as an inspiration for the movement.[72] The explicit connection made in Nordman's writings between feminism and vegetarianism was unusual in the Russian context, but had parallels in, for example, Britain, where women activists, like Nordman, drew parallels between the victimization of animals and of women, and also emphasized the contribution made to social change by the alteration of diet and culinary practices.[73]

Equally, when Nordman extolled the joys of sleeping naked in a well-aired room, as practised in 'modern European sanatoriums', then leaping energetically from your bed in order to do 'Dr Miller's [*sic*] gymnastic exercises',[74] she was simply giving idiosyncratic expression to the spirit of a generation when many well-off people, perturbed by the incidence of what they took to be diseases of superfluity, such as gout, dyspepsia, and obesity, were becoming increasingly concerned with prophylactic medicine. The need for machine-like efficiency (an idea that was to be taken to the point of absurdity in advice literature of the early Soviet period) was only one, rather minor, motif in pre-revolutionary fitness manuals. Many books on exercise advocated a body-centred culture that was reactive rather than proactive (that is, it was designed to avoid illness rather than generate fitness), and that was based on an aesthetics of personal purity rather than a pragmatics of exercise to a certain end (participation in the 'struggle for existence'). Not for nothing did such religiously coloured fitness systems as yoga and ju-jitsu have currency.[75] Rather than formidable programmes of physical jerks, books generally prescribed moderation in eating, in drinking, and in sexual activity, regular exercise, and especially, abundant draughts of fresh air. Sub-genres of advice material set out the

[71] *Vegetarianskoe obozrenie* began publishing in 1909, *Vegetarianskii vestnik* in 1914. On the *stolovaya*, see *Vegetarianskoe obozrenie* 9–10 (1910), 61.

[72] See *Vegetarianskii vestnik* 2 (1914), 3, and *Vegetarianskoe obozrenie* 6–7 (1914), 204–20.

[73] See L. Leneman, 'The Awakened Instinct: Vegetarianism and the Women's Suffrage Movement in Britain', in *Women's History Review* 6 (1997), 271–88. My thanks to Melanie Ilic for drawing this article to my attention.

[74] *Raiskie zavety*, 69.

[75] See e.g. Garman and Gankok, *Dzhyu-dzhitsu* (1908). This appears to be a version of H. I. Hancock, *Jiu-Jitsu Combat Tricks: Japanese Feats of Attack and Defence in Personal Encounters* (New York and London, 1904).

rules of healthy housekeeping and of 'rational dress' (that is, loose, comfortable clothing), explicitly opposing themselves to those books which emphasized 'elegant taste' and 'comfort' more than 'the hygienic idea', and 'fashion' more than sensible simplicity. P. P. Andreev's *House Management: A Handbook for Housewives* asserted: 'Economy, simplicity, tidiness, order, and constant concern for the hygiene of one's dwelling are what is needed to furnish one's house in the best way.' His kitchen inventory, unlike Redelin's, was limited to the bare essentials—only twenty-nine items, of which the vast majority are multi-functional—and his advice on skin and hair care stressed above all the need for frequent washing (hair was to be washed no less than once a week).[76]

The conditions obtaining in Russian cities around 1900 were generally acknowledged to be especially threatening to health. Unregulated industrialization meant that the proliferating chimneys of factories and foundries (some of which were placed right in the centre of conurbations) filled the air with noxious fumes. Moreover, unlike their fellows in some Western cities, such as Berlin, Paris, and London, Russians did not tend to take refuge year-round in the suburbs; living in a city apartment (or, for the very well-off, mansion) remained the norm. Most particularly St Petersburg, where even reasonably well-off individuals often inhabited small, cramped, dark flats, and which had a notoriously dank climate, was seen as a site of putridity and disease. All this meant that advocacy of fresh air and healthy living customarily focused on a site beyond the city limits: the *dacha* or summer-house.

As every reader (or spectator) of Chekhov's *The Cherry Orchard*, or his story 'The Dacha People' (Dachniki) knows, the 1890s and 1900s were the era when purchasing a dacha became something approaching a mass phenomenon.[77] Certainly, a dacha, or even a hut or allotment, remained beyond the reach of factory workers, but many Russians who were only just comfortably off could afford to build, or at the very least rent, a small house for summer visits. Originally a term signifying 'gift' or 'portion', and meaning a parcel of land awarded by royalty to favoured courtiers (for example, Lanskaya-Villiamova, who was given land north of St Petersburg), the word 'dacha' had in the late eighteenth and early nineteenth centuries been applied to quite grand buildings (some of the early generation of dachas, two- and three-storeyed with outbuildings, can still

---

[76] Andreev, *Domovedenie* (1893), 31. Andreev, who stated that the main inspiration for his books came from Western manuals (p. i), also provided (p. 224) a list of about a dozen comparable Russian publications, of which I could track down only Antonov, *Obshchedostupnaya gigiena* (1889), and Al'medingen, *Na vsyakii sluchai!* (a book of handy hints on housekeeping and gardening).

[77] A detailed historical study of the dacha is given in Stephen Lovell's forthcoming book on the subject. On the late imperial era, see Chs. 3 and 4.

be seen in the Kamennyi Ostrov area of St Petersburg). As the dacha cult spread, however, humbler dwellings became available. In Turgenev's *First Love*, set in the 1840s, the narrator's family have rented an outbuilding which stands next to a wallpaper factory on the edge of the city. And a satirical poem published in *Satirikon* in 1909 purported to celebrate a dacha that was still less exclusive:

> Что за миленькая дача!
> «Тридцать в месяц» — очень рад.
> Справа лавка, слева прачка,
> В сажен сад.
>
> На купальню вид с балкона,
> Танцовальный близок круг,
> А из чайной граммофона
> Слышен звук.[78]

> What a pretty little dacha!
> 'Thirty for the month' Great! Done!
> Here a grocer's, there a laundry,
> Garden measures three by one.
>
> You can peer at the bathers from the balcony,
> The dance-hall's just across the way;
> The gramophone inside the tea-rooms
> Belts loud music out all day.

Some, at least, of the readers of *Satirikon* could afford to smile disdainfully at this; in the same year that the poem was published, the magazine was advertising two dachas at Terioki (now Zelenograd) with seven and ten rooms respectively, set in 80 desyatins of parkland, with a *banya*, fishing rights, a boat-jetty, and tennis courts (no rent specified, but clearly substantially more than 30 roubles a month).[79]

The very wide variety of different dachas naturally meant that, in practice, there was no one kind of 'dacha life'. Some dacha-dwellers were heirs to the old country estate tradition of perpetual idleness (*vechnaya prazdnost'*), lazing in hammocks or on the verandah all day, smoking, and drinking endless cups of tea (or consuming more decadent brews), or to the established upper-class tradition according to which the only exercise taken was climbing into a carriage to go visiting.[80] But for at least some summer

---

[78] 'A. R.', 'Dacha', *Satirikon* 14 (1909), front cover.

[79] *Satirikon* 25 (1909), 10.

[80] The earlier dacha life is described, for instance, in M. G. Nazimova's memoir 'Babushka Razumovskaya', *Istoricheskii vestnik* 75 (1899), 848: 'Life at the dacha was almost the same as in town: the landeau was put to at two in the afternoon, and then there was the usual round of visits till five, then a promenade to listen to a concert, at which more invitations were issued, this time to tea after the concert. The only difference was that at the dacha it was easier to ask people over than it was in the town.'

visitors, a stay at the *dacha* was treated as the British middle classes of the same generation treated a seaside holiday: as the opportunity for mental recovery through physical exercise. And by the 1900s, dachas had attracted their own 'hygienic' advice literature encouraging readers to see them in exactly this way. *How to Spend Your Summer at the Dacha* (1909) advises its readers to choose a well-ventilated spot on sandy soil, preferably on a slight rise, and certainly away from factories and other pollutant sources. Furniture should be simple (leather bags stuffed with hay were recommended instead of armchairs) and dress also (no corsets, dark jackets, or heavy hats). Diet should be plain, and consist mainly of vegetables. And there should be no lazing about: instead each day should be organized according to a specific plan, with plenty of exercise. After getting up at six, the *dachnik* should go for a walk, before consuming a light breakfast, after which some sedentary, but improving, occupation such as chess or reading would be permissible. More exercise was advised before lunch, and then, when a suitable space had elapsed to facilitate digestion, a bathe, preferably without the impediment of a swimming costume, was in order. The rest of the day might be spent engaging in relaxing activities such as walking, rowing, playing tennis, croquet, and skittles. The brochure concluded: 'In such a way, even if your means are not large, you may if you really wish spend your time profitably and pleasantly till autumn and return to town with plenty of energy and a sense that you have not spent your time in vain.'[81]

It is in the context of dacha life that Nordman's hygienic ideas are best understood. The house into which she and Repin had moved in the early 1900s, 'Penaty', was set in one of the most fashionable St Petersburg dacha settlements of the early twentieth century, Kuokkala in the Gulf of Finland.[82] While very much at the top end of the dacha hierarchy—an elaborate villa with a studio running the full length of the house, a spacious study, a drawing-room and a dining room—it was also a typical dacha, wooden, with a shingled roof, a large terrace for sitting out of doors, and an *uchastok* (stretch of wood) instead of a formal garden (albeit with pavilions in a sort of Finno-Russian-Red Indian style). The entire complex bespoke concern for healthy living. The situation of 'Penaty' is ideal for those who wish to lead a bracing existence. A five-minute stroll from the beach, it is shady and cooled by sea breezes even on the hottest summer day. In winter icy winds blow off the Baltic, and must have found out every crack in the

---

[81]   V-v, *Kak provodit' leto na dache* (1909), 21.

[82]   The popularity of woodland and seaside sites such as Kuokkala is itself an indication of the association of dachas with healthy living: early 19th-cent. dacha settlements, such as Kamennyi ostrov and the Karpovka river in St Petersburg, were much closer to the city centre and the houses were designed for elegance, rather than fresh air and the outdoor life.

wooden walls had the windows not been left open deliberately in order to let in the maximum of fresh air.

Not only the 'Penaty' site, but every aspect of the regime organized by Nordman there was in harmony with guides such as *How to Spend Your Summer at the Dacha*. To be sure, 'Penaty' was used all the year round, winter as well as summer, and so straw-stuffed armchairs would not have been practical. However, the furniture there was simple and functional: no malachite, no ormolu, and only the plainest of upholstery: days included bathing, walks, and (in winter) cross-country skiing. And at meals, healthy and simple dishes were set before guests. On 24 March 1910, for example, (before Nordman's conversion to a milkless diet), the following meal was served:

> Mixed appetisers [zakuski]
> Vermicelli
> Herb and curd cheese buns [*vatrushki*]
> Braised celery
> Cabbage
> Salad
> Ice cream
> Coffee[83]

Certainly, the fare was was anything but punitive, bearing out Nordman's own concern that rational diet should not necessarily involve only renunciation: 'Why should vegetarianism not make its entry into our lives triumphantly, with music, flowers, and wine?' she asked in *The Cookbook for the Hungry* (1). But the informality of the meal, with its lack of hierarchization into hors d'oeuvre, soup, main dish, and pudding, was striking, by contemporary standards; so, too, was its lack of richness (not a hint of the cream sauces and egg-enriched emulsions recommended by cookery writers of the 1900s, and listed on surviving menus of the day).

The regime at 'Penaty' drew not only on the resonance of the dacha as a place for healthy living, but also on its association with alternative forms of social organization. As *How to Spend Your Summer at the Dacha* advised its readers, 'At the dacha, more than anywhere else, it is possible to withdraw from fashion and etiquette; even eccentricities will be excused.'[84] In particular, by living at 'Penaty' rather than in St Petersburg, Nordman was able to give full rein to one of her main concerns: the desire to

[83] RGALI f. 1018, Arian, P. N., op. 1, ed. khr. 169, l. 4.
[84] *Kak provodit' leto na dache*, 15. Though Nordman and Repin lived at 'Penaty' throughout the year, Nordman definitely considered the place a 'dacha'; cf. a facetious postcard, 'Otkrytka dlya lentyaev', which she sent to Arian on 20 June 1911: of the various options to be ticked by the lazy postcard-writer, those Nordman selected included 'Dacha s protektsiei' as well as 'Pitaemsya senom' (RGALI f. 1018 op. 1 ed. khr. 169 l. 8 verso).

improve the lot of domestic servants. A regime of 'self-service' obtained at the house. Guests were greeted by a notice placed on a gong-stand which announced the specifities of the household with the abundant use of exclamation marks that was one of Nordman's favourite devices:

> SELF HELP
> Take your coat and galoshes off
> YOURSELF!
> Open the door into the dining room
> YOURSELF!
> Hit the Tam-Tam cheerfully and loudly
> YOURSELF!!!
> (see Fig. 10)[85]

In the dining-room, the table had been adapted so that dirty plates were slid into special shelves, while a revolving dish-stand allowed guests to help themselves, so that service at table was not required. The timetable of the house was also organized to be sparing in terms of servant labour. The main meal was served in the early afternoon, so that the cook-general could finish work at five on ordinary days; no live-in servants were employed.

'Penaty', then, was a model of 'rational housekeeping' not only in the sense that the house was clean, airy, and bare of superfluous decoration, but also because the regime there was designed to save on female labour. The arrangements reflected the important connection between 'rational house-keeping' and the feminist movement, the contemporary view that the performers of domestic labour were, in the words of Charlotte Gilman's Russian translator, 'the most wretched she-dilettantes, the Egyptian labour of whom is at best unhelpful to the cause of progress'.[86] And in her tracts, Nordman preached as she practised, while also eagerly emphasizing the moral superiority of vegetarianism. On the one hand, a diet free of meat and milk products had the attraction of avoiding the inhumane treatment of animals (in *Testaments of Paradise* (1913), she argued that the production of milk represented 'the profanation of motherhood', underlining the fact that feminist appreciations were at work here too). On the other, it made a direct contribution to the well-being of the poor. This was partly because it lightened the load of servants, whose 'disenserfment' (*raskreposhchenie*) was

---

[85] According to one affectionately deprecating account of Penaty, facetious exhortation did not stop at the front door. The painter V. V. Verevkina recorded that 'in a certain solitary place' [i.e. the lavatory], 'there was another poster with exclamation marks'. Slightly irritated by the constant nagging, Verevkina pencilled at the bottom of this some instructions of her own: 'Respect the solitude. Feel no regrets for the deeds you have committed'—to Repin's vast amusement. (See Grabar' and Zil'bershtein, *Repin*, ii. 196.)

[86] See Sh. Stetson-[Gil'man], *Ekonomicheskoe rabstvo zhenshchiny*, trans. M. Mamurovsky (Moscow, 1903), p. v. My thanks to Christine Holden for this reference.

Fig. 10. The hall at Penaty, Kuokkala (now Repino),
showing the self-service instructions and gong.

always a burning concern of Nordman's.[87] But it was also because self-restraint on the part of the rich meant that more food would be available for those living in penury. In *A Cookbook for the Hungry* (1913), and *Testaments of Paradise*, Nordman argued that, if the rich adopted a diet based on cooked vegetables, broth, bread, and sunflower or olive oil, the waste products not used in their kitchens (for instance, the outer leaves of cabbages, the peelings of potatoes, carrots, apples, and so on) could be collected at the kitchen door and then used to make nourishing vegetable

[87] See e.g. *Sleduet raskrepostit' prislugu! Posvyashchaetsya Kukharkam, Gornichnym i Lakeyam* (St Petersburg, 1911). On this subject, see further Catriona Kelly, 'Manners for the *menšaja bratija*: the case of Natalija Nordman', in G. Ritz, C. Binswanger, and C. Scheide (eds.), *Nowa świadomość płci v modernizmie* (Cracow, 2000).

stocks, which were wholesome and satisfying to the poor when boiled up with chopped vegetables and herbs to make *shchi* (cabbage soup), or borshch.

This informal recycling system was too much for some of Nordman's contemporaries, such as the staff of the St Petersburg humorous magazine *Satirikon*, which published a cartoon in 1910, 'A Brilliant Solution to the Famine Problem (According to Madame Nordman's System)'. It showed a pair of obese bourgeois straining to complete their vast dessert. One says to the other: 'It's a hard life, old chap! Don't forget it's Sunday tomorrow. If we want to treat the poor folks who are going to turn up at the kitchen door tomorrow wanting their fruit peel dessert, then we'd better eat another dozen or so pears, a couple of dozen apples, and half-a-dozen oranges' (Fig. 11). But if the *Satirikon* cartoon was an effective encapsulation of the failure of Nordman's preaching to convert the sceptical and cynical to her views, its appearance also indicates the extent of her notoreity.[88] And while her attempt to demonstrate the correlation between self-restraint and the well-being of the poor may have been zany in itself, the correlation itself was a central tenet of the Russian vegetarian movement. Self-betterment, it was held, should not simply contribute to individual well-being (which would have been a form of transmuted self-indulgence), but also to the common good. As S. P. Poltavsky put it, with magnificent tautology, in 1913, 'Personal self-perfection only has social value when the good of society at large is its goal.'[89] Accordingly, the extremely wide range of issues on the agenda for the Second Vegetarian Congress, held in 1914, included not only 'Vegetarianism and Hygiene', 'Vegetarianism and the Sex Question', 'The Practical Realization of Vegetarianism in One's Personal Life', and 'The Defence of Animals', but also 'Vegetarianism and Economics', 'Vegetarianism and Life Ideals', and 'Vegetarianism and the World in General'.[90]

---

[88] Few women writers were given the back-handed compliment of being pilloried in *Satirikon* or its successor, *Novyi Satirikon*: those who were included such very well-known figures as Anastasiya Verbitskaya, Anna Akhmatova, and Nordman's own 'sister' from the Znanie movement, Izabella Grinevskaya.

[89] S. P. Poltavsky, 'Imeet li lichnoe samosovershenstvovanie obshchestvennuyu tsennost'?', *Vegetarianskoe obozrenie* 2 (1913), 49–53.

[90] See *Vegetarianskii vestnik* 1 (1914), 3.

FIG. 11. 'A Brilliant Solution to the Famine Problem (According to Madame Nordman)'. Cartoon by Re-Mi (1910).

RATIONAL LIVING FOR 'THE RUSSIAN PEOPLE':
TOLSTOI AND NORDMAN

One characteristic concern of the Russian vegetarian movement was 'how to make the ideas and practice of vegetarianism accessible to the labouring classes' (discussion of this topic was scheduled to take place at the Second Vegetarian Congress, in the session under the title 'Vegetarianism and the World in General'). Indeed, for many Russian reformers of daily life, reshaping of the lives of the educated took second place behind a concern to better the lot of those at the bottom of society, who had suddenly emerged as a potential audience for advice literature. Here again, the pioneer and towering figure was Tolstoi, whose many pamphlets on vegetarianism for educated readers were accompanied by at least as many publications directed at workers and peasants. And here he displayed a knowledge of the market that would have done credit to any commercial publisher, beginning with his selection of one of the most popular genres for disseminating conduct guidance, the daily calendar, in order to propagandize his views. From the late 1880s, he published a whole series of almanacs in 'thought-for-the-day' style, including *A Calendar of Proverbs for 1887* (1886), *The Thoughts of Wise People for Every Day* (1903–4), and *For Every Day* (1909–10).[91] The publications (as their titles suggest) adopted the compilatory pattern familiar in advice literature since the eighteenth century, and manifested an equally traditional contempt for the integrity of original texts (thinkers as disparate as John Ruskin, St Francis of Assisi, Confucius, Marcus Aurelius, St Augustine, and Jeremy Bentham were plundered for quotations, and these pieced together into a moralizing text whose import would certainly have amazed and disconcerted some of those cited). The themes, too, included ones familiar in traditional advice literature—the need for truthfulness, modesty, serenity, tolerance—though with some Tolstoyan agitprop directed at the official Church and the wealthy alongside.[92]

The explicitly religious character of Tolstoi's guidance, which emanated from his idiosyncratic version of Christianity, a fusion of Orthodox sectarianism and Protestant fundamentalism, might seem at first sight to put him outside the scope of this book. In tracts such as *Think Again!* (1904, published in Russia in 1906), or *On Moral Education* (1909), Tolstoi's primary point was to emphasize the importance of belief above all else. In the former he contended that the ills of modern times were attributable to the fact that people live without 'true religion', which means not church observance, but 'the religion that fixes a man's relationship to God'; in the latter he argued that instruction in the answers offered by religious and moral thinkers to 'universal questions' was the only worthwhile kind of schooling that can be given.[93] Tolstoyanism was, then, a form of religiously coloured popular utopianism akin to *bezpopovshchina* (priestless Old Belief) that looked forward to a time when 'there will be no rich men, no landowners, no officials, no priests, no bishops. Or if

<hr/>

[91] *Kalendar' s poslovitsami na 1887 god* (PSS xl); *Mysli mudrykh lyudei na kazhdyi den' sobrany L. N. Tolstym* (PSS xl); *Na kazhdyi den'* (PSS xliii). A similar publication is *Nedel'noe chtenie*, see Tolstoi, *PSS* xlii.

[92] Some of the latter was, however, censored out of editions published in the Russian empire.

[93] Tolstoi, *Odumaites'!* (1906): *PSS* xxxvi. 122; *O vospitanii*, *PSS* xxxviii. 62–9.

there are, they will feed themselves and the people will suffer no oppression from them'.[94]

For all that, the brilliance of Tolstoi's work lay in the fact that, unlike official Orthodox or indeed sectarian advice literature, it proposed a detailed model of behaviour in the secular world.[95] Rather than branding 'the world' as inherently sinful, to be recuperated by religious experience only in a transformative or redemptive sense (because the transcendence of sin is the fundament of theological enlightenment and higher wisdom), Tolstoyan doctrine saw appropriate behaviour in this world as the foundation of true virtue. *How Can Working People Free Themselves? A Letter to Peasants* (1906) is a systematic (indeed relentlessly systematic) explication of the abstract commandments of the Old and New Testaments in order to produce detailed rules for everyday life:

'Thou shalt not kill.'
   This means: it is not only forbidden to kill, but to quarrel, to swear, to bear ill will against each other. . . .
'Thou shalt not commit adultery.'
   This means not only that you must not engage in debauchery, but you must live honestly [*chestno*], one man with one wife, one wife with one husband, and avoid all that inflames lust. . . .
   'Do not bear false witness'.
   This means: do not give your word in a court of law, or to swear fealty to the Tsar, or to undergo military service.[96]

What is more, Tolstoi's tracts also offered advice on practical matters, such as the fact that land held in common ownership should be worked according to the allotment system.[97] And Tolstoi's combination of a suspicion of Western capitalism with a reconfiguration of the Enlightenment code of rational behaviour (hygiene, self-restraint, egalitarian social interaction) led him to an all-out assault on traditional behaviour, with its residue of (in his eyes) unthinking superstition and unquestioning reverence for extant practice. This assault was as characteristic of left radicalism in the 1890s and 1900s as his celebration of *byt* had been typical of Slavophile conservatives in the 1850s, 1860s, and 1870s.

The most interesting of his calendars, *A Calendar of Proverbs*, included not only the promised selection of proverbs, but also agricultural advice (hints

[94] Tolstoi, *Kak osvobodit'sya rabochemu narodu? Pis'mo k krest'yaninu* (1909), PSS xc. 69–76.
[95] Contrast e.g. Anon., *Kak zhit' po Evangeliyu* (1905), a collection of scriptural quotations ('Self-love is an indication of want of faith', 106, etc.). Some advice on secular behaviour is contained in Old Believer publications such as Karabinovich, *Kratkoe khristianskoe uchenie*, e.g. on the need to wear 'Christian, Old Russian, long [clothes]', but there is nothing, say, on conduct in daily business.
[96] Tolstoi, *Kak osvobodit'sya*, PSS xc. 70–1.
[97] Tolstoi, *Gde vykhod?*, PSS xxxiv. 127.

on the work timetable for each month, given under 'Raboty v mae', etc.),
and a section assaulting traditional peasant rituals and beliefs. The custom
according to which women did not work on Fridays out of reverence for
St Paraskeva was attacked as 'meaningless [*pustoe*]. Friday is a day in the
week and nothing more' (*PSS* xl. 13). Of Shrovetide, Tolstoi observed,
'Why eat pancakes and drink vodka for a week?' (*PSS* xl. 18). Other
customs attacked included witchcraft (*PSS* xl. 32–3), expensive weddings
('spending 50 roubles on drink and getting the whole village drunk . . .
playing fanfares on washtubs [*v tazy bit'*], tossing the young couple in the
air [*molodykh klast' i podnimat'*], baking karavai loaves [*karavai podnimat'*]—
that's a pagan wedding, and very disgusting too' (*PSS* xl. 55–6) and
drunken Christmases (Christ should be commemorated with 'humility,
purity, and good deeds', *PSS* xl. 66). Though Tolstoi's critique of village
life was based, he claimed, upon the dictates of 'true Christianity', the
calendar was otherwise a striking prefiguration of the materials that would
be issued by Soviet propagandists in the 1920s and 1930s. Tolstoi does not
use the term 'cultured' (*kul'turnyi*), but his emphasis on industriousness and
rational leisure (work in September includes 'reading', *PSS* xl. 51) was
replicated in the Soviet *kul'turnost'* ethos, for which these were the primary
requirements.[98]

But Tolstoi was hindered from reaching the mass reader of his own day
by obstacles not of his own making: the tsarist censorship suppressed
many of his advice pamphlets, for example *What is the Way Out?*, or *How
Should Working People Liberate Themselves?*, which could circulate freely in
Russia only after the Revolution (the latter pamphlet was reprinted ten
times between 1917 and 1919).[99] Others were allowed to be published
only in those of Tolstoi's books that were beyond the pockets of the
common people, such as the various editions of his *Collected Works*.[100] So
far as the 'mass reader' went, perhaps most widely disseminated in
Tolstoi's time were his didactic tales, which adopted apparently innocent
forms, such as the folk tale, in order to convey their message. A notable
contribution to this kind of 'fictionalized conduct literature' was *What
People Live By*. This fable of great limpidity and beauty about an angel
punished for his transgression by being sent to earth, and spending some

---

[98] See Ch. 4 below.

[99] See *PSS* xc. 376–7. Even as late as 1929, Tolstoyanism required denunciation to the Soviet
mass reader as 'the banner of kulaks and nepmen, the replacement of clear class slogans by foggy
statements about humanity in a general sense' (V. Aramilev, *Tolstovstvo i etika rabochego klassa*
(Moscow, 1929), 80), a clear indication of its continuing popularity. This does not of course
mean that Tolstoi reached no working-class readers before the Revolution (his reception by these
will be discussed below).

[100] E.g. *Odumaites'!* appeared in vol. xix of the 12th edn. of Tolstoi's *Sobranie sochinenii* (see
commentaries to *PSS* xxxvi).

years living in the family of a poor cobbler, appeared in the children's magazine *Detskii otdykh* (Children's Leisure) in 1881 before being brought out by the popular publishing house Posrednik (The Intermediary) in 1885.[101]

The restricted circulation of his writings is one reason why Tolstoi (for all the centrality of his ideas to Russian intellectual culture) was not the most typical of populist advice-literature authors. Other reasons included the fact that he (like Nataliya Nordman) was an enthusiastic amateur without ties to official post-reform organizations such as the *zemstvo* (in late Imperial Russia, it was increasingly common for writers to have a position in some official body).[102] But the most idiosyncratic feature about Tolstoi was his mistrust of education in an intellectual sense, his vehemently expressed conviction that intellectual self-improvement was a mere distraction from the true task in hand, moral self-perfection. In 'On Education', he asserted, 'the most educated people are those that in reality are the most ignorant', and attributed this to the neglect of 'the most important subject of education, without which there can be no sensible acquisition of knowledge of any kind': that is, the 'answers' that have been provided by 'wise men' to 'the questions that ineluctably stand before everyman: one, what am I . . . and two, how am I to live in accordance with my view of the world?'[103] This attitude had become marginal even among conservatives by the late nineteenth century; it was certainly totally out of step with the views of liberals and radicals, who were in turn the most assiduous composers of 'alternative' advice literature aimed at the lower classes.

Of these, by far the most influential was N. A. Rubakin. Rubakin was himself the end result of a prolonged, intensive, and stunningly successful campaign of self-education. Born into an Old Believer family straight out of one of Ostrovsky's plays, he had removed himself from school as an adolescent and prepared single-handedly for the university examinations, which he then passed with flying colours before graduating simultaneously, and *summa cum laude*, from two faculties—History and Philology, and

[101] On Posrednik see Ruud, *Russian Entrepreneur*, 30–4. Tolstoi's involvement had more or less ceased by 1888, and in 1892, Ivan Sytin was forced to stop placing his powerful distributive network at the aid of the publishing house. On the currency of *What People Live By*, see e.g. R. E. Johnson, *Peasant and Proletarian: The Working Class of Moscow in the Late Nineteenth Century* (Leicester, 1979), 187 n. 41, referring to a copy found in a house search upon left radicals in 1894.

[102] More typical figures include Ekaterina Averkieva, née Sorokina (1852–?), a professional gardener and wife of the chairman of the *zemskaya uprava* in Klin District, whose publications include a series of 'practical hints on market-gardening'. (See Vengerov, *Russkie knigi*, i. 30–1.)

[103] *PSS* xxxviii. 65–6. Cf. Tolstoi's evident contempt, in 'Master and Man', for the son of a peasant household who prides himself on reading 'Pul'son' (i.e. I. I. Paul'son (1825–98), autodidactic son of a tailor and author of numerous basic grammars and of a reading-book for beginning readers).

Mathematics and Physics. His fiction for beginning readers had a huge readership among Russian peasants and workers, but it was his non-fictional treatises, such as *Letters to Readers on Self-Education*, which propagandized the rationale and methodology of self-education to others like himself. Asserting, 'Anyone who wants to can turn himself into a person who is educated in the genuine sense,' he offered readers an intellectually ambitious programme reflecting the concerns, and literary tastes, of the left intelligentsia in the 1900s: from Chernyshevsky to Kropotkin, from Byron to Goethe, from Bebel to George Sand, as well as one or two more idiosyncratic choices, such as Pascal and the religious works of Tolstoi.[104]

While encouraging readers to develop their own interests (he distinguished between 'intuitive, deductive, concrete, abstract, speculative and practical' types of personality), Rubakin was by no means permissive in his prescriptions for self-betterment in other respects.[105] He was careful to distinguish 'true education' from self-improvement in a material sense:

A genuinely educated person is not someone who considers himself 'educated'. Even illiterate shop-assistants and *uryadniki* [minor officials in the rural police force] and many of the kind of people who have the resources to buy themselves 'German [i.e. Western] clothes' and so be accounted part of the 'refined public' [*chistaya publika*]—even people of that kind consider themselves 'educated', though their minds are about as enlightened as a pitch-dark tunnel.[106]

Rubakin's use of the term *intelligentnyi* as an alternative to *obrazovannyi* points to his concept of education's goal: to become a member of the intelligentsia, someone of broad knowledge and high ideals: 'A member of the intelligentsia [*intelligentnyi chelovek*] is someone who knows and understands life, how life works, what it requires; knows and understands it so well that at any moment he can truly express all that life means.' (p. 41) In itself, this definition was so vague as to be almost meaningless, but by distinguishing the *intelligentnyi chelovek* from the 'narrow specialist' and the 'careerist', Rubakin clearly conveyed that education should not be employed simply in order to further one's own success.

---

[104] N. A. Rubakin, *Pis'ma k chitatelyam o samoobrazovanii* (1913): quotation p. 28. Other works by Rubakin with reading lists include *Praktika samoobrazovaniya* (1914) and the bibliography *Sredi knig* (3rd edn., 3 vols., Moscow, 1911). Cf. A. V. Panov, *Domashnie biblioteki* (1903). On the background to the work of such didactic bibliographers as Rubakin, see Mary Stuart, '"The Ennobling Illusion": The Public Library Movement in Late Imperial Russia', *SEER* 76 (1998), 401–40.

[105] Cf. Stuart, '"The Ennobling Illusion"', 425: 'The educated élite and the government shared a belief that the lower classes could not be left to their own devices and certainly could not be allowed to choose their own reading matter.' This 'culturalism' on the part of the intelligentsia is extensively analysed in Brooks, *When Russia Learned to Read*.

[106] Rubakin, *Pis'ma k chitatelyam*, 161–5, 39.

Rubakin's resolutely anti-consumerist, and anti-functionalist, view of self-betterment was typical of intellectual Russian populists, who, on the whole, saw the encroachment of capitalism as necessarily threatening the integrity of culture, and believed that peasants and workers who displayed an interest in acquisitions, such as fashionable 'German' dress, had tumbled over the boundary into the despised *meshchanstvo*. Similarly, intellectual magazines such as *Satirikon* mocked excessive politeness as a trait characteristic of the *meshchanstvo* (an example is a cartoon by A. Yakovlev in which a shop assistant asks a customer, 'And just where would the gracious lady be pleased to have her honourable little vest delivered?'), and it is impossible to imagine commentators such as Tolstoi or Rubakin lowering themselves to offer advice on etiquette. It was generally left to foreign writers to propound refinement as a synthesis of extensive reading and good manners. The author of a manual translated from the English in 1912 argued that 'the essence of character' (in a positive sense) lay not only in 'kindness, renunciation of self, considerateness and self-control, but also refined manners, *bon ton*'.[107]

There were, though, occasional Russian writers who saw what was now known as *kul'turnost'*, 'the cultured life', in broader terms than the devouring of book-lists. Here again, Nataliya Nordman is an idiosyncratic but characteristic figure. In *Testaments of Paradise*, she described parasites such as bedbugs, allegedly unknown in the vegetarian household, as 'the left-overs of a savage and uncultured lifestyle' [*dikoi, nekul'turnoi zhizni*],[108] thus indicating that for her, cleanliness was as important a trait of 'culturedness' as was reading or visiting the theatre. And in her writings for the lower classes, she combined a Russian emphasis on education with a stress on cultivation of the self in a broader sense that was more characteristic of British or American advice literature of the day.

A model contract for servants drawn up by Nordman in 1913, for instance, was not solely concerned with welfare in a material sense (hours to be worked and wages to be paid), though the details of these were specified.[109] It was also intended to help the servant regard her labour as that of a free labourer rather than a serf:

---

[107] Klauston, *Gigiena uma*, 125. for the Yakovlev cartoon, see *Satirikon* 22 (1911), 4.

[108] *Raiskie zavety*, 29.

[109] Fifteen roubles was a reasonably generous salary even for a servant who did not have a guaranteed eight-hour working day, and the payment of overtime to servants was very unusual (servants were normally expected to work such hours as the employer chose to specify from day to day, all for the basic salary). On servant wages and work conditions generally, see A. Rustemeyer, *Dienstboten in Petersburg und Moskau, 1861–1917* (Stuttgart, 1996), 118–34. S. Voskresenskaya, *Drug khozyaiki* (St Petersburg, 1909), bk. 8, sect. ix, sets out a 'typical' family budget of 3,600 roubles disposable income, of which 144 roubles is anticipated to be spent on the 'servants' (while travel, gifts, newspapers and books total 250 roubles).

I, Nataliya Borisovna Nordman and you, Avdot'ya Fedorovna Zinina, put our hands by mutual agreement to the following contract:

I, N. B. Nordman, will pay you 15 roubles a month for an eight-hour working day, with four completely free days a month, two Fridays and two Sundays. In return you are obliged to carry out all the housework: cooking, ironing, tidying the rooms, sewing, darning, cleaning, trimming, and filling the lamps, fetching the shopping, and so on and so on.

The normal hours of your working day will be 8 till 5, excluding time spent having breakfast and lunch. However, these hours can be altered by mutual consent, so that you, Avdot'ya Fedorovna, have the morning free, especially during the bathing season.

For every guest who visits you will receive 10 kopecks.

For every extra hour of work over and above the ordinary load, you will receive 10 kopecks.

For every mouse caught and released into freedom outdoors in the fields, you will receive 10 kopecks.

With the exception of towels [aprons has been crossed out], you will supply all your clothes.

We will provide you with a vegetarian breakfast and tea, and a vegetarian lunch at three pm. You can have breakfast and lunch with us or on your own, as you wish. After work you will go back to your own home, into your own personal life [*lichnaya zhizn'*] and interests.

You have the right to make use of our newspapers, magazines and books and also our medicine chest.

On Wednesday, our 'at home' day [*priemnyi den'*], from 5 p.m. in the evening you will be treated as our guest and we will invite you to have dinner with us and spend the evening with us.

You, Avdot'ya Fedorovna, are obliged to carry out your tasks energetically and joyfully [*bodro i radostno*]; if you should ever wish to leave your employment for some family reason, you are obliged to give me due notice so that you are able to train a new person to take over your employment.

With mutual respect for each other's rights and duties, before two witnesses we sign our names hereto,

Penaty, 1913, Kuokkala.[110]

The wording of the contract is significant. In some respects, it propounds traditional populist notions, placing the self-improvement of the servant under the control of the employer. There is no space in this contract for an employee whose idea of spending a free moment was to lounge about with a doughnut and a penny dreadful, or whose idea of self-improvement was to save money and then buy her way out of service altogether: there is a distinctly coercive ring to the reference to free mornings 'especially during the bathing season', and 'the right to make use of our newspapers,

[110] RGALI, f. 1018 Arian, P. N. op. 1 ed. khr. 169 l. 22. The contract was also published in *Zhenshchina* 7 (1914), 30–1, and in *Vegetarianskoe obozrenie* 9 (1913), 357–9.

magazines and books'. In this sense, Nordman's contract for her servants bears out Angela Rustemeyer's assertion that wealthy Russian servant employers who were concerned for their servants' well-being 'aimed at the creation of a personal utopia in microcosm'.[111] Yet at the same time, there is some concern for the personal autonomy of the servant. Nordman's wage structure was designed to avoid the need for the servant to expect tips from visitors, and she carefully avoided using the term *rabota* (derived from *rab*, 'slave') to refer to the servant's employment, and instead emphasized the dignity of domestic labour by naming it as *delo* and *trud*. Where contemporary legislation and formulae for writing letters of recommendation still stressed the old patriarchal requirement of servants that they be 'loyal' (*vernye*),[112] she required 'efficiency' from her employee (even if the more elusive, and intrusive, requirement of 'good humour' was also made). Her statement that, after work, the servant was to return to 'her own personal life and interests' departed from the traditional perception of employees as members of the family, and encouraged the servant to perceive her own existence as autonomous and separate, independent of that of her employers. The contract, then, is a paradoxical document, at once placing servants' behaviour under the control of employers, and encouraging servants to break free from that control. To borrow the equally contradictory formulation used by Nordman in the address to employers that accompanied her contract, mistresses were supposed to 'pour into their [the servants'] souls the delights of a personal life'.[113] The ambiguity of the formulation, representing the servant as at once passive and potentially autonomous, reflected Nordman's double status as mistress of 'Penaty'. On the one hand she was very much the salon hostess in the early twentieth-century manifestation of the role, holding court in the *gostinaya* (drawing-room) where she also kept her writing-desk. But on the other, she organized other, more unusual, parties at 'Penaty', cross-class festivals at which servants, baronesses, industrialists, peasants, and factory workers jointly participated in improvised carnivals of spontaneous entertainment: 'The cook brings her lady [*barynya*] along, the lady brings her maid. A philosopher and his laundress together carry the poles of a huge banner celebrating cooperation. . . . All is still and quiet,

---

[111] Rustemeyer, *Dienstboten in Petersburg und Moskau*, 196.

[112] The legal requirements of servants even in the late imperial era were that they be 'faithful, obedient, and respectful' (*vernye, poslushnye i pochtitel'nye*) to their employers, and the typical reference formula was 'so and so has carried out his/her tasks zealously and honestly [*s userdiem i chestno*], and has behaved with fidelity and sobriety [*vel sebya verno i trezvo*]'. See D. Mordukhai-Boltovsky, *Svod zakonov Rossiiskoi Imperii* (St Petersburg, 1912), x. 165–6, and Sazonov and Bel'sky (comp.), *Russkii pis'movnik* (1890), 340.

[113] RGALI, f. 1018 Arian P. op. 1 ed. khr. 169 l. 17. See also *Zhenshchina* 7 (1914), 30, and *Vegetarianskoe obozrenie* 9 (1913), 357.

but for the words of love and respect for work and freedom [*trud i svoboda*].'[114]

Another product of Nordman's mixture of condescension and genuine concern to inculcate self-respect in working people was her etiquette book for the working-class reader, *To My Dear Brothers and Sisters (Instead of a Governess)* (1913).[115] The book represented an extraordinarily interesting foray by a Russian intellectual into the new world of mass-market publications. It stood somewhere between Tolstoi's use of popular advice literature, such as the annotated calendar, to propagandize his beliefs[116] and the mainstream tradition of the etiquette manual. Much of the advice in the book repeated the commonplaces of etiquette books from the late eighteenth century onwards. Don't stick your hands in your pockets, whistle or snigger in public; greet your host and hostess first, then the oldest people in the room. Don't belch during meals, or put your elbows on the table; use a napkin to wipe your moustache, not your hand; spit in your handkerchief, not on the pavement. Naturally, Nordman also pays tribute to the novel elements in etiquette literature of her time. For instance, she provides meticulous guidance on the need for personal cleanliness. Before visiting, one should, if possible, visit the bathhouse or, failing that, have a wash and put on clean underwear (this is especially important for working people who may sweat a lot). Clean skin, clean teeth and clean nails are essential when visiting ('You must ensure that no bad smell comes from anywhere'). Two clean handkerchiefs should be taken along: 'One becomes hot with shame when a person drags out from his or her pocket a handkerchief that has turned into a crumpled tatter, or worse still, one that has become brown in colour' (p. 6). Clothes are to be treated carefully, hung on hangers when not in use and kept away from kitchen fumes and damp.[117] Also characteristic of her age was Nordman's recognition of the need to give guidance on how to behave on public transport. Rather optimistically, she instructed her readers that they should never push into a crowded tram or argue with the conductor, and that they

[114] N. B. Severova[-Nordman], 'Kooperativnye voskresen'ya Narodnogo Sobraniya v "Penatakh"', in her *Intimnye stranitsy* (St Petersburg, 1910), 183–4.

[115] *Dorogim sestritsam i tovarishcham.* The book was privately printed, and seems to have been distributed by Nordman herself, no doubt at her lectures, and to the domestic staffs in her own and her acquaintances' houses. All references to this edition in text.

[116] *Kalendar' s poslovitsami na 1887 god*, *PSS* xl; *Mysli mudrykh lyudei na kazhdyi den'*, *sobrany L. N. Tolstym*, *PSS* xl; *Na kazhdyi den': Uchenie o zhizni izlozhennoe v izrecheniyakh*, *PSS* xliii, xliv. See above for a discussion of these.

[117] Earlier behaviour books had provided very general instructions on the need for cleanliness—for example, Anon., *Pravila uchtivosti* (1779), had ordered that it was quite improper to bite one's nails, blow one's nose without a handkerchief or inspect the contents thereof, but this advice occupies only an insignificant part of a treatise that is above all concerned with gesture: not wrinkling one's face, not gesticulating in conversation, not fiddling, the doffing of hats, etc.

should give up their places to elderly ladies and to invalids.[118] But perhaps the most important novelty was advice on polite speech. Nordman informed her readers that a good upbringing gave one the confidence 'not to make scandals', and to learn to stop using 'strong expressions, coarse language, and curses'. She also suggested using the genteelism *kushat'* when speaking to or of others (rather than the plain *ya em,* said of oneself).[119] To be sure, this was nothing compared with the lists given in, say, *The Rules of Social Life and Etiquette: Bon Ton* (1889), whose long list of forbidden phrases included *beremenna* (pregnant: the correct term was 'v interesnom polozhenii', 'in an interesting condition'), *chugunka* (a colloquial term for the railway), *kozyryat'* (to salute or to show off), *admiral'sky chas* ('the admiral's hour', a colloquial term for a midday drinking session), *lebezit'* (to butter someone up), and a host of others.[120] But it was new compared with the conduct literature of earlier generations.[121]

While all of this could be matched in other conduct treatises of the day, Nordman differed from most other Russian etiquette regulators in explicitly anticipating a reader who had spent 'half a life in someone else's kitchen, next to a boiler or in a stuffy izba with flies and cockroaches' (p. 1), and in encouraging that reader to see *samovospitanie,* 'self-education in manners', as a means to self-respect. Her Rule Number One was that behaviour should be no respecter of hierarchies: 'If you are always the same [*raven*] with everyone, you will not get muddled and you will never offend anyone' (p. 4). Self-respect should be inherent not only in a person's address to others, but also in his or her dress. It is vital, Nordman argues, to

---

[118] On etiquette for public transport users, cf. Brodersen, *Khoroshii ton,* 107, which advises readers not to sprawl about train carriages or put their feet on the seats; Svetozarskaya, *Zhizn' v svete,* 139, tells men that they may keep their hats on *na omnibuse.* Public transport etiquette was also the subject of cartoons in *Satirikon* and *Novyi Satirikon:* for an example, see Fig. 12. For similar advice to Nordman's in a Western book, see Anon., *Complete Etiquette for Ladies and Gentlemen: A Guide to the Rules and Observances of Good Society* (London, 1900), section for 'gentlemen', p. 47: 'It is hardly necessary to add that, while legally a man has no call to do so, yet the commonest courtesy would prompt anyone possessed of a particle of manliness to offer his seat to a woman, if he saw her compelled to stand.' By the early 20th cent., a more egalitarian attitude was evident than in earlier books, such as *Zhiteiskaya mudrost'* (1871), which was particularly concerned with the fact that 'railways and steam-boats unite on a single bench persons of different social estates and of different levels of education' (p. II). On the shock effect of the railways for mid-19th cent. aristocrats used to travelling in their own carriages, cf. E. N. Trubetskoi's account of his grandfather: *Iz proshlogo: Vospominaniya. Iz putevykh zametok* (Newtonville, Tenn., 1976), 19.

[119] N. B. Severova-Nordman, *Dorogim sestritsam i tovarishcham. 'Zamesto guvernantki'* (St Petersburg, 1913), 4, 6.

[120] *Pravila svetskoi zhizni i etiketa,* 134, 149.

[121] E.g. Sokolov, *Svetskii chelovek* (1847), does not include any advice on language for its reader of 'middling society', while the translated *Pravila svetskogo etiketa dlya muzhchin* (1873), contains only a very general warning against slang (*argo,* p. 19). 18th-cent. conduct literature instructed readers to avoid locutions that might be perceived as impertinent (see Ch. 1), but otherwise left the subject of language alone.

FIG. 12. How not to behave on public transport:
cartoon by Nathan Altman, 1916. The dialogue
reads: 'Young lady, are you tired?' 'Yes, yes,
exhausted!' 'Well, change hands then!'

have a set of special clothes for Sundays and holidays. 'Abroad, especially in
America and Switzerland, you would never recognize a poor person or a
workman on a festival day. They're clean-shaven and spotlessly clean, and
their clothes look as if they came straight out of a bandbox.' (p. 6). At the
end of the pamphlet, she emphasized that 'dignity', 'self-respect', the
striving towards 'ideals' and 'perfection' were more important than mere
outward *vospitannost'*; but in fact her model for appropriate behaviour laid
some emphasis on the latter as well.

Whence, though, did Nordman derive this unusual set of concerns?
Very evidently, her writings for the educated public owed much to
Tolstoi, the inspiration of her commitment to vegetarianism, if hardly of
her desire to see meatless meals piped in with trumpet fanfares and washed
down with wine. But her tracts for a popular audience, with their strictures

on clean handkerchiefs and the advantages of Sunday best, have nothing in common with Tolstoi's writings. Rather, their sources seem to lie in Western tradition: on the one hand in a formative visit made by Nordman to America as a young woman, where she had herself worked as a servant and been struck by the egalitarianism with which she was treated,[122] and on the other, in the work of Western ideologues of self-improvement such as Samuel Smiles.

Smiles was a mid-nineteenth-century British publisher and prolific author of guides to self-betterment that popularized the views of rational and utilitarian philosophers in Britain, across Europe, in the Middle East, and in Japan.[123] His works were immensely successful in Russia: *Self-Help* had at least seventeen Russian editions between 1866 and 1914 (under various titles and in various translations). *Character* was issued at least eleven times from 1872 to 1909; there were six editions of *Duty* between 1882 and 1914, and even the relatively unpopular *Thrift* managed three editions between 1876 and 1905. Other books by Smiles that got translated included *The Life of the Scottish Naturalist Thomas Edward*, which was issued ten times between 1877 and 1917; and also *Lives of the Engineers*, translated into Russian in 1870 as *Heroes of Labour* (this seems to be the earliest usage in Russia of what was later to become a classic Soviet collocation).[124]

In the many countries where he was read, including Russia, Smiles was an influential popularizer of self-education, and of the ideology of 'nature's gentleman', the 'self-made man' who attained his social position by application and upright character rather than by birth: '[The Gentleman's] qualities depend not upon fashion or manners, but upon moral worth—not

---

[122] This experience is described in Nordman-(Severova), *Eta* (St Petersburg, 1901), 242–77.

[123] See A. Jarvis, *Samuel Smiles and the Construction of Victorian Values* (Stroud, 1997); Tim Travers, *Samuel Smiles and the Victorian Work Ethic* (New York, 1987); Asa Briggs, introduction to Smiles, *Self-Help, with Illustrations of Conduct and Perseverance* (London, 1958), 7–35. On Smiles's popularity in Japan, see Travers, *Samuel Smiles*, 43–4; in Egypt, where quotations from 'Smeelis' were even used to direct the Khedive's Palace, see Briggs, *Self-Help*, 7. As is pointed out by A. St George, *The Descent of Manners: Etiquette, Rules and the Victorians* (London, 1993), 12, the books of Martin Tupper were more popular than those of Smiles in America; but so far as I have been able to establish from library catalogues, these do not seem to have reached Russia. Slightly better known were the works of William Channing (whose *O samovospitanii* appeared once, in 1912).

[124] *Self-Help* was issued as *Samodeyatel'nost'* in 1866 (twice), 1867, 1868, 1872, 1875, 1881, 1902, *c.*1907, 1914; as *Samopomoshch'* (Khar'kov, 1867); as *Samorazvitie umstvennoe* in 1895, 1900, 1901, 1910; as *Samostoyatel'naya deyatel'nost'* in 1882 (twice). *Character* appeared as *Kharakter* in 1872 (twice), 1873, 1874, 1880, 1882, 1883, 1889, 1895, 1900, and 1909; *Thrift*, under the title *Berezhlivost'*, in 1876, 1905, and as *Raschetlivost'* in 1876; *Duty* came out as *Dolg* in 1882, 1893, 1901, 1904, 1914 (twice); *The Life of the Scottish Naturalist Thomas Edward*, as *Vechnyi truzhenik: zhizneopisanie shotlandskogo naturalista Tomasa Eduarda* in 1877, 1888, 1898, 1911; as *Zamechatel'nyi rabotnik. Zhizn' i priklyucheniya shotlandskogo naturalista-bashmachnika Tomas Eduarda*, 1877, 1879, 1914; as *Neumolimyi rabotnik Tomas Eduard*, 1911; as *Neumolimyi truzhenik*, 1877; as *Neumolimyi truzhenik Tomas*, 1879. *Lives of the Engineers* as *Geroi truda: Istoriya chetyrekh angliiskikh rabotnikov*, in 1870, 1902; as *Zhizn' i trud: kharakteristika velikikh lyudei*, 1904, 1915; as *Trud i ego geroi*, 1901.

on personal possessions, but on personal qualities.'[125] Smiles argued that 'even the humblest person, who sets before his fellows an example of industry, sobriety, and upright honesty of purpose in life, has a present as well as future influence upon the well-being of his country' (*Self-Help*, p. 5). He emphasized the importance of directed reading: 'Reading for pleasure is a distraction and corruption' (*Self-Help*, p. 325). But at the same time, Smiles also underlined the importance of etiquette by including in *Self-Help* a section on how to behave, while distinguishing between 'true manners' and 'genteel' pretension, in much the same way that Nordman had between *vospitannost'* and *dostoinstvo*: 'There is a dreadful ambition abroad for being "genteel". We keep up appearances, too often at the expense of honesty; and, though we may not be rich, yet we must seem to be so. We must be 'respectable', though only in the meanest sense—in mere outward show' (*Self-Help*, p. 301).

That Nordman was convinced of Smiles's efficacy as a source of advice is indicated by a passage in *That One*, in which a formidably determined young German woman, Karolina, reveals that she has learned music 'from Smiles's *Self-Help*. It is only in your [i.e. privileged] social environment that you think one has to have teachers to ram knowledge by force into your passive brains.'[126] For all that, though, her standpoint in her discussion of behaviour was in some respects quite different to Smiles's. As an advice author, she emphasized her access to privilege, to the live 'governess' whose tuition on manners her book was supposed to replace. Similarly, the 'cooperation' that was celebrated at the 'Penaty' festivals had little to do with the 'Rochdale Movement' of co-operative trading partnerships, which began to have a not inconsiderable following in late imperial Russia.[127] What Nordman had in mind was a reinterpretation of traditional gentry philanthropy, in which the socially advantaged shared some of their worldly goods with those less fortunate than themselves. She makes this particularly clear in her article 'Women Traders' (1913), which suggests that the appalling conditions in which small traders selling house-to-house were forced to labour could be ameliorated if their customers changed their own habits. Purchasers of vegetables, berries, and other items peddled at the door should refuse to buy on a Sunday (hence, according to Nordman, allowing the traders a day off); they should club together in neighbour-hoods, and buy handcarts so that the women traders could transport their goods more easily; they should press for legal changes at the Duma, in

[125] Smiles, *Self-Help, with Illustrations of Character, Conduct and Perserverance* (London, 1866), p. 398. Citations henceforth in text as *Self-Help*.

[126] See Nordman, *Eta*, 74.

[127] On the Rochdale movement, see Kheisin, *Chto takoe potrebitel'skoe obshchestvo i kakaya ot nego pol'za* (1916).

order to protect street traders from exploitation by middle-men [*nanima-teli*]; and they should take care to treat women street traders 'kindly' [*laskovo*], and always offer them a cup of hot soup if they called at lunchtime.[128] Here, as in many of her writings, Nordman pushed to extremes attitudes characteristic of the campaign to *vospityvat' narod* (educate the people) on the part of the Russian intelligentsia as a whole. An egalitarian ideal was propagandized in a manner that underlined the enormous gulf between the disseminator of *kul'turnost'* and his or her audience.

To be sure, pre-First World War Russian society was less 'exquisitely graded according to a hierarchy of ranks' than British society of the same period, where 'the clergyman's widow, in reduced circumstances, would not make friends with the elementary school teacher, though she might have her round to tea . . . the academic in cap and gown would hardly mix with the shirt-sleeved, chain-smoking journalist'.[129] A liberal landowner's daughter (to name someone with approximately the same social status as a 'clergyman's widow', a category of person with a totally different resonance in Russia), was far more likely to associate with the 'elementary school teacher' than his or her counterpart in Britain. A Russian Jude the Obscure would not have been treated with the crushing hauteur shown to Hardy's protagonist by the Oxford academic with whom he tried to make contact. But at the same time, the inaccessibility of elementary education in Russia meant that the structures by which the disadvantaged bettered themselves, such as the 'Sunday Schools', or indeed Nordman's own series of popular lectures, were quite different in character from the organizations where Smiles had made his name, such as the 'Mechanics' Institutes' of Northern England. Rather than groups that had sprung from *within* the working class, they were philanthropic endeavours organized by privileged outsiders. And because the community of the educated was dominated (to a far greater extent than in Britain, France, or Germany) by members of the socio-economic elite, those who entered it from outside were expected to adjust their patterns of behaviour to fit dominant modes. Vulgar manners grated on refined sensibilities just as much in Russia as they did elsewhere in Europe, and the gentle but implacable correction of Natasha by Ol'ga, Masha, and Irina in the early scenes of *Three Sisters* illustrates the confidence that Russian gentlewomen and gentlemen felt in imposing their own standards of behaviour upon those whom they admitted to their houses.

---

[128] Severova[-Nordman], 'O torgovkakh', *Raiskie zavety*, 52–5; on gentry philanthropy at this period, see A. Lindenmeyr, *Poverty is not a vice: Charity, Society, and the State in Imperial Russia* (Princeton, 1996), ch. 9.

[129] See Raphael Samuel, *Theatres of Memory*, ii (*Island Stories: Unravelling Britain*) (London, 1998), 256.

THE RECEPTION OF ADVICE LITERATURE:
A CASE-STUDY OF SELF-HELP TEXTS

As has become clear, between 1880 and 1917 a very wide variety of material was published under the 'how to' rubric. It included books aimed at moneyed Russians keen to establish their social status, as well as texts encouraging the paternalistic instincts of the well-off; guides to self-betterment through education as well as etiquette manuals for the socially insecure; keep-fit manuals and guides to fashionable dress. It is tempting to posit a stratification by readership according to which members of the intelligentsia read keep-fit manuals and literature on the humane treatment of their inferiors, while literate members of the working classes concentrated on guides to self-education and Smilesian self-help tracts, and the new middle classes devoured material on house management, fashion, and etiquette.

To some extent, evidence on reading patterns bears this out. The fact that health literature enjoyed a wide currency among educated Russians is clear not only from memoirs,[130] but also because guides to salubrious living were seldom, if ever, the targets of the sort of scathing parody that intelligentsia writers loved to lavish on advice literature of other kinds (see below). And there was indeed an audience for self-education materials and self-help guides among working-class Russians. The Soviet poet Dem'yan Bedny, who rose from a peasant background to train as a ward orderly, and from there managed to progress to a course in philology at St Petersburg University, recalled that Samuel Smiles had been an inspiration to him: in 1924, he recommended *Self-Help* to a conference of worker-correspondents for newspapers. Though he might be scorned by 'feeble and puny little intellectuals' (*dryablye intelligentiki*), Smiles provided 'brilliant examples of what is meant by consistent and systematic labour'.[131]

---

[130] E.g. Nabokov records in *Speak, Memory* that his father, the prominent Kadet politician V. D. Nabokov, who was imprisoned by the tsarist government in July, 1906, 'spent a restful, if somewhat lonesome, three months in solitary confinement with his books, his collapsible bathtub, and his copy of J. P. Muller's [*sic*] manual of home gymnastics.' (V. Nabokov, *Speak, Memory* (Harmondsworth, 1969), 25.) Conversely, it is impossible to imagine that Nabokov's mother was the owner of a household manual, given that 'not only were the kitchen and the servants' hall never visited by [her], but they stood as far removed from her consciousness as if they were the corresponding quarters in a hotel' (ibid. 37).

[131] See *Rabkor i stennaya gazeta* (1924), 31. It is not clear whether Bedny was aware of Nadezhda Krupskaya's hostility to Smiles's work (as mentioned in the Introduction to this book, he was on the first version of her blacklist of texts to be withdrawn from Soviet libraries): this would have made the observation about 'feeble intellectuals' particularly pointed. On the audience for Smiles among politically conscious workers, see also Semen Kanatchikov's memoirs (R. E. Zelnik (trans. and ed.), *A Radical Worker in Tsarist Russia: The Autobiography of Semen Ivanovich Kanatchikov* (Stanford, Calif., 1986), 166), which mention borrowing a copy of 'Smails' from a friend.

But if there was an audience for books on 'rational living' and on 'self-improvement' in the Russian intelligentsia and worker intelligentsia, the question of who subscribed to the 'taste of luxury' is rather more complicated. While books such as Voznesenskaya's *The Housewife's Friend*, with its emphasis on the housewife's duty to create a 'cosy nest' to which her husband could return after a hard day's work, or journals such as *The Lady's World*, certainly do reek of 'bourgeois' taste, that does not prove that only the spouses of bankers and middle-ranking civil servants necessarily read them and subscribed to their values. On the contrary, some pluralism seems to have been possible, as is suggested by the fact that *Zhenskoe delo* (Women's Affairs), a magazine generally committed to the cult of hygiene, and which included material on literature and culture, was also able to carry articles on fashion and on cosmetics. Just so did the *Lady's Calendar* accompany its articles on dainty teas and lacy blouses with advice on diets, spas, efficiency at work, and supplementing the income by raising rabbits, while *Vol'f's Book News*, an advisory catalogue produced by one of Russia's largest publishers and booksellers at the turn of the century, not only educated readers about the biographies and writings of its featured authors, but also taught them how to care for the book as a precious object (a task considered so important that it was left to male members of the household).[132] What is more, at least some intellectuals were aware of the creative potential of advice literature as the inspiration of surreal whimsy. Elena Guro's collection of poetry and prose pieces, *The Little Camels of the Sky*, opened with a mock newspaper advertisement advising the reader how to construct 'extremely warm jerkins, underpants, stockings and stomachers from camel hair':

You set up a corral and catch some young shining spirits, lanky and kind, and resembling golden-haired, long-legged baby camels, covered by the down of sacred radiance. You drive them into a herd by thrashing the air with a whip, and the tender, kind-hearted creatures, which are too kind to realise how much they are going to be hurt, will crowd together, stretching out and interlacing their necks, pressing themselves to the rough fence and rubbing the tender down off themselves as they press together.

You then collect this sky-camel down, which is especially warm because full of life-giving spring warmth, and you spin it and make jerkins from it.[133]

Nor did Russian intellectuals' condemnation of the *meshchanstvo* in the abstract necessarily signify a commitment to asceticism in the abstract. Though Chekhov's plays and fiction mercilessly exposed the pretensions

---

[132] See Beth Holmgren, *Rewriting Capitalism: Literature and the Market in Late Tsarist Russia and the Kingdom of Poland* (Pittsburgh, 1998), 124.

[133] Elena Guro, 'Gazetnoe ob"yavlenie', in *eadem*, *Sochineniya*, ed. G. K. Perkins (Berkeley, 1996), 219. Guro also has a health piece, 'Solnechnaya vanna', ibid. p. 251.

of the new bourgeoisie (particularly memorable is the sickeningly over-elaborate party dinner in *Kingdom of Women*: shellfish topped with Branston's pickles and *sauce provençale*), the writer's own correspondence from Yalta, with its fretting over seed catalogues, and worrying about where to acquire a decent piano, is neither more nor less 'bourgeois' in terms of its construction of daily life than Redelin's domestic manual.[134] And even Marina Tsvetaeva, whose hostility to *byt* (domestic life) was later to be expressed everywhere in her poetry, was forced to resort to manuals of household management when ordering food from the cook in her father's Moscow household once she was the senior female living there, while her sister, Anastasiya, nostalgically recalled childhood days spent visiting Moscow's most opulent emporium of bourgeois delights, the department store Muir and Merrilies.[135] Conversely, newly wealthy industrialists were not necessarily more 'arriviste' in their ways than the aristocracy of the late eighteenth and early nineteenth centuries, many of whose expensively refined pursuits (hunting, bibliophilia, and the collection of paintings) they now pursued, or indeed than the well-off *dvoryane* of the early twentieth century, whose memoirs record details of formidably extensive and elaborate breakfasts, dinners, suppers, and teas, flourishing foreign brand-names as metonyms of sophistication and refinement.[136] By the late nineteenth century, most Russians who were comfortably off

[134] The *gostinaya* in Chekhov's house in Moscow even observes Redelin's preference for yellow walls and fabrics ('which harmonize with the yellowish tones of artificial light': *Dom i khozyaistvo*, i. 19). For a photograph, see E. Gaynor and K. Haavisto, *Russian Houses* (New York, 1991), 171.

[135] A. Tsvetaeva, *Minuvshee* (Moscow, 1991).

[136] On the last point, see e.g. Sof'ya Volkonskaya [as Princess Peter Wolkonsky], *The Way of Bitterness: Soviet Russia 1920* (London, 1931), 45–6, whose belongings when she returned to Russia to rescue her husband from prison included 'toilet things, a new fountain pen, a small electric torch and a bottle of Guerlain scent', or Nabokov, *Speak, Memory*, 63, where the longer and more imaginative list of objects recalled from childhood includes 'Pears Soap' and 'Golden Syrup'. On vast meals, see e.g. I. Skariatina, *A World Can End* (London, 1931), 57: at the Skaryatin property of Troitskoe, an English-style country-house breakfast of cereals, bacon and eggs, cream and milk, bread and butter, coffee and tea was followed, at 10, by a 'pick-me-up' of sherry and sandwiches; dinner at 1 lasted for an hour and a half, beginning with *zakuski* and continuing with five main courses; after tea and cakes at 4 followed a vast supper at 7 and then more tea and cakes at 10, with finally an 'emergency supper' left out by the servants in the bedrooms. On the thoroughly 'aristocratic' life led by some members of the *haute bourgeoisie* in Russia, see Tamara Talbot-Rice (1904–93), *Tamara: Memoirs of St Petersburg, Paris, Oxford, and Byzantium* (London, 1996), 7–41. Tamara's father, Boris (Israel) Abelson, was a merchant of the first guild, but her family led a life indistinguishable from that of rich *dvoryane* such as the Nabokovs, with summers on the family estates, a house on the elegant Mokhovaya Street in St Petersburg, children's parties for forty at a time, a staff of dozens of servants, and an entire railway-carriage rented for the frequent trips to resorts. Much interesting incidental detail on the transformation of life in late imperial Russia is available in James L. West and Iurii A. Petrov, *Merchant Moscow: Images of Russia's Vanished Bourgeoisie* (Princeton, 1998). See especially Karen Pennar, 'Daily Life Among the Morozovs', 73–81, and the many superb illustrations to the volume.

frequently decorated their households more elaborately, and owned more objects, than Russians of a comparable income might have done in the mid-nineteenth century.[137] And even among the less wealthy *dvoryane*, comfort had now begun to play a far larger role than previously. Zinaida Zhemchuzhnaya, who grew up in the small Urals town of Alapaevka during the 1890s, was the daughter of the chief doctor in the local hospital, a fervent and rather unworldly liberal who refused to take fees from his patients. On his government salary alone, however, the family were able to afford a house with a dining-room seating fifty as well as a smaller family dining-room, a drawing-room with two sets of soft furnishings and a grand piano, a large study and parental bedroom, a 'clean kitchen' used for making special cakes and puddings as well as an outdoor one for everyday use, and a separate small children's library. The enormous garden had larch and lime alleys and glasshouses for growing fruit as well as a pond and mound with swings on it.[138]

If the *dvoryanstvo* and intelligentsia in no sense lived 'by books alone', the much-despised *melkoe meshchanstvo*, or petty bourgeoisie, was quite capable of nurturing intellectual aspirations. The rare memoirists who admitted belonging to this despised class, such as Mandelstam in *The Noise of Time*, may have excoriated their backgrounds, but they still recorded the possession of cultural objects—the first mass-produced *Collected Works* of Pushkin, volumes of *Niva* magazine—among the *style russe* sideboards and lace curtains. And N. A. Rubakin's informal survey of the letters which he received from readers in response to his writings on self-education indicate that the audience for these among the *meshchanstvo* was not much smaller than the audience among workers; there was a far larger audience among *meshchane* than among peasants.[139] Striking, too, is the case of a lonely-

---

[137] Compare e.g. pl. 54 in Chloe Obolensky, *The Russian Empire: A Portrait in Photographs* (London, 1980), which shows an officer's family sitting at a table covered with a braided plush cloth, and alongside a handsome mahogany glass-fronted bookcase topped with a skeleton clock under a glass dome, with a mantelpiece crowded with china ornaments in the background,=; and the setting of mid-19th-cent. paintings such as G. S. Myasoedov, *Congratulation of the Newly-Weds in a Landowner's House* (1861), V. G. Perov, *Arrival of a New Governess in the House of a Merchant Family* (1866), or V. I. Sternberg, *At Kachanovka, the Estate of G. S. Tarnovsky* (1838). (The first two paintings are available in M. N. Shumova, *Russkaya zhivopis' serediny XIX veka* (Moscow, 1984), [this edn. has no page nos.], and the last one in *eadem, Russkaya zhivopis' pervoi poloviny XIX veka* (Moscow, 1978), 121.)

[138] *Puti izgnaniya: Ural, Kuban', Moskva, Kharbin, Tzyantsin: Vospominaniya* (Tenafly, NJ, 1987), 3–5.

[139] Rubakin, *Pis'ma k chitatelyam o samoobrazovanii*, 376–7. 5,506 readers had written to Rubakin between 1911 and 1914, and of these 955 were workers (256 from villages and 699 from towns), 101 skilled workers (*tekhniki, mastera, mashinisty*); 55 from villages and 46 from towns): i.e. 1,056 in all. 387 were peasants (in a village/town proportion of 172: 215). If one assumes that all the 'town peasants' were in fact workers, and that a proportion of the city-dwelling individuals who described themselves as 'representatives of circles and societies' (63 individuals in a village/ town proportion of 13:50) may have been, the figure for workers was around 1,300 and for

hearts advertisement published in 1909, in which an 'individuum' (*sic*) of 28, 'a small trader and craftsman by profession', attempted to lure his bride (who was to be of a 'generally humanitarian' character as well as the possessor of a dowry 'if possible') by boasting not only of his 5,000 rouble capital and salary of 600 roubles per year and his handsome looks, but also of his achievements in self-improvement:

I have a humanely delicate soul, an idealistic heart full of vivacity, I am a cosmopolitan, atheist, vegetarian, with an energetic and original mind. I am an *intelligentnyi* auto-didact, I am preparing myself for serious self-education and research on the problems of today's world.

My ideal is of a progressive and evolutionary world-view [*sic*], and my motto is to learn everything and become a better person.[140]

This touching, if ungrammatical, self-description was by no means exceptional. But in turn-of-the-century Russian culture, it was less the factual character of the *meshchanstvo* than its mythic status that counted. According to the process termed by Roland Barthes *défection du nom* (concept evasion),[141] intelligentsia commentators used *meshchanstvo* and *meshchanskoe* as terms of abuse (interchangeably with *poshlost'* and *poshloe*) in order to indicate that they themselves did not belong to the bourgeoisie, but to the 'classless' intelligentsia.[142] The practice was widespread not only among intellectuals from the *dvoryanstvo*, but also among self-improved members of the Russian *meshchanstvo* in the strict legal sense (free urban lower class). In March 1886, for instance, the 26-year-old Chekhov, who was just beginning to make his name as an author of comic stories, turned a letter to his younger brother into an entire mini conduct book on how to escape the promptings of what he described as 'the fleshly existence of

peasants 172. Traders, shop-assistants, and clerks (*torgovtsy, prikazchiki, kontorshchiki*) together made up 1,008 individuals (in a village/town proportion of 231:777).

[140] *Literaturno-brachnaya gazeta 'Amur'* 1 (1909), 1. My thanks to Stephen Lovell for this reference.

[141] R. Barthes, *Mythologies: Œuvres complètes* i (Paris, 1993), 706: 'The *défection du nom* of the bourgeois is no illusory, accidental, ancillary, natural or insignificant phenomenon, it is the very heart of bourgeois ideology, the process according to which the bourgeoisie transforms the reality of the world into image.' Cf. Béatrix Le Wita, *French Bourgeois Culture*, trans. J. A. Underwood (Cambridge, 1994), 24: 'By depreciating the words *bourgeois* and *bourgeoisie*, individuals of that [kind] are in effect forbidding you to call them such.' This strategy was common outside the intelligentsia as well. For example, the very interesting memoir of S. F. Svetlov, *Peterburgskaya zhizn' v kontse XIX stoletiya (v 1892 godu* (ed. A. M. Konechnyi) (St Petersburg, 1998), 62, recalls that it was customary in his circle (middle-ranking civil servants) to set out the *gostinaya* furniture 'gracefully' (i.e. place it in groups across the floor), since, by the late 19th cent., lining it up along the walls was considered fit only for the *meshchanstvo*.

[142] See e.g. Nabokov's comment on his father in *Speak, Memory*, 144: 'Belonging, as he did by choice, to the great classless intelligentsia of Russia'. For his part, the plebeian Kornei Chukovsky regarded V. D Nabokov as *both* a service grandee *and* an intellectual (*Dnevnik 1901–1929* (Moscow, 1991), 205, entry for 29 Mar. 1922.)

meshchanstvo [*meshchanskaya plot'*]'. His recommendations on how to do this were not only moralistic (show real concern for others, not just kittens and beggars, pay your debts, be truthful and avoid sentimental outbursts and preying on other's sympathy, help others to improve their ways), but also hygienic. Well-bred (*vospitannye*) people must not sleep in their clothes, regard bedbugs with indifference, breathe dirty air, step on to a spit-covered floor, or over-indulge themselves sexually with women. They must regard women as 'mothers, not tarts', and their motto should be 'mens sana in corpore sano'.[143]

For all his much-vaunted lack of didacticism, and saving sense of irony, Chekhov retained the beliefs set out in this letter as absolute values throughout his life: in his fiction and plays, sloppiness is as obvious a pointer to moral failure as is self-indulgence. (Take, for instance, Dr Gromov in *Ward Number Six*, a man whose dereliction of duty at work is matched by his willingness to drink beer out of a bottle and eat off a greasy paper.) Equally stern criticism of *meshchanstvo* could be found in the work of other notable representatives of the self-bettered lower classes, such as Gor'ky, Fedor Sologub, and Kornei Chukovsky. For all these commentators, it was obvious on first principles that anything 'vulgar' would be enjoyed by representatives of the *meshchanstvo*, whether these were millionaire factory owners or back-street hairdressers and shop-assistants, and that the *meshchanstvo* would have vulgar tastes, and customs that were, in the broadest sense of the word, unhygienic.[144] It is an indicative touch when Varvara, the fat, bone-headed girlfriend of the ghastly Peredonov, the eponymous Low-Grade Demon of a 1902 novel by Sologub, is discovered 'in the sitting-room, book in hand (not something that happened at all often). It was a cookbook, the only kind she ever opened, old, battered, in a black cover.'[145] If the nature of the readership for household manuals and advice on cosmetics has to be considered 'not proven', they were certainly a type of manual from which the intelligentsia actively sought to distance itself when representing the world.

One important method of so doing, as in the early nineteenth century, was parody, in the production of which the energetic group of writers associated with *Novyi Satirikon* magazine were particularly noted specialists. In 1914, for example, the group published its own version of a popular formula, the 'calendar almanac' for the housewife. Like the genuine article (for instance, *The Lady's World Calendar*), the *Novyi Satirikon* publication

---

[143] A. P. Chekhov, letter to N. P. Chekhov, *PSS Pis'ma*, i. 223–4.

[144] See e.g. Kornei Chukovsky, 'Verbitskaya' (1910), *Sobranie sochinenii v 6 tomakh* vi (Moscow, 1966), 10–21.

[145] F. Sologub, *Melkii bes* (Letchworth, 1966), 158 (ch. 10). Peredonov, it should be noted, takes the book for quite another kind of advice literature—a 'black book' of witchcraft.

combined a calendar proper (a list of dates, with religious festivals and state occasions in red) with selections of 'handy hints' setting out the obvious with sepulchral solemnity. A section for the agriculturally inexperienced warned its readers that, in order to start a milk business, 'it is a *sine qua non* to acquire some good dairy cows', while 'The Rules of Using the Post' verbosely counselled readers on such difficult and complex operations as folding a sheet of paper, placing it in an envelope, and inserting it in a letter-box. However, it was the 'household hints' whose surreal impracticality best captured the eccentricities of the original genre. The housewife needing to remove a spot was advised to 'dab it with rice wine and place the tablecloth on a bollard in the street; the spot will soon disappear' (likewise, no doubt, the tablecloth itself). And the hostess caught on a Sunday with nothing in the house to serve to unexpected guests was advised: 'Do not despair. Take a joint of veal, roast to a turn, allow to get cold and garnish. Serve up with a ten-pound trout dressed *à la provençale*. It is quite in order to limit oneself to bottled and tinned hors d'oeuvres, and ice-cream for pudding.'[146]

The *Novyi Satirikon* team also produced a *Very Latest Letter-Writer, Combined with the Art of Conduct in Society and of Writing Album Verse, Guide to Dancing and Conversation* (1916). Here they indulged in a good deal of fun at the expense of the epistolary manual, the target of their particular scorn being the slimy letter addressed to a superior. The usual oleaginous formulae were rendered ridiculous by being applied to incongruous situations. In one letter, an elderly official was congratulated on the fact that his child had taken a whole four years to arrive after the wedding, an indication of his 'attention to detail':

The especial demands made by the difficult time that the country is living through presently, however, speeded the results of Your activities, which reached the most productive phase of their development at exactly the moment when two cavalry divisions happened to be stationed in the locality.

Your Excellency!

We, your subordinates, are happy to cluster in our thoughts round the cradle, and, without paying any heed to differences in age, opinions and nationalities, to pour out before You and Your Spouse, and Your Excellency's most gracious Little One, the overflowing torrent of the warmest and most respectful good wishes which is now filling our bosoms and which we hope will bedew His first sweet young footsteps and excursions into the outside world.

We remain, Your Excellency, Your Excellency's Very Humble Servants.[147]

---

[146] *Izdatel'stvo 'Novyi Satirikon': Khudozhestvenno-yumoristicheskii kalendar'-al'manakh na 1914 god*, 63, 95–100, 81, 113. Was this last joke the remote source of a supposed quotation from Elena Molokhovets's cookbook which circulated in Soviet intellectual folklore in the 1960s, 1970s and 1980s, which ran: 'When unexpected guests arrive, descend to the cellar, take out a whole cold turkey, have dressed and sent to table'?   [147] *Samonoveishii pis'movnik* (1916), 7.

Since the original letter-writing manuals that were the targets of this satire already parodied themselves so effectively, they made easy meat. A more creative type of mockery was evident in Chekhov's provision, in a sketch under the title, 'The Latest Letter-Writing Manual' (1884), of a type of letter definitely not included in the manuals: the rebuke from a senior official to his junior. Chekhov's spoof also provides interesting evidence of the fact that politeness was, at least in official contexts, a perquisite of powerlessness:

Two days ago, while you were handing our galoshes to me and to my wife, you were pleased to stand in a draught. I now hear that you have caught cold and have been failing to report for work. Your dreadful negligence with regard to your own health gives me no option but to ordain that you should receive a formal reprimand...[148]

Not only the habit of giving peremptory dressings-down to one's juniors, or of bowing and scraping to small-fry officials by writing to them in tones more suitable for the royal household (and perhaps excessive even then) was mocked, but also the 'advice for every occasion' format. In an article printed at the back of the *Very Latest Letter-Writing Manual*, Arkady Averchenko suggested that it was odd that compilers had somehow forgotten to include letters apologizing for missing a social occasion because 'grandfather just fell into a cauldron of boiling soap down at the factory', or inviting an acquaintance to come and taste kitten pie. However, if the preposterous formulae of the letter-writing guides inspired amusement, a more serious note was sounded when Averchenko evoked what he saw as the likely reader of such trash: 'After all, will this literature not do much to ennoble the Il'yushka Trynkins of this world, who will be relieved to know that they can find the right formula for calling a member of high society out to a duel, or sending Baroness F. an invitation to *le fif o'clock*?'[149] Averchenko's disgust at the incongruity of offering such material to a popular audience was typical of intelligentsia attitudes to mass-market culture; but to be fair, it was also shared by some of the workers exposed to this area of the popular market. The autobiography of Semen Kanatchikov illustrates the case of a reader who bought advice literature on purely practical grounds, and spurned it when it did not measure up to his needs.

---

[148] *PSS* iii.125. The original uses the informal second person singular (which is generally considered extremely rude when talking to another adult who is not an intimate). The practice of using the form to subordinates—junior officers or rank-and-file in the army, and Party juniors— persisted in official circles during the Soviet period. (Personal communication from informant in St Petersburg, 1998.) On Chekhov's fascination with letter-writing manuals, see the memoir of A. S. Lazarev quoted in *PSS* iii. 564, which recalls how the writer kept two friends entertained for the whole of a rainy day with a recital of 'incredible rubbish' from his *pis'movnik* collection.

[149] *Samonoveishii pis'movnik*, 149.

Having purchased a book under the title *Teach Yourself Dance and Good Manners*, Kanatchikov discovered that the book was pretty well no good to him:

It said that when seated at table, one should not wipe one's nose with the napkin, roll the bread into little balls, eat fish with a knife, or gnaw at the bones of a goose. In short, the book dealt with subject matter I had never even encountered; in fact, I did not know if these things belonged to the animal, vegetable, or mineral world.

The only part of the book of any value to me was the one that contained some pointers on the 'theory' of the art of dance. But it did not make me any less timid or more resourceful in my relations with women, notwithstanding the intensive assistance of my friend Stepka.[150]

Yet it would be a mistake to extrapolate too much from the case of a 'conscious' worker writing up his memoirs in the Soviet period. Some of the 'Il'yusha Trynkins' who bought such books may have found them more useful; others probably valued them less as practical advice manuals than for the entertainment which they afforded, treating them as information about the delights of life in society, as consumers did Verbitskaya's novels or Evgeny Bauer's films. So much is suggested, for instance, by the immense popularity of guides to writing love-letters, some examples of which, such as 'Uncle Serge's' *Complete Love-Letter Writer*, ran into many editions. It is difficult to imagine an Il'yusha from the pattern workshop copying any of the model letters here to send to Mashka from the sweet factory, given that they are composed in the flowery style of an early nineteenth-century three-decker novel:

Incomparable Liza!
Yes, I think that I have the right to call You 'incomparable', because the most sublime days of my life have been spent with You, since the time when I became Your zealous admirer, o precious Liza.[151]

It is more likely that such material was read because it afforded a glimpse of a fascinating and extraordinary world where people actually did sit down and write letters like that.

[150] Zelnik (trans. and ed.), *A Radical Worker*, 59–60. No book under the title *Samouchitel' tantsev i etiketa* is listed in the RNB general catalogue, but books of this kind were widely available in the late 19th and early 20th cents. In his amusing study of Moscow markets at this period, *Metkoe moskovskoe slovo: Byt i rech' staroi Moskvy* (Moscow, 1985), 155, E. P. Ivanov recalls pedlars tempting buyers with *The Complete Teach-Yourself Ballroom Dancing* (Polnyi samouchitel' salonnykh i bal'nykh tantsev) and *Teach Yourself Bon-Ton* (Samouchitel' khoroshego tona).

[151] 'Dyadya Serzh', *Polnyi lyubovnyi pis'movnik* (1916), 15. It is difficult to calculate the number of editions that a popular book of this kind had gone through, but it was certainly constantly in print between 1909 and 1917. See also 'Nikolini', *Polnyi pis'movnik dlya vlyublennykh* (1909), 29: 'Cast but one fleeting glance of Your heavenly eyes upon the lines of my latest composition and sweeten the last minutes of the death-agony of my dying heart!' A book from an earlier generation is Anon., *Lyubovnaya pochta* (1863).

By an amusing historical irony, it turns out that the Helsinki University Library's copy of the *Satirikon* circle's *Very Latest Letter-Writer* itself once fell into the hands of an 'Il'yusha Trynkin'. The flyleaf of the book is signed, in a half-literate hand, 'Ivan Mikhailovich Fadeev, 16 August 1917, Shamarino Village, Simbirsk Province'. Of course, Ivan Mikhailovich (who was a sailor) may have bought the book simply for its blank pages (on which he wrote up his laconic diary of life at sea and his accounts). It may have been the nearest available thing to a notebook at a time of wartime shortage. But if he did read the book, did he get the joke? Or was he so used to reading advice manuals as fantasy in any case that the parody one slipped down like the rest? Whichever way, his ownership of the book makes it possible that working-class Russians had more ways of reading advice manuals than the Satirikon jokers supposed: that they saw them not just as sources of practical information or of insight into the lives of the rich, but found them entertaining in the sense of laughable as well.

If working-class readers treated commercial advice literature ironically or sceptically, it is possible to assume by extension that they were quite capable of doing the same with the worthy publications produced for their consumption by members of the intelligentsia. And there is actual evidence of this from the cases of Tolstoi and of Nataliya Nordman. Both writers, with a refreshing lack of the humourlessness sometimes considered essential to zealots (and zealots they certainly were), themselves recognized the presence of opposition to their ideas. Tolstoi, for instance, described a meeting with a peasant from a village close to the Yasnaya Polyana estate who would have none of the writer's pacifism, terming the armed uprisings of 1905 'a tragic necessity' (*pechal'naya neobkhodimost'*).[152] And Nordman acknowledged in *A Cookbook for the Hungry*, that a working-class audience in St Petersburg had been stony ground for the seeds of vegan propaganda. When a cook slyly wondered what kind of food Nordman herself preferred, she played into the lecturer's hands by giving her the chance to outline the menu for the week: Monday, a *rassol'nik* (sour soup) made from hay, then barley porridge and cabbage fried up with salted cucumbers and potatoes; Tuesday, a puree of oats (the husks were fed to the family horses), fried beet in breadcrumbs with onion, and fried celery; Wednesday, lentils, herb borshch, and compote, etc. But not all the questions were so easy to deal with. 'Are we cattle, to be fed on hay and waste food?' asked one man, and another woman enquired how long Nordman thought it would take to scrub all those vegetables.

Yet at the same time, Nordman and Tolstoi make clear that responses from those they addressed were by no means always hostile. Tolstoi, who

---

[152] 'Chto zhe delat'?' *PSS* xxxvi. 366.

seems to have been the first Russian advice-book author to include responses from readers, cited, in *Odumaites'!*, a letter from a sailor serving at Port Arthur who enthused about what he had read and asked for more of the same.[153] Similarly, Nordman recalled, in an afterword to her pamphlet on the liberation of servants, a visit from a servant, alerted by a lecture that Nordman had given, who wanted the writer to publicize the appalling treatment of womenservants in orphanages. And though there is some evidence that Nordman's determination to override social barriers occasionally shocked working-class Russians, there is no reason to disbelieve Repin's assertion that, 'incomprehension at the behaviour of this peculiar lady [*chudnaya barynya*] was very soon replaced by straightforward delight . . . and by feelings of closeness that never faded'.[154] Certainly, it is significant that Nordman's correspondence and memoirs never record the sort of unhappy conflict with servants and rapid turnover of staff that were commonplaces in the writings of educated Russians in the late nineteenth and early twentieth centuries.[155] And the assertion by some educated visitors to the house that Nordman's servants disliked dining at her table probably speaks more about their own boredom and embarrassment when forced to make conversation to 'oiks' than it does about the feelings of the servants themselves.[156]

These cases, though, concern not so much the conscious absorption and enactment of the tenets of behaviour propaganda as a positive reaction to its contents in the abstract, which was probably dictated as much by admiration for the radiant goodwill of Nordman and Tolstoi as by an acceptance of the ideas that he or she was expressing. The question of the

---

[153] 'Вотъ и четалъ ваше сочинение оно для меня оченъ была четать Преятна я очень любитель Былъ четать ваше сочинение такъ Левъ никалаевичъ унасъ теперь Военая дество какъ Припишите Мне пожалуста Угодна оно Богу ил нетъ [. . .] Пришлите мне такихъ книжек сколка это будетъ стоеть я заплачу.' (*PSS* xxxvi. 147–8: spelling follows original).

[154] I. Repin, 'Sestritsa Natal'ya Borisovna', *Vegetarianskoe obozrenie* 6–7 (1914), 204. Cf. Nordman's own account of a meeting with a visiting footman in a note to the feminist activist Praskov'ya Arian: 'I went up to him and stretched out my hand. He covered his hands with his fur hat and looked at me very expressively, but without saying anything, then said clearly: 'You must be mistaken, can't you see I'm an oik, I'm scum' [kham, svoloch']. That look on his face haunts me still. . . . But I insisted on having my way. 'Give me your hand, comrade!' . . . He turned out to be the most upright [*pochtennyi*], and worthiest [*dobreishii*] of souls, he's been in service so many years!' (RGALI, f. 1018, op. 1, ed. khr. 169, l. 24.)

[155] See e.g. I. Goncharov, 'Slugi starogo vremeni', *Sobranie sochinenii v 8 tomakh*, vii. 316–83, or the entries made by Aleksandr Blok in his diary during the 1910s (A. Blok, *Dnevniki 1901–1921, Sobranie sochinenii v 8 tomakh*, vii (Moscow and Leningrad, 1963), 19–426; idem, *Zapisnye knizhki 1901–1920* (Moscow, 1965): on these see also C. Kelly, '"Who'll Clean the Boots Now?": Servants and Social Anxieties in Late Imperial St Petersburg', *Europa Orientalis*, 16 (1997), pt. 2, 18–19.

[156] See e.g. Tat'yana Shchepkina-Kupernik, 'the conversation did not much interest them' (quoted in Grabar' and Zil'bershtein, *Repin*, ii. 266).

extent to which precept actually succeeded in altering world-view is much more problematic. Perhaps the best way of exploring its complex ramifications is to examine the after-history of one type of book that had a particularly large and socially varied readership: Samuel Smiles's guides to self-help.

Not only publication data, the sheer numbers of editions of his works, but evidence from memoirs, indicate that the circulation for Smiles was huge. Already by the 1870s, he had considerable currency among Russian radicals, as Repin recalls in his memoir (cited in Chapter 2) of a visit to one of the musical soirées held at the Serov household in St Petersburg. His hostess, Valentina Serova, besides cutting her hair short, and spurning society ways, earnestly acquired familiarity with a series of sacred texts of the radical movement, 'mighty works of Russian publicistics and literature forbidden at the time', including Chernyshevsky, Pisarev, Dobrolyubov, Shelgunov, Antonovich, Georg Büchner, Jakob Moleschott, Feuerbach, Mill, Lassales, and Samuel Smiles.[157]

Smiles's works never constituted 'forbidden literature' as represented by Chernyshevsky or Feuerbach, though it is indicative that Repin should have supposed that they did. Indeed, the extraordinary thing about Smiles is that the reception of his work (unlike that of Feuerbach or Chernyshevsky) bridged the gap between state and radical values. The many editions of his work indicate official approval for the dissemination of his ideas, no doubt as part of the Russian establishment's commitment to modernizing ideologies in the late 1890s and early 1900s.[158] But Smiles was just as popular among opponents of autocracy, and, unlike his contemporary and tutelary genius John Stuart Mill, was read as widely in worker circles as in intelligentsia circles.

But what did Russian readers learn from reading *Self-Help* and its companions? On the face of it, the popularity of Smiles's creed would seem to bear out the hypothesis advanced by several historians of late imperial Russia during recent years, and which emphasizes the growth of individualist discourses on the construction of identity during the late nineteenth and early twentieth centuries, along with the development of a 'civic' ideal, stressing each citizen's disinterested participation in social life.[159] But scrutinized more closely, the case of Smiles in fact demonstrates

---

[157] Repin, 'Serov', *Dalekoe i blizkoe*, 353.

[158] Propaganda for self-help was among the material carried in *Sel'skii Vestnik*, the official newspaper for the peasantry published by the Interior Ministry from 1881. See J. S. Krukones, *To the People: The Russian Government and the Newspaper Sel'skii Vestnik ('Village Herald'), 1881–1917* (New York, 1987); R. Wortman, *Scenarios of Power*, ii (Princeton, 2000), 211.

[159] On individualism, see Brooks, *When Russia Learned to Read*, 271–94; McReynolds, *The News Under Russia's Old Regime*; on civic consciousness see Mark Steinberg, *Moral Communities: The Culture of Class Relations in the Russian Printing Industry, 1867–1907* (Berkeley, 1992); idem,

that the influence of individualistic dogma remained superficial, failing to effect a wide-ranging shift in cultural paradigms. Especially interesting here is the case of 'self-reliance', which along with diligence and organization formed one of the three central elements in Smiles's ideology of self-help. This all-important point was underlined in the first paragraph of the book:

'Heaven helps those who help themselves' is a well-tried maxim, embodying in small compass the results of vast human experience. The spirit of self-help is the root of all genuine growth in the individual, and exhibited in the lives of many, it constitutes the true source of national vigour and strength. Help from without is often enfeebling in its effects, but help from within invariably invigorates.[160]

Via a patriotic fanfare to 'Englishness' ('The spirit of self-help, as exhibited in the energetic action of individuals, has in all times been a marked feature of the English character, and furnishes the true measure of our power as a nation'), Smiles moved on to a hymn of praise for self-education, which he favourably contrasted to the passive absorption of knowledge in educational institutions:

Daily experience shows that it is energetic individualism which produces the most profound effects upon the life and action of others, and really constitutes the best practical education. Schools, academies, and colleges, give but the merest beginnings of education in comparison with it. Far more influential is the life-education given daily in our homes, in the streets, behind counters, in workshops, at the loom and the plough, in counting-houses and manufactories, and in the busy haunts of men. (p. 4)

Smiles's message was unambiguous: self-help was dependent upon individual action, and upon the crucial Victorian virtues of 'backbone', and ability to 'stand on one's own feet'. However, early Russian translations of *Self-Help* do not convey this simple message with absolute clarity. In N. Katernikov's version of 1866, the first paragraph is rendered faithfully:

«На Бога надейся, а сам не плошай» — вот истинная пословица, заключающая в немногих словах вывод из огромного числа жизненных опытов. По отношению к отдельной личности, дух самодеятельности служит основанием всякого действительного развития, а в приложении к жизни масс составляет настоящий источник национальной бодрости и силы. Внешнее пособие часто только рассла-

'Worker-Authors and the Cult of the Person', in S. Frank and M. D. Steinberg (eds.), *Cultures in Flux: Lower-Class Values, Practices, and Resistance in Late Imperial Russia* (Princeton, 1994), 168–84. My argument here is closer to that in Charters Wynn, *Workers, Strikes, and Pogroms: The Donbass-Dnepr Bend in Late Imperial Russia, 1870–1905* (Princeton, 1992), which emphasizes the persistence of traditional elements in the mentality of Russian industrial workers at the turn of the century.

[160] Samuel Smiles, *Self-Help, with Illustrations of Character, Conduct and Perseverance* (London, 1859), 1.

бляет, тогда как помощь, основанная на внутренней силе, непременно укрепляет.[161]

But other sections of the text departed more radically from the original in terms both of omissions and of additions. For example, in translating Smiles's statement about the importance of self-reliance to national greatness, Katernikov played up, rather than toned down, the specificity of the English case, turning Smiles's sentence about 'our power as a nation' into the formulation 'этот дух самодеятельности . . . был всегда отличительной чертой характера англичан' (p. 6) (this spirit of self-reliance . . . has always been a distinguishing feature of the English). And in adding Russian examples of men who raised themselves from humble beginnings by dint of self-help (Smiles's had included Humphrey Davy, Milton, George Stephenson, Cardinal Wolsey, and many others), Katernikov did not always pick individuals who perfectly exemplified Smiles's vision of 'nature's gentlemen'. One of the examples selected for the first chapter was the early nineteenth-century statesman Mikhail Speransky, of whom Katernikov observed: 'The distinguishing characteristics of Speransky even at this early stage of his life were, apart from unremitting diligence, extraordinary quickness and facility, and also stealth, the ability to please those in authority.' (p. 28). To be sure, Katernikov then adds disapprovingly, 'which was later to put a blot on Speransky's life, successful as this was' (ibid.). But by leaving open the question of quite how self-advancement might have been possible, in the context of the Russian civil service of Speransky's time, without sacrificing some of the principles of self-help (self-reliance and uprightness), Katernikov stopped short of complete condemnation.

Katernikov was not alone in his less than whole-hearted appropriation of the idea of self-reliance. The variety of ways in which the word 'self-help' was translated—*samodeyatel'nost'*, or 'doing things by oneself', *samostoyatel'naya deyatel'nost'*, or 'independent activity', and *samorazvitie umstvennoe*, as well as *samopomoshch'*, literally 'self-help'—is some indication of the concept's unfamiliarity (in the case of Smiles's other one-word titles, it was only 'Thrift' that threw up similar uncertainty, appearing both as *berezhlivost'*, or 'prudence', and as *raschetlivost'*, or 'calculation'; 'Duty' and 'Character' made their way smoothly into the Russian language). One of the variants of 'self-help', *samorazvitie umstvennoe*, or 'intellectual development', pointed to an emphasis on self-education. This was underlined by a passage in Katernikov's rendering of *Self-Help*. Where he had emphasized the 'Englishness' of self-reliance, its centrality to 'their' culture, he Russified the passage in which Smiles spoke of the inferiority of formal

---

[161] Smail's, *Samodeyatel'nost'*, 1–2.

education as compared with education on the streets, turning Smiles's 'schools, academies, and colleges' into 'shkoly, akademii i gimnazii'. The rendering of 'colleges' (by which Smiles had meant universities) as *gimnazii*, the elite high schools of the Russian empire, was, technically speaking, an error, but it emphasized the topicality of Smiles's views in terms of the Russian context.[162] Equally, a thoroughly Russian resonance was given to the phrase 'in our homes, in the streets, behind counters, in workshops, at the loom and the plough, in counting-houses and manufactories, and in the busy haunts of men', which became, in Katernikov's version:

дома, на улицах, за прилавками, в мастерских, за ткацким станком и за плугом, в конторах и на фабриках, и вообще в всех центрах общественной деятельности.

This retained the rhetorical force of the original, but substituted the sociologically coloured *obshchestvennaya deyatel'nost'* (public activity) for the quasi-biblical, 'the busy haunts of men'.

Smiles's emphasis on self-improvement in an intellectual sense was bound to strike a chord with his Russian audience. Already in the 1860s, Chernyshevsky had stressed the importance of reading (in a strictly controlled manner!) to the end of enlightenment: his model revolutionary Rakhmetov, who 'had read Thackeray's *Vanity Fair* with enjoyment . . . shut *Pendennis* when he had reached page 20: "Thackeray said everything he had to say in *Vanity Fair*: one can tell there's nothing new here, so there's no point in reading on." "Every book I have read saves me from having to read twenty other books," he said.'[163] And Smiles's insistence on probity was absolutely in tone with Russian intellectual populism: Rubakin asked rhetorically, in the third edition of his *Letters to Readers on Self-Education* 'Can a man who contravenes the elementary rules of propriety (*poryadochnost'*) be termed *intelligentnyi*?'[164] The link between self-education and propriety was not in itself problematic, then. What created difficulties was the linking of these two qualities with the notion of self-betterment in another sense: that of improving one's social position. The relative unpopularity of *Thrift* illustrates that one aspect of this last concern, the desirability of material self-betterment, failed to take hold much in Russia. But there was an equally muted response to Smiles's criticisms of 'help from without', to his intolerance of patronage and of the use of connections in order to achieve results.

---

[162] Cf. the passage in Rubakin, *Pis'ma k chitatelyam*, 39: 'A really educated person is not necessarily one who has completed a course of formal education in some institution, even one at a university: after all, plenty of ignoramuses, narrow specialists, or careerists emerge from there!'

[163] N. Chernyshevsky, *Izbrannye proizvedeniia v 3 tomakh* (Leningrad, 1978), i. 286.

[164] Rubakin, *Pis'ma k chitatelyam o samoobrazovanii* (1921), 38. This edition also contained a new chapter (xiv) under the title 'A True Intellectual is a Deeply Moral Personality'.

Among intellectuals, the reason for this lay in the commitment to utopian collectivism characteristic of the late imperial Russian intelligentsia at large, a commitment evident not only among thinkers of a post-Slavophile colouration, such as Vyacheslav Ivanov, with his Dostoevskian attachment to *sobornost'*, the community of Orthodox believers, but also in Russian socialists, such as Petr Kropotkin, whose famous essay, *Mutual Aid as a Factor in Evolution* (1902),[165] could be read as a riposte to the tradition of Smilesian *samopomoshch'* as well as to Social Darwinism. But among Smiles's less privileged readers, it is traceable to the persistence of the collective principle in Russian peasant and working-class life; to the dependence upon 'help from without' if people were to survive at all.

It is important not to see this collectivity as all-embracing, suffocating to any notion of the private self. The concept of privacy in the sense of boundaries between individuals did exist in peasant and working-class Russian life (its non-existence is as tenacious, and as misleading, a cliché as the supposed lack of preoccupation with *byt* among intellectuals).[166] Both peasants and workers had strict codes of propriety controlling the forms of behaviour on the part of individuals that were acceptable in public. Il'ya Repin, who was brought up in a post-station in the steppes, recalled in his memoirs the tortuous manoeuvres that had to be executed when cabbies needed to leave the table while eating:

Every society has its own rules of propriety, its own etiquette. Among cabbies, it was considered improper to leave the table before finishing one's supper. However, people who have travelled thirty or forty miles on foot in the frost, then thawed out by sitting in a warm room eating hot food, and above all by methodically working their way through a large quantity of soup and other sorts of food with a high liquid content, inevitably sooner or later feel the need to nip 'into the fresh air' for a moment [to relieve themselves].

And so it was customary for a man to nudge his neighbour in the ribs, so that the latter could say:

'Hey, Akhremka, I just remembered, your gelding's torn a hole in his haynet and he's trampling the hay, making a real mess—I'd go and have a look if I were you.'

Akhremka scrambles off the bench as fast as he can and rushes off in the direction of the horses.

---

[165] The text was originally published in English, and appeared in Russian translation in 1904 as *Vzaimopomoshch' sredi zhivotnykh i lyudei* (St Petersburg, 1904).

[166] See e.g. Svetlana Boym, *Common Places: Mythologies of Everyday Life in Russia* (Cambridge, Mass., 1994), 73: 'The closest to the word "privacy" is the concept of *chastnaia zhizn'* (literally, particular (partial) life).' The concept of 'particularity' is, of course, not indigenous to Russia: *chastnaya* is simply a calque of the French *particulaire*, as is clear from Karamzin's remark in a letter to his wife, 'I'd rather throw my *History* straight in the fire than take 50 thousand roubles [as a subsidy] from a private individual [*partikulyarnyi chelovek*]' (*Neizdannye sochineniya* (St Petersburg, 1862), 143).

Ten or fifteen minutes later, when he gets back, he hears Nikita cough discreetly and says,

'Eh, Nikita, I think your roan's near out of hay, isn't it time you gave him some more?'

Nikita dashes off in his turn, and Akhremka sits down and finishes his soup.

We children knew perfectly well what all this meant; we would exchange glances and try not to laugh.[167]

And Aleksandr Dorokhov, the author of a Soviet guide to etiquette, has set down a revealing outsider's account of traditional communal eating practices dating back to the early 1920s, when working-class life still maintained forms close to those that had been evident before the Revolution. Assigned, as a student, to do vacation work with an *artel'* of lumberjacks, Dorokhov found himself (to his consternation) criticized for bad manners because he had helped himself too freely to meat from the communal bowl, and failed to hold a piece of bread under his spoon when helping himself to soup from the common pot, so that the table became speckled with drops of liquid.[168]

But clearly as these stories demonstrate the importance, in worker and peasant circles, of 'privacy' in the sense of self-restraint, they equally clearly illustrate a collective enforcement of conformity that was based less on self-consciousness than on external status (as underlined by the saying 'Where's honour when you've nothing to eat?' (*Chto za chest', esli nechego est'?*)[169] The powerful term *obida*, 'insult', was applied to those who disrupted the ethos of *prilichie* (decency, literally 'what is fit to be seen'): as one proverb had it, 'People live in closeness, but in insult they go under' (*V tesnote zhivut lyudi, a v obide gibnut*).[170] In such circumstances 'indecent' behaviour failed to impair the status of its perpetrator only when turned back upon someone whose behaviour was itself offensive: peasant or worker who wished to insult someone whom he or she disliked might, without loss of respect, employ bad language (*mat*) or even, as a still more deadly sanction, bare his or her backside and thrust it at the antagonist. The specific ways in which the boundaries between private and public behaviour were drawn meant that tarring and feathering were used as a very public punishment for adultery, but that Russian peasant communities were notoriously reluctant to intervene in cases where domestic violence erupted in individual households (not just because such intervention would have threatened male authority, but because it would have violated the notion of the *izba* as

---

[167] I. E. Repin, 'Vpechatleniya detstva 1844–1854', in *Dalekoe blizkoe* (Leningrad, 1982), 42.

[168] Dorokhov, *Eto stoit zapomnit'*, 4–5.

[169] V. Dal', *Tolkovyi slovar' zhivogo velikorusskogo yazyka* (2nd edn., 4 vols.; Moscow, 1880–1882), iv. 599, lists a number of variants of this proverb, including 'Khudaya chest', koli nechego est'', 'Chest' dobra, da s''est' nel'zya'.

[170] Ibid. ii. 583.

personal space—a term that is absolutely appropriate here, given the proverb 'one's little hut is one's own wide space' (*svoya izbushka, svoi prostor*)).[171] Equally, premarital intercourse was tolerated so long as it remained furtive, and there was widespread acceptance of infanticide as a means whereby a young woman might remove the tangible evidence of her 'loss of honour'.[172]

Above all, the concept of *prilichie* was based on the idea of *common decency*, upon the perception that personal needs should give way before the needs of the community at large. The same principle applied to other instances of collective engagement, such as the various forms of 'mutual aid' found in Russian peasant and working-class culture. In Russian villages, 'help from without' was formalized through the practices of *pomochi* and *toloka*, respectively the northern and southern dialect words for gatherings of neighbours to help bring in the hay, spread manure, or harvest quick-spoiling crops that ripened in bulk (for instance, cabbages or peas), or to carry out any other such jobs that were beyond the resources of a single family group.[173] Convention demanded that households benefiting from *pomochi* should themselves take part in helping others, and that the householder who received aid should also provide reciprocation in the form of hospitality. The realization that *pomochi* were part of an exchange system was expressed in the proverb, 'Darom kormyat, tak na pomoch' zovut' (meaning roughly, 'There's no such thing as a free lunch'), and also in a standard formula used for inviting neighbours to take part in a pomoch' session: 'Come over to us and eat our bread and salt; there'll be plenty of nice vodka and beer for our guests; but please heed our plea; help us and other Orthodox folk to cope with the work we have to do.'[174] Other, similar, patterns of collective reciprocity included *magarych*, a word applying to a wide set of practices, including the 'treats' that were supposed to be provided by an employer to workmen, and the drinks stood by a new employee to workmates. In Russian cities, the custom of *zemlyachestvo*, or

---

[171] On violence and adultery, see particularly Barbara Engel, *Between the Fields and the City: Women, Work and Family in Russia, 1861–1914* (Cambridge, 1994), 24–5. For this and other proverbs relating to the sanctity of the 'hut' (e.g., 'Every hut has its own roof', *vsyakaya izbushka svoei krovlei kryta*), see Dal', *Tolkovyi slovar'*, ii. 10.

[172] See particularly David Ransel, *Mothers of Misery: Child Abandonment in Russia* (Princeton, 1988); on attitudes to sexuality generally, see Barbara Engel, 'Peasant Morality and Pre-Marital Relations in Late Imperial Russia', *Journal of Social History* 23 (1990), 49–64.

[173] M. M. Gromyko, *Traditsionnye normy povedeniya i formy obshcheniya russkikh krest'ian XIX veka* (Moscow, 1986), 31–62.

[174] Quoted in ibid. 26. For 'Darom kormyat' see V. Dal', *Tolkovyi slovar'*, ii. 274, headword *pomogat'*. This entry also gives general information on the *pomochi*; on *toloka*, see ibid. iii. 412, headword *toloch'*. For a fuller discussion of mutual aid and its relationship with corruption, see C. Kelly, '"Self-Interested Giving": Bribery and Etiquette in Late Imperial Russia', in A. Ledeneva, S. Lovell, and A. Rogachevsky (eds.), *Bribery and Blat in Imperial Russia* (London, 2000).

'regional networking', meant that incomers from the village could turn to those from the region from which they came in order to find help with seeking accommodation or jobs, and factory workers would band together into *arteli*, 'gangs', in order to hire themselves out to factories or to pool resources in order to mitigate the costs of accommodation and food.[175] (In practice, these two kinds of 'help from without' often intersected, since an *artel'* was likely to be formed among *zemlyaki*, thereby both facilitating and formalizing the practice of *zemlyachestvo*.)

The various practices that can be grouped together as 'mutual aid' were not 'spontaneous', but strictly controlled. They were not expressions of the innate generosity of the Russian soul,[176] but forms of 'self-interested giving' in which favours were calculated according to the likelihood of a perceived return. Moreover, in the late nineteenth and early twentieth centuries, this 'return' was increasingly often in cash or goods rather than in labour or favours. In the 1890s, an informant from Vologodskaya province complained that the rise in land ownership among peasants there had had pernicious effects on cooperation. 'Those admirable survivals of the past, the *pomochi*, are beginning gradually to take on a totally different appearance,' he wrote, explaining this by the fact that the householder receiving help now had to provide such expensive treats that it was sometimes cheaper simply to get in hired labour.[177] And by the 1920s, job-seekers at cotton mills in some parts of the Ivanovo *guberniya* 'distributed vodka to foremen and onlookers in order to secure places', rather than relying on the obligations of *zemlyachestvo*.[178] In such cases, the boundary between 'self-interested giving' and bribery was extremely narrow.

For Smiles, refusal of bribes was a *sine qua non* of 'nature's gentleman' (*Self-Help*, 399), and the writer devoted an entire chapter of one of his

---

[175] See Johnson, *Peasant and Proletarian*, 68–70, 72, 91–2.

[176] Gromyko has distinguished three kinds of *pomochi*: aid rendered routinely for big jobs (carrying out manure, harvesting, sewing, etc.); aid given in a crisis (e.g. when a cottage burned down or a family was stricken by sickness); and aid directly requested by the head of a household himself (say, in the case of an unexpected crop glut). She asserts that aid given in a crisis was obligatory for everyone, while in the first and third cases, a return was expected (*Traditsionnye normy*, 61–2). However, even in the second case, one may doubt whether total disinterest was always preserved. As another historian of Russian peasant culture, Christine Worobec, has put it, 'households whose destitution was the result of an irresponsible or alcoholic patriarch received neither sympathy nor help'. (*Peasant Russia: Family and Community in the Post-Emancipation Period* (Princeton, 1991), 7.) Judgements of this kind were based at least partly on an appreciation that improvident individuals were not only 'beyond help', but incapable of contributing to the community in return for aid received.

[177] Anonymous informant's report to the Tenishevskoe byuro: quoted in Gromyko, *Normy povedeniya*, 59.

[178] See Chris Ward, *Russia's Cotton Workers and the New Economic Policy* (Cambridge, 1990), 93.

sequels to *Self-Help*, *Duty* (1880), to 'Men who Cannot be Bought'. Before preceding to eulogies on role models, such as Sir Humphrey Davy, William Pitt, Sir Thomas Outram, Meyer Anselm (founder of the Rothschild dynasty), and Lord Macaulay, whose upright probity and independence are intended as models for the reader, Smiles offers a ringing denunciation of those who fall below the standards of 'nature's gentlemen':

First, there are men who *can* be bought. There are rogues innumerable, who are ready to sell their bodies and souls for money or for drink. Who has not heard of the elections which have been made void through bribery and corruption? . . . The men who sell themselves are slaves; their buyers are dishonest and unprincipled. . . . [*The Times* says.] 'It is all important that the public service should be pure, and that no suspicion should rest on the name of any official in a post of confidence. It would be an evil day if it were generally suspected that civil servants took backsheesh or *pots de vin*.' . . . In Russia, the corruption of civil servants, even of the highest grade, is most gross. You must buy your way by gold. Bribery in every conceivable form is practised.[179]

These passages appeared, translated with word-for-word accuracy, in both Russian translations of *Duty*.[180] Many of the Russian workers who read Smiles would undoubtedly have endorsed his denunciation of official venality, and regarded the institution of bribery as appalling. Yet at the same time, conscious workers such as Semen Kanatchikov and Petr Moiseenko recorded their participation in practices such as *zemlyachestvo* without question or embarrassment,[181] though these would certainly have struck Smiles as improper, and—in some of their transmutations—verged on, or indeed crossed the border into, bribery. It is not so far, after all, from the case of a bottle of vodka handed to a foreman in return for a job to the case depicted in Chekhov's story *In the Ravine*, where a peasant patriarch presents the warder of his jailed son with a silver tea-glass holder ornamented with the inscription, 'Moderation in everything'. In both cases, the gift's purpose was coercive; in neither case was this considered inappropriate. There is abundant evidence that workers (like most other Russian citizens) condemned the recipient of bribes far more strongly than the purveyor of bribes.[182]

Not only did self-help ideologies do little to combat traditional non-individualist patterns of social organization that depended on exchange of

---

[179] S. Smiles, *Duty* (London, 1880), 70–2.

[180] See Smail's, *Dolg*, trans. S. Maikova (1882), and Smail's, *Sobranie sochinenii*, iv. 79–82.

[181] P. A. Moiseenko records how, visiting a textile mill to look for work, 'I had a look for *zemlyaks*. It turned out the under-foreman was one. I sent for him and we got talking. It turned out there were plenty of other *zemlyaks* at the plant too. I got a job and got fixed up in an *artel'* of *zemlyaks*' (*Vospominaniya starogo revolyutsionera* (Moscow, 1966), 15).

[182] For example, the derogatory verb *mogarychnit'*, 'to live off presents', 'to scrounge' did not have an equivalent describing bribe-taking.

favours, then, but they also failed to impede the transmutation of those types of exchange into assymmetrical relationships in which favours were traded for gifts or money. The Russian workers who read Smiles in translation were as eager to broaden their minds as the British workers that he described in the preface to the 1859 edition of *Self-Help*, and they had their own and firm concepts of 'decent behaviour'—in class outsiders as well as in themselves. In the late nineteenth and early twentieth centuries, abusive or impolite address on the part of foremen and other factory officials, or of customers in taverns, inspired strong resentment on the part of working-class Russians.[183] But the brutal conditions of life in Russia were such that self-reliance, in the pure terms demanded by Smiles, was simply not feasible. A villager who arrived in St Petersburg or Moscow without contacts could not turn to an agency for a job, or rely on impressing factory foremen with his self-improved personality: he or she was—without help from *zemlyaki*—certain to end up unemployed, half-starved, and sleeping on the streets or in a doss-house, or else pushed into some kind of criminal activity (petty theft, prostitution).[184] Equally, mutual aid systems in villages—while in no sense inflexible and beyond change—survived because they were essential to those who could not afford to hire labour or purchase machinery or draught animals. Prudence demanded that networks were used, and the persisting inadequacies in the rural and urban infrastructure meant that they continued to be well into the twentieth century. As the 'community spirit' broke down under the pressure of urbanization, and as exchanges hardened so that they became commercial transactions rather than expressions of goodwill, workers were often sucked into relationships that crossed the border between 'self-interested giving' and bribery. Here too, necessity was almost certain to be the mother of conformity.

Illuminating evidence about the persistence of the culture of 'self-interested giving' in the late imperial era, and its possible transmutation into bribery, can be drawn from the work of Smiles's Russian imitators. These imitators, while emphasizing the virtues of self-education and other aspects of Smiles's creed, tended to take a less stern attitude to bribery than he. *Self-Education as the Path to Wealth*, for example, gives advice about presents that is based on expediency, rather than on strict adherence to moral absolutes:

---

[183] See S. A. Smith, 'The Social Meanings of Swearing: Workers and Bad Language in Late Imperial and Early Soviet Russia', *Past and Present* 160 (1998), 183–5; and Introduction above.

[184] After being accepted in the *artel'*, Moiseenko observed: 'Completely saved from hunger. A shared flat, a shared table, and all my workmates (*tovarishchi*) young people.' (*Vospominaniya starogo revolyutsionera*, 17).

There is a saying: 'little gifts cement a friendship'. Like all proverbs, this is only correct up to a point. In reality, friendship has nothing at all to do with presents. . . . It is better neither to give, nor to receive presents. In any case, if you cannot get by without gifts, then adopt the rule: give, rather than receive.[185]

The softening of tone apparent here—it is better to give than to receive—is evident in the continuation, which suggests that there are circumstances in which it is all right to accept favours (so long as the person extending them is your superior): 'Having done a favour for someone, we will continue to take an interest in him out of the self-indulgent feeling that he ought to be grateful to us. And therefore the same holds in reverse: if a person who might be useful to you later on does you some kindness, do not refuse the kindness.'[186] In other words, it was less stigmatizing to be a bribe-giver than a bribe-taker, unless the 'bribe' came in the form of a downward trickle of patronage, a 'noblesse oblige' gesture of condescension. Here the audience addressed is a more privileged one than the workers Smiles himself had in mind (petty officials or white-collar workers appear to be the readers in view), but the code of 'self-interested giving' held good. Indeed, informal networks were characteristic not just of Russian working-class and peasant culture, but at considerably higher educational levels. As late as 1902, it was perfectly natural for Mariamna Davydova, a woman from the old, though impoverished, gentry family of Lopukhin, to contact an acquaintance when her husband needed a new job.[187] And a law setting out the proper attributes of Russian officials (originally composed in 1720, but still in force in 1912), condemned bribe-taking, yet imposed on officials the duty of exercising the 'patronage' that was the root of arbitrariness, *proizvol*:

The general qualities of every person who occupies a position in the civil service, and the general duties, which must always be a looking-glass of his behaviour, are: 1) common sense; 2) goodwill with regard to his subordinates; 3) love of humanity; 4) fidelity to the service of His Imperial Majesty; 5) zealous pursuit of the common weal; 6) energy in the performance of his duties; 7) honesty, selflessness and *abstinence from bribe-taking*; 8) just and disinterested judgement of all, independent of their social standing; 9) *patronage to the innocent and injured*.[188]

It is scarcely surprising that, while bribery was frowned upon by many officials, it remained endemic: as one upright official, Sergei Svetlov,

[185] *Samoobrazovanie—kak put' k bogatstvu*, i. 42.

[186] ibid. i. 43.

[187] See *On the Estate: Memoirs of Russia before the Revolution* (London, 1986), 59: 'I wrote to the vice-governor of Warsaw, Krevsky, who was married to the sister of a good friend of ours. He promised to give Lev a post as a regional director.'

[188] D. Mordukhai-Boltovsky, *Svod zakonov Rossiiskoi Imperii* (St Petersburg, 1912), iii, *Ustav o sluzhbe po opredeleniyu ot pravitel'stva*, article 705; my emphasis.

recalled, 'The vast majority [of civil servants] conduct themselves in an orderly and honest manner [*dobroporyadochno i chestno*], but there are some bribe-takers too, especially in certain departments [*spetsial'nye vedomstva*]. In this respect, a melancholy notoriety is enjoyed by quartermasters in the armed forces, by railway engineers, and by economists and supervisors working in state institutes.'[189] For its part, a special issue of *Novyi Satirikon* devoted to bribery was to confirm this last point, lambasting in particular diocesan schools (*eparkhial'nye uchilishcha*) and the consistory courts, which latter were described as 'a veritable academy, a Sorbonne of bribe-taking'.[190]

There was also another area where Smiles's individualist views made little headway. His attempt to see self-enrichment as inseparable from upright behaviour meant that, as well as manuals of self-education, his books were pioneering guides to business ethics: 'Attention, application, accuracy, method, punctuality, and despatch, are the principal qualities required for the official conduct of business of any sort' (*Self-Help*, 270). Though the most popular, they were by no means the only sources on conscientious business practice. R. Marden's *Success in Life*, translated into Russian in 1903, emphasized the role not only of 'strength of will', 'persistence', and 'enthusiasm', but also of 'self-respect', 'reading', 'good manners', 'honesty and a sense of fairness'.[191] And in 1917, The 'Lady's World' Calendar printed a list of the so-called 'American Rules of Life', which spelled out these abstract requirements into a list of concrete actions:

1. Brief yourself thoroughly on a subject.
2. Stick to one opinion and don't chop and change between tasks.
3. Be efficient, but don't rush things.
4. Be systematic in everything that you do.
5. Finish whatever you start. One 'today' is worth two 'tomorrows'.
6. Don't listen to too much advice. Be independent.
7. Stick to every decision you make and be punctual to the minute.
8. Don't ever sit doing nothing; always give something useful to do to your hands and your head; they can rest while you're asleep.
9. Be gentle in everything, be generous in what you say and what you do; help others along the thorny path.
10. Always start by being gentle.
11. Anyone at the top had to start at the bottom.
12. Don't try to get rich quick; a small reliable return will ensure your well-being.
13. Remember that your thoughts are your own, but your words belong to others.[192]

[189] *Peterburgskaya zhizn'*, 21.
[190] E. Vensky, 'Tekhnika vzyatki', *Novyi Satirikon* 35 (1915), 3.
[191] Marden, *Uspekh v zhizni*, *passim*.
[192] *Kalendar' 'Damskii mir' na 1917 god*, 255.

But it is significant that translated material of this kind did not initiate a native tradition (an echo of the emphasis on efficiency can be heard in post-revolutionary advice literature, but without the appeal to high moral tone). Pre-revolutionary advice literature was polarized between material advancing an ideology of self-advancement through education, and an ideology advancing self-assertion at all costs: as *Self-Education as a Path to Wealth* put it, 'Away with old prejudices! Influence people and bend them to your will!'[193]

Again, the reason for this lies in the new context into which Smiles was absorbed. The 'entrepreneurial intelligentsia', as Mark Steinberg has termed it[194]—in other words, the community of self improving business men—was small compared with its counterpart in, say, Britain or America. Conversely, ambitious peasant entrepreneurs made up a substantial proportion of the Russian merchant class by the late nineteenth century. Russian criticism of corruption and proto-corruption, and insistence on the need for probity in human transactions, emanated above all from sectors of society which were hostile to trade and commercialism, and, indeed, in some cases, *Realpolitik* in a general sense. A typical instance is Tolstoi's attack on peasant networking in *A Calendar of Proverbs*:

[Taking part in the *skhodka*] is not hard for people who do not think about how to judge according to God's law, but only about how to do well by a connection, a brother, a croney. . . . But it is hard to forget your connections, your relations, your cronies at the *skhodka*, and to remember only truth and justice, and to judge by God's way, and to consider how as little harm as possible may be done.[195]

The very point of this guidance, though, was that it flew in the face of contemporary practical reality: a village commune without interest groups was as much an impossibility as a code of 'Tolstoyan business ethics' would have been (commercial activity being perceived by Tolstoi and his followers as immoral per se). Equally, Russian radical groups, such as the Social Democrats, could not conceive of capitalist business activity as compatible with probity in any sense; hence, they were no more successful than the Tolstoyans in evolving a model for ethical commercial practices.

The difficulty in absorbing Smiles came not because his work was insufficiently known, or because his attitude to self-reliance was incomprehensible in itself, but because the conditions in which the statement had been formulated by him was very different to those operating in turn-of-the-century Russia. Like the participants in the Protestant sects that Max Weber, famously, saw as the pioneers of capitalism, Smiles accorded a

[193] *Samoobrazovanie kak put' k bogatstvu*, iii. 64.
[194] Steinberg, *Moral Communities*, 38–48.
[195] Tolstoi, *Kalendar' s poslovitsami na 1887 god*, *PSS* xl. 22.

strictly controlled role to 'mutual aid'.[196] But though the rigidity of his code helps explain its appeal to moral absolutists such as the Russian radicals, it also made it peculiarly ill-suited to the circumstances actually prevailing in Russian everyday life, where reliance upon others, even in ways that would have been considered morally questionable by some of those involved, was a prerequisite of survival in villages and cities, where high moral tone had little impact upon the market-place, and where 'looking after one's relations' was serenely assumed to be proper by many educated members of the gentry (such hostile terms as 'nepotism' or 'croneyism' would not have been used).

CONCLUSION

In the late nineteenth and early twentieth centuries, advice literature became more varied than ever before. Material concerning etiquette often rehearsed familiar clichés about cleanliness and respectfulness, but a new literature of hygiene, parading its own expertise and authority, exhorted readers to care for the physical body more intensively than they had in the past, and housekeeping manuals propounded extremely elaborate inventories of necessary possessions.

As well as a proliferation of genres, there was a proliferation of contradictions. The rise of codes of 'rational living' was countered by an upsurge of sources propounding consumerism; the same sources (for example, magazines and calendars aimed at the well-off) often contained material that pulled in both directions. Reception, too, was haphazard: intellectual sources criticized and parodied the vulgarity and vacuousness of advice on etiquette and on house management, yet well-off members of the intelligentsia themselves often lived in a manner perfectly congruent with the recommendations set out in advice on refinement.

So far as the new readership groups that began to emerge in the late nineteenth and early twentieth centuries went, matters were equally unpredictable. There was a market for self-education books among the despised petit-bourgeoisie, and even conscious workers did not necessarily prove fertile soil for the ideas about individual probity, self-reliance and internal self-regulation set out in Samuel Smiles's extremely popular self-help books. To be sure, the proponents of Smilesian individualism were

[196] M. Weber, 'The Protestant Sects and the Rise of Capitalism', *Essays in Sociology* trans. H. H. Gerth and C. Wright Mills (London, 1993), 303. Smiles's own views have been plausibly linked to his Calvinist background (he was a Scot whose father was a member of an exclusive Presbyterian sect). See A. Jarvis, *Samuel Smiles and the Construction of Victorian Values* (Stroud, 1997), and T. Travers, *Samuel Smiles and the Victorian Work Ethic* (New York, 1987).

less frank in acknowledging their creative adaptation of borrowed material than the Russian editors of Baden-Powell's *Scouting for Boys*, who, after introducing scouting as 'a form of first-aid against the deficiencies of the modern upbringing', with its emphasis on 'rationalism' and 'careerism', emphasize the unfamiliarity of *skautizm*, and suggest that its values will trickle through only gradually: 'Don't be too stern and demanding. Scouting in Russia is too young, too new an activity for us to be able to set our demands of it too high.'[197] But in practice, Smiles's 'demands' were reduced, and the wide implications of the self-help ethic contracted to mean, in the first instance, self-betterment through education; in the second (as used by Nordman at Penaty, for example), the renunciation, by an intelligentsia committed to enhancing the well-being of 'the Russian People', of certain privileges, such as that of escaping all domestic labour; and in the third, economic self-advancement at all costs. However, the last was a considerably less popular interpretation than the first two. And the figure most readily evoked in the Russian mind by the term 'self-made man' was a 'man of the people' who had escaped his origins and transformed himself into a member of the intelligentsia. One such was Kornei Chukovsky, as hostile to Russian commercial culture as he was to the patronizing endeavours of Nordman and her like;[198] another Maksim Gor'ky. Intellectuals of their convictions were to play a major part in shaping cultural policy in the post-revolutionary era, when an ethos of *kul'turnost'* embracing intellectual self-betterment, hygiene, and respect for high culture began to be propagandized still more assiduously than before, and when conscious attempts were made to distinguish the Soviet campaign to 'educate the people' (*vospityvat' narod*) from the pre-revolutionary intelligentsia's philanthropic efforts to do the same. At the same time, the traditions of 'self-interested giving'—of official *proizvol* on the one hand, of peasant collectivism warped by its recontextualization in the harsh world of the Russian city on the other—were to bear poisonous fruit after the Revolution, when Soviet leaders fulminated against 'backward' practices such as *zemlyachestvo*, yet presided over a further degeneration of 'proto-corruption' into all-out corruption.[199]

---

[197] *Boi-skauty*, 275.

[198] On the former, see e.g. Chukovsky, 'Tretii sort', (*Sobranie sochinenii v 6 tomakh*, vi (Moscow, 1966), 75). On the latter, cf. his assertion that Nordman was only polite to the servants when there were others around to see it: *Dnevnik 1901–1929* (Moscow, 1991), 57 (entry for 10 Apr. 1913).

[199] On the relationship of 'proto-corruption' to 'corruption', see James C. Scott, *Comparative Political Corruption* (Englewood Cliffs, NJ, 1972), 7–11.

CHAPTER FOUR

'The Personal Does Not Exist': Advising the Early Soviet Mass Reader, 1917–1953

Лозунг:
                    — В ногах у старья не ползай! —
Готов
        ежедневно
                    твердить раз сто:
изящество —
                    это стопроцентная польза,
удобство одежд
                            и жилья простор.
        (Mayakovsky, '"Give Us an Elligant Life"', 1927)[1]

Tables and benches
Radio set
Portraits of the leaders
Magazines
Newspapers
Slogans
Board games—chess and draughts
Football, volley-ball, skittles
Socialist competition noticeboard
Wall newspaper
Shower
Cauldrons for heating water
Wash-tub for laundry
Washing line

('Equipment for Culture and Daily Life' at a *kolkhoz* in
        Kabardino-Balkar: *Nashi dostizheniya*, 1935).

In Soviet literature and film of the 1930s and 1940s, representatives of the *partiinaya znat'* (Party aristocracy) figured commonly enough. But the deepest and most striking portrayal of the pampered upper echelons of the

---

[1] The slogan: | 'Don't bow down to the past!' | I'll repeat every day | a hundred times: | 'elegance' means | what's totally useful, | enough living space | and comfortable clothes. V. Mayakovsky, 'Daesh' izyachnuyu zhizn''. (*PSS* viii. 35).

Party hierarchy during the Stalin era is to be found in a historical novel written more than ten years after the dictator's death, Solzhenitsyn's *The First Circle*. One of the three central figures in the narrative, the diplomat Innokenty Volodin, is a high-ranking Soviet diplomat who inhabits a closed world of enclosed information, dynastic marriages, and long stays in Paris. His career has its stresses (such as the need to work deep into the night because that is Stalin's own work-pattern) but also its compensations: Western clothes and luxuries, and—through his wife—access to a circle of powerful and influential politicians and cultural figures. A culminating scene of the novel shortly before Innokenty's arrest represents a cocktail party with Western jazz playing in the background, an opulent spread of food and drink, and undercurrents of intrigue and treachery below the small talk. Itself the parody of a civilized gathering, it stands in grotesque contrast to a number of other social events in the novel—the Christmas party in the *sharashka* (research institute for political prisoners) in the opening scenes, and the celebration of solidarity among the former *sharashka* inmates going to the camps—just as Alevtina Makarygina's preference for antique crystal to the Soviet product, 'squint-sided and passed down the conveyor of indifferent hands', clashes with Innokenty's derivation of spiritual solace from the pre-revolutionary journals left to him by his mother.[2]

The plausibility of Solzhenitsyn's portrait of Innokenty has been challenged by at least one reasonably well-qualified observer. Solzhenitsyn's friend Lev Kopelev regarded the character as an example of 'those homunculi who perforce are conceived in newspaper and archival test tubes'. Michael Scammell, Solzhenitsyn's biographer, comments, 'Kopelev had a right to criticize because he knew [Soviet high society and intelligentsia circles] far better than Solzhenitsyn (indeed was a member of them) and understood how they worked . . . some of Solzhenitsyn's simplifications sprang from ignorance of his subject matter.'[3] One could object with reference to, say, Larisa Vasil'eva's group biography *The Kremlin Wives*, which shows that there was a variety of different 'high society circles' in Moscow, some not too unlike those depicted in Solzhenitsyn's fictional portraits. But the main point is that mimesis is not (Solzhenitsyn's conscious aims notwithstanding) the most important artistic principle in *The First Circle*. The novel is, rather, one whose strength, like that of Dostoevsky's *The Idiot*, depends on its creation of a nightmarish imagined reality whose relation to the real one is tangential. Innokenty succeeds as a fictional figure because the 'circle' that he inhabits represents an artistically adequate alternative world to that in which the

[2] Aleksandr Solzhenitsyn, *V kruge pervom* (Paris, 1989), 91 (ch. 62).
[3] Michael Scammell, *Solzhenitsyn: A Biography* (London, 1984), 500.

prisoners dwell. Its strangeness does not so much attest the verisimilitude of the latter by contrast (according to the familiar realist technique used by Tolstoi when balancing Levin and Anna in *Anna Karenina*) as indicate that there *is* no normal reality.

A kind of bizarre confirmation of the symbolic truth of Solzhenitsyn's imaginary universe comes from one of the few genres of advice literature dating from the Stalin era that was specifically aimed at the Soviet elite: guidebooks for Soviet diplomats. The perverted world of the late 1940s had its share of curious ironies, but few were odder than the concatenation by which, as Party ideologues lambasted 'kow-towing to the West', 'rootless cosmopolitanism' and 'foreignism' (*inostranshchina*), a secret and extreme pleasure was taken in Western products. Audiences flocked to 'trophy films', the products of the Third Reich cinema confiscated by Soviet forces in the aftermath of the Second World War.[4] Meanwhile, diplomats were exposed to translations of two Western textbooks on protocol in which the diplomat was represented as a combination of eighteenth-century *honnête homme* and Jesuitical dissembler.

The books in question were Jules Cambon's *Le Diplomate* and Ernest Satow's *A Guide to Diplomatic Practice*. In Satow's book, the link with the tradition of the *honnête homme* is quite explicit. 'Counsels to Diplomats', a chapter dealing with the diplomat's personality, begins with a long quotation from Callières' *De la manière de négocier avec les souverains* (Paris, 1716). The diplomat is the perfect courtier. Restrained, tactful, yet urbane, he is possessed of:

un abord toujours ouvert, doux, civil, agréable, des manières aisées et insinuantes qui contribuent beaucoup à acquérir les inclinations de ceux avec qui on traite, au lieu qu'un air grave et froid, et une mine sombre et rude, rebute et cause d'ordinaire de l'aversion.

всегда открытый подход к человеку, мягкость, учтивость, приятность обращения, непринужденная и располагающая манера, которая очень помогает снискать расположение тех, с кем имеешь дело, тогда как холодный и важный вид, грубая и мрачная манера обычно отталкивают и внушают отвращение.[5]

---

[4]   See M. Turovskaia, 'The Tastes of Soviet Movie-Goers during the 1930s', in T. Lahusen and G. Kuperman (eds.), *Late Soviet Cultures: From Perestroika to Novostroika* (Durham, NC, 1993), 104.

[5]   'an approach that is always open, softness and civility, pleasantness in his address, an easy and ingratiating manner that is helpful to attaining the favour of those with whom one deals; at the same time a cold, haughty air, a coarse and morose manner generally repel and awaken repulsion.' E. Satow, *A Guide to Diplomatic Practice* (2nd revi. edn.; 2 vols., London, 1922), i. 131 [French spelling modernized]; Satou, *Rukovodstvo po diplomaticheskoi praktike* (1947), 103. Further refs. to these edns. in text. The fact that this edn. was issued by the 'Red Proletarian' publishing house proliferates the ironies of the venture.

He is at once self-controlled (the diplomat needs 'un esprit attentif et appliqué, qui ne se laisse point distraire par les plaisirs' ('внимательный и прилежный ум, не позволяющий себе отвлекаться удовольствиями и фривольными забавами', Satow, i. 130/Satou, 103), and open-handed, though never without due calculation of the impression which he intends to make on the circles of distinguished foreigners in which he moves:

Il faut que celui qui en est revêtu, soit liberal et magnifique, mais avec choix et avec dessein, que sa magnificence paroisse dans son train, dans sa livrée et dans le reste de son equipage; que la propreté, l'abondance, et même la délicatesse, regne sur sa table; . . . qu'il tâche d'entrer ses parties de divertissements, mais d'une manière agréable et sans le contraindre, et qu'il y apporte toujours un air ouvert, complaisant, honnête et un désir continuel de lui plaire. (Satow, i. 132)[6]

чтобы поддержать достойнство, связанное с этим занятием, надо, чтобы тот, кому оно поручено, был щедр и блестящ, но с толком и расчетом, чтобы в его блеске можно было судить по его свите, по его прислуге и вообще по его окружению; чтобы за его столом царила опрятность, изобилие и даже утонченность . . . чтобы он и сам участвовал в устраиваемых для него развлечениях, но с приятностью и без принуждений, чтобы он сохранял при этом открытый, честный и довольный вид и выказывал постоянное желание быть приятным монарху. (Satou, 104)

Above all, he is conscious of his place in the social hierarchy, 'juste et modeste dans toutes ses actions; respectueux avec les princes, complaisant avec ses égaux, carressant avec ses inférieurs, doux, civil et honnête avec tout le monde' (Satow, i. 135) ['справедлив и скромен во всех своих действиях, почтителен с государями, любезен с равными себе, ласков с низшими, кроток, учтив и честен со всеми' (Satou, 105)].

The fact that ethics plays a lesser role than the acting out of refinement is underlined by Callières' treatment of the question of spying. The spy is described as 'un honorable Espion' (*pochetnyi shpion*: Satow i. 133/Satou 104), whose duties include 'discovering the secrets of the court' where he is placed. Intelligence-gathering is seen as a necessary condition of diplomatic activity. And another questionable practice in ethical terms, bribery, is

---

[6] 'A person dignified by this name must be munificent and keep a splendid establishment, but in a way that manifests nicety and good sense; his splendidness must be visible in his staff, in his servants, and in everything that surrounds him; good order, opulence and even sophistication must be evident at his table . . . he should take care to put in an appearance at [court] entertainments, but in an agreeable manner that does not constrain others, always maintaining an open, complaisant and honourable manner and showing a constant desire to amuse [the monarch].'

accepted by Satow himself as a perfectly acceptable manner of gaining access to necessary information:

There are many cases recorded in history of such proceedings being practised on a large scale, and with considerable effect. (Satow, i. 142)

История знает немало случаев, когда цдача взятокъ практиковалась в широком масштабе, и с большим успехом. (Satou, 162)

It is remarkable that none of this, one would have supposed, totally antipathetic material is presented with any emphasis on its remoteness from Soviet practice. Indeed, the 1947 edition of the text brings the material closer to Soviet reality than the 1941 edition, by rendering Callières' term, *négociateur*, by the modern term *diplomat* rather than *negotsiant*. And the translator's introduction to *Rukovodstvo k diplomaticheskoi praktike* underlines the relevance of the traditional diplomatic model to the present day: 'If the diplomat possesses the essential knowledge, intelligence and tact, all the underwater rocks that he may encounter will be swum past safely, and in the end his efforts will be crowned by success' (A. A. Troyanovsky in Satou, 22). A curious sense emerges of the Soviet diplomat as courtier to some latter-day Roi Soleil, as polished a master of the intrigue behind the gobelin as he is of elegant picnics and *fêtes champêtres*.

If the diplomat in Satow's account is above all a cosmopolitan figure, easily at home among the elite of any country, Cambon, for his part, places more emphasis on the need for self-conscious shaping of the identity to reflect that of the country in which one resides:

Every nation has customs, prejudices and sentiments that are peculiar to itself. An ambassador does not put off the old Adam merely because he happens to live abroad; but as it is his duty in the interests of his country to avoid arousing enmity, he naturally tries to adapt himself as far as possible to social customs and a mental attitude that are not his own.

У каждой нации — свои нравы, свои предрассудки, своя манера выражать чувства. Живя за границей, послы не отрешаются от всего этого, но так как их задача заключается в том, чтобы служить своей стране, не создавая вокруг себя враждебного настроения, то они, естественно, стараются приспособиться к чужому образу жизни и мыслей.[7]

This chameleonism, Cambon admits, may offend some, but only those who are naive and unaware of the demands of the profession:

---

[7] Jules Cambon, *The Diplomatist*, trans. C. R. Turner (London, 1931), 1; Kambon, *Diplomat* (1946), 11. Further references to these editions in text.

Diplomatists are often a puzzle to the man in the street, who is unable to realize the difficulties of their position and accordingly judges them very severely. (Cambon, 2)

Это часто сбивает с толку широкую публику, которая не понимает, как сложна роль дипломатов, и склонна без снисхождения осуждать их. (Kambon, 11)

Striking, again, is the fact that the translation brings the book closer to Soviet perceptions, rather than attempting to distance it. The rendering of Callières invokes such characteristic Stalinist values as *izobilie* (abundance) and *izyashchestvo* (elegance); the Soviet version of Cambon uses the Stalinist phrase *shirokaya publika* in order to name the mass of the population. And in his Introduction to Cambon's book, A. A. Troyanovsky, though criticizing Cambon for his naive trust in the efficacy of the League of Nations and for his unawareness of the historical dialectic, all the same endorses Cambon's ideal of the diplomat as suave and cultivated: 'A limited and dried-up person can hardly be a good diplomat' (Ограниченный, сухой человек вряд ли может быть хорошим дипломатом) (Kambon, 8).

The extent to which these books affected the reality of Soviet diplomatic practice is questionable. Certainly, the Ministry of the Interior's trainee diplomats passed through courses on deportment, conducted by remnants of the old Russian gentry, at the Ministry's Academy. The sister of the famous critic Dmitry Sviatopolk-Mirsky was one of those employed at the Academy in the 1940s, her duties including the teaching of French, and instruction in proper conduct at diplomatic receptions.[8] However, ambassadors of the late Stalin era were by no means always career diplomats as such. Some were Party functionaries promoted from other parts of the apparatus (a case in point being Andrei Gromyko, who made his way up from teaching in the provinces to postgraduate work at the annexe to the 'Red Academy' in Minsk, before being transferred to Moscow, and then nominated for diplomatic work in 1939).[9] Rather than polished citizens of the world, Stalinist diplomats were more likely to be, as evoked in Nabokov's disdainful description,

ruthless, paste-faced automatons in opulent John Held trousers and high-shouldered jackets, those *Sitzriesen* looming at our conference tables, whom—or shall I say which?—the Soviet State began to export around 1945 after more than two decades of selective breeding and tailoring, during which men's fashions abroad had begun to change, so that the symbol of infinitely available cloth could

[8] Information from an interview given by her to Gerry Smith, to whom I owe this recollection.
[9] See his *Memories*, trans. H. Shukman (London, 1989).

only provoke cruel derision (as occurred in postwar England when a famous Soviet team of professional soccer players happened to parade in mufti).[10]

However, even this caricature shows how important the symbolism of *propreté* and *abondance* was to the Soviet *corps diplomatique*; the failure came in the practical realization of this symbolism before a Western audience whose own tastes had been constrained by wartime shortages and by rationing. Even if they themselves chose not to behave like 'gentlemen', members of the Soviet elite thought that they recognized what the concept embodied, and a fantasy of 'Western diplomacy' as an exotic and feline combination of manipulative courtesy, love of luxury, and devious unreliability had a powerful hold over the Soviet architects of the Cold War.

It is to this imaginative reality of the West as both a civilizing and a corrupting force that Solzhenitsyn's Innokenty is true. 'Innokenty' is a 'speaking name' certainly, but one that articulates in a mixture of tongues. Semantically, it may be connected with 'innocence', but the derivation is from Latin, not Church Slavonic; at the level of register, it sounds unusual, even pretentious, to a Russian native speaker, much as 'Innocent' would to a modern Anglophone ear. Innokenty's place in the novel is equally ambiguous. His position as diplomat gives him the opportunity to see beyond his own situation. Significantly, he is the only character in the novel who senses that the symbolism of 'the first circle' might stand for more than his own immediate state, representing Russia's national isolation:

> 'Life has fallen apart.'
> 'But how, Innk? How has it fallen apart?' Klara blurted in desperation. 'You promised to explain everything, but you're not explaining anything!'
> He looked at her, eyes wide, then took a broken stick to serve as a pencil. He drew a circle on the damp earth.
> 'You see this circle? It's Russia [lit.: the fatherland]. That's the first circle. And here's the second circle.' He drew another circle round the outside of the first. 'That's humanity. So you think the first circle is connected with the second? Not a bit of it! There are whole fences of prejudice in between. Barbed wire with machine-gun posts, even. You can hardly break through in body or soul. So the result is that there's no such thing as humanity: only separate state after separate state after separate state... [lit.: fatherland after fatherland after fatherland].[11]

Innokenty draws his diagram on the 'damp earth', which in folk tradition is the maternal medium (*mat' syra zemlya*), and hence the symbol of

---

[10] V. Nabokov, *Speak, Memory* (Harmondsworth, 1969), 204.
[11] Solzhenitsyn, *V kruge pervom*, 348–9, ch. 44.

transcendental and unchanging values, the ultimate truths of birth and death, as opposed to the expedient immediacy of the 'fatherland'. While unconsciously in touch with this symbolism and these truths, however, Innokenty is at the same time a dissembler, the representative of the distorted and perverted national identity of the 'fatherland' which he so agonizingly criticizes. Not only in the terms of the 'broad public' and of Soviet law, but in the terms of international law, he is guilty of an act of treachery, and a bungled one at that. Certainly, the world in which he lives is one in which 'loyalty' in the usual sense (for instance, the determination of Lev Rubin to undertake the duties that have been assigned to him), is a morally problematic category; however, the question of whether *active* infidelity is permissible is left open. At once the instrument of the regime and its victim, Innokenty is a symbol of Western influence as both salutary and insidious, embodying a division in perception that was especially painful and acute in the historical world that Solzhenitsyn took as his starting point.

The diplomatic manuals of the Stalin period are exceptional in resonating with such a complex literary representation as Solzhenitsyn's novel; what is more, these conduct guides for the *verkhushka* (Soviet elite) have no parallels elsewhere in the culture. Though pamphlets aimed at the 'middle management' of the Soviet regime were published throughout the early Soviet period,[12] instruction for high-ranking officials was scanty, and almost invariably of a negative kind. The crucial term here was *komchvanstvo* ('communist arrogance'), condemned by Lenin in 1922 as one of the three main threats to the new Soviet state (the other two were bribery and illiteracy).[13] Throughout the first decades of Soviet power, this heinous compound of faults was denounced in official statements such as *Pravda* editorials, and excoriated in satirical portraits such as cartoons in *Krokodil*. *Komchvanstvo* embraced both insensitivity to higher Party authority, a misreading by an official of his place in the chain of command, and also an insensitivity to the needs of the general public, a failure to heed 'signals from below'. Naturally, it was particularly the second aspect that was most frequently exposed in material intended for lay readers. Themes regularly exposed in *Krokodil* cartoons during the 1920s, 1930s, and 1940s included the length of time that petitioners were expected to wait while presenting their problems to officials, brusqueness and lack of sympathy towards

---

[12] See e.g. *Nastol'naya kniga volostnogo rabotnika* (Moscow: izd. NKVD, 1925), cited in *Programmy i metodicheskie zapiski edinoi trudovoi shkoly* (Moscow and Leningrad, 1927), vi. 92 (as recommended reading for the 'co-operative' vocational section in Russian city schools). For a discussion of some material of this kind, see Oleg Khakhordin, *The Collective and the Individual in Soviet Russia: A Study of Practices* (Berkeley, 1999).

[13] Lenin, 'Doklad na II vserossiiskom s"ezde politprosvetov', *Sochineniya* (4th edn., Moscow, 1941–67), xxxiii. 55.

members of the public, and the persistence of croneyism and nepotism in official institutions.[14]

But if *komchvanstvo* became associated with a clear set of negative qualities, there was a good deal less clarity about the positive attributes of the 'responsible official' (*otvetstvennyi rabotnik*), who, like the tsarist official of legal codes, that impossible combination of patronage and disinterest, was a mixture of incompatible qualities. On the one hand, he or she was 'simple', 'modest', and ever-sensitive to 'signals from below': 'To be straightforward and modest [*prostym i skromnym*] means to be sensitive in your dealings with people, to make efforts to satisfy their needs and desires, to fight with red tape [*volokita*], with soullessness and callousness [*cherstvost'*],' as a *Pravda* article had it in January 1953.[15] But on the other, the official was granted wide-ranging powers of surveillance over the behaviour of his subordinates. As the same article went on, 'It is impossible to remain indifferent if it becomes known that an employee [*rabotnik*] is behaving badly in his domestic life [*v bytu*], that he is immodest in his private life, has dirty and impure habits and behaves in a self-serving manner. No matter what the achievements of an employee, if he behaves in an unworthy manner, he must be brought to his senses in time.'[16] In other words, modesty was always requisite, but not when dealing with immodesty, a paradox that allowed for a good deal of self-assertion in day-to-day actions and behaviour. *Proizvol*, 'caprice', was criticized where it occurred, but the power accorded by official codes to responsible officials meant that in practice *proizvol* was an ever-present hazard, particularly since subordinates' capacity to scrutinize the behaviour of their superiors was recognized only in so far as it did not threaten the principles of top-down governance and the authority of the Party.[17]

A paradigmatic text was Gladkov's massively popular *Cement* (1925), at once an adventure novel and a 'novelized conduct book' for rank-and-file

[14] Nepotism came under particular scrutiny in 1952, after a speech by Ekaterina Furtseva at the Nineteenth Party Congress naming particularly crying cases, such as the Academy of Sciences Institute of Physics, where no less than 102 workers were related to each other. See e.g. E. Gorokhov, 'S kumovstvom pokoncheno', *Krokodil* 20 (1952), 6; N. Semenov, 'Semeistven-naya idilliya', *Krokodil* 31 (1952), 8–9. The struggle with *komchvanstvo* was also carried on by institutional means (e.g. through the establishment of the Central Control Committee (TsKK) in 1922); see Khakhordin, *The Collective and the Individual in Russia*, ch. 1.

[15] 'Na partiinye temy: prostota i skromnost'', *Pravda*, 9 Jan. 1953, 2. An earlier guide for Party activists, Toporkov's *Kak stat' kul'turnym* (1929), depends on an equally significant contrast between the responsible official's capacity to 'work with men and machines', and his ability to dominate his environment (p. 39, p. 6).

[16] 'Na partiinye temy', 2.

[17] The obvious precedent here is military discipline: cf. *Ustav vnutrennei sluzhby Raboche-Krest'yanskoi Krasnoi Armii* (1922), Article 1 of which required of the rank and file soldier not only 'honourable and conscientious behaviour', but 'revolutionary discipline and unquestioning response to the orders of his commanders and commissars'.

Party members. The chairman of the Party executive at the cement factory where the novel is set, Bad'in, is indeed a real baddie in many respects (the terms *byurokrat*, *babnik* (womanizer), and *bandit* are all alliteratively expended on him by other characters). However, the novel makes clear that, whatever his personal failings, his ideological direction must not be questioned. It is Bad'in's speech at a meeting of the factory workers, rather than his wife Dasha's exhortations, that incites Gleb Chumalov, the worker protagonist and ex-Red Army hero, to put aside his violent sexual jealousy of Bad'in and declare his allegiance to the utopian ideal to which he and others are 'called by the Party and by Lenin'. By a different route, Gleb absorbs the dogma also ingested by Sergei, the intellectual Party member who realizes that the question of his own reinstatement to Party membership is of less consequence than the life of the Party *in toto*: 'This means that one thing and only one thing is necessary: the Party and work for the Party. The personal does not exist.'[18] If the novel produced an extremely clear message for the Party rank-and-file, what lessons the Bad'ins of the early Soviet world were supposed to derive from *Cement* remained unclear— except perhaps that ideological rectitude and incisive command was in the end more important than private propriety. A Soviet 'responsible worker' or 'supervisor' (*rukovoditel'*) was supposed to cultivate a 'tone that allowed no doubt in his authority', as employed by Pavel Korchagin, the exemplary hero of Nikolai Ostrovsky's *How the Steel was Tempered* (1935).[19]

In the absence of clear-cut positive guidance, the tendency was for responsible officials to model themselves on the behaviour of those at the top of the ladder, a tendency which had decidedly mixed effects, since when doing so they might, for instance, imitate not only the 'practicality and directness' and 'sense of responsibility' that Bukharin held to be exemplary traits in Lenin,[20] but also the leader's brusqueness in dealing with his subordinates, and his habit of resorting to abusive language when vexed. The likelihood of this was further increased after the 'show trials' of 1937–8, at which the State Prosecutor, Vyshinsky, apostrophized the defendants as 'a foul-smelling heap of human garbage' at 'the very limit of human vileness', and described Trotsky's pamphlet of 1904, *Our Political Tasks* as 'squirt[ing] venomous saliva at the great ideas of Marxism-Leninism'—so that an overt

[18] F. Gladkov, *Tsement*, *Krasnaya nov'* 1–2, 5–6 (1925) (this quote is 6. 64). The passage also appears in later redactions of this much-revised text (see Gladkov, *Tsement* (Moscow, 1964), 244, which reprints the text first published in Gladkov's *Sobranie sochinenii*, iii (1930).) Cf. M. I. Kalinin's speech to a conference of Leading Members of the Komsomol, May 1934: 'A real Communist's personal troubles occupy a *subordinate* place in his mind.' (Quoted from *On Communist Education: Selected Speeches and Articles* (Moscow, 1949), 37: emphasis original.) Thirteen years later, Kalinin's *O kommunisticheskom vospitanii* (1947) was a textbook exposition of such views on behaviour for ordinary members of the Party and Komsomol.

[19] *Kak zakalyalas' stal'* (Moscow, 1943), 202.

[20] See N. Bukharin, *O rabkore: sbornik stat'ei* (Moscow, 1924), 5.

connection was made between invective and the castigation of those who had crossed the boundaries of permissible behaviour.[21] The courtesy of some Old Bolshevik officials in the early 1920s had come as a surprise to their political opponents.[22] The officials who replaced them in the late 1920s and early 1930s, however, were of quite a different type, and brusque authoritarianism was now the norm in anyone who considered himself a *nachal'nik*, or 'boss'.[23] According to an eminently plausible anecdote, one British diplomat in Russia during the 1930s survived his entire stay on just one sentence of Russian: 'Vy svoloch', daite samoe vysshee nachal'stvo' (You're a bastard, take me to the big boss).[24] The entire Soviet population was now exposed to forms of verbal bullying that had characterized the behaviour of tsarist officials in strictly defined contexts: to their inferiors within the military or civil hierarchy, or to members of what they saw as the 'lower orders'.[25]

The behaviour patterns of 'bosses' or self-styled 'bosses' (*nachal'niki*) emerged, so to speak, by default, then; the case of intellectuals was somewhat analogous. There were assaults on 'unacceptable' forms of behaviour, notably on 'bohemianism' and 'inflexibility' during the Cultural Revolution—but criticism of aberrant behaviour is not the same as the establishment of a norm, and it cannot be said that Soviet ideology was successful in creating a single and unified model of 'the Soviet intellectual', let alone in bringing intellectual models of behaviour in line with those of the bulk of the population. There was tacit acceptance of the fact that

[21] *Report of Court Proceedings in the Case of the Anti-Soviet 'Block of Rightists and Trotskyites' Heard Before the Military Colloquium of the USSR, Moscow, March 2–13 1938* (New York, 1988), 631, 659, 467.

[22] See e.g. S. Volkonskaya (as Princess Peter Wolkonsky), *The Way of Bitterness: Soviet Russia, 1920* (London, 1931), recalling Medvedev's 'quiet courtesy' and 'absence of all needless words' (95). Cf. Ol'ga Adamova Sliozberg's account of her first husband, a fire-eating radical whose favourite phrase was 'you can't make a revolution in white gloves', but also 'a refined [*rafinirovannyi*] intellectual and polymath . . . it [was] impossible to imagine him swearing or jostling anyone.' (*Put'*, (Moscow, 1993), 140).

[23] Mary Britnieva, who knew Russia well, recalled the 'hopeless muddling and rudeness of the illiterate officials we came across' in 1930 as something new (*One Woman's Story* (London, 1934), 238). At a higher level of officialdom, the diplomats Vladimir and Evdokiya Petrov remembered that Kollontai 'was always reasonable and polite in her dealings with staff, even when reproving them. When she was away, the rude, hectoring manner of her deputy, Semenov, made everyone appreciate the Ambassador's courtesy' (*Empire of Fear* (London, 1956), 190). For a concrete example from 1930, see V. Bedin, M. Kushnikova, and V. Togulev (eds.), *Dokumental'noe nasledie kuznetskogo kraya* 4 (1999), 57: a village soviet chairman writes, 'Fuck your mother, you stupid fuckface, why did you go and do that?'   [24] My thanks to Ronald Hingley for this story.

[25] On the first, see Chekhov's parody letter from an official to his subordinate (quoted in Ch. 3 above); for the second, cf. Kuprin's story *Poedinok* (1905), in which a colonel bawls out a junior who has been caught drinking ('This isn't a regiment, it's a b—y whorehouse!') (*Sobranie sochinenii v 7 tomakh*, iv (Moscow, 1964), 71). On the third, cf. E. M. Almedingen's memory of the abrupt and 'nauseating' change in the manner of a beat policeman (*gorodovoi*) when he realized she was a *dvoryanka* and not an ordinary citizen (*I Remember St Petersburg* (London, 1969), 41).

writers, actors, composers, artists, university professors, and research scientists were entitled to a rarefied existence, and almost the only kind of behaviour guide that was aimed at intelligentsia readers was the manual on 'the hygiene of intellectual labour' (*gigiena umstvennogo truda*): that is, the compendium of keep-fit exercises aimed at those in sedentary pursuits.[26] On passing into the intelligentsia, therefore, the socially mobile tended either to retain their proletarian identities, or (and more often) to subscribe to the model of self-sacrifice (hard work and rational living) that they inherited from their radical predecessors.[27] This model was at once useful to Party authority and tangential to it, as is suggested by the case of the writer Vera Inber. At her examination for full Party membership in 1943, Inber was asked, 'Are you not daunted by the thought of strict Party discipline?' She responded, 'No. I'm a very organized person.' Though 'discipline' was in practice not at all the same thing as mere 'organization', the case illustrates how a loyal Soviet intellectual could assimilate the former to the latter, and perceive the Party as the fountain-head of modern values such as efficiency and application.[28] The personal tastes of Lenin, an anti-smoking hygiene fanatic and workaholic, and of Stalin, who shared at least the last of his predecessor's preferences, were fundamental to this sort of perception.

The continuing existence of models of behaviour that had characterized the pre-revolutionary intelligentsia, albeit in diluted form, was aided by the accommodation of these in Party ideology, a process that became notable from the mid-1930s. The 1930s also saw a reversion to pre-revolutionary tradition in other ways: the nuclear family, now seen as the best bulwark

[26] For example, Kekcheev, *Gigiena umstvennogo truda* (1948), or Korablev, *Ezhednevnaya gimnastika dlya lyudei umstvennogo truda* (1950).

[27] For examples of the second type, see Adamova-Sliozberg, *Put'*, which recalls how *intelligenty* consigned to prison camps retained their belief that 'hard work was humane and pure' (102), or Yury Lotman, 'Prosmatrivaya zhizn' s ee nachala', *Vyshgorod* 3 (1998), 38: 'After they chucked us out of the library (I never lived in a hostel, and that was a big stroke of luck because it meant I had my own room to work in) I would, naturally, work all night. We were used to sleeping 3 or 4 hours. That was perfectly normal.' The reference to not living in a hostel as 'luck' is interesting in the context of the 'collective' norms operating for the Soviet masses (see below).

[28] See V. Ya. Brainina and E. F. Nikitina (eds.), *Sovetskie pisateli: avtobiografii*, i (Moscow, 1959), 477. Marietta Shaginyan is another case of a conformist intellectual whose submission to the new system was combined with a decidedly traditional view of cultural leadership. Humiliated over her attempt to stand down from the Union of Writers in 1936, she declared, 'Hearing [this criticism . . .] has been very useful for me, because in our country being worked over in this way is a form of Party education.' (See D. L. Babichenko (ed.), *'Schast'e literatury': gosudarstvo i pisateli 1925–1938. Dokumenty* (Moscow, 1997), 212.) However, as Mikhail Lifshits pointed out in 1954, the writer's *Diary* showed her taking a decidedly bossy line with everyone she encountered on official tours round the Soviet Union, from *kolkhozniki* up to directors. ('Dnevnik Marietty Shaginyan', *Novyi mir* 2 (1954), 206–15). The official Soviet writer might be an instrument of the state, but s/he was also a 'master of minds' (*vlastitel' dum*) as 19th-cent. writers had been.

against social atomization, was reasserted, and a growing licence was accorded to consumption—in ideology if not in fact. During the mid-1930s, Soviet cities and towns began to acquire large, prominent, handsomely appointed (albeit inadequately stocked) department stores, and in 1939, the Third Five-Year Plan expressed a determination to 'broaden the available range of food products, particularly high-quality food products'. Larger quantities of tinned and frozen foodstuffs were to be produced, and 'cultured' alcoholic drinks such as wine, beer, and champagne made available.[29] Significantly, too, the mid-1930s also saw a covert rehabilitation of domestic service. Though the employment of servants (now known as *domrabotnitsy* rather than *prisluga*) had never been banned after the Revolution, a war of attrition had been carried on against it by such means as the active recruitment of domestic servants to literacy classes.[30] Legal regulation of the profession, on the other hand, remained vestigial. Hours were limited to the extent that employers were supposed to allow a *domrabotnitsa* one free evening per week (ostensibly in order that she could attend classes in literacy and political consciousness-raising). However, there was nothing to stop an employer assigning very long hours on other days, or to force him or her to make an adequate allocation of living space (cases of *domrabotnitsy* who shared a single room with their employers and employers' families were not infrequent). And even these far from adequate provisions to some extent lost their force with the reintroduction of the internal passport system (suspended in 1918) in 1932. *Kolkhoz*-dwellers, who were not normally entitled to passports, could leave their place of residence only with difficulty; yet hardship in the villages made migration to cities attractive. Domestic service provided a reasonably safe means for a peasant woman to reside in the city illegally (she was protected by her employers, who would not denounce her to the authorities since they were themselves dependent on her labour). On the other hand, the illegal *domrabotnitsa*'s marginal position meant that she could not herself complain to the authorities if badly treated.[31] The result was to enforce low wages and subservience, and make domestic service of one kind or another

---

[29] See 'Tretii plan razvitiya narodnogo khozyaistva SSSR (1938–1942)', *Pravda*, 21 Mar. 1939.

[30] See Z. A. Bogomazova, *Kul'turnaya rabota sredi domashnikh rabotnits* (Moscow and Leningrad, 1929).

[31] Conditions for *domrabotnitsy* who were employed legally were still strictly regulated. The memoir of Valentina Bogdan, *Mimikriya v SSSR* (Frankfurt am Main, *c.*1975), excerpted in S. Fitzpatrick and Yu. Slezkine (eds.), *In the Shadow of Revolution: Life Stories of Russian Women from 1917 to the Second World War* (Princeton, 2000), records that she had to persuade the local trade union office she genuinely needed domestic help, and to guarantee two weeks' paid holiday, a six-day week, and time off to attend union meetings. The salary paid was 30 roubles per month, generous by comparison with the wages paid to factory workers at the time. For material on illegally employed *domrabotnitsy*, see Elena Bonner, *Dochki-materi* (Moscow, 1994).

available (according to the evidence of memoirs and oral histories) to quite large numbers of better-off Soviet families.

Those of Left Bolshevik convictions, including most famously Trotsky in his *The Revolution Betrayed*, were to see the events of the 1930s as a backsliding from Bolshevik values. Their view of circumstances has been replicated in the classic interpretation of the high Stalinist era as a 'Great Retreat', a capitulation to the tastes of 'a privileged new elite whose values would have been labelled "bourgeois" a decade earlier'.[32] But much though the hypothesis of a 'Great Retreat' has to recommend it (as we shall see, some of the advice literature published in the 1930s and later was indeed directly aimed at nurturing the tastes of a comfortably-off 'new elite'), it is also flawed in significant ways. One problem is that it takes an outsider's view of Soviet society, failing to take into account the fact that Stalin and his associates did all they could to avoid having mid-1930s policy change understood by those who witnessed it close up as a 'retreat'. The second, and more important, point is that the 'Great Retreat' hypothesis— like Stalinist myth itself—glosses over the social divisions within Soviet society. Phenomena such as the more frequent construction of separate apartments or the increase in the production of double beds are adduced as evidence for a move, by Soviet society as a whole, towards a 'cult of privacy', without adequate consideration being given to the question of who had access to apartments or double beds.[33]

Even in the much more straightforward domain of ideology, there is a

[32] Quotation from S. Fitzpatrick, 'Becoming Cultured: Socialist Realism and the Representation of Privilege and Taste', *The Cultural Front: Power and Culture in Revolutionary Russia* (Ithaca, NY, 1992), 216. On the 'Great Retreat', the standard sources are N. Timasheff, *The Great Retreat: The Growth and Decline of Communism in Russia* (New York, 1946), and V. S. Dunham, *In Stalin's Time: Middle-Class Values in Soviet Fiction* (Cambridge, 1976) (for a detailed commentary on this latter, see the opening to Ch. 5 of the present volume).

[33] See particularly V. Papernyi, *Kul'tura '2'* (Ann Arbor, 1985), 120, 122, 125; and cf. Blair A. Ruble, 'From Palace Square to Moscow Square: St Petersburg's Century-Long Retreat from Public Space', in W. Brumfield (ed.), *Reshaping Russian Architecture: Western Technology, Utopian Dreams* (Cambridge, 1990), 39: 'Just as elsewhere in the industrial world, Soviet society was turning in on itself by midcentury.' Ruble adduces this view from the architecture of Moskovsky Prospekt in Leningrad; yet it is impossible to overestimate the importance of public spaces—such as Parks of Culture and Rest—in working-class areas such as this, where living conditions remained cramped and unpleasant well into the 1960s (see below). There were also significant variations between the kind of 'private space' to which those lucky enough to enjoy the concept at all had access. This might be a partitioned room in a communal flat, while separate flats also varied hugely in terms of their space and appointments. In the words of an official history of interior decoration in the first decades of Soviet power: '[In the Stalin years] expensively decorated fitted furniture was employed only in one-off projects [*unikal'nye doma*] built to special commission—e.g. for Glavsevmorput' officials or for artistes in the Bol'shoi theatre . . . In run-of-the-mill apartment blocks [*tipovye doma*] fitted furniture was purely utilitarian in design.' (See G. M. Bocharov, V. P. Vygolov, 'Inter'er', in *Sovetskoe dekorativnoe iskusstvo, 1917–1945: ocherki istorii* (Moscow, 1984), 250; for an outline of elite housing projects, Timothy J. Colton, *Moscow: Governing the Socialist Metropolis* (Cambridge, Mass., 1995), 337–9).

need to consider the specific case of material addressed to 'the Soviet masses' (a construct that was, in some ways, the counterpart of the old intelligentsia myth of the *narod*, embracing all those beyond the Party hierarchy and lacking the intelligentsia's prestige: not only peasants and factory workers, but the lowest grades of white-collar workers, such as typists and filing clerks, and indeed rank-and-file Party members).[34] Advice literature specifically aimed at this group or groups makes clear that there was a concerted effort to generate an integrated model of behaviour, *kul'turnost'*, or 'culturedness' from the early days of Soviet power, and that this model in fact underwent remarkably little change during the mid-1930s. A salient point is that the Stalin cult, so assiduously disseminated in Soviet culture from the late 1930s, was nearly invisible in *kul'turnost'* propaganda. Though permeated by politics, the propaganda of daily life was at the same time politically marginal. It would be absurd to suppose that advice literature provided definitive evidence that the 'Great Retreat' or 'the cult of personality' went unnoticed by the Soviet masses. However, in a society where ideological reversals and shifts of political symbolism were frequent, the transcendental idea of the *kul'turnyi chelovek* (cultured person) worked as an important force for stability and homogeneity.

Advice literature was, of course, only one of a whole range of methods by which the Soviet masses were supposed to be 'made cultured', turned into the efficient and docile workforce required by the accelerated modernization that was the target of the regime. Though literary specialists have perhaps been too inclined to take on trust the supposition that literature was the *only* vehicle for the dissemination of behaviour models, the role of Soviet plays, novels, and poems in influencing behaviour was certainly extremely important.[35] From the beginning, Soviet newspapers carried a huge responsibility for the dissemination of ideology.[36] Still more vital, in the 1920s, when literacy, outside the major cities, remained low,

---

[34] Even in the 1920s, the concept of 'proletariat' was often extended to include not only poor peasants, but also craftsmen and 'labouring people' [*trudyashchiesya*) in general: see Lynn Mally, *Culture of the Future: the Proletkult Movement in Revolutionary Russia* (Berkeley, 1990), 66. For an extension of mass-market behaviour models to low-level Party officials, see Toporkov, *Kak stat' kul'turnym*.

[35] Cases in point were *Cement* and also Nikolai Ostrovsky's *How the Steel Was Tempered* (1935), which are mentioned in many memoirs as inspiring and enthralling reading. See K. Clark, *The Soviet Novel: History as Ritual* (Chicago, 1981) for a classic study of this subject. In his *Sex in Public: The Incarnation of Early Soviet Ideology* (Princeton, 1997), 19, Eric Naiman argues, 'The unfolding of historical events (and the perception of that unfolding) may be *uniquely* dependent on literary models' (my emphasis), and goes on to take literature as the basis of his study. But the question of literature's importance in events and perceptions in Russia still needs proper investigation, as does that of the relative weight carried by literature there as opposed to anywhere else.

[36] See the important recent study by Jeffrey Brooks, *Thank You, Comrade Stalin! Soviet Public Culture from Revolution to Cold War* (Princeton, 2000).

and where book and newspaper distribution were vexed problems,[37] was the work of visual and aural forms of propaganda: the poster, the cinema, and, from the late 1920s, the radio.[38] And behaviour codes—as communicated in texts such as pro formas for character references, membership cards, and oaths of fealty for the Party, Komsomol, and Pioneer movements, and instructions to schoolchildren and students—were another vital way of drawing the population's attention to behaviour standards.[39]

From time to time, the regime made clear its suspicion that publishing hortatory material was not the optimal way of regulating behaviour. In 1929, Gor'ky argued that workers were unimpressed by 'skinny brochures', preferring 'a nice thick book with something in it'.[40] In 1937, a newspaper article mocked local administrators in the town of Zhizda, who had attempted to prevent people walking home after 1 a.m. at night: 'If the authors of the old manuals delicately admonished, Comrades Belov [and Belov] "institute" and "prohibit".'[41] Just so in 1941, a contribution to the campaign for better service ridiculed the idea of commands *in vacuo*:

What does poor service consist in? . . .

It's a poster saying 'Shop assistants and customers, be polite to each other' rather than simple respect for the customer. It's a poster saying 'Respect the work done

---

[37] In an overview of book distribution in the 1920s, Jeffrey Brooks has suggested that 'journalism, more than books and pamphlets, was the medium for communicating the Bolshevik message to the common people' ('The Breakdown in Production and Distribution of Printed Materials, 1917–1927', in A. Gleason, P. Kenez, and R. Stites (eds.), *Bolshevik Culture: Experiment and Order in the Russian Revolution* (Bloomington, Ind., 1985), 151–74; this quotation 161). Roger Pethybridge, however, points out that there were difficulties with newspaper circulation too: in 1922, 90 per cent of newspaper circulation was in Petrograd and Moscow. (*One Step Backwards, Two Steps Forward: Soviet Society and Politics in the NEP* (Oxford, 1990), 215.)

[38] On posters, see S. White, *Bolshevik Posters* (New Haven, 1988); V. Bonnell, *Iconography of Power: Soviet Political Posters under Lenin and Stalin* (Berkeley, 1997); on the cinema see P. Kenez, *The Birth of the Propaganda State* (Cambridge, 1985), and D. Youngblood, *Movies for the Masses: Soviet Popular Cinema in the Twenties* (Cambridge, 1992); on the media see F. Ellis, 'The Media as Social Engineer', in Kelly and Shepherd (eds.), *Russian Cultural Studies: An Introduction* (Oxford, 1998), 192–208. Advice literature was sometimes published to accompany radio programmes: see e.g. *Gimnastika po radio* (1946).

[39] The official *Polozhenie ob attestovanii* (Regulation on the Writing of References) current in the Red Army during the 1930s, for example, required the reference-giver to comment on the subject's 'loyalty to the Party of Lenin and Stalin and the Socialist Motherland', 'political and moral stability', 'watchfulness and ability to keep military secrets', as well as the level of their political education, 'personal discipline', and health as well as military skills. (Quoted in V. Zenzinov (ed.), *Vstrecha s Rossiei: Kak i chem zhivut v Sovetskom Soyuze: Pis'ma v Krasnuyu Armiyu 1939–1940* (New York, 1944), 584–5.)

[40] M. Gor'ky, 'O meshchanstve' (1929), *PSS* xxv. 28.

[41] See *Izvestiya* 21 Aug. 1937: quoted from 'Chronicle of the Year 1937 as Recorded by the Newspaper *Izvestiya* and Collective Farmer Ignat Danilovich Frolov', in V. Garros, N. Korenevskaya, and T. Lahusen (eds.), *Intimacy and Terror: Soviet Diaries of the 1930s*, trans. C. A. Flath (New York, 1995), 39. Cf. the discussion of rule-making in Sheila Fitzpatrick, *Everyday Stalinism: Ordinary Life in Extraordinary Times: Soviet Russia in the 1930s* (New York, 1999), 33.

by the cleaners' in a filthy corridor covered in spit. **It's posters rather than action.**[42]

Behind such statements lay not only a preference for 'actions' over 'words', but also an anxiety that public statements about the need for good behaviour might be seen as pointing to the fact that behaviour fell below the required standard (an anxiety that was not in fact ill founded).

Abstract admonitions, then, were often associated, in official ideology, with pre-revolutionary backwardness. The Soviet central administration tried to ensure that written precept at least appeared to be accompanied by 'action'. Sometimes this took the form of legislation, as in the labour decree of 1938 which reintroduced *trudovye knizhki*, work records for those employed in plants and factories, and imposed penalties for absenteeism.[43] Sometimes it took the form of 'agitation', the dissemination of ideology via direct contact. Soviet citizens were at least as likely to be urged to change their ways by visits and addresses from activists as by an encounter with a brochure. Platonov's 1934 novella *The Sea of Youth* has a characteristically idiosyncratic, but nonetheless convincing, representation of such an encounter:

In the very first peasant hut that Federatovna visited, abnormality hit one in the eyes: on the stove stood two overflowing pots of watery mess, and the woman of the house was sitting on her shelf-bed above the stove with her wooden ladle, taking no steps.

'You ain't got no education, you ignorant devils!' Fedoratovna, in a fury, said to the woman. 'You see, you half-witted heifer, you, the water expands when it heats up, so why the hell do you pour it in at the sides and make the fat boil away? And now you've wormed your way into the kolkhoz! How're we supposed to teach you education, you bugaboo, unless we smother the demon inside you first?[44]

At other stages of Soviet history, Federatovna might well have relied not merely on eloquence: during the collectivization campaign, as an OGPU official complained in 1930, the 'basic means of persuasion' used by many officials was 'a revolver'.[45] However, agitation was not always so confrontational. Besides employing direct force, the Soviet authorities also carried out their assault upon consciousness through education, and

---

[42] 'Khorosho li vas obsluzhivayut?' *Ogonek* 8 (1941), 1. Emphasis original.

[43] The decree was followed by a second decree of 1940 criminalizing absenteeism. See Sarah Davies, *Popular Opinion in Stalin's Russia: : Terror, Propaganda, and Dissent, 1934–1941* (Cambridge, 1997), 43–4.

[44] A. Platonov, *Kotlovan. Yuvenil'noe more* (Moscow, 1987), 168. 'Bugaboo' in the original is *domovaya*, a feminization of the word *domovoi*, or 'house spirit', which was traditionally held responsible for sabotaging domestic activities.

[45] See the report of the Ryazan' district division of OGPU, 10 Mar. 1930, in L. Viola, T. MacDonald, S. V. Zhuravlev, and A. N. Mel'nik, *Ryazanskaya derevnya v 1929–1930 gg. Khronika golovokruzheniya* (Moscow, 1998), 411.

through public meetings and 'demonstrations'. Crucial, too, were the activities of elite organizations such as the Komsomol, which had an 'agitation and propaganda' brief from the earliest days of its existence. Later, the *obshchestvennitsy*, groups of 'socially-active' women, mostly the wives of skilled workers and of engineers, were to aid the spread of *kul'turnost'* in its 1930s variant by such activities as hanging curtains in factory canteens and organizing welfare and childcare services.[46] The presentation of plays and agitprop sketches (*agitki*) and 'live newspapers' dedicated to ideologically central issues, and collective performances such as gymnastic spectacles, sessions of 'mass song', and public festivals, all contributed to the task of civilizing the Soviet people.

An intriguing sense of the priorities for cultural construction is given by the diary of Mikhail Il'in, one of the engineers responsible for building the Soviet new town of Komsomol'sk-on-Amur. The first boat-loads of Komsomol members began arriving in March 1932, and in early May, work started in earnest. A bread oven was built on 18 May, the construction of the hospital began in late May (though the side-wall collapsed on 1 June), and the local newspaper, *The Amur Shock-Worker*, was founded on 1 July. On 7 November, the fifteenth anniversary of the October Revolution, the cinema opened (it was also called *The Shock-Worker*). A laundry began to be built on 1 December, and the *banya* was ready for use on 3 December. A temporary water main was laid on 5 April 1933, and the first restaurant opened its doors on 6 November 1934. The work was accompanied by large numbers of agitational events—a 'ten-day cleanliness drive' (*dekadnik chistoty*) from 1 July 1932; the award of a booby prize for insufficient effort ('the slacker's medal', *orden shlyapy*), on 13 September 1933; and a competition for the best canteen on 1 January 1934. But before a spade had been turned, a mop dipped in a bucket, or a wall flyposted, on 15 May 1932, came the founding of Komsomol'sk-on-Amur's *militsia* station.[47]

[46] See C. Kelly and V. Volkov, '*Kul'turnost'* and Consumption', in C. Kelly and D. Shepherd, *Constructing Russian Culture in the Age of Revolution* (Oxford, 1998), 297–8; S. Fitzpatrick, 'Becoming Cultured: Socialist Realism and the Representation of Privilege and Taste', *The Cultural Front: Power and Culture in Revolutionary Russia* (Ithaca, NY, 1992), 232–3, and *eadem*, *Everyday Stalinism*, 156–62; M. Buckley, 'The Untold Story of *Obshchestvennitsa* in the 1930s', *Europe-Asia Studies* 48/4 (1996), 569–86; R. Maier, 'Die Hausfrau als *kulturtreger* im Sozialismus', in G. Gorzka (ed.), *Kultur im Stalinismus: Sowjetische Kunst der 1930er bis 1950er Jahre* (Bremen, 1994), 39–45; J. Hessler, 'Cultured Trade: the Stalinist Turn towards Consumerism', in S. Fitzpatrick (ed.), *Stalinism: New Directions* (London, 2000), 182–209; and my brief discussion later in this chapter.

[47] Yu. Zhukov, *Lyudi tridtsatykh godov* (Moscow, 1966), 320–1. The *militsia* station was necessary, apart from anything else, because the Komsomol'sk-on-Amur workers included prisoners, dispossessed kulaks, and other unwilling participants in the project. See J. A. Bone, 'A la recherche d'un Komsomol perdu: Who Really Built Komsomol'sk-na-Amure, and Why', *Revue des études slaves* 71/1 (1999), 59–91.

Of note here is the relatively muted role played by propaganda as such. To be sure, the local edition of *Komsomol'skaya pravda* regularly published cartoons and articles assaulting *nekul'turnost'*, and exhorting Komsomol'sk-on-Amur's inhabitants to dedicate themselves fully to the task of implanting culture in the city. But it was above all institutions and public spaces that carried the thrust of the *kul'turnost'* drive. Similarly, in Moscow, which, as the Soviet capital, was meant to be the model for the aspirations of all other cities, a massive campaign of architectural reconstruction, beginning in the mid-1920s, created new squares and arterial thoroughfares for parades and promenades, new parks, and new venues for decorous entertainments (ice-cream cafés, outdoor theatres for variety shows, cinemas, department stores). The new, 'cultured', environment was intended to have an immediate impact upon behaviour: to shame the uncultured into giving up their old ways as inappropriate.[48]

Propaganda, then, had acknowledged limitations; undue reliance on it was also somewhat heretical in terms of the Marxism-Leninist dogma 'being determines consciousness', that is, the notion that psychological phenomena are dependent upon the material environment.[49] Yet printed appeals to reason persisted. It was, after all, cheaper and simpler to bombard the population with pamphlets on the dangers of contaminated water than it was to lay on mains drainage, and faster to issue public-health warnings about TB and trachoma than to provide adequate medical care or improve living standards.[50] Advice literature could also help reassure the population that the regime cared about problems, even if, in practical terms, little was done about solving them; and it transferred the balance of guilt, when a new society was not immediately achieved, from party elite to recalcitrant masses. who had, after all, been told in words of one syllable how to be cultured.[51]

---

[48] On Moscow, see Colton, *Moscow*; Hessler, 'Cultured Trade'; and cf. an item on the Dzerzhinsky Builders' Club, 'Obstanovka menyaet lyudei', published in the flagship *Nashi dostizheniya* 3 (1935), 94. For an exemplary case-study of an integrated 'civilizing project' in a new Soviet town, see S. Kotkin, *Magnetic Mountain: Stalinism as a Civilization* (Berkeley, 1995).

[49] As Stalin himself argued, 'In public life . . . external conditions change first, and then, in response to this, people's way of thinking, customs, and world-view also alter.' (A. Ya. Zis', *O kommunisticheskoi morali. Stenogramma publichnoi lektsii, prochitannoi v Tsentral'nom lektorii [Vsesoyuznogo] Obshchestva [po rasprostraneniyu politicheskikh i nauchnykh znanii]* (Moscow, 1948), 7 (citing Stalin's *Sobranie sochinenii*, i. 316).)

[50] S. G. Solomon has pointed out ('Social Hygiene and Soviet Public Health, 1921–1930', in *eadem* and J. F. Hutchinson, *Health and Society in Revolutionary Russia, 1921–1930* (Bloomington, Ind., 1990), 177), that 'throughout the 1920s, investment in health care was, at best, modest'. The low level of investment may be instructively contrasted with the energy devoted to pamphlet publishing at the time. For an excellent study of another equally important kind of propaganda, health and fitness posters, see F. L. Bernstein, 'Envisioning Health in Revolutionary Russia: The Politics of Gender in Sexual-Enlightenment Posters of the 1920s', *RR* 57 (Apr., 1998), 191–217.

[51] For an interesting exposition of the guilt and gratitude principle in Soviet culture generally, see Brooks, *Thank You, Comrade Stalin.*

To be sure, many of the 'how to' brochures published were intended to reinforce knowledge transmitted by other means: at meetings or 'seminars', or in the workplace. Without guidance, novice readers would not necessarily have turned to a brochure called *How to Read a Book*, and might simply have started out on whatever raw reading material came to hand, some of it, quite possibly, of an ideologically questionable kind.[52] The work of reading groups, public libraries and, in the 1920s, also of official 'book pedlars' (*knigonoshi*) was vital in directing mass readers to the kind of literature that the regime considered would improve the simple-minded.[53] But the circulation also worked the other way round, with pamphlets used in order to teach activists what they should think and how they should address the population.[54] And the sheer number of advice literature titles published in the first decades of the Soviet Union's existence—on subjects from dirigible production to the avoidance of malaria—is some indication of the regime's confidence that the genre could contribute to social change. In any case, the material published in the how-to guides is interesting and significant because it represents official ideology in a lucid, simplified, and homogeneous form, showing what 'the Soviet way of life' was, in its essence, supposed to be.

In part this homogeneity derived from the fact that *kul'turnost'*, the 'cultured behaviour' that Soviet advice literature sought to construct, reflected many constants of the 'civilizing process'. Though Soviet modernization had institutional differences from the modernizing pro-grammes in Western countries (notably the high degree of state ownership and state co-ordination, and the extent of compulsion applied on the masses, including forced labour and public calling to order or shaming—the Russian verb for this activity is *pristydit'*—of the 'uncultured'),[55] the practical end in view—the construction of a literate, clean, sober, and

[52] This did indeed happen. Z. A. Bogomazova, *Kul'turnaya rabota sredi domashnikh rabotnits* (Moscow and Leningrad, 1929), 25–7, remarks that left to themselves, *domrabotnitsy* will get distracted by 'any old junk' which their employers give them to stop them visiting the library, such as the works of Verbitskaya or dream divination guides (*sonniki*).

[53] Brooks, 'The Breakdown', 155, quotes a Soviet source of 1928 in support of a claim that the book-pedlar system had been a total failure. However, Bogomazova, *Kul'turnaya rabota*, 23, refers to the system as a viable entity in 1929.

[54] See e.g. Primakovsky, *Kak rabotat' s knigoi*, which provides a five–point agitational plan for Komsomol meetings, beginning with the formulation, 'The Soviet Union is the greatest country in the world' (14–16); and the huge number of pamphlets under the title *Pamyatnik agitatora* published in the first three decades of Soviet power. D. Ransel, *Village Mothers: Three Generations of Change in Russia and Tataria* (Bloomington, Ind., 2000), 44–8, discusses pamphlets in the work of child-care activists in the 1920s and 1920s.

[55] Ways that shaming was carried out included denunciation at public meetings and use of the so-called *doska pozora* (Board of Shame), the mirror-image of the *doska pocheta* (Board of Honour) on which the photographs and biographies of Party activists and outstanding workers were displayed. (An isolated example of the *doska pocheta*, a once-ubiquitous Soviet sight, survives in the Kuzminki district of Moscow, on a thoroughfare still called Young Leninists' Street.)

FIG. 13. Distributing books to the Soviet peasantry. *The Fusion of Town and Country* (poster by Boris Kustodiev, 1927).

reliable workforce—was the same as in industrializing countries the world over. Much of the rhetoric used was also very far from novel. The model citizen depicted in *On the Duties of Man and of Citizen* (1783)—patriotic, tidy, hard-working, open to innovation—was a family ancestor of the Soviet ideal, an ideal which was also foreshadowed in *Friendly Advice to a Young Man Beginning to Live in the World* (1765):

Combine cleanliness with order and method in all that you do . . . Avoid distractions. It is a very rational rule of life that you should spend all your time on carrying out your duties . . . Those who read only in order to pass the time, and to boast about how many books they have read, are unworthy to hold a good book in their hands.[56]

    [56] [Grabinsky], *Druzheskie sovety*, 52, 63.

In the same way, the character of Lenin, a potent and influential mixture of industriousness, rational time management, early rising, cold bathing, and detestation of smoking, reflected traits that Lenin had in common with 'civilized man' in his late nineteenth century, 'Victorian', variant, 'the man of backbone'. Whatever their manifest dissimilarities in other ways, Nicholas II and Lenin were alike in their taste for exercise, fresh air, and days divided between bureaucratic toil and wholesome domestic pursuits.[57]

Even the characteristic of Soviet behaviour guides that was most radical in terms of Russian tradition—their fervent egalitarianism—was not, in an overall sense, unique. Many contemporary Western behaviour books also sanctioned the overt display of superiority.[58] If there was nothing path-breaking about egalitarianism, in one other important respect Soviet books were actually rather conservative. The fascination of the post-Freudian West with what Nickolas Rose has termed 'psy', in other words the scientific or quasi-scientific exploration and manipulation of a putative inner self by 'experts of experience', and the attempt to prescribe and regulate difference through the supposedly objective imposition of categories such as intelligence, made little impact upon material for the Soviet masses, even in the 1920s, before psychoanalysis had been branded un-Soviet.[59] Rather, the Soviet 'experts of experience' propounded a different kind of normative collectivism, one based not on an assumption of necessary and containable divergence, but on a dream of harmonious integration. In this sense, there is considerably more resemblance between *On the Duties of Man and of Citizen* and a Soviet pamphlet such as Kerzhentsev's *Organize Yourself!* than there is between the latter and Dale Carnegie's *How to Win Friends and Influence People*. In Soviet *kul'turnost'*, an

[57] Compare R. Service, *Lenin: A Political Life*, 3 vols. (London, 1991–4), and D. Lieven, *Nicholas II* (London, 1993).

[58] See Cas Wouters, 'Etiquette Books and Emotion Management in the Twentieth Century', *Journal of Social History* 29 (1995–6), which argues that normative sources in America, the Netherlands, Britain, and Germany became 'more lenient, more differentiated and varied' over this period (p. 107). Wouters cites the 1937 edn. of Emily Post's classic etiquette guide, which dropped references to 'the Best Society' and 'old-world cultivation', and referred instead to 'nature's nobleman' as the ideal (p. 111). In behaviour books published in Germany under the Third Reich, on the other hand, use of titles and deference *were* advocated. See Horst-Volker Krumrey, *Entwicklungsstrukturen von Verhaltstanden. Eine soziologische Prozessanalyse auf der Grundlage deutscher Anstands- und Manierbücher von 1870 bis 1970* (Frankfurt on Main, 1970), 421–2.

[59] See N. Rose, 'Assembling the Modern Self', in R. Porter (ed.), *Rewriting the Self: Histories from the Renaissance to the Present* (London, 1997), 224–8. In 1930, the psychologist Aron Zalkind lamented the fact that although 'the supervisory organs of our Party carry out work with cadres and campaigns of moral education, science [i.e. psychology] does not give positive guidance in this sphere [for the mass reader].' ('Psikhonevrologicheskie nauki i sotsialisticheskoe obshchestvo', *Pedologiya* 3 (1930), 309–22: quoted in A. Etkind, *Eros nevozmozhnogo: Istoriya psikhoanaliza v Rossii* (St Petersburg, 1993), 330. For a biography of Zalkind (1888–1936), see ibid. 326–7.

Enlightenment myth of social consensus through shared behaviour rules lived on.

All in all, the originality of Soviet behaviour tracts lay less in the base metal of their stipulations than in the use of the term 'Soviet' to gild these. Truisms of post-Enlightenment behaviour literature all over Europe were presented as new and exciting discoveries (just as the aspirations of people in all Western capitalist societies to better their material conditions acquired an illusory specificity when named as 'the American dream'). Even in the most internationalist phase of Soviet history (1917–35), the distinction between this new society and the capitalist West was constantly em- phasized, and undesirable phenomena represented as 'survivals of the past'. For example, a lengthy lament on the poor conditions in co-operative canteens and shops published in 1930 saw the deficiencies of trading etiquette as 'capitalist':

> Buyers get short weight, and short measure; they are treated coarsely; the assistants don't even want to speak to them or show them the goods, and when they do they pretend they're doing the buyers a favour. All these things are signs of our lack of culture (*nekul'turnost'*), which we have received as an inheritance from the capitalist system.[60]

Everything possible was done to distance Soviet reality, in ideological terms, from the negative manifestations of Western culture, such as fashion and the accumulation of material possessions. There was a revival of the traditional assaults on Gallomania. Women susceptible to the lure of French fashion and cosmetics were known as 'mamzelles' (*mamzeli*), and an admiration for the products of the French cosmetics company Coty was held emblematic of a self-serving, petit-bourgeois obsession with softening and scenting the body.[61] If French culture was still fatally associated with false civilization, artificiality, and decadence, German culture retained (at least until the rise of Fascism in 1933) its traditional connotations of integrity as well as exactitude and reliability. This explained why, having attributed the problems of Soviet co-operatives to 'the capitalist system', the author of the article just quoted could go on to argue: 'Other cultured peoples, for example the Germans, treat shoppers in co-operatives differently—with unfailing attentiveness and

---

[60] A. R–l', 'Rabotu kooperatsii—pod kontrol' trudyashchikhsya!', *Zhenskii zhurnal* 7 (1930), 3.

[61] See Anne Gorsuch, 'Soviet Youth and the Politics of Popular Culture during NEP', *Social History* 17 (1992), 199. On Coty see Naiman, *Sex in Public*, 245–6. One notable satirical treatment of a *mamzelle* is in agitprop versions of the traditional puppet play *Petrushka*: see Catriona Kelly, 'A Stick with Two Ends', in Jane Costlow, Stephanie Sandler, and Judith Vowles (eds.), *Sexuality and the Body in Russian Culture* (Stanford, Calif., 1993), 73–96. Aleksandr Tarasov-Rodionov's well-known novel *Shokolad* (1922) was a notably vehement attack on consumerism.

courtesy, in a manner that keeps them satisfied and makes them want to visit the shop again.'[62] The 'culture/artificiality' and 'German/French' binary oppositions were supported by a third distinction, between 'capitalism' on the one hand, and 'modernity' (*sovremennost'*) on the other. This allowed, for instance, the appropriation of work practices ('Taylorist' principles of rational management in particular) from the capitalist world in the conviction that they would be purged of their exploitative nature once they were integrated in Soviet reality.[63] And a fourth contrast, between 'Soviet' and 'bourgeois' (*meshchanskoe*) was perhaps the most useful of all, since the term 'meshchanskoe' gave weight to stern puritanical fulminations about what Mayakovsky termed 'canarified cosiness' (*kanareechnyi uyutik*), while at the same time glossing over the uncomfortable resemblance between the constituents of *kul'turnost'* and the values of the 'bourgeois world'.

To be sure, left intellectuals such as Mayakovsky or Sergei Tret'yakov applied the term *meshchanskoe* far more widely than the authors of mainstream advice literature. Mayakovsky's pioneering revolutionary masque, *Mystery-Bouffe* (1918), lambasted capitalist oppressors as 'the clean ones', suggesting that an undue emphasis on cleanliness was unproletarian; such ideas were also common among the fierier activists in the Komsomol.[64] Advice literature authors, by contrast, only occasionally even mentioned the view that cleanliness might be considered 'bourgeois', and then in order vehemently to oppose it.[65] Equally, Mayakovsky's poem 'The Stabilization of Everyday Life' (1927) listed instances of vulgarity that included not only the lust for fashionable clothes, trashy films (above all the notorious were-bear melodrama *The Bear's Wedding*) and sentimental romances, but also—more controversially—the collection of photographs of 'geniuses'.[66]

That said, the tension between the avant-garde and the mainstream was in the end not very consequential, given that left intellectuals' contributions to advice literature were so obviously eccentric and idiosyncratic.

---

[62] A. R–l', 'Rabotu kooperatsii', 3. That said, German culture was sometimes now also assigned to the 'artificiality' part of the binary opposition: Gor'ky, for instance, saw it as a place where feminism ran riot and where 'same-sex "love" is almost accounted a natural phenomenon' ('O meshchanstve', *PSS* xxv. 26).

[63] See Lenin, 'Ocherednye zadachi sovetskoi vlasti', *Sobranie sochinenii*, xxvii. 229–30, arguing that the 'extraordinarily rich scientific achievements' of the Taylor system needed to be separated from the 'refined barbarism of bourgeois exploitation'. See also H. Braveman, *Labour and Monopoly Capital: The Degradation of Work in the Twentieth Century* (New York, 1974), ch. 4; Steve Smith, 'Taylorism Rules OK? Bolshevism, Taylorism, and the Technical Intelligentsia in the Soviet Union', *Radical Science Journal* 13 (1983), 3–27, esp. 10–14.

[64] On the latter, see Gorsuch, 'Soviet Youth', 195.

[65] See e.g. Semashko, *Iskusstvo odevat'sya* (1927), 18.

[66] Mayakovsky, 'Stabilizatsiya byta', *Izvestiya* 16 Jan. 1927: *PSS* viii. 7–10.

Mayakovsky's *How to Make Verses*, while undoubtedly one of the most brilliant and original books ever published under the guise of how-to literature, was in fact not a manual but an anti-manual, written as a riposte to guides for writers such as G. A. Shengeli's *How to Write Essays, Verses and Stories*,[67] N. Abramov's *Complete Russian Rhyme Dictionary*, and even (rather belatedly) N. Grech's *Textbook of Russian Verse Composition* (1820). Such books, Mayakovsky asserted, were only of use because a reader could learn from the advice contained in them what was *not* worth repeating, and hence eschew the labour of a 'qualified copyist':

> Knowing the rules is not, in itself, the purpose of poetry; otherwise a poet degenerates into a scholast who keeps himself occupied composing lists of rules for non-existent or useless activities and conditions. For example, there would be no point in inventing rules about how to count stars while riding a bicycle full-tilt. (*PSS* xii. 84).

For Mayakovsky, there were no positive rules for writing poetry, only negative ones (don't heed other people's guidance). Just so, the 'useless' or 'non-existent', and also indescribable, activity of 'counting stars while riding a bicycle full-tilt' emerged as his definition of the poet's art—a definition which, for all its brilliance, was scarcely encouraging to the novice writer. Even in 'A Guide for Beginning Slimeballs' ('Obshchee rukovodstvo dlya nachinayushchikh podkhalim', 1927, *PSS* viii. 140–3), a decidedly broad satire upon cringing Party careerists, any straightforwardly didactic function was subverted in the culminating lines: 'Don't do like this verse, but quite the reverse' (*Postupaite ne po stikhu, a naoborot*).

   Few authors of advice literature, though, would have undermined their own authority so lightly. For the most part, guides were mini-oracles, brooking no contradiction, demanding the reader's total attention and compliance. To be sure, the authorial voice in advice literature had in any case always spoken *de haut en bas*, the writer taking the position of a teacher in possession of information that readers were assumed to lack, but urgently require. But in the early Soviet period, power asymmetry was more evident than usual. The authors of literature on hygiene usually flourished their medical qualifications, emphasizing the expertise upon which their recommendations were based. While this had been the practice before the Revolution as well, the activity as advisory authors of such figures as Nikolai Semashko, People's Commissar of Health, Lenin's consort Nadezhda Krupskaya, or Z. N. Lilina, wife of Zinoviev, underlined the point that the state was now—as it had not been in the late imperial era—the sponsor and controller of

---

[67] Shengeli, *Kak pisat' stat'i, stikhi i rasskazy* (1926).

behaviour literature.[68] Where pamphlets appeared anonymously, this suggested not the free-for-all of a commercial print market in which titles mattered more than writers, but the fact that such titles carried the impersonal authority of the state itself.[69] And the gap between author and readers was widened, rather than bridged, by their patronizing use of the informal second person singular in order to address the reader—*Organizui samogo sebya!* (Organize Yourself!)—where pre-revolutionary guides had preferred impersonal and indirect formulae such as 'prinyato . . .' (it is customary), 'molodaya zhenshchina dolzhna . . .' (a young woman ought . . .).[70] Even at the point when, officially, the Soviet nation was governed by 'dictatorship of the proletariat', and when 'bourgeois experts' were loudly denounced in some quarters, advice literature continued to be written by 'bourgeois experts', some of whom had been the authors of advice literature well before the Revolution. For instance, Mariya Zarina, a prolific author of guides to house management in the first sixteen years of Soviet power, was an expert on domestic science whose textbook for the training of professional cooks, first published in 1910, had been reprinted in 1918, still with the imprimatur of the tsarist education ministry on the front page.[71]

Just as importantly, the authority of Soviet advice books came from their uniformity in setting out a model of good behaviour that was consistent, well-regulated and (at least supposedly) specifically 'Soviet'. To be sure, a 'Soviet advice literature' did not emerge immediately after the Revolution. Though advice literature as a genre is characteristically quick to reflect social change and cultural pressure, the remarkable events of 1917 had at first next to no impact on this branch of the popular book market. No brochures entitled *How to Survive an Apartment Search by Armed Anarchists* were forthcoming; instead, the 1917 run of *Knizhnaya letopis'* indicates that publishers such as Sytin maintained their fidelity to time-honoured modes such as the love-letter manual.[72] However, from early

---

[68] Semashko's works on prophylactic health were part of the drive for 'social hygiene' of which he was the most powerful advocate in the 1920s. See Solomon, 'Social Hygiene', *passim*. Krupskaya's and Lilina's stemmed from their activities in Glavpolitprosvet, the propaganda section of Narkompros, the education and culture commisariat.

[69] As e.g. in the case of a batch of pamphlets for demobilized soldiers produced after the 1941–5 War, e.g. *Demobilizovannym ryadovym i serzhantam Krasnoi Armii* (1945); or that of *The Book of Tasty and Nutritious Food* (see below).

[70] See e.g. Svetozarskaya, *Zhizn' v svete, doma* (1890), *passim*.

[71] See *Uchebnik kulinarii* (1910); eadem, *Uchebnik kulinarii* (1918). In the former edition, Zarina is described as 'head of practical knowledge at the Aleksandro-Mariinskii Institute, the Ekaterinskii Institute, the Usachevsko-Chernyavskii and Nikolaevskii Professional Institutes. The latter carries the statement 'Approved by the Ministry of the People's Enlightenment for use in women's professional institutes where the culinary arts are taught'.

[72] For example, *N. I K-sky, *Polnyi pis'movnik dlya vlyublennykh* (Moscow, 1917), edn. of 15,000; or a re-edn. of *'Dyadya Serzh', *Polnyi lyubovnyi pis'movnik* (Moscow, 1917), and the tract

1918, with the establishment of Soviet censorship and control over the book market, advice literature, like other types of self-declaredly commercial literature, began to be squeezed out of existence. Though one or two frivolous publications apparently sneaked through in 1918 (including N. Mikhailov's *An Indispensable Book for Young Persons: A Letter-Writing Manual for Lovers*, and the anonymous *Secrets of the Female Toilette*), stocks of books in the possession of 'capitalist enterprises' were confiscated in 1918 and again in 1919, and in 1920, all remaining such stocks were confiscated.[73] The NEP period saw vigorous activity on the part of small presses so far as the publication of poetry and belles-lettres was concerned, but there was no large-scale revival of an autonomous, market-driven advisory literature.[74] Advertisements in Soviet magazines such as *Ogonek* point to the appearance of occasional author-published advice titles, such as two booklets called *The Care of the Skin* and *The Care of the Hair* in the late 1920s, but such titles were by all indications rare.[75] They were commoner outside the Soviet Union, in cities with a sizeable population

for sufferers from venereal disease (*V. T. (psevdonim), *Obshcheponyatnyi lechebnik sekretnykh boleznei muzhskikh i zhenskikh* (Petrograd, 1916). A poignant exception from the general lack of concern with topicality, however, is the publication of a few books on small-scale food production: see especially *P. Gorsky, *Dovol'no golodat'! Komnatnyi ogorod* (Petrograd, 1918); and the occasional 'crisis cookbook': see e.g. Anon., *Nastavlenie dlya khoroshego i zdorovogo pitaniya* (1918). (See *KL* 1917, 1918.)

[73] *N. Mikhailov, *Neobkhodimaya kniga dlya molodykh lyudei: Pis'movnik dlya vlyublennykh* (Moscow, 1918); *Anon., *Tainy zhenskogo tualeta* (Moscow, 1918) (see *KL* 1918). The print-run of the latter was announced as 10,000. On confiscation, see Brooks, 'The Breakdown', 154. The Bolsheviks' suspicion of entrepreneurial capitalism made them reluctant to use the established networks of popular book distribution even when this would have the task of disseminating material easier: e.g., attempts by Ivan Sytin to cooperate with the state publishing house Gosizdat were constantly snubbed and frustrated. (See C. A. Ruud, *Russian Entrepreneur: Publisher Ivan Sytin of Moscow, 1851–1934* (Montreal, 1990), 174–220.)

[74] It is safe to assume that this was at least partly because the Soviet censorship would not tolerate the revival of the genre. Recently published archival documents indicate that toleration of advice literature was directly related to the extent that it was seen to contribute to the *kul'turnost'* programme. For instance, Brokgauz and Efron publishers was allowed to survive until 1930 because it was felt to be 'pursuing cultural ends' (*presleduyushchaya kul''urnye tseli*), and other publishers were pressurized into issuing or suppressing advice literature according to whether they were held to be serving such ends. In 1922, an advisory calendar for schoolchildren issued by Petrograd publishers was confiscated, and in the same year, the self-education specialist house Kolos was refused permission to reprint the works of the populist thinker Mikhailovsky and told that they should be devoting their efforts to 'agitational literature'. (See A. V. Blyum, *Za kulisami 'Ministerstva pravdy': Tainaya istoriya sovetskoi tsenzury 1917–1929* (St Petersburg, 1994), 146, 50, 77.)

[75] *A. Stantsevich, *Ukhod za kozhei* and *Ukhod za volosami* (Kiev?, 1928?), though not held in any library to which I had access, were regularly advertised in *Ogonek* in 1929–30. R. Rothstein and H. Rothstein, 'The Beginnings of Soviet Culinary Arts', in M. Glants and J. Toomre (eds.), *Food in Russian History and Culture* (Bloomington, Ind., 1997), 188–9, deal with the cases of two cookbooks published privately in the 1920s, *A. Markov's *Bliny, blinchiki, blintsy, i olad'i* (Moscow, 1925), and *A. I. Nikishova, *Povarennaya kniga—rukovodstvo domashnego stola, zapasov i zagotovok* (Moscow, 1929).

of Russian émigrés.[76] While by no means all émigré books were practical, many were, and give a strong sense of cultural pressures, particularly those affecting upper- and middle-class Russian women, who now needed to find 'respectable' work and to run the household without servants. Few if any émigrés, on the other hand, believed that they required initiation into the requirements of gentility: the almost universal view of the Soviet Union as a monstrous case of government by ignorance and vulgarity, as well as by tyranny, was matched by a proud belief that émigrés alone conserved pre-revolutionary traditions of politeness and refinement.[77]

Soviet advice literature was in many respects the mirror-image of émigré literature: here the dissemination of practical information (how to ride a bicycle, how to knit a sock) was definitely not the main concern. Though large numbers of work guides on subjects from welding to animal husbandry to crop-sowing were published, how-to manuals for the private sphere were few and far between, and were mostly limited to the induction of 'cultured' pastimes such as chess, draughts, and playing the accordion, and—in the 1920s—to advice on labour legislation and family law.[78] From the early days of Soviet power, the recently founded State Publishing House and associated presses gave priority to conduct guides that were mouthpieces of ideology, and intended to construct the citizen required by the new order: literate, politically aware, orderly, committed to hard work and to the support of the regime. At no period since Catherine II's legalization of private presses in 1783 had advice literature been so closely

[76] See e.g. Chunikhin, *Kak imet' krasivye ruki* (?early 1930s); Adov, *Uchebnik lyubvi* (1924)—not a sex manual, but a guide to love-making, with advice on the different characters of men and women, and on chat-up conversations; Merezhkovskaya, *Sovety khozyaikam* (mid-1930s); the book was based on a series in the newspaper *Vozrozhdenie* by M. N. Merezhkovskaya-Yakubovich; Kurennov, *Russkii Narodnyi Lechebnik* (1955). There is also some evidence in memoirs and belles-lettres that there was an avid audience for advice books in foreign languages among some émigré(e)s: see e.g. the reference in Ekaterina Bakunina's scandalous novel *Lyubov' k shesterym* (Paris, 1934), in which the heroine monitors her colonic movements according to 'the Kellogg system', i.e. the dietary and excretory regimen advocated by J. H. Kellogg, inventor of the cornflake, and author of dozens of publications including *The Home Hand-Book of Domestic Hygiene and Rational Medicine* (2nd edn., London, 1896), in which he stresses the need to 'establish a regular habit of relieving the bowels daily at a certain hour' (337). And Tamara Talbot Rice, the distinguished art historian, consoled herself when suffering osteoporosis with thoughts of Dr Coué's formula: 'Every day in every way, I am getting better and better' (see E. Talbot Rice's afterword to *Tamara: Memoirs of St Petersburg, Paris, Oxford and Byzantium* (London, 1996), 253). (E. Coué's books included *Self-Mastery through Conscious Auto-Suggestion* (London, 1922), and *Better and Better Every Day* (London, 1922).)

[77] For an especially eloquent expression of such views, see the writings of Vladimir Nabokov, especially *Zashchita Luzhina*, *Pnin*, *Pale Fire*, and the famous expostulation on *poshlost'* in *Nikolai Gogol'* (Norfolk, Conn., 1944), 70.

[78] See *Knizhnaya letopis'* and *Ezhegodnik knigi*. A good idea of the span is given in V. Mayakovsky and S. Tret'yakov's rhymes for book-peddlars, 'Chastushki dlya knigonosh' (1926), which recommend to buyers books on pig-raising, poultry-rearing, agricultural pests, legislation on military service and on divorce. See V. Mayakovsky, *PSS* vii. 384–90.

monitored and regulated by the country's government as it was after 1918. The late imperial Russian state's sponsorship of the agricultural newspaper *Sel'skii Vestnik*, its single important foray into this field, pales into insignificance by comparison.[79]

It is a truism that Soviet culture aimed at creating a rational collective, and that the governing concept of individual identity was entirely constrained by this collective ideal. As one recent commentator puts it: 'Although the Soviet ideal person was the opposite of the Russian personality on the grounds of religious idealism, the constructs were structurally similar: self-sacrificial, anti-individualist, and ascetic.'[80] In an overall sense, such views are simplistic not only because of their reductive understanding of 'Russianness', but also because they obscure the manner in which 'self-sacrifice', 'anti-individualism', and 'ascetism' could be modulated in Soviet ideology according to the social roles of those discussed. 'Self-sacrifice' and 'ascetism' were not the same for Gladkov's Bad'in as they were for Gleb and Sergei, and 'anti-individualism' did not preclude the assumption that there existed heroic individuals whose contribution was unlike anyone else's. The genre of 'model lives'—as manifested in the popular biographical series *The Lives of Remarkable People* aimed at adults,[81] and texts such as Mikhail Zoshchenko's 'Stories about Lenin' for children—emphasized that the virtues encapsulated in the lives of the great were universal, but that these virtues were more purely manifested there than they could be in ordinary people. In Zoshchenko's stories, Lenin is not only implacably opposed to smoking and convinced of the virtues of bathing in cold water (which health propaganda propounded as beliefs for everyone), but is able to swim better and further than other people, to be more resolute in his self-denial; he is cleverer, more hard-working and (here if nowhere else the stories owe something to folk tales) more benevolently crafty.[82] From 1935, the 'culture of labour' acquired its own supermen too, as the Stakhanovite movement raised selected workers

---

[79] See J. S. Krukones, *To the People: The Russian Government and the Newspaper Sel'skii Vestnik ('Village Herald'), 1881–1917* (New York, 1987).

[80] Svetlana Boym, *Common Places: Mythologies of Everyday Life in Russia* (Cambridge, Mass., 1994), 89.

[81] The series *Zhizn' zamechatel'nykh lyudei* was founded in 1933, with Gor'ky as its moving spirit. As early as 1929, the writer had suggested that *Ogonek* should inaugurate a series of biographical articles on the pattern of the model lives published by F. F. Pavlenkov's press at the turn of the century. (See *Zhizn' zamechatel'nykh lyudei: Seriya biografii osnovana v 1933 godu M. Gor'kim: Katalog 1933–1985* (Moscow, 1987), 6.) The genre of 'model life' of course went back much further than the 1890s. The bias towards lives of famous Westerners evident in the ZZL series between 1933 and 1948 gave these biographical studies an affinity to the collections by imitators of Plutarch published in Russia during the late 18th cent. (see Ch. 1), and the popularity of such texts with Russian readers was undoubtedly partly traceable to the prominent role played in grass-roots Orthodoxy by lives of the saints.

[82] Zoshchenko, 'Rasskazy o Lenine' (1940).

to the pantheon of Soviet over-achievers, stressing the superhuman numbers of hectares ploughed, tons of steel manufactured, bricks and hammers turned out, by the efforts and ingenuity of extraordinary individuals.[83] Moreover, the ethos of *kollektivizm* always depended upon the demonstration of loyalty by individual members of the *kollektiv*.[84] In practice, too, individuals were expected to manifest a high degree of self-reliance, if not necessarily initiative. A Soviet citizen who broke his or her ankle falling out of a train, rather than being encouraged to mount litigation against the railway company (as would have been the case in late twentieth-century Britain or America), would instead have been upbraided for negligence (and probably suspected of drunkenness into the bargain). The principle of *penyai na sebya* ('you've only yourself to blame') was pervasive.

Yet if the notion of 'ideal collectivism' has to be invoked with more care than it sometimes is, there is no doubt of its centrality to propaganda aimed at mass readers. A case in point is G. Ya. Bruk's *What Every Peasant Going to Town to Find Work Should Know*, a pamphlet of 1930 aimed at *sezonniki*, temporary migrants from the village who dwelt in the city while undertaking seasonal work as labourers on construction sites. The pamphlet represents the worker hostel (*obshchezhitie*) as an ideal community which not only indoctrinates incomers in urban values, but also turns them into missionaries for *kul'turnost'* once they reach the village: 'You must bring about a fusion [*smychka*] of city and village. After all a seasonal worker is one-half peasant and one-half city-dweller. The seasonal worker is the element in the peasant population who should bind city and village together into a coherent whole.' The suggestion that a hostel existence in itself offered the opportunity to lead a civilized existence was unwittingly undermined by the writer, though, when he emphasized the necessity of hygienic behaviour on the part of the hostel's inhabitants: 'If the lavatories in hostels are kept in an untidy condition, if the *sezonniki* 'relieve themselves' at night wherever they feel like it, rather than in the lavatory, flies will start breeding in huge numbers.' While representing the hostel as the well-spring of *kul'turnost'*, Bruk makes it clear that the conditions in real hostels were usually such as to encourage the very insanitary and anti-social practices that the hostels were designed to combat.[85]

[83] See esp. L. H. Siegelbaum, *Stakhanovism and the Politics of Productivity in the USSR, 1935–1941* (Cambridge, 1988).

[84] See Khakhordin, *The Collective and the Individual*, esp. ch. 5.

[85] Bruk, *Chto nado znat' krest''aninu*, 30, 11. Cf. the anxieties about hostels as breeding grounds of 'dirty and uncultured habits' expressed by party officials behind closed doors: see N. Lebina, *Povsednevnaya zhizn' sovetskogo goroda. Normy i anomalii. 1920–e i 1930–e gody* (St Petersburg, 1999), 57 9.

In ideological terms, though, there was no contradiction here, since the hostel appealed to Soviet ideology above all as a locus of collectivism (a point suggested also in the primary meaning of the Russian word for hostel, *obshchezhitie*—social life). Hostels, that is, were seen as 'hygienic' not because they actually were clean and sanitary, but because the values of cleanliness and sanitation might be propagandized within them:

By living in a hostel you will learn not to be shy of others—that is the first thing. And the second thing is that you will learn to participate in social activities, you will go through a good school of moral education, so to speak.

That is why it is so important that seasonal workers should go and live in a hostel.[86]

In the central areas of early Soviet propaganda—hygiene, self-education, rational dress, and house management—the importance of conformity to social norms was stressed again and again. Certainly, oddity in behaviour had seldom previously been encouraged by the purveyors of advice (even Gogol''s splendidly crazy *Selected Passages from Correspondence with Friends* had been intended by the writer as a work of unimpeachable conservatism). But even the limited ideals of differential self-development that had been expounded in pre-revolutionary behaviour literature were now discarded. Soviet mass readers were urged to think of the amelioration of self exclusively as a contribution to the task of building a rational society. Though the term *kul'turnyi* continued to be used by Soviet intellectuals to name a desirable behaviour pattern along the lines of the one invoked by their pre-revolutionary predecessors when using the word, the link between the concept and political conformity was something quite new.

FORMULATING THE IDEAL: PROPAGANDA FOR
KUL'TURNOST', 1918–1930

The genre of Soviet behaviour literature that developed earliest, apart from the political pamphlet as such,[87] was, following on from pre-revolutionary

---

[86] Bruk, *Chto nado znat' krest'yaninu*, 8. On *obshchezhitie* as social life, cf. the entry on Countess Shuvalova in I. M. Dolgorukov, 'Kapishche moego serdtsa, ili slovar' vsekh tekh lits, s koimi ya byl v raznykh otnosheniyakh v techenii moei zhizni', *Russkii arkhiv* 9 (1890), 391: Shuvalova's house is described here as 'samaya luchshaya shkola obshchezhitiya' for young people. A comparable case to the hostel was the communal canteen: on the failure of these, see Rothstein and Rothstein, 'The Beginnings of Soviet Culinary Arts', in Glants and Toomre (eds.), *Food in Russia: History and Culture*, esp. 183–4.

[87] On political pamphlets see P. Kerzhentsev (comp.), *Biblioteka kommunista: Sistematicheskii ukazatel' sotsyalisticheskoi literatury* (4th edn., Moscow, 1919).

tradition, the guide to self-education. In the first year of Bolshevik power (1918), no fewer than twenty-nine brochures on this subject were issued: they included Vsevolod Flerov's *An Alphabet for Adults*, issued in an edition of no less than 200,000, and a reissue of Tolstoi's *New Reading Book*.[88] As pre-Enlightenment reading primers had introduced the newly literate first of all to the Catechism, Soviet reading books and guides were invariably also inductions in political education. Reading texts were not only linguistically graded to the capabilities of novices, but were also, to borrow the title of a political pamphlet of 1918, 'alphabets of Leninism' which pounded into the heads of their readers the benefits of political participation, and underlined the contract between the new regime and the workers.[89] This was in tune with the broader aims of Bolshevik educational policy, whose primary aim was to inculcate solidarity with the regime. In his speech inaugurating the Komsomol, 'The Tasks of the Youth Leagues' (2 October 1920), Lenin had emphasized that the need to 'absorb the sum of information set out in communist textbooks, brochures, and essays' was only one requirement: practical knowledge and respect for 'communist morality' were also essential.[90] Similarly, in a piece on 'Social Education' (1922), Krupskaya had insisted that Soviet schools should be places not only for education in an intellectual sense, but also for social engineering: pupils should be kept in touch with 'village and factory youth' in order to prepare them for a life of useful labour.[91]

As in the education of children and adolescents, so in adult education, the acquisition of intellectual skills was not an end in itself, but one part of a package of measures aimed at producing an exemplary worker, a mission that had been initiated after the promulgation of the 1918 decree on workers' control of industry. In an article first published in *Pravda* in 1923, Trotsky had addressed the particular problem involved in reaching the

[88] *V. Flerov, *Bukvar' vzroslykh* (Moscow, 1918); *L. N. Tolstoi, *Pervaya russkaya kniga dlya chteniya* (Moscow, 1918) (see *KL* 1918). For the 1873 original of this publication, see *PSS* xxi. 3–100.

[89] *P. Kerzhentsev, *Azbuka leninizma* (Petrograd, 1918); idem,*Pamyatka bol'shevika: Posobie dlya novykh chlenov partii i dlya samoobrazovaniya* (Petrograd, 1918) (*KL* 1918); M. Gremin, *Azbuka politgramoty* (Moscow and Leningrad, 1925). N. Bukharin and E. Preobrazhensky's *Azbuka kommunista* (Moscow, 1920), which was regularly reprinted in the early 1920s (see *KL*, 1920–4), and translated into English by the British Communist Party in 1922 (*The ABC of Communism*, trans. E. and C. Paul, London, 1922), was a more substantial and complex document which beginning readers managed with difficulty and found deadly dull. (On this, see the memoir of a former literacy tutor for the Red Army, Ivan Fedoryuk, in L. S. Petrusheva (ed.), *Deti russkoi emigratsii* (Moscow, 1997), 278.)

[90] *Sobranie sochinenii*, xxxi. 260–1, 264–5.

[91] N. Krupskaya, 'Obshchestvennoe vospitanie', in her *Izbrannye pedagogicheskie sochineniya* (Moscow, 1955), 201–5. On the school syllabus and history of education in practical terms, see the excellent study by L. E. Holmes, *The Kremlin and the Schoolhouse: Reforming Education in Soviet Russia, 1917–1931* (Bloomington, Ind., 1991).

non-Party workers who, though 'not altogether "apolitical"', were 'nonpolitical'. How were these workers to be induced 'to connect their individual productive work with the interests of socialism as a whole'? The answer was not to bombard them with explicitly political material, but to address 'matters of production and technique':

What we really want is a series of new handbooks—for the Soviet locksmith, the Soviet cabinetmaker, the Soviet electrician, etc. The handbooks must be adapted to our up-to-date techniques and economics, and must take into acount our poverty, and on the other hand, our big possibilities; they must try to introduce new methods and new habits into our industrial life.[92]

The new 'methods' for which Trotsky called were addressed in particular by the propagandization of Taylorist techniques of 'rational management', or 'the scientific organization of labour'. The Central Institute of Scientific Labour in Moscow, founded in 1920, had produced over 2,000 publications by 1924, among them Aleksei Gastev's guide for in-factory trainers, *The Principles of Labour*, illustrated with drawings of the right way to use a hammer and the ergonomic method of operating a lathe, as well as with rousing proclamations of the efficacy of this system.[93] But apart from professional guides of this kind, which are outside the scope of my discussion here, there was also material aimed at altering mentality: at propagandizing new 'habits', rather than publicizing new 'methods'. It included *Organize Yourself!* (1925) by Pavel Kerzhentsev, a compendium of three brochures originally published separately, 'Organize Yourself', 'The Fight for Time' (i.e. the struggle to spend it wisely), and 'How to Read a Book'.[94] *Organize Yourself!* insisted that every worker must acquire 'method, system, a capacity for exactitude and for accurate analysis' (metodichnost'', sistema, tochnyi raschet, pravil'nyi analiz). It proclaimed an assault on inefficiency and sloppiness, which were labelled (in traditionally Russian style) as 'traditionally Russian', here through the use of colloquial terms such as *avos'* (let's give it a go), *oblomovshchina* (from Oblomov, the hero of Goncharov's novel), and *koe-kak* (any old how):

---

[92] L. Trotsky, 'Not By Politics Alone', *Problems of Everyday Life: Creating the Foundations for a New Society in Revolutionary Russia* (New York, 1973), 21–2.

[93] Gastev, *Trudovye ustanovki*, (1924). On Gastev and the Central Labour Institute, see Kendall E. Bailes, 'Aleksei Gastev and the Soviet Controversy over Taylorism, 1918–1924', *Soviet Studies* 29 (1977), 373–94.

[94] One of these brochures, probably the first, is mentioned with approval in Lenin's 'Luchshe men'she, da luchshe' (4 Mar. 1923), *Sobranie sochinenii*, xxxiii. 451 (as 'Kerzhentsev's recent book'). Kerzhentsev (1881–1940) was a former foreign correspondent for *Pravda* who held a series of high-level posts in Soviet propaganda organizations (e.g. ROSTA 1919–20, the Propaganda Section of the Central Committee 1928–30) as well as heading the Soviet legation to Sweden in 1921–3 and to Italy in 1925–6.

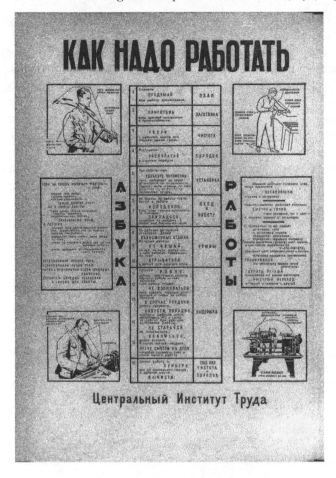

FIG. 14. *How to Work*. Poster published by the Scientific
Institute of Labour (NOT), 1926.

Down with the bumpkinism of Poshekhon'e [a place invented by the satirist
Saltykov-Shchedrin to symbolize backwardness], the dreamy sloth of Oblomov,
slovenliness, slackness!

Instead of 'let's give it a go'—exact calculation.

Instead of 'any old how'—the scientific method.

Instead of 'any old when'—20.35 pm on 15 October.

Forward to communism via the struggle to economize time and the scientific
organization of labour![95]

[95] Kerzhentsev, *Organizui samogo sebya!*, 73, 74.

Kerzhentsev's pamphlet offered not only sententious abstractions of this kind, but also more detailed advice. Like Trotsky in an article of 1921, he called for 'attention to trifles'.[96] Workers should introduce an 'English day' (at this stage of his career Kerzhentsev was a vehement Anglophile), with lunch at 12–1 precisely, and tea at 4.30. They should acquire an appointments book and an address book, to be scrupulously kept in alphabetical order. And they should maintain a chart of the time spent on various activities every day (a method borrowed from Gastev), in order that minutes devoted to eating, smoking and talking breaks, sleeping, and visiting the lavatory could be pared down to the minimum.[97] Gastev's own *How to Work*, first published in 1921, was similarly detailed, using fashionable typographical cues (capital letters, different sizes of print, bold type) in order to highlight its central demands: cleanliness, tidiness, method, organization, and physical self-control:

DON'T FORGET!
YOUR FIRST STEP
WHEN REORGANIZING FACTORIES AND OFFICES MUST BE TO ESTABLISH CLEANLINESS . . .

Usually people 'get cracking' with a piece of work; where possible, taking things gradually is a better idea. . . .
The cultured worker is easy to distinguish from the uncultured worker because he always has everything to hand. . . .
You should never eat while working. It is not only bad for your stomach, but it is very bad for a person's character, since it causes him to lose all self-restraint, and it is worst of all for the work being done, since this will certainly be carried out in a sloppy manner [*neriashlivo*].[98]

As this last example suggested, one of the most important aspects of *kul'turnost'* was physical fitness. Kerzhentsev, too, emphasized this: 'A man will only be worthy of the revolutionary era, and a genuine communist, when he not only has brains that have been worked over in a Marxist way, but also a healthy body, the strong muscles of the warrior, the skilled hands of the worker.'[99] Though no specific guidance was given here on how to go about acquiring a 'healthy body' and 'warrior's muscles', this was a

---

[96] Trotsky, 'Attention to Trifles!' *Pravda*, 1 Oct. 1921. See L. Trotsky, *Problems of Everyday Life: Creating the Foundations for a New Society in Revolutionary Russia* (New York, 1973), 73–6.

[97] Toporkov, *Kak stat' kul'turnym*, 83, also recommends keeping a chart, and gives a sample one for Party officials: arrive 8.48, discussions with colleagues till 9.52, correspondence till 11.35, work on article till 12.51, etc.

[98] Gastev, *Kak nado rabotat'* (1926). Quoted from Gastev, *Kak nado rabotat'* (Moscow, 1966), 112, 117, 119, 128–9.

[99] Kerzhentsev, *Organizui samogo sebya!*, 7.

theme so widely dispersed in Soviet advice literature that Kerzhentsev could assume his readers would be familiar with it from other sources. Indeed, throughout the Soviet period, propaganda for physical culture, and health education more generally, was perhaps the single most significant genre of advice literature, with the working classes now inducted into a 'cult of the body' that had some resemblances to the body-cult in the pre-revolutionary Russian upper and middle classes, but which was much more explicitly linked with the industrialization drive and the propagandization of *boevaya gotovnost'*, civil defence.[100]

The health cult was so pervasive that it led to the absorption into mainstream Soviet culture of some rather odd material where this could be presented as 'scientific': for example, the graphological hypotheses of D. M. Zuev-Insarov, author of *Handwriting and the Personality*.[101] The book underlines the scientific credentials of graphology not only by linking this type of analysis with hypnosis and psychoanalysis, but also by printing complimentary responses by various famous people, including health commissar Semashko and Maxim Gor'ky, to graphological analyses of their handwriting. The author also conveyed his respectability by publishing a photograph of the 'popularized graphological display table' in the foyer of the Moscow Experimental Theatre (p. 103). Equally improbably, a further rationale for graphology was stated to be its usefulness to the collective. 'To know oneself, to carve out the niche in life that one deserves, means to save society from the morbid experiments performed by a social unit that has not found itself'—so ran the incongruously pompous epigraph to Zuev-Insarov's book, a lurid blend of social Darwinism, Platonic philosophy, and utilitarianism. And eugenics, too, sometimes made its fashionable presence felt in the humble field of advice literature, most incongruously, perhaps, in Aleksandr Mendel'son's 1928 brochure aimed at combatting shyness, which advised timid readers that they should avoid perpetuating the condition by marrying one of their own kind (advice that, for the extremely timid, was perhaps easy to carry out).[102]

Such oddities apart, though, literature on hygiene was as unoriginal as every other branch of Soviet advice literature. The Soviet 'new man', as reflected in advice literature, represented a pared-down version of the pre-revolutionary 'new man': possessed of toned muscles and 'moral fibre' (or

---

[100] For hygiene pamphlet publication statistics, see Appendix 4 Table 1. On the institutionalized 'fizkul'tura' movement, see J. Riordan, *Sport in Soviet Society* (Cambridge 1977), ch. 2; K. Petrone, 'Parading the Nation: Physical Culture Celebrations and the Construction of Soviet Identities in the 1930s', *Michigan Discussions in Anthropology* 12 (19996), and *eadem*, *Life Has Become More Joyous, Comrades: Celebrations in the Time of Stalin* (Bloomington, Ind., 2000), 30–9.

[101] Zuev-Insarov, *Pocherk i lichnost'* (1929). This rare, self-published book is held in RGB at P 105/121.

[102] Mendel'son, *Zastenchivost' i bor'ba s neyu.*

in the Russian term, 'steeliness', *zakal*), resolute and determined in the workplace if not in 'business' (financial success was certainly not part of the new code of values). The difference was that care of the body was now seen as a civic, as well as personal, duty. It underwrote the commitment of the Soviet medical establishment to 'social hygiene', the doctrine that 'health was not simply the absence of disease; it was the active promotion of the well-being of the population at large'.[103]

One area where prophylactic medicine was very actively propagandized was in advice on dress and grooming, which promoted 'rational dress': simple and 'natural' garments allowing maximum freedom of movement. Pamphleteers might hold back from endorsing nudism, but they did so ostensibly on grounds of hygiene, rather than of morality (as L. D. Ul'yanov put it in *Clothing and Health* (1929), 'When a naked person appears on the street wearing a banner saying "Down with Shame", then his health gains nothing from this activity; on the contrary, it is detrimental to health, since he risks catching cold as a result (even in the summer), or else of wounding or damaging his body in some way').[104] By far the larger share of their bile was reserved for what Nikolai Semashko's *Art of Dress* called 'the most wanton imitation of the supremely idiotic, harmful and depraved fashion of the bourgeosie'.[105] As Semashko argued, the main requisites were that clothing be discreet, comfortable, and above all clean and tidy:

An extremely unpleasant impression is made by a person (especially by a woman, since we have come to expect more neatness from a woman than a man) in rusty-coloured down-at-heel shoes, with buttons torn off their clothing, with an undarned hole on their coat, looking dirty, shabby and ugly. On the other hand, what a pleasant impression is made by clothes that may be cheap and old, but are neat and carefully mended![106]

Contemporary advice on skin care was also entirely consonant with the 'hygienic' approach; commentators were insistent that skin should be kept clean and 'cared for', but little detailed advice on care routines was given, and cosmetics were not touched on at all.[107]

House management manuals of the 1920s, too, were above all concerned with basic hygiene and the rational organization of labour, and they, too, resolutely opposed superfluous ornamentation. As the most widely published author of the 1920s, Mariya Zarina, wrote in her *House Management: Food, Accommodation, Clothes* (1928), the best 'decoration' was 'cleanliness and order':

---

[103] Solomon, 'Social Hygiene', 175.   [104] Ul'yanov, *Odezhda i zdorov''* (1929), 46.

[105] Semashko, *Iskusstvo odevat'sya*, 3.

[106] Ibid., 17: cf. Ul'yanov, *Odezhda i zdorov'e*, 28.

[107] However, Soviet magazines did carry advertisements for cosmetics, notably 'Metamorfoza' vanishing cream (see e.g. *Zhenskii zhurnal* 8 (1930), inside front cover).

The purpose of hygiene and of house management is one and the same—to create a healthy life. . . . The ultimate purpose of studying house management is to further the prosperity and health of new generations and the intellectual and moral development of the population . . . Cleanliness and order are the best decorations of any dwelling-places.[108]

Zarina's detailed advice was in accordance with these principles. Rooms should have white walls and as few items as possible should be set out, since 'every object that takes up space reduces the quantity of air in the room . . . and requires looking after, which makes it more difficult to keep living quarters clean' (ibid. 77–8). Diet was expected to be similarly streamlined, with the emphasis placed on choosing food that was nutritious and reasonably fresh, keeping it properly, and cooking it successfully when only makeshift resources were available (the use of a primus and thermos flask was carefully explained). This was a world where pianos, pictures, and rugs were seen as things the reader would only need to know about because she might be required to help with cleaning communal facilities: 'Apart from knowing about how to look after simple furniture, one should also know how to care for luxurious items which are used to decorate and furnish clubs, Lenin corners and other public places' (ibid. 91). The recipes given in *House Management*, and in Zarina's other books, were similarly modest: they included soups, roasts, kashas, kisels, egg dishes, fried fish, and vegetables. The diet was, in fact, almost identical to that proposed in Zarina's pamphlet on mass catering, *At the Common Table*.[109]

The emphasis on 'hygienic living' was so strong as to be a major factor in the rehabilitation for propaganda purposes of the dacha, seen in the 1920s as a shibboleth of pre-revolutionary middle-class Russian life (the conversion of 'petit-bourgeois dachas' to use as proletarian holiday homes was regularly hymned in the 1920s Soviet press).[110] A brochure of 1930 extolled the advantages for town-dwellers of exposure to time in the country: the opportunity to enjoy 'easy and pleasant work in one's own miniature garden' was held certain to ensure all sorts of prophylactic benefits, including even the lowering of the crime rate (perhaps on the grounds that people who had spent all day digging the allotment were unlikely to have the energy left to engage in house-breaking).[111]

Thus far, 'rational living' was something taken over wholesale from the

[108] Zarina, *Domovodstvo* (1928), 5, 7, 83. Cf. Prigradov-Kudrin, *Ukhod za zhil'em* (1927), or *Domovodstvo: khrestomatiya* (1929), or the instructions in *Drug rabotnitsy*, a supplement to the newspaper *Golos tekstilei* published in 1929.

[109] Zarina, *Za obshchim stolom* (1933).

[110] See e.g. I. Babel' (as K. Lyutov), 'V dome otdykha', *Zarya vostoka*, 24 June 1922 (repr. in Babel', *Zabytaya proza* (Ann Arbor, 1979), 130–2).

[111] Plotnikov, *Deshevoe dachnoe stroitel'stvo*, 41.

revolutionary past. Rather more novel was the constant iteration of the instrumentality of self-improvement: it was to be seen as a means to an end, not an end in itself. 'The thing of greatest importance in the campaign for self-education,' declared Anatoly Lunacharsky in his introduction to the first issue of the journal *Aid to Self-Education* in 1923,

should of course not be the transformation of oneself into a specialist of some kind, not the aim to acquire knowledge that is needed for personal ends, for making a success of one's career. . . . No: the thing of greatest importance is to turn oneself into a conscious citizen, to evolve the ability to comprehend complex questions of internal politics, economics, and to grasp the most essential cultural issues.[112]

Equally, physical culture was in no sense to be understood as a hedonistic appreciation of the body for its own sake. Instead, fitness was a means of making the individual citizen a functional and obedient instrument of the new state. As V. Gorinevsky put it in a pamphlet under the title *The Repair and Tempering of the Human Organism* (1925): 'The weak, feeble, intellectually undeveloped, ideologically and politically indifferent person cannot become the professionally qualified worker of the kind now essential for Soviet economic development.'[113] The procedures for achieving the requisite fitness included not only the fresh air and balanced diet recommended by pre-revolutionary authors, but also sunbathing, and above all the abundant use of cold water (the term *zakalivanie*, or 'steel tempering', describing a series of procedures ranging from rubbing oneself with a cold damp towel to the taking of cold showers and baths, sometimes in alternation with hot ones, was used *ad nauseam*).[114] The ethos was that of 'mens sana in corpore sano', with pamphlets on physical exercise matched by material on 'the hygiene of intellectual labour'. The 'ten commandments' of the latter (the 'ten commandment' format being another cliché of early Soviet propaganda) were set out by Aleksandr Mendel'son in *Improving Your Memory* (1930). They included the need to keep the room well aired and briskly chilly, and to sit in reasonable light, as well as taking regular breaks, removing distractions, and keeping activities well varied.[115]

Physical and mental labour were seen as complementary forces, each equally purposive, each contributing to the development of the ideal citizen, who would be at once firm-willed and subordinate to the direction

---

[112] A. Lunacharsky, 'Znachenie samoobrazovatel'noi raboty', *Pomoshch' samoobrazovaniyu*, no. 1 (1923), 4. Or, as the painter Yury Annenkov alleged Lenin to have told him when sitting for his portrait in 1921, 'The only reason why it's worth "liquidating illiteracy" is so every peasant and worker can read our decrees and appeals for him- or herself. Our purpose is entirely practical' (*Dnevnik moikh vstrech: tsikl tragedii* (Moscow, 1991), 269–70).

[113] Gorinevsky, *Remont i zakalivanie organizma*, 5.

[114] On sunbathing, see e.g. Sarkizov-Serazini, *Lechites' solntsem!* (1927); on *zakalivanie* see for example Gol'dfail', *Lechenie vodoi doma, na kurorte i v lechebnom uchrezhdenii* (1930), 19.

[115] Mendel'son, *Ob ukreplenii pamyati*, 33.

of the governing state. One customary analogy expressing the relationship between citizen and state was that of the person as machine. As well as signifying that the body could be mended as easily as a broken lathe—an idea invoked, for example, in a pamphlet under the title *The Repair of the Human Machine* (1927) by V. S. Muralevich[116]—the analogy also evoked the disinterested obedience that was characteristic of machines as inanimate servants of production. But in another, less familiar, and in some ways more interesting analogy, the time-honoured concept of the 'body politic', the state as organic entity, was reversed, and the body came to be understood as a well-governed republic:

[The body is] the most ideal republic, constructed of millions of microscopic entities—that is to say, the cells, which live in perfect harmony and purposive adaptation one to the other, rationally carrying out their duties with regard to the preservation of life in the given organism.[117]

It followed that the most convenient analogy for illness and death was subversive behaviour on the part of the 'citizens', or indeed rebellion.

Again, there was nothing particularly 'Soviet' in much of this; some of the rhetoric could easily have emanated from the average sports master at a British public school of the 1920s or 1930s, right down to the obligatory analogies with Ancient Greece as a justification for sanitized homo-eroticism:

Scarcely any time had passed [after the Revolution] when the streets of Moscow and other cities began to be bestridden by detachments of marching youths, half-naked, with bronzed skins and with firm strong muscles. And sometimes on public holidays it seemed that the fairy-tale world of Hellas had descended upon our city squares, and that crowds of long-dead Greeks had come to life among the extraordinary bustle of contemporary life.[118]

As with the British public school, or indeed Catherine II's educational institutions, such as Smol'nyi, too, any retreat from this neo-Enlightenment utopia into solitude could only be seen as pathological. In *Shyness and the Fight to Combat It* (1928), the tireless Aleksandr L. Mendel'son, one of the most prolific popularizers of the hygiene code, insisted that shyness was a side-effect of 'self-love'; it was imperative that it be cured, which could be effected by determination and commitment to a programme of 'self-education' (notably, practice in public speaking). The split between a 'bad self' (the object of self-love, disgracefully lurking in private) and a

[116] Muralevich, *Remont chelovecheskoi mashiny*, 6. The book is an enthusiastic description of experiments in rejuvenation therapy, including an operation performed on a 16-year-old mongrel dog in Leningrad in May 1923 (perhaps the real-life forerunner of the grisly procedures in Bulgakov's 1925 story *Heart of a Dog*?).

[117] Sarkizov-Serazini, *Lechites' solntsem!*, 31.

[118] Ibid. 19.

'good self' (inert material that had been transformed by the active principle of re-education and took a full part in public activities) was entirely characteristic of the times.[119]

A signal case illustrating the ideology of hygiene-as-socialization is that of masturbation, the subject of a number of cautionary pamphlets published during the the 1920s. The authors of these diatribes against onanism were eager to dismiss the popular myths current at the time—that masturbation could provoke physical traumas such as failing eyesight, impotence, and so on. Their own arguments against the practice were not so much medical as sociological. Masturbation was unacceptable first and foremost because it was a 'solitary form of self-pleasuring' (odinokoe samoudovletvorenie), in the phrase of Aleksandr Mendel'son, author of a pamphlet under the title *Onanism and the Fight Against It* (1924).[120]

Not only mistrust of solitude, but also, of course, mistrust of pleasure itself was at the root of this condemnation of 'illicit' sexual activity. Some advice literature even took a wary stand on the only kind of sexual practice endorsed by Mendel'son, the union of one male with one female. In a study of sexual continence published in the late 1920s, Yakov Golomb concluded that the main argument in favour of sexual intercourse was a hygienic one: frustration was detrimental to health. However, if properly sublimated, sexual energy could be channelled into more useful activities than intercourse itself: 'Creating a reservoir of higher energy and firing the first salvo in the successful battle with ulcerous social ills of all kinds, sexual continence plays a valuable role in the task of bettering the human race and furthering the cultural process.'[121]

Suspicion of pleasure also emerges particularly strongly in studies of another activity approved so long as it was socially useful—reading. (No doubt fear of what one writer called 'psychic onanism', i.e. the clandestine reading of pornography, played some part in this.)[122] For example, a

---

[119] Mendel'son, *Zastenchivost' i bor'ba s neyu*. The catalogue of RNB states that M. held a position (*privat-dotsent*) at a Leningrad medical institute (Gos. Institut dlya usovershenstvovaniya vrachei), but gives no other biographical details. The fight against shyness was not, of course, a Soviet invention (on its pre-revolutionary history, see above, Ch. 3), but again, the emphasis on its perniciousness as an impediment to harmonious collectivity was something new.

[120] Mendel'son, *Onanizm i bor'ba s nim*, 8; cf. Fronshtein, *Onanizm* (1930), and the comments of Naiman, *Sex in Public*, 120–3. The 'sociological' criticism of masturbation contrasts sharply with the attitude taken by pre-revolutionary pamphlets on onanism: e.g. L. A. Zolotarev, the Russian translator of Anton Nystrom's *The Laws of Sexual Life*, rebukes N. for not including more on this dangerous practice, but is prepared to countenance onanism in youth, when 'if individual development proceeds correctly, sexual intercourse should not take place' (Nistrom, *Polovaya zhizn' i ee zakony* (1909), 39).

[121] Golomb, *Polovoe vozderzhanie: za i protiv* (1927), 30. Note the extraordinary mixed metaphors, suggesting that continence is at once prophylactic (the 'sores' that it heals suggest syphilitic sores), and simultaneously conserves potency (the 'reservoir') and expresses sexual puissance (the 'salvo'). [122] Fronshtein, *Onanizm*, 9.

pioneering Soviet guide to rational reading, Pavel Kerzhentsev's *How to Read a Book* (1924), was firm on the need to dissociate reading and pleasure. Readers should prepare themselves for systematic reading by making sure they had a quiet, well-aired space in which to work, and should adopt a posture that made their readiness for energetic and thorough activity clear:

If you aren't able to read in a library, find the best-lit and quietest corner that you can. Check whether the room needs airing. . . . If the weather is at all tolerable, read outside in the fresh air. . . . It is best to read sitting at a table, having selected a comfortable chair or bench. A low table which forces you to bend over your reading is no use. Incidentally, it is vital to cure yourself of the habit of lolling on a bed during the day or reading in bed at night.

Of course, while reading you should change your position every now and again—you can read for a while standing up, and then you can sit down again.

While reading, have the book directly in front of you, preferably in an inclined position (on a rest of some kind).

If you need to make extracts while reading, lay the paper or note book to the right of your book, and place the inkwell alongside. Have your dictionary of foreign words, your encyclopedia or other such reference books (which you may find helpful) on the left-hand side.[123]

Though Kerzhentsev's suggestion that the reader shift his posture from time to time while reading is consonant with ergonomics, his preference for standing over lying down is traceable to moral, rather than physical, appreciations. Reading must not be a passive, pleasurable activity, but an active, useful one: an upright posture signified the reader's readiness for serious work. (This signification resonated even decades later in Russian intellectual culture. At the end of the twentieth century too, a *pis'mennyi stol*, or 'writing table', was seen as a prerequisite for reading and writing. The absence of desks from many Western homes and hotels, equipped with what Russian observers considered luxurious inessentials (for instance, hair-dryers and ironing-boards), inspired bemusement. Since reading and writing are physically possible without a desk, the perception that access to one was essential to these activities was no doubt traceable to a culturally specific belief that reading and writing should be serious, focused activities. It is instructive to contrast Kerzhentsev's advice to the reader with C. S. Lewis's advice to young British students of literature, issued in the 1960s, that they should *not* treat reading as work.)[124]

Kerzhentsev's advice, to work systematically as one reads, to pose

---

[123] P. Kerzhentsev, *Kak chitat' knigu* (Moscow, 1924): quoted from *Organizui samogo sebya!*, 77–8.
[124] C. S. Lewis, *An Experiment in Criticism* (Cambridge, 1961). Cf. H. Lee, *Reading in Bed: An Inaugural Lecture Delivered before the University of Oxford on 21 October, 1999* (Oxford, 2000).

questions, to make notes, was duplicated in a host of other guides published in the 1920s and 1930s, as well as the advisory essays which came out in self-education magazines such as *Pomoshch' samoobrazovaniyu* (1923–31) and *Uchis' sam!* (1926–9). Nadezhda Krupskaya's 'Advice to a Person Beginning Self-Education', first published in 1922, and frequently reprinted thereafter, tabulated the procedure as a list of seven rules: 1. Read slowly and thoroughly. 2. Choose good, useful books that are at your own level. 3. Stop reading regularly and ask yourself questions. Write down anything you don't understand. 4. Write a summary of each chapter. 5. Note down any particularly striking thoughts. 6. Note down important facts. 7. After finishing, ask yourself what you have learned from the book.[125] (Interestingly, Gladkov's *Cement* provided a near variation on the model:

In his little roomlet in the House of Soviets, Sergei sat by the lamp reading [Lenin's] *Materialism and Empiriocriticism*. He carefully underlined whole paragraphs with pencil lines and made illegible dashes and squiggles in the margins.[126]

But here Sergei's underlining of 'whole paragraphs' and making of 'illegible dashes and squiggles' suggested the morbid lack of intellectual focus and susceptibility to distraction by trivial private concerns that must be over-come before he was to be a fully worthy communist. Indicative of these faults was also the fact that Sergei kept pacing about between 'his corner and the washstand', and could not 'formulate his thoughts'. And when he retired to sleep, instead of enjoying a refreshing and healthful rest, he would be disturbed by the sounds of Bad'in and Polya copulating in the next-door room.)

The stress on the need to 'formulate one's thoughts' when reading, and to learn from books, meant that self-education manuals not only provided lists of further reading, but routinely printed comprehension questions at the end of each section so that material might be rehearsed and re-rehearsed. Sometimes, but not always, bold type was used (as in Soviet newspapers of the day) so that the most important points could be grasped all the more easily.

The practice of testing knowledge represented one important strategy for bringing reading, potentially a dangerous activity in that it was carried out in solitude, under state control. Comprehension questions took a catechistic, rather than Socratic, attitude to knowledge: that is, the issue of

[125] N. Krupskaya, 'Sovety nachinayushchim zanimat'sya samoobrazovaniem', *O samoobrazo-vanii: Sbornik stat'ei* (Moscow, 1936), 10–14. The material was originally published in her *Kakie znaniya nuzhny molodomu rabochemu, krest'yaninu, krasnoarmeitsu (Moscow, 1922).

[126] Gladkov, *Tsement*, ch. XVI, pt. 3: *Krasnaya nov'* 6 (1925), 49. The passage appears in almost identical form in later editions of the text.

the value of information was not raised. Rather than encouraging the questioning of received ideas, or emphasizing that reading was a contribution to self-discovery, they conveyed the sense of a corpus of essential facts that must be acquired by every member of a society and by all the members of that society. They supplemented the reading lists that were also an essential part of directing new readers to use their knowledge wisely. As a book under the title *Self-Education by Means of Reading Belles-Lettres: What to Read on Holiday* (1929) argued, many readers supposed that literature was simply a means of entertainment. But they were wrong:

[The book], if read thoughtfully and systematically, can be the source of something far more important [than pleasure]. Modern writers constantly represent the most important moments of [Soviet] construction, depict life in its various manifestations, and touch on the most important moments in contemporary life and in the recent revolutionary past.[127]

There followed a list, thematically laid out, of materials by authors such as Nikolai Nikitin, Panteleimon Romanov, Vera Ketlinskaya, and Anna Karavaeva on subjects ranging from the Struggle with Religion, the Civil War, the New Way of Life (*byt*) and the Struggle with the Threat of War. The list was dominated by recently published Soviet fiction, all of it of a straightforwardly realist kind. This was in sharp contrast to Nikolai Rubakin's pre-revolutionary manuals of self-education, with their demanding reading lists and their constant suggestions that readers should follow up their own interests, rather than conforming to standards imposed from outside, and their emphasis upon the existence of different types of reader. Indeed, even in a manual published during the early Soviet era, Rubakin had emphasized that 'checking facts, studying them and holding opinions about them is not enough. It is also necessary to *evaluate these facts and opinions*.'[128] In most manuals published at this period, though, unilateral 'evaluation' of this kind was definitely not encouraged. Rather, the point was to absorb material generally perceived as useful. The tight relationship between 'education' (*vospitanie*) and 'political education' (*politvospitanie*) had among its effects the fact that questioning *any* material

---

[127] *Samoobrazovanie putem chitki belletristiki*, 1.

[128] Rubakin, *Pis'ma k chitatelyam o samoobrazovanii* (1913), 91, 161–86; idem, *Kak i s kakoi tsel'yu chitat' knigu*, 37 (emphasis original). Significantly, Rubakin's writings were specifically discounted by the author of an ancillary bibliography of books on self-education published in 1923: they were 'not suitable to contemporary needs' because self-education was represented in them as 'a complex individual, intimate process with a very broadly defined sphere of tasks; a lifetime would not be enough to get through them' (Z. Bogomazova, *Literatura po samoobrazovaniyu* (Moscow and Leningrad, 1927), 16). For analysis of the constructs of readership that shaped the composition of such manuals, see S. Lovell, *The Russian Reading Revolution: Print Culture in the Soviet and Post-Soviet Eras* (Basingstoke, 2000), ch. 2, and J. Brooks, 'Studies of the Reader in the 1920s', *Russian History* 9 (1982), 187–202.

presented for instruction meant mounting an indirect challenge to political authority.[129]

The fact that the purpose of gathering information was related to the broader social good, and to the maintenance of social discipline, was underlined in many other ways as well. Most 'how to' books for new readers stressed the efficacy of collaboration, encouraging those acquiring literary skills to form a *kruzhok* (association).[130] But the authors of self-education manuals also ordained that a sense of the social ramifications of reading skills, its applicability to the needs of the collective, be maintained even by those who had perforce to work in solitude. 'Genuine self-education is hammered out not in studies, but in the process of active participation in collective life,' wrote Nadezhda Krupskaya in 1919.[131]

Once a reader had acquired the ability to read correctly (namely, for the *right* information), the next step was to bring the material that he or she had gleaned from reading into the public domain. One way of doing this was, of course, by reading aloud. Evgeny Katsman's 1928 genre painting *Kalyazin Lace Makers* shows a young girl—whose rational clothing (a simple knee-length shift and pale scarf to keep her hair tidy) immediately mark her out as a member of the new generation—reading aloud from a brochure to two older women in peasant clothing and two girls as they sit over their lace pillows.[132] But this was only the simplest method of enacting a new skill and of disseminating information. The custom of making notes while reading was a preparation for the ultimate end of literacy skills: making a contribution to political culture. The two main methods of doing this were the *doklad* (spoken presentation) and the article or note written for a newspaper. *How to Work on a Presentation*, a brochure of 1929, stressed the need for thorough planning, and also for collaborative work: the audience must be involved by appropriate seating and by having questions addressed to them.[133] The presentation-giver was seen as an

---

[129] Cf. Kalinin's comments on the acquisition of political knowledge: 'To study Marxism does not mean to read through Marx, Engels, and Lenin . . . To learn Marxism means to know after mastering the Marxist method how to approach the problems connected with your work. . . . It means being able to adopt the correct line.' (From a speech to the Seventh Congress of the Komsomol, 11 Mar. 1926, *On Communist Education*, 16.)

[130] 'It is useful and desirable for those studying to unify themselves into groups', stated one text-book for distance learning' (*Rabochii fakul'tet na domu*, 45). In her writings, Nadezhda Krupskaya emphasized *vzaimopomoshch'* (mutual aid) rather than *samopomoshch'* (self-help).

[131] N. Krupskaya, 'Kak uchit'sya?, *Yunyi kommunist* 4–5 (1919): see *eadem, O samoobrazovanii* (1936), 6.

[132] See M. Cullerne Bown, *Socialist Realist Painting* (New Haven, 1997), pl. 103.

[133] Petrov, *Kak rabotat' nad dokladom*. A rather different set of guides was aimed at training the speaker's rhetorical skills. See e.g. *E. Khersonskaya, *Molodym propagandistam i oratoram* (Petrograd, 1918); Rozhitsyn, *Kak vystupat' na sobraniyakh* (1920); Mirtov, *Umen'e govorit' publichno* (1925); Kreps and Erberg, *Praktika oratorskoi rechi* (1931). For a full study of such

intermediary between the newspapers and books that he read and the audience; he himself was expected to complete comprehension tests in order to facilitate the understanding of those who listened to him. Public speaking was thus presented as a skill that was accessible to all by diligent labour.

Similarly, guides on how to write for the newspapers stressed that newspapers were accountable to their readers, to the mass of the Soviet population. They encouraged contributions from 'worker-correspondents', who, they emphasized, did not need to be representatives of any elite. Any Soviet citizen could become a 'worker-correspondent' simply by publishing material in a newspaper:

Anyone can write. Our press is a proletarian press. Anyone can participate in the press, even someone who is hardly literate. . . . The editors of the wall newspaper or printed newspaper will correct a [badly expressed and ungrammatical] note, will print it and will demand that the note is acted upon in the necessary way.[134]

In her book *Common Places*, Svetlana Boym has used the loaded term 'graphomania' to name the Soviet cult of mass participation in the publishing industry, and has argued that its key point was the Stalin period: 'Socialist Realism refined and "corrected" the concept of graphomania. . . . Everyone is encouraged to be an artist, to write or compose in an effort to reveal his or her great patriotic talent.'[135] But in fact the refinement of 'graphomania' began well before the term 'Socialist Realism' had been invented. Even before the Revolution, manuals such as N. Abramov's *The Gift of Words* (1901) had given encouragement and practical advice to those seeking to hone their skills as public speakers, narrators of anecdotes, or the authors of fiction and poetry.[136] In the decade after the Revolution, additional impetus came from the Proletkul't movement, which, like German Expressionism, looked with suspicion on the Romantic cult of innate ability, 'talent', or 'genius'. As 'Metal Worker Zasim' put it, writing for the journal *Rabochii korrespondent* in 1924: 'If a worker-correspondent has it [talent], so much the better. But if he

---

material, see M. S. Gorham, 'From "Charisma" to "Cant"': Models of Public Speaking in Early Soviet Russia', *Canadian Slavonic Papers* 38/3–4 (1996), 331–56.

[134] *Kak i o chem pisat' v gazetu?* (1928), 1. On the worker-correspondent movement, see V. N. Alferov, *Vozniknovenie i razvitie rabsel'korovskogo dvizheniya v SSSR* (Moscow, 1970); M. S. Gorham, 'Tongue-Tied Writers: The *Rabsel'kor* Movement and the Voice of the "New Intelligentsia" in Soviet Russia', *RR* 55 (1996), 412–29; J. Brooks, 'Competing Modes of Popular Discourse: Individualism and Class Consciousness in the Russian Print Media, 1880–1928', in M. Ferro *et al.* (eds.), *Culture et Révolution* (Paris, 1989), 71–81. Alferov, *Vozniknovenie*, 91, 118, and Kenez, *The Birth of the Propaganda State*, 235, suggest that the numbers involved had risen from a few hundreds in 1923 to half a million by 1928.

[135] Boym, *Common Places*, 200.

[136] Abramov, *Dar slova*.

doesn't, that's no bad thing either. Anyone can learn to write for the newspaper.'[137]

Yet, despite their encouragement of mass participation in the writing process, at the same time the brochures and articles advising potential authors and journalists were keen to underline that not just any copy was of interest to the Soviet press. The primary requirement was ideological rectitude: 'Our press . . . expresses the judgements and the moods of the best section of the working class, the conscious and advanced section, which correctly understands the interests of the working class as a whole.'[138] But it was not the only requirement. Writers should also be aware of the right forum in which to air their comments. The *stengazeta* (wall newspaper, or home-produced newssheet displayed on a noticeboard in a place of work or educational institution) was the place for matters of purely local interest, printed newspapers for broader issues.

Advice was also given on stylistic matters. 'Worker-correspondents' were urged to be concrete, rather than abstract, and above all, to use their newly acquired writing skills in order to bring specific local incidents and problems to the attention of the Soviet public. The structure of the *zametka*, 'note', the expected contribution from a worker-correspondent, was set out paradigmatically in *How to Write for the Newspaper and What to Write About* (1928). 1. Describe the incident. 2. Say where and 3. when it happened. 4. Say what was done to put it right on the spot. 5. Explain why it happened. 6. State what should be done to put it right.[139]

Other sources offered guidance on more detailed aspects of style, for example, register and choice of lexis. In one textbook, *The Culture of Language in Examples and Exercises*, the development of 'cultured use of language' is described as 'the evolution of linguistic sensitivity, a recognition of linguistic norms, and of the strategies needed for constructing an exact, clear and expressive form of speech, the ability to employ these in practice, in one's own way of expressing oneself both orally and in written form, and to become more sensitive towards others' ways of expressing themselves'. A fundamental method of acquiring such 'cultured use of language' was 'creative work by analogy' (*tvorcheskaya rabota po analogii*), that is, the acquisition of literary style by the imitation of models in different genres: the letter, the diary, the memoir, the story.[140] When the Lef writer V. Trenin vented his spleen at the tireless poetasters who inundated journals such as his with their miserable exudations ('these

---

[137] 'Slesar' Zasim', 'Zametki iz zapisnoi knizhki rabkora', *Rabochii korrespondent* 1 (1924), 27–8.

[138] Pilatskaya and Zuev, *Kruzhok rabkorov i stennaya gazeta* (1925), 13; cf. Dokunin, *Kak rabotat' rabkoru* (1925), 17–19.

[139] *Kak i o chem pisat' v gazetu*, 2.

[140] Gurevich, Svetlova, Sokolova, and Yanchevskaya, *Kul'tura rechi v obraztsakh i zadaniyakh* (1929), 3.

poems are not a literary phenomenon, they are a physiological one'), excoriating in particular the writers' imitativeness ('the one thing that you can call "literary" is the fact that they slavishly imitate well-known poetic models').[141] he was voicing a rather unusual view: exactly this imitativeness was what most guides to writing encouraged. Equally unusual was the Lef group's insistence that writing poetry was difficult and that worker writers should stick to different genres ('The comrade who sent us his verses ought to recognize that his very valuable material about life in Zyryansk should not be tarted up with Russian rhymes . . . that he should write his diary or his autobiography').[142] For the most part, guides propounded a view of the poetry writer (one cannot say 'poet') not as someone offering an extraordinary new vision, but as a workaday craftsman; they stressed basic literacy in metrics rather than the desirability of originality or adventurousness.[143]

The *kul'turnyi chelovek* propounded in 1920s advice literature, then, was someone who set him- or herself modest goals, practising intellectual as well as physical self-restraint, and leading a life balanced between work and rational leisure. So far as self-education and the communication of its results went, the targets set out for worker readers and writers were uniformly unambitious. The astonishing history of auto-didacticism in Russia—the emergence, from intellectual obscurity, of such figures as Lomonosov, or more recently, Kornei Chukovsky, or the peasant poet Nikolai Klyuev—somehow got ignored in the advice guidance.

In advice on manners, too, the rule was simplicity rather than sophistication. Guidance on *kul'turnost'* took care not to teeter too far towards what Sergei Tret'yakov contemptuously described as 'bon ton for toffs'.[144] To be sure, Trotsky might admonish workers that 'a person who spits on the floor is a dissolute slob', and Pavel Kerzhentsev insist that speakers at meetings should learn to express themselves '*without undue harshness* towards other orators'.[145] But no one suggested that workers should keep their elbows off

---

[141] V. Trenin, 'Pochtovyi yashchik Lefa', *Novyi Lef* 5 (1928), 39. Cf. Mayakovsky's lecture 'How to Write Poetry' (1926): 'They retrieve worn-out poetic images from old-style gentry culture and use them in exactly the same way that the gentry poets used to.' (Report from *Sel'kor Ukraini* 1 (1926): Mayakovsky, *PSS* xii. 486.)

[142] Trenin, 'Pochtovyi yashchik', 40. It was exactly such material—e.g. a diary about a provincial worker's visit to Moscow in 1928—that *Lef* and *Novyi Lef* were prepared to accept from beginning writers. (Isaak Slutsky, 'Zapiski provintsiala o Moskve', *Novyi Lef* 10 (1928), 17–30.)

[143] A case in point was the very book vilified by Mayakovsky in his *Kak delat' stikhi*, Shengeli's *Kak pisat' stat'i, stikhi i rasskazy* (1926), which not only equated writing poetry with the composition of essays and stories, but represented writing above all as technique ('A writer must study technique as a violinist does', p. 10).

[144] S. Tret'yakov, 'Khoroshii ton', *Novyi Lef* 5 (1927), 28–30.

[145] Trotsky, *Problems of Everyday Life*, 75; Kerzhentsev, *Kak vesti sobraniya* (1919), 32 (emphasis follows original).

the table while eating or employ the verb *kushat'* rather than *est'*. It was one thing to admonish peasants and workers about the dangers of communal eating-vessels, since that was considered beneficial to hygiene, and quite another to instruct them that it was rude to eat peas off their knives. And hand-kissing figured in activists' diatribes as an example of the worst kind of 'bourgeois survival'.[146] Like the French Revolutionaries, who had preferred straightforward *civilité* to refined *politesse*,[147] the Russian revolutionaries distinguished sharply between *kul'turnost'* and the old-fashioned ideal of *vospitannost'* or *uchtivost'*: too much of the latter was an obstacle to attainment of the former, rather than a sign of its presence.

CLEAN TEETH AND WHITE TABLECLOTHS: *KUL'TURNOST'* IN THE 1930S AND 1940S

> Culture is a very broad conception, ranging from the washing of one's face to the furthest reaches of human thought.
>
> (M. I. Kalinin, 1938)[148]

Coherent in synchronic terms, advice literature also maintained a high degree of coherence over time. Health, self-improvement, efficiency, and self-discipline remained the fundamental qualities propagandized, after 1935 as before. A statement of the purpose of fitness made in 1925 was closely paralleled in a guide to physical exercise published in 1953:

The resolution [of the question of the production of the forces of labour] will demand much effort from the Soviet government. But it will also demand conscious effort from all workers and peasants, as well as well-considered action and initiative, above all in order to realize the most basic and important stage of the production of the forces of labour—*cure of the self and restoration of one's own capacity to work*.

The Communist Party of the Soviet Union has always seen physical culture not only as a means of physical education and a path to health, and as one part of the campaign to prepare our youth for cultural, economic and military activity, but also as one of the means towards the moral education [*vospitanie*] of the masses, as a

---

[146] For instance, a Komsomol member wrote to the wall newspaper in the clinic where he worked in 1925 to complain of hand-kissing by doctors and other educated people, signing off with the lament, 'I should of thought we could have finished with this after seven and a half years of revolution.' See Leningrad District State Archive, City of Vyborg, f. r-2908, op. 1, d. 326, l. 51 (my thanks to Stephen Lovell for this and further references from Vyborg).

[147] See Peter France, *Politeness and Its Discontents: Problems in French Classical Culture* (Cambridge, 1992), 58.

[148] From a speech at the Conference of Best Urban and Rural Schoolteachers, 28 Dec. 1938, *On Communist Education*, 81.

method of involving the broad masses of workers and peasants with Party, Soviet and professional organizations, through which the labouring people of the Soviet Union are drawn into social and political life.[149]

The sense that physical self-improvement was more than an individual goal was enhanced by the propagandization, first and foremost, of collective forms of exercise: the participation in programmes of physical jerks (*zaryadka*) organized by *fizkul'tura* groups at places of work, or broadcast over the radio,[150] or, during vacations, in the extremely strenuous activity known as *turizm*. This had nothing to do with 'tourism' (which, confusingly, also became known in late twentieth-century Russian as *turizm*), but referred to athletic forms of hiking and, most particularly, the scaling of mountain peaks. In the words of a manual published in 1951, *turizm* was 'one of the methods of ideo-political education of the Soviet working people, which develops a sense of pride in our great Mother-land'.[151]

There was a similar continuity in the propaganda for self-education, whose goals, despite rising literacy, remained humble. Emphasis upon the need to acquire socially useful knowledge was further strengthened by the employment of a new tool: the quiz, or 'test your knowledge' contest, covering a variety of areas (basic mathematics, geography, high culture, and Soviet achievements) with which the *kul'turnyi chelovek* was supposed to have a nodding acquaintance. As a ten-point test printed by *Ogonek* in 1936 put it:

1. Recite by heart at least one poem by Pushkin. 2. Name and describe five plays by Shakespeare. 3. Name at least four rivers in Africa. 4. Name your favourite composer and his three major works. 5. Name five Soviet automobiles. 6. Convert $\frac{3}{8}$ into a decimal. 7. Name the three most important sports tournaments of the last year and their results. 8. Describe the three paintings which you liked most at last year's exhibitions. 9. Have you read Stendhal's *Scarlet and Black* and Turgenev's

---

[149] Gorinevsky, *Remont i zakalivanie organizma* (1925), 3 (emphasis original); Korablev, *Fizicheskaya kul'tura i zdorov'e* (1953), 5.

[150] See e.g. *Gimnastika po radio* (1946).

[151] Khrisanfov and Trakhtman, *Pamyatka turista*, 3. Cf. Pogrebetsky, *V pomoshch' turistu* (1935); *Turizm zimoi* (1935). (These two brochures were among many published by OPGE (The Proletarian Tourism Society), founded in 1930 in order to propagandize collective expeditions). Organized hiking was not, of course, unique to Russia. It had its parallels not only in the German passion for *Wandern* (a passion much encouraged during the Third Reich), but also in the 'revolutionary romanticism' of British socialists and communists of the 1920s and 1930s, which was to be expressed, for instance, in the alternative children's movement, the Woodland Folk. For a fascinating first-hand account of this strand in British culture, see Raphael Samuel, 'Country Visiting: A Memoir', *Island Stories: Unravelling Britain* (London, 1998), 132–52. A more specifically 'Russian' form of exercise (at least, as a mass activity) was hunting and shooting (*okhota*). This began to be promoted in the 1930s. The excellent bibliography of Gusev, *Lyubitel'skaya okhota* (1997), 247–50, lists no less than thirty-eight publications between 1930 and 1953.

Fathers and Children? 10. Explain why the Stakhanovite movement became possible in our country.[152]

Like comprehension tests, quizzes not only set out a body of requisite knowledge, but also encouraged individual readers to take an instrumental and performative view of this: to limit learning to facts that might be aired in the public domain.

As for efficiency and discipline, the main development was that 1930s and 1940s advice literature became, if anything, still more insistent about the need for these. An important development was the posting of rules in public places in order to ensure correct behaviour—for example, in the Moscow Metro, where smoking, eating, and drunkenness were forbidden, where travellers were marshalled into orderly lines on the escalator, and encouraged to give up their seats to those in need. Other codes—for example, the sets of rules on decorous behaviour for schoolchildren imposed in 1935 and 1943, and pasted, in the 1943 case, into identity documents[153]—reminded Soviet citizens that appropriate conduct was a duty in the workplace. And from the second half of the 1930s, as paranoia about foreign-sponsored 'Trotskyite saboteurs' replaced the former emphasis on 'class enemies', Soviet citizens were exhorted to supervise each other with a new zeal. While those in upper ranks exercised *rukovodstvo*, 'supervision' or 'guidance', those in the lower ranks were encouraged to manifest *bditel'nost'*, vigilance: that is, to be constantly on the alert for 'enemies of the people' who might have infiltrated their organization.[154]

In similar vein, the model child represented in literature aimed at parents was now a tidy, clean, respectable conformist whose absolute obedience to adults was reinforced at all times. So far as babies were concerned, the enforcement of discipline was nothing new: right back to Catherine II's didactic tales in the eighteenth century, advice literature had underlined the importance of regular feeding and the avoidance of indulgence. When

---

[152] *Ogonek* 1 (1936), 2. Quoted in C. Kelly and V. Volkov, '*Kul'turnost'* and Consumption', C. Kelly and D. Shepherd (eds.), *Constructing Russian Culture in the Age of Revolutions* (Oxford, 1998), 301.

[153] See *Kopii postanovlenii Byuro TsK VLKSM po rabote sredi pionerov: shkol'nikov 1929–1935* (typescript held in TsKhDMO Reading Room), 203–5; N. Grant, *Soviet Education* (Harmondsworth, 1979), 69.

[154] The turning point here was Stalin's speech at the 13 April 1928 meeting of the Plenum of the Central Committee, in which he referred to 'the public opinion of the working class as a lively and watchful [*bditel'nyi*] moral control' (*Sochineniya* xi (Moscow, 1949), 32). When 'class war' was terminated in 1931, *bditel'nost'* became required of the entire 'Soviet people': see. e.g. the slogan 'Bditel'nost' nuzhno usilit' na lyubom uchastke raboty!' (*V pomoshch' stengazete: Lektsii, opublikovannye v zhurnale 'Raboche-krest'yansky korrespondent' za 1935 i 1936 gg.* (Piatigorsk, 1937), 6.) For an excellent study of horizontal surveillance, based to a large extent on advice sources such as Party guides to *samokritika*, see Khakhordin, *The Collective and the Individual.*

Stalinist guides, such as B. A. Arkhangel'sky and G. N. Speransky's *Mother and Child: A School for Young Mothers* (1951) stressed the need to avoid rocking, and to carry out a programme of *zakalivan'e*, toughening the child by exposure to air and to cold water, their strictures were anything other than original.[155] But in the 1920s, more liberal treatment had often been advocated for older children.[156] On the other hand, the most important pedagogue of the Stalin era, A. A. Makarenko (1888–1939), whose writings, publicized by the journal *Sovetskaya pedagogika*, also appeared in many individual editions from the mid-1930s,[157] stipulated a rigid regime for older children too. Any violation of the rules was to to be corrected immediately, for, 'in the matter of upbringing, there is no such thing as a trivial detail' (*Besedy s roditelyami*, 19). Upbringing had to be be first and foremost an education for citizenship: good parents set their child an example through 'work, civic identity [*litso*], behaviour', while bad ones displayed a range of weaknesses including unduly repressive behaviour, insufficiently caring behaviour (consigning the child to a grandmother 'or even a *domrabotnitsa*'), 'the arrogance of office' (*chvanstvo*), pedantry, attempting to reason with the child (*rezonerstvo*), authoritarianism, too much love, too much kindness, treating the child as a friend, or attempting to bribe it (*podkup*: 'the most immoral kind of authority').(*Besedy s roditelyami*, 56, 52–5.) Parents were supposed to treat their own children much in the manner of a kindly supervisor at a well-run kindergarten.[158] In the words of the canonical Stalinist baby book, the raising of children was never merely an individual matter, but a national one, with parents looking

---

[155] Arkhangel'sky and Speransky, *Mat' i ditya* (1951), and cf. Catherine II, 'Tsarevich Fevei', (*Sochineniya Imperatritsy Ekateriny Vtoroi: proizvedeniya literaturnye*, ed. A. I. Vvedensky (St Petersburg, 1893), 375), emphasizing that the young prince was 'not swaddled or wrapped up or sung lullabies to or rocked in any way or ever; he was fed correctly and regularly'; or Anon., *Nastavlenie materyam.* (1884), which warned 'A child should not be given the breast as something to comfort him, but systematically, at a fixed time', and advised vehemently against rocking (sections 1 and 5); or Ida S. Katsenel'son, in her *Advice to Mothers* (1927), directing readers that they should leave a baby to cry if they could find no obvious reason why it should be crying ('the consciousness of how good for the baby this "stern" form of upbringing is will aid the mother in putting it into practice') and that they should train the infant to control its bodily functions as early as possible, placing it on the pot from the age of three months (31, 32). Western literature of the period is entirely congruent: cf. the work of F. Truby King, the famous early 20th-cent. propagandist of 'scientific motherhood', who also advocated that babies be left to 'cry it out' and that 'pampering' should be avoided. (See *Feeding and Care of Baby* (London, 1913), and *Mothercraft* (8th edn.; Sydney, 1942).)

[156] See e.g. Babina, *Kak organizovat' dosug detei*, 7.

[157] For example, Makarenko, *Besedy s roditelyami* (1941); *Kniga dlya roditelei* (1937); *Izbrannye pedagogicheskie sochineniya*, 4 vols. (Moscow, 1949). Khakhordin, *The Collective and the Individual*, and Fitzpatrick, *Everyday Stalinism*, have excellent short discussions of Makarenko's work.

[158] There is a striking similarity between advice for parents and advice for professional carers: see e.g. *Kak organizovat' detskii kollektiv v detskom sadu* (Moscow, 1935), which also emphasizes the need to *vospityvat' kollektivista* (p. 2).

forward to the 'sight of sons or daughters who have become worthy citizens of their great Motherland'.[159]

In sum, then, the themes of health, self-education, discipline, and conformity to collective norms underpinned the *kul'turnost'* ethos right through the early Soviet period: the Stalinist era, rather than seeing a 'retreat' from this position, saw it advocated with increasing fervour and represented with growing clarity. But that is not to say that there were no discontinuities between advice literature of the 1920s and of the 1930s. One remarkable difference is the decline in the number of titles of advice literature published after 1930 (a decline not only absolute, but proportionate, given that the overall numbers of book titles were significantly larger in the 1930s than in the 1920s) (see Appendix 4, Table 1).

This decline in the publication of pamphlets had a number of different causes. One cause was 'professionalization' in various forms. Self-education was now increasingly presented as the responsibility of those in 'nurturing' positions, in particular librarians: guides on 'how to read' were replaced by systematic catalogues in libraries, and lists of literary texts on educative subjects such as 'What the Soviet Person Should Be Like' took the place of brochures such as *How to Organize Yourself.*[160] Similarly, the expansion of the service industries was accompanied by a transfer of printing resources into guides for the workplace rather than the home: pamphlets on hair-styling, for example, were now aimed at professional hairdressers rather than women who wanted to do their own hair.[161] But another, and perhaps still more important cause for the decline in the importance of pamphlets was the streamlining and unification of propaganda in all its various forms, from films to belles-lettres to posters, that took place in the 1930s. On the one hand, this involved a switch from breadth to depth, from a concentration on proliferation of different titles to a concentration

[159] Arkhangel'sky and Speransky, *Mat' i ditya*, 5. Cf. F. Vigdorova, *Diary of a Russian Schoolteacher*, trans. R. Prokofieva (New York, 1960); original *Moi klass* (Moscow, 1949), which emphasizes above all consideration for others and not standing out: e.g. 'Dima Kirsanov', 162–77 describes the conversion to collective values of an intelligent, aloof boy, who at first despised his unintellectual class pen-pal, but after a stay in hospital realized the latter's human worth. The collective, public nature of the model upbringing is also made piquantly clear by L. Raskin, 'Vospitanie khoroshikh privychek i kul''urnykh maner', *Obshchestvennitsa* 11 (1940), 34, which suggests to parents that 'a domestic *stengazeta*' should be kept.

[160] See Evgeny Dobrenko, *The Making of the State Reader: Social and Aesthetic Contexts of the Reception of Soviet Literature* (Stanford, Calif., 1997), ch. 7, esp. 257–61.

[161] E.g. *Bytovoe obsluzhivanie naselenie: Banno-prachechnoe i parikmakherskoe delo* (Moscow? 1947). See *Ezhegodnik knigi*, 1947. Of the thirty-seven publications listed under 'Obshchestvennoe pitanie. Kulinariya' in *Ezhegodnik knigi*, 1949, three at most were aimed at general readers (one book on vitamins in food, one on hygiene in food, and one recipe book). It is instructive to compare publication figures in another so-called totalitarian society, the Third Reich. According to a graph in Krumrey, *Entwicklungsstrukturen von Verhaltstanden*, 25, the number of etiquette titles published in Germany was lower between 1930 and 1940 than at any other time between 1870 and 1970: but it still amounted to forty to fifty titles per year.

on expanding copies in circulation of certain targeted titles. Though the number of book titles printed in the RSFSR more than doubled between 1934 and 1956, from 19,300 to 39,500, the average print-run over the same period rose more than fivefold, from 3,900 to 22,500. The result was the creation of what Evgeny Dobrenko has termed an 'official anthology' of key texts—a canon of necessary cultural information for the ordinary Soviet reader.[162]

Alongside the concentration on certain highly specific titles (a concentration evident in the field of advice literature too, as we shall see) went a growing emphasis on the popular magazine as the main vehicle for advisory texts. To be sure, magazines such as *Rabotnitsa* and *Krest'yanka* had already offered their readers some material in the 1920s, such as cookery columns. But in the 1930s, new publications, such as *Sovetskaya zhenshchina*, and *Obshchestvennitsa*, joined the old ones, while general magazines, such as *Ogonek*, carried a wide variety of materials, from fashion sketches to programmes of exercises meant to accompany radio *fizkul'tura* programmes.

The use of magazines as forums had two advantages. The first was that it worked as a unifying mechanism for the advice purveyed, so that what might otherwise have seemed disparate and haphazard concerns were easily perceived as interlocking parts of the 'Soviet way of life' (*sovetskii obraz zhizni*). Moreover, the layout of the magazine was employed in order demonstratively to subordinate advice on *byt* to more 'serious' considerations, such as political ideology or industrial productivity. *Bytovye* items were almost always placed towards the back (typically, on pp. 18 and 19 of a twenty-page magazine such as *Rabotnitsa* or *Krest'yanka*) and their normal length was a half-page, as opposed to the multiple-page spreads on forthcoming elections, jubilees of political figures or famous writers, or the deeds of shock workers, Stakhanovites, and prize-winning milkmaids.

The second and equally important advantage of using magazines was that it facilitated targeting of advice literature by readership. In 1940, for example, *Obshchestvennitsa* and *Rabotnitsa* offered their readers rather different advice on upbringing. Readers of *Rabotnitsa* were counselled on the need to inculcate in children a respect for 'cleanliness and order', 'honesty and fairness'.[163] Readers of *Obshchestvennitsa*, on the other hand,

[162] Dobrenko, *The Making of the State Reader*, 170; statistics on p. 169.

[163] See D. Ioffe, 'Priuchaite rebenka k chistote i poryadku', *Rabotnitsa* 20 (1940), 19; B. L. Barash, 'Vospitanie chestnosti i pravdivosti u detei', *Rabotnitsa* 33 (1940), 18. It was assumed that teaching manners to working-class children would be the responsibility of carers and school-teachers: cf. *Kak organizovat' detskii kollektiv*, 9, which instructs kindergarten staff to 'ingrain good habits [*navyki bytovogo poryadka*] such as saying hallo, goodbye, and thank you; not to interrupt others and to listen carefully, not to answer rudely, to do good turns, to speak in the usual way without any yelling, to wait one's turn, not to snatch toys from other children, etc.'.

were treated to a lengthy article by L. Raskin which urged that children should not only be taught to be clean and orderly, but also polite: 'The habits of true politeness speak of nobility of character; on the other hand, bad manners, which manifest themselves in coarseness and lack of respect for those around, are a quite accurate manifestation of negative qualities.' Raskin went so far as to argue that parents should deliberately drop things in order that children could get into the habit of deferentially picking them up, a suggestion that would have been anathema to members of the Russian avant-garde, for whom grovelling after handkerchiefs had been as abject a manifestation of toadying attitudes to authority as hand-kissing.[164]

The relatively rare publications of advice books that took place after 1935 also contributed to this stratification. The year 1939, for example, saw the publication of two very different cookbooks. The first, *A Cookbook: 200 Dishes for the Home Table*, was, as its title suggests, a modest affair: a small-format, low-priced publication apparently aimed at readers who were provided with most meals in a works canteen: breakfast is emphasized over other meals.[165] However, the second, *The Book of Tasty and Nutritious Food*, was an altogether different publication. Dedicated 'To the Housewife— from the People's Commissariat of the Food Industry', the book began, in the established Soviet way, with advice on 'rational diet'. Yet it was far from being merely a functional publication. The recipes included game, carp stuffed with kasha in sour cream, roast veal, friture of brains, a variety of ice-creams and of rich sauces, such as hollandaise and sabayon. Mikoyan, quoted in the book's introduction, boasted that this was 'the first big cookbook published in the Soviet Union',[166] and though this was in a sense misleading, given the publications by Zarina and others discussed earlier, *The Book of Tasty and Nutritious Food* was beyond question and comparison the most opulent manual of food preparation produced by any publishing house since the existence of Soviet power. Even the title, giving the first place to 'taste' rather than 'nutrition', had symbolic force. As well as *chistota* and *poryadok*, key words were now *izyashchnost'* or *izyashchestvo* (elegance), *priyatnost'* (pleasantness), *udobstvo* and *uyut* (comfort). The reader, was for example, advised on the necessity of ensuring 'the comfort, pleasantness,

[164] Raskin, 'Vospitanie khoroshikh privychek', *Obshchestvennitsa* 11 (1940), 34. On the avant-garde attitude to hanky-dropping, see e.g. Lev Shiffers's sketch for a 'living newspaper', 'Sluzhebnoe prodvizhenie', *Zhivaya gazeta 'Sovtorg sluzhashchii': Sbornik materialov dlya vystuplenii zhivykh gazet*, 1 (1928), 64, which shows a servile official addressing his superior in the following terms: Kuz'ma Ivanych, ooh whoops, *you've dropped your hanky...* | *Kuz'ma Ivanych, just let me dust your shoulder ...* | *Kuz'ma Ivanych, may I just mention something?* | *Kuz'ma Ivanych, might I... dare I, sir.. ask about a promotion, sir? (My emphasis).*

[165] Tsyplenkov, *Povarennaya kniga.*

[166] *Kniga o vkusnoi i zdorovoi pishche* (1939), 3. Reprinted in a much reduced edition in 1946 and 1948 (when post-war food rationing was still in force), the book was restored to its original opulence in the edition of 1952.

and pleasingness to the eye of the dinner- or tea-table' (*udobstvo, priyatnost'
i priyatnaya dlya glaza vneshnost' obedennogo ili chainogo stola*, pp. 19–20); and
the inset panels of the book included items that were supposed to guarantee
such 'pleasingness to the eye', for example the elaborate silver-plated fish
slice (*lopatochka dlya ryby*) emblazoning page 95.

The intended audience for *The Book of Tasty and Nutritious Food* is
suggested by the fact that extracts from it were carried in *Obshchestvennitsa*
in 1940.[167] In the same year *Rabotnitsa*, on the other hand, carried a
cookery column that was strictly practical in character, largely concerning
itself with the production of bottled food to be put by over the winter,
while items connected with the culture of the body covered such subjects
as physical culture, personal hygiene, and childcare.[168] And other articles,
too, continued to propagandize the old principles of 'rational living' and
self-education. For instance, Nikolai Semyashko's 'Towards Comfort,
Order, and Cleanliness in the Home' (1940) could equally well have
been published in the 1920s, as could a contribution from women workers
at the Stalin factory under the title 'Organize Excursions to Your Local
Museum!', and an agitational piece on the 'culture of labour', 'Let's
Tighten up Work Discipline!'.[169] To be sure, occasional references to
material possessions that were not strictly functional did sometimes occur.
An article on 'How to Decorate Your Home' in 1935, for example,
suggested that the reader might go so far as decorating a 'toilet table' with a
mirror, comb-case, sewing box, vase of fresh flowers, and even 'little
animals made of Urals marble'. But a bookcase remained 'an essential for
every cultured home', and stern warnings were given against artificial
flowers and gaudy hangings (which might 'attract bugs'), embroidered
pillows, and elaborate bedspreads.[170] And a profile of model woman
worker F. I. Korytova not only inventoried the personal possessions that
had accrued through her diligence ('a wardrobe in the Slavonic style, a
divan, tables, beautiful chairs . . . an embroidered tablecloth', and pot
plants), but also the books that she had read (Marietta Shaginyan's
production novel *Hydrocentral*, Sholokhov's *Virgin Soil Upturned*, and
Questions of Leninism), and the Bol'shoi performances and films that she
had seen (Tchaikovsky, Verdi, *Chapaev*). The profile also dwelt on the fact
that 'cleanliness—the essential of a cultured life' was 'strictly observed', and
that 'the cultured life helps Korytova to work better'.[171]

[167] *Obshchestvennitsa* 4–5 (1940), 63.

[168] See e.g. *Rabotnitsa* 4 (1940), 20; 10 (1940), 19; 24 (1940), 29.

[169] See *Rabotnitsa* 11 (1940), 19; 17–18 (1940), 5; 27 (1940), 3–4.

[170] Fomina [first name not given], 'Kak ukrasit' zhilishche', *Rabotnitsa* 34–5 (1935), 30; 36
(1935), 15.

[171] See *Rabotnitsa* 6 (1935), 32. Cf. the items that appear in a poster of 1934 by Konstantin
Zotov: 'Every Peasant-Collective Farm Worker Now Has the Chance to Live A Decent Human

If 1930s advice literature for the masses in some ways maintained the character of 1920s advice literature for the same audience, it was equally the case that the divide between 'masses' and more privileged sectors of the population had occasionally made itself felt in the 1920s as well. For example, 1930s fashion magazines for the better-off reader, such as *Zhurnal mod*, were exact successors to similarly entitled magazines of the 1920s, which offered rather ambitious outfits to their female readers.[172] Even at its height, during the Cultural Revolution, the campaign for the 'collectivization of *byt*' had always been aimed primarily at the masses rather than the educated population, as is demonstrated by the fact that in 1930, the magazine *Zhenskii zhurnal* predicted that by 1932–3 75 per cent of manual workers and 50 per cent of their families would be catered for by public facilities. The projected proportion of white-collar workers having access to such facilities, on the other hand, was placed at only 35 per cent, and a figure for their families was not given (it was presumably too insignificant to be worth recording).[173] The absence of any comment on the need to rectify this discrepancy indicated that the concept of *byt* was status-differentiated, with white-collar workers (who were tacitly assumed already to enjoy an acceptable standard of *kul'turnost'*) left to direct their own lives, while factory workers were exposed to communal life as a civilizing measure. A description, dating from 1940, of the welcome extended by metallurgists' wives in Siberia to the wives of new colleagues made clear the persistence of the 'collective life/private life' divide through its reference to a 'cosy home' (enjoyed by the metallurgists) on the one hand, and 'a cosy canteen' (enjoyed by the workers) on the other:

What do they talk to them about? Life. Husbands. Work. Leisure. *Making a cosy home*. About the handkerchief that should be placed in a husband's pocket if he's forgotten to do it himself, about the button that should be sewn back on for him— a missing button could make a man feel fretful when he's at work, and

Life'—a record-player (upon which Stalin speeches and patriotic songs might be listened to), a shelf-full of tractor-maintenance books and literary classics, and an electric light with a functional shade. (Reproduced in Bonnell, *Iconography of Power*, pl. 4: see also discussion, pp. 118–19.) On distinctions between Soviet magazines in their propaganda for consumption, see also Hessler, 'Cultured Trade', 197.

[172] Compare the issues of *Mody* for 1927 with those for 1936: if anything, indeed, the models in the 1927 issues are more attractive, with bold red lips, glamorous bobs, and bias-cut flapper dresses. On the 1920s, see also Gorsuch, 'Soviet Youth', 197. On competing views of domestic design in the 1920s, see Kettering, '"Ever More Cosy and Comfortable"', 119–21; on cookery literature, H. Rothstein and R. A. Rothstein, 'The Beginnings of Soviet Culinary Arts' in M. Glants and J. Toomre (eds.), *Food in Russian History and Culture* (Bloomington, Ind., 1997), 177–94. An example of a relatively elaborate cookbook is Uvarova's *Sputnik domashnei khozyaiki* (1927).

[173] A. R—l', 'Rabotu kooperatsii—pod kontrol' trudyashchikhsya!', *Zhenskii zhurnal* 7 (1930), 2–3.

Stakhanovite output depends on organization, on strict method in everything, large or small. . . . An *obshchestvennitsa*, a member of the wives' committee, is attached to the section dealing with appointment and dismissal of cadres. She and her colleagues meet new people as they arrive. The Siberian climate is harsh and the frosts fierce. It's important that a new worker should feel good from the moment he first arrives, that he should be placed in a *clean hostel* and eat in a *cosy canteen*.[174]

While a minority of workers (those who achieved Stakhanovite work targets) were, from 1935, rewarded with privileges such as their own 'cosy home', the expectation as well as the reality was that the majority would continue to be housed, as they had been before the Revolution, in hostels, factory barracks, and shared tenements.

Yet at the same time, once the ideology of 'class war' was suspended in 1935–6, there were consistent attempts to present Soviet society as a unified whole. Though the number of Soviet citizens with money to spend on silver fish-slices and champagne, and the leisure to cook four-course meals of hors d'oeuvres, soup, meat, ice-cream, and cake, was decidedly small, *The Book of Tasty and Nutritious Food* proclaimed that it was intended 'for the very broadest public'. Should any member of the 'Soviet masses' stray across a copy of the book (perhaps while working in the kitchen of a restaurant), he or she could rest assured that in time such luxuries and delicacies would be available for all. The point was reinforced in the late 1940s, when the mass-market *Rabotnitsa* began to carry material on domestic culture that emphasized 'beauty' (*krasota*) as well as hygiene, when decoration began to be recommended for even the humblest Soviet dwellings, the houses of *kolkhoz* dwellers, when *Ogonek* approvingly quoted a reader's words, 'every Soviet woman now has the chance of taking trouble over her toilettes [*tualety*]', and when readers were advised that upbringing should include training in politeness as well as in the sterner virtues, such as 'honesty'.[175]

But even at this stage, the principles of 'rational life' had not completely vanished. The families of chief engineers in Stalin-prize-winning novels might have their grand pianos, and Party officials their high heels and silk dresses, but excessive interest in appearance on the part of rank-and-file

[174] Z. Borisov, 'Dela i dni zhen metallurgov', *Obshchestvennitsa* 7 (1940), 13. (My emphasis.)

[175] See Z. Chalaya, 'Khotim, chtoby mebel' byla krasivaya', *Rabotnitsa* 2 (1952), 29–30; 'Pogovorim o mode', *Ogonek* 11 (1948), 29; Ryabov, *Kakim dolzhen byt' blagoustroennoe selo* (1947), 34, recommending 'cornices', folksy window-surrounds, and shutters; and V. Aleksandrov, 'O chutkosti i vnimatel'nosti k lyudyam', *Rabotnitsa* 12 (1948), 14–15, which asserts: 'A mother's duty is to firmly inculcate in the child all the habits of cultured behaviour, to which polite manners and a polite attitude to others are absolutely essential.' The recipes provided also became richer: compare the beef in jelly (*studen'*), Ukrainian borshch and roast lamb in *Rabotnitsa* 8 (1952), 32 with the stuffed cabbage, carrot puree, potato bake, and potato croquettes, *Rabotnitsa* 32 (1935), 13.

women was still discouraged (for example, Vera Panova's novel *The Train* contained the very moralistic example of a young woman whose attempts to pluck her eyebrows ended in disaster).[176] And an article published in *Rabotnitsa* in 1947 began with the enquiry: 'What qualities do we require in our clothes? They should be warm and hygienic. And clothes should be comfortable, should not hinder our movements.' Only then did it observe: 'And they should look nice and conceal our physical defects.'[177]

It is important, too, not to exaggerate the esotericism of the material possessions that were labelled as legitimate by Soviet advice literature. Compared with the readers of women's magazines in the West, Soviet readers (including the more privileged ones) were offered only limited advice on dress and grooming; they were not invited to explore such esoteric areas of the 1930s and 1940s dress code as how to match your shoes, handbag, and gloves to an outfit, or how to select toning stockings and choose the right shade of lipstick and powder. And while the spreads of 'consumer goods' (*tovary shirokogo potrebleniya*) that were advertised to the public in books such as *The Book of Tasty and Nutritious Food* or spreads in *Ogonek* and *Rabotnitsa* included some luxuries (cars, toys, cosmetics, radiograms, silverware), there was a heavier emphasis on functional items such as cots, saucepans, prams, and beds.[178] Advice on *kul'turnost'* created a matrix of appropriate possessions, mostly with a hygienic resonance: sheets and underwear, curtains, tablecloths, bookcases, lampshades.[179] The ideal Soviet citizen might—indeed, was supposed to—own a sufficiency of these, but only a *meshchanin* would have possessed such objects as artificial flowers or imitation crystal vases, let alone a canary or an Angora cat, which remained as loathsome to the Soviet sensibility as ever they had been in the 1920s.[180] The selection of objects was far more than a personal matter: this was a world where 'something as innocuous as a scrolled, gilded handle on

---

[176] V. Panova, *Sputniki* (Moscow, 1947). It is not clear whether Panova had subconsciously remembered the scene in Madame de Ségur's famous 19th-cent. didactic tale for small girls, *Les Malheurs de Sophie*, in which the heroine disfigures herself by cutting off her eyebrows.

[177] M. K. Abramova, 'O kul'ture proizvodstva tovarov shirokogo potrebleniya', for example, *Rabotnitsa* 6 (1947), 16. Cf. Ryabov, *Kakim dolzhen byt' blagoustroennoe selo*, which begins with the need for a *kolkhoznik*'s house to be 'comfortable, cosy, and create the best facilities for rest and recuperation after work' (33).

[178] See e.g. *Ogonek* 4 and 5 (1941), *Rabotnitsa* 4–5 (1946), or *Rabotnitsa* 2 (1947).

[179] See Kelly and Volkov, '*Kul'turnost'* and Consumption', 298–9.

[180] See e.g. E. Sergeev, 'V znak blagodarnosti: fel'eton', *Ogonek* 14 (1949), 28, in which a *meshchanin*'s character is revealed by his admiration for the fake silver forks, mock crystal vases, and imitation fur rugs that he has encountered on war service in Berlin; or K. Eliseev's cartoon 'A gody prokhodyat', *Krokodil* 2 (1949), 4, which shows a Party member snoring under his newspaper while lying on a Karelian birch divan; opposite him, an Angora cat plays on a matching birch armchair under an orange silk lamp. On canaries, kittens, etc. in the 1920s, see e.g. Mayakovsky's 'O dryani' (On rubbish, 1922) and 'Daesh' izyachnuyu zhizn'' (Give Us an Elligant Life), and the general discussion of the topic in Boym, *Common Places*, 34–8.

a teacup was not dangerous because it diminished the owner's taste, but because it could lull the user into a bourgeois, counter-revolutionary outlook contravening the Party's political struggle'.[181] Excessive decoration was to be avoided at all costs. The exemplary Soviet home, even in the late 1940s, offered its inhabitants only modest comforts:

In our home everything has its place . . . We treat our things with care. Our principle is not to shorten the life of anything which it has taken hard work to make. . . . We all keep the flat tidy, because cleanliness is the best decoration for a dwelling place. Before public holidays my husband and my son put fresh lacquer on the furniture. . . . The cleanliness of a home starts in the hallway, and so I clean that up more often than anywhere else.[182]

The passage nicely encapsulates the intermediate location of *kul'turnost'*. As in the 1920s, its counter-signifiers were not only *meshchanstvo*, 'petit-bourgeois ways', or excessive refinement and undue interest in material possessions, but also *nekul'turnost'* or *bezkul'ture*—illiteracy, dirt, inefficiency, apathy. Indeed, the two could sometimes come together, as in a *Krokodil* cartoon of 1946 (Fig. 15), which showed a secretary prancing around in an astrakhan coat with a poodle, observed by two disapproving, quietly dressed women. The caption read: 'Look, that woman is dressed head to foot in astrakhan [*v karakulyakh*]' 'Yes, she even writes in scribbles [*karakulyami*].' As the pun on two meanings of *karakul'* indicated, in the end, *meshchanstvo* and *bezkul'tur'e* were the same thing—a point doing much to foster cultural insecurity and the need to look to 'superiors' for guidance. In Mikhail Kalinin's words, 'a considerable level of culture and political insight' (for which read, closeness to the Party elite) was needed in

---

[181] Karen Kettering, ' "Ever More Cosy and Comfortable": Stalinism and the Soviet Domestic Interior, 1928–1938', *Journal of Design History* 2 (1997), 126.

[182] A. G. Zueva, 'Organizovannyi byt pomogaet vospitaniyu detei', *Sovetskaya zhenshchina* 2 (1946), 39. The phrase 'cleanliness is the best ornament of the home' appears to be a direct quotation from Zarina's *Domovodstvo* of 1929. Cf. the advice in Vaintsvaig, *V nashem dome* (1950), or a 1948 photograph of an exemplary dwelling, the flat owned by a senior steel worker and family, reproduced in Victor Buchli, 'Khrushchev, Modernism, and the Fight Against Petit-Bourgeois Consciousness in the Soviet Home', *Journal of Design History* 2 (1997), 165, which resembles the environment of a late 19th- or early 20th-cent. schoolteacher, with bookcase and framed portrait of Pushkin to the fore. Part of the background to this was of course the state's inability to supply more than the most basic 'kit' of consumer goods, coupled with a renewed assault, from 1948, upon small-scale private enterprise: on the latter point, see J. Hessler, 'A Postwar Perestroika? Toward a History of Private Enterprise in the USSR', *SR* 57 (1998), 516–42. Until the publication of the new Civil Code of 1964, 'luxury items' (not specified) were explicitly stated *not* to be heritable by descendants or other beneficiaries of a will after their owner's death. Compare *Grazhdanskii kodeks RSFSR* (Petrograd, 1923), art. 421, and *Grazhdanskii kodeks RSFSR* (Moscow, 1948), art. 421, and *Grazhdanskii kodeks RSFSR* (Moscow, 1954), art. 421, and contrast *Grazhdanskii kodeks RSFSR* (Moscow, 1964), art. 533, which rephrases to allow the inheritance of 'objects of the usual domestic interior' rather than precluding the inheritance of 'luxury items'.

Рис. И. Семёнова

— Посмотри, эта гражданка вся в каракулях.
— Это наша секретарша. Она даже пишет каракулями.

Fig. 15. 'Look at that woman, all dressed up in astrakhan!'
Cartoon from *Krokodil*, 1946.

order to 'draw the boundary between philistinism [*meshchanstvo*] and real cultural progress'.[183]

If representations of domestic life continued to emphasize hygiene, the rehabilitation of etiquette literature was also at best only partial. The extremely small amount of advice on this topic (no books, only very occasional articles) concerned itself with the behaviour of children, not of adults, and it did not touch on the subject of how to address people further up or further down the social ladder than oneself. Indeed, there was no indication that such a ladder existed: politeness was represented in very abstract terms such as 'concern for others', 'respect for other members of

---

[183] See 'Speech to a Conference of Best Urban and Rural Schoolteachers', 28 Dec. 1938, *On Communist Education*, 81. Cf. a pre-revolutionary article by Kornei Chukovsky, 'Meshchanin protiv meshchanstva' (1908), *Sobranie sochinenii*, 6 vols. (Moscow 1962–6), vi. 173–4, which uses the work of the writer Anatoly Kamensky as an instance of 'the high level of perfection *meshchane* have attained in falsifying anti-*meshchanstvo* ideas'. In circumstances where even condemning *meshchanstvo* did not prove immunity, literally anyone could be accused of suffering from the vice.

the collective', terms such as 'deference' or 'impudence' were never used, and cartoons in popular magazines such as *Krokodil* lambasted instances of servility where this occurred.[184] To be sure, the growing emphasis, in manuals intended for the mass reader, upon the need to make political discourse decorous and celebratory[185] stood in rather vivid contrast to the actual use of violent and putrid rhetoric by highly placed officials (most notably, as mentioned earlier, State Prosecutor Vyshinsky in the 1937–8 show trials). But this contrast was not underlined in advice literature, and discussions of *kul'tura rechi*, 'cultured speech', retained a relativistic flavour right through the Stalin era (outright breaches of propriety, such as swearing, were strongly discouraged, but breaches of grammatical rules were treated more hesitantly).[186] Therefore, the myth that all were equal could persist unchallenged. Equally, though manuals aimed at waiters in 'restaurants of the first class' made clear that the ideal of service practised there was a distinctly old-fashioned one—obsequious discretion,[187] material aimed at mass readers encouraged them to see good service as the prerogative of all Soviet citizens. A campaign begun by *Ogonek* in 1940, for example, listed a very wide range of Soviet institutions in which service had to be improved, including not only such relatively exclusive places as hotels and restaurants, but also such universally visited ones as post offices and railway stations:

[184] See e.g. K. Eliseev, 'Obsluzhivanie i samoobsluzhivanie', *Krokodil* 8 (1948), 10, which shows an official being crawled to by his underlings: 'The porter took off his coat. His secretary picked a bit off dust off his suit. The only thing he disposed of himself was his responsibility for getting anything done.'

[185] On this, see Gorham, 'From "Charisma" to "Cant"', 348–56, and the discussion of the *stengazeta* below.

[186] The crucial text for the 1920s is G. Vinokur, *Kul'tura yazyka* (Moscow, 1925), which saw all 'purism' as class-marked. V. L. Vorontsova and A. I. Sumkina, 'O knigakh po kul'ture rechi', *Voprosy kul'turi rechi* 1 (1955), 208–2 published at the start of a reinterpretation of the term *kul'tura rechi* from an evaluative point of view in the mid-1950s (on which see further Ch. 5), rebukes guides of 1952–3 for their failure to ram home the distinction between 'correct' and 'incorrect' speech, and their emphasis on 'sincerity' rather than grammatical accuracy.

[187] For example, Tsyplenkov, *Obsluzhivanie v restorane* (1945), 36, insists: 'The waiter must be cultured [*kul'turen*] and polite. He must have perfect command of himself when carrying out his duties.' The book also offers a startling window on the leisure life of the Soviet elite, describing as it does an establishment with *otdel'nye kabinety* (*chambres particulières*) as well as public halls, decorated with 'chandeliers' or 'shaded lights', 'evergreen plants, bay trees or palms', 'silk curtains', and 'brightly coloured parquet floors', and where the waiter was required to offer an elaborate silver service for a menu consisting of such delicacies as freshwater crayfish soup with fish dumplings and slices of sturgeon, or roast quail accompanied by Tsinandali or Mukuzani wine. The discreet loucheness of the setting suggests the kind of place where a highly placed Party official might have taken a favourite ballerina to dine, or factory managers met to negotiate deals with planning bosses. A slightly less over-the-top publication in the same vein is Pisarev, *Organizatsiya i tekhnika raboty ofitsianta* (1949). The facilities offered to top Soviet officials were sometimes satirized in the press of the day, e.g. in a cartoon in *Krokodil* 1 (1949), 7, which shows a salesman saying to a smartly dressed buyer: 'Can I tempt the citizeness to a little sausage today? A smidgen of Gourmet's Choice (*Lyubitel'skaya*), perhaps? Or Polish salami (*Krakovskaya*)?'

What is good service?

It's exactitude, politeness, the ability to keep one's word, an understanding of the value of other people's time, pride in the production process [*proizvodstvennaya gordost'*], in the 'brand name' [*marka*] of the railway, hotel, restaurant, post office or whatever else that one works for.

But what is poor service?

It's indifference ('they'll lap it up anyway'), rudeness, dirt, sloppiness. It's cold tea served with the sugar already put in and no spoon. It's an endless queue in the waiting room. . . . It's a swinish attitude to other people—citizens of the socialist society—in general.

Do I serve other people well?

Everyone should ask themselves this question.[188]

And, as the last sentences suggest, the amelioration of facilities was seen as a universal project, not one in which the 'us' of the consumers was pitted against the 'them' of shop assistants.[189] The stick of the 'book of complaints' (*kniga zhalob*) and the denunciatory newspaper article was accompanied by the carrot of the wage bonus and, in the late 1940s, 'prizes for good service' competed for by Soviet shops.[190] As for domestic service, that might as well never have existed so far as Soviet advice literature was concerned. There were no articles in *Sovetskaya zhenshchina* advising professional women on how to cope with uppity *domrabotnitsy*, or even evoking the indebtedness of prominent scientists to their trusty nannies (rather, prominent professional women always emphasized that they were also exemplary housewives). Still less were there pamphlets telling peasant women how to become exemplary *domrabotnitsy*.[191] The readers of *Krest'yanka* and *Rabotnitsa* were never encouraged to consider domestic service as a career possibility: the only work that was assigned value in mass-market magazines of this kind was work for public institutions.

Considerably more evident than the rehabilitation of class distinctions in the 1930s was the restoration of rigidly defined gender roles. To be sure, gender essentialism was by no means absent from material published in the first decade of Soviet power: the rhetoric of 1920s advisory literature, like

---

[188] 'Khorosho li vas obsluzhivayut?' *Ogonek* 8 (1941), 1.

[189] Compare a Socialist Realist fairy story which appeared in *Rabotnitsa* 4 (1952), 27–8, in which a new 'senior saleswoman' (*starshaya prodavshchitsa*) heroically sets to rights a shop with rude assistants, poorly displayed goods, and a spider's web on the wall newspaper. On shop staff's part in the *kul'turnost'* campaign, see A. E. Randall, '"Revolutionary Bolshevik Work": Stakhanovism in Retail Trade', *RR* 59 (2000), 425–41, esp. 440.

[190] On these prizes in the late 1940s, see R. Parker, *Moscow Correspondent* (London, 1949), 269.

[191] The only guidance aimed at *domrabotnitsy* after 1930 was pep-talks encouraging them to report subversive activities on the part of their employers: on this see Bogdan in Fitzpatrick and Slezkine, (eds.), *In the Shadow of Revolution*, 407. Domestic service was mentioned only in a negative context, in e.g. sardonic cartoons published in *Krokodil* in the 1930s (see Fitzpatrick, *Everyday Stalinism*, 100).

the symbolism of public discourse more generally, was strongly masculinist in tone. The ideal of the campaign for *zakalennost'* was a muscular male body, that of the fit young 'warrior'; the assault on 'fashion' was overtly aimed at transforming the behaviour of women, rather than men.[192] Much of the literature on house management addressed itself explicitly to women. But at the same time, attempts to propagandize gender egalitarianism were fairly frequent. The constitution of 'domestic economy circles' attached to village *izby-chital'ny* in the 1920s, for example, specifically stated that 'not only a woman, but also a man, can be a member of the circle'. It went on to argue that such membership might be very beneficial to men in terms of social engineering: 'Knowledge and skills acquired by men at the courses organized by the circles will be very helpful to them in daily life, and also during military service; a few may also be aided in a choice of career.'[193] In the 1930s, on the other hand, house management was almost always the concern of the woman in the house: at the very most, a man might help 'put fresh lacqueur on the furniture', but only the most criminally neglectful wife would expect him to sew on his own buttons.[194]

This is not to say that 1920s advice literature exactly encouraged the formation of model 'new men' in the late twentieth-century sense. Childcare models, for instance, placed quite strict boundaries round the involvement of the male. Even a book specially aimed at fathers, N. F. Al'tgauzen's *Father and Child* (1929), which criticized earlier books for looking at a father only as 'producer' of the child, rather than a partner in upbringing, still advocated that he maintain a rather distant and remote attitude to the relationship: 'In [his child a father] should see not only his own child . . . from the very beginning he should teach himself to treat the child as a person and as a citizen.'[195] But the image of the 'remote father' here has to be seen in the context of the 'hygienic' model of upbringing then generally fashionable, which did not encourage great warmth in mothers either.[196] During the 1930s, however, the gender comple-mentarity of parental roles was reinforced, with the father becoming responsible for *distsiplina*, while the mother (in a reversion to the traditional

---

[192] Ul'yanov e.g. argued that women were especially 'susceptible to fashion', *Odezhda i zdorov'e*, 15.

[193] *Kruzhok domovodstva v izbe-chital'ne* (1925), 37; cf. the reminiscences on working with *domrabotnitsy* by A. Manuilova in *Zhenshchiny rasskazyvayut: Vospominaniya, stat'i (1918–1959)* (Smolensk, 1959), 102–4.

[194] See the quotations from Borisov, 'Dela i dni', and Zueva, 'Organizovannyi byt'. A rare exception was a pamphlet on domestic science circles in schools, *Kruzhki domovodstva v srednei shkole* (Moscow, 1945), which suggested that in 'mixed schools' boys might also participate in such circles (p. 3). However, parental participation was to be encouraged only in mothers (ibid.).

[195] Al'tgauzen, *Otets i rebenok*, 33.

[196] Cf. Al'tgauzen's advice to women, 'we insist that a healthy child should never be picked up and held in the arms at all': *Besedy s devushkami o materinstve* (1929), 167.

post-Enlightenment pattern) became responsible for *vospitanie*, the direction of a child's moral education.[197]

The *distsiplina/vospitanie* divide was also carried over into the public domain. The task of female disseminators of culture, such as the *obshchestvennitsy*, was to contribute to public culture in self-evidently 'feminine' ways: doing volunteer work in the canteens of worker hostels, qualifying in first aid, taking part in cook-offs to select the best pel'meni recipe for food factories, 'morally educating' those who failed to work productively, and so on.[198] As tabulated in an article of 1940, the functions of '*obshchestvennitsa* soviets' could be divided into four categories: political consciousness-raising among wives, including the organization of lectures and special interest circles; involvement of housewives in the productive process (i.e. the recruitment of housewives to advisory or part-time work in industrial enterprises); the improvement of *byt*, including the setting-up of canteens, 'American cafés', and sewing workshops; and childcare (e.g. the organization of day-care centres for children).[199] And if the female duty was to bring private values (where required) into the public world, the ideal of private male behaviour eschewed any hint of effeminate concern with the domestic. Male politeness (where recognized at all) was assimilated to *distsiplina*. As one commentator put it: 'The smartness of appearance among our military men, their emphatic *kul'turnost'*, neatness, concern for others, and politeness is a model for our children, adolescents and young people.'[200] The exemplary family was presented in a photo-reportage of 'a day in the life' of M. A. Kozhevnikova, a production controller at the Second Moscow Ball-Bearings Factory and winner of the Stalin prize. Kozhevnikova's husband appeared only once in the reportage, in a shot where he was shown standing up and giving his wife advice on how to handle things at work.[201] By subordinating the female 'educative' role to the male 'disciplinary' role, Soviet ideologues underlined women's social and political subordination to a male command, thus attempting to avoid the danger that *kul'turnost'* would be seen as a form of 'petticoat rule'.[202] At the same time, the integration of women's roles as arbiters of

---

[197] Cf. the increased emphasis on the role of mothers in Krupskaya's articles of the 1920s, e.g. 'Zhenshchina, vospitatel'nitsa novogo pokoleniya' (1935): *Pedagogicheskie sochineniya*, 607–9; 'Vospityvat' dostoinuyu smenu' (1938), ibid. 742–54.

[198] See M. Matsova, N. Koroleva, 'Sdelaem kul'turnym nash byt: Stolovaya v dome', *Obshchestvennitsa* 3 (1940), 24–5; E. G. Erina, 'Sumeem okazat' pervuyu pomoshch'', *Obshchestvennitsa* 1 (1940), 34; L. Zaritovskaya, 'Pel'meni po moim retseptam', ibid. 33; Tov. Serova, 'Protiv letunov i progul'shchikov', *Obshchestvennitsa* 9 (1940), 11–12.

[199] A. Lazutina, 'Kak organizovat' sovet obshchestvennits', *Obshchestvennitsa* 3 (1940), 27.

[200] Raskin, 'Vospitanie khoroshikh privychek', *Obshchestvennitsa* 11 (1940), 34–5.

[201] Anon., 'Na zavode i v sem'e', *Rabotnitsa* 6–7 (1946), 8.

[202] Like status differentials, this gender division was observable in the early days of Soviet culture. In the 1920s, women were also exhorted to exercise 'moral vigilance', and to be 'the

morals into the collectivizing project of Soviet society as a whole now made women representatives of the slippery ethos of 'communist morality': *vospitanie* was separated from *samovospitanie*. The ideal woman no longer began by examining her own behaviour and finding it wanting, but spent her entire energy on monitoring her family—seeing that her children had clean handkerchiefs and had prepared their homework, and making sure her husband did not drink or swear.[203]

The history of *kul'turnost'* propaganda in the 1930s and 1940s, then, is one of both continuities and discontinuities. Emphasis upon hygiene, self-education, and discipline remained central; at the same time, there was a rehabilitation, albeit at a subsidiary level, of status differentials and of the notion that women and men had distinct roles in the family and in society. And qualities such as *uyut* and *elegantnost'*, upon which scorn had been poured by some commentators during the 1920s, began to be invoked positively. Yet to summarize the total effects of all this as a 'Great Retreat' would distort the Stalinist regime's efforts to renuance 'culturedness' without appearing to negotiate a u-turn, their constant insistence that ideological changes were not backslidings, but refinements of the struggle to build a new reality. For example, Mikoyan asserted, in his introduction to the 1939 publication of *A Book of Tasty and Nutritious Food* (p. 24), that the book was a radical *break* with the past, rather than a return to tradition: 'We must put an end to old habits!' In this way, a manual of what could from some points of view be described as Soviet *cuisine bourgeoise* was repackaged as a guide to the ideal diet of socialist man.

All in all, then, the 1930s and 1940s interpretation of *kul'turnost'* reflected not so much a denial or subversion of the 1920s interpretation, as a clarification and expansion of this. On the one hand, 'white noise' was cleaned out of the cultural air-waves with the disappearance of the more unusual kinds of health literature, such as graphology treatises. On the other, *kul'turnost'*, especially after 1946, could mean having the odd

"conscience" of the revolution, to bring their "sharp eyes" to its defense'. See Elizabeth A. Wood, *The Baba and the Comrade: Gender and Politics in Revolutionary Russia* (Bloomington, Ind., 1998), 61, and ch. 2 *passim*.

[203] The pre-revolutionary upbringing of upper-class girls had underlined the dictates of conscience (*sovest'*), often with reference to the biblical narrative of the 'Fall'. In her memoir, *Moe otrochestvo* (St Petersburg, 1893), for example, Vera Zhelikhovskaya related how she was forced to confess to her entire family that she had taken and eaten an apple without permission. (My thanks to E. O. Putilova for this information.) For a discussion of 'anti-Edenic' narratives in women's life histories, see Pamela Chester, 'Painted Mirrors: Women's Visual and Verbal Texts' in C. Kelly and S. Lovell (eds.), *Russian Literature, Modernism and the Visual Arts* (Cambridge, 2000), 287–305. It seems likely that this tradition of upbringing lies behind Susan K. Morrissey's intriguing discovery that 'women students [unlike their male colleagues] had displaced the ideal of *studenchestvo* with the concept of an ethical individual' (*Heralds of Revolution: Russian Students and the Mythologies of Radicalism* (New York, 1998), 88).

'tasteful' ornament and a crêpe-de-chine dress, as well as reading Lenin, Pushkin, and Gor'ky.[204] And 1930s and 1940s behaviour literature, while in some respects modelling a stratified society, also did its best to create a myth of harmonious social unity. If, according to the false, but seductive, logic of Gor'ky's formulation in 1928, the reappearance of *meshchanstvo* would be the first step in the resurgence of class inequality,[205] then it followed that the elimination of *meshchanstvo* spelled egalitarianism. In constructing their myth of egalitarianism, the Soviet creators of propaganda were also helped (whether they were aware of it or not) by the post-Enlightenment tradition of seeing women's moral activities as horizontally, rather than vertically, denominated.[206] The traditional idea that women's morality was 'above class' facilitated the perception, among members of the intelligentsia themselves, that the 'educating' project executed by Soviet women was something radically different from the 'bourgeois philan-thropy' of pre-revolutionary days, or from the equally 'bourgeois' self-indulgence of the NEP era.[207]

READING ADVICE LITERATURE: THE *KOLLEKTIV* AND COLLECTIVE PRACTICES

The vision of the efficient, rational, patriotic masses set out in advice literature was a notable contribution to Soviet 'Potemkinism': the

[204] Cf. the observations of Fitzpatrick in 'Becoming Cultured', 218: 'Becoming cultured had always been a proper and necessary individual goal in Bolshevik terms. In the 1930s the term was simply expanded to include acquisition of the means and manners of a lifestyle appropriate to the new masters of the Soviet state.' I would add to this only that the audience for the *kul'turnost'* ideology included the Soviet 'masses' as well as 'masters', and that 'becoming cultured' was a goal embracing far larger sections of pre-revolutionary Russian society than the Bolsheviks, including self-improving workers as well as liberal and indeed conservative intellectuals (see Chs. 2 and 3 above).

[205] 'It is essential to propagandize an active attitude to reality and the education of the will to live . . . if we do not want to return to *meshchanstvo* and through *meshchanstvo* to the resurrection of a class society.' (*Kak ya stal pisatelem* (1928: edn. of Moscow, 1959), 14.)

[206] See Ch. 1 above. The sense that the *obshchestvennitsa* movement was not bourgeois was also helped by the participation of the wives of skilled workers. Indeed, *Rabotnitsa's* reporting on the *obshchestvennitsa* movement in the early 1930s concentrates exclusively on *zheny rabochikh* (see e.g. 18 (1930), 13; 33 (1930), 10–11). And Z. M. Rogachevskaya (ed.), *Zhena inzhenera (Avtorskii kollektiv zhen ITR 'Zaporozhstali)'* (Moscow, 1936), despite its title, includes memoirs by nine wives of skilled workers, as well as seven officials' wives and eleven engineers' wives. Significantly, the workers' wives are represented quite differently in their photographs, with much simpler dresses, hair-dos, etc. Less privileged workers, though, were not deceived by attempts to downplay the 'bourgeois' credentials of the wives' movement: on this see Davies, *Popular Opinion in Stalin's Russia*, 64; Fitzpatrick, *Everyday Stalinism*, 158.

[207] The memoirs in Rogachevskaya (ed.), *Zhena inzhenera* are insistent on this point: see e.g. N. P. Ivanova (p. 16) or E. K. Rabinovich (p. 25), who contrast their socially useful existence after the *obshchestvennitsa* movement with the idle purposelessness of their lives before it.

dissemination of incentive visions of the 'bright future', of a world where clean, tidy, upright citizens worked and played in modern, well-equipped collective and state farms with plump, placid cattle, contented inhabitants, and a comprehensively stocked and well-frequented library, or in orderly cities with neatly asphalted streets between straight, regular rows of trees.[208] To an even greater extent than in advice literature generally, reality only impacted in a negative way—when the authors of books drew attention to failures that needed correction. Material published during the so-called 'Cultural Revolution' of 1928–32 was especially frank about instances of persisting *bezkul'tur'e*—as in the following description by Z. N. Lilina of a hostel housing workers at the Staro-Glukhovskaya factory on the Klyaz'ma River, not far from Moscow:

Noise, racket and swearing are coming from the kitchen. At one end of the corridor late revellers are strumming on an accordion, at the other a worker who has just drunk away his pay packet is swearing in the choicest terms at his wife, emphasizing his words with blows from his fists. The corridor is filthy and stinking.[209]

Indications of malaise might become more oblique with the supposed restoration of 'order' and 'discipline' after 1932, but they did not disappear altogether. A 1940 article on 'Services for the Home', for example, pointed to cases such as an apartment block in Bol'shoi Sukharevskii pereulok, Moscow, which was left with puddles on the floor and peeling walls even *after* a major overhaul, and where the common parts were always filthy because the women in the block could not agree a schedule for cleaning.[210] A melancholy picture was painted also by a 1945 pamphlet under the title *Towards Healthy Living Space*; even after nearly thirty years of post-revolutionary indoctrination on hygiene, Leningrad residents still had to be told that they should not leave dirty clothes lying round their dwellings or spit on the floor.[211] Revealing, too, was the modesty of the positive achievements recorded. For example, *The Culture of Passenger Service* (1950), a collection of essays intended for railway workers, commended the model practices of the Western Railways. The guard of a passenger carriage took

[208] On the image of the collective farm in official propaganda, see Sheila Fitzpatrick, 'The Potemkin Village', in her *Stalin's Peasants: Resistance and Survival in the Russian Village after Collectivization* (New York, 1994), 262–85. The image of the 'Potemkin city' would be an excellent subject for a similarly detailed analysis.

[209] *Roditeli, uchites' vospityvat' svoikh detei* (1929), 5.

[210] O. Matorina, 'Okhrana zhilishchnogo fonda', *Obshchestvennitsa* 12 (1940), 17.

[211] *Za zdorovoe zhilishche!*, *passim*. There are also more indirect reflections of the survival of what the regime saw as 'uncultured practices'. The unremitting hostility to corporal punishment in Soviet behaviour tracts even after *distsiplina* had become the governing principle of upbringing is surely a reflection of the persistence of physical chastisement of children among many working-class and peasant parents.

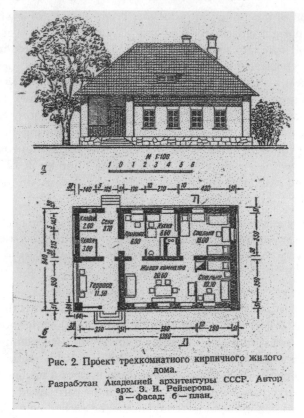

FIG. 16. The Potemkin village. Model design for a
brick-built cottage (Ryabov, *What a Well-Ordered Village
Should Be Like*, 1947).

care to ensure her uniform was clean and ironed and that the passenger
tickets were checked 'quickly, without any delay'. 'My rule is to be caring
and polite to passengers; I make sure everything is clean, warm, and cosy.'
And the manager of a station described how she and her team had
transformed it by 'Bolshevik desire', so that 'there are no queues and
pushing and shoving by the ticket offices', and 'the baggage invariably goes
off with the train the traveller is booked to travel on'.[212]

To be sure, the acknowledged successes of the Soviet regime in some
areas of education (the reduction of illiteracy) and of primary health-care
(notably, the reduction of infant mortality)[213]—may indicate that advice

[212] *Kul'tura obsluzhivaniya passazhirov*, 22, 48. Similarly modest in its aspirations was a 'cultural
barracks' contest run in Kemerovo (1933): the winner was the barracks with least excrement
outside its windows. (See Bedin, Kushnikova, and Togulev (eds.), *Dokumental'noe nasledie*, 87.)
[213] In European Russia, the death rate for infants under 1 was 273 per 1,000 in 1913; this had

literature had a role in increasing public awareness of new facilities and in inculcating desirable practices. But the spread of ideas by example or word of mouth, and socio-economic pressures (particularly, the difficulty of securing employment without elementary literacy skills), are just as likely to have counted here. Certainly, it is remarkable that sources such as private letters often reveal a very low penetration of the ideology of *kul'turnost'*. In letters from working-class and peasant Russians to relations serving at the front during the Soviet-Finnish War of 1939–40, for instance, 'Soviet identity' was expressed primarily in terms of quotations from popular song and the citing of garbled patriotic slogans ('we wish you suksess in feerless protekshun of the borders' [*tebe zhylaem zarika Akhranyat nashu granitsu*]). Most correspondents were concerned with telling their sons, fathers, and uncles that they were 'getting by somehow', and it was only a very occasional letter-writer who found time even to pass on that her baby had 'clean warm clothes I bought him a few new things'.[214]

Significantly, too, the ideas about hygiene that stuck most deeply were often those which bore some relation to extant beliefs. The successful dissemination of the notion that it was possible to 'temper oneself' by washing in cold water, and so avoid catching cold through changes of temperature, probably owed as much to traditional practices in the Russian bathhouse (rolling in the snow after using the steam-room) as it did to a familiarity with the popular literature on hydrotherapy.[215] Equally, the curious obsession of women's magazines with advice on how to get rid of freckles may be less a reflection of concerns with hygiene as such than of the ingrained suspicion of red-haired people (*ryzhie*) that is attested in proverbs and in folklore.[216] And attempts to inculcate suspicion about *meshchanstvo*

fallen to 184 per 1,000 in 1940, 81 per 1,000 in 1950, and 35 per 1,000 in 1960. (See *Zhenshchina i deti v SSSR: statisticheskii sbornik* (Moscow, 1961), 61.) Though this information was published under Soviet censorship, it tallies well with post-glasnost figures from 1987, which quote a rate of 26.2 per 1,000 for rural areas in 1970, and 21.7 per 1,000 for rural areas in 1985. However, in Central Asia and other parts of the Soviet Union with an underdeveloped health infrastructure, progress was less impressive: figures from 1987 indicate deaths of 55 per 1,000 in Central Asia, and over 40 per 1,000 in the Chechen-Ingush Republic. (See Mary Buckley, *Women and Ideology in the Soviet Union* (Hemel Hempstead, 1989), 205, 222 n. 14.) For information on literacy figures, see J. Dunstan, *Soviet Schooling and the Second World War* (London, 1997), 18–19, Table 2.1: by 1939, the rate in European Russia ranged between 79.3 per cent (women in rural areas) and 98.1 per cent (men in cities).

[214] Zenzinov (ed.), *Vstrecha s Rossiei*, letters 4, 117, 107.

[215] The intersection between popular belief about the *banya* and medical literature goes back to Sanches, *O parnykh rossiiskikh banyakh* (1779). It is possible that acceptance of *zakalivanie* was also related to its dependence upon a binary opposition (here that between 'hot' and 'cold') of the kind characteristic of Russian traditional culture. For a wide-ranging study of such oppositions, see A. D. Baiburin, *Ritual v traditsionnoi kul'ture: strukturno-semanticheskii analiz vostochnoslavyanskikh obryadov* (St Petersburg, 1993).

[216] On freckles see e.g. *Rabotnitsa* 11 (1939), 18 and 15 (1940), 18. Among proverbs listed by Dal' is e.g. 'S ryzhim druzhby ne vodi, s chernym v les ne khodi', 'Ryzhii da krasnyi, chelovek

could draw on the world-view expressed in popular sayings such as *pod podolom fal'bala, pod podolom pud govna* (nothing but frills and furbelows, with a shitty arse below),[217] which set out the luxury = *beskul'tur'e* equation a good deal more graphically than Soviet propaganda ever did.

If attempts to persuade Soviet citizens into better practices were not always successful, more draconian methods were not necessarily any more effective. Indeed, as the regulation of behaviour became stricter, so the Soviet population became more adept at bending the rules. For instance, rehearsals for grand parades organized to mark National Physical Culture Day in July, 1939, turned into a fiasco because large numbers of the gymnasts from Moscow (members of the Institute of Physical Culture of the Name of Stalin, no less) simply failed to show up.[218]

Yet if official behaviour regulation was frequently ignored or openly flouted, this does not necessarily indicate that it had no effect whatever on the Soviet population. There were some notable successes: for example, the Parks of Culture and Rest might not have combatted drinking in worker hostels, but they were widely used by the population for 'cultured' activities such as walking, skating, playing games, reading, and healthful (but not immodest) sunbathing. In this sense, the new society indeed bore out a eulogy composed by the unofficial poet laureate of the early 1930s, Dem'yan Bednyi, in his poem 'Worker Leisure Then and Now':

> Кто мог представить в годы оны
> Рабочий отдых наших лет:
> Музеи, парки, стадионы,
> Театры, музыку, балет.
>
> Все виды радостного спорта,
> Парадов мощную красу,
> Уют приморского курорта,
> Дома для отдыха в лесу!
>
> Рабочий отдых стал культурным
> И оздоровленным насквозь...

> Who could imagine, in those times,
> A worker's leisure, nowadays?
> Museums, parks, and stadiums,
> Theatres, music, the ballet.

opasnyi', 'Ryzhikh i vo svyatykh net' (*Tolkovyi slovar' velikorusskogo yazyka* (Moscow 1880–2), iv. 117.

[217] Bonner, *Dochki-materi*, 102, remembers the family *domrabotnitsa* using this expression.

[218] See TsKhDMO f. 1 op. 23 d. 1364 ll. 81–2, letter from the Commissar of the Parade, I. K. Frolov, to the Secretary of the Central Committee of the Komsomol, N. A. Mikhailov. As many as 100–140 participants were failing to turn up for rehearsals, Frolov complained, the doctors gave out sick notes 'for every scratch', one Komsomol member had been sacked after forging his own sick note, and there was gambling and drinking in the hostel.

All joyful sports the world has known,
Military parades, with their brave show,
Resorts, all cosy, by the sea,
Or rest homes standing in the trees!

Now workers' leisure is *kul'turnyi*
And clean and wholesome through and through . . .[219]

In any case, practicalities aside, the question of the extent to which the ideals preached in the behaviour struck home—their contribution to the construction of mentality, if not the reform of day-to-day behaviour—deserves further examination.

An initial issue here is readership: how large an audience did advice books have? The strict control over publishing established by the Soviet regime in its early days meant that statistics of categories of books printed and titles reprinted are indications of the regime's priorities rather than of grass-roots interest. The fact that the works of Makarenko, or Arkhan-gel'sky and Speransky's *Mother and Child*, were regularly reissued during the 1930s, 1940s, and early 1950s, points to the canonicity of these books, rather than to 'consumer demand' as that would be understood in a market economy.[220] Moreover, the fact of issuing a book by no means guaranteed an audience. The distribution difficulties that afflicted the Soviet book market during the 1920s bedevilled the reception of advice literature as they did other categories, such as belles-lettres. In an excoriating denunciation of the inefficiency of the state-run publishing industry that appeared in 1926, Mayakovsky quoted a letter from Zakkniga (the book ordering agency) in Tiflis, lamenting the lack of foresight in the supply of agricultural pamphlets:

We cannot emphasize too strongly that the current selection of literature for peasants and the popular readership generally is perfectly useless to us. The local peasants cannot read Russian and in any case the literature that is sent to us takes no account whatever of our objective requirements and local conditions . . . For

---

[219] 'Rabochii otdykh v starinu i teper'', *Stikhotvoreniya i poemy* (Moscow and Leningrad, 1965), 258–9.

[220] Detailed exploration of advice literature planning is frustrated by the patchiness of archive documentation (TsKhDMO has dedicated files on the crucial *Molodaya gvardiya* publishing house only from the post-1941 period, when publications in this category were relatively scanty). However, already by the 1920s, a two-way process of creating publishers' lists had been evolved. Editorial collectives in state houses forwarded their suggestions (based on an appreciation of key policy issues as articulated in decrees, circulars, etc.) to Party and Komsomol authorities, and the latter not only critiqued these (as well as keeping close scrutiny on material actually published), but also issued instructions and directives about important publishing areas. (For a 1925 document including observations on plans and publications in the area of literature for Pioneer leaders, see TsKhDMO f. 1 op. 23 d. 388 l. 7, l. 9, l. 21; for a directive (also in this area), see *Kopii postanovlenii Byuro TsK VLKSM po rabote sredi pionerov i shkol'nikov 1936–1942* (held in TsKhDMO Reading Room), pp. 8–9.)

example, you send us a brochure called *How to Make Your Own Horse-Collar* (when the peasants round here use bulls to plough—you just try putting a horse-collar on one of them!) Or one called *A Simple Way to Double Your Harvest of Winter Rye* (no one plants rye round here), or *Water-Dowsing Made Simple* (there's plenty of water round here, so dowsing is not exactly necessary), or *The Uses of Peat* (we don't have any), and so on. We hope that you will agree that sending literature of that kind to us is about as much use as sending a consignment of bicycles to Venice.

Mayakovsky himself recorded that one of the few editions widely available in Baku was the magazine *Lyzhnyi sport* (Skiing), whose appeal locally was, not surprisingly, rather limited. No doubt such books suffered a similar or worse fate to the one which, as Kornei Chukovsky recalled, overtook any books about socialist construction that reached the Black Sea resort of Eupatoria—they were torn up and used to wrap grapes for sale at the market.[221]

But not all titles seem to have been as contemptuously received by the Soviet population. For instance, state-produced books on health and house management were regularly reprinted during the NEP period, when the government did not have the resources to subsidize large runs of unpopular books, and when state titles had to fight off competition from private ones. Sarkizov-Serazini's *Cure Yourself with Sun!* had run to five editions by 1930, Mendel'son's *Onanism* to eight by 1930, and Zarina's *At the Common Table* to five by 1933.[222] And, like their pre-revolutionary predecessors, surviving copies of early Soviet advice books and pamphlets often show signs of heavy use and intent readership. Particularly striking is the instance of a copy of Kerzhentsev's *Organize Yourself!* now in the Russian State Library, where one of the few sentences that has *not* been underlined by a reader or readers is the stern warning, 'It goes without saying that those who take it into their heads to scribble underlinings and question marks on books that

[221] Mayakovsky, 'Podozhdem obvinyat' poetov', *PSS* xii. 76; Chukovsky, *Dnevnik 1930–1969* (Moscow, 1994), 79, entry for 26 Aug. 1932. Mayakovsky's objective in his essay was to undermine the widespread argument that poetry did not sell, but his article offers fascinating information about the chaotic state of the Soviet book trade in the mid-1920s. In most bookshops, card-indexes of stock were only introduced in early 1926, and even once they had appeared, assistants had little idea of which books were in stock, and little interest in selling them (advice was not provided and displays were remarkably uninviting). The task of supplying consumer demand was also bedevilled by the fact that shops had no control over numbers of a particular edition supplied (a consignment might be made up of ninety-five copies of an unpopular book and five copies of a popular one, and the latter could only be reordered if the former also was, a disincentive to restock even if books sold out). (See *PSS* xii. 73–4.)

[222] There is other evidence as well of a popular market for health literature. In 1921, 'Klavdiya Semenovna D.', who had read a pamphlet on onanism by L. Ya. Leibovich, a pathologist working for the People's Commissariat of Health, came to Moscow to ask the advice of its author about her abnormal secondary characteristics. (Cited in Daniel Healey, '"Man or Woman?": Hermaphroditism as a Medical Problem in Tsarist and Soviet Russia', paper presented at CREES, University of Birmingham, Nov. 1999.) However, Ransel, *Village Mothers*, 147, argues that even this material reached peasant readers only in the 1960s.

are not their own deserve severe punishment.'[223] Underlinings not only show beginning readers trying to absorb new material; they also show them putting into practice the reading techniques that they had been taught, learning to 'read in a cultured manner' as it was propagandized by books on *How to Read*.

Workers also learned to 'write in a cultured manner', celebrating in their own words the glories of the *kul'turnost'* ideal. The diary of Isaak Slutsky, a young provincial worker who visited Moscow in 1928, reflects enthusiasm for the bustle of the town, its modern structures ('a ten-storey building with a restaurant on top'), its glamorous women, and its 'cultured' citizens:

I've noticed that when you visit a hospital, a theatre, a cinema, anywhere you go, people are reading books and newspapers (mostly they've brought them along themselves). They're cultured (*kul'turnye*). Film shows start at 7, just like the posters say they will. It's not like in the provinces. I saw a troop of firemen riding their engine down Tverskaya. They looked good, real smart.

Cultured.[224]

Slutsky's own itinerary was such as to have pleased any adherent of Soviet self-improvement: it included visits to the theatre, where he saw *Man with a Briefcase* (Chelovek s portfelem) and *The Proletarian* (Proletarii); to the cinema, where he saw Eisenstein's *October*; to the Museum of the Revolution and the Polytechnical Museum. And he was indignant at the instances of 'uncultured' behaviour that he came across: actresses at the Bol'shoi with 'damn make-up plastered all over their face', dirty streets, pedestrians crossing themselves as they passed a church. Slutsky and observers like him were the successors to the pre-revolutionary self-improving worker intelligentsia, for whom culture was far too hard-won to be treated lightly, and who were particularly resentful about behaviour that smacked of self-indulgence.[225] Such attitudes could only be enhanced during the 1930s, as years of participating in 'self-criticism' meetings, or exposure to education, inducted workers and self-made intellectuals into the new values of Soviet ideology.

[223] Kerzhentsev, *Organizui samogo sebya!*, 98: the copy is at shelfmark W 247/883.

[224] 'Zapiski provintsiala o Moskve', *Novyi Lef* 10 (1928), 20.

[225] The Red Guard Eduard Dune, for example, poured contempt on intellectuals who filched books from the Yusupov estate at Arkhangel'skoe ('An incomprehensible book was as mysterious as an icon, not something to be read as a way of passing the time. Such things had become "ours". Who would think of stealing them?') And he bitterly recalled seeing Ekaterina Gel'tser, a ballerina, disgrace herself by licking caviare off an entire pile of canapés and piling the discarded pastry shells on a plate: 'In any other company she would not have dared to take such liberties, but among us... "Imagine! Such boorish people! What do they know about good manners? Robbing the robbers!"' (E. Dune, *Notes of a Red Guard*, trans. and ed. Diane P. Koenker and S. A. Smith (Urbana, Ill., 1993), 85–6.)

An illustration of the success of the new behaviour models is to be found in the diary of Leonid Potemkin, the son of a provincial postal official studying in Moscow in the 1930s. Acquiring a love of Beethoven and Tchaikovsky for their expression of 'iron will', Potemkin prided himself upon his own exercise of will in intimate matters, noting in May 1936 that 'tender ecstatic love' was spurned by 'the iron discipline of the mind as an obstacle to my goal' of self-improvement.[226] The most earnest self-improvers even kept notebooks in which they recorded progress: books read, facts assimilated, and Lenin quotes learned.[227] Those who had been entirely educated under the Soviet regime were particularly likely to see aspiration to self-improvement and respect for culture as central to Soviet identity.[228] Even the complaints in a letter sent by a provincial schoolboy to *Komsomol'skaya pravda* in 1950 were 'cultured' ones: the light in his classroom was too dim to read by, and there was insufficient access to newspapers:

Mezmai Settlement [in Krasnodarskii krai] is little, but we have a narrow-gauge railway link, a saw-mill, a radio land-line, a club, a post office, and a shop, and everything else has been done for Mezmai Settlement.

But the factory school is a real mess. The lighting's very bad, it burns so dimly in the daytime you can't see to write or read a newspaper, there's no radio in the school. They only give out the papers twice a week, and not all the issues even then. We only have one paper to a class of thirty-five, and there aren't any communal readings.[229]

Yet the ability to spout 'Sovietese' in certain well-defined cultural contexts (such as letters to newspapers, or diaries composed as class assignments)[230] did not necessarily mean that 'Sovietese' constituted the sole expressive vocabulary of Soviet subjects. For Soviet intellectuals, as Oleg Khakhordin has argued, a 'schizophrenic split' between private and

---

[226] 'Diary of Leonid Alekseevich Potyomkin [sic]', in Garros, Korenevskaya, and Lahusen (eds.), *Intimacy and Terror: Soviet Diaries of the 1930s*, 285. For an instructive discussion of a similar case, see J. Hellbeck, 'Fashioning the Stalinist Soul: the Diary of Stepan Podlubnyi, 1931–9', in Fitzpatrick (ed.), *Stalinism: New Directions*, 77–116.

[227] An instance is the pocket book published by Zenzinov (ed.), *Vstrecha s Rossiei*, 563–8.

[228] On the 'Soviet' identity, cf. the interesting observations of J. Scott, *Magnitogorsk* (New York, 1942), who relates that in early 1938, 'in spite of the purges, the town was still full of rough and earnest young Russians—working, studying, making mistakes and learning, reproducing to the tune of thirty-odd thousand per year. They were also writing poetry, going to see remarkably good performances of *Othello*, learning to play violins and tennis' (p. 253). Davies, *Popular Opinion*, 69, indicates that decrees of 1935 and 1940 abolishing 'positive discrimination' in favour of worker and peasant applicants to higher education, and introducing fees for education beyond elementary level, were deeply unpopular at the grass roots, which is yet a further indication of how the educational ethic had penetrated.

[229] TsKhDMO f. 1 op. 32 d. 624 l. 27.

[230] Potemkin, for example, recorded that, to his embarrassment, he was directed to read his diary at a class he was attending. See Garros, Korenevskaya, and Lahusen, *Intimacy and Terror*, 253.

public self often obtained: a model member of the collective in public life was likely to be 'an unconstrained egoist' at home.[231] The much-mythologized and villified *kommunalki*, communal flats with a family to a room, such as were inhabitated by many members of the intelligentsia, at least allowed a door to be shut on strangers, even if noise, or still more disagreeably, vomit and urine, sometimes leaked through or under the barrier.[232]

To be sure, this binary model is of questionable relevance to the lives of many working-class Russians, among whom 'privacy' was constructed rather differently. A communal flat was a relatively luxurious place compared with a bed in a hostel or a factory barracks, or with a rented 'corner' of a room; in each of these cases, a room had to be shared with at least three other people, not all of whom were likely to be friends or relatives.[233] Departure to some out-of-the-way nook such as a blind corridor or staircase in search of solitude would have seemed as peculiar and suspicious a manoeuvre as failure to participate in demonstrations and factory meetings. Because far more of working-class life took place 'in public', tensions sometimes blew up there as well as in the company of trusted friends; without the safety valve of private criticism, open or semi-open dissent seems to have been more common among peasants and factory workers than among intellectuals. Conversely, self-improving Soviet workers, who set themselves out to assimilate the private self into public values (in line with official policy), did not necessarily draw a firm divide between criticism in a diary (even one not composed as an official work assignment), and expressed out loud—

[231] Khakhordin, *The Collective and the Individual*, 204; cf. E. Zubkova, *Russia after the War: Hopes, Illusions, and Disappointments, 1945–1957*, trans. and ed. H. Ragsdale (New York, 1998), 201. An amusing account of the public/private divide at a later period of Soviet history is given in Ronald Hingley, *The Russian Mind* (London, 1977), 158–9 (on the contrast between public prudery and private bawdy in Soviet male officials). Russian intellectuals had been practised in observing it well before the Revolution: the writer Yury Smolich, for example, recalled how his parents had been entirely conformist in public during the 1910s, but had drawn the curtains and closed the doors in order to read dissident literature and have critical discussion of the tsarist regime in public. (See Brainina and Nikitina (eds.), *Sovetskie pisateli: avtobiografii*, ii (Moscow, 1959), 370.)

[232] See Boym, *Common Places*, ch. 2, 'Living in Common Places', for a particularly vivid description of life in a communal apartment.

[233] Between 1935 and 1937, 34 per cent of new building in Moscow was still in the form of *baraki* (euphemistically known as *standartnye doma*), while 60 per cent of workers at the prestigious Serp i molot factory still inhabited hostels. See Colton, *Moscow*, 342. In the worst cases, such as a 'hellhole at Cherkizovo, for Elektrozavod', a single room held fifty people sleeping on the floor, and even so inhabitants had to use the beds in shifts (ibid.). To deal with a pool of vomit or urine in the corridor is bad enough: far worse when someone urinates over your clean clothes in the wardrobe, as happened to some students in the hostel where I lived in Voronezh in 1981. An absorbing collection of articles on worker daily life is T. Vihovainen [as Vikhovainen] (ed.), *Normy i tsennosti povsednevnoi zhizni* (St Petersburg, 2000), see esp. 27–150.

statements of the former kind might already be seen as belonging in the public domain.[234]

The fact that complaints from the proletariat and peasantry, whose supposed support was the central plank of Soviet rule, were such a volatile entity, as well as potentially such a disruptive one, made Soviet propaganda institutions attempt to direct disaffection into sanctioned channels—for example, readers' letters to newspapers, and complaints to government agencies. But these forms were not always used in ways desirable to the authorities. This was less a question of direct subversion (though this was not unknown),[235] than of a misfit between official notions of how genres should be used and how they functioned on the ground. An interesting case in point is the *stengazeta*, or wall newspaper. Evolved as a local and parochial version of the official printed newspaper, as 'a lever of the new *byt*', and subject to strict censorship by the editorial committee, the factory administration, and the Party hierarchy, as well as by the censorship authorities themselves, and to regulation via the officially sponsored movement of 'worker correspondents' (the semi-official 'stringers' who supplied copy for printed newspapers as well as for manuscript journals),[236] the genre sometimes worked to express the collective practices that Soviet propaganda sought to stamp out, rather than the rational relationships it was supposed to implement. So much is clear not only from the (extremely rare) surviving copies of manuscript wall newspapers, but also from asides in advisory literature of the 1920s and 1930s, which, when informing readers how *not* to write for the wall newspaper, were forced to include citations of inappropriate materials from real wall newspapers.[237]

The difficulty for the authorities in controlling the *stengazeta* stemmed from the ambiguous function of the genre. It was supposed to be at once an instrument of *vospitanie*, and a forum for mass creativity and mass expression; the content was supposed to be of local interest, yet also to reflect the effective dissemination of Party ideology at grass-roots level. To use the jargon of the time, the *stengazeta* was meant to be not only *zlobodnevnaya*

[234] For an interesting discussion of this kind of mentality, see Hellbeck, 'Fashioning the Stalinist Soul'.

[235] For instance, the parodying of official slogans and agitational verse by disaffected workers. See Davies, *Popular Opinion*, 52–3.

[236] The phrase 'a lever of the new *byt*' is used in *Rabkor i stennaya gazeta* (1924), 10. For a lucid exposition of the mechanisms of control within the collective, see *Rabkor i gazeta*, 55–69, 148–9). On external censorship, cf. the decision by the Leningrad district censorship office (Gublit), 15 Mar. 1927, that wall newspapers in apartment blocks should be registered with the censorship authority and 'those responsible for them' vetted by that authority. (Blyum, *Za kulisami*, 89).

[237] A fuller exposition of the argument below is given in C. Kelly, '"A Laboratory for the Manufacture of Proletarian Writers": The *Stengazeta* (Wall Newspaper), 1924–1940' (publication forthcoming).

(topical), but also *operativnaya* (politically effective).[238] Copy published in the journal *Rabochii korrespondent* (later *Raboche-krest'yanskii korrespondent*), and in many individual brochures aimed at *stengazeta* editorial committees during the 1920s and 1930s, indicates that in practice this fusion of interests proved extremely problematic. The *stengazeta* often functioned more like a parish magazine or student newsletter than a vehicle of Soviet ideology. As a brochure of 1928 complained: 'Three-quarters of the space is taken up by reports about the youth team's victories at football matches, about how hooliganism at meetings is a bad thing, or about "flirtatiousness" [*ukhaz-herstvo*].'[239] Worse, *stengazety* often filled their columns with tattle (*spletni*) or 'ribbing' (*zvon*) of the sort that was associated among educated observers with the 'backward' masses in general.[240] Copy of this sort made it painfully clear that workers often wanted to bring workmates into line not so much because of ideological failings, but because they were seen as 'stuck up'. A January 1926 issue of a *stengazeta* from a village in the Urals carried a typical item of this kind:

Praise for Nothing
In our village, there's a certain N. S. Tryastsin who's been praised to the skies in the wall newspaper, he's their number one blue-eyed boy. But he's not got anyone signed up in the club. Quite the opposite: he just sneers at all the young people. For instance, if any lad wants to dance the quadrille or something, this N. S. Tryastsin's so well dressed that all the girls only have eyes for him. He grabs hold of one of the girls and he dances a polka [krakovlyak] or a waltz. Whereas the lad who wanted to dance with her has to go and sit on a bench bright red with shame, and the next time he don't dare ask. If we follow that example, then we all ought to take advantage of people and poke fun at them. That's number one blue-eyed boy N. S. Tryastsin—his father's a wealthy peasant, by the way.[241]

---

[238] These interpretations were thrashed out in the Resolutions of the Second All-Soviet Congress of Worker-Correspondents in December 1924: see *Itogi i perspektivy rabsel'korovskogo dvizheniya: stenograficheskii otchet Vtorogo Vsesoyuznogo soveshchaniya rabkorov, sel'korov, voenkorov i yunkorov pri 'Pravde'* (Moscow, 1925), 355–9. They were repeated in the various guides to writing for the *stengazeta* published in the mid-1920s (e.g. Charnyi, *Gazeta na stene* (1924), and *Rabkor i stennaya gazeta*).

[239] Polotskaya and Dokunin, *Redkollegiya stennoi gazety i kruzhok rabkorov*, 36.

[240] On 'ribbing', see D. P. Koenker, 'Men and Women on the Shop Floor in Early Soviet Russia: Gender and Class in the Soviet Workplace', *American Historical Review* 100/5 (1995), 1438–64. An article under the title 'Dikie nravy', *Pechatnik*, 22 Nov. 1928, 28, commented, '"Ribbing" your comrade used even to be considered "good form" (*khoroshii ton*) in the past. Now we are struggling with it. But it has still not disappeared in the setting room.' The example given is of a 'keen sportsman and enthusiast for culture (*zavzyatyi kul'turnik*) who was the subject of cruel teasing from his comrades. (My thanks to Steve Smith for this reference.)

[241] From *Yunye bortsy*, Guban village, Sarapul'skii okrug Ural'skoi ob., no. 2, Jan. 1926: signed 'Terepug'. Quoted in A. Nasimovich, 'Stengazetnyi yumor', *Pechat' i revolyutsiya* 6 (1927), 29. The article also quotes a riposte by the wall newspaper organizer defending Tryastsin as 'honest and not at all rich' (ibid. 30).

Despite all the efforts of manual-writers, worker-correspondents, and the factory and Party authorities to enforce good *stengazeta* practices, copy of this kind continued to be produced well into the 1930s. The following poison-pen item appeared in 1935 in *Instrumental'shchik*, the wall newspaper of the instrument workshop of the Moscow Car Factory:

In our shop, in foreman Shulman's group, there's a certain workman called Semen Katz. He's a wise one if you like. Thinks the world of himself and has nothing to do with anyone else. I should say straight out that Katz has got very lax about his work. After dinner he wiped down his lathe and went off to the dance hall. We must incite public opinion about him and call him to order.[242]

To be sure, writing for the *stengazeta* could be a way of learning 'to talk Bolshevik', in Stephen Kotkin's phrase.[243] But what was learned was a kind of political Creole, in which the linguistic formulae of the public denunciation ('we must incite public opinion...' 'so and so must be called to answer...' 'judgement must be passed'), jostled with colloquialisms ('he's a wise one if you like'). Further, workers did not interpret the 'wall newspaper' as a medium of 'self-criticism' in the official sense: that is, for integration of local behaviour regulation with commands coming out from the centre. Rather, they saw it as a medium for criticism *within* the collective, for punitive action against those who disobeyed its rules, and also as a way of directing gripes at the factory management from a position of relative safety.[244] While writing for the *stengazeta* was a practice that contributed to community solidarity, it did so in a very different sense from that anticipated by the Party authorities.

It is scarcely surprising that from the late 1930s the *stengazeta* began to be downplayed as a forum for the expression of opinion. The journal *Raboche-krest'yanskii korrespondent* was closed down in 1941, and not revived until 1957; though guides continued to be produced, these stressed the 'educative' role of the genre rather than its 'topicality' in terms of the issues that interested workers.[245] And in Anatoly Levitin and Yury Tulin's

---

[242] *V pomoshch' stengazete* (1937), 81.

[243] Kotkin, *Magnetic Mountain*: see e.g. p. 217: 'The very fact that [in their memoirs] workers sometimes "erred", and had to be corrected, both for grammar and content, shows how they were implicated in a process of adapting the official method of speaking about themselves.' A similar view is taken in Matthew E. Lenoe, 'Letter-Writing and the State: Reader Correspondence with Newspapers as a Source for Early Soviet History', *Cahiers du monde russe* 40/1–2 (1999), 139–69.

[244] An example of the latter kind of use is a complaint in 1925 to a wall newspaper under the title *Proletarskoe delo* that the overseer (*ekspeditor*) of the packing workshop in one factory was making physical threats to his subordinates when he considered their work shoddy (see Leningrad District State Archive, City of Vyborg, f. 2908, op. 1, d. 236).

[245] See e.g. A. Alekseev, 'Stengazeta v kolkhoze', *Raboche-krest'yanskii korrespondent* 3 (1939), 8; Topchan, *Den' za dnem* (1946); Gorelik, *Kak organizovat' rabotu kolkhoznoi stennoi gazety* (1946); Boiko, *Stennaya gazeta i boevoi listok* (1949). Only the last includes any examples of 'bad'

painting of 1952, *A Fresh Issue of the Works Newspaper* (1952),[246] the emphasis is not on the content of the paper itself (the board on which it is placed is turned away from the viewer's gaze), but on its consumption by the spectators as a gesture of social solidarity and an instrument of political education (a young attractive blonde woman gazes reproachfully at a handsome, but sulky, young man who has, evidently, just been the target of criticism in the paper).

CONCLUSION

This chapter has shown that early Soviet advice literature was, taken on its own terms, and aside from the complicated question of its reception, eloquent propaganda: coherent, consistent, yet flexible enough to absorb material of 'bourgeois' origin and to present this as a necessary part of a distinctive Soviet identity. It might have been at times (at most times) dull, pompous, and narrow-minded, but in this it differed little from advice literature of other eras and other countries, and its message was—compared both with pre-revolutionary advice literature, and with the post-Soviet advice literature that will be examined in my next chapter—clear and direct. But the success of early Soviet advice literature as an ideological medium came largely in familiarizing some sectors of the population (above all those living in cities and those educated under the Soviet system) with the idea of what a 'Soviet person' was in the abstract (a person committed to self-betterment, strong-willed, patriotic, and egalitarian). It altered the contours of ideals, rather than changing practices on the ground.

Moreover, though emphasis upon the individual's duty to conform and to monitor deviations from normal behaviour on the part of fellow citizens was superficially an effective way of ensuring social solidarity and curbing outward expressions of disaffection, the attempt to establish rational *kollektivizm* was bedevilled by pre-existing collective practices that Soviet ideology considered uncultured (such as gossip and 'ribbing'). Worker collectives were often inimical not only to 'petit-bourgeois' self-betterment, but to self-improvement of the kind that the state attempted to

stengazeta copy, a piece of 'vicious mockery' (*zuboskal'stvo*) aimed at a sentry who spent his time on duty either dozing or 'doodling pictures of cockerels and puppies' (p. 34). Evidently, the genre was still far from always an ideal means of collective regulation, even in a relatively disciplined military environment.

[246] See Cullerne Bown, *Socialist Realism*, pl. 337. By the end of the 1930s, demands for higher standards in the *stengazeta* had meant that the material was sometimes bought in. Yury Lotman recalls earning money as a student by producing artwork for *stengazety* ('Prosmatrivaya zhizn'', 38).

foster.[247] A zealous *kul'turnik* was just as likely to come in for hostility as was a worker with an excessive interest in fashion—indeed, perhaps more likely. Living in conditions of nineteenth-century squalor, resenting their immediate superiors and those who did well out of the system, existing in rough-and-ready communities that were not at all like the rational collectives envisaged by Soviet propaganda, most members of the 'Soviet masses' could only in a very approximate sense be considered the 'ideal citizens' envisaged in conduct literature. At the same time, the inadequate control that was exercised over the high-handed behaviour of officials (a far more public matter than their access to special food supplies or to glamorous restaurants),[248] meant that the 'elite' whom the masses were supposed to consider their role models were often very far from manifesting the 'civilized values' that *kul'turnost'* was supposed to embody, a fact that further increased cynicism at the bottom of Soviet society.

Often, then, the Soviet campaign for *kul'turnost'* ended up by reinforcing the *nekul'tur'e* that the state sought to root out and destroy. This process was not just the result of accelerated modernization.[249] It was also a consequence of defects in the *kul'turnost'* ideology itself. Like the secular morality propounded by Emile Durkheim in 1903, this emphasized discipline and collectivism; however, it neglected what Durkheim had seen as a third and equally important element of an effective moral system, autonomy, or the construction of a rational sense of why rules functioned as they did.[250] Fundamental, too, was the sentimental populism of a regime that gestured towards its popular mandate as legitimation while doing all it could to deny the masses the opportunity to exercise actual political leverage.[251] The result was to perpetuate the survival strategies learned

[247] The same could be true of petty officials. When attending military college in 1941, Yakov Kozlovsky was sent a letter of rebuke by his commander, who had seen an article written by Kozlovsky in the paper: 'You didn't oughter be messing round with no skribling, nor no artickles neither seeing as you ain't a schoolboy no more' (a ne fil'kinoi gramotoi, raznymi fel'etonami ibo vy ne shkol'nik). See Ya. Kozlovsky, 'Iz moei rodoslovnoi', E. Ya. Brainina and A. N. Dmitrieva (eds.), *Sovetskie pisateli: avtobiografii*, v (Moscow, 1988), 285.

[248] 'Sovet power is *blat* [corruption], plus bureaucratism, boorishness, and vandalism', stated one anonymous letter of the mid-1930s (Davies, *Popular Opinion*, 134). For similar evidence from the 1940s, see Elena Zubkova, *Russia After the War: Hopes, Illusions, and Disappointments, 1945–1957*, trans. and ed. H. Ragsdale (New York, 1998), esp. 74–87.

[249] As argued e.g. by M. Peris, *War on the Heavens: The Soviet League of the Militant Godless, 1918–1932* (Princeton, 1998), 98.

[250] E. Durkheim, *Moral Education* (London, 1973). For a useful discussion of Soviet morality in the context of this model, see F. O'Dell, *Socialisation and Children's Literature: The Soviet Example* (Cambridge, 1978), ch. 9.

[251] One should not, of course, exaggerate the freedoms obtaining in participatory democracies in this period, at any rate between 1918 and 1939. As Mark Mazower argues in *Dark Continent: Europe's Twentieth Century* (London, 1998), 7, 23–4, an emphasis upon social welfare as opposed to political and civil liberties was evident Europe-wide at this period, and 'fear of communism, in particular, drew many liberals towards authoritarian solutions'; the trust of conservatives in

under authoritarian rule in the pre-revolutionary era, to strengthen what Robert Johnson has termed the 'web of relationships and routines . . . not foreseen or regulated by the employer'.[252] And even at the level of an ideal, *kul'turnost'* was to prove less useful to the Soviet elite in the long term than in the short term. The fact that the homogeneity of behaviour models was an important force of continuity as policy and symbolism changed also meant that alteration of behaviour models had the potential to suggest discontinuity, and by extension to destabilize the idealistic patriotism of ordinary Soviet citizens. This potential was to be fully realized, as we shall see, during the decades that followed the death of Stalin, when the development of a broader and more permissive understanding of *kul'tur-nost'* was one factor behind the decline of social consensus, and the decay of Party authority, that culminated in the collapse of Soviet power in 1991.

parliamentary democracy was still smaller. However, the brutality with which dissent was suppressed, and the intolerance of open disaffection, under Soviet rule were matched only in other one-party states, such as Italy, Germany, and Spain. Terror, moreover, was an explicit mechanism of authority: cf. Aleksandr Afinogenov's play *Strakh* (Fear, 1931), where an exemplary enlightened character of proletarian origins declares: 'We live in the era of magnificent fear' [*my zhivem v epokhu velikogo strakha*: the phrase would also translate as 'of great terror']. A. Afinogenov, *Izbrannoe v 2 tomakh* , (Moscow, 1997), 230.

[252] *Peasant and Proletarian: The Working Class of Moscow in the Late Nineteenth Century* (Leicester, 1979), 94. When Mikhail Kalinin asserted that Soviet collectivism was founded on 'mutual aid' ('On Communist Education: Speech at Meeting of Leading Party Workers of the City of Moscow, 2 October 1940', *On Communist Education*, 155), he was, at one level, completely accurate—but the 'mutual aid' concerned was of the self-serving variety described in Ch. 3, easily spilling over into bribery and corruption, rather than of the elevated Kropotkinian variety that was no doubt at the back of Kalinin's mind. (For further discussion of *blat* (favour networking/corruption) in the Soviet era, see A. Ledeneva, S. Lovell, and A. Rogachevsky (eds.), *Bribery and Blat in Russia* (London, 2000).)

CHAPTER FIVE

Negotiating Consumerism: The Dilemmas of Behaviour Literature, 1953–2000

A well-bred hostess never says: 'Let's have the cognac when Ivan Ivanovich gets here.' For her, all guests are equal, no matter what posts they hold.

(M. Khodakov, *How Not to Behave*, 1975)

In 1976, the Russian émigré writer Vera Dunham published an extraordinary and eloquent study of Soviet culture, *In Stalin's Time: Middle-Class Values in Soviet Fiction*. She argued that the Soviet system had lasted not because of its commitment to radical idealism, but because Soviet leaders had been able to manipulate popular opinion by crafting a new kind of social contract, one based, unlike Rousseau's, on the cultivation of materialist self-interest rather than the assurance of basic human rights. This social contract, which Dunham, in parodistic reference to Roosevelt's programme for combating the Great Depression, nicknamed 'The Big Deal', rested less on the leaders' abilities to supply the Soviet masses with their material wants, than on the constant repetition, in ideological statements and propaganda representations, of the idea that the regime was committed to providing these. Soon, in the 'bright future', Soviet citizens would have the radio sets, lipsticks, tailored suits, champagne, and ice-cream that were celebrated in Soviet advertising and popular magazines. This was a world where, as Dunham puts it, 'petunias in imaginary gardens or printed on imaginary fabrics acquired promissory significance'; that is to say, where the comfortably furnished apartments in Soviet plays and novels came to represent what the average citizen soon might have.[1] Not only 'fiction' as such, but more humdrum publications, such as articles and advertising in the popular illustrated magazine *Ogonek*, catalogued the new world just over the horizon, one in which Soviet citizens would have their own *Pobeda* (Victory) motor cars, walnut-clad radio sets, and bathroom cabinets full of cosmetics, as well as being able to eat their fill of ice-cream in spotless, shining cafés.

In an epilogue to her chronicle of *meshchanstvo*, Dunham argued that the

[1] V. Dunham, *In Stalin's Time: Middle-Class Values in Soviet Fiction* (Cambridge, 1976), 54.

post-Stalin era had seen an intensification of materialism, and an extension of its beneficiaries. It is worth quoting at length from this epilogue, since it not only encapsulates her argument, but also captures her forceful and sardonic character as a chronicler of Soviet history:

At some point the regime began to respond to the people's need for a better life, the dream which had been shaped long before by middleclass aspirations. Consumer goods became available and improved; their Excellencies the Refrigerator, the Washing machine, the Television set, the Record player, and, most coveted, the 'Volga', made their appearance. More and more people began to worship the goods in showrooms and strained to think them now, perhaps, within their reach. Cookbooks with tempting color plates, featuring jellied sturgeon festooned in radish rosettes and live daisies, were followed by chapters on kulturnost. Lessons in manners, featured in popular magazines and summarized in calendars, go well with recipes for partridges in sour cream. The total style of meshchanstvo's desires has been accepted so thoroughly that it has stimulated the beginnings of a counter culture. This is polarized among the young; between cynics who look for loopholes and shortcuts and, if frustrated, become aggressive; and, on the other hand, genuine dissidents.[2]

The model of Soviet history that this account sets up runs as follows. First, the regime creates 'a need for a better life', then it satisfies it. Ideology gives way to pragmatism, fantasies of consumption to a consumption-led system of industrial production. The transition is seamless, and materialism creates an unshakeably stable social consensus, a society where 'the goals at the top and at the bottom are the same; acquisitiveness reigns'.[3] So successful is the stereotyping that only young cynics 'become aggressive' when denied exactly what they want, and only 'genuine dissidents' (whom Dunham, like many other commentators, saw as the heirs of the real Russian intelligentsia) question the materialist desires fostered by officialdom.

Dunham's model was, of course, a product of its time, the Brezhnev years, or 'era of stagnation' (*period zastoya*). In 1976, no one could have imagined that the Soviet system had only another fifteen years of life; the central task was to rationalize its survival, rather than to explain its entropy. Hindsight has now imposed a greater sensitivity to the contradictions and difficulties in Soviet society, the factors that may be supposed to have caused collapse. As a matter of fact, even at the stage when Dunham's book was written, it was clear that shortages, not only of goods, but of basic foodstuffs, had become a major problem for the Soviet regime, and that aggression was a much more widespread symptom than she suggests. This was partly because Party policy proved more effective in 'creating' needs than in fulfilling them. Though successive Party congresses, especially from

---

[2] Ibid. 244.   [3] Ibid. 242.

the Twenty-Second Congress in 1961 onwards, iterated the intention to increase production of consumer goods, Soviet industry remained notoriously deficient both in terms of the quantity and of the quality of its output. The result, as everyone knows, was mushrooming of the 'shadow economy', and of a substantial black-market trade in Western goods and scarce Soviet items, plus a boom in corruption, recognized as early as 1962 by the enactment of new legislation increasing the penalties for receiving a bribe from two years to between ten and fifteen years, and for giving one from five to between eight and fifteen years.[4]

Yet to see conflict in the post-Stalin years in terms only of a distinction between 'ideology' and 'practice' would be as simplistic as to see it in terms of a conflict between 'bourgeois' and 'intellectual' values. The ideological objectives of the regime were in themselves problematic and ambiguous. At the most straightforward level, there was a contradiction between the regime's new commitment to consumer-led production, and its continuing fidelity to a system of centralized planning that privileged the so-called 'military-industrial complex' (*voenno-promyshlennyi kompleks*). But there was also a host of lesser contradictions, some of which were evident in the regulation of day-to-day living outside the workplace via advice literature. The confused signals sent out by this material seem to indicate that Dunham was profoundly wrong to see this society as one where 'lessons in manners, featured in popular magazines and summarized in calendars, [went] well with recipes for partridges in sour cream'.

To be sure, the Twenty-Second Congress had attempted to suggest harmony between communist ideology and material comfort. On the one hand it promised that 'for the first time in history, shortage and want will be ended once and for all [*likvidiruetsya maloobespechennost' lyudei*] . . . all layers of the population will have access to good, high-quality food . . . all the Soviet population will be able to obtain adequate supplies of consumer goods.'[5] On the other, it attempted to underline ideological rectitude, setting before the population the 'Moral Code of the Builder of Communism', which stressed that the collective virtues of the past were still to be retained. The Code is worth quoting in full, since it was to remain in force until the end of Soviet power, and was immensely important as background for the advice literature published in the three decades that followed its promulgation. The characteristics of 'The Builder of Communism' were:

---

[4] See *Ugolovnyi kodeks RSFSR* (Moscow, 1964), articles 173, 174, and 174[1]; and compare *The Penal Code of the Russian Socialist Federal Soviet Republic [1926]* (London, 1934).

[5] 'Rech' N. S. Khrushcheva na XXII s"ezde KPSS', Section III part 3, *Komsomol'skaya pravda*, 19 Oct. 1961, 5.

1. Devotion to the cause of Communism, love for the Socialist Motherland, and for the Socialist countries in general.
2. A commitment to conscientious labour on behalf of society. Whoever does not work does not eat.
3. A concern on the part of everyone for the preservation and proliferation of public property.
4. An elevated consciousness of social duty, an intolerance of any disruption of the interests of society as a whole.
5. Collectivism and mutual aid. All for one, one for all.
6. A humane relationship and mutual respect between people. Man is the friend, comrade and brother of his fellow man.
7. Honesty and fairness, moral purity, simplicity and modesty in one's social and personal life.
8. Mutual respect within the family, concern for the proper upbringing of children.
9. An intolerance of injustice, parasitism, dishonesty, careerism.
10. Friendship and brotherhood of all the peoples in the USSR, an intolerance of nationalism and racial hatred.
11. An intolerance of the enemies of Communism, of peace, and of the freedom of nations.
12. Brotherly solidarity with the peoples of all countries, and with all nations.[6]

Here 'the interests of society as a whole' were kept firmly to the forefront, and 'social' and 'personal' life, as in the 1930s and 1940s, were seen as mere subdivisions within the unitary whole of 'communist morality'. Yet if the Code and Khrushchev's promises are taken together, an incipient contradiction emerges. Soviet citizens were encouraged to expect 'adequate supplies of consumer goods', yet informed that they must cultivate 'simplicity and modesty' in their lives. If Socialist Realism had, in Boris Groys's words, 'market[ed] not things but ideology',[7] now 'things' were supposed to take a much larger place in Soviet culture. This destabilization of ascetism was to bedevil late Soviet 'lessons in manners' and advice on daily living, which expressed a high degree of confusion on all sorts of issues, ranging from the question of whether 'recipes for partridges in sour cream' really were suitable fare for the Soviet citizen, to what kinds of 'lessons in manners' should be given, or indeed whether concern with etiquette might represent an undesirable backsliding to the 'bourgeois past'. The central problems can be summarized thus. How was universal plenty (*obespechennost'*, the opposite of 'shortage and want', *maloobespechennost'*), to be guaranteed while retaining the moral elevation and material disinterest that was supposedly traditional in Soviet society? How could a greater

---

[6] 'Programma KPSS' section V part 1, *KP* 2 Aug. 1961, 2.

[7] B. Groys, *The Total Art of Stalinism: Avant-Garde, Aesthetic Dictatorship, and Beyond*, trans. C. Rougle (Princeton, 1992), 11.

degree of autonomy be allowed to individual citizens while still leaving the collective ideal undamaged?[8] And how, in a culture where advice literature increasingly, and with growing explicitness, drew on non-Soviet models, was even vestigial allegiance to the original model of the 'new man and woman', characterized by his or her unique selflessness, 'Soviet patriotism', to be preserved? And this is leaving aside a difficulty that could not be addressed directly in print. The most coherent civilizing campaigns of the past—those of the late eighteenth century, or of the first decades of Soviet rule—had depended upon a close association of political authority and civiliing power. Catherine II, Lenin, and Stalin were all at some level the embodiments of the dominant behaviour ideologies of the day. Khrushchev, on the other hand, described by an eyewitness as 'rumbustious, impetuous, free-wheeling',[9] and Brezhnev, his successor, themselves manifested the contradictions of the new behaviour ethos. In a culture where superficial impressions were crucial (given the dearth of factual information about Soviet leaders' personalities), their spherical silhouettes, awkward gestures, provincial accents and—in Khrushchev's case—deliberate violations of propriety made them into something approaching the anti-type of 'cultured behaviour'; moreover, their taste for the luxurious perks of office made official attacks on the deadly sin of *meshchanstvo* seem more than a little hypocritical.

Dunham's account, then, needs taking to task on the grounds of its failure to record conflict within Soviet ideology and official policy; it also badly needs historicizing. The sweeping impressionism of *In Stalin's Time* (which adds immensely to the book's imaginative force) obscures intricate delineation of detail. For a start, the idea that the accommodation of consumerism 'just happened' will not stand up: the fact is that the easing of top-down repression in 1956 allowed officials to pay greater attention to the enormous number of complaints made by ordinary people about the often appalling conditions in which they were forced to live. A file of materials forwarded by the editors of *Komsomol'skaya pravda* to the Komsomol Central Committee in 1956, for example, revealed deep dissatisfaction with living conditions in important industrial regions, including the Donbass and the Soviet Far East. A miner from the Stalinskaya province reported that it was not uncommon to wait twenty minutes for a lift to the coal-face or the surface, that there was often no water to wash with after work, so that people's bed-linen became black

[8] Especially in the early 1960s, the Stalinist view of collectivism was occasionally subjected to direct criticism: 'The reasons behind the widely recognized timidity and lack of initiative [in Soviet citizens] obviously lie in the recent past, when people brought themselves to believe that they were mere cogs in a vast mechanism: "The bosses'll come, the bosses'll fix it!"' (T. Gromova, 'Kak vy provodite svobodnoe vremya?', *KP* 27 Mar. 1963, 2).

[9] William Hayter, *The Kremlin and the Embassy* (London, 1966), 107.

with dust, and that the food in the buffet was disgusting, the queues huge, and the staff dishonest. Reporting similar conditions in the Kamenskaya province, another worker added: 'A cultured worker has nowhere to relax here. There are no chess-sets in the club, no dominos, no newspapers.' For her part, a woman worker at Bratsk Hydro-Electric Power Station reported that no warm clothes were supplied even at times of extreme cold, while the workers spent their leisure time drinking (females as well as males), 'using foul language . . . and smoking . . .'. Promiscuity was rife: 'It's unbearably dreary here [*zdes' uzhasnaya skuka*]. The girls are treated like dirt. And many of them don't value themselves at all.'[10]

Even the surface of history is represented in Dunham's account only partially. It would be hard to tell by reading *In Stalin's Time* just how much of a watershed the Khrushchev era represented not only in terms of proliferating behaviour models, but even in terms of the burgeoning production of advice literature. Already in 1954, the union catalogue of Soviet new book titles, *Ezhegodnik knigi*, records a marked increase in the production of treatises dealing with behaviour (most particularly the regulation of family life). Khrushchev's de-Stalinizing speech at the Twentieth Party Congress of 1956 was followed by a marked rise not only in the number of titles of books in this area, but also in the numbers of titles of books on household management (see Appendix 5 Table 1). These figures reveal very different priorities from those of the Soviet regime during its first three and a half decades. During the 1920s and 1930s, hygiene and self-education had been the most important categories; though some books on house management were published in the late 1920s, the genre rapidly fell out of favour again, while the only titles devoted to behaviour that got published were those relating to 'communist education' (*kommunisticheskoe vospitanie*) and upbringing more generally.

Apart from an expansion of titles relating to private life, the table reveals interesting differences between the publishing profiles of the two categories of advice literature that I have identified, household manuals and behaviour books. In the very first years of the Khrushchev regime, the government gave priority to household manuals, perhaps because this genre had been represented by scattered examples in the Stalinist era too, notably *The Book of Tasty and Nutritious Food* (1939). Reprinted in 1953, the book was reissued in full and abridged editions almost annually thereafter, and in far larger editions than during the Stalin years (running to hundreds, rather than tens, of thousands).[11]

[10] See the untitled overview of readers' letters to *KP*, 4 Dec. 1956, by D. Gorynov, TsKhDMO f. 1 op. 32 delo 821 l. 176, l. 178.

[11] On *Kniga o vkusnoi i zdorovoi pishche* see Ch. 4; on the history of the manual in the post-Stalin era, also G. P. Piretto, 'Gryaznoe i vonyuchee kukhonnoe prostranstvo v Peterburge-Leningrade', *Europa Orientalis* 2 (1997), 399–428.

But if household manuals dominated in 1953, 1954 manifested a rash of behaviour books. And, though the production of household manuals reached its peak a year earlier than that of behaviour books, in 1960 rather than 1961, numbers of such titles declined quite sharply thereafter. This might seem on the face of it odd, given the Party's commitment, at the Twenty-Second Congress, to encouraging the production of consumer goods, a step that had considerable implications for the Soviet material culture that is modelled in household manuals. However, on closer scrutiny, a degree of logic emerges. Many of the pre-1961 titles in the 'domestic manuals' category were collections of 'handy hints': that is, they represented a 'make do and mend' ethos which depended on stretching the capacities of old possessions and traditional materials, rather than exploring the possibilities of new ones.[12]

In the late 1970s, the numbers of home management books started to rise again, with most of the rise being attributable to an increase in the number of cookbook titles published (including not only reprints of the classic *Book of Tasty and Nutritious Food*, but also many specialist titles on the preparation of different foods). (See Appendix 5 Table 2.) At this point, the logic of publishing policy becomes more elusive. Some of the titles were certainly aimed at ameliorating food shortages by propagandizing foodstuffs not in short supply, such as fish and tinned goods (*konserry*), so that householders might be induced into accepting these as substitutes for scarce items, such as fresh meat. In the 1970s, for example, *Gifts of the Ocean* (*Dary okeana*, Kaliningrad, 1975), '[attempted] to convert the reader to using a fish paste made from shellfish which has been available for many years now, but has failed to catch the people's imagination'. However, other titles did not have such a clear practical rationale: a book on vegetables published in Moscow in 1978 included 'recipes for asparagus and artichokes, which most Russians today have never even seen, let alone tasted or prepared'.[13] Material of this kind fulfilled the time-honoured Soviet tradition of representing visions of the elegant life as a way of allowing the population an escape in fantasy from deprivation. But the appearance of gastronomic titles containing recipes for meals so elaborate they could only have been

[12] See e.g. some sections of *Domovodstvo* (see below); *Kniga poleznykh sovetov* (1958); Fedorova, *300 poleznykh sovetov po domovodstvu* (1958); *Bytovye sovety* (1958); *Sovety po domovodstvu* (1959): print-run 100,000; *Poleznye sovety* (1959: print-run 500,000) (The catalogue of the Russian National Library in St Petersburg lists twenty-five books under the title *Poleznye sovety* alone). Such books appear in smaller numbers after 1961; instead there is a concentration on substantial publications, such as *Kratkaya entsiklopediya domashnego khozyaistvo* (first edn. 1959, repri. 1962 and 1966), which provide detailed guidance on the nature and functions of the new consumer durables.

[13] See Pamela Davidson, 'Russia', in Jane Grigson, *The Observer Guide to European Cookery* (London, 1983), 228.

served on high days and holidays was now also meant to underline the ritual significance of eating, and in particular of family eating, in an effort to consolidate family relations, which were felt to be under threat from atomization because of high divorce rates,[14] The rehabilitation of culinary enthusiasms can also be seen as part of a wide-ranging movement to propagandize secular festivals and rites of passage that had been initiated by Khrushchev, and continued by Brezhnev, and which was intended to assault the continuing authority of organized religion.[15] Conversely, once Orthodox Christianity began to become more acceptable, in the late Soviet period, some cookbooks reflected this too: a collection of recipes from Elena Molokhovets's *Gift to Young Housewives*, published in 1989, consisted of fast day and Easter dishes.[16] But there are some cookbook titles so bizarre as to elude convenient rationalization: the first prize should perhaps be awarded to a 1985 translation into Armenian of a book on classic Irish cooking.[17]

Apart from numbers of titles, another factor that illustrates the priority that the Soviet authorities were giving advice manuals from the late 1950s is the very high print-runs of many titles (all fixed by centralized planning). For example, re-editions of *The Book of Tasty and Nutritious Food* ran to a million copies, while books of 'handy hints' (*poleznye sovety*) had runs of up to half a million.[18] Runs of 100,000 plus were also common for etiquette manuals: A. Dorokhov's *It Does Matter!* (1961) had a run of 350,000; the anonymous *Aesthetics of Behaviour* one of 300,000, and B. V. Busheleva's *Let's Have A Little Talk about Good Breeding* one of 200,000.[19]

Apart from the fact that all this activity was generated by a publishing industry which remained under rigid state control until the late 1980s,[20] there were other notable similarities between the context in which these new guides to etiquette and daily life were produced and that of the Stalinist *kul'turnost'* campaign. A second industrialization drive had brought

[14] So much is suggested, for instance, by the publication of a book specifically entitled *The Family at the Dinner Table* in 1960. (Grigor'ev and Semenova, *Sem'ya za obedennym stolom*: the publication had a print-run of 200,000.)

[15] See e.g. *Za novye obryady, obychai, traditsii* (Perm' 1964); Emel'yanova, *Pervyi v strane* (1964) on the *dvorets brakosochetaniya* has a lengthy description of ritual that was obviously supposed to be exhortatory (i.e. to get couples to come along and take part).

[16] See Joyce Toomre (trans. and ed.), *Classic Russian Cooking: Elena Molokhovets' A Gift to Young Housewives* (Bloomington, Ind., 1992), 4. This continued in the post-Soviet period: KL 1995 lists *Semeinaya postnaya kukhnya: V pomoshch' pravoslavnoi khozyaike* (Obninsk, 1995). Note also *Z. M. Evenshtein, Evreiskaya kukhnya: Kulinariya, ratsional'nost', dietetika* (St Petersburg, 1995).

[17] *D. L. Tomson [sic], Irlandskaya traditsionnaya kukhnya* (Erevan, 1985). See *EK*, 1985.

[18] See e.g. *Poleznye sovety* (1959).

[19] Dorokhov, *Eto ne melochi!* (1961); *Estetika povedeniya* (1963); Busheleva *Pogovorim o vospitannosti* (1980).

[20] See Gregory Walker, *Soviet Book Publishing Policy* (Cambridge, 1978): see esp. pp. 20–2.

a wave of new immigrants to Russian cities, many of whom, the so-called *limitchiki*, had been granted the right to reside only in grim satellite developments outside the official borders of the major cities.[21] As in the Stalin era, the regime attempted to cope with the practical consequences of social upheaval by offering hortatory advice on morality and conduct, a cheaper and quicker solution for the short term than improving living conditions or raising wages. At the same time, the needs of the Soviet middle class were borne in mind; some publications, such as *The Culture of the Apartment Interior*, a 1966 collection of essays,[22] represented handsome modernist furniture ensembles that could have been within the reach only of the most privileged members of society (and indeed the model flats illustrated were all owned by architects, writers, and painters).

But if the overall context of this *kul'turnost'* campaign was roughly similar to that of its Stalinist predecessor, it is fair to say that the sheer size of the post-1953 torrent of publications, compared with the much smaller flow of books and brochures issuing in the 1930s and 1940s, was a major difference. Where the Stalinist *kul'turnost'* campaign—though supported by propaganda in the Soviet media—had been heavily dependent on *agitatsiya*, and particularly on the efforts made by groups such as the *obshchestvennitsy*, the Khrushchev and Brezhnev eras placed a heavier emphasis on the printed word (and later, began to exploit the new medium of television). This signalled a new emphasis on independent acquisition of knowledge, on self-help, rather than on education by collective means.

The expansion of advice provision also went with an increasing complexity of information. Specialist books and brochures once again challenged magazines, so that the notion of '*homo sovieticus* as complete package' came under threat, and more and more areas of knowledge became requisite for the new Soviet citizen. By the late 1950s, the priorities of the second wave of *kul'turnost'*, 'cultured behaviour', were less easy to sort out than the first wave's had been. The two areas targeted in the 1920s, 1930s, and 1940s were hygiene and self-education; etiquette books had disappeared as a genre after the nationalization of the publishing industry in 1918. While Soviet literature and popular magazines did begin, in the mid-

---

[21] Between 1939 and 1959, the rural population of the USSR declined from 66 per cent to 52 per cent of the total population; between 1959 and 1970 it declined from 52 per cent to 44 per cent, and between 1970 and 1980 to 38 per cent. (See S. Fitzpatrick, *Stalin's Peasants: Resistance and Survival in the Russian Village After Collectivization* (New York, 1994), 319.) This equates to a 20 per cent drop over twenty years between 1939 and 1959, and a 30 per cent drop over the following two decades. Even without correcting for wartime losses, it is clear that out-migration rose steeply after 1959. On the *limitchiki*, see D. Filtzer, *Soviet Workers Under Stalinization: The Consolidation of the Modern System of Production Relations, 1953–1964* (Cambridge, 1992), 29–30.

[22] *Kul'tura zhilogo inter'ra* (1966).

1930s, to offer their readers a supply of material about domestic regulation and good behaviour, care was taken to emphasize the importance of the public sphere over the private sphere; Soviet citizens were constantly reminded of the need for self-restraint (*skromnost'*, or modesty) in their ambitions, and attacks on those who manifested their materialism too obviously were common in the press and in literary satire. If the 'cultured person' possessed sheets, a lampshade, and a bookcase, he or she most emphatically was not the proud owner of an angora cat, and concerned him or herself little about issues such as where to put the stress in a word or which fork to eat with.[23]

From the mid-1950s, on the other hand, according to the brochures and guides on offer, the 'new Soviet man or woman' was supposed to be distinguished not only by an informed familiarity with electrical goods and household chemicals, but by a developed taste in curtains and wallpaper, an eye for elegant dress, good table manners, and refined speech.[24] The most inclusive publication, the *Concise Encyclopedia of Home Economy*, was an exhaustive alphabetical inventory of Soviet material culture, from *abazhur* (lampshade) through *billiard* to *oboi* (wallpaper) and onwards. Articles covered not only the new accoutrements of domestic life, but also social phenomena from *alimenty* (alimony) to *turizm* (a term that now referred to the passive consumption of attractive cityscapes as well as to energetic hiking about in the wild), and beyond. Between the first edition in 1959, and the second in 1962, 272 new articles were added; the decoration of the 'cultured home', with its patterned wallpapers, pot plants, ornaments, showpiece radio sets, rugs, and even pedigree cat (an article on cat breeds was included in volume 1 of the second edition) was becoming increasingly elaborate.[25] To be sure, some of the new Soviet 'ideal home's' acquisitions were labour-saving devices, 'convenient refrigerators, washing-machines, different sorts of electric and gas appliance that make many domestic tasks significantly easier'.[26] This was in tune with Khrushchev's commitment, at the 1956 Party Congress, to lightening women's domestic

---

[23] See Ch. 4 of the present study.

[24] A single brochure on household chemicals appeared as early as 1951 (see *EK* for that year), but the genre became firmly established in the mid-1950s (e.g. *P. E. Kazaryan, *Khimiya v bytu*, , was reprinted four times between 1955 and 1957: see *EK* 1955, 1956, 1957). Publications on electrical appliances included *Elektricheskie bytovye pribory* (Moscow, 1955); *Elektropribory v bytu* (Moscow, 1956) (see *EK* 1955, 1956). The late 1960s saw the birth of a specialist advice literature encouraging readers to purchase books and to treat these as a commodity (they should be kept in handsome glass-fronted bookcases, etc.). See e.g. Osipov, *Kniga v vashem dome* (1967).

[25] For a similar argument, based on a comparison of two reference books of consumer goods, the *Tovarnaya entsiklopediya* of 1927 and the *Tovarnyi slovar'* of 1956–61, see J. Hessler, 'Cultured Trade: The Stalinist Turn Towards Consumption', in S. Fitzpatrick (ed.), *Stalinism: New Directions* (London, 2000), 182–3.

[26] Quoted from *Kratkaya entsiklopediya domashnego khozyaistva* (1962), i. 8.

ВНИМАТЕЛЬНЫЕ ТЕЛЕЗРИТЕЛИ.
Фотолюбитель С. Григорьяни.
Ленинград.

FIG. 17. The Attentive Viewers. Amateur photograph, *Ogonek,* 1960. The image demonstrates
the rehabilitation of pet animals in the post-Stalin
era.

burden so that their representation in prestigious forms of employment
could be improved.[27] But the liberation of women from housework was by
no means the only message; indeed, this message was largely undercut by

[27] See Mary Buckley, *Women and Ideology in the Soviet Union* (Hemel Hempstead, 1989),
140–5. The 1961 edition of *Kniga o vkusnoi i zdorovoi pishche,* 410 anticipates that the streamlining
of housework will allow women to take a greater share in *obshchestvennyi trud* (socially useful
work).

an emphasis on acquisitions that could only add to the burden of domestic existence (such as carpets and display cabinets requiring dusting, or pets needing to be fed, watered, and kept clean).

Not only housekeeping manuals, but also guides to behaviour were becoming increasingly prolix. The snappy lists of books to read or facts to learn with which 1930s magazines had furnished their readers were replaced by wide-ranging quizzes drawing on all manner of esoteric information. In a 'Viktorina' run by *Ogonek* during 1967, for example, readers were asked to identify hairstyles that would have been worn in Ancient Greece and in medieval Europe, to explain the physiology of yawning, to say which synthetic fabric was most like the human skin, and to state how many centimetres longer a giraffe's forelegs were than its hind legs.[28] But above all, the scanty hints on the need for 'sensitivity' and 'honesty' were replaced by expansive advice on 'etiquette for every occasion'. The books all contained sections on table manners, receiving guests and paying visits, conduct in public transport, at the theatre, and in reading rooms, and some also had advice on important rites of passage (weddings and funerals). Hence, though it was a cliché among etiquette writers to state that the mere externals of behaviour were less important than the inner spirit of conduct, in practice this formulation rang rather hollow. And, bearing in mind the fact that possessions such as pedigree cats had been considered, in the 1920s and 1930s, infallible indicators of their possessors' unculturedness and vulgarity, a degree of confusion about what possessions one might safely own was inevitable. Nor was the question of the standards of taste that should apply in popular responses to the arts any easier. Facile condemnations of 'bourgeois abstractionism' might persist, but mass readers were also informed that they had only themselves to blame if they were alienated by the complex modernist poetry of Velimir Khlebnikov, or pre-Columbian Mexican sculpture. 'In order to have a more profound understanding of the world of art and beauty, it is essential to attend concerts and plays as often as possible, to read as widely as possible and to compare the impressions gained from different art works.'[29] A self-improving worker was now in a quite different world from that of *Ogonek* in the 1930s or 1940s.

At the same time, continuity with the past was also underlined in various ways. Popular women's magazines, such as *Rabotnitsa* and *Krest'yanka*, and

[28] *Ogonek* 10 (1967), 18–19, 13 (1967), 22–3 (the giraffe question was sent in by a reader). For comparison's sake, in issue 10, 18–19, the magazine printed some questions from 1928, when readers had been asked where the banners of the Parisian communards were preserved and what the plural of the word *dno* was.

[29] Razumnyi, *O khoroshem khudozhestvennom vkuse*, 52. Confusion is evident too in Razumnyi's argument that great art requires effort to be understood, but is also immediately comprehensible (see pp. 20–1).

calendars aimed at a mass market, continued to emphasize production, and heroic deeds of the Soviet past, and to dole out leaden abstractions about 'honesty' and 'fairness', while also offering handy hints on home care, sewing, and health.[30] And alongside the new genres, publications on health and hygiene went on occupying an important niche in the Soviet publishing market. As Appendix 5 Table 3 indicates, numbers of titles remained roughly similar to the levels recorded in the 1930s and 1940s, with women's health and 'the protection of maternity and childhood' still prominent areas of concern. At a detailed level, however, there was a lessening of the Stalinist emphasis on control of infectious disease, and a still greater stress than before on prophylactic medicine, as was perfectly consistent with the propagandization of the private responsibility of citizens for their behaviour that was evident in advice-book publishing generally.

The ramifications of the new ethos can be clearly seen in one of the most significant titles of the post-Stalin era, *House Management*, whose first edition in 1957 was a landmark of advice-book publishing. By 1965, this monumental book (over 1,000 pages) had already gone into four editions; material from it was also published in abridged adaptations by provincial presses, sometimes with explicit reference in their introductions to the insatiable demand for the more comprehensive original.[31]

House Management, despite its unimaginative title, was the nearest Soviet equivalent to Elena Molokhovets's *A Gift to Young Housewives* (1861), the most famous pre-revolutionary guide to home economy. In other words, it was an encyclopedically inclusive manual in which the concept of 'house-keeping' was interpreted in the broadest sense, so that the book became, in effect, a guide to Soviet private life in all its diverse aspects. The book's thirteen sections embraced not only domestic hygiene, cooking and preserving, sewing, household repairs, the care of houseplants, animal husbandry and gardening for the allotment holder, but also childcare, the upbringing of children, etiquette, hygiene for women, and skin care.

Much of the material provided in *House Management* was 'Soviet' only in terms of its omissions. The recipes were for straightforward family food (partridges in cream emphatically did not figure!), and there were no instructions on how to deal with servants (though there could have been: what were still euphemistically known as *domrabotnitsy*, 'house workers', were beginning to disappear from Soviet families in the 1960s, but the second edition of the *Concise Encyclopedia of Home Economy* contained information for employers on the legal regulation of their profession).

---

[30] See e.g. *Kalendar' dlya zhenshchin na 1982 god* (this publication had a print-run of 15 million).
[31] *Domovodstvo* (1957): this edn. had a print-run of 800,000. The 2nd edn. (Moscow, 1965) had risen to a million copies. For an example of a shortened spin-off edn., see e.g. *Poleznye sovety* (Yuzhnosakhalinsk, 1960).

Generally, though, what was most striking was the resemblance between the advice provided here and the topoi of post-Enlightenment conduct literature. On hygiene, for example, the reader was told that everything boiled down to cleanliness, sleep, fresh air, and diet (though little detailed advice was given on the last). On 'elevated culture' (*vysokaya kul'tura*), he or she was reminded of the need to 'observe punctuality and exactitude [*tochnost' i akkuratnost'*]', to take care to dress well and to keep one's body and underwear clean, and one's clothes and shoes tidy, as well as to manifest self-control and reliability [*postoyannost'*].[32] A daily routine was advised, as was a quick check on one's appearance before leaving the house. Conspicuous behaviour of all kinds (staring, pushing, talking or laughing too loudly, wearing striking clothes, making conversation about personal problems, appearing nervous or irritable, using 'crude words') was held to be a sign of a person's 'low culture'.[33]

There were only two specifically Soviet touches in all this, the first of which was the preference for the term *vysokaya kul'tura* over *khoroshii ton*, the pre-revolutionary term of approbation for good behaviour, with *nizkaya kul'tura* rather than *durnoi ton*, *poshlost'*, or *vulgarnost'* as its opposites.[34] The second, and far more important, Soviet element was the emphasis on the need for the collective regulation of good behaviour:

An indifferent attitude to the disrupters of public order is quite impermissible. It is the duty of every Soviet person to struggle with those who disrupt the law. The slogan 'I'm all right, Jack' [*moya khata s krayu*] expresses a form of morality that acts as a cover for cowardice and petit-bourgeois smugness [*obyvatel'shchina*].[35]

In the introduction to her study of Russian peasant culture, Christine Worobec pointed to this monitoring of others' public behaviour as a survival of Russian peasant culture: 'When you . . . have been rudely upbraided by a passing *baba* for not wearing proper clothing, you know

[32] *Domovodstvo*, 87. For a similar spread of information, see the house management page started by *Ogonek* in 1960, 'Zhenshchiny, eto dlya vas!' (in nos. 24, 26, 27, 29). The introductory article in 24, p. 32 promised advice to the housewife from experts: 'They will give you hints about how to make your home cosier, your food tastier, your child healthier and better brought up, oh, and how to make yourself more attractive too. You will find out how concerned for your welfare industries and trading organizations are, and how they do all they can to make housework and caring for your family simpler and easier for you.' However, in 1961 the page more or less petered out, appearing rarely (e.g. in no. 35), and only in the form of a spread of fashion photographs.

[33] *Domovodstvo*, 88–9.

[34] Though the term *khoroshii ton* was occasionally invoked directly during the post-Stalin era, as in the wonderfully tautologous title of a brochure listed by *EK* 1958, *O manerakh khoroshego tona* [The Manners of Bon Ton] (Moscow, 1958), it did not come back into regular usage till the late 1980s. The 17-vol. Academy of Sciences dictionary (*Slovar' sovremennogo yazyka*) labels *moveton* as 'obsolete' and as a term characteristic of 'aristocratic and bourgeois society'.

[35] *Domovodstvo*, 88–9.

peasant Russia is very much alive today.'[36] However, behaviour books of the Khrushchev era indicate that such vigilantism should not be seen simply as an organic residue of traditional peasant custom, but also as a quality that was recognized, and fostered, by official ideology. The war on *bezrazlichie* (indifference) can be seen as a milder and less threatening version of the campaign to inculcate *bditel'nost'* (watchfulness) carried out by the Stalinist press during the 1930s and 1940s.[37]

If one looks beyond official ideology, however, there is plenty of evidence that exhortations to others to mend their ways already made at least some intellectuals uncomfortable by the early 1960s, in other words, not long after *House Management* was first published. In their collaborative memoir of Moscow life in the post-Stalin years, *We Lived in Moscow*, Raisa Orlova and Lev Kopelev recalled that Kopelev took issue with Evgeniya Ginzburg when she upbraided some guests who had chosen to play cards, rather than making conversation or engaging in some other such civilized pursuit, at a party. Kopelev felt that Ginzburg's frankness was overly dictatorial, a 'Bolshevik' imposition of her tastes on others. Her riposte—that the Bolsheviks were not wrong about everything—neatly encapsulated the clash between different points of view, the interventionist and the non-interventionist (as between the different generations espousing these perspectives).[38]

A comparable clash is evident in a discussion that took place in the early 1960s between two writers, the poet and *Novyi Mir* editor Aleksandr Tvardovsky, and the novelist Yury Trifonov, about how to approach a neighbour who was plaguing their dacha settlement by playing his radio noisily.

That summer, the first we spent at Pakhra, we were delighted with everything: the forest, the fresh air, the path to the river, the river itself, the girl delivering milk on her bicycle. The only thing that spoiled everything was the radio. The sounds came floating over from the lot next to us. The sounds of the radio voices and music rending the still air were torture. I spent many days in agony, quite unable to work. To have approached Aleksandr Trifonovych and asked him to turn his

[36] C. Worobec, *Peasant Culture: Family and Community in the Post-Emancipation Period* (Princeton, 1991), 14–15. In the same way, it would be possible to see the sort of moral surveillance to be found in British towns during the 1950s and early 1960s (as manifested in a neighbour of my mother's who telephoned in 1963 to complain that my sister and I—then aged 3 and eighteen months—were disporting themselves naked on the lawn in company with two boys of the same age) as a hangover from the bossy vigilance encouraged during the Second World War, not just as a manifestation of age-old British puritanism.

[37] On *bditel'nost'*, see Ch. 4 above; on the propaganda for surveillance in the post-Stalinist era, see Oleg Khakhordin, *The Collective and the Individual in Russia: A Study of Practices* (Berkeley, 1999), ch. 3. However, in mounting the case that 'the disciplinary grid became faultless and ubiquitous' in the 1960s (ibid. 303), Khakhordin ignores the substantial evidence of unease about the surveillance process manifested at the time (see my discussion below).

[38] R. Orlova and L. Kopelev, *My zhili v Moskve* (Ann Arbor, 1986?), 326.

radio down would, I thought, have been dreadfully tactless. Finally, though, I could stand it no longer, and one morning when the radio started playing and at the same time I heard the familiar sound of branches crunching, I went up to the corner of the fence, greeted him, and said:

'Aleksandr Trifonovych, that wouldn't be your radio playing, by any chance?'

'No,' he replied; he seemed embarrassed even to be asked. 'We never have the radio playing. We never even switch it on.'

It turned out that the radio was playing on a plot somewhere beyond the Tvardovskys. Aleksandr Trifonovych was even more irritated by it than I was. So why not ask those people to turn it down?

He shrugged.

'How can I ask? I don't know them. And it's kind of awkward—we're all adults, after all...'[39]

Trifonov's shyness in approaching his neighbour was partly derived from hierarchical promptings (though a respectable writer, he was not a powerful functionary in the way that Tvardovsky was). But Tvardovsky's own hesitancy cannot be explained away by considerations of this kind; he could certainly have made use of his own authority had he chosen to. Even for some of those in the Soviet elite, the old, collective Soviet tradition of 'watchfully' commenting upon, which is to say, homiletically denouncing, others' behaviour, and the new 'politeness and delicacy', which demanded that faults be passed over in silence, could sometimes come into conflict.

Tvardovsky and Trifonov's dilemma made itself felt in at least one normative source as well. In the mid-1980s, Academician Dmitry Sergeevich Likhachev, a cultural historian of immense authority, made an unexpected, but highly significant, excursion into the field of advice literature. His *Letters on Goodness and Beauty* was composed as a series of epistles to 'young people' (the colophon of the publisher, Detskaya literatura, said that it was aimed at 'schoolchildren in the middle and senior years' (*srednii i starshii shkol'nyi vozrast*, i.e. 12–18-year-olds). The book combined a number of advice manuals in one. Instructions on the appreciation of art, landscape and literature (particularly those of a broadly defined Russia, including 'our native Caucasus'), were combined with strictures on morality (and especially on the family as a 'circle of moral settlement' (*krug nravstvennoi osedlosti*).[40] Much advice on manners in a more straightforward sense was also given, and here Likhachev's book represented an entirely conventional, though particularly carefully argued, statement of positive and negatives: for example, swearing was as usual not permissible, but here the argument was not so much that it was offensive, as

---

[39] Yu. Trifonov, 'Zapiski soseda', *Kak slovo nashe otzovetsya* (Moscow, 1985), 163–4.

[40] Likhachev, *Pis'ma o dobrom i prekrasnom*, Epistle 17. (Likhachev's book reached a second edition in 1995).

that it infringed the personal dignity of the speaker. But the most crucial comments on the ethics of behaviour came in two sections entitled 'A person should behave like a member of the intelligentsia' (*Chelovek dolzhen byt' intelligenten*), and 'On being well bred' (*O vospitannosti*). The latter section set out, in a sentence emphasized by being placed in its own short paragraph, the central maxim of good behaviour: 'At the foundation of all good manners is one concern—a concern that people should not intrude on each other, that everyone should feel comfortable with everyone else.'[41]

The advice given by Likhachev, and the attitudes that it reflected, became more and more important as *intelligentnost'*, behaving like a member of the intelligentsia (a term that had gone under wraps since 1917), started to rise in the esteem of Soviet society. Numerous sources point to the progressive abandonment, during the Brezhnev years, of the symbolic dominance that the 'proletariat' had still enjoyed, in however vestigial a sense, during the Khrushchev era. The term *plebei* (plebeian), for example, began to be used quite widely in unofficial discourse in order to signify a member of the Soviet working classes.[42] Increasingly, too, Soviet citizens took pride in their own, or their friends', descent from the 'old' (i.e. pre-Soviet) intelligentsia: Kopelev and Orlova, for example, attributed Andrei Sakharov's extraordinary probity to his 'old intelligentsia' background, while none other than Boris Yeltsin was to pay tribute to the ancestry of his son-in-law, 'a pilot. He comes from a family with traditions, with some very fine manners, and these best qualities were passed on to Valera.'[43] For his part, despite insisting that intelligentsia values were available to everybody, Likhachev very definitely addressed himself to readers outside the mainstream of Soviet culture, a fact indicated not only by the preference for the adjective 'Russian' over 'Soviet', but also by the fact that the cultural institutions which he named as crucial arenas for the display of refinement in *Letters on Goodness and Beauty* were elite ones: concert halls, art galleries, and museums, rather than cinemas and theatres.

The direct articulation of intelligentsia non-interventionist values was not merely an underground or marginal tendency in the post-Stalin years: it can also be found in mainstream sources going back to the 1960s. For

[41] Likhachev, *Pis'ma o dobrom i prekrasnom*, 33.

[42] For example, 'plebei' is used in this sense in Ol'ga Novikova's story, 'Strogaya dama'; and in Dmitry Savitsky's novel *Niotkuda s lyubov'yu* (1978), the narrator and a friend plan to issue a Soviet girlie magazine under the punning title *Plebei* (from *Playboy*).

[43] Kopelev and Orlova, *My zhili v Moskve*, 390: B. Yeltsin, *The Struggle for Russia*, trans. Catherine A. Fitzpatrick (New York, 1994), 10. A less exotic example is the Pushkinist Dmitry Blagoi's emphasis, in his autobiography, on his gentry origins and connections with the Blagovo family (see E. Ya. Brainina and A. N. Dmitrieva (eds.), *Sovetskie pisateli: avtobiografii*, iii (Moscow, 1966), 85).

example, *Komsomol'skaya pravda*, while campaigning regularly against 'social indifference' and *obyvatel'shchina* (petit-bourgeois indifference to things of the mind) where it purported to encounter these in Soviet society, at the same time frequently protested against busy-bodying on the part of officials and of ordinary members of the Soviet population. In October 1961, the paper took up the case of V. Gogin, whose poetry reading in Tambov had been disrupted by members of the local Komsomol committee, and attributed the incident to the lack of culture prevalent in this provincial outpost.[44] Three years later, the paper reported on a number of cases where citizens had taken the law into their own hands. The first was when a woman had reported another to the police for alleged fraud in a trolleybus (putting three kopecks instead of four into the honesty box when she bought a ticket). The second was when a police investigator had treated some schoolgirls to a tirade because they had made a bonfire in a courtyard, and the third, when local residents had stopped a man from fishing. In each case, the paper expressed a view *against* those who had interfered. What is more, the article included an astonishing outburst of sarcastic 'anti-advice' directed at such vigilance: 'Dear reader, surely you agree that the stranger just coming towards you is bound to be a forger of banknotes? No? . . . Well, aren't you rather too trusting? Keep your eyes well open. It can't possibly be the case that a person isn't a scoundrel.' The conclusion was that 'Petit-bourgeois suspicion continues to stalk our streets. Hard-heartedness against one's fellow man intoxicates the unwary; it is searching for official forms of expression [*organizatsionnykh form*] . . .'. Referring to the phrasing of the Moral Code of the Builder of Communism, it concluded, 'Petit-bourgeois suspicion is quite incompatible with the principle: "Man is the friend, comrade and brother of his fellow man."'[45]

The division between these two interpretations—dutiful vigilance versus 'petit-bourgeois suspicion'—derives ultimately from the regime's uncertainties about how best to maintain conformity in a society where individual family housing was now the goal, and, increasingly, the reality.[46] The conflict between a stern emphasis on duty to the collective

[44] See L. Arkhipova, 'Dvesti "shalopaev" slushayut stikhi', *KP*, 1 Oct.1961, 2. Arkhipova's article attracted a furious response on the part of the officials involved, who asserted they had no prejudice against poetry as such ('we are not against . . . entertaining and well-organized forms of leisure activity'), but that the audience and poet had desecrated 'with spittle and cigarette-ends' a monument to the partisan heroine Zoya Kosmodem'yanskaya ('which, every spring, young and old in our town decorate with the first living flowers'). See TsKhDMO f. 1 op. 32 delo 1047 l. 148.

[45] Leonid Likhodeev, 'Kak byt' s khoroshimi lyud'mi?' *KP*, 12 Oct. 1964, 4.

[46] The proportion of *tipovye doma*, blocks of 'discrete living cells' as opposed to 'unpartitioned barracks', rose from 20 per cent of new buildings in 1954 to 85 per cent in 1958 and 98 per cent in 1962. Although 20 per cent of the Moscow population were still living in communal

and a 'live and let live' attitude was ubiquituous in advice literature during the 1970s and 1980s. For example, Iina Aasamaa's *How to Behave* combined an impeccably orthodox statement of communist society's unitary morality ('there is only one culture of behaviour, a culture of behaviour that is the same for all members of society, and which is subordinated to the higher morality of the communist society') with verbatim citation of the Moral Code of the Builder of Communism ('all for one, one for all', etc.). But the familiar sentiments about 'implacability' and 'intolerance' as the ultimate virtues were undermined by the gloss which Aasamaa herself put on the Moral Code: 'Every member of society is obliged to comply with the norms of behaviour that obtain in our country, and which are founded on the principle: *respect and take heed of society and of your fellow citizens and behave as you would like others to behave with you.*'[47] The phrase 'behave as you would like others to behave with you' reads like nothing so much as a clumsy paraphrase of Christ's injunction in the Gospels 'do as you would be done by'. To adapt evangelical tradition just as clumsily, the question of who was to 'cast the first stone' in Soviet society was now under dispute, given that scolding others was an option (by implication) counselled only to those who would not mind being the recipients of scoldings themselves. And so, while still 'Soviet' in a way that Likhachev's book no longer was, Aasamaa's treatise (no doubt unintentionally) expressed a highly ambivalent attitude to the correction of behaviour. For its part, *Domovodstvo* had not only advised its readers to comment vocally and forcefully on all breaches of behaviour, but had also warned that tact and discretion were required in some cases, for example, in advising people that their dress required adjustment.[48]

Also noticeable in many of the advice manuals was a growing emphasis on the centrality of personal dignity. In Aleksandr Dorokhov's *This is Worth Remembering* (1961), the importance of not appearing 'ridiculous' (*smeshnym*) was emphasized every bit as insistently as it was in Likhachev's book twenty-four years later, though here it was given a specifically Soviet rationale: 'Only in labour and in struggle does a person develop completely', the author asserted, and unflatteringly compared the panda eyes of a young *frantikha* (she-dandy) with the appearance of a miner returning

---

accommodation in 1988, the figure of 292,000 hostel-dwellers in the entire city should be compared with the 1940 figure of 50,000 people in barracks in the Leningradskii raion alone. (See Timothy J. Colton, *Moscow: Governing the Socialist Metropolis* (Cambridge, Mass., 1995), 371, 493, 343.)

[47] Aasamaa, *Kak sebya vesti* (1974), 8: emphasis original.

[48] *Domovodstvo*, 88. Cf. Khodakov, *Kak ne nado sebya vesti* (1975), 89, denouncing busy-bodies who criticize others' dress on the street. The presence of the two contradictory moral imperatives would leave advice-book readers in something of a dilemma about how to deal with a case of sexual exhibitionism, for instance.

from work, whose soot-ringed lids were at least the badge of honest labour, if not of the precise attention to a clean efficient appearance that was the Soviet ideal.[49]

The contradictions of advice literature captured a society now torn, even at the level of ideology, between the values of 'communist education' (collective solidarity, the dignity of labour) on the one hand, and those of personal dignity on the other. In her fine story 'Words' (Slova), written in the 1970s, Lyudmila Petrushevskaya brought out the confusing ambiguity of behaviour rules. The piece is a monologue by a young woman whose rapport with two male strangers met by chance on a suburban train ends abruptly when she suddenly joins in a chorus of voices telling them not to smoke:

And then I said to those two, 'Well, maybe you really shouldn't smoke?'

Then they both got up and left, and I didn't see them again. And the idiot next to me kept pestering me for the whole journey.

Perhaps they went off to smoke between the carriages and stayed on there, maybe they went and sat down in another carriage or got off at some station somewhere.

But I was left with the feeling there was some law I had broken, that I'd done something I shouldn't have done.[50]

Another, and less subtle, representation of such conflicts was Nikolai Gubenko's 1983 film *Life, Love and Tears*, in which the chief doctor working at an old people's home attempts to introduce a less 'Soviet' regime, and finds herself at loggerheads not only with the home's administrator, a man of little education who has risen through the Party ranks, but also with some of the old people, notably the 'floor monitors' responsible for enforcing discipline on their neighbours.

The tension between social activism and polite non-interference as ideals during the post-Stalin era is also evident in the publication statistics for guides to good behaviour that were not intended as self-help manuals: that is, tracts for Party activists and the coordinators of agitprop. The numbers of these observe much the same trajectory in the post-Stalin years as those in the two categories of self-help manual. That is, the numbers of titles published start to rise steeply in the late 1950s, reach a peak in 1961, and begin to decline thereafter (see Appendix 5 Table 4). In the Stalin era, and particularly after 1940, titles for activists outstripped all categories of advice

---

[49] Dorokhov, *Eto stoit zapomnit'*, 50–1.

[50] L. Petrushevskaya, *Bessmertnaya lyubov'* (Moscow, 1988), 166. The date of composition was given to me by the author, London, 1996. Bringing others into line was still common when I was in the USSR in the early 1980s, yet on one occasion I manage to 'win' a conflict with an old woman who told me off for being improperly dressed while I was standing in line next to her in a post office (my 'crime' was not wearing a *kombinatsiya*, or petticoat, under my blouse). When I asked her what business she thought it was of hers, other people joined in, taking my side.

literature intended for personal consumption (with the exception of titles on health and hygiene) many times.[51] The post-Stalin years saw a growing equilibrium between behaviour guides aimed at those responsible for the public direction of private behaviour, and those devoted to telling citizens how to order themselves from within. Hand in hand went contradictory attempts by the authorities to allow more expression to voices 'from below', yet also reinstitutionalize social control by revamping extant institutions such as student sovets (Komsomol patrols in student hostels) and zhensovety (official women's groups), and by creating new ones, notably the *druzhinas* (popular militias).[52]

The druzhinas were founded in 1959 by a decree of the Central Committee (2 March): the brief was to involve workers in the maintenance of public order (*obshchestvennyi poryadok*). Allegedly, the stimulus for the creation of the new organizations came from a society that had been founded spontaneously by workers at a factory in Leningrad earlier in the same year. The organizations were jointly managed by the police (militsiya, i.e. ordinary rather than secret police), the Komsomol, and the Party. A second decree of 23 July 1959, 'On Measures for Combating Criminality', increased the powers of the druzhinas. During the 1960s, 1970s, and 1980s, medals and money prizes were awarded to zealous druzhinniki, and by 1970, there were more than 100,000 workplace associations, ostensibly recruiting those of exemplary character. The Criminal Code of the Russian Federation, articles 191–2, levelled heavy penalties on those who interfered with the work of druzhina members, who were mandated to 'take part in the preservation of public order', and to 'participate in the struggle with hooliganism, drunkenness, illegal distilling of spirits, misappropriation of state and social property, and also of the personal property of citizens, with misappropriation of the regulations relating to trade, with speculation and other infringements of law (*pravonarusheniya*)'.[53]

Collective regulation of behaviour in the post-Stalin era by no means always had a punitive character, however. New consultative bodies set up in the post-Stalin period often emphasized support and guidance rather than correction and punishment. Certainly, those responsible for marital misdemeanours and other offences against 'Communist morality' could still be arraigned at their place of work or residence and subjected to public

[51] For example, in 1950, 158 'agitation and propaganda' titles were published, in 1952, 90, and in 1953, 94. In the same years, titles on house management, 'communist education' and self-education amounted to 8, 6, and 4 respectively.

[52] On *zhensovety*, see Browning in Buckley (ed.), *Perestroika and Soviet Women*. On *druzhinas* see *BSE*, 3rd edn., viii. 512; *Svod zakonov SSSR*, x. 248. Remarkable also in terms of public organization of behaviour was the continuing role of the Pioneers, and more particularly the Komsomol (see e.g. the incident with the low-cut dress cited below).

[53] *Svod zakonov SSSR*, x. 248. See also Khakhordin, *The Collective and the Individual*, ch. 7.

harangues.[54] But official response to the rising divorce rate began, from the late 1970s, to include the provision of ante- and post-marital counselling services. The 'Young Family' and 'Young Marrieds' clubs, and the rather pompously named 'Faculties of Family and Domestic Culture', offered lectures and 'consultations' to couples. Advice provided included contraception and baby-care, and sometimes (though official sources were muted in their advertising of this) even sex therapy. An introduction to the clubs' work by V. A. Sysenko, published in 1986, indirectly points to the authorities' uncertainty about whether the face-to-face method of directing behaviour via counselling, or the provision of advice on a 'distance learning' basis, was the system to be preferred. The book quotes a survey which had established that 66 per cent of men and 35 per cent of women wanting to marry had got their information about marriage from literature and the media, as opposed to 'only' 10 per cent of both sexes who had been briefed by the new clubs (and these tended to be drawn from the best-educated section of the population). The inference was that work needed to be done to publicize the clubs; the fact that Sysenko's book was itself chosen as a method of doing this indicates the continuing doubt about how best to reach the Soviet population—directly or by means of printed texts.[55] It is also notable that advice books on family relationships were among the most frequently published types of conduct guide throughout the post-Stalin era; the genre was in no sense edged out by the arrival of counselling. But conversely, the authorities' commitment to the publication of advice books in this and other areas in no way indicated a complete abandonment of traditional methods of 'agitation'.

The division between collectivist and individualist solutions to social malaise was not by any means the only division that post-Stalin discourses on behaviour reflected. The attitudes to class and status difference were also bewilderingly contradictory. On the one hand, manuals still insisted that proper Soviet citizens should behave in exactly the same way to everyone. In an instruction manual of 1962 devoted to 'service culture' in Soviet shops, shop assistants were ordered not to discriminate between customers on grounds of dress or appearance: 'In the circumstances of our Soviet society it is imperative that a salesperson should not treat a customer according to external appearance, but be equally polite to everyone.'[56] On

[54] For a fictional depiction of this (stressing the intrusiveness of the procedure), see Natal'ya Baranskaya, 'Lyubka', *Otritsatel'naya Zhizel'* (Moscow, 1977), 124–84.

[55] Sysenko, *Molodezh' vstupaet v brak*, 200–20; 215 ff. prints the questionnaire.

[56] Strogov, *Kul'tura obsluzhivaniya pokupatelei*, 21–2. Cf. N. Kruzhkov, 'Chto takoe poryadochnost'?' in *Ogonek* 38 (1960), 13: 'I'm sure we've all seen a smug man with smart clothes come into a restaurant, and how a real hubbub starts all round him: the tables are rearranged, the normally stern faces of the waiters become all vitality and servility: "Sergei Ivanovich has arrived!" . . . He's not even such a big fish, but when he goes to the restaurant, he wants to be a

the other hand, the same shop assistants were also exhorted to observe rules of behaviour which, in the early Soviet period, would have been considered revoltingly servile and bourgeois. Not only were they to display 'an attentive, considerate attitude to every customer, a concern for his individual peculiarities' as opposed to the generalized 'care for others' advocated in the 1940s, but they were also to use such forms of speech as 'May I help you to choose your purchase?' 'Please tell me what you would like' (*Pozhaluista, chto vam ugodno*), and all this while standing up straight, not 'lolling on the shop fittings'. When asked by customers whether certain goods were available, it was out of the question to say, 'Use your eyes,' or 'Can't you read what it says?' If goods that were out of stock were requested, an assistant should explain the situation courteously. The correct answer to questions such as 'Have you any elasticated socks?' was not a flat 'No,' but 'Not at the moment, we've sold right out; however, we're expecting some more next week.'[57]

As anyone who ever entered a Soviet store during the post-Stalin era could testify, such advice was seldom, if ever, observed by real shop assistants, any more than the advice in another improbably named manual, *Etiquette and Tact of the Soviet Policeman* (1977), which instructed its readers, 'You must speak to citizens using the polite form of address (*na vy*), eschewing over-familiarity, false bonhomie and undue directness (*uproshchennost'*).'[58] But the fact of its being given was new and significant. After all, the correspondents quoted by Kornei Chukovsky in a book on *kul'tura rechi* (cultured linguistic usage) published in 1963 still held the innocent polite cliché of telephone conversation, 'vas bespokoit...' (the person disturbing you is...) to be 'obsequious'.[59]

The subject of *kul'tura rechi*, first broached in 1952–3, became extremely topical from about 1960, inspiring both serious sociolinguistic discussions (as in *Kul'tura russkoi rechi v natsional'nykh respublikakh* (Kiev, 1984), a collection of scholarly articles on miners' work slang and so on), and normative treatments of linguistic etiquette, the latter forming a kind of sub-genre of behaviour manuals more generally. Again, attempts to emphasize the classless nature of Soviet society increasingly came into contact with what one can only describe as a burgeoning of class snobbery. Though

gentleman, not a citizen: caliph for an hour! In any case, the caliph is a thoroughly decent sort of fellow, generous with tips.'

[57] Strogov, *Kul'tura obsluzhivaniya pokupatelei*, 5, 11, 18.

[58] *Etiket i takt sotrudnika militsii*. The book, subtitled a 'textbook', was published by the Interior Ministry Academy (Akademiya MVD), and would have been used for classes on the subject of dealing with the public.

[59] Chukovsky, *Zhivoi kak zhizn'*, 217–18. Chukovsky himself, while more equivocal about the need for politeness than the letters he cited here, still referred to the use of this phrase as a 'bad habit' (p. 217).

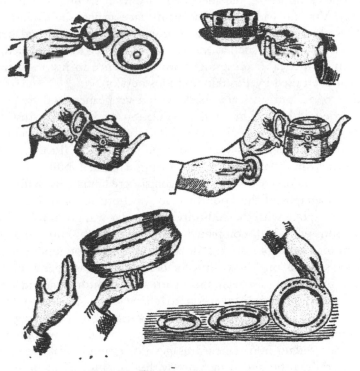

Рис. 20. Приемы показа посуды

FIG. 18. How to show the customer china. Diagram from N. I. Strogov,
The Culture of Customer Service (1962).

the prominent lexicographer S. I. Ozhegov had argued that Soviet
linguistics conceptualized norms on the basis of general usage rather than
'purism', in practice (as he himself admitted), 'purism' was everywhere to
be found.[60] To some extent, this had been true in the earlier periods of
Soviet history too: for example, G. Vinokur's classic study *The Culture of
Language* (1925), attacked various formulations popular at the time of
writing, such as 'women demand to be emancipated from cooking and
changing nappies', on the grounds of their alleged absurdity in practical

[60] *Osnovy kul'tury rechi: khrestomatiya*, ed. L. I. Skvortsov (Moscow, 1984), 215. On the origins
of the *kul'tura rechi* drive, see V. L. Vorontsova and A. I. Sumkina, 'O knigakh po kul'ture rechi',
Voprosy kul'tury rechi 1 (1955), 208–20. Interestingly, the authors of this article show a
considerable sensitivity to the class-marked character of the advice given in popular normative
sources, but their call for more neutral and better-informed pronouncements on correct speech
and writing went unheeded.

terms (one cannot be 'emancipated' from a nappy, he thought).[61] However, Vinokur had for all that set his face against the exclusivity that he saw as characteristic of pre-revolutionary manuals, and had defended some colloquial usages, such as 'ya izvinyayus'' (I beg to be excused) rather than 'izvinite menya' (excuse me) with a reference to historical tradition (both had been used by Pushkin and Dostoevsky).

In the 1960s, 'purism' came back with a vengeance, and frequency of usage carried little weight in the regulation of standards. Instead, the practices of educated speech were laid down as models for emulation. Typical of the new trends was a 1963 book by B. N. Pronsky, *Are We Speaking Correctly?* (Pravil'no li my govorim?), subtitled 'Notes of a Writer'. The author reinforced his old-intelligentsia credentials by stating in the opening paragraphs of the book that he was born in 1899, the son of an engineer; he spoke with the authority, the reader was given to understand, of a person who had completed his education by the time of the Revolution. The book, an anecdotal compilation not unlike Aleksandr Dorokhov's books on 'the culture of behaviour', was openly prejudiced against various forms of speech, most particularly youth slang and swearing. Pronsky also displayed an aversion to characteristically Soviet locutions such as 'a master of linen sewing' (*master poshiva bel'ya*), preferring the pre-revolutionary term 'seamstress' (*beloshveika*). Though he was prepared to countenance certain non-standard usages (for example dialect and sailor's cant), and though he ended his tract with a ringing call to preserve 'our precious national treasure, our native language', which is 'part of the general culture of the Soviet person, the builder of communist society', his ideal Russian language was one in which no attempt was made to dignify those in low-status professions (in however clumsy a way), and in which intelligentsia usage became the only yardstick of correct language use, with those from outside the intelligentsia anxiously minding their os and as, chs and shchs. There was a strange continuity here with the behaviour of members of the 'first wave' Russian emigration, who had mocked Soviet citizens for using supposedly coarse phrases like *skol'ko vremeni* (what time is it?), or describing dishes of cooked liver as *pechen'* (used before the Revolution for human liver only), rather than *pechenka*, and poked fun at the monstrous language of Soviet regulations.[62]

---

[61]   *Kul'tura yazyka*, 49.

[62]   These observations are drawn from personal contacts with Russian émigrés in the age range 60–80 during the 1970s. The language of Soviet regulations was also the subject of émigré humour: an especially distinguished example is the set of rules for prisoners in Nabokov's novel *Invitation to a Beheading* (1938), including gems such as 'It is strictly forbidden to leave the prison building' and 'It is desirable that the prisoner should attempt at all costs to avoid dreaming'. (See V. Nabokov, *Mashen'ka. Zashchita Luzhina. Priglashenie na kazn'. Drugie berega* (Moscow, 1988), 261–2.)

Very similar prejudices were displayed by other post-Stalinist com-mentators, notably Kornei Chukovsky, who was just as fierce about pretension, youth slang and 'vulgarity' as Pronsky, and whose prohibi-tions also extended to dialect usage.[63] For his part, I. V. Uspensky, in *Kul'tura rechi* (1976), proclaimed that 'speech should always be preserved from coarse popular speech [*gruboe prostorech'e*] and unnecessary vulgar-isms'. Among these latter he classed the innocent and widely used phrase 'mne do lampochki' (literally, 'I couldn't give a light-bulb'), meaning, 'it's all the same to me'. Among other crusades carried out by the King Canutes of *kul'tura rechi* were those against supposedly incorrect placings of stress and purportedly aberrant grammatical forms, including such near-universal usages as the zero-ending genitive *kilogramm*, or the idiomatic phrase *skol'ko vremeni* (what time is it), not to speak of the regulators' old friend, *izvinyayus'* (first condemned as a vulgar neologism in the 1900s, and in use for at least a hundred and fifty years by the 1960s).[64]

Literature aimed at children, too, reflected some of the ideological tensions. Manners were now propagandized more actively than before. In Samuil Marshak's 'If You're Polite' (*Ezheli vy vezhlivy*, 1953), for example, children were instructed to stand up for old people on public transport and help them in and out of vehicles, not to interrupt their elders, and to be silent and attentive in classes. At the same time, though, 'politeness' was defined here to include traits broadly associated with *kul'turnost'*, such as being careful with library books, keeping tidy, and defending the weak from the strong. And both here and in a companion piece, 'A Lesson in Manners' (*Urok vezhlivosti*, 1956), Marshak drew a sharp (and conventional) distinction between external (that is, superficial and insincere) forms of politeness, and true courtesy. The anti-hero of 'A Lesson in Manners' was a bear-cub who had acquired the manifestations of the former rather than the latter:

[63] See Chukovsky, *Zhivoi kak zhizn'*, *passim*.

[64] Uspensky, *Kul'tura rechi* (1976), 60. For *kilogramm* see e.g. Strogov, *Kul'tura obsluzhivaniya pokupatelei*; for the latter two instances, e.g. Kolesov, *Kul'tura rechi—kul'tura povedeniya* (1988). An article on *Kul'tura rechi* was added to the third edn. of *Kratkaya entsiklopediya domashnego khozyaistva* (Moscow, 1966), cols. 621–8. An interesting exception to the general line of argument is V. Novikov, 'Nobless oblizh: o nashem rechevom povedenii', *Novyi Mir* 1 (1998), 139–53, which not only displays sensitivity to the class resonance of customary advice on 'cultured speech' and argues for a compartmentalization according to which popular speech would be allowed to follow its own rules since 'simple people have an excellent command of language—of their own language' (p. 142), while intellectuals, especially writers, would be required to pay close heed to linguistic convention: on pp. 147–53 Novikov discusses linguistic etiquette as part of the necessary *blagorodnaya intelligentnost'* to which all Russian intellectuals should subscribe.

> Он кланялся соседям —
> Лисицам и медведям,
> Знакомым место уступал,
> Снимал пред ними шляпу,
> А незнакомым наступал
> Всей пяткою на лапу.

> He bowed to his neighbours—
> Foxes and other bears,
> Made way for his acquaintances,
> And raised his hat to them,
> But plonked his heel right down
> On strangers' paws.[65]

Here again there was the strong sense of a return to the pre-revolutionary past, as Soviet intellectuals brought into the public domain the standards underpinning their own upbringing, whether this had taken place before the Revolution, or after it, at the hands of surviving practitioners of traditional manners.[66]

To sum up: post-Stalinist conduct guides revealed interesting tensions. On the one hand, they championed the role of the intelligentsia; on the other, they voiced an unchanged commitment to a classless society. Equally contradictory was the combination of a new emphasis on the importance of private values, such as dignity and self-restraint, with a continuing stress on the collective regulation of behaviour via the activities of politically and morally aware citizens, as well as through those of officially sponsored bodies, from the *druzhiny* to counselling groups. And not least, vitriolic denunciations of *meshchanstvo*, and emphasis upon Lenin as the figurehead of revolutionary asceticism,[67] sat alongside warm exhortations to the Soviet population to acquire such (in terms of early Soviet ideology) dangerously 'petit-bourgeois' items as pot plants, fluffy cats, elaborate vases, and china tea-sets.

---

[65] S. Marshak, *Sobranie sochinenii v 8 tomakh*, i (Moscow, 1968), 232; see also ibid. 228–30.

[66] The writer David Samoilov recalled, for instance, that he was given private tuition in subjects not offered at Soviet schools in the late 1930s (languages and manners) by a graduate of an Institute for Daughters of the Nobility. (See E. Ya. Brainina and A. N. Dmitrieva (eds.), *Sovetskie pisateli: avtobiografii*, v (Moscow, 1988), 414.)

[67] See e.g. Bardin, *Pogovorim o skromnosti* (1959); or L. Kunetskaya, K. Mashtakova, and Z. Subbotina, *Kabinet i kvartira Vladimira Il'icha Lenina v Kremle* (Moscow, 1969), which emphasizes the character of the leader's flat as an expression of 'an undemanding but truly cultured person' (88), leading a life characterized by discipline, self-sacrifice, and hostility to chatter and smoking. On this strand in Soviet culture generally, see Victor Buchli, 'Khrushchev, Modernism, and the Fight Against Petit-Bourgeois Consciousness', in *Journal of Design History* 2 (1997), 161–76 (Buchli points out that an item of especial vilification was the set of *sloniki*, elephants of graduated size, or the Soviet equivalent of flying ducks, p. 170); and Susan E. Reid, 'Destalinization and Taste, 1953–1963', ibid. 177–201. On *meshchanstvo* in literature, see Mary Seton-Watson, *Scenes from Soviet Life: Soviet Life Through Official Literature* (London, 1986), 103–5.

The tension between different perceptions of appropriate 'Soviet' behaviour could only be increased by the gradual leakage of material of non-Russian origin into discussions of behaviour after 1960. Even the bare data in *Ezhegodnik knigi* make clear that there was some degree of cross-fertilization between Russian culture and other ethnically distinct cultures within the Soviet Empire. That Russian books were translated into other Soviet languages, such as Georgian, Kirghiz, Uzbek, Komi, etc. is wholly predictable, given the *primus inter pares* role played by the Russian nation since the mid-1930s.[68] Equally to be expected is the insistence of some etiquette books on the need to propagandize a 'unified' (i.e. Europeanized) code of behaviour.[69] Rather more surprising is the fact that the behaviour books published in Russian from the late 1950s included a number of publications translated from other Soviet languages, and also from the languages of the so-called 'friendly nations' or *sotsstrany* (socialist countries), particularly Germany and Poland. Among these titles were Aasamaa's *How to Behave*, translated from the Estonian, and also Akhmet Mal'sagov's *Fables of Mountain Etiquette*, and Karl Smolka's *The Rules of Bon-Ton*, translated from the German.[70]

The occasional Western behaviour book also sneaked through. An important early example was the first translation, in 1970, of Benjamin Spock's *Baby and Child Care*. Though the publication of the book was justified in the introduction by reference to Spock's opposition to the Vietnam War, the translation itself was for the most part ideologically neutral. The odd corrective note was added by the editors, as, for example, when readers were informed that Soviet doctors (in line with the usual theories of *zakalennost'*, one may assume) did not recommend drying babies after a bath, or when the editors took issue with Spock's assertion that aggression was a useful quality in a future citizen, and suggested correcting manifestations of it gently. But generally the original text was left to stand—even when Spock suggested that there was little point in paying attention to small children's use of swear-words, or that bad manners should be interpreted as a sign that the child did at least recognize the code against which he was transgressing.[71]

---

[68] e.g. *Kniga dlya roditelei* (Tashkent, 1963): (in Uzbek); *V. E. Drozdova and N. E. Shchadrina, *Sovety rabotayushchei zhenshchine* (publ. in Moldavian, 1990): see *EK* 1963, 1990.

[69] e.g. A. S. Agaronyan, *Kul'tura povedeniya. Sotsial'no-prakticheskie aspekty* (Tashkent, 1979), 8: 'Here in the Soviet Union we have created all the conditions for developing unified rules for the culture of behaviour of all nations and nationalities.'

[70] Mal'sagov, *Pritchi o gorskom etikete* (1989), and Smolke, *Pravila khoroshego tona,* (1980) (the print-run of the latter edn. was 300,000).

[71] Spok, *Rebenok i ukhod za nim,* 128, 263. According to the catalogue of the Russian National Library in St Petersburg, the book had gone into thirty-seven editions by 1995, most of them, however, post-1990. Another book by Spock, *Razgovor s mater'yu*, appeared in 1987, but has proved less popular: according to the RNL catalogue, only seven editions had appeared by August 1997.

Nor was foreign influence limited to the production of translations. Even books originally published in Russian occasionally showed awareness of non-Russian norms. They referred, for instance, to the legendary generosity of hospitality in the Caucasus, or to the exemplary politeness of the French or the English. A particularly striking example of the fetishization of the foreign was to be found in *This is Worth Remembering*, where Aleksandr Dorokhov informed his readers: 'English people say that real manners are indicated less by the fact that you yourself don't get things wrong, than by the fact that you overlook mistakes made by others.'[72] As a matter of fact, Chekhov gave voice to very similar views, in his famous letter to his brother of March 1886;[73] that Dorokhov chose to use a foreign example rather than cite Chekhov was an indication of the growing prestige of Western practices.

A particularly important source of non-Russian material was the guide to diplomatic protocol. While this was the only type of etiquette manual that had continued to be published in the Stalin period (see Chapter 4), the 1960s manuals are rather different from their 1940s predecessors. Rather than abstract ruminations on the duties and personality of the diplomat, they are strictly practical guides to the rules of protocol, embracing also the niceties of official hospitality. The books laid down that bad manners on the part of a diplomat (or his wife) impaired his country's prestige; they set out the procedures for official entertainment (to be organized by the diplomat's wife), with seating plans, and advice to serve national food, while taking account of guests' preferences, such as vegetarianism, and so on. In one book, F. F. Molochkov's *Diplomatic Protocol and the Practice of Diplomacy*, the advice on behaviour made explicit its relation to Western norms. An appendix, 'The most widespread regulations on behaviour abroad', told diplomats that they should arrive at receptions on time, take off their coats before entering the drawing-room, not seat themselves before the 'ladies' (*damy*) in the party did, or before instructed to by the hostess; that they should not read letters or documents at table, dominate conversation, or make physical contact with interlocutors. When leaving, they should not take flowers away with them unless specifically invited to by the host and hostess.[74] Instructions were also given on appropriate dress, and on behaviour while travelling

[72] Dorokhov, *Eto stoit zapomnit'*, 23.

[73] 'Well-bred people . . . are indulgent, gentle, polite, unassuming . . . they don't make a scene over a missing hammer or rubber band' (*PSS, Pis'ma*, i. 223–4: on the letter generally, see Ch. 3 above).

[74] This strange instruction had nothing in the behaviour norms of intellectual or working-class to justify it. Had some eccentric member of the Soviet *corps diplomatique* created an international incident in the 1970s (while in his cups, perhaps) by helping himself to the floral decorations when leaving a reception?

and walking in the street.[75] With the exception of the guidance on precedence, much of the advice here could have been taken from many Soviet conduct manuals; again, the fact that Molochkov chose to emphasize the 'foreign' nature of this material, rather than to play it down, is significant. It is equally intriguing that one of the readers used for English teaching in the prestigious Institute of International Relations during the 1960s was an abridged edition of the 1956 edition of Emily Post's classic guide to American *bon ton*.[76]

Of course, increased familiarity with Western manners was not always understood so positively. Books for teenagers in particular regularly expressed anxiety about the dubious blandishments of Western popular culture. In sections of his *It's a Question of Taste* aimed at adolescents and young people, the children's writer Lev Kassil' vehemently denounced 'those sickening convulsions and monotonous rhythms . . . which sometimes drive spectators and dancers to the point of frenzy, and can even spill over into mass hysteria'—that is, dancing to rock and other forms of fashionable Western music. Yet at the same time he poked fun, using the composer Dmitry Kabalevsky as authority, at a provincial schoolteacher who had attempted to perpetuate the Stalinist view of jazz as 'cultural imperialism', and he observed that Yves Montand was infinitely preferable to home-bred popular singers such as Vertinsky and Leshchenko.[77]

Equally, while a spate of Soviet travelogues published in the 1960s and 1970s emphasized the superiority of the 'Soviet way', the tone adopted was now considerably more conciliatory than in the 1940s or even the 1950s. For example, Larisa Vasil'eva's lightly fictionalized account of life in England, *Albion and the Secrets of Time*, sketched two different types of dinner party as a way of representing, in time-honoured manner, Russian spontaneity and immediacy lined up against English frigid calculation. Humour and a fair degree of accurate observation, however, overlaid ideological rigidity as she described how she and her husband had entertained an English 'lord and lady' in the Russian style: table heaped with food and drink on cheery patterned plates, and conversation about intellectual matters. Only later did she learn, from the advice of a neighbour and exposure to an extraordinarily costive formal dinner in a private house, that the tone cultivated by the upper middle classes was

[75] Molochkov, *Diplomaticheskii protokol* (1979), 236 ff. Other such manuals included Nikiforov and Borunkov, *Diplomaticheskii protokol v SSSR* (1985).

[76] *Etiquette (after Emily Post)* (1961). The sections included were Introductions, Greetings, Visiting-Cards and Visits, On the Subject of Invitations, The Clothes of a Gentleman, The Clothes of a Lady, Table Manners, Luncheons, Teas, Cocktails, and Other Afternoon Parties, Formal Dinners, Telephone Courtesy Test, Etiquette for the Smoker, Formal Correspondence, and Funerals. My thanks to Wojciech Jajdelski for presenting me with a copy of this book.

[77] *Delo vkusa*, 49, 48, 53.

drinks before dinner with conversation about the weather, and a stereo-typically 'Russian dish', beef stroganov (in fact a speciality of third-rate restaurants in the USSR) served on gilded Wedgwood. The piece concluded with Vasil'eva describing (tongue well in cheek) how she had decided to try this kind of entertaining out on her Moscow friends:

When I arrived home on holiday, I asked my closest friends round, and decided to carry out a little experiment. I made them all sit in different corners of the room and said to them, 'What are you having to drink?

Looking a little taken aback, they started to pour themselves drinks. I had put out a light hors d'oeuvre in four little bowls.

My dear friends exchanged glances, but said nothing. In about a minute flat, one of them had tipped the contents of one bowl onto his plate, another had grabbed a second bowl, and so on; guests numbers five and six ended up with nothing. Breaking the total silence, guest number six raised his glass above his empty plate, and said:

'Well, I know you've been through an economic crisis there in England, and I don't suppose there's much to eat, but thank God, you're at home now. So why don't we run round the corner to the Komsomolets store and get you something? OK, it's late now, and the choice isn't great at the best of times, but they can always manage a bit of salami and a few things in tins.'

I chuckled happily and rushed into the kitchen to fetch the quantities of delicious food that I'd carefully hidden away.[78]

The vignette clearly expresses a sense, present in etiquette manuals too, that 'abroad' was once again understood as the sphere of refinement and luxury—whether for better or for worse. A revival of the mid-nineteenth-century Slavophile representation of Russia as the home of 'barbarous' brutalism, but also of sincerity and human warmth, versus the West as the home of elegance, but at the cost of falsehood and spiritual emptiness, was well under way.

The rehabilitation of pre-revolutionary behaviour patterns via etiquette books was rather less explicit. During the Khrushchev and Brezhnev eras, an undue admiration of these was frequently criticized as a means of emphasizing the 'Soviet' behaviour ideal. I. S. Runova's *We Must Struggle with Petty-Bourgeois Vulgarity* (1962), for example, warned against the acquisition of 'lumpy great beds with a super-abundance of nickel-plated knobs', plush table-cloths, oversized sideboards, and the like, all of which were simply markers of 'backwardness'.[79] And M. Khodakov's *How Not to*

---

[78] L. Vasil'eva, 'Befstroganov na zolotom drakone', *Al'bion i taina vremeni: rasskazy* (Moscow, 1978), 35–6.

[79] Runova, *S meshchanstvom nado borot'sya*, 57. Cf. the round table 'O vospitanii vkusa' in *Novyi Mir* 2 (1955), 247–54, and lambasting *inter alia* the vulgarity of greetings cards showing kissing couples: 'It is hard to believe that these so-called "artistic" efforts are intended for people of our time, and not for satisfying the petit-bourgeois tastes of the family of some pre-revolutionary merchant called Epishkin', 253.

Behave lambasted not only the coarse kind of bad manners, but also the over-refinement of a young man who had learned up his behaviour patterns from a pre-revolutionary etiquette book.[80] It was not until the late 1980s that pre-revolutionary conduct guides began to be reprinted. Important pioneering steps here were the appearance of Svetozarskaya's *Life in Society, At Home and at Court* in 1990 (the centenary of its first appearance), and the reissuing of *Bon-Ton* (1892) in 1989. *Women's Magic*, an uncredited compilation of 'women's interest' material—from feminism to 'astrocookery'—which came out in Moscow during 1990, includes a section under the title, 'What being comme il faut means'. This reprints material from a late nineteenth-century advice manual, apparently without any desire to provoke the reader's laughter.[81]

Prior to this very late stage of Soviet history, sources other than etiquette books were more significant in resurrecting awareness of the past. For the intelligentsia, the major conduits for a new and more nostalgic view of history, based on a myth of elegance and refinement rather than the previous (and equally reductive) Soviet myth of pre-revolutionary reality as characterized by brutal class exploitation, were the historical novels of Bulat Okudzhava, and the writings and lectures of Yury Lotman, both of whom dedicated themselves above all to the Pushkin era. Lotman's evocation of the architecture, costume, and etiquette of upper-class Russia in the late eighteenth and early nineteenth century underlined not only the self-conscious artifice of this vanished world, but also its tranquillity: he showed a society riven by intellectual debates, rather than by political malaise, and characterized by poise and self-awareness, rather than Romantic agony.[82] Appreciations of this kind were aided, above all, by a selective reading of memoirs by Pushkin's contemporaries such as had also, a century earlier, inspired Tolstoi's very similar eulogy to upper-class life in *War and Peace*.

For many readers, though, the way into the past was not historical

[80] Khodakov, *Kak ne nado sebya vesti*, 7: 'His behaviour struck me as in some way bogus (*narochitoe*), calculated to "please his audience".'

[81] Svetozarskaya, *Zhizn' v svete, doma i pri dvore*; *Khoroshii ton* (Moscow, 1989); *Zhenskaya magiya* (1989). Contrast the explicitly humorous character of reprints of historic advice books in post-war Britain: see e.g. Anon, *Hints on Etiquette, and the Usages of Society, with a Glance at Bad Habits* (London, 1947), the reissue of an 1836 manual with witty modern drawings by Brian Robb.

[82] See e.g. B. Okudzhava, *Puteshestvie diletantov* (1976–8), *Druzhba narodov* 8–9 (1976), 9–10 (1978); and the popularizing essays collected in Yu. Lotman, *Besedy o russkoi kul'ture* (St Petersburg, 1994). This selective interpretation of the late 19th cent. made it seem easily accessible, despite the enormous historical changes of the 20th cent. Cf. Tat'yana Tolstaya's assertion in 1989: 'For cultured Russians the early nineteenth century is very close. Pushkin is still alive for them.' (Andrew Wilson, 'Something in the Air [interview with Tolstaya]', *Observer*, 21 May 1989, p. 52.)

commentary of this kind, or Okudzhava's intellectual fiction, but historical novels aimed at the mass market, which also gained much of their attraction from the fact that they represented an alternative world, at once more refined and more brutal than that of the present. Exemplary here was the work of perhaps the most prominent late Soviet popular novelist, Valentin Pikul', whose work included a dropsically vast account (it stretches to 900 pages!) of the court of Catherine II, *The Favourite* (1984). Employing a dualism that ultimately went back to Pushkin's 1836 novel *The Captain's Daughter,* Pikul' juxtaposed the manipulative petticoat-government of Catherine herself and bluff masculine directness (here embodied in the military genius of the eponymous 'favourite', Grigory Potemkin). But where Pushkin employed a characterized narrator, Grinev, through whom he ventriloquized, with eerie accuracy, the voice of a middle-of-the-road eighteenth-century gentleman, Pikul's omniscient narrator used the language of the author's Soviet contemporaries. The young Catherine, 'Fike', had, the reader was informed, been brought up with careful attention to the details of conduct:

Fike's mother wanted to turn her into an elegant and well-mannered creature, like a porcelain statuette, in the mode of Watteau's refined paintings, and even at the dinner table she had her legs placed in special leg-irons meant to train them into 'the third position'—the start of the affected minuet.

'The main thing in life is bon ton! [*khoroshii ton*]', Fike was told over and over again.[83]

'Affected' (*zhemannyi*) might be a concession to the usage of Catherine's time (though the word was more characteristic of the 1780s than the 1750s), but 'khoroshii ton' was a definite anachronism. Indeed, Catherine occasionally spoke as though reading directly from a Soviet conduct book, as when she argued with her son Pavel about his first wife Natalie: 'Upbringing has to stand the test of time . . . manners should not be confused with empty playing at politeness [*manernichan'e*]'.[84] And where Pushkin's Catherine, whatever her ruthlessness in putting down rebellion, always perfectly exemplified eighteenth-century good-breeding, Pikul's Catherine, never a 'porcelain statuette' at the best of times, was overheard scolding at Count Orlov like a Soviet fishwife: 'Legless again, you drunkard! Now I suppose you'll lie around sleeping it off till dinner time!'[85] As with the invocation of 'Western' behaviour patterns in Soviet

---

[83] V. Pikul', *Favorit,* 2 vols. (Moscow, 1984), i. 34.   [84] Ibid. i. 543.

[85] 'Ty nagulyalsya, p'yanitsa, teper' budesh' spat' do obeda', ibid. i. 213. While Orlov's brother Aleksei was notoriously foul-mouthed (according to E. Dashkova, *The Memoirs of Princess Dashkova,* trans. K. Fitzlyon, ed. J. Gheith (Durham, NC, 1995), 93), he 'wrote like a stevedore'), it is difficult to imagine Catherine herself scolding, or allowing herself to be scolded, in these terms.

discussions of the day, the familiar was simultaneously represented as exotic; the distorting prism of historicism rendered the present alien. By emphasizing the accuracy of his alternative reality (via footnotes, an explanatory preface, and the Tolstoyan device of mixing up real and fictional characters), yet lapsing into obvious anachronism, Pikul' lent historical respectability to an eminently topical issue, the question of 'true' versus 'false' politeness.[86] At the same time, he produced a vision of historical reality that the average Soviet reader could feel comfortable in, one where gilt and stucco rooms accommodated the behaviour patterns of the communal apartment.

The more or less overt recuperation of pre-revolutionary Russian behaviour patterns was yet another blow to the attempt to modulate the old Stalinist ideal of *kul'turnost'*, which had gained authority above all from its status as a nationally and historically exclusive entity, a badge of affiliation to a uniquely Soviet ideal. It is scarcely surprising that the effort to contain such a major shift in perception within a mythologization of Soviet history that emphasized continuity and uniformity became acutely problematic. Georgy Kublitsky, author of an English-language brochure intended for foreign readers, *Peoples of the Soviet Union: Traditions and Customs*, indicated some of the dilemmas felt by loyal Soviet citizens as new attitudes worked their way through. Kublitsky lamented the drabness of 1950s Soviet life, when a wedding meant no more than a brief visit to a city registrar to have one's passport stamped, yet also criticized the ostentatious luxury thought necessary for a wedding ceremony thirty years later. He mourned the vanished 'self-reliance' that was expected from his generation, when young people did not depend on their parents for accommodation and financial support, yet also praised the strong extended family that he saw as existing in Georgia, where parents and children lived harmoniously together.[87] As Kublitsky's book shows, the dilemmas of correct behaviour could make themselves felt even in a piece of propaganda aimed at a foreign audience, whose supposed purpose was to portray the harmonious coexistence that characterized the Soviet Union.

Normative sources on conduct not only registered the conflict between different layers of the past: they occasionally commented on them directly. Lyudmila Aleshina's frequently reprinted *On Politeness, Tact and Delicacy* (1975), recorded the following dialogue which allegedly took place after the author had given a talk about etiquette in a Soviet factory:

[86] A parallel may be seen in one of the most popular films of the 1960s, *Gusarskaya pesn'*, an openly anachronistic account of the 1812 partisan campaign (the actors wore synthetic fabrics in pastel shades, and a bottle of Soviet champagne stands in for Ai) which at the same time alluded constantly to the 'aristocratic' nature of the world that it evoked.

[87] G. Kublitsky, *Peoples of the Soviet Union: Traditions and Customs* (Moscow: Novosti Press Agency, 1990), 20–1, 25, 59.

'You keep talking about "work etiquette" [*sluzhebnyi etiket*]... The rules of behaviour... The rules of propriety... But is that really the main thing? It's responsibility and discipline that we need.'

'But, Sergei Sergeevich,' a younger worker protests, 'say two men are talking. The whole brigade is listening. The boss is angry. "Is that a head you have on your shoulders, or a pot of porridge? People like you should be thrown out on your necks! You messed that job up good and proper!" And they're both disciplined and responsible, though, aren't they?'

'If you do your work responsibly, you don't mess things up,' answers Sergei Sergeevich.

'That's true, but all the same, isn't it better if one makes observations in a businesslike way, without wasting words, tactfully?'

'It's better to work so that the brigade-leader doesn't have to make any observations. Whether loudly or softly.'

'But you can't get by without hitches at work, or in life generally,' says the other worker. 'And that's where the culture of behaviour comes in.'[88]

Aleshina also cited the instance of an *obshchezhitie* meeting at which various workers were criticized for their lack of consideration towards others on the street, or at home. A voice from the floor questioned stridently, 'What are you talking about tact for when the five-year-plan is going to pot!' (*Kakaya tam delikatnost', kogda plan gorit!*)[89] Once more the 'innovators' carried the day, though. Not only the resolution, but the very phrasing of the conflict was hardly such as to reassure any diehard Stalinist: the participants in the dialogues themselves accepted that 'discipline' and 'etiquette' must in some sense be traded off against each other, and the valuing of the two codes was directly opposite to that which had obtained in the 1930s and 1940s.

Aleshina's imaginary discussions also highlighted, though without her underlining the point, another persistent feature of behaviour guides at this period: their insistence on polarized gender roles. This imaginary world was one in which men adhered to the 'old' values of discipline and work tempo above all else, while women preached the importance of *delikatnost'* and etiquette. On the surface, this represented an entirely conventional opposition of private and public values, an opposition maintained also in instructions on the regulation of private space, such as household management books, which addressed themselves explicitly to an audience of

---

[88] Aleshina, *O vezhlivosti, o takte i delikatnosti* (quote here from edn. of 1986), 15–16. Vladimir Voinovich's famous novel *Zhizn' i neobychainye priklyucheniya soldata Ivana Chonkina* (Moscow, 1990), 176–8 (pt. 1, ch. 25), includes an extremely funny parody of this kind of discussion, 'The Rules of Bon Ton: Are They Really Necessary?' The theme was a great deal more characteristic of the time when *Chonkin* was actually written (the early 1960s) than of the time when it is set (in 1941–2).

[89] Aleshina, *O vezhlivosti*, 10.

women. *House Management*, for example, contained sections on hygiene for women, and information on the use of cosmetic preparations, but had no material on hygiene directed at men. Remarkable, too, was the fact that the section on household repairs concerned itself exclusively with odd jobs that women might ordinarily have been expected to do: that is, advice was given on glueing broken furniture, but not on carpentry; plumbing and electrical wiring did not figure, and so on. In other words, this was in no sense a 'do it yourself' manual of the kind familiar in contemporary Britain. On the evidence here, Khrushchev's concern about the exploitation of Soviet women, as voiced at the 1956 Congress of the Communist Party, had not resulted in an attempt to correct the division of labour along gender lines within the Soviet household, but in the offering of more guidance to women on how to perform 'feminine' tasks efficiently.

Yet at the same time, the public/private dichotomy was threatened by the fact that the new *kul'turnost'* ethic, unlike the old, explicitly sought to impose on men the 'private' qualities of 'tact' and 'delicacy', and to see these observed in the 'work collective' as well as in the home. The message was that good behaviour was only good behaviour if the same values were practised both in private and in public. One of the women workers that Aleshina introduced, 'Galya R', cited the case of Vadim, generally considered 'cultured', but in fact failing in signal respects: 'He keeps his workplace tidy, fulfils his quota, gives flowers to all the girls, goes to exhibitions and new plays. But he couldn't give a toss for anything that doesn't concern him personally. For instance, when he hears people swearing on the street, with little children right next to them...'[90] In this 'feminized' perception of Soviet life, self-improvement that affected only the public sphere was now seen as selfish, and the treatment of women had become a yardstick of 'cultured' behaviour. From the late 1950s, a crop of books began impressing upon men the need for a due observation of family duties. As V. Benderova's *Filial Duty* put it in 1959: 'Those five little letters on the breast of a Komsomol member. Five letters, sanctified by the name of "the most human human being"—as Mayakovsky called Lenin. Is a man who has breached the most sacred of Lenin's commandments, who has forgotten another human being, forgotten his mother, worthy to wear that badge?'[91] For their part, etiquette books constructed a world in which politeness was enacted by men as a tribute to women. They laid much emphasis on the desirability of treating women politely. Guidance on

[90] Ibid. 9.

[91] Benderova, *Synovnii dolg: Ocherki o sem'e*, 9. Cf. N. A. Lisitsyn, *Kak zhivesh', mama?*, 3: 'She gave you life. The first thing that you ever pronounced was that little word. You muttered it unconsciously, still not knowing all the sacred meaning it contained. She pressed you to her bosom, beaming with happiness. "Listen!" she wanted to shout. "My son has begun to speak! He just said: "Mama".'

behaviour in public transport, for instance, stated that men should give up their seats to women, allow them first into train carriages, buses, and trams, and help them descend from vehicles upon arrival. In the words of *House Management*, 'Handing a woman her coat is a duty of male politeness'; according to Karl Smolka, 'Equality does not exclude gallantry.'[92]

That such gestures accorded women symbolic rather than real power was sometimes underlined. Likhachev, for example, suggested that men should defer to women, but that women should not allow men to feel that they were deferring, or insist on their superiority:

My reader has probably noticed that I address myself in the first place to a man, to the head of the family. This is because one really should give way to a woman... and not only in a doorway.

But a clever woman will immediately realize exactly what she should do in order that, while always accepting gratefully from a man the right that has been accorded to her by nature, she should compel him to surrender priority to her as infrequently as possible. Which is much more difficult![93]

The tortuous phrasing of this passage reflected a signal lack of logic in Likhachev's argument (for if women have a 'natural right' to be deferred to, why should they be grateful to men for deferring? and why should men have to be compelled into deference?) But the essential point was communicated clearly enough: refinement required a courteous recognition of women's superiority.

The corrolary of this ethic, in which women were expected to act as symbols and arbiters of refinement, was of course that especial restrictions were placed on their own behaviour. It was customary to consider so-called solecisms of speech especially offensive in women. Here, for instance, a commentator fastens on the use of the diminutive suffix '-ka' appended to personal names as a sign of familiarity. This perfectly harmless and universal habit is lambasted as a sign of extraordinary female coarseness:

I don't know how you feel about this, my young friends, but I always feel jangled when some nice little girl talks in a derogatory, coarse way about her friends, calling them 'Val'ka', 'Tanka', 'Sonka'. She immediately sounds like a nineteenth-century female landowner speaking about her serfs.[94]

The guides which were most insistent on gender difference were, not surprisingly, those devoted to family relationships. For example, V. A.

---

[92] *Domovodstvo*, 88; Smolka, *Pravila khoroshego tona*, 19. Occasionally, this motif is found in Stalinist materials as well—e.g. 'A Theorist of Politeness', *Krokodil* 12 (1948), 11, showed a man on a bus reading the newspaper and saying 'I agree that we should give way to women at every point!' while a woman alongside observed, 'Excuse me, then why don't you give up your seat to me?' But such motifs were much more insistently rehearsed after 1953.

[93] Likhachev, *Pis'ma o dobrom i prekrasnom*, 32.

[94] Dorokhov, *Eto stoit zapomnit'*, 65.

Sysenko's *Family Conflicts* (1983) suggested that the difficulties alluded to in the title of his book could only be avoided if there were explicit sexual dominance on the part of one gender or the other (inevitably, the dominance of the male was preferred):

In intimate life some one person, usually the husband, takes upon himself the initiative, and gradually, tactfully and carefully overcomes the shyness, embarrassment and reserve of his young wife. Without a doubt, equality is rarely evident in the case in question. Someone always has to take the initiative on himself. . . . In certain marriages, sexual hegemony on the part of the woman is in force; this can have a negative effect on the male psyche.[95]

If he was lucky, the husband would not be faced, when performing his sexual tutorials, with a recalcitrant wife, one belonging to the three pathological types of the touch-me-not, the 'Brünnhilde' (i.e. the termagant), and the 'Queen Bee' (the philoprogenitive man-hater), whose symptoms could only be cured by resort to a psychiatrist.

Sysenko's representation of marriage involved a reversion to the early nineteenth-century Russian tradition of the 'tutelary husband', who inducted his malleable and innocent wife in the appropriate behaviour codes, exerting his own command of etiquette ('tact') in order to keep her sexual expression within the limits required by propriety.[96] Other books on family relations laid rather more stress on the conditioning of women from childhood. Fundamental here was the work of the Ukrainian pedagogue V. A. Sukhomlinsky (1918–70), whose *The Birth of a Citizen* laid much stress on the need to condition women into their future duties as mothers. 'In the well-conducted child collective the small girl takes heed of what the educator [*vospitatel'*] says about her being a future mother; she realizes that nature and many centuries of human experience have laid upon her the responsibility for the entire human race.'[97] The same author's *On Education*, which described the experimental school run by the author, indicated how 'responsibility for the human race' was to be instilled in girls. Alongside its art room, radio workshop, photographic workshop, and model garden, there was a separate reading room for girls with books and brochures on human biology, feminine hygiene, and motherhood.

The production of books about relationships between the genders, and about the need to incorporate rigid gender stereotyping in the socialization

[95] Sysenko, *Supruzheskie konflikty*, 85–6. Cf. Vladin and Kapustin, *Garmoniya semeinykh otnoshenii* (1988).

[96] But Sukhomlinsky was more conventional than some 19th-cent. writers, for instance Pushkin. In *Kniga o lyubvi* (1982), 129–30, he told girls that they should not express love until sure it was reciprocated. Pushkin's Tat'yana (a favourite role-model in Soviet schools since the 1930s) should not be imitated in this respect, he warned.

[97] *Rozhdenie grazhdanina*, 75.

of children, has been plausibly linked by Lynne Attwood to the onset of the so-called 'demographic crisis' in the Brezhnev era; that is to say, the shortfall of live births in the Russian Federation that threatened to reduce the numerical dominance of ethnic Russians in the Soviet population.[98] At the same time, such books were one of the earliest categories of advice literature to begin appearing after the death of Stalin, and the earlier publications emphasize gender distinctions just as insistently as the late ones. This suggests that the first prompting for the publication of such material was less concern about falling birth rates than anxiety about the breakdown of the Soviet family, and the erosion of gender norms which was felt to underlie this.[99] Whichever way, the insistence on the need for 'true femininity' and 'true masculinity' became more and more strident from the early 1960s onwards.

At the same time, the propaganda about gender roles went a considerable way towards undermining its own aims. Fears about the 'emasculation' of Soviet men could only be enhanced by the depiction of an ideal according to which men's moral qualities were so restrictively defined that behaviour towards women became almost the only criterion for virtue. It was quite clear what femininity meant in the post-Stalin era:

In our perception, the word *femininity* means the combination of outer and inner beauty. As a result of different factors—moral, aesthetic, historical—female beauty embodies all the most captivating traits of human beauty. . . . It is impermissible to do any harm to a woman by virtue of the fact that she is a woman.[100]

The definition of 'masculinity' that emerged by subtraction from this, however, was one founded on the 'less captivating traits of human beauty', with an anti-social potential that had to be suppressed by contemplation of the feminine as ideal on the one hand, self-denial on the other. The distinction was reinforced by the floods of pamphlets on negative forms of behaviour, in particular alcoholism, which represented these as masculine perversions destructive of a home environment regulated by women: take, for example, a cartoon that appeared in Aleshina's book, and showed a red-nosed husband, cigarette dangling from his mouth, deserting his wife, daughter, and baby for Vodka, personified as a vulgar hussy in headscarf and high heels. (See Fig. 19.)[101]

---

[98] L. Attwood, *The New Soviet Man and Woman: Sex Role Socialization in the USSR* (Basingstoke, 1990).

[99] The effect of the 'demographic crisis' on behaviour literature is more evident at the level of books on women's health: the advice on contraception given in 1960s studies of 'women's hygiene' is perfectly sensible, where as that given in the 1970s can only be described as disinformation.   [100] Sukhomlinsky, *Kniga o lyubvi*, 132.

[101] See e.g. the 'from a glass of vodka to the hospital morgue' horror stories related in Zenevich, *Vrednaya privychka ili bolezn'?* (1972), and Blinov and Danyushevsky, *Skazhi sebe 'net!'* (1973).

Fig. 19. 'She Split Them Up.' Cartoon from L. Aleshina, *On Etiquette, Tact, and Delicacy* (1976), showing a personified Vodka as marriage-breaker.

Since Soviet schools had no rooms where boys might learn about their bodies, and males were not taught domestic science (while girls were tutored in woodwork), almost the only space for construction of masculinity in a more positive sense was education in *boevaya gotovnost'* (civil defence). By extension, the compulsory military service to which most Soviet young men were subject became a vital site for the construction of male identity. Here the rules were very much the reverse of those that applied in civilian life: acquisitiveness was severely discouraged, and reliability and discipline underlined. A handbook for young conscripts, *Advice to the Soldier*, emphasizes the need for hygiene (soldiers should be clean-shaven and have short, tidy hair, visit the *banya* once a week and change their underwear when bathing there). The clinical anonymity of barracks life is underlined: family photographs are banned from conscripts locker-tops because they 'disrupt order in the detachment dormitory. It is sensible to keep such photographs in a personal album.'[102]

Yet such representations of military discipline, while utterly consistent with early Soviet tradition, had changed their meaning significantly in the context of a culture where martial imagery no longer occupied the central place that it had in the first three and a half decades of Soviet rule. Military

---

[102] *Poleznye sovety voinu*, 397.

experience had now become marginal to a society where private life was championed. At the same time, men were kept remote from induction into domestic matters, and learned to associate with women only according to the artificial principles of *kul'tura povedeniya*, which had an increasing presence in post-Stalinist Soviet schools. Teachers might use Dorokhov or Aleshina's guides as reading material, or exercise their own initiative (at least one teacher proceeded by assigning every boy in the class a girl, whom he was expected to look after at the end of each day, by helping her on with her coat, opening the door, etc.).[103] The obvious danger was the one foregrounded by the discussions in Aleshina: that men would detach the concepts of 'home' and 'etiquette', regarding domestic duties as beneath their dignity, but ostentatiously helping a girlfriend on with her coat, or gallantly handing her out of the tram, when they went out for the evening. And the idealization, in popular literature, of 'romantic love' (*lyubov'*) rather than 'friendship' (*druzhba*), not only emphasized male-female relationships over male-male relationships, but also implied that *lyubov'* was for courtship, and some other and less attractive emotion reserved for married life.[104]

Rather than resolving conflict over opposing concepts of good behaviour by introducing certainty on at least one issue, then, the rigid gender stereotyping set out in conduct manuals added to the tension because of the failure to provide adequate models for boys. Reference to established codes of masculinity, such as *zakalennost'*, or the heroic self-sacrifice of the revolutionary pioneers, was of no avail because these codes had been concerned with public rather than with private behaviour.[105] The assertion of the importance of the domestic sphere challenged the prominence of 'masculine' qualities such as 'citizenship' and 'discipline'; at the same time, the continuing emphasis on domesticity as 'feminine', without a 'do it

---

[103] Related by a Russian woman informant to Stephen Lovell: private communication to CK, 6 Jan. 1997.

[104] A sentimental publication under the title *Lyubit—ne lyubit* (Moscow, 1969), a collection of readers' letters to *Komsomol'skaya pravda*, demonstrates exactly this in its efforts to prove otherwise. For example, it quotes (pp. 3–5) a letter from a certain Andrei S. in Tyumen': 'Me and my Inna have been married for ages. Nearly ten years. But I love her just as much as I did on our honeymoon. We have three little daughters: Lada, Larisa and Nastya, who look just like their mum.' The letter's careful picture of married bliss is called into question not only by the writer's curious view that ten years represents being married for 'ages', but also by his revelation that he and his wife were living hundreds of miles apart while he worked on the oil rigs. Friendship was by no means absent from Soviet representations of human relations (e.g. it figures largely in post-Stalinist movies, such as *Ya shagayu po Moskve*), but advice literature seldom, if ever, deals with it directly.

[105] On *zakalennost'* see e.g. Ivanchenko, *Tainy russkogo zakala* (1985); Shenkman, *My—muzhchiny* (1980). The introduction to the Shenkman book has material on male mortality. V. Sukhomlinsky, *Pis'ma k synu* (1976) is a presentation of the pedagogue's private letters to his son, written in the Stalin era, as a conduct manual for the Brezhnev era.

yourself' ethos of complementary roles (he fixes a washer, she cooks a meal), enhanced the alienation of men from home and family. Sensitivity to this hiatus began to affect official publishing policy in the Brezhnev era, being reflected, for instance, in the appearance of a compendium of home management for men, *The Man at Home*, translated from a French publication of 1976. The introduction to the Russian edition saw the book as an aid to the re-establishment of male authority in the home: 'The practical usefulness of this book comes from the fact that all the information about running the home is addressed directly to the man, the head of the house [*muzhchina-khozyain*], which will help many men to attain this role in reality.'[106] A guide to the organization of home management circles for Pioneer groups published in 1978 also sought to draw males into domestic activities, suggesting that boys, as well as girls, might enjoy taking part in the circles.[107] But such initiatives were few in number, made in a self-conscious sense of swimming against the tide, and often incongruous in effect. Perhaps the most signal example of this incongruity was *A Thousand Hints 'To Your Health'* (1971), whose title awkwardly punned on a traditional drinking toast. The advice provided included not only the usual exhortations to get plenty of fresh air and exercise, but also information about 'manly cosmetics' (*muzhskaya kosmetika*), a collocation which to Soviet Russian ears sounded not only comical, but verging on the indecent.[108]

READING CONDUCT GUIDES

The ubiquity of advice literature during the post-Stalin period tells us very little in itself. The continuation of centralized cultural planning meant that print-runs were still fixed 'from above'; therefore, they were as likely to reflect what the regime saw as ideological priorities as they were genuine grass-roots enthusiasms. (To use the jargon of Soviet planning, 'need', *potrebnost'*, was more important than 'demand', *spros*.)[109] But at the same

---

[106] Beneze *et al*, *Muzhchina u sebya doma* (1980). The publication of such books appears to have been a growth area in the post-Soviet period: see e.g. Verzhbovich, Ivanov, and Sidorov, *Muzhchina v dome* (1991), which has sections on house maintenance, caring for books, building a dacha, looking after your clothes, quick and easy recipes, putting food by (including game), home-made wine, making oddments for the desk-top etc., good manners, and conduct generally (including what to do about looking after yourself when your wife is in hospital having a baby).

[107] *Kruzhok kulinarii i kul'tura byta*.

[108] Kol'gunenko, 'Krasota kozhi', *Tysyacha sovetov 'na zdorov'e'*, 171–3.

[109] Similarly, publication of advice material in newspapers continued to proceed at Party dictate: in 1956, e.g., the Central Committee of the Komsomol decreed that a number of periodicals should carry materials on young people's leisure activities. See N. Mesyatsev, 'Ob osveshchenii organizatsii letnego otdykha molodezhi v gazetakh *Komsomol'skaya pravda*, *Trud* i *Sovetskaya kul'tura*', TsKhDMO f. 1 op. 32 delo 821, ll. 19–23.

time, the post-Stalin era did see hypotheses about consumer demand (if not always demand in a practical sense) begin to affect the production of books, as it did the production of other kinds of commodity. In a recent article, Stephen Lovell has traced the various stages of the process, which included the growing toleration of private book collection from the late 1950s, and the concomitant growth of *knizhnyi golod*, or 'book hunger'. Once it began to be felt appreciably, 'book hunger' became a self-generating mechanism, stimulating a highly profitable black market in 'wanted' titles, and placing pressure on the state-regulated publishing and bookselling industries, which were unable to subsidize loss-making titles by turning a profit on popular books. One result of this situation was the gradual incursion of price differentials: these reflected not only the cost of the book, but also its subject matter. Decisions about which types of book should have their prices increased were related to consumer demand, since they pinpointed areas where scarcity was most prevalent. It is therefore of some interest that books on house management and leisure pursuits were two of the categories on which prices were raised in 1977.[110] What is more, many of the introductions to post-1953 books on etiquette and house manage-ment stated directly that these books were produced in response to reader pleas: according to the second edition of the *Concise Encyclopedia of Home Economy*, more than 4,000 readers' letters were received by the publisher, Sovetskaya entsiklopediya, after publication of the first edition.[111]

Published letters in newspapers are another source of information about reception, though one that has to be used with caution. To be sure, the widely held belief in the Soviet intelligentsia that such letters were made up by members of newspaper editorial staffs (in other words, that they were disguised newspaper articles credited to non-existent readers) is not well founded. The post-bags of newspapers were so large (in July 1956 alone, *Komsomol'skaya pravda* received more than 8,000 letters, and newspapers and magazines were regularly used by readers as a clearing-house for complaints and problems of all kinds) that the invention of letters would have been unnecessary. It would also have been dangerous, given that it was not unknown for Party authorities to carry out inspections in order to check how effectively complaints and suggestions had been followed up.[112]

---

[110] Stephen Lovell, 'Publishing and the Book Trade in Russia, 1986–1992: A Case-Study in the Commodification of Culture', *Europe–Asia Studies* 50 (1998), 679–89; Walker, *Soviet Book Publishing Policy*, 9–11; App. 2 p. 133 in the latter indicates that 'literature for parents' was priced at less than half the rates for 'domestic economy' and 'hobbies'.

[111] 'Ot redaktsii', *Kratkaya entsiklopediya domashnego khozyaistva* (1962), i. 8–9. 'Zhenshchiny, eto dlya vas!', *Ogonek* 24 (1960), 32, invited responses from readers, but so far as I can find, none was ever printed.

[112] On the number of letters, see 'Spravka o pis'makh, otklikakh, kriticheskikh zametkakh i predlozheniyakh, poluchennykh redaktsiei *Komsomol'skoi pravdy* ot chitatelei v iyule 1956 goda',

However, the letters selected for publication represented only a tiny fraction of those submitted (1,339 of 88,364 letters submitted to *Komsomol'skaya pravda* in January–October 1956, for example),[113] and they were often edited before appearing, sometimes heavily. The manipulative practices catalogued at a *Komsomol'skaya pravda* editorial meeting in 1950 remained in force throughout the Soviet period. Letters would be selected for editing if they dealt with an issue that the newspaper staff wished to publicize in the first place. They would then be 'improved' by rewriting, which might consist of cutting out irrelevant (or potentially subversive) material, rephrasing, or 'embellishment' (*obogashchenie*: that is, the addition of extra material with or without consultation with the letter-writer), or a combination of all three. Or sometimes a letter might be printed 'in the context of' an explanatory article (that is, short quotations from it would be used in order to spice up, and lend authority to, a text written by a professional journalist).[114]

These procedures went a considerable way towards eroding the boundary between 'ideology' and 'reception'—a circular process was at work according to which letters were combed for evidence of ideology's successful penetration, and then used as a foundation for further policies that were supposedly responsive to popular opinion. In any case, readers who wrote to Soviet newspapers often held positions of low-level cultural authority (teachers, Komsomol activists, brigade leaders in factories, and so on), and the propaganda encouraging Soviet citizens to police each other meant that the original impulse for writing a letter was often a desire to regulate others' behaviour. Therefore, letters were in a sense a sub-genre of conduct literature rather than an independent expression of opinion about official behaviour manifestos. But for all that, readers' letters—particularly those published in the early 1960s—often made quite vivid and unconsciously revealing contributions to debates on issues of the day. Both *Ogonek* and *Krokodil*, for instance, ran consumer columns to which readers sent their moans about subjects from the mendacity of canteen menus to the unreliability of agency cleaning women, and where local issues such as

TsKhDMO f. 1 op. 32 delo 821, ll. 35–7; for an example of an inspection of letters, see 'Akt o sostoyanii raboty s pis'mami molodezhi v redaktsii gazety *Komsomol'skoi pravdy*' (26 Nov. 1956), TsKhDMO f. 1 op. 32 delo 821, ll. 106–21. Even in the Stalin era, it was not considered appropriate for journalists to produce fake 'readers' letters'. The chairman of an editorial meeting of *KP* on 17 Apr. 1950 stated 'It would of course be inappropriate to depute people to write letters on behalf of someone else', while the head of the newspaper's correspondence section regretfully noted that it had been impossible to plan a pre-election spread under the title 'Za Stalina, za schast'e nashe' 'because we didn't know how our reader was going to see things'. See 'Zasedanie partiino-proizvodstvennoi konferentsii redaktsii KP, posvyashchennoi redaktsionnoi rabote s pis'mom', TsKhDMO f. 1 op. 32 delo 624 l. 11, l. 23.

[113] 'Akt o sostoyanii', l. 106.

[114] See 'Zasedanie partiino-proizvodstvennoi konferentsii', l. 25–37.

the replacement of a children's playground by private garages generated fierce disputes about the rights of car owners versus the rest of society.[115] And between 1962 and 1964, *Komsomol'skaya pravda* published some extraordinarily interesting discussions of public morality that directly reflected the ramifications of contradictory ideologies at the grass roots. On the whole, the readers of the newspaper (or those who were allowed to voice their views) supported an active, rather than a passive, attitude towards misdemeanours.[116] But there were some instructive exceptions, indicating confusion among readers as to which offences were and were not 'actionable' on the part of friends, neighbours, and colleagues, and sometimes pointing to deeper uncertainties as well.

A particularly striking case emerged in the early months of 1964. In January, Vasily Russkikh, a builder from Kemerovo province, wrote to complain that his attempts to stop work-time drinking in his brigade had provoked a rebuke from his *brigadir* ('What are you going against the collective for? After all, it's "all for one, one for all", innit?'). When Russkikh refused to quieten down, he was ostracized by his workmates. This dispute over two different interpretations of the Moral Code of the Builder of Communism attracted an extremely mixed bag of follow-up letters. Some of the readers supported Russkikh's actions; but a number did not. One reply, from a worker in Severodvinsk signing himself 'Savin', for example, wondered: 'What did he go against his mates for?', and added, 'The brigade was right to give him the cold shoulder. . . . I think V. Russikh wrote to the paper so his bosses would read his letter,think he was a "patriot", and assign him a higher-grade job [*povysit' v chine*]'. This letter in its turn provoked a bitter controversy, with some correspondents attacking Savin for his lack of idealism and sense of 'Communist duty', and others defending his honesty. A construction worker from Orel province observed: 'At least Savin wrote what he thought. But that letter from Belyaev [one of his opponents] reads like he sat down and read a whole batch of agitprop pamphlets before he wrote it. . . . Savin's quite right: only a toady could go against the collective. . . . And when Belyaev says, "We don't work because of the money," what the heck does he think he *does* work for, then?'[117]

If this exchange showed the subversive collectivism which had flour-

---

[115] See e.g. N. Pchelyakov, 'Pel'meni s....', *Krokodil* 1 (1960), 2; V. Podol'skii, 'Dobraya usluga', *Krokodil* 25 (1964), 4; *Ogonek* 3 (1964), 30. The 'Byt ili ne byt?', 'Khorosho li vas obsluzhivayut?' and 'Byuro medvezhikh uslug' slots running in *Ogonek* during 1962 and 1963 were regular forums for readers' complaints of this kind.

[116] For example, five out of five responses to a reader who had intervened to chide a youth who was vandalizing a pine-tree approved the decision to take action: see 'Chitatel' prodolzhaet razgovor', *KP* 165 (17 July 1962), 2.

[117] See *KP* 24 Jan. 1964, 2; 5 Feb. 1964, 2; 20 Feb. 1964, 2.

ished underground since the early 1940s asserting itself with new boldness, and even claiming official slogans as licence for its actions, other cases indicated that the tolerance of formerly prohibited activities and behaviour sometimes met resistance at the grass roots. In June 1962, for example, a young woman from Novokuznetsk, a brigade leader at the Kuznetsky metal factory, wrote in to report an incident at a local dance. A member of the Komsomol *druzhina* supervising the occasion had expelled her from the room, complaining that her low-cut dress was 'disgusting':

The next day, I took a copy of *The Concise Encyclopedia of Home Economy* and went to the district committee [of the Komsomol] to see Il'nitsky. I tried to show him that the kind of dress I was wearing had the approval of the Ministry of Culture. . . . Il'nitsky didn't mince his words: 'I couldn't care less who's approved it. You're not wearing that in our club. Suppose some hooligan pulled off your shawl? After all, you've got nothing on underneath it, have you?[118]

On the whole, though, it was less common for women to complain about undue strictness in enforcing behaviour standards than to lament laxity in upholding these. An example was a controversy which erupted at the end of 1964, about whether it was, or was not, appropriate for young men to proposition young female strangers on the streets or in other public places. A young woman from Leningrad who had complained that she was bored with being 'pestered' by groups of men provoked widely differing responses. Two respondents (both men) suggested that she was a prude to be upset about the matter ('Who doesn't want to talk to a pretty looking girl? But I can see that you just *look* pretty: inside, you're really awful'); however, a letter from a group of young women took the complainant's side. An alternative reply again came from one young man defensively suggesting that girls who wore short skirts, did sexy dances and 'smiled when young men talked to them very freely, using all kinds of bad language [*mat*]' ought to take part of the blame, though he admitted that the behaviour described had not been acceptable either.[119]

As well as reflecting the general contours of controversy at, or close to, the grass roots of Russian society, the letters in *Komsomol'skaya pravda* occasionally gave direct evidence of the circulation of advice texts—and not just the Moral Code of the Builders of Communism, which was ground into Soviet citizens at schools, Komsomol meetings, and by official

---

[118]   *KP* 24 June 1962, 2. Cf. a denunciation of his colleagues by A. Peterson, political instructor of the magazine *Estonskaya molodezh'*, in 1961, on the grounds that the periodical had not only reviewed two advice books for young people on sexual development, *A Boy Becomes a Man* (Yunosha prevrashchaetsya v muzhchinu) and *A Girl Becomes a Woman* (Devushka prevrash-chaetsya v zhenshchinu), but far worse, had dared to recommend them to its readers. (TsKhDMO f. 1 op. 32 d. 1047 l. 182).

[119]   *KP* 10 Jan. 1965, 2.

propaganda generally. The piquant case of the woman metal-worker taking her copy of *The Concise Encyclopedia of Home Economy* to remonstrate with her Komsomol boss (as though it had been a copy of the Gospels, the Koran, or the Talmud) is a case in point. On the whole it seems to have been practical guides, such as this, that enjoyed the greatest popularity among working-class Soviet readers; there is little to suggest that guides to the 'culture of behaviour' had much currency.[120] And much the same obtained at the other end of the social scale, among highly educated intellectuals, who might purchase a recipe book, or collection of 'handy hints', but did not generally feel the need for guidance on how to (or how not to) behave. Reprints of *The Book of Tasty and Nutritious Food* and similar cookbooks were still on view in many intelligentsia households in the late 1990s, but seldom, if ever, in the company of manuals such as *On Etiquette, Tact, and Delicacy* or *How to Behave*.

To be sure, Lyudmila Aleshina and Aleksandr Dorokhov, authors of two of the most popular behaviour books published after 1953, referred (when introducing later editions of their works) to the encouragement that they had received from readers: the fact that etiquette books, like household manuals, generated correspondence indicates that they did not remain wholly unread. However, it is significant that most of the the letters quoted came from a very specific group of individuals—middle-aged men and women professionally involved in the business of moral indoctrination, such as teachers. Equally, most were devoted to one particular problem: the regulation of young people's behaviour. In the words of a letter quoted by Aleshina in the 1986 edition of her book, 'As soon as I take your book in my hands, I feel great respect for you. You do so much good with your writing.... *Your work is so important for young people*. Delicacy, politeness, tact help us to sustain friendship, love, work, and build the family.'[121]

The sense that the prime readership for advice on behaviour consisted of the socially conscious middle-aged is also brought out by a capsule library of 1960s advice literature once owned by a self-improving communist of peasant origins living in the village of Klyaz'ma outside Moscow. It

[120] Questionnaires from the post-Stalin era suggest that factory workers and peasants were more likely to spend their very limited leisure time at the cinema, watching television, or engaging in sporting activities (especially fishing) or domestic activities (sewing, playing with the children) than they were to spend it reading, and that the most popular categories of reading material were popular fiction and practical literature—including periodicals such as *Za rulem*, *Futbol*, *Okhota*, *Rabotnitsa*). (See e.g. a survey of workers at the Astrakhan railway engine repair factory, July 1964, TsKhDMO f. 1 op. 32 d. 1175: of the fifty-one workers who responded, forty-three had been to the cinema at least once during the previous two months, thirty-nine at least five times, while only eight had read more than five books during the same period, and only seven specified that reading was their favourite activity, as opposed to fourteen sport and five various forms of domestic activity (sewing, home furnishing).

[121] Aleshina, *O vezhlivosti, o takte, o delikatnosti*, 3–5. My emphasis.

included a Stalinist publication on reading, A. Primakovsky's *How to Work with Books* (*Kak rabotat' s knigoi*, 1951), and a number of more recent publications: S. Antonova's *Learn to Control Yourself* (*Uchites' vlastvovat' soboyu*, 1975), a collection of letters from famous people to their children and younger relations; the self-explanatory *Upbringing: A Dictionary for Parents* (*Semeinoe vospitanie, slovar' dlya roditelei*, 1967); a rather nauseating series of uplifting tales for the young, N. Dolinina's *A Person Speaking to People* (*Chelovek—lyudyam*, 1961); and S. M. Bardin's *Let's Have a Little Talk about Modesty* (*Pogovorim o skromnosti*, 1959). Several of the books were heavily underlined, sometimes in a way that suggested the material was to be used for giving pep-talks to teenagers. Alongside a passage in Bardin complaining of how the 'immodesty' of young people manifested itself in 'the incapacity to behave properly in public places, showing-off, bad manners, and the blind imitation of the worst customs of young people in bourgeois places', the book's owner noted in the margin 'Rasskazat'' (Be sure to tell them this).[122]

If advice literature undoubtedly appealed to authority figures from the older generation, it may be doubted how successful it was in targeting 'young people' themselves, whether at first or second hand, and in fighting its battle against the rising tide of immorality and laxity, and the devious aims of Western powers to propandize 'their menu of consumerist dishes served up in a musical sauce'.[123] Adolescents 'corrupted' by the values of Western popular music were unlikely to respond very positively to, say, the pious sentiments of Karl Liebknecht to his children: 'Onward and upward—walk the straight road, no matter how difficult it seems.'[124] From the early 1960s, recognition of this, and of the fact that Komsomol clubs were increasingly thinly attended by young people, prompted attempts to meet the new generation half-way by setting up cultural institutions and practices that were intended as innocuous alternatives to dangerous Western blandishments. Clubs organized entertainments such as 'question-and-answer evenings, live newspapers, discussions, theoretical conferences and political quizzes', and 'youth cafés' were set up, where young people could enjoy non-alcoholic refreshments and 'cultured' pastimes such as poetry readings or debates on political issues of the day.[125] There were even embarrassing campaigns to disseminate alternative 'Soviet' versions of youth trends. For instance, anxiety about the spread of 'the Charleston' and 'the Twist' in the early 1960s led to the invention, by

[122] See the copy of Bardin, *Pogovorim o skromnosti* in my possession, p. 52. My thanks to Ralph and Oxana Cleminson for making this material available to me.

[123] Motyashov, *Moda, prestizh, lichnost'* (1986), 38.

[124] Antonova (comp.), *Uchites' vlastvovat' soboyu*, 27.

[125] On the Komsomol clubs and on 'question-and-answer evenings', see TsKhDMO f. 1 op. 23 d. 1047 l. 29; on *molodezhnye kafe*, KP 29 Mar. 1961, 2 Apr. 1961, 20 May 1961.

a middle-aged composer, of a dance called the 'Terrikon'. But, as *Komsomol'skaya pravda* admitted, the dance turned out to be aptly named: it was indeed so absolutely terrible that bands attempting to play the accompaniment became incapacitated with laughter when they saw the antics of couples on the dance floor.[126]

Disasters such as this may have been one reason why it was common for advice literature authors to set their faces against any accommodation with what was actually popular among young people, such as the fashions of the *stilyagi* (Soviet mods). 'Of course,' as a publication entitled *Clothes for Young People* put it in 1959,

fashionable dress in the understanding of Soviet people has nothing to do with the lurid, glaring [*kriklivye*] costumes of the *stilyagi*, their imitation of the worst tendencies in foreign fashion.

In our country fashion is the expression of the taste of working people, of people who study or have jobs; they are able to discriminate between being attractively dressed and making a show of originality [*pokaznoe original'nichan'e*].[127]

The book's solution was to dress young people in miniature versions of adult attire, for example fitted wool dresses with knife-pleat hems and matching hat and gloves, or a décolleté black dress with shawl for the theatre and concerts.

Dilution and prohibition were, in the end, equally ineffective. Expostulation against the 'demonic music' of the Beatles only intrigued teenagers, helping the band to the extraordinary popularity that it enjoyed in Russia throughout the 1970s and 1980s.[128] Even if it did not achieve the precise opposite of what it intended, advice literature was seldom successful in convincing its target readers. The fundamental misconception of much solemn pontification on 'the culture of behaviour' in terms of these is plausibly suggested by Natal'ya Baranskaya's story 'A Negative Giselle', in which a working-class young girl attending the ballet for the first time is made deeply uneasy by the fact that her only sources of information on how to dress, her mother's books *Good Taste* and *The Art of Dressing Well*, recommend styles wholly unsuitable for her age.[129] Among young Soviet people brought up in more privileged circumstances than Baranskaya's character, publications such as this, or treatises on etiquette, were more likely to be seen as high comedy than as repositories of useful advice.

---

[126] 'Iskusstvo tantsa', *KP* 6 Sept. 1964, 4.

[127] *Odezhda dlya molodykh*, 1.

[128] For the condemnation, see Kassil', *Delo vkusa*, 57. I can confirm from my own experience that bootleg tapes of the Beatles circulated widely even in the Russian provinces in the late 1970s and early 1980s, having spent many an hour translating the lyrics for the benefit of monoglot fans.

[129] N. Baranskaya, *Otritsatel'naya Zhizel'*, 45–56. The titles of the books mentioned by Baranskaya appear to be invented, but the point still carries.

According to a Russian informant of mine born into the Leningrad creative intelligentsia in the late 1950s, she and other members of her class at school used to read Aasamaa's *How to Behave* aloud to each other for pure entertainment—they found the book 'hysterically funny'.[130]

Mockery of indoctrination in good manners was also behind the emergence of two forms of narrative joke very popular with younger adolescents from the early 1960s to the early 1990s. One type had as its protagonist the double agent Stirlitz, a Soviet officer stationed in Germany and posing as a highly placed Nazi. In the original novels by Yulian Semenov, Stirlitz is an enigmatic and urbane individual who comes under threat of exposure only when betrayed by an informer. In his role as the hero of *anekdoty*, though, he forever teeters on the edge of discovery, not only because of a Soviet patriotism hyperbolized to the point of absurdity (he is physically incapable of sitting down during the Soviet national anthem, has the hammer and sickle on his underpants, and so on), but because he commits such startling breaches of etiquette as falling face-downwards in his food when drunk, licking his plate, or picking his ear with a fork:

Scene: the Reichskanzlerei. A meeting of Germany's top officials is in progress. Stirlitz is present. At one point everyone is bent over a map of Europe unrolled on the table, and Stirlitz, seizing his chance, quietly blows his nose on the curtains. The voice-over is heard saying: 'Of course, Stirlitz knew that doing this was terribly dangerous. But he badly, oh so badly wanted, right here, in the very nerve-centre of Fascism, to feel himself for once.'[131]

Similar is another anecdotal hero, Cornet Rzhevsky, loosely based on a character from *The Hussar's Song*, whose *faux pas* acquired additional resonance because they played on the clichéd perception of the early nineteenth century as the quintessential era of refinement and elegance:

Cornet Rzhevsky had heard that the correct way of getting to know a lady was to go up to her, begin making light conversation about the weather, and then introduce yourself. When he was out walking once, he met a young girl out with her pug-dog. He walked up and gave the dog a great kick, so it went flying, then said to the girl:

'Flying low today. Means we're in for rain, I expect. Oh, by the way, allow me to introduce myself: Cornet Rzhevsky at your service, ma'am!'[132]

A rather more sophisticated anecdote derived from the manners fetish is the following parody guide on how to write a Soviet historical novel:

[130] Personal information, St Petersburg 1997.
[131] A. F. Belousov, 'Mnimyi Shtirlits', *Uchebnyi material po teorii literatury: zhanry slovesnogo teksta: anekdot*, ed. V. N. Neverdinov (Tallinn 1989), 105.
[132] V. F. Lur'e, 'Materialy po sovremennomu leningradskomu fol'kloru', *Uchebnyi material po teorii literatury*, 140.

An author went into a Soviet publishing house and said, 'I've written a historical novel.' The editor began reading the manuscript. '"My love, should we perhaps partake of a little coffee?" said the count to the countess.' 'That's not a bad start. But you need to work a little sex into the plot to keep the reader's interest up.' A day later, the author brought in the continuation of the first scene: 'The count and the countess lay down on the windowsill and began making love.' 'That's much better,' said the editor, 'but now you need to get in a reference to the production situation.' The author inserted: 'Just at that moment, some iron object was being beaten out down in the yard.' 'Brilliant,' said the editor, 'now all you need is a sense of perspective, of striving to the future.' The author thought for a while, then scribbled down, '"To f... with it, I'll finish the job tomorrow!"' [133]

The joke is a wickedly accurate encapsulation of the technique used by Pikul': racy eroticism, a voyeuristic fly-on-the-wall view of aristocratic life, and bogus pastiche, given a spurious respectability by means of a leaden reference to Soviet historiographical formula (cf. the aside in *Favorit*, 'The so-called "Golden Age" of Catherine was never at all "golden" so far as the Russian people was concerned').[134]

Besides inspiring these frivolous reactions, however, the genre of behaviour literature had some more serious spin-offs (all, once more, beyond the margins of official culture). One of these was the first cookbook of any character to be published since 1917, Petr Vail' and Aleksandr Genis's *The Russian Kitchen in Exile* (1987), which offered its readers no bland assemblage of quasi-scientific lists of ingredients and methods, but an opinionated and extremely informative guide to how to cook *à la russe* with American ingredients. Punctuated by reminiscences of Soviet life and by ironic asides ('Cheese comes at the end of the meal, of course; but pardon the banality'), the book was preceded by the poet Lev Losev's robust defence of the place of cooking in Russian culture: 'The vulgar utilitarianism of the Bazarovs and the Rakhmet'evs, who, rather than eating, simply ingested proteins and carbohydrates, coincided with the decline of Russian poetry.'[135] While this book remained unique, advice literature and creativity also began going together in another way: cookbooks and other manuals were one of the key forms of intertext in unofficial Soviet literature of the 1960s and 1970s. Take, for example, the killer cocktail recipes offered by the narrator of Venedikt Erofeev's brilliant novel *Moskva-Petushki*, which read like obscene parodies of the alcohol-free and wholesome 'milk cocktails' (i.e. milkshakes) propagandized in Soviet cookbooks. But a more extended use of parody is evident in the writings of Sergei Dovlatov (1941–90), a writer carried off by drink

[133] Borev, *Farisei*, 212.
[134] Pikul', *Favorit*, ii. 81.
[135] Vail' and Genis, *Russkaya kukhnya v izgnanii*, 132, 17.

even younger than Erofeev, whose montages of anecdotes, such as *Solo on an Underwood* (1967–78) and *Solo on an IBM* (1979–90) are among the most creative reworkings of official maunderings on morality to emerge from *samizdat* culture.

The threadbare term 'counter-cultural' is baldly inadequate to Dovlatov's subject position. His aphoristic miniatures, like the fragments of Novalis, Schlegel, or Vyazemsky turned inside-out, are patchworks of Russian bohemian life in the post-Stalin era. Dovlatov inventories a world of 'self-contained communal flats', round-the-clock binge drinking, libidinous attempts at sex, clandestine listening to the BBC Russian service (so that Dovlatov's daughter thinks the word 'bibisi' means a radio), idolization of literature and jazz (the title 'solo on an Underwood' metaphorically links these outpourings and jazz riffs).[136] Dovlatov's fictional *alter ego* and his companions are self-conscious practitioners of a neo-Romantic 'anti-behaviour', steadfastly opposing themselves not only to the official Soviet virtues of sobriety, punctuality, clean living, and reliability, but to the elitist idealism of old intelligentsia ideologues such as Likhachev. Dovlatov's own former life as a mediocre Soviet writer (evoked in his writings), and his occasional decision to adopt a moralizing position himself, or to show one of his heroes, such as Joseph Brodsky, teaching *homo sovieticus* a lesson, made the crusade for independence that he later pressed forward seem piquantly ambiguous. At times, the humorous deflation of Soviet pomposity was achieved in a manner that drew directly on official guidance about how to behave. Here, for example, is *kul'tura rechi* translated into the language of the barrack room:

A sergeant from Moscow was posted to our division. He was a cultured person, a writer's son, even. He didn't feel too happy among us boors. But he really did want to be 'one of the boys'. So as to make us trust him, he swore all he could. Once, he bawled out Corporal Gaenko:
'Ty chto, ebnúlsya?' [Fucked up again, have you?]
  That's exactly where he put the stress—'ebnúlsya'.
  What Gaenko replied was this:
  'Comrade Sergeant, you've got that wrong. In Russian you can say yóbnulsya. You can say ebanúlsya. You can even say naebnúlsya. But ebnúlsya—I'm sorry, there's just no word like that in the Russian literary language.[137]

The obsession with correct stress that haunted Soviet linguistic policemen is turned into a weapon against authority, not one supporting the cause of official regulation, and a patent 'vulgarism' is elevated to the status of the

---

[136] S. Dovlatov, *Zapisnye knizhki* (St Petersburg, 1992): phrases quoted are on p. 31. On Dovlatov as satirist (particularly his 'family chronicle' *Nashi* (Ann Arbor, 1983), see Karen L. Ryan-Hayes, *Contemporary Russian Satire: A Genre Study* (Cambridge, 1995), ch. 4.
[137] Dovlatov, *Zapisnye knizhki* (St Petersburg, 1992), 12.

'Russian literary language'. This idiosyncratic value-exchange system is also seen operating in another vignette, where a visitor is rebuked for bringing the gift of a cake ('what sort of old-fashioned manners is that?') but redeems his reputation by promising marijuana next time. The relationship to Romantic anti-behaviour codes (where knowledge of the conventional pieties is required in order to subvert these) is at times more than simply functional. The characters in Dovlatov's world relish Pushkinian expressions such as 'lovelace' (for 'rake'), and despise the busloads of Soviet trippers to Pushkin's estate whose knowledge of the poet's biography is such that they are capable of asking why Pushkin fought a duel with Lermontov, or whether Anna Kern (one of Pushkin's better-known lovers) was 'Esenin's mistress'.[138]

Attachment to the Romantic period may well have helped foster the marked impatience with women's moralizing role that was widespread in the alternative Russian intelligentsia of the post-Stalin era. However, self-congratulatory male 'bad behaviour' extended to a far wider sector of society than bohemian painters and writers, which suggests that the character of Soviet propaganda itself was a more important factor in provoking it than was unofficial writing. The point was that, once alcoholism began to be seen as an endemic male trait, it could also come to seem one which was beyond the powers of self-help; it could, moreover, be understood as the expression of an alternative masculinity all the more attractive because it was subversive. Recording conversations with Muscovites just before the collapse of Soviet power, the ethnographer Nancy Ries noted that the subjects of manners and order came up far more frequently when women were speaking than when men were. She registered a widespread belief that 'men are bad, but women are the real totalitarians'. Where women's genres of self-expression included blame, lament, and tales about negligent or incompetent husbands, men inclined more to cursing, bragging, and the relation of 'sexual and drinking epics'. Ries concluded: 'While alcoholism as a bio-medical/social phenomenon is a serious and tragic problem in Russian families and for the polity as a whole, alcoholism as a performative/narrative phenomenon offers endless possibilities for an elaboration of iconic resistance to the mundane, practical disciplines of family, community, and state.'[139] Because it was so evidently not for 'real men', the ideology of 'cultured behaviour' enhanced the prestige not only of drinking binges, but also of other oppositional forms of

---

[138] Dovlatov, *Zapisnye knizhki*, 28–9, 31–2.

[139] Nancy Ries, *Russian Talk: Culture and Conversation during Perestroika* (Ithaca, NY, 1997), 60, 37. Cf. Andrei Siniavsky's aphorism: 'Vodka is the Russian man's white magic; he decidedly prefers it to black magic—the female sex' (*Mysli vrasplokh* (New York, 1966), 79: quoted in Rosalind Marsh, 'An Image of Their Own?', in *eadem* (ed.), *Women and Russian Culture*, 24).

activity, such as the gang-culture of racketeers. These became attractive not merely because they were pleasurable (in the first case) and profitable (in the second), but because they were glamorous.[140]

For all that, late Soviet intellectuals, so far from always maintaining an ironic distance from the process of dictating refinement, often directly involved themselves in it. As we have seen, a good many of the behaviour books of the post-Stalin era (particularly Likhachev's *Letters on Goodness and Beauty*) drew their authority from the intellectual background of their writers. What was more, the provision of advice on behaviour was an activity that also leaked into other kinds of writing, with one particularly popular form being the short sermon for young people. In the 1980s, for example, Joseph Brodsky composed an address to freshmen at Williams College in which he set out some cherished views on appropriate behaviour:

To put it mildly, nothing can be turned and worn inside out with greater ease than one's notion of social justice, civic conscience, a better future, etc. One of the surest signs of danger here is the number of those who share your views, not so much because unanimity has the knack of degenerating into uniformity as because of the probability—implicit in great numbers—that noble sentiment is being faked.

By the same token, the surest defence against Evil is extreme individualism, originality of thinking, whimsicality, even—if you will—eccentricity. That is, something that can't be feigned, faked, imitated: something that even a seasoned imposter couldn't be happy with.[141]

One might choose to take issue with the notion that there is no such thing as bogus eccentricity (a form of behaviour on view in most post-Romantic European societies), or raise one's eyebrows at the notion of preaching individualism as a pedagogical means of generating non-conformity (given the tendency of teaching to achieve the opposite ends to those desired by the teacher), but that is not the point. The association of 'extreme individualism' with righteous behaviour had been elevated by the post-Stalinist Russian intelligentsia to the status of a dogmatic truth. The *idée reçue* that moral rectitude was attainable only inside the collective had been replaced by the *idée reçue* that moral rectitude was attainable only outside it.

If Brodsky's piece self-consciously set its face against Soviet moral

---

[140] It is surely significant that the 1970s and 1980s also saw a re-evaluation, among some male writers, of the traditional 19th-cent. and Socialist Realist emphasis on women as moral educators: as Svetlana Carsten argues, women were often represented as intellectually inferior, philistine, unreliable, and obsessed with domestic trivia (see 'In the Shadow of a Prominent Partner: Educated Women in Literature on the *Shestedesyatniki*', in Marsh, *Women and Russian Culture*, 259–74.)

[141] J. Brodsky, *Less than One: Selected Essays* (London, 1986), 385.

discourse in terms of its expression (hence the ironical reference to 'bright future'), some other statements by Russian intellectuals, such as Sergei Dovlatov's description of the ideal reader for the New York Russian newspaper with which he was involved, *Novyi amerikanets*, seem almost an echo of Soviet statements on etiquette:

It's a person of no matter what creed, but who loathes tyranny, demagogy and stupidity.

Who has a broad outlook in the sphere of politics, science, art.

Who likes good literature, but also a good read.

Who isn't a snob, who likes chess and football, gossip about Hollywood stars and astrology columns.

It's a person who worries about the hostages in Tehran but who also likes doing the crossword.

It's a person who's grasped the main thing—the world will be saved by valour, kindness and nobility [*otvaga, dobrota i blagorodstvo*].

In short, it's an ordinary person, simple and complicated, sad and cheerful, calculating and insouciant.

I hope you recognize yourself, reader?[142]

The resemblance between the Romantic aphorism and Dovlatov's text was here only typographical; the structuring of the latter was, at a deeper level, characteristically Soviet. Significant, for example, was the dependence on triads of abstract nouns (the formula *otvaga, dobrota i blagorodstvo*, or 'valour, kindness and nobility', has all the resonant vacuity of its Soviet predecessors. Easy enough to reify these qualities in the abstract: what about how to identify or express them in a complicated world?) This chiming of formal patterning and lexis lent an unintended irony to Dovlatov's assertion (on the very page that this passage is taken from) that Soviet propaganda produced the opposite effect on its recipients to the one its proponents had in mind.

Not only treatises on the 'culture of behaviour', but guides to domestic living sometimes found a curious kind of echo in serious literature of the 1960s and 1970s. An example was Solzhenitsyn's eulogy to improvised *intelligentsia byt* in *Cancer Ward*:

They don't have any furniture, so they got old Khomratovich (another exile) to make a parallelepiped-shaped arrangement of logs in one corner. That's their double bed—look how wide it is! How comfortable! What bliss! Then they get a big sack made out of ticking and stuffed with straw. The next order from Khomratovich is a table, and it must be a round one. . . . The next job is getting hold of an oil lamp, not a tin one, a glass one, on a tall stem, and it mustn't have seven facets, it must have ten, and it must still have the glass in place . . . And here,

---

[142] S. Dovlatov, *Marsh odinokikh* (Holyoke, Mass., 1983), 13.

in Ush-Terek, in 1954, when people in the capitals are rushing round buying torchères and when the hydrogen bomb has already been invented—this lamp on a home-made round table turns their mud hut into a luxurious drawing-room straight out of the nineteenth century.[143]

The reading lamp, the double bed, and the round table appeared as alternatives to the *torchère* as a metonym of 'Soviet luxury'; yet Soviet advice on taste in furnishing itself depended upon just this kind of contrast between acceptable and unacceptable possessions. And the resurrection of pre-revolutionary taste ('a luxurious drawing-room straight out of the nineteenth century') as a model for cultured behaviour was also in the spirit of at least some post-Stalinist official guides to furnishing domestic space.

Even the boldest critics of the post-Stalinist 'culture of behaviour', then, often phrased their moral statements in ways that owed something to the official discourses of the time. Growing pluralism in the latter bedevilled opposition to 'Soviet culture' as a unified whole, even as it diluted the hegemony of early Soviet *kul'turnost'*. However paradoxical the intellectual effects of pluralism, though, its impact at the level of day-to-day behaviour was unambiguous: the emergence of a more permissive ethos of behaviour and consumption gave a leeway to variation in individual taste that had not existed since the NEP era. A well-informed observer who visited Russia in the 1960s as well as in the 1940s noticed a considerable difference even in public manners. Street behaviour had become less rough-edged, and there was more eccentricity on display, not only in the case of *stilyagi*, but also of young men who 'sport Pushkinesque side-burns and affect the manner of a nineteenth-century guardsman', or 'men, by no means elderly, who greet a lady with old-fashioned bows and kissing of the hand'.[144] Attentive observers of public spaces in the late 1960s, 1970s, and early 1980s recorded similar diversity. In private, a still greater variety of behaviour patterns became noticeable, as broadening access to separate living space placed neighbours at a greater distance, as interference with others' behaviour became a controversial possibility, rather than an explicit duty, and as the increased availability of material goods turned asceticism, for some Soviet citizens, into a counter-cultural choice, rather than an inescapable norm.[145]

---

[143] Solzhenitsyn, *Rakovyi korpus* (Paris, 1970), 231 (ch. 20).

[144] See W. Miller, *Russians as People* (London, 1962), 136.

[145] For sensible journalistic accounts of the post-Stalin era, see H. Smith, *The Russians* (London, 1976) and *The New Russians* (London, 1990). The daily life of the post-Stalin era has yet to receive systematic historical treatment. An outstandingly imaginative account by an insider is S. Boym, *Common Places: Mythologies of Everyday Life in Russia* (Cambridge, Mass., 1994), ch. 2. V. Shlapentokh, *Public and Private Life of the Russian People: Changing Values in Post-Stalin Russia* (New York, 1989), argues for a decline in the work ethic (43), a rise in consumer goods ownership and the importance of family life (163), and an increase in the value placed on privacy (181–2).

BEHAVIOUR BOOKS IN POST-SOVIET RUSSIA:

A CODA

> It's hardly worth trying to mend people's ways during a short visit to
> their homes.
>
> (*Encyclopedia of Etiquette*, 1996)

Deregulation of the publishing industry in Russia began in the late 1980s. As part of Mikhail Gorbachev's commitment to establishing a mixed economy in the Soviet Union by the propagandization of *khozraschet* (independent budgeting), and legalizing the formation of 'co-operatives', i.e small-scale private enterprises (at first mostly in the service and retail sectors), publishers were allowed to negotiate prices for their editions with booksellers from 1987, and independent publication (*izdanie za schet sredstv avtora*) was allowed from 1988. The reluctance of many state publishing houses to take the risk of bringing out sponsored editions led to the emergence of 'co-operative' (i.e. private) publishing.[146] To begin with, most of these were minnow-sized ventures, but popular literature and advice guides were two of the genres in which they specialized at an early stage. This material was bought by the public avidly, and state publishers began to adjust their lists in order to cash in on the boom. Advice literature maintained its hold on the market through the mid-1990s, and until the late 1990s its popularity showed little signs of abating.

Commentary on the post-Soviet advice book is made problematic by the fragmented nature of the book market generally after 1991. With the demise of the preventative censorship (*predvaritel'naya tsenzura*) to which they were adjuncts, the weekly serial bibliography, *Knizhnaya letopis'*, and the annual, *Ezhegodnik knigi*, lost their authority as inclusive sources; even at the end of the twentieth century, there was still no post-Soviet equivalent of commercial Western directories such as *Books in Print*. The catalogues of major libraries were no longer wholly reliable guides to new publications either: private publishers did not necessarily always comply with the legal requirement to supply a copy (the *obyazatel'nyi ekzemplar*) of any publication to the Lenin/State Russian Library in Moscow, and the Public/Russian National Library in St Petersburg. Bewildering, too, was the sheer quantity of advice literature printed, and its vast range, embracing everything from cat-breeding to palm-reading, and including not only mindless trivia, but also serious and helpful books—guides to crime prevention, advice for the victims of crime, particularly sex crime,[147]

---

[146] See Lovell, 'Publishing and the Book Trade in Russia'.
[147] See e.g. *Kak ne stat' zhertvoi prestupleniya* (1991); *Kto zashchishchaet zhenshchin* (1996).

information on legal issues, telephone directories, *Who's Who* collections of the biographies of prominent Moscow businessmen, and so on and so on. The parsimonious trickle of practical books under Soviet power swelled to a vast deluge. A complete survey of this material would demand a separate book in itself: what follows, therefore, concentrates on tracing developments during the 1990s in a few of the genres of advice literature that were represented in Soviet times, so that some sense of historical evolution emerges.

It has become a commonplace to state that the deregulation of publishing totally altered the character of Russian book publishing, replacing a readership based on consumption of serious literature with a market driven by lust for sensational ephemera.[148] In fact, this interpretation misrepresents the situation more than a little. As the earlier part of this chapter has shown, Soviet readers manifested a considerable appetite for popular and ephemeral publications, such as advice books, throughout the post-Stalin era. Nor did books published in Soviet times necessarily go straight into the 'dustbin of history' after 1991. Just as post-Soviet readers continued to enjoy popular novels by the likes of Pikul', so some Soviet conduct guides remained in print, and went on circulating in the new era.[149] What is more, genres such as house management and cookery books remained as productive as before, at any rate until the mid-1990s (See Appendix 5, Table 5). However, they now came to embrace a variety of sub-genres (for instance, guides to home furnishing and curtain-making) which were quite unknown in the days before the collapse of Soviet power.[150]

Something comparable came about in the case of books about health. As early as 1990, publications listed under 'hygiene' in *Ezhegodnik knigi* included seventeen guides to cosmetics and slimming for women, and no less than forty-nine sex manuals. Among the latter were abridged translations of Robert Street's *Modern Sex Techniques* (first published in 1955), F. M. Rossiter's *The Torch of Life: A Key to Sex Harmony* (first published in 1925), and *Xaviera on the Best Part of a Man*, by Xaviera Hollander, author of *The Happy Hooker*. These were followed, in 1991, by a large-format luxury edition of Alex Comfort's *The Joy of Sex*, with full-page

---

[148] See e.g. N. Condee and N. Padunov in N. Condee (ed.), *Soviet Hieroglyphics: Visual Culture in Late Twentieth-Century Russia* (Bloomington, Ind., 1995), 141–2.

[149] See e.g. the bibliography to Chinennyi and Stoyan, *Etiket na vse sluchai zhizni* (1996), 148–9. Soviet-published books were quite often to be seen on the book-stalls (*lotki*) of Moscow and St Petersburg in the late 1990s.

[150] General books on domestic economy, e.g. Nikiforova and Kaganovskaya (eds.), *Domovodstvo* (1998) also included new materials—in this case on Christian festivals such as Christmas and name-days and the desirability of reading the Bible aloud to children, the care of small animals (guinea pigs and hamsters as well as cats, birds, and fish), and the keeping of a family photo album.

colour illustrations.[151] The familiar process by which material from radically different phases of Western history was absorbed at one and the same time meant that the Soviet and post-Soviet reader was presented with a bewildering variety of conflicting advice on sexual behaviour. While Street and Comfort's books (aimed at men) stressed the importance of ensuring mutual pleasure, Xaviera Hollander's laid emphasis on pleasing men above all. Vastly different repertoires of sexual activity were also advocated: Comfort's book (translated from the revised 1986 edition of the English-language original) warned against anal sex on the grounds that it was a means of communicating AIDS, Hollander warmly advocated the practice, and Rossiter's and Street's books passed over it in silence. The sheer variety of advice on offer may help to explain why no one manual of sexual etiquette established dominance over the market, or even made a particular impact on it. Though the introduction to Comfort's book by Igor' Kon anticipated that sales of the book in Russia would be commensurate with those worldwide (more than 8 million copies), the fact that the first Russian edition, of only 50,000 copies, was not reprinted suggests that this anticipation was wrong.[152] Additionally, the character of home-produced materials such as the tabloid newspaper *AIDS-Info* (SPID-Info) (which offered luridly illustrated selections of erotic materials and general hints on sexual practices rather than medical counsel about safe sex) suggests that what the Russian readership often wanted from sex manuals was the kind of titillation inhibited by Soviet censorship, rather than advice on sexual hygiene. Conversely, the persistence of disapproving attitudes to sex manuals as mere smut was suggested by the continuing practice, in some libraries, of shelving them in the 'special sections' (*spetskhrany*), along with incunabula and rare books of the eighteenth and early nineteenth centuries.[153]

More popularity, in the long run, was enjoyed by two other Western-dominated areas of advice literature: the self-help guide in the modern sense (i.e. the manual of popular psychotherapy), and the guide to success in business. One of the specialists in the first area was Nikolai Kozlov, a Moscow psychotherapist, whose *How to Relate to Yourself and Others, or*

---

[151] Rossiter, *Vse o sekse* (1989); Strit, *Tekhnika sovremennogo seksa* (1990); Khollander, *Kak stat' seksual'noi zhenshchiny* (1990); Komfort, *Radost' seksa* (1991).

[152] It is possible that the opulency and cost of the Comfort translation was off-putting to Russian readers, but the failure of the book to make much headway even with the Russian 'new rich' (whose numbers in Moscow alone should have been sufficient to ensure a reprint) is still significant.

[153] On a visit to the Russian National Library in St Petersburg in May 2000, I saw one reader, in evident embarrassment, collecting his copy of a book called *The Secrets of Chinese Sex* (Tainy kitaiskogo seksa). Having myself, when scanning the Russian translation of *The Joy of Sex* in 1996, endured the inquisitive stares of other readers, most of whom were assiduously transcribing notes from dusty leatherbound volumes, I felt a good deal of sympathy for this person.

Practical Psychology for Every Day had reached a third edition by 1996. Kozlov, who peppered his account with nauseatingly cheery pieces of information about himself and his family, such as the fact that he called his wife Wonderwoman (Chudo) and she liked to refer to him as Sunshine (Solnyshko), or that his standard response when she asked whether he liked her new dress was, 'Yes, but I prefer you with nothing on at all,' drew heavily on self-help tomes by American authors of the 1980s. He presented his readers, for example, with a quiz in order to establish whether they were a Hawk, a Dove, or an Ostrich, and emphasized self-assertion to a degree unprecedented in Russian conduct guides: 'I don't know what guilt is'; 'If a person lacking conscience is one who doesn't allow that stupid and inhumane old bag Conscience to torment him, then I'm proud of having no conscience at all.' Apologies were only worth countenancing, he asserted, as a means of assuaging others' feelings.[154] In this propaganda for guilt-free existence, interpersonal relations (to invoke an appropriate cliché), and most particularly sexual relationships, were now validated to the exclusion of anything else; all conceptualization of 'the collective good' had disappeared. Morality was no longer at issue: any relationship or situation that 'felt good' was to be welcomed.

Though Kozlov's book went through several editions, the runaway success in the genre of individualistic self-help books was a far older publication, Dale Carnegie's *How to Win Friends and Influence People*. This American classic, first published in 1937, went through no less than sixty-eight editions in Russian from 1989 to 1997. An introduction to a provincial edition of the book, published in Kemerovo in 1990, summed up the importance of the material to the new economic situation:

Today, when the Kuzbass is on the verge of economic independence, of the transition to self-finance and financial responsibility [*samookupaemost'*], when international business relations have become a reality, Dale Carnegie's advice has acquired a special value for us; after all, he demonstrates how 'they' carry out their business affairs, the principles according to which our Western business partners operate.[155]

Anxiety about how to deal with Western businessmen seems to have been a motivating factor in the publication not only of Carnegie's book, but also of other self-help guides for new Russian *kommersanty*—at any rate judging by the emphasis given on the importance of not offending foreign customs in the books themselves. Readers were warned, for example, not to go on the razzle when abroad, not to overestimate their importance in terms of their business partners, and not to attempt fixing deals 'through the back

[154] Kozlov, *Kak otnosit'sya k sebe i lyudyam*, 10, 253, 54–6, 93.
[155] Karnegi, *Kak zavoevyvat' druzei* (1990), 6.

door', as none of these strategies was likely to go down well with foreigners.[156] But the point was not simply or even mainly 'knowing one's enemy'. Like the books for diplomats published in the 1940s, books for Russian businessmen published in the 1990s emphasized the Western businessman as an appropriate model for emulation in an absolute sense. They propagandized a distinctly idealistic image of the Western business-man as representing a time-honoured package of efficiency and organ-ization plus morality, good taste, and good manners. As D. V. Beklashov put it in *Manners and Conduct for the Businessman,* 'business ethics' embraced honesty, the willingness to take responsibility, the ability and desire to find compromises, professional knowledge (of the product, of commercial relations, of foreign languages), plus 'a profound internal culture', 'a good level of physical preparation' (i.e. fitness), 'the ability to be elegant, self-controlled and organized', good manners, and knowledge of proto-col.[157]

Yet again the *honnête homme* reconstituted himself (though this time in his early twentieth-century manifestation), and once more, material that was stunningly unoriginal was presented as radically new. In their introduction to the maunderings of Dale Carnegie, for example, two Soviet specialists in psychology asserted (with confident disregard for the facts), that 'advice literature' (*zhanr pouchenii*) was 'an unfamiliar genre for our [i.e. Soviet] readers'. And they asserted the high intellectual value of this material, presenting Carnegie as 'a serious specialist in the human factor', who was never guilty of 'slipping into mere entertainment and banality', and even (still more flatteringly) as the heir to William James's theory of pragmatism.[158]

At the same time, the novelty of some aspects of the guides for businessmen, in terms of their cultural context, must be acknowledged. In an abstract sense, they attempted to find a justification for values such as 'honesty' without appealing either to the need to respect the social hierarchy, or to the old Soviet myth of a jealously vigilant collective. Instead, they took the utilitarian view that trust, co-operation, and good-will were to be advocated because they were successful in terms of business relations. They offered a kind of practical morality which, however limited

---

[156] See e.g. Venediktova, *O delovoi etike i etikete* (1994), esp. 6–12.

[157] Beklashov, *Manery i povedenie delovogo cheloveka,* 4. Other books of this type include Maksimovsky, *Etiket delovogo cheloveka* (1994).

[158] See Karnegi, *Kak zavoevyvat' druzei* (1989), 8, 7, 10. Another popular Western author given an incongruously 'academic' treatment is C. Northcote Parkinson: editions of *Parkinson's Law* (for example, *Zakony Parkinsona* (1989)), customarily appear without the humorous cartoons by Osbert Lancaster that lightened the tone of the original, but prefaced by ponderous ruminations upon the wisdom of Parkinson's advice on dealing with the 'Alice-in-Wonderland world of bureaucracy' (*byurokraticheskoe zazerkal'e*).

its horizons and questionable its suppositions, was at least more far-reaching than the 'rational egotism' proposed in guides to individual happiness such as Kozlov's. The extent to which these books succeeded in filling the moral vacuum left by the collapse of Soviet concepts such as 'the collective' or 'conscience' (in the sense 'social conscience') is questionable (certainly, 'business ethics' were generally agreed to be in short supply among Russian entrepreneurs in the late 1990s). But they were an interesting phenomenon in that they were the first indigenous Russian sources to combine, in a code of business ethics, such national values as 'deep internal culture' with advocacy of an enlightened commercialism respectful of laws and of business partnerships.

In terms of their relation to post-Stalinist models of gender identity, the businessmen's guides also worked to consolidate, as well as challenge, the past. But here their role was rather more ambiguous. To be sure, the representation of etiquette as essential to career success broke down the Soviet opposition between 'distsiplina' and the 'feminized' aspects of *kul'turnost'*, 'tact' and 'delicacy'. 'Tact' was now seen (in Carnegie, for instance) as an effective form of manipulating opponents, particularly when combined with sudden and unpredictable fits of aggression (rule 12 is 'Make sure you grab them', *zadevaite za zhivoe*). There was no reason, therefore, why etiquette should be seen as a specifically feminine property. Yet at the same time, the guides propounded an absolute division between work and home. The role of the family, if considered at all, was simply to support the career of the main bread-winner, who was invariably assumed to be male. For Dale Carnegie, the most important rules for a wife were, 'Don't nag' (*ne pridiraites'*) and 'Don't try reforming your husband' (*ne pytaites' peredelat' svoego supruga*); similar advice was offered in the complementary guides of Dorothy Carnegie, expounding the duties of a 'perfect wife' at greater length, which started to appear in Russia in the late 1990s.[159] If manuals of 'business etiquette' ever did acknowledge the existence of 'businesswomen', this was normally only in order to offer advice on dress (no fancy patterns or short skirts), or on the exercise of 'feminine wiles'; no specific guide to 'success at work for women' had appeared before 2000.[160]

Here, rather than running ahead of social practices, advice literature (perhaps fortuitously) reflected them. With very few exceptions, the new entrepreneurs of the 1990s were male; to have a stay-at-home wife was

[159] An abridged translation of Dorothy Carnegie's *How to Help your Husband be Successful at Work* was published in 1990 as an appendix to the Kemerovo edition of *Kak zavoevyvat' druzei* (see n. 109); a full translation was on the bookstalls in Moscow in the summer of 1997.

[160] Venediktova, *O delovoi etike i etikete*, 88–90. On 'feminine wiles' see *Shkola etiketa*. The only exception to this generalization is Western-style glossy magazines (see below), which did occasionally offer advice on dealing with stereotyping at interview, etc.

fashionable since it was a sign of high earning power and of a 'modern' ability to break with Soviet norms. Given that most 'stay-at-home wives' had been brought up to expect to have their own careers, there could be friction of a kind that the Carnegies, writing in 1930s America, had utterly failed to anticipate. In July 1997, for example, a woman calling herself 'Tat'yana' wrote to the Petersburg women's weekly *Damskii ugodnik* lamenting that she had complied with her husband's wish that she give up work, having not known how dreary and frustrated she would feel:

His way of life has completely changed. The car and the mobile telephone are his best friends, they're always at his side. It's nothing but meetings with 'useful people', restaurants, drinking. Going out drinking is something he has to do for work, and then he drinks to wind down afterwards. And then, in order to live up to his new status, he's started going to 'prestigious' places. Night clubs, casinos, expensive restaurants. I don't go with him. There's the baby and the house to keep me busy, for a start, and then he doesn't really seem to want me to go anyway.[161]

Women in this position were beyond the reach of advice literature of any kind. Women's organizations naturally gave first emphasis to cases of actual domestic violence and of economic hardship; mere loneliness and boredom of this kind naturally did not seem so important. The businessman might be seen as an important and novel form of reader in need of new kinds of advice, but the particular needs of his wife were not recognized or assuaged.

Apart from representations of the businessman in the abstract, another growth area of post-Soviet behaviour books was in the area of what was now called *imidzh*: dress, hospitality, and personal demeanour. It was here where departure from the past was most heavily emphasized. The direction to smile frequently—never given in Soviet etiquette books—was one striking feature. One of Carnegie's 'rules' of conduct, the smiling imperative, was also underlined in the 1993 edition of Borunkov's guide for diplomats; the author saw a ready smile as essential now that the world was no longer made up of 'comrades and misters', but of citizens equal in urbanity.[162] But the need for more relaxed and friendly behaviour was by no means invariably assumed. The practical advice given in *The School of Etiquette*, an opulent hardback aimed at 'new Russians', suggests, for example, that 'crude, vulgar mimicry' (i.e. excessively demonstrative 'body language', to use a term employed elsewhere in the book), was to

---

[161] 'Pis'ma v *Damskii ugodnik*', *Damskii ugodnik* 35 (July, 1997), p. 26.

[162] Borunkov, *Diplomaticheskii protokol v Rossii i diplomaticheskii etiket*, 72. The same writer's *Diplomaticheskii protokol v Rossii* (1999), 161–8, warns readers that Soviet sources on diplomacy are now somewhat 'outdated', and recommends instead books from the post-Soviet period and a selection of Western manuals.

be avoided, and recommended such tortuous exercises in the higher levels of table manners as the dissection of apples with a knife and fork:

Push the skin that you have peeled off with your knife to the edge of your plate (the one furthest from you), and place the peeled apple in the centre of your plate. Having wiped your left hand on your napkin, cut the apple in half with your knife and fork. Place one half of the apple slightly to the side, and cut the second half into quarters. Holding each quarter on your fork, cut the core out with your knife and place it on top of the discarded peel. Then, with the aid of your knife and fork, eat the peeled and cored segment and move on to the next, and then to the next half-apple, proceeding with it in the same way that you have with the first...[163]

—though one suspects that by this stage most readers would have quite lost their appetite for fruit.

Not only guides for professionals, but some publications aimed at the private citizen were insistent on the need for manners that traditional Russian perceptions would have branded as impossibly *choporny* (stuffy), and which would have seemed undesirably stiff in many Western circles of the 1990s as well. For example, *Etiquette and Us* (1993), represented even the entertaining of friends at home as something of an ordeal: ad hoc dropping in was to be discouraged, and every meal dictated several changes of an already elaborate place-setting, along with multiple courses and a variety of different wines. Conversation, the reader was told, should be sober and frigid, with personal remarks and intrusive questions avoided, and also 'jokes about other people's surnames, complexions, bald patches or hair colour, height, nationality, place of origin, education, or serious motor accidents' (in other words, pretty well any jokes at all); the weather (that infamous British ice-breaker) was recommended as a safe topic. The time-honoured custom of drinking toasts to *Bruderschaft* (brotherhood) in order to mark a rite of passage to the use of the informal second personal plural was censured, and so, too, was the eminently practical custom of giving visitors *tapochki* (slippers or house-shoes) to replace their footwear as they enter the flat. The ethos of reserve and self-control was supposed to extend beyond public occasions as well: with a sense of understatement not apparently intended humorously, the reader was advised, 'to threaten suicide in the midst of a family quarrel is most ungentlemanly'.[164]

Remarkable in these publications was their indiscriminate and exaggerated struggle to counteract any spontaneity and humour in human

---

[163] *Shkola etiketa: poucheniya na vsyakii sluchai* (1996), 186–7, 331–1. A significantly simpler instruction is given in the 1961 Soviet abridgement of Emily Post, *Etiquette*, 34: 'Apples and pears are quartered usually with a knife. The core is then cut away from each quarter and the fruit is eaten in the fingers. Those who do not like the skin pare each quarter separately.'

[164] *Etiket i my* (1993), 33–8, 51–3, 36, 28.

relations. A greater degree of courtesy in public was seen by them as necessarily matched by self-restraint in the private sphere. This was a world in which slopping round in a dressing-gown at home was as rude as placing a used tea-bag in a restaurant ashtray, and where making a crude joke among friends was as unforgivable as answering a telephone at work with the phrase 'Who's that?' Though etiquette manuals of the 1960s and 1970s certainly sought to regulate private behaviour, they were less whole-hearted in their propagandization of a supposedly neutral, undifferentiated, brisk and formal behaviour pattern for all occasions. Well might *The School of Etiquette* emphasize the fact that there was an increasing standardization of behaviour worldwide, since it and similar volumes propounded a code of behaviour as lacking in individuality as the contents of the average international chain hotel bedroom, or, indeed, as the monotonously luxurious homes envisaged by translated publications such as the *Formation of the Domestic Interior* series (1997).[165]

At the same time, if the Russian manuals are compared with the translations of Western behaviour manuals that began appearing in the early 1990s, some discrepancies do emerge. An opulent, two-volume Russian edition of Amy Vanderbilt's *New Complete Book of Etiquette: The Guide to Gracious Living*, published in 1996, more than three decades after the American original, revealed an astonishing degree of inertia in the reproduction not only of information that was hopelessly out of date (for instance, the suggestion that Europeans bathed only once a week, or that the correct manner of asking for the lavatory in 'England' was to say, 'May I wash my hands?'), but also information that was totally redundant for a Russian reader (such as the statement that the sign for a women's lavatory in Russia (in fact the letter Ж for женский) 'resembles a spider').[166] However, the attraction of the publication may well have been that it included material not generally covered in Russian advice literature, such as the problem of how to address your servants; the question of whether it was polite to send Christmas cards to a Jewish friend; the etiquette of a divorce; and the art of visiting your children when they were going through their American college education. This last topic in particular was likely to be of importance to those few privileged members of Russian society who, taking refuge from the financial starvation of educational institutions in their home country, began, in the mid-1990s, to have their

---

[165] The first five parts of the series *Oformlenie domashnikh inter'erov*, were *Ubranstvo spal'ni* (How to Decorate Your Bedroom), *Ukrashaem stol i prinimaem gostei* (Table Decorations and Entertaining Guests), *Ukrashaem okna: sorok pyat' stilei, opisannykh shag za shagom* (Window Decorations: A Step-by-Step Guide to Forty-Five Different Styles), *Ubranstvo gostinoi* (Decorating Your Living-Room) and *Ubranstvo kukhni* (Decorating Your Kitchen).

[166] Vanderbil't, *Etiket*, ii. 253.

children educated abroad. And for those lacking such privileges, the very curious information about Western European practices was no doubt taken on trust, coming as it did from a Western author, so that a conduct book— in familiar mode—was seen as the source of intriguing details about the peculiarity of foreigners, rather than as a fount of practical information about how to behave in their presence. Similar sources of luridly impractical information were translated household manuals, offering advice that could only have been useful to the very well-off. Even the simplest designs in one American compendium of 'window treatments'— for example, plain french-pleated curtains without ruffles, blinds, or pelmets—required a formidable amount of material and specialist purchases (tapes, interlinings, hooks, cords, curtain-rails) compared with the simple unlined oblong of material suspended from five or six metal clips that was still the standard Russian curtain at the time.[167] Yet it is none the less possible that some readers of more modest means purchased copies of these books as a way of escaping into fantasy—assuming that the relatively high prices charged even for the book did not act as a complete deterrent.

Not surprisingly, the original Russian behaviour manuals (if one can use the word 'original' about a genre where plagiarism remained so common) were considerably closer to the world of the average Russian reader than this. What is more, they resembled their Soviet predecessors extremely closely in terms of the format in which advice was given. *Etiquette and Us* contained the usual series of sections on behaviour at work, on holiday, at home, at exhibitions and the theatre, and in public transport, along with advice on dress and conversational topics, while *The School of Etiquette* presented the new cultural information in the time-honoured Soviet form of round-up quizzes: 'Do You Know the Rules of Bon-Ton?' 'Let's Get Acquainted', and 'When People Pay You Compliments', among others.[168]

Despite some underlying continuities with the Soviet past, though, most manuals had, by the mid-1990s, become explicitly anti-Soviet in terms of their outward standpoint. The point of the quizzes, for example, was now self-betterment that was not intellectual in character, and had a competitive edge ('How Good a Businesswoman Are You?'). Where participation in

---

[167] See *Ukrashaem okna*, 37. Fabric and notions for dress-making and home decoration became more widely available in the late 1990s (there was a particularly well-stocked bazaar for such items in south-west Moscow), but fancy drapes would still have required a great deal of money and effort to make.

[168] Much the same format is observed in two recent books for adolescent girls, Rukavchuk (ed.), *Entsiklopediya etiketa* (1996), and the nauseatingly entitled *Entsiklopediya dlya malen'kikh printsess* (1996). Though the latter shows signs of Western influence too, recommending to the reader tampons (228) and 'sheiping' (i.e. body-shaping, 340), it includes a quiz on 'self-observation' (see below), while the former combines advice on pet-care and napkin-folding with a list of 'Qualities the Modern Girl Should Have' ('a well-meaning character' and 'a healthy appearance' are nos. 1 and 2, 'intelligence' no. 3, p. 171).

the social collective was advocated, this was according to a quite different model from that set out in Soviet behaviour guides. Readers were now exhorted to acquire the ability to please those with whom they associated, rather than to implement the principles of an abstract code (albeit one as vague as 'The Moral Code of the Builders of Communism'). One guide for adolescent girls, *The Little Princess's Encyclopedia*, for example, suggested a 'self-observation' exercise in which the performer scrutinized her own table-manners, conversational skills, ability to 'carry out little services for others', and 'behaviour when in company'. Further, an acute embarrassment about what the books themselves presented as stereotypically 'Russian' traits—spontaneity, lack of self-control, ignorance of the 'rules of Bon-Ton'—was frequently evident.[169]

This at times uncritical idolization of the foreign was paralleled by an equally uncritical celebration of the national past. Ol'ga Muranova's *How the Russian Gentleman Was Brought Up* (1995) was ostensibly a sub-Lotmanish history of nineteenth-century behaviour patterns, but the author's sententious tone and moralizing asides made explicit that her purpose was mainly to resurrect the past as model for the present, rather than representing it as a vanished curiosity. She argued that the *dvoryanstvo* behaviour code had been 'an organic unity of ethical and etiquette norms'. It had given 'full space to the expression of personality; a person who was in command of the rules of *bon ton* not only did not feel oppressed by these, but acquired genuine freedom in his relations with other people thanks to them'. Such assertions oversimplified the difficulties of some historical subjects, such as Pushkin or Anna Tyutcheva, when living within the behaviour codes that Murav'eva described; but they facilitated Muranova's task of propagandizing an alternative, 'non-Soviet', behaviour model for her own contemporaries. In Muranova's words, 'Along with the word *lyubeznost'* [amiability] has vanished from daily life everything which that word expressed; along with bows and other "trifles" have disappeared shades of feelings and relationships, which only those "trifles" were capable of expressing.' In Muranova's impassioned representation, 'the manners of the Russian gentleman' stood for everything that the author considered desirable in modern society, from arriving punctually at the theatre to adaptability and practicality. She eulogized aristocratic women who worked as seamstresses to keep their families in Soviet times, and related, as a clinching anecdote, the tale of a Russian aristocrat's impeccable reaction to a customary hazard of Soviet life, a rebarbitive privy:

---

[169] *Entsiklopediya dlya malen'kikh printsess*, 424. Similarly, advice on the home library (pp. 424–5), rather than suggesting a canon of texts to be owned, instructed the owner to set the books out in alphabetical order within subject category. Tidiness had replaced knowledge as the focus of advice-giving.

At the end of the 1940s, a permanent camp used for geological expeditions boasted an exceptionally filthy public toilet. It goes without saying that this circumstance in itself would not have attracted anyone's attention; however, one of the expedition parties arriving at the camp most unfortunately contained among its members the descendant of an ancient princely family. 'Well, it's all right for us,' the geologists thought; 'but what's His Highness going to make of it?' When 'His Highness' arrived, what he did made many people feel really small. He got hold of a bucket of water and a mop and scrubbed the dirt-encrusted lavatory clean.[170]

Though Muranova ended her book with a question about the value of a *dvoryanstvo* upbringing, this and other vignettes had ensured that the question had been answered in advance.

The tradition of *vospitanie* to which Muranova looked back in her work was, of course, a Westernized one, so that the nationalism of her text was diluted. A much stronger and more overt celebration of Russian tradition resounded in the work of some other commentators on behaviour. Particularly striking in this respect was a low-budget soft-cover effort, by A. I. Chinennyi, and T. A. Stoyan, *Etiquette for Every Occasion*, published in 1996—three years, as it happens, after the reissuing of Gogol's *Selected Passages from Correspondence with Friends*, brought out by a Moscow publisher in 1993.

Unusually for an etiquette book, Chinennyi and Stoyan's book provided some information about its authors' biographies, which was significant enough to be worth repeating. Chinennyi (born in 1924), described himself as a retired military man, who served in the Second World War and was decorated with the For Valour (Za otvagu) medal. He later joined the staff of the Yury Gagarin Air Force Academy where he rose to be head of the Social Sciences Department—that is, the section responsible for communist indoctrination). Stoyan, who was much younger (born 1955) than her co-author, had an equally predictable background for a nationalist, being from the Russian-speaking community in Ukraine. A graduate in history who had studied social sciences (in the Soviet sense) at postgraduate level, she was, at the time the book was published, a 'senior instructor [*starshii prepodavatel'*] in the history of the Fatherland' at Kiev State Pedagogical University.

Etiquette for Every Occasion was eminently characteristic of the new nationalism. On the one hand, it harked back to the Soviet past, as, for example, in the following definition of *kul'turnost'*, stereotypical right down to its invocation of an exact (if also highly questionable) statistic:

[170] O. Muranova, *Kak vospytivali russkogo dvoryanina* (Moscow, 1995), 7, 102, 237–8. For similar attitudes in an etiquette book, see e.g. *Etiket: umen'e zhit' i vesti sebya doma v sem'e*, 2: 'this book will help you to remember what was lost by our society during the years of Soviet power'. Much of the material is plagiarized from 19th-cent. sources, as the phrasing indicates—'Prilichno kushat' sostavlyaet tseluyu nauku' (27).

[*Kul'turnost'* is] the fusion of intellectual education, moral self-education and moral education, innate *intelligentnost'*. Much benefit is also derived from friendship with books, wide reading. The only pity is that a person can only read five thousand books in his conscious life, out of a total of millions of cultural treasures. Having books in your home is a sign of culture.[171]

Yet at the same time, the book devoted a substantial section to Orthodox rituals (weddings, christenings, funerals); advocated a return to pre-revolutionary military protocol (appending a reading list of books on *The Code of Honour of the Russian Officer*, etc.); and, above all, abandoned the Soviet regime's ostensible commitment to egalitarianism before all else. Etiquette, the authors argued, was necessary not so much because it ensured equal treatment for all, as to facilitate the smooth articulation of the social hierarchy:

The rules of etiquette are essential in order to mute the 'animal principles' buried in each individual, to oppose the norms of reserve and decency to instincts and emotions. The tokens of etiquette are essential, finally, to maintain a relative degree of equality between people, and mutual respect, in a society that is full of 'objective inequality'. After all, the objective legal status of men and women, old and young, junior and senior, superior and inferior, parents and children, acquaintances and strangers, is not at all the same. And everyone should know his place, his rights and his duties.[172]

The book harked back to the past most explicitly in setting out its recommendations for relationships between men and women. The patronizing celebration of superior femininity characteristic of the late Soviet period was abandoned, and the authors went so far as to resurrect the pre-Petrine ideal of the virtuous and obedient wife:

In many situations, a woman's eye sees more clearly and sharply than a man's. At the critical moment, her perspicacity saves the situation. The virtues of a wife— patience, submissiveness, kindness—create the conditions for inner *bon ton*.

Such a combined image of a wife and mother is formed by upbringing and must become a woman who possesses all virtues. Among the traits of woman, eight good qualities stand out: honesty, fidelity to her husband, modesty, shame, cleanliness, thrift, kindness, industry. . . . The wife is responsible for the *bon ton* that reigns in any harmonious household. . . . The *Domostroi*, to which we have already referred, was composed in the sixteenth century, but it is still useful at the end of the twentieth century, and in it a portrait of a wife distinguished by modesty, respect and self-sacrifice [*smirenie*] is to be found. The wife should only be pleasing to her husband, and therefore cosmetics are pointless and to be

[171] Chinennyi and Stoyan, *Etiket na vse sluchai zhizni* (1996), 80. This book certainly found at least one avid reader: it arrived in my hands having been well-thumbed by a 21-year-old male from a technical college (my thanks to his flatmate, Stephen Lovell, for this information).

[172] Chinennyi and Stoyan, *Etiket na vse sluchai zhizni*, 5–6.

condemned. After all, the husband knows his wife without any decorations. The wife should know how to bake, boil, and do every kind of women's handiwork, and she should 'not be at all fond' of intoxicating drink. And a wife should not be gloomy; after all, a cheerful wife is always more beautiful.[173]

Later in the book, the authors suggested that this patriarchal idyll should not altogether absolve the husband from conjugal responsibility (the importance of a marriage's 'intimate aspects' was stressed—though no practical advice was given—and a quiz for husbands was included, which implied that men who help with shopping and child-minding (though not cleaning, cooking, and clothes-washing) made better husbands). But on the whole, a man's main duties were perceived as lying in the public sphere— behaving with respect to those in authority, and avoiding drunkeness, debauchery, and spitting in the street. A certain distance was to be maintained between a father and his family. Relations between father and daughter, in particular, were to be characterized by 'respect' rather than 'tenderness': 'For instance, a daughter should be respectful to her father, rather than over-affectionate. For his part, a father must be extremely reserved in the presence of his daughter.'[174] Though some Western advice had leaked in even to this treatise—for instance, in the instruction to the reader on p. 93 to follow Dale Carnegie's advice and hold his [sic] head high—the general effect of the book was that of a desperate attempt to shore up the sandbank of Russian tradition against the tidal wave of newfangled Western ways.[175]

The drabness of *Etiquette for Every Occasion* (another aspect that harked back to the Soviet past!), with its orange-speckled paper cover decorated with a line drawing of a gentleman, dressed in an approximation of the fashions of the 1910s, raising his hat, and its poor-quality paper, suggested an appeal to a quite specific section of a market which was now as elaborately stratified as the pre-revolutionary market for behaviour books. Other publications, such as *The School of Etiquette, The Formation of Domestic Interiors*, and most particularly Vanderbilt's book, had significantly more luxurious production values. However, in the same way as before the Revolution or indeed in the 1930s, it was magazines rather than

---

[173] Ibid. 9–10. [174] Ibid. 14–15, 19.

[175] Comparable low-budget publications with a strongly nationalist and moralistic feel are those in 'Do it Right' (Delaite eto pravil'no), a series issued by Bukmen of Moscow. In Kuz'menko (comp.), *Delaite eto pravil'no: Svad'ba* and *Delaite eto pravil'no: Pokhorony*, for instance (Fig. 20) readers were advised to serve traditional foods, and provided with instructions for carrying out Orthodox ceremonies and traditional rituals. Nothing was said about appropriate dress, or about the materialist aspects of the ceremony (presents, etc.); there was not even advice on how to acquire coffins, or how to make a booking for a ceremony. Other titles in the series, apart from those on rituals (e.g. christenings), included manuals on mushroom-hunting and on home brewing.

FIG. 20. *Do It Right: Funerals* (front cover of advice
manual, 1996).

books that most sharply reflected the new class distinctions. *Imidzh* for the
relatively well-off was propagandized above all by the new Western-style
glossy magazines. These were mostly, with occasional exceptions such as
Domovoi (House Spirit), a lifestyle magazine run by the Kommersant
publishing group, simply Russian editions of titles circulating in the
West. A forerunner in the field, *Cosmopolitan*, which began publishing in
1994, was later joined by numerous other titles, including *Elle*, *Marie-
Claire*, *World of Interiors*, and *Vogue*, whose launch took place under rather
blighted circumstances during the financial crisis of August 1998). All these
magazines carried large amounts of advice coverage on fashion, cosmetics,
interior design, cookery, travel, and leisure activities. Their street price was
at least 5 dollars a copy in the summer of 1997 (more than ten times the cost

of a ride on the metro, or of an issue of the newspaper-style magazines). In the autumn of 1998, after the financial crisis had hit, the price in dollars had dropped slightly, but represented a still larger chunk of an income earned in roubles. The esoteric character of the advice material presented was indicated by, for instance, the issue of *Domovoi* for July 1997, which included articles on remote-controlled toys, the spa facilities in Baden-Baden, and on yachting in the Volga; an item on styling your bathroom to suit your astrological sign; and another on having your picnic catered by professional restaurateurs (at a cost of around 100 dollars per head). At the same time, the fact that the readership of these magazines perhaps extended outside the plutocratic elite was suggested by the fact that their print-runs were reasonably large (especially in the case of *Cosmopolitan*, whose debut issue went to nearly half a million copies).[176]

A second tier of magazines, printed on rather less glossy paper, and at a lower cost, offered material that was slightly less fabulous in terms of those who were not dollar millionaires. Foremost in this category was *Ogonek*, which after its revamp in the mid-1990s more or less abandoned investigative journalism in favour of gossip, sensational news, and features on bodily hygiene, furniture, and food.[177] Not surprisingly, middle-market women's magazines also carried huge amounts of advice coverage. These included the former Soviet titles *Rabotnitsa* and *Krest'yanka*, which switched, early in the 1990s, from running articles about prize-winning milkmaids to carrying fashion, grooming, cookery, and astrology columns, as well as magazines founded in the post-Soviet period, such as *Liza* (first published in 1996), which offered its readers extensive advice on subjects ranging from the right choice of wineglasses to the best selection of resorts in Cyprus, from how to make sure your pot plants stayed watered when on the beach in Cyprus, to how to catch and keep hold of your man.[178] A cohort of young women's magazines, notably *Rovesnik*, *Shestnadtsat'*, and *Shtuchka*, counselled its readers (in the manner of Western products such as

---

[176] N. Kozhevnikova in 'The Style Council', *Pulse* 9 (1998), 27, quotes print-runs as follows: *Cosmopolitan* 480,000 (July 1994); *Elle* 200,000 (Spring, 1996); *Marie Claire* 100,000 (Mar. 1997).

[177] See e.g. 'Shtora, eto obraz zhizni', *Ogonek* 12 (Mar. 1996), 24–5; article on toothcare 16 (Apr. 1996), 24–5 (the piece includes advertisement pictures of French gel dentaire, though presented as editorial); 'Iskusstvo byt' bogatym', by Yury Oleshuk (*Ogonek* 18 (Apr. 1996), 21–23; Viktoriya Tokareva's culinary advice, with the somewhat misleading title 'Est' veshchi vazhnee edy', *Ogonek* 11 (Mar. 1996), 81. After the 1998 crisis, the emphasis on items of this kind diminished somewhat in favour of 'soft' features, especially celebrity profiles.

[178] *Liza* 31 (1996) had, for instance, a 'colour psychology' piece ('Kakogo tsveta vash kharakter?', 12), tips on how to keep your plants watered while away (20) and how to serve drinks (23), as well as material on travel, cooking, fashion, a quiz on 'Do you over-protect your child?' ('Ne slishkom li vy opekaete rebenka', 24), as well as advice on health (19), childcare (22) and an agony column ('O samom intimnom', 25). According to Kozhevnikova, 'The Style Council', the circulation for the 'deeply provincial and sincere' *Krest'yanka* was 450,000 in 1998.

Sugar) on dilemmas such as 'how to make him put a condom on' or 'how to be a bitch'.[179] More modest in terms of their production values, but equally assiduous in offering advice, were newspaper-style magazines such as *Damskii ugodnik*. Similarly, the previously august weekly newspaper *Nezavisimaya gazeta* began in the mid-1990s to run supplements on health and family life (*Zdorov'e, Sem'ya i byt*) which brought readers advice on subjects such as 'dress for success' according to typecast colour-coordination, elegant living, and the avoidance of *faux pas* on social occasions.[180]

Magazines, still relatively few and far between as late as 1993, had, by 1996, turned into one of the most dynamic areas of the Russian print market. In an article published in *Elle* in May 1997, and modelled on the 'what's in and what's out' coverage beloved of Western glossies, Gennady Ustiyan listed magazines, along with whisky, unisex perfumes, skiing and tampons, as the fashion hits of the 1990s. He pointed to magazines' advice coverage as a key factor in readership interest:

The fat novels with their exhaustingly detailed descriptions of a life that seems very alien to us, however interesting it may be, have been replaced by the more functional 'new' magazines. These are to be welcomed because they come out regularly, because they are full of beautiful pictures, and finally because you can learn many useful and practical things by reading them.[181]

Though there were indeed occasional practical items in these publications—for example, *Damskii ugodnik* was running a sensible and informative column about women's legal rights in 1997—'functional' is perhaps not the word that would first spring to mind in attempting to describe them. The world they represented was one where outward appearance really did count for everything, where a nineteenth-century ruler could be summed up in the sentence, 'The Russian Emperor Nicholas I was very sensitive to sounds and colours; he could not stand the colour black.'[182] Compared with material of this kind, the content of early twentieth-century lifestyle magazines such as *Damskii mir* could be described as verging on the profound.

Some of the advice, too, was compromised in its neutrality and helpfulness by the fact that the barrier between advertising and editorial copy was disconcertingly porous. The St Petersburg women's magazine *Natali*, for example, was, in 1997, running front covers that were to all

---

[179] On these, see Elena Omel'chenko, 'New Dimensions of the Sexual Universe: Sexual Discourses in Russian Youth Magazines', in C. Corrin (ed.), *Gender and Identity in Central and Eastern Europe* (London, 1999), 124–8.

[180] See e.g. Klavdiya W. Stylish [*sic*], 'Seks kak dieta: Prochti i peredai drugomu', *Nezavisimaya gazeta: Zdorov'e* 21 Nov. 1996, 30.

[181] G. Ustiyan, 'Kak my lyubili odno i polyubili drugoe', *Elle* 5 (1997), 71.

[182] Tat'yana Zabozlaeva, 'Tsvet obedennogo stola', *Modnyi bazar* 9 (1997), 18–19.

intents and purposes advertisements for clothing companies. An item under the title 'We Like Real Men!' turned out on close scrutiny to be an advertisement for an agency that aimed to find Russian wives for American men.[183] What is more, the new-style image advice was, at least before the autumn of 1998, restricted to enthusing about the availability of enticing Western goods and experiences; information about value, and guides to enable consumers to discriminate between different versions of the same product, were extremely hard, if not impossible, to find. Nadezhda Kozhevnikova's conclusion that, 'even if they fill their pages with good, honest advice, the Russian glossies never lose sight of their role as a status symbol in their own right' was more accurate in the second part of its formulation than the first.[184] The quality of advice was also compromised in another direction, since many advertisements played upon post-Soviet readers' enthusiasm for conduct guidance, styling themselves on household manuals or etiquette tracts. A series of posters advertising ready-prepared cocktails under the title *Pravila khoroshego dzhin-tonika* (The Rules of a Good Gin and Tonic, punning on *The Rules of Bon Ton*) could have deceived only the least sophisticated. But the practice according to which weather forecasters on NTV turned to camera at the end of their broadcasts in order to extol the virtues of mosquito repellents made by the programme sponsor represented a more insidious kind of commercial propaganda.[185] Material of this kind represented a curious conjunction between the paternalist heritage of Soviet journalism and the unregulated free-market values that triumphed during the Yeltsin era.

The explosion of advisory genres represented only one facet of the transformation of behaviour regulation during the post-Soviet era. Soviet institutions such as the *druzhina* might have disappeared, but private reading was by no means the only method by which advice was disseminated. Indeed, advice bureaux and consultancies of all kinds proliferated in the early and mid-1990s. In July 1996, for example, a Petersburg free newspaper carried advertisements for an 'Academy of Experimental Psychology and Hypnosis', and a 'centre of parapsychology' ('the oldest in St Petersburg) run by 'a specialist in practical magic, Aleksandr Viktorovich Orlov'), alongside advertisements for quack pills and the services of a clairvoyant, as well as for relatively banal (but in Russia, still novel) items such as computers and bathroom tiles.[186]

One boom type of advice office was the marriage agency, which, in

---

[183] 'My rady nastoyashchim muzhchinam!', *Natali* 6 (1997), 26–7.

[184] Kozhevnikova, 'The Style Council', 27.

[185] The posters were displayed in the Moscow Metro in May–June 2000; the weather forecast puffs date from the same period.

[186] *Astok-press* (declared circulation 400,000), 12 July 1996.

Russia, not only facilitated introductions, but also helped clients with phrasing lonely-hearts advertisements, obtaining newspaper box-numbers, and even with conducting the relationship itself. In the event that marriage was achieved, clients were able to return to the agency to receive advice on housework and grooming, and even counselling on dealing with difficult issues, such as how to get on with a new husband's relatives. In this branch of the advice industry too, the emphasis was on teaching women that they should downgrade their ambitions. For example, a representative of the so-called 'Russian Institute of the Family at the International Academy of Information', Tamara Shkunova, warned 'on the shelf' [*zasidevshiesya*] women in their late twenties that they should think of themselves as 'Christmas cake': luscious and of high quality , but destined to dry up soon. She blamed the situation not only on the social ambitions of parents, who wrongly taught children that getting fixed up with a boyfriend or girlfriend could wait till studies were finished, but also, and particularly, on domineering mothers ('major-generals in skirts'), who had 'lost out on the domestic front themselves', and rejected their daughters' suitors, while at the same time teaching them to despise men in general.[187] Shkunova's words not only betrayed the well-established tendency in those offering advice to oversimplify the ramified and wide-ranging causes behind social phenomena, but also gave a negative view of women's moral role within the family that was a new theme of the late 1990s, and yet another aspect of the reaction against 'the Soviet way of life'.

Indeed, the reaction against perceived Soviet norms was a unifying feature in all the different genres of post-Soviet advisory practice—books, magazine columns, and bureaux. Though the precise points at issue, and the extent of the reaction, might vary, materialism was rarely, if ever, criticized in itself. (Even a guide to hunting stressed first and foremost the consumerist attractions of the activity—it ensured a supply of healthy and delicious meat, and of fur for personal use and resale, and meant the hunter had plenty of attractive trophies with which to decorate the home.)[188] The disapproving term *meshchanstvo*, applied to an excessive interest in personal possessions, had largely fallen out of use, except among members of the intelligentsia expressing their dissatisfaction with mass-market genres for a narrow audience of their peers.[189] Along with the dethroning of asceticism as an ideal had gone a ditching of the assumption of social equality; social stratification was taken for granted. Allegiance to the Soviet past was evident only in certain small points of presentation: in the manner of structuring information (a penchant for an authoritative tone, and for forms

---

[187] See Elena Perevedentseva, 'Ya odinokaya ovtsa', *Ogonek* 1 (1996), 47–8.
[188] Gusev, *Lyubitel'skaya okhota* (1997), 3–4, back cover.
[189] See e.g. R. Gal'tseva, 'Zapiski prikhozhanki', *Kontinent* 95 (1998), 286.

such as the quiz remained), and in the reuse (probably unconscious) of clichés such as 'the domestic front'.

These general and incidental features aside, though, advice material had, by the late 1990s, become so varied that it is very difficult to systematize overall tendencies. Indeed, one and the same publication often threw up glaring contradictions, as is piquantly illustrated by the 'Health' supplement to *Nezavisimaya gazeta*, which in January 1997 ran a column on dealing with an alcoholic husband directly opposite one giving recipes for 'seductive cocktails' (cause and effect?)[190] The details of behaviour advocated in different places conflicted still more wildly. For example, where *The School of Etiquette* directed readers to eat an apple with a knife and fork (see above), *Etiquette for Every Occasion* suggested handling it with a knife alone; and while the latter book suggested that presents should always be disinterested, the former's section on business etiquette argued that it was perfectly all right to give presents out of self interest; only in England were they likely to be badly received. Just as important was the fact that there was no longer any attempt to fit contradictory materials into an overarching ideological framework. Soviet behaviour discourses, while riven with internal contradictions, none the less constantly evoked social consensus as legitimation; post-Soviet discussions of behaviour, on the other hand, often had no sense of broader purpose at all, and where they did, presented this in terms of correcting a social atomization whose existence was now taken for granted. Though every form of guidance exhorted readers or participants to obey behaviour rules, the total disappearance of harmonization between specific sets of these made the achievement of a homogeneous society still more elusive than it was in the 1960s, 1970s, and 1980s. At this point, too, the political elite abandoned any attempt to offer overall direction in this area. Boris Yeltsin, president between 1991 and 2000, not only outdid Khrushchev and Brezhnev in terms of offences against *kul'turnost'*, and rivalled their negligent attitude to financial probity, but, unlike any Soviet leader, did not even pretend to be interested in moral leadership. Where Khrushchev, Brezhnev, and later Gorbachev, had pompously inveighed on subjects from the importance of the family to the evils of drinking, Yeltsin became, through the efforts of his entourage, an advertisement for the power of *imidzh* (his behaviour might at times be erratic and his speech inarticulate, but at least his suit was of high quality and his haircut sharp).

The bewildering profusion of advice literature is certainly one reason why parodies and creative reworkings of behaviour texts were scarcer in the post-Soviet era than before 1991. To be sure, parodies of *Soviet* advice

[190] 'Vernite libido sami!', *Nezavisimaya gazeta: Zdorov'e*, 16 Jan. 1997, 25; 'Kak pobedit' zelenogo zmiya', ibid. 24.

literature and moral guidance flourished. Yury Borev's anthology of post-Stalinist *anekdoty* contained a post-Soviet joke in the 'First catch your hare...' style, 'Recipe from the *Book of Tasty and Nutritious Food*, 1992 edition: "First stealthily unlatch the gate [of your neighbour's vegetable garden]...".[191] And an episode of the television situation comedy *Strawberry* (Klubnichka), set in a privately-run café, showed children and grandchildren exhorting the grandmother of the family not to leave for a fortnight's holiday in Paris that she had won in a scratch-card competition by appealing to 'the general good' (*nashe obshchee delo*), a Soviet phrase that sounded ludicrously inappropriate in the thoroughly capitalist setting of a family business.[192] But newer types of advice material were taken more seriously: indicative is the appearance, for the first time since the mid-nineteenth century, of serious reviews of such material.[193] Such ironic responses as did appear were usually jejune, an example being Oleg Solod's joke recipe for a failsafe slimming remedy: 'three teaspoons of lard and six laxative tablets'.[194]

    That said, the shift towards an extreme emphasis on *imidzh* and external behaviour values did evoke at least one interestingly bizarre literary response, in the shape of Ol'ga Novikova's story *Strogaya dama* (A Strict Lady, 1995). The story's protagonist, Zoya, was a young woman descended on the one side from the pre-revolutionary Russian aristocracy, and on the other from the communist elite (Party nomenklatura).[195] This highly improbable ancestry already underlined the fact that Zoya, like the vast majority of her female fictional contemporaries (for example, the heroine of Viktor Erofeev's novel *A Russian Beauty* (Russkaya krasavitsa), was meant to be understood not as a 'type' in the realist sense (that is, a metonym of a particular social group), but as a symbol of a nation in crisis. The plot of the story worked to some extent as a reversal of the notorious early 1990s trash film *The International Girl* (Interdevochka), in which a prostitute makes a disastrous marriage to a Swedish client. Having lost both

---

[191] Yu. Borev, *Fariseya* (Moscow, 1992), 277. The joke puns on the first line of a famous Russian romance, 'Otvorite potikhonuchku kalitku' (where the gate-opening occurs in a romantic context). 1992 was a particularly bleak year of food shortages.

[192] This episode was broadcast on TV-Tsentr on 23 Oct. 1998.

[193] Notably, in *Knizhnoe obozrenie*. See e.g. no. 49 (1992) 5, 'Budem uchit'sya bodi lengvidzhu!' (on a guide to body language); no. 51 (1992), 10, 'Kniga, kotoraya dolzhna byt' v kazhdom dome' (on a home medical book); and no. 32 (1992), 2, 'Znakom'tes': MP *Imidzh-Vest*' (on a press specializing in advice texts). See also Lovell, *The Russian Reading Revolution*, 95.

[194] O. Solod, 'Sekrety pokhudaniya', *Damskii ugodnik* 35 (1997), 30. A more interesting item with a tongue-in-cheek flavour was Efim Shenkin, 'Poprobui sdelat' sam: Ne budu ya tebya uchit'', *Den'gi* 15 (1996), 20–23, advertised on the magazine's front cover as 'The Bribe: How and When to Give It, Who Should Get It', which contained lists of 'going rates' for getting telephones installed and businesses set up, and advice on which officials should and should not be bribed.

[195] O. Novikova, 'Strogaya dama', *Znamya*, 6 (1995), 1–18.

parents in a car crash, and become dissatisfied with her job as an Intourist guide (though 'the people you had to deal with were pretty civilized, no one used crude language' (p. 3)—the first instance of a 'civilization' motif that recurs insistently through the text), Zoya takes up a friend's invitation to visit Germany, evades an offer of marriage, and gets acquainted with a German woman who has worked as a prostitute, specializing in sado-masochistic dominance rituals. On returning to Moscow, Zoya sets herself up as a dominatrix [*domina*], which, despite a hiccup with one client whose personal hygiene is as lax as his sexual desires are unusual, provides her, fairy-tale style, with financial independence, self-respect, and a sense of refinement that is underlined by the reiteration, time and again, of the word 'dama', 'lady'. By becoming not just any prostitute, but one who abuses her clients and refuses penetrative sex, Zoya demonstrates that she has found a sure path to feminine authority in a situation where, as one client puts it, 'Russia can't survive without a strong hand . . . so that hand had better be a woman's' (p. 17).

There was little sense of distance in the way that Zoya's story was presented by Novikova. Indeed, the juxtaposition of her narrative with a second plot strand recounting the melancholy history of another Zoya, a pupil at an 'institute for daughters of the nobility' where chastisement is meted out by sadistic perverts, underlined the fact that women's choices were polarized: the alternatives were to beat, or to be beaten. 'A Strict Lady', then, was not a fable about the dangers of a narrow-minded refinement blind to larger questions of morality: this was not a twenti-eth-century reworking of a nineteenth-century radical narrative, centred on the distinction between manners and morals. Rather, the story interpreted refinement as the triumph of female resourcefulness over adversity: gentility was a way of transcending exploitation in a world that offered few ways of so doing. That Novikova's story did not seem particularly controversial when it first appeared illustrated not only that Russian readers and critics had started to come to terms with relatively explicit representations of sexual activity, but also the extent to which the desirability of living a 'civilized' life, in the sense of a wistful striving for material well-being, and elegance, was generally accepted in post-Soviet society, even if disagreement about the ways of achieving that ideal persisted.

CONCLUSION

In his study of illicit literature in the last days of the French *ancien régime*, Robert Darton has suggested a pivotal role for pornography and subversive political writings in hastening the collapse of the old order: 'Nothing sapped legitimacy more effectively than the literature of libel.'[196] According to such a view, popular literature is accorded a power that was formerly credited to the writings of 'great men', such as Voltaire and Rousseau; the genre of printed text has altered, but the fundamental point (that written material is the primary force in changing cultural history) has not. Appreciations of this kind—attractive as they may be to specialists in verbal texts, myself included—without doubt oversimplify the complexity of historical processes. After all, the capacity of popular literature to attain its effects depends on (at the very least) the expansion of elementary education; the growth of prosperity and/or reduction in the cost of printed materials (so that the purchase of these becomes possible among wider sectors of society); and the increase in time free from work, domestic responsibilities, and other activities essential to the continuance of life. Certainly I would not wish to make unduly sweeping claims on behalf of the subversive potential of Soviet advice literature *on its own*. But in Chapter 4 of this book I hypothesized that the advice literature of the early Soviet years made its modest contribution to the success of the regime, by producing a relatively coherent model of Soviet citizenship, and I would like to argue here, in the same way, that the chaotic character of late Soviet advice literature likewise had a role, however minor, in the collapse of the post–Stalin regime.

To be sure, the mechanics of this were rather different from the triumph of libertarianism hazarded by Darnton for France. The behaviour books of the late Soviet period were all officially published; unlike, say, *Thérèse-philosophe*, they did not lay bare the working of half-secret ideologies at the margins of society, but rather a ruling elite's attempt to neutralize hostile material (here, the consumerist ethos) by permitting it to circulate within official culture. The failure of this attempt may be attributable in part to Michel de Certeau's suggestion that the power of any belief system depends above all upon what it can withhold from believers, upon the fact that it excites desires that can patently not be satisfied because they are clearly a matter of fantasy.[197] This would suggest the converse: that it is extremely

---

[196] R. Darnton, *The Forbidden Best-Sellers of Revolutionary France* (New York, 1995), 216.

[197] 'By a paradox that is only apparent, the discourse that makes people believe is the one that takes away what it urges them to believe in, or never delivers what it promises', M. Certeau, *The Practice of Everyday Life*, trans. S. Rendall (Berkeley, 1984), 105. Certeau applies this argument to the 'local authorities' that he sees as *undermining* totalitarian discourse, but it fits the mythopoeic powers of the latter equally well.

dangerous for any belief system to begin attempting to satisfy the practical requirements of believers. This indeed seems to have been the case with the post-Stalinist leaders' shift from the 'marketing of ideology' to 'the marketing of things'.[198] The mechanism of *defitsit* depended not only upon scarcity in terms of sheer numbers of goods, but also upon awareness in the Soviet population that goods were potentially available, which excited a desire to obtain them. Advice literature, like the tentative excursions made by the post-Stalinist Soviet administration into advertising, contributed to this process by disseminating practical information about the supposed availability of certain items, so that they came to seem not luxuries (as in the 1940s), but necessities.[199] In turn, the increasing importance of material conditions impacted to a fatal degree upon the ideal of Soviet collectivism that had been essential to maintaining unity in the Stalin days. Attempts to assert the importance of good behaviour without taking account of immediate practical factors had always had a certain absurdity; but this absurdity was made particularly obvious by the coinage, in the late 1980s, of the term 'politeness deficit' to encapsulate the Soviet Union's social problems, given that the extent of the economic deficit was now openly discussed.[200]

During the late Soviet era, then, the notion that the primary problems of society lay within its citizens, who should simply try harder to transform themselves, began to collapse from inside. And just as conflicts in the ideology of behaviour reflected a crisis within the Soviet symbolic order, so the uncertainty about what was and was not permitted jeopardized the regulation of society because it made the drawing of boundaries round asocial behaviour more difficult. 'Enemies of the people' no longer had a clear identity: those who boozed at street corners, skived off work, or dabbled in illegal economic activities had an ambiguous status, to the romanticization of which even propaganda literature, with its vacuous celebration of 'the feminine', indirectly contributed. In a society where real power generally lay in the hands of men, the assumption that transgressors were likely to be men made their transgression seem more glamorous than social conformity.[201] Indeed, conformity could seem almost equivalent to

---

[198] I borrow these terms from Groys, *The Total Art of Stalinism* (see n. 7 above).

[199] On advertising in the 1960s and 1970s, see P. Hansen, *Advertising and Socialism: The Nature and Extent of Consumer Advertising in the Soviet Union, Poland, Hungary and Yugoslavia* (London, 1974).

[200] V. Tkachenko, 'Rozy i zhaby', quoted in Trofimenko and Volgin, *Pogovorim ob etikete*, 22: 'defitsit vezhlivosti utupil nashi chuvstva'.

[201] This assumption held good in the post-Soviet period as well, as can be seen, for instance, in the fact that both Yeltsin and his sometime rival Vladimir Zhirinovsky exploited the 'bad boy' stereotype in their memoirs. See B. Yeltsin, *Against the Grain*, trans. M. Glenny (New York, 1999), esp. 25–6; V. Zhirinovsky, *Poslednii brosok na Yug* (Moscow, 1993).

emasculation, the more so since low-level regulators of behaviour (whether in ideology or fact) were so often women.

The years after the breakdown of Soviet power saw the Westernization of behaviour guides that was already evident in the late Soviet period expand out of all recognition. While the term *kul'turnost'* was still occasionally used, it became much less common than *khoroshii ton, etiket*, or the newest linguistic import, *imidzh*. Also evident was a stratification of material according to the expected purchasing power of the readership (as in the early twentieth century). This stratification was particularly obvious in the case of magazines, but sensitivity to the divergence of earning levels had some effects on the cost of books as well. By the late 1990s, treatises on etiquette ranged from slim softcover books, hardly more than brochures, up to glossy hardbacks, with the latter costing up to fifty times the price of the former; periodical publications from humble newspapers up to magazines the size of small-town telephone directories. Given that the book market was now consumer-driven to a much higher extent than it had been even in the final decades of Soviet power, the proliferation of advice literature indicated its currency with a wide and varied reading public, a currency also suggested by the most desultory observation of book stores, book stalls, and buying practices in the major cities. As in the late eighteenth century, in the 1900s, and in the 1920s, social upheaval had generated a hunger for guidance of all kinds. The severe economic crisis of August 1998 appeared to have a slightly inhibitory effect upon book production,[202] but did not dampen enthusiasm for advice presented in other forms. Within days, newspapers were carrying new kinds of material, such as recipes advising on the confection of 'crisis cutlets'. Indeed, in some ways advice had become a still more urgent matter than before the financial collapse. For those at the bottom of society, the columns that began to be printed by free newspapers in the autumn of 1998, and which detailed how shoppers might save a few roubles by buying foodstuffs in one region of the city rather than another, now offered information that had become, quite literally, a matter of life and death.

At the same time, some aspects of the Soviet behaviour ethos, most particularly the notion of self-improvement as a contribution to collective rather than individual well-being, continued to enjoy a curious after-life in the decade after Party authority collapsed. For instance, a 1997 article in *Ogonek* revealed that Russian tourists in mediterranean seaside resorts such

[202] This statement is based on the systematic catalogue of RNB (see App. 5). However, the number of glossy magazines on sale in kiosks in 1999 had not significantly declined by comparison with 1998, and advice literature of various levels of ambition continued to appear, ranging from an opulent complete reprint of Molokhovets, *Podarok molodym khozyaikam* to modest brochures dealing with etiquette in cemeteries and at church (*Kak vesti sebya na kladbishche; Chto dolzhen znat''kazhdyi prikhodyashchii v pravoslavnyi khram*).

as Malta, in between downing formidable amounts of alcohol, nude sunbathing, ogling topless women, and partaking in oratorios of swearing, still considered it obligatory to pay their tribute to the requirements of *kul'turnost'* by means of cultural excursions. 'If a visit to a museum is part of the package, then on no account can this be missed.'[203]

To a British reader of the day, such behaviour seemed not only incongruous, but unlikely. It was difficult to imagine the participants in a 'Club 18–30' trip to Mykonos demanding a visit to the local museum or an early-morning trip to Delos, or a coachload of soccer fans going from a World Cup match in Rome to visit the church of St John Lateran. Certainly, the self-education ethic still existed—it was represented, for instance, by Ruskin College, the Worker Education Association, and the Open University. But though facilities were in some ways superior to those available in Russia, self-education occupied a more muted place, being primarily the occupation of a determined minority rather than of a vocal majority. What is more, it was seen as a contribution to individual rather than collective self-improvement: the idea of visiting a museum *only* because, and if, a group excursion was laid on would have struck Britons (indeed, Western Europeans generally) as extremely curious. That self-education, albeit in diluted form, was still the ambition of most Russian citizens at the end of the twentieth century, and that a nodding acquaintance with high culture was still considered requisite for all, and regarded as a contribution to social cohesion, was a belated and unexpected tribute to the success of the Soviet system in constructing symbolic reality, whatever its failures in achieving practical goals.

[203] Yu. Kolesova, I. Petrova, and A. Barni, 'Russkie edut!', *Ogonek* 24 (1997), 23.

Afterword

Don't you realise that caring about people *is* national pride?[1]

At first sight, this book may seem to have set out two different, and contradictory, narrative lines. The first, a grand history of ideals and aspirations, chronicled the development of propaganda for refinement between the late eighteenth and the late twentieth century. The second, pieced together from fragments of memoirs, letters, and annotations, related the constant failure of sermons about civilized conduct to change the behaviour of readers. From early nineteenth-century landowners who bought cashmere shawls and diamond necklaces rather than didactic fiction, to Soviet *meshchane* spending their money on gramophones and fur coats as well as (or instead of) the complete works of Lenin, moneyed Russians resisted messages about principled self-restraint. Just so, less privileged individuals failed to turn into the sober, zealous, and efficient automatons that advice literature writers imagined to be common in Western societies. The admission by advice literature writers that refinement was *also* about consumption was frequently interpreted as a message that refinement was *only* about consumption; the desperate insistence with which advice writers repeated their strictures about punctuality and reliability pointed to just how ineffective such strictures were. Given the propensity of successive leaders to associate themselves directly with propaganda for gentility, but also to tolerate or even encourage the formation of venal and self-serving social elites, it is possible to draw a direct connection between high-level promotion of the 'civilizing process', and surly resistance to this on the part of subordinate human material.

Striking, too, was the persistence of glaring contrasts at the level of public culture: the new stone centres of eighteenth-century cities, surrounded by wooden huts; the *fasadnost'* of early twentieth-century Muscovite apartment blocks,[2] turning their stucco fronts upon unimproved courtyards of cottages with earth closets for sanitation; the exemplary cleanliness of certain privileged urban spaces in the Soviet period versus the muddy neglect of others; or the splendour of post-Soviet banks and

[1] Russian contributor to a telephone discussion programme in the wake of the Kursk disaster, quoted in *The Independent on Sunday*, 20 Aug. 2000, 3.

[2] For this term, see M. Nashchokina, *Sto arkhitektorov russkogo moderna: tvorcheskie portrety* (Moscow, 2000), 11.

restored churches standing alongside shoddily built market stalls in under-passes. Here, the literal meaning of the Russian word for 'decency', *prilichie*, 'what is fit to be seen', was directly enacted, with efforts expended only upon those sectors of the city that were visible to a privileged gaze.

In some senses, then, the account of cultural change I have given here supports a 'neo-traditionalist' interpretation of Russian history,[3] offsetting short-lived modernizing campaigns and the doughty survival of the extant cultural patterns that these were meant to change. The case of the salon, which inspired ridicule and suspicion as a place for artistic self-expression by women, but later became an arena where the wives of conservative thinkers could contribute to political discourse by voicing the ideology of sanctified domesticity, or of the wall newspaper, which was supposed to be the mouthpiece of the rational collective, and which became the voice of community intolerance, are particularly inviting instances for such an interpretation. Yet traditions were just as likely to be invented as to seep through into new practices—a striking case of this was the late nineteenth-century discovery of pre-Petrine Russia as a model of civilized culture.[4] And we should also not assume that the survival of traditional elements in Russia is anything peculiar in itself: such elements can be found in most modern societies. If a decline in religious belief is seen as modern, then the United States is neo-traditional compared with, say, France, and if it is modern to avoid urinating in public, then many British towns could provide examples of neo-traditional behaviour every Friday and Saturday night. Most late twentieth-century urbanized societies shared the anxieties about control and order which beset Soviet society in the post-Stalin era, and sometimes the solutions suggested were strikingly similar to those already tried (and found wanting) in the Soviet Union. In 1999, the British Home Secretary, Jack Straw, spoke about the need for all communities to have 'capable guardians' (rather like the Khrushchev *druzhinas*, perhaps?) who would help stamp out drug-dealing and theft. Employing hortatory tones that any General Secretary of the Communist Party would have approved, he continued, 'It is about all of us realising that we have a role to play, in our everyday lives, in confronting the low-level disorder and disrespect that leads to more serious crime.'[5] In this perspective, it is perhaps less the persistence in Russia of 'neo-traditional' features that is remarkable than the pervasiveness of anxiety about the aberrancy of these.

---

[3] For a recent discussion of 'neo-traditionalism' in the Soviet context, see T. Martin, 'Modernization or Neo-Traditionalism? Ascribed Nationality and Soviet Primordialism', in S. Fitzpatrick (ed.), *Stalinism: New Directions* (London, 2000), 348–67.

[4] Mentioned briefly in the discussion of Klyuchevsky (Ch. 3 above): for a fuller discussion, see R. Wortman, *Scenarios of Power: Myth and Ceremony in Russian Monarchy*, ii (Princeton, 2000), chs. 7–8.

[5] Speech to the Social Market foundation, quoted in the *Guardian*, 19 Feb. 1999, 6.

The survival of patronage networks into the late twentieth century was evident also in Italy or Spain: what was more peculiar was the agonized assumption on the part of many Russians themselves that this survival pointed to national backwardness (though this could be matched in Ireland, another country filled with uncertainty about its relationship to 'European civilization').[6]

In any case, the history of polite culture in Russia amounted to far more than a conflict between 'ideologies' and 'practices', 'myth' and 'real life', 'traditional' and 'modern', or indeed 'Russian' and 'Western'. The very existence of a translated literature about hygiene, self-improvement, and etiquette, was proof of receptivity to new ideologies (such as Smiles's idea of 'nature's gentleman'). Subtle distinctions in phrasing between original and translated text spoke not only of misunderstanding, but of attempts to negotiate between one cultural context and another. New ideologies made themselves felt not only in the controlling legislation of rulers committed to reshape Russia (in the period considered here, Catherine II, Nicholas I, Lenin, Stalin, and Khrushchev were the most significant examples), and in the institutional regulations of tsarist and Communist Party functionaries, but in the, at times painful, self-scrutiny of Russians measuring themselves against new standards. Even deliberate subversion of the accepted standards of good behaviour pointed to absorption of these standards. When the young Romantics of Pushkin's circle engaged in mischievous parodies of moralistic literature, or the Slavophiles strove to find a 'Russian' way in which refinement could be expressed, they displayed how much at home they felt with the behaviour codes that they affected to despise. Already by the early nineteenth century, the upper levels of the *dvoryanstvo* belonged to what was, by the standards of the day, a recognizable 'polite society'; by the late 1960s, the Russian working classes had, from most points of view, more in common with their counterparts in Western Europe, in terms of their household furnishings, dress, and leisure practices, than they did with their ancestors in early twentieth-century Russia.

In these, and in many other ways, ideals became part of lived reality for

---

[6] In Ireland also, qualities such as 'efficiency', 'uprightness', and self-education were associated with patriotism between the 1920s and the 1960s (see e.g. the memoirs of Sean Kelly and Gerald Bartley in P. Gannon (ed.), *The Way it Was* (Renvyle, Connemara, self-published, 1999), 171, 302, or Sean Ó Ciaráin, *Farewell to Mayo: An Emigrant's Memoirs of Ireland and Scotland* (Dublin, 1991), *passim*), an association that also came under threat with the onset of a consumerist and individualist ethos in the last three decades of the 20th cent. Of course, in Ireland modernization never involved industrialization or urbanization on the scale of that in Russia, but the two countries shared certain underlying structural features (high levels of state ownership in industry, the construction of paternalist programmes in health and education), and had in common also the persistence of traditional forms of collectivism (cronyism, hostility to outsiders and to non-conformity) that were very different from the visions of peaceful harmony and co-operation invoked in official ideology.

historical subjects. Where ideals and reality conflicted, individuals some-times blamed themselves, rather than the exacting demands set out in advice literature. For example, many young mothers in the 1920s and 1930s (like those in other modern, literate societies) had absolute faith in contemporary childcare literature: instructed that 'it is wrong to breast-feed at night', Raisa Orlova made herself and her infant wretched rather than break the rule.[7] Even if members of the Russian intelligentsia mocked some kinds of behaviour tracts (for instance, etiquette manuals), they usually subscribed to the idea that *vospitanie*, or moral education, was an appropriate activity for educated people. *Consuming* advice literature (and, by extension, trusting too much in the written word) was sometimes seen as foolish; *producing* such literature (or authoritative writing more broadly) was regarded as a responsible and laudable activity.

For their part, at least some Russians not born to educational and cultural privilege, whatever their hostility to 'the bourgeoisie', shared the determination to create a 'cultured life' in the face of huge practical difficulties. Exemplary workers measuring themselves against ideal stan-dards represented one aspect of this; another made itself felt in the outrage expressed by a factory 'wall newspaper' in the 1930s, when the manage-ment deployed funds collected by workers to create flowerbeds in the factory yards to another purpose, or in the grim canteen at an oil refinery in 1960 where a rubber plant whose pot had been dressed up in a white skirt 'embodied warmth and comfort, was the single oasis in a cold, shambolic room with a wretched counter for food and a rack of coats in full view of those having their meals'.[8] In this perspective, the efforts expended by generations of Soviet attendants in eating establishments, theatres, and museums to get visitors to remove outer wear could be seen as principled as well as ridiculous. The insistence in a student dining-room in 1980s Voronezh that visitors remove their coats (the only protection against a circling flock of incontinent sparrows) was based, after all, on a conviction that the place *should* have been clean.

This defiant assertion of values in impossible conditions is one reason why, contrary to the expectations or intentions of those in power, the revolution of daily life during the Soviet era had more lasting effects than the grandiose economic, political and social reforms of the day. Post-Soviet society, then, was by no means the 'moral vacuum' routinely lamented by intelligentsia commentators (who confused the decline in automatic respect for writers pontificating about moral standards with a disappearance of all such standards). Rather, it was the 'resilience and residual sense of duty' of

[7] *Vospominaniya o neproshedshem vremeni* (Ann Arbor, 1983), 126.
[8] On the first, see *V pomoshch' stennoi gazete* (1937), 36; on the second, 'Obshchestvennoe pitanie', *Ogonek* 7 (1960), 30.

the post-Soviet Russian population which explained why public institutions continued to function as salaries went unpaid and working conditions deteriorated in the Yeltsin years.[9] Whatever one's (certainly my) sneaking admiration for improvisation and creative mess, or secret preference for the red nose of the carnival to the little finger extended from the handle of the tea cup, to brand the agonized and often doomed quest for cleanliness, politeness, and good taste as 'petit-bourgeois' (*meshchanskoe*) or 'twee', would not only be condescending, but a suspension of the historical imagination. If the sonorous absolutism of behaviour books sometimes seems worthy only of laughter, the attempt to realize their impossible demands, in conditions of material deprivation and official indifference, has more often been the stuff of tragedy.[10]

[9] This point is made by Anatole Lieven in *Chechnya: Tombstone of Russian Power* (2nd edn.: New Haven, 1999), 21.

[10] Cf. Mikhail Prishvin's agonized rhetorical question in his diary for 1 Jan. 1927: 'Why should the abstract be sacred, and that be the place for human tragedy, while the everyday is left to comedy?' (See 'Dnevnik 1927 goda', *Rossiya* 7 (1997), 30.)

Appendix 1

TABLE 1. Publication of advice literature, 1750–1850 (summary of title nos. in specific genres)

Genre	1750–99	1800–50
Rules of *bon-ton*	11	16
Moral education	31	39
Practical ethics	7	3
Manuals on the art of love	15	12
Moral instruction	62	36
Recipes and handy hints	15	28
House management	6	6

Source: Classified catalogue (*sistematicheskii katalog*) of RNB.

Appendix 2

TABLE 1. Advice literature, 1834–1838: titles per annum

Subject	1834	1837	1838
Estate management	9	34	25
House management	–	18	11
Upbringing	11	7	1
Etiquette	–	1	1
Home medicine	7	10	9

Sources: (1835) 'Obozrenie knig, vyshedshikh v Rossii v 1834 godu', *Zhurnal ministerstva narodnogo prosveshcheniya* 8 (1835) and 9 (1835).
(1837–8) 'Ukazatel' vnov' vykhodyashchikh knig', *Zhurnal ministerstva narodnogo prosveshcheniya* 2 (1837)–1 (1838) (published as suppl. to each issue in those years)

Appendix 3

TABLE 1. Publication of advice literature, 1907–1915: titles per annum

Subject	1907	1910	1912	1915
Health	102	119	97	105
Mother and child	15	27	11	15
Self-education	24	14	36	14
Etiquette	4	1	1	–
Hobbies	2	22	22	16
House management	13	68[a]	41	69[b]

[a] Including 51 titles on gardening and market gardening (*sadovodstvo, ogorodnichestvo*).
[b] Including 47 titles on gardening and market gardening.

Source: *KL* for the relevant years.

Appendix 4

TABLE I. Advice literature statistics, 1918–1953

Year	Hygiene[a]	Mother and child[b]	House management[c]	Self-education[d]
1918	2	—	10	29
1919	7	4		20
1920	22	10	5	13
1921	20	7	2	19
1922	27	11	12	21
1923	46	12	2	28
1924	51	17	7	27
1925	20	10	—	4
1926	25	21	—	4
1927	30	51	22	47
1928	42	39	13	14
1929	33	73	13	4
1930	159	128[e]	10	15
1935	3	63[e]	—	—[f]
1939	161	91[e]	2	19
1946	4	41[g]	—	—
1948	20	40	1	—
1950	37	74[g]	1	1
1952	48	94	4	2
1953	39	59	3	1

[a] Heading (from 1925) 'Lichnaya gigiena' or 'Obshchaya gigiena'.
[b] Heading (from 1925) 'Gigiena detstva. Okhrana materinstva i mladenchestva'.
[c] Heading (from 1925) 'Domovodstvo. Kulinariya'; (from 1935) 'Obshchestvennoe pitanie: kulinariya', and 'Bytovoe obsluzhivanie naseleniya. Kul'tura byta'.
[d] Heading 'Samoobrazovanie'.
[e] This figure includes books under the heading 'Vospitanie v sem'e' (37 in 1930, 16 in 1935, 21 in 1930, 4 in 1939).
[f] The category 'Samoobrazovanie' is not listed in this year; however, a number of textbooks for distance learning (*zaochnoe obrazovanie*) were published.
[g] Figures include books under the heading *Kommunisticheskoe vospitanie* (12 published in 1946, 4 in 1950).

Source: EK for 1925–9, 1935, 1946–52; KL for 1918–24, 1930, 1939.

Appendix 5

TABLE 1. Publication of advice literature, 1950–70: titles per annum

Year	Behaviour[a]	Household management[b]
1950	1[c]	2
1951	3[c]	6
1952	2[c]	7
1953	–	10
1954	14	9
1955	18	6
1956	16	8
1957	10	20
1958	32	21
1959	44	29
1960	57	63
1961	72	36
1962	61	20
1963	56	26
1964	58	15
1965	59	24
1966	110	20
1967	70	29
1968	45	15
1969	60	19
1970	50	4

[a] The category here is 'Home and domestic life' (Sem'ya i byt).
[b] The categories here are 'Bytovoe ustroistvo i obsluzhivanie naseleniya. Banno-prachechnoe i parikhmakherskoe delo' (1960–64); 'Kommunal'noe-bytovoe obsluzhivanie. Tekhnika v bytu. Domovodstvo' (1965–70); 'Obshchestvennoe pitanie. Kulinariya' (1950–70). Professional manuals for the service industries (hairdressing, catering, etc.) are excluded from the figures.
[c] In these years, behaviour books are also listed under *kommunisticheskoe vospitanie* (a category which disappears in 1953): 1950: 4; 1951: 13; 1952: 3.

Source: *EK* for the relevant years.

TABLE 2. Advice literature 1970–1990: titles per annum

Year	Behaviour[a]	Household management[b]
1975	$c.101^{c}$	3
1980	$c.93^{d}$	35
1985	$c.104^{e}$	73
1990	$c.70^{f}$	237

[a] In the early 1970s, the category 'Sem'ya i byt' disappeared, and behaviour books began to appear in a number of different categories (see nn. e–f for details).
[b] Categories 'Bytovoe obsluzhivanie naseleniya. Domovodstvo' (1975–87); 'Obshchestvennoe pitanie. Kulinariya' (1975–87). As before, professional manuals for the service industries are excluded. From 1987, 'Domovodstvo' and 'Bytovoe obsluzhivanie naseleniya' became separate categories, and catering manuals etc. were listed under 'Vnutrennyaya torgovlya'.
[c] Made up of roughly 70 books in the category 'Etika' (which also included school textbooks, discussions of Darwinism, etc.) and 31 in the category 'Semeinoe vospitanie'.
[d] Made up of roughly 80 books from category 'Etika' (see n. c above) and 13 on 'Kul'tura byta'.
[e] Made up of roughly 84 books from category 'Etika' (see n. c above) and 18 on 'Kul'tura byta'.
[f] Made up of roughly 70 books from category 'Etika'.

Source: EK for the relevant years

TABLE 3. Health and hygiene literature, 1956–1990: titles per annum

Year	General	Women's health and childcare
1956	34	63
1960	64	84
1965	48	44
1970	23	28
1975	36	24
1980	63	43
1985	112	63
1990	144	56

[a] Heading 'Gigiena i sanitariya'.
[b] Headings 'Ginekologiya' and 'Akusherstvo' (but not including professional manuals for doctors, midwives, etc.).

Source: EK for the relevant years.

TABLE 4. Manuals for Party activists, 1950–1970: titles per annum[a]

Year	No. of manuals
1950	158
1951	100
1952	90
1953	94
1954	70
1955	73
1956	72
1957	98
1958	127
1959	179
1960	230
1961	259
1962	190
1963	203
1964	163
1965	104
1966	81
1967	80
1968	99
1969	102
1970	94

[a] The categories are 'Propaganda i agitatsiya. Partiinoe prosveshchenie' (1950–6); 'Ideologicheskaya rabota. Propaganda i agitatsiya' (1957–65), and 'Ideologicheskaya rabota' (1966–70).

Source: *EK* for the relevant years.

TABLE 5. Advice literature 1991–1998: titles per annum

Year	Recipes and handy hints	House management
1991	28	12
1992	35	15
1993	37	29
1994	15	10
1995	5	7
1996	7	8
1997	7	2
1998	2	1

Source: Classified catalogue (*sistematicheskii katalog*) of the RNB for the relevant years.

Select Bibliography of Advice Literature

I. A NOTE ON THE PUBLISHERS OF ADVICE LITERATURE

The only period before 1917 when there existed anything resembling specialist publishers for advice literature was the late nineteenth and early twentieth centuries (they included the populist house Posrednik (see Chapter 3), which issued various titles on self-education and self-improvement). Etiquette books, health books, letter-writing manuals etc., on the other hand, were brought out by a wide variety of different houses, including not only mass-market specialists such as Sytin, but also general publishers such as A. F. Marks (publisher, for instance, of Mariya Redelin's *Dom i khozyaistvo*). The historically more widespread pattern was one where how-to books emanated from a bewildering variety of different publishers and printers, including the typographies of Moscow University, the Academy of Sciences, and various military and naval academies and philanthropic societies (for example, the Society for the Dissemination of Moral Brochures among the Common People, operating in St Petersburg in the 1830s), as well as commercial publishers (for instance, the typographies of A. Reshetnikov, the Lazar'ev Brothers, of Vasily Polyakov, N. Stepanov, and I. Smirnov in Moscow). This mode prevailed from the late eighteenth to the late nineteenth centuries. (The involvement of 'respectable' presses, until at least the mid-nineteenth century, in the publication of advisory texts is an indication of the seriousness with which these were taken. At the same time, such editions also stood a fair chance of turning a profit—for example, according to a survey published in *Zhurnal ministerstva narodnogo prosveshcheniya* 8 (1835), 464, a book under the title *Istinnyi sposob byt' zdorovym, dolgovechnym i bogatym . . .*, published by Moscow University, had reached a third edition by 1835.)

Printing at the initiative of authors or translators was another feature that persisted throughout the pre-revolutionary era. In the late eighteenth and early nineteenth centuries, this was no doubt often a money-making strategy (as perhaps in the case of Nadezhda Nikiforova's translation of Fénelon's *Traité de l'éducation des filles*); in the late nineteenth and early twentieth centuries, on the other hand, at least some such publications had philanthropic aims (as with Nataliya Nordman's *Povarennaya kniga dlya golodayushchikh*).

After 1917, the situation changed significantly. To be sure, private publishing and self-publishing continued until the end of NEP (1928). However, the field was now dominated by state-sponsored publications. Soviet presses absorbed the functions of commercial publishers in the West, while also acting as a mouthpiece for government policy (compare the Stationery Office in the UK). There was no such thing as a specialist advice literature publisher—most Soviet houses had some publications of this kind on their lists, while no single house ever issued such material to the exclusion of anything else. However, many Soviet newspapers and magazines had a line in how-to books, especially during the 1920s (*Pravda* and its regional offshoots, *Bednota*, *Krasnaya gazeta*, and *Gigiena i zdorov'e* for example), and quasi-autonomous divisions of the State Publishing House which had higher than average outputs of how-to books included *Zdorov'e* (Health), *Sovetskaya entsiklopediya*, *Moskovskii rabochii*, *Kolos*, and above all the Komsomol press, *Molodaya gvardiya*. Given the very wide briefs of Soviet presses (*Molodaya gvardiya*, for instance, published belles lettres and agitational pamphlets as well as books on 'communist education', while even such august cultural houses as *Khudozhestvennaya literatura* or *Iskusstvo* had the odd advice title on their lists), the title of the series in which a book or brochure was published ('Bibliotechka agitatora', 'Zaochnye kursy molodoi materi', 'Populyarnaya biblioteka po estetike', etc.) was often more revealing about its mass-educational aims than the imprint under which it appeared. Information about series affiliation, where available, has accordingly been supplied in the Bibliography.

With the opening up of the print market in the late Soviet and post-Soviet eras, the situation once again came to resemble that in the early twentieth century. A few advice-specific houses existed, now almost always with explicitly commercial aims (1990s examples included *Bukmen* and *MK-Servis*, both based in Moscow). Advice literature was, however, also published (no doubt primarily for economic reasons) by a large number of different houses—which included former state publishing houses such as *Kolos*, *Moskovskii rabochii*, and even the Academy of Sciences imprint *Nauka*, which, according to its catalogue for that year, brought out a translation of Emily Post's etiquette classic in 1997.

2. BIBLIOGRAPHIES OF, OR INCLUDING SIGNIFICANT AMOUNTS OF, ADVICE LITERATURE (SEE ALSO *EK*, *KL*, *SK*, *SKKIYA* IN THE LIST OF ABBREVIATIONS)

Anon., 'Obozrenie knig, vyshedshikh v Rossii v 1835 godu', *Zhurnal ministerstva narodnogo prosveshcheniya* 8 (1838).

Anon., 'Ukazatel' vnov' vykhodyashchikh knig', *Zhurnal ministerstva narodnogo prosveshcheniya* 2 (1837)-1 (1838) (published as suppl. to each issue in those years).

BOGOMAZOVA, Z. (comp.), *Literatura po samoobrazovaniyu* (Moscow and Leningrad, 1927).

GENNADI, G. N. *Spravochnyi slovar' o Russkikh pisatelyakh i uchenykh umershikh v XVIII i XIX stoletiyakh i spisok russkikh knig s 1725 po 1825 g.* (2 vols.; Berlin, 1876–8).

KERZHENTSEV, P. (comp.), *Biblioteka kommunista: Sistematicheskii ukazatel' sotsialisticheskoi literatury* (4th edn.; Moscow, 1919).

MEZHOV, V. I., *Sistematicheskaya rospis' knigam, prodayushchimsya v knizhnom magazine A. I. Glazunova v Moskve* (St Petersburg, 1867–89).

MONTANDON, ALAIN (ed.), *Bibliographie des traités de savoir-vivre en Europe du Moyen age à nos jours* (2 vols.; Clermont-Ferrand, 1995).

ROBERTSON-HODGES, DEBORAH (ed.), *Etiquette: An Annotated Bibliography of Literature Published in English in the US, 1900 through 1987* (Tanglewood, Mass., 1988).

RUBAKIN, N. A., *Sredi knig* (3rd edn.; 3 vols.; Moscow, 1911).

3. ADVICE BOOKS ARRANGED BY ERA

Only the editions actually consulted by me are included, except in the case of well-known works by major writers—for example, Mayakovsky's *Kak delat' stikhi* –where I have cited first editions for the sake of completeness. Republications in collectaneous form are cited only where they were aimed at an advice literature market (e.g. Rubakin's *Kak zanimat'sya samoobrazovaniem* of 1962 is included, but Makarenko's *Izbrannye pedagogicheskie sochineniya* of 1949 is not). Where it has been possible to establish this, the original title of a translated work follows the Russian title in curly brackets { }; the details are those of the first edition, unless it is certain that another edition was used by the Russian translator (as in the case of e.g. Spock, *Mother and Child Care*), in which case full publication details of that edn. are given. In the case of eighteenth-century books, the immensely long titles of the originals have occasionally been slightly abridged (with omissions indicated in square brackets): the full citations are available in *SK*. Equally, the names of some French authors appear in contracted form—e.g. Louise d'Épinay, rather than the strictly correct Louise-Florence-Pétronille Tardieu d'Épinay.

Names of publishers and printers are given only in the case of Russian-language advice literature. The following abbreviations are used:

MU   typography of Imperial Moscow University
IAN   typography of Imperial Academy of Sciences
npg   no publisher or printer given
tip.   tipografiya (typography)

To reflect the different character of anonymity before and after 1917 (see opening section of Chapter 4), books without an author credited on the title-page are listed under 'Anon.' if published before the Revolution, but under their titles if published by official Soviet presses thereafter. (This follows standard practice in Western bibliographies.)

1700–1800 (SK inventory number follows in square brackets)

Anon., *Dolzhnosti zhenskogo polu [. . .] S nemetskogo* (Moscow: MU, 1760). [*SK* 1959]. {?Desmothes, J., *Les Devoirs des filles chrétiennes pour une vie chaste et vertueuse dans le monde* (Paris, 1719).}

Anon., *Gespräche von Haussachen/Razgovory o domashnikh delakh/Conversations domestiques* (5th edn., Riga: J. F. Hartknoch, 1784) [*SK* 1975].

Anon., *Kakim obrazom mozhno sokhranyat' zdravie i krasotu molodykh zhenshchin*, trans. A. Tikhomirov (Moscow: tip. A. Reshetnikova, 1793) [*SK* 2746].

Anon., *Karmannaya, ili Pamyatnaya knizhka dlya molodykh devits, soderzhashchaya v sebe nastavleniya prekrasnomu polu, s pokazaniem, v chem dolzhny sostoyat' uprazhneniya ikh* (Moscow: MU/tip. N. Novikova, 1784) [*SK* 2851].

Anon., *Nastavlenie, kak sochinyat' i pisat' vsyakie pis'ma k raznym osobam, s priobshcheniem primerov iz raznykh avtorov* (Moscow: MU, 1765) [*SK* 4472].

Anon., *Nauka byt' uchtivym*, trans. from the French by Ivan Kryukov (St Petersburg: IAN, 1774) [*SK* 4495].

Anon., *O dolzhnostyakh cheloveka i grazhdanina: kniga k chteniyu opredelennaya v narodnykh gorodskikh uchilishchakh* (St Petersburg: IAN, 1783) [*SK* 4739].

Anon., *Pravila uchtivosti*, trans. P. Kalyazin (St Petersburg: tip. Morskogo shlyakhetskogo korpusa, 1779). [*SK* 5599]. {?Anon., *Règles de la bienséance, ou la civilité moderne qui se pratique parmi les honnêtes gens [. . .]* (Strassbourg, 1754).}

Anon., *Sovety ot vospitatel'nitsy k vospitannitse*, trans. I. Sipyagin (Moscow: tip. Ponomareva, 1787) [*SK* 6654].

Anon., *Yunosti chestnoe zertsalo, ili pokazanie k zhiteiskomu obkhozhdeniyu. Sobrannoe ot raznykh Avtorov. Napechataetsya poveleniem Tsarskogo Velichestva [. . .]* (St Petersburg: IAN, 1717) [Repr. in 1740, 1742, 1745, 1767: see *SK* 8732–5].

Anon., *Zertsalo zhenskoi drevnei uchenosti, ili Opisanie zhizni drevnikh filosofok [. . .]*, trans. F. Bakhteyarov (Moscow: tip. A. Reshetnikova, 1800) [*SK* 2343].

Bakherakht, A. G., *Sobranie raznykh poleznykh lekarstv* (St Petersburg: Senatskaya tip., 1779) [*SK* 6642].

[Bel'gard, M. de], *Rassuzhdeniya o tom, chto mozhet nravit'sya i ne nravit'sya v svetskom obrashchenii, napisannye g. Abbatom Beligardom. Perevedeny s frantsuzskogo* (Moscow: tip. Ponomareva, 1795) [*SK* 476] {Bellegard, Morvan de, *Réflexions sur la politesse des moeurs [. . .]* (Paris, 1696)}.

Betskoi, I., *Ustav vospitaniya dvukhsot blagorodnykh devits uchrezhdennogo e. v. gosudaryneyu imp. Ekaterinoi Vtoroyu [. . .]* (St Petersburg: Senatskaya tip., 1765) [*SK* 556].

——, *Sobranie uchrezhdenii i predpisanii kasatel'no vospitaniya v Rossii oboego pola blagorodnogo i meshchanskogo yunoshestva* (St Petersburg: tip. I. K. Shpora, 1791) [*SK* 555].

Bogdanovich, P. I., *Novyi i polnyi pis'movnik, ili podrobnoe i yasnoe nastavlenie kak pisat' kupecheskie, kantselyarskie, prositel'nye, zhalobnye, odobritel'nye, druzheskie, uveshchatel'nye i voobshche vsyakogo roda delovye pis'ma; takzhe ob"yavleniya, raznye dogovory, zapisi, svidetel'stva, veruyushchie, obyazatel'stva, zaveshchaniya i proch. [. . .]* (St Petersburg: tip. P. I. Bogdanovicha, 1791) [*SK* 646].

Bud'e de Vil'mer, P., *Drug zhenshchin, ili Iskrennee nastavlenie dlya povedeniya prekrasnogo pola* (Moscow: MU, 1765) [*SK* 764]. {Pierre Boudier de Villemert, *L'Ami des femmes* (Hamburg, 1758).}

[Catherine II], *Rossiiskaya azbuka dlya obucheniya yunoshestva chteniyu. Napechatannaya dlya obshchestvennykh shkol po Vysochaishemu poveleniyu* (St Petersburg: IAN, n.d.) [*SK* 2176].

[de Kur, R.], *Istinnaya politika znatnykh i blagorodnykh osob*, trans. from the French by V. Trediakovsky (St Petersburg: IAN, 1737) [SK 2677]. {Des Cours, Rémond, *La Véritable politique des personnes de qualité* (Paris, 1692).}

[EPINE, L.: misattributed to Bomon, M. Leprens de], *Uchilishche yunykh devits, ili Razgovory materi s docher'yu [. . .] sluzhashchaya prodolzheniem Detskogo uchilishcha*, trans. A. M. (Moscow: tip. I. Lopukhina, 1784) [SK 3641]. {Épinay, Louise de, *Les Conversations d'Émilie* (Paris, 1774).}

Épinay's book appeared in Russian under its own name in 1798: *Rassuzhdenii [sic] nravouchitel'nye i lyubopytnye, materi s docher'yu. Iz sochinenii gospozhi la Liv Epinati [sic]*, trans. P. Pushchin (St Petersburg: Imperatorskaya tip., 1798) [SK 8652]

ERAZM ROTERDAMSKII, *Erazma Roterodamskogo [sic] Molodym detyam nauka kak dolzhno sebya vesti i obkhodit'sya s drugimi; i Ioanna Ludovika Rukovodstvo k mudrosti. Dlya pol'zy obuchayushchagosya v Moskovskoi slavyano-greko-latinskoi akademii yunoshestva*, trans. A. Mel'gunov (Moscow: tip. Ponomareva, 1788) [SK 8663]. (For the version with Latin parallel text, see SK 8664). {Erasmus, Desiderius, *De civilitate morum puerilium* (1530).}

[ESPINASI, G-zha], *Opyt o vospitanii blagorodnykh devits, sochinennyy g-zheyu ***, trans. M. Semchevsky (St Petersburg: tip. Artilleriiskogo i inzhinernogo shlyakhetnogo kadetskogo korpusa, 1778) [SK 5012]. {Espinassy, Mademoiselle de, *Essai sur l'éducation des demoiselles* (Paris, 1764).}

FENELON, F., *O vospitanii devits*, trans. N. Tumansky (St Petersburg: tip. Sukhoputnogo kadetskogo korpusa, 1763; repr. 1774, 1778) [SK 7703–4]. {Fénelon, F., *De l'éducation des filles* (1687).}

Another version, F. Fenelon, *O vospitanii devits: sochinenie g. Fenelona, arkhiepiskopa gertsoga Kambriiskogo. Novoe izdanie, s pribavleniem pis'ma ego k odnoi znatnoi Gospozhe otnositel'no do vospitaniya eya edinorodnoi docheri*, trans. Nadezhda Nikiforova (Tambov: Vol'naya tip., 1794), includes 'Lettre à une dame de qualité' [SK 7705]. It was perhaps trans. from the edn. of *De l'éducation des filles* (Paris, 1719), and including this text.

——, *Obshchiya pravila zhizni, vzyatyya iz knigi, nazyvaemoi Istinnaya politika blagorodnykh lyudei* (Moscow: MU, 1779) [SK 7706]. {Trans. of Fénelon's poem *La Sagesse humaine ou Le Portrait d'un honnête homme*.}

GRASIAN I MORALES, B., *Gratsian. Pridvornyi chelovek s frantsuzskogo na rossiiskii yazyk pereveden [. . .] A napechatana siya kniga po vsevysochaishemu poveleniyu, i vo vtoroe litso bogomkhranimoi derzhavy Vseprosvetleishiya Derzhavneishiya Velikiya Gosudaryni ELISAVETY PETROVNY Imperatritsy i Samoderzhitsy Vserossiiskoi*, trans. S. Volchkov (2nd edn.; St Petersburg: IAN, 1742) [SK 1613]. {Gracián y Morales, B., *El oráculo manual y arte de prudencia* (Husca, 1647).}

[GRABINSKY, I.] *Druzheskie sovety molodomu cheloveku, nachinayushchemu zhit''v svete* (2nd edn.; Moscow: MU, 1765). {Grabiensky, J., *Conseils d'un ami à un jeune homme qui entre dans le monde* (Berlin, 1760) [SK 2038].}

GULEN, Dzh., *Damskii vrach v trekh chastyakh, soderzhashchikh v sebe nuzhnye predokhraneniya, sluzhashchie k soblyudeniyu zdraviya, s prisovokupleniem Venerina tualeta*, trans. K. Mukovnikov (Moscow: tip. A. Reshetnikova, 1793) [SK 1665]. {Goulin, J., *Le Médecin des dames* (n.p, n.d.: Paris, 1775?.)}

KOMPAN, SHARL', *Tantsoval'nyi slovar', soderzhashchii v sebe istoriyu pravila i osnovaniya tantsoval'nogo iskusstva, s kriticheskimi razmyshleniyami i lyubopytnymi anekdotami, otnosyashchimisya k drevnim i novym tantsam* (Moscow: MU/tip. V. Okorokova, 1790) [*SK* 3084]. {Compan, Charles, *Dictionnaire de danse* (Paris, 1787).}

KURGANOV, N., *Pismovnik [sic], soderzhashchii v sebe nauku rossiiskogo yazyka so mnogim prisovokupleniem raznogo uchebnogo i poleznozabavnogo veshchesloviya* (5th edn., St Petersburg: IAN, 1793; repr. Würzburg, 1978) [*SK* 3370].

[LA SHETARDI, TROTTI DE], *Nastavlenie znatnomu molodomu cheloveku, ili Voobrazhenie o svetskom cheloveke*, trans. Ivan Murav'ev (St Petersburg: tip. Artilleriiskogo i inzhinernogo shlyakhetnogo kadetskogo korpusa, 1778) [*SK* 3488]. {La Chetardie, Trotti de, *Instructions pour un jeune seigneur ou l'idée d'un galant homme* (2 vols.; Paris, 1683).}

[LAMBER, A. DE], *Pis'ma gospozhi de Lambert k eya synu o pravednoi chesti i k docheri o dobrodetelyakh prilichnykh zhenskomu polu* (St Petersburg: IAN, 1761) [*SK* 3425]. {Lambert, Anne de, *Avis d'une mère à son fils et à sa fille* (Paris, 1728).}

——, *Rassuzhdeniya o druzhestve*, trans. S. Smirnov (St Petersburg: IAN, 1777) [*SK* 3427]. {*Traité de l'amitié* (Paris, 1736].}

LEPRENS DE BOMON, M., *Detskoe uchilishche, ili Nravouchitel'nye razgovory mezhdu razumnoyu uchitel'nitseyu i znatnymi raznykh let uchenitsami sochinennye na frantsuzskom yazyke gospozheyu Le Prens de Bomont [sic]*, trans. P. S. Svistunov (4 parts; St Petersburg: tip. Sukhoputnogo kadetskogo korpusa, 1761–7; repr. 1776, 1788) [*SK* 3624–7].

{LEPRINCE DE BEAUMONT, Marie, *Magasin des enfans, ou dialogues d'une sage gouvernante avec ses élèves de la première distinction, dans lesquels on fait penser, parler, agir les jeunes gens suivant le génie, le tempérament, et les inclinations d'un chacun [. . .] par Madame Leprince de Beaumont* (Lyon, 1758).}

Also trans. as: *Detskoe uchilishche, ili Razgovory blagorazumnoi nastavnitsy [. . .]* (St Petersburg: tip. I. K. Shnora, 1792), repr. 1794, 1800. Parts of this book also appeared separately in 1763, 1767, 1784, and 1795, and an edition in French was published in Moscow, 1795. [See *SK* 3629–31, and *SKKIYa* 1714.]

——, *Yunosheskoe uchilishche, ili Nravouchitel'nye razgovory mezhdu razumnoyu uchitel'nitseyu i mnogimi znatnymi uchenitsami, sochinennoe na frantsuzskom yazyke g-zheyu le Prens de Bomont [. . .]*, trans. I. Kharlamov (4 vols.; [Moscow]: MU, 1774; repr. 1788) [*SK* 3642–3]. {*Magasin des adolescentes, ou dialogues entre une sage gouvernante et plusieurs de ses élèves de la première distinction, par Madame Le Prince [sic] de Beaumont, pour servir de suite au Magasin des enfants* (London, 1764].}

——, *Nastavlenie molodym gospozham, vstupayushchim v svet i brachnye soyuzy, sluzhashchee prodolzheniem Yunosheskomu uchilishchu, gde iz"yasnyayutsya dolzhnosti kak v rassuzhdenii ikh samikh, tak i v rassuzhdenii ikh detei. Sochinenie gzhi le Prens de Bomont*, trans. from the French by E. Runich (4 vols.; Moscow, tip. N. Novikova, 1788). [*SK* 3633]. {*Instructions pour les jeunes dames qui entrent dans le monde, et se marient. Leurs devoirs dans cet état, et envers leurs enfants. Pour servir de suite au Magasin des adolescentes. Par Mad. Leprince de Beaumont [. . .]* (London, 1764).}

Also translated as: *Pravila dlya obshchezhitiya, ili Nastavlenie devitsam, soderz-hashchee svyashchennuyu i svetskuyu istorii i geografiyu, sochinenie g. de Bomont.* Trans. from the French by [Miss] M. M. T. (5 vols.; St Petersburg: tip. Vil'kovskogo, 1800–1). A trans. of vol. i only appeared as *Uchilishche devits. Sochineniya g. Bomonta [!]. Perevedeno s frantsuzskogo na rossiiskoi* (St Petersburg: tip. Galchenkova, 1784) [*SK* 3640].

LEVSHIN, V. A., *Vseobshchee i polnoe domovodstvo, v kotorom yasno, kratko i podrobno pokazyvayutsya sposoby sokhranyat' i priumnozhat' vsyakogo roda imushchestva, s pokazaniem sil obyknovennykh trav i domashnei apteki i proch. i proch.* (3 vols.; Moscow: MU/tip. Khr. Ridigera i Khr. Klavdy, 1795) [*SK* 3534].

LOKK, Dzh., *O vospitanii detei gospodina Lokka,* trans. Nikolai Popovsky (2nd edn.; 2 vols.; Moscow: MU, 1760. {Locke, John, *Some Thoughts Concerning Education* (London, 1690)} [*SK* 3720].

OSIPOV, N. P., *Starinnaya ruskaya khozyaika, klyuchnitsa i stryapukha, ili Podlinnoe nastavlenie o prigotovlenii nastoyashchikh starinnykh kushan'ev [. . .]* (St Petersburg: Imperatorskaya tip., 1790) [*SK* 5048].

——, *Karmannaya kniga sel'skogo i domashnego khozyaistva [. . .]* (St Petersburg: Imperatorskaya tip., 1791) [*SK* 5032].

[PENINGTON, S.] *Sovety neshchastnoi materi ee docheryam [. . .],* trans. (from the French!) N. Yatsenkov (Moscow: Senatskaya tip., 1788) [*SK* 5149].

{PENNINGTON, SARAH, *An Unfortunate Mother's Advice to Her Absent Daughters; in a Letter to Miss Pennington* (London, 1761).}

RUSSO, ZH. ZH., *Emil' i Sofiya, ili khorosho vospitannye lyubovniki,* trans. P. I. Strakhov (St Petersburg: MU, 1779). [*SK* 6234]. {Partial translation of Part V of ROUSSEAU, J. J., *Émile, ou de l'éducation* (Paris, 1762).}

——, *Emily i Sofiya, ili blagovospitannye lyubovniki,* trans. I. Vinogradov (2 vols.; St Petersburg: tip. Gosudarstvennoi meditsynskoi akademii, 1799–1800) [*SK* 6235]. {Vol. i contains another partial trans. of Part V of *Émile.*}

SANCHES, A. N. R., *O parnykh rossiiskikh banyakh, poeliku spospeshestvuyut one ukrepleniyu, sokhraneniyu i vosstanovleniyu zdraviya [. . .]* (St Petersburg: tip. Imperatorskogo sukhoputnogo shlyakhetnogo korpus, 1779) [*SK* 6313]. [Also included in Betskoi, *Sobranie uchrezhdenii i predpisanii . . .* above.]

STRAKHOV, N., *Karmannaya knizhka dlya priezzhayushchikh v Moskvu starichkov i starushek, nevest i zhenikhov, molodykh i ustarelykh devushek, shchegolei, vertopra-khov, volokit, igrokov i proch. ili Inoskazatel'nye dlya nikh nastavleniya i sovety, pisannye Sochinitelem Satiricheskogo Vestnika* (2nd edn.; 2 vols.; Moscow: MU, 1795) [*SK* 6885].

VITZMANN, A., *Nastavleniya poleznye dlya slug, kotorye tak zhe ne budut bespolezny i dlya samikh khozyaev* (St Petersburg: npg, 1799) [*SK* 1010].

ZHANLIS, S., *Adeliya i Teodor, ili Pis'my [sic] o vospitanii, soderzhashchie v sebe pravila, kasayushchiesya do trekh razlichnykh sposobov vospitaniya [. . .],* trans. P. Sumarokov (Tambov': Vol'naya tip., 1793) [*SK* 2209]. Another trans., as *Adeliya i Feodor,* appeared in 1794, [*SK* 2210]. {S. de Genlis, *Adèle et Théodore, ou lettres sur l'éducation, contenant tous les principes relatifs aux trois differens plans d'éducation, des princes, des jeunes personnes, et des hommes* (Paris, 1782)}.

1800–1880

Anon., *Beregis' pervoi charki!* (St Petersburg: tip. Iversena/Obshchestvo, rasprostranyayushchee nravstvennye listki dlya chteniya prostolyudinov, 1835)

Anon., *Domashnyaya spravochnaya kniga: sobranie postavlenii, retseptov, i—tak nazyvaemykh—sekretov po raznym otraslyam khozyaistva i domovodstva* (2 vols.; St Petersburg: tip. Shtaba otdel'nogo korpusa Vnutrennei strazhi, 1855).

Anon., *Lyubovnaya pochta, ili obraztsy pis'mennykh iz"yasnenii v lyubvi: s prilozheniem al'bomnykh stikhov, s politipazhnymi risunkami v tekste. Posvyashchaetsya khoroshen'kim zhenshchinam* (St Petersburg: tip. P. Golike, 1863).

Anon., *Podarok sluzhankam* (St Petersburg: tip. Iversena/Obshchestvo, rasprostranyayushchee nravstvennye listki dlya chteniya prostolyudinov, 1835).

Anon., *Postaraisya eshche raz!* (St Petersburg: tip. Iversena/Obshchestvo, rasprostranyayushchee nravstvennye listki dlya chteniya prostolyudinov, 1834).

Anon., *Prakticheskii khozyain, ili Kniga dlya vsekh soslovii, izlagayushchaya Polnoe sobranie noveishikh opytov i otkrytii, sdelannykh izvestnymi v Evrope agronomami po vsem otraslyam estestvennykh nauk, tekhnologii, zemledel'cheskoi promyshlennosti, sel'skogo khozyaistva, iskusstv i proch. Vybrano iz sochinenii luchshikh pisatelei M. M.* (Moscow: tip. Lazarevykh Instituta Vostochnykh yazykov, 1838).

Anon., *Pravila svetskogo obkhozhdeniya o vezhlivosti: Polnaya karmannaya knizhka, soderzhashchaya pravila, nastavleniya, primeneniya, i primery kak predstavit' sebya v obshchestvo, i kak obrashchat'sya v nem, sochinennaya izdatelem nastavlenii UBORNOGO STOLIKA* (Moscow: tip. N. Stepanova, 1829).

Anon., *Pravila semeinye* (St Petersburg: tip. Iversena/Obshchestvo, rasprostranyayushchee nravstvennye listki dlya chteniya prostolyudinov, 1835).

Anon., *Pravila svetskogo etiketa dlya dam: S angliiskogo* (St Petersburg: tip. Sankt-Peterburgskikh teatrov, 1873). {Anon., *Routledge's Etiquette for Ladies* (London, 1864).}

Anon., *Pravila svetskogo etiketa dlya muzhchin: S angliiskogo* (St Petersburg: tip. Sankt-Peterburskikh teatrov, 1873). {Anon., *Routledge's Etiquette for Gentlemen* (London, 1864).}

Anon., *Put' chesti, ili Sovety molodomu ofitseru* (Moscow: MU, 1837).

Anon., *Zhiteiskaya mudrost', ili pravila vezhlivosti i svetskikh prilichii* (St Petersburg: pechatnya V. Golovina, 1871).

AVDEEVA, E. A., *Karmannaya povarennaya knizhka* (St Petersburg: tip. Departmenta Vneshnei torgovli, 1846).

——, *Ruchnaya kniga russkoi opytnoi khozyaiki, sostavlennaya iz sorokoletnikh opytov i nablyudenii dobroi khozyaiki russkoi, Kateriny Avdeevoi* (1842: 8th edn., Moscow: tip. Vedomstva Moskovskoi gorodskoi politsii, 1854).

——, *Rukovodstvo k ustroistvu ferm i vedeniyu na nikh khozyaistva* (St Petersburg: Shtaba Otdel'nogo korpusa vneshnei strazhi, 1863).

——, *Vkusnyi i deshovyi stol. Povarennaya kniga. Rukovodstvo k izgotovleniyu deshovogo i vkusnogo stola. Sostavlennaya Ekaterinoyu Avdeevoi* (4th edn., St Petersburg: tip. i litografiya knyazya V. V. Obolenskogo, 1877).

——, *Zapiski dlya gorodskikh i sel'skikh khozyaev, soderzhashchie v sebe opytnye pravila o skotovodstve [. . .] Sobrany sochinitel'nitsy ruchnoi knigi Opytnoi Russkoi khozyaiki* (St Petersburg: tip. I. Glazunova, 1842).

BOGDANOVICH, I., *O vospitanii yunoshestva* (Moscow: tip. P. Beketova, 1807).

CHARUKOVSKY, A., *Narodnaya meditsyna, primenennaya k russkomu bytu i raznoklimatnosti* (St Petersburg: tip. Voenno-uchebnykh zavedenii, 1844).

CHESTERFILD, Lord, *Dukh Lorda Chesterfilda, ili Izbrannye mysli iz nravouchitel'nykh ego sochinenii [. . .]*, trans. I. Livitov (St Petersburg: IAN, 1815). {Chesterfield, P. D. S., *Lord Chesterfield's Maxims, or A New Plan of Education, on the Principles of Virtue and Politeness* (London, 1786).}

DYMMAN, EFIM, *Nauka zhizni ili kak molodomu cheloveku zhit' na svete* (St Petersburg: tip. E. Pratsa, 1859).

GOGOL', N. V., *Vybrannye mesta iz perepiski s druz'yami* (St Petersburg: tip. Departmenta Vneshnei torgovli, 1847).

GRUM, K. , *Rukovodstvo k vospitaniyu, obrazovaniyu, i sokhraneniyu zdorov'ya detei* (2 vols.; St Petersburg: tip. Ministerstva Vnutrennikh del, 1843–4).

GUMILEVSKY, S., *Nastavlenie otsa synu—molodomu voinu, otpravlyayushchemu v pokhod protiv nepriyatelei, o vazhnosti voennogo zvaniya i ispolnenii prisyagi. Sochinenie Glavnogo svyashchennika Kavkazskoi Armii Protereya Stefana Gumilevskogo* (Tiflis: npg, 1866).

LAMBER, A. de, *Rassuzhdeniya o vospitanii devits. S nemetskogo [sic.!]* (St Petersburg: Senatskaya tip., 1814). (A. de Lambert, *Avis d'une mère à son fils et à sa fille* (1728].)

LEVSHIN, V. A., *Polnaya khozyaistvennaya kniga, otnosyashchayasya do vnutrennego domovodstva kak gorodskogo, tak i derevenskogo zhitelei, khozyaev i khozyaek* (Moscow: tip. S. Selivanovskogo, 1813).

——, *Ruskaya povarnya, ili Nastavlenie o prigotovlenii vsyakogo roda nastoyashchikh Ruskikh kushan'ev i o zagotovlenii v prok raznykh pripasov* (Moscow: S. Selivanovsky, 1816).

MOLOKHOVETS, E., *Podarok molodym khozyaikam* (Kursk, 1861: tip. Gubernskogo pravleniya).

——, *Podarok molodym khozyaikam. Domashnee, gorodskoe i sel'skoe khozyaistvo, gigiena i meditsyna, zaklyuchayushchaya v sebe 3000 domashnykh sredstv ot razlichnykh boleznei vzroslykh i detei i 1000 ukazanii na ukhod, otkarmlivanie i bolezni domashnykh ptits i zhivotnykh*, iii (St Petersburg: tip. Gibermana, 1881).

——, *Prostaya obshchedostupnaya kukhnya* (St Petersburg: npg, 1884).

——, *Russkomu narodu: Sobranie gigienicheskikh i poleznishikh, prostykh domashnykh vrachuyushchikh sredstv ot razlichnykh boleznei vzroslykh i detei* (St Petersburg: tip. Doktora M. A. Khana, 1880).

MUKHANOV, P. A., *Portfel' dlya khozyaev, ili kurs sel'skoi arkhitektury* (2 vols.; St Petersburg: tip. Lazarevykh Instituta Vostochnykh yazykov, 1840).

PESTALOTSTSI, I. G., *Kniga dlya materei, ili sposob uchit' ditya nablyudat' i govorit'* (St Petersburg: tip. Shpora, 1806). {Pestalozzi, Johann Heinrich, *Buch der Muetter, oder Anleitung fuer Muetter, ihre Kinder bemerken und reden zu lehren* (Zürich and Bern, 1803).}

RADETSKY, I. M., *Al'manakh gastronomov, zaklyuchayushchii v sebe sostav blyud tridtsati polnykh obedov, oznachennykh zapiskami russkimi i frantsuzskimi [. . .]* (St Petersburg: tip. shtaba Otdel'nogo korpusa Vnutrennei strazhi, 1852: 2nd, expanded edition, containing 'ninety full menus' (*devyanosta polnykh obedov*), 1877.)

, *Khozyaika, ili polneishee rukovodstvo k sokrashcheniyu domashnikh raskhodov* (St Petersburg: M. O. Vol'f, 1868; reprinted 1883).

RUDOL'SKY, A., *Arkhitekturnyi al'bom dlya khozyaev, soderzhashchii v sebe bolee 100 arkhitekturnykh chertezhei, nuzhneishikh dlya sel'skikh stroenii [. . .]* (Moscow, 1839).

RUSSO, DZH. DZII., *Emil'*, trans. Elizaveta Fersal' (4 vols.; Moscow, tip. S. Selivanovskogo, 1807). {First complete translation of Rousseau, *Émile, ou de l'éducation.*}

SOKOLOV, D. N., *Svetskii chelovek, ili Rukovodstvo k poznaniyu pravil obshchezhitiya* (St Peterburg: npg, 1847).

STEPANOV, G., *Poslednii trud sleptsa-startsa Gerasima Stepanova, izdatelya pyati knig [. . .]* (2nd edn.; tip. V. Got'e, Moscow, 1851).

VARLAMOVA, R., *Semeinyi magazin sovremennykh usovershenstvovanii k rasprostrane-niyu mezhdu vsemi klassami lyudei izyashchnogo vkusa, poryadka i udobstva v domashnei i obshchestvennoi zhizni [. . .]* (Moscow: A. Everennov, 1856).

VOLOSHINOV, P., *Otets pouchayushchii pis'menno syna svoego zhitiyu dobromu i ne zazornomu. S prisovokupleniem synovnego otcheta v svobodnom vremyani, soderzhash-chem v sebe rozmyshleniya o raznykh predemetakh* (St Petersburg: Imperatorskaya tip., 1810).

V–v, B., *Entsiklopediya molodoi russkoi khozyaki* (2 vols.; St Petersburg: tip. A. Voeikova i Ko., 1839).

1880–1917

ABRAMOV, N., *Dar slova* (10 issues; St Petersburg: tip. V. Ya. Mil'shteina, 1913).

ALEKSANDROVA-IGNAT'EVA, P. P., *Prakticheskie osnovy kulinarnogo iskusstva* (8th edn.: Ya. Trei, St Petersburg, 1911).

AL'MEDINGEN, A., *Na vsyakii sluchai!* (St Petersburg: F. Pavlenkov, 1891).

ANDREEV, P. P., *Domovedenie: Rukovodstvo dlya khozyaek doma, domashnikh uchitel'nits* (St Petersburg: tip. brat'ev Panteleevykh, 1893).

Anon., *Damskii ugodnik: Sbornik al'bomnykh stikhotvorenii na vsyakoe zhenskoe imya* (St Petersburg: Vladimirskaya parovaya tip., 1898).

Anon., *Gigiena krasoty: Neobkhodimaya kniga dlya zhenshchiny* (Moscow: Skoro-pechatnya Levenson, 1909).

Anon., *Izdatel'stvo "Novyi Satirikon": Khudozhestvenno-yumoristicheskii kalendar'-al'manakh na 1914 god* (St Petersburg: Novyi Satirikon, 1914).

Anon., *Kak zhit' po Evangeliyu* (Moscow: izd. Moskovskoi sinodal'noi tip., 1905).

Anon., *Khoroshii ton* (St Petersburg: Rodina, 1907).

Anon., *Khozyain-domovod. Prakticheskie sovety* (Moscow: I. D. Sytin, 1904).

Anon., *Kurs sokol'skoi gimnazii: posobie dlya rukovoditelei*, trans. N. V. Manokhin (St Petersburg: Gimnasticheskoe obshchestvo 'Sokol', 1911).

Anon., *Nastavlenie materyam* (Moscow: npg, 1884).

Anon., *Samonoveishii pis'movnik: s prilozheniem: Kak derzhat' sebya doma i v obshchestve. Iskusstvo pisat' v al'bom. Rukovodstvo k tantsam i k svetskim razgovoram. A takzhe nauchnaya stat'ya Arkadiya Averchenko 'O pis'movnikakh voobshche'* (Petrograd: Novyi Satirikon, 1916).

Anon., *Samoobrazovanie kak put' k bogatstvu* (3 parts; St Petersburg: Dvadtsatyi vek, 1908–9).

Anon., *Zhenshchina i ee obyazannost': Kak sokhranit' zdorov'e, molodost', krasotu i byt' lyubimoi* (Moscow: tovarishchestvo skoropechatni A. A. Levinson, 1909).

Anon., *Zhenshchina-vrach. Zhena, mat' i ditya. Intimnye sovety zhenshchine. Ukhod za soboyu v razlichnye periody zhizni. Sostavlena pod redaktsiei doktora-meditsiny S. M. Ershova* (St Petersburg: npg, 1909).

Antonov, A., *Obshchedostupnaya gigiena* (St Petersburg: A. Suvorin, 1889).

Baden-Poel', R., *Boi-skauty: rukovodstvo samovospitaniya molodezhi po sisteme "skauting" sera Roberta Baden Poelya primenitel'no k usloviyam russkoi zhizni i prirody. V pererabotke V. A. Popova i V. S. Preobrazhenskogo* (Moscow: tip. I. D. Sytina, 1917). {Baden-Powell, R., *Scouting for Boys: A Handbook for Instruction in Good Citizenship* (rev. edn.; London, 1908).}

[Brodersen, G.], *Khoroshii ton: Nastol'naya kniga dlya zhenshchin* (St Petersburg: Modnyi svet, 1884).

Channing, V., *O samovospitanii i drugie izbrannye stat'i*, trans. P. A. Bulanzhe (Moscow: Posrednik, 1912).

Dragomirova, S., *V pomoshch' khozyaikam* (St Petersburg: tip. V. Berezovskogo, 1909).

'Dyadya serzh', *Polnyi lyubovnyi pis'movnik: sobranie lyubovnykh pisem dlya vsekh vozrastov, razlichnogo soderzhaniya* (Moscow: tovarishchestvo I. D. Sytina, 1916).

Dyuga, L., *Zastenchivost' i ee lechenie* (St Petersburg: tip. V. I. Gubinskogo, 1899). {Dugas, Louis, *La Timidité, étude psychologique et morale* (Paris, 1898).}

Edvards, D., *Ideal'naya kul'tura tela. Naibolee vernye i deistvitel'no obezpechivayush-chie zdorov'e uprazhneniya dlya kazhdogo cheloveka* (St Petersburg: Sotrudnik, n.d. [c.1910]).

Fisher-Dyukel'man, Anna, *Zhenshchina—domashnii vrach. Nastol'naya kniga dlya zhenshchin. Znachitel'no dopolnennyi perevod s nemetskogo*, ed. I. A. Litinsky (St Petersburg: A. F. Marks, ·1909). {Fischer-Dückelmann, A., *Die Frau als Hausärtztin (Das goldene Frauenbuch). Nachschlagebuch der Gesundsheitspflege und Heilkunde der Familie [. . .]* (Stuttgart, 1908).}

Garman [Harman?], N., and Gankok [Hancock], I. *Dzhyu-dzhitsu: metod yaponskoi atletiki*. Trans. from the French [!] (St Petersburg: tip. Yu. Mansfel'd, 1908). {?H. I. Hancock, *Jiu-Jitsu Combat Tricks: Japanese Feats of Attack and Defence in Personal Encounters* (New York and London, 1904).}

Iur'ev and Vladimirsky, *Pravila svetskoi zhizni i etiketa: Khoroshii ton* (St Petersburg: tip. V. A. Tikhanova, 1889).

Izvol'sky, S. *Interesnye zapiski dlya molodykh, zhelaiushchikh sdelat'sia v obshchestve razvyaznymi, lovkimi, obrazovannymi, umnymi i lyubeznymi kavalerami: S prilozheniem pis'movnika dlia molodykh liudei i nekotorykh privetstvii* (Moscow: Mysl', 1912).

Kalendar' 'Damskii mir' na 1915 god (St Petersburg: Damskii mir, 1915).

Kalendar' 'Damskii mir' na 1917 god (St Petersburg: Damskii mir, 1917).

KARABINOVICH, G. M., *Kratkoe khristiianskoe uchenie. Uchebnik po zakonu Bozhiyu dlya staroobryadcheskikh shkol* (Moscow: Moskovskaya staroobryadcheskaya knigopechatnya, 1916; repr. Moscow, 1997).

KHEISIN, M. L., *Chto takoe potrebitel'skoe obshchestvo i kakaya ot nego pol'za* (3rd edn.: Moskovskii soyuz potrebitel'skikh obshchestv, Moscow, 1916).

Khudozhestvenno-yumoristicheskii kalendar'-al'manakh na 1914 god (St Petersburg: Novyi Satirikon, 1914).

KLAUSTON, T. S., *Gigiena uma* (Moscow: tip. i litografiya L. Lyundorf, 1910). {?Clauston, T. S., *Mental Hygiene*: original not located.}

LEINARD, B., *Sekrety krasoty, zdorov'ya i dolgovechnosti* (2nd edn.; Moscow: tip. A. P. Poplavskogo, 1909). {Laynard, B., *Secrets of Beauty, Health and Long Life* (London, 1900).}

LEVI, P. E., *Ratsional'noe vospitanie voli: Prakticheskoe rukovodstvo k dukhovnomu samolecheniyu i samovospitaniyu* (St Petersburg: tip. O. Bogdanova, 1912). {Levy, P. E., *L'Education rationelle de la volonté* (Paris, 1898).}

LORI, A., *Kak uvelichit' i ukrepit' zhenskii byust* (St Petersburg: Zhizn', 1909).

LOZINsky, E., *Vegetarianstvo i vospitanie* (Moscow: tip. Vil'de, 1912).

MARDEN, R. [sic] *Uspekh v zhizni*, trans. T. V. Babenkova (St Petersburg: tip. i litografiya V. A. Tikhanova, 1903). {Marden, Orison Swett, *Good Manners: A Passport to Success* (New York, 1900).}

MARTEN, A., *O vospitanii kharaktera*, trans. V. Revyakin (Moscow: tip. A. A. Kartseva, 1888). {Martin, A., *L'éducation du caractère* (Paris, 1887).}

METUZALA, P. F., *Dzhentl'men: nastol'naya kniga izyashchnogo muzhchiny* (St Petersburg: P. F. Metuzala, 1913).

MIKHAILOVA, E. A., *Fizicheskoe vospitanie zhenskoi molodezhi zhenshchiny-vracha E. A. Mikhailovoi. Lektsii, chitannye avtorom v Istoricheskom muzee v yanvare 1904 goda* (Moscow: tip. Obshchestva rasprostraneniya poleznykh znanii, 1905).

MILLER, I. P., *Moya sistema: 15 minut ezhednevnoi raboty dlya zdorov'ya*, trans. G. M. Romm (St Petersburg: Sotrudnik, 1909). {Müller, Jørgen Peter, *My System: Fifteen Minutes' Work a Day for Health Sake, from the Fifth Edition of the Danish Original* (London, 1905).}

MOLOKHOVETS, E., *V zashchitu pravoslavno-russkoi sem'i* (St Petersburg: tip. Chelovekolyubivogo obshchestva, 1908).

'NIKOLINI', *Polnyi pis'movnik dlya vlyublennykh i rukovodstvo k izucheniyu zhiteiskoi mudrosti* (7th edn.; Moscow: Torgovyi dom E. Konovalova i Ko., 1909).

NISTROM, A., *Polovye zhizn' i ee zakony*, trans. L. A. Zolotarev (Moscow: M. A. Zolotarev, 1909). {Nystrom, Anton: original not located.}

[SEVEROVA]-NORDMAN, N., *Sleduet raskrepostit' prislugu. Posvyashchaetsya Kukharkam, Gornichnym i Lakeyam* (St Petersburg: Skoropechatnya Ya. Krovitskogo, n.d. [c.1909]).

[SEVEROVA]-NORDMAN, N., *Povarennaya kniga dlya golodayushchikh: posvyashchaetsya presyshchennym. Zametki s natury* (St Petersburg: Skoropechatnya Ya. Krovitskogo, 1911).

——, *Dorogim sestritsam i tovarishcham. "Zamesto guvernantki"* (St Petersburg: Skoropechatnya Ya. Krovitskogo, 1913).

——, *Raiskie zavety: stat'i i zametki* (St Petersburg: Skoropechatnya Ya. Krovitskogo, 1913).

'OLIMPIETS, VILLI', *Kul't tela: krasota i sila* (St Petersburg: npg, n.d. [*c.*1910]).

PANOV, A. V., *Domashnie biblioteki: Opyt sostavleniya sistematicheskogo ukazatelya knig dlya samoobrazovaniya* (Saratov: V. K. Sampsonov, 1903).

PEIO, ZH., *Vospitanie voli* (St Petersburg: F. Pavlenkov, 1913). {Payot, Jacques, *L'éducation de la volonté* (1894).}

REDELIN, M., *Dom i khozyaistvo: Rukovodstvo k ratsional'nomu vedeniyu domashnego khozyaistva v gorode i v derevne* (3rd edn.; 2 vols.; St Petersburg: A. F. Marks, 1900).

RUBAKIN, N. A., *Pis'ma k chitatelyam o samoobrazovanii. Kak nachinayushchie chitateli dolzhny pristupat' k nemu i kak vesti ego* (St Petersburg: N. P. Karabasnikov, 1913).

——, *Praktika samoobrazovaniya: Sredi knig i chitatelei* (Moscow: Nauka, 1914).

Samonoveishii pis'movnik: s prilozheniem: Kak derzhat' sebya doma i v obshchestve. Iskusstvo pisat' v al'bom. Rukovodstvo k tantsam i k svetskim razgovoram. A takzhe nauchnaya stat'ya Arkadiya Averchenko 'O pis'movnikakh voobshche' (Petrograd: Novyi Satirikon, 1916).

SAZONOV and BEL'SKY [no first names given] (comp.), *Russkii pis'movnik. Sbornik obraztsovykh pisem, delovykh bumag i kommercheskoi perepiski* (6th edn.; St Petersburg: P. F. Voshchinskaya, 1890).

SHTEINBERG, P., *Kak eto samomu sdelat'?* (St Petersburg: npg., n.d.; *c.*1910).

SMAIL'S, S., *Samodeyatel'nost'*, trans. N. Katernikov (2nd edn., St Petersburg: Kolesov and Mikhin, 1868). {Smiles, S., *Self-Help, with Illustrations of Character, Conduct and Perseverance* (London, 1859).}

——, *Dolg*, trans. S. Maikova (St Petersburg: K. N. Plotnikov, 1882). {Smiles, S., *Duty* (London, 1880).}.

——, *Kharakter*, trans. S. Maikova (2nd edn.; St Petersburg: K. N. Plotnikov, 1874). {Smiles, S., *Character* (London, 1866).}

——, *Sobranie sochinenii v 6 tomakh pod redaktsiei M. N. Nikol'skogo* (St Petersburg and Moscow: tovarishchestvo M. O. Vol'f, 1903).

STAFF, BLANSH, *Chto dolzhno znat' kazhdoi zhenshchine* (Moscow: tip. V. P. Bykova, 1912). {Staffe, Blanche, *Instructions pratiques pour obtenir un brevet de femme chic* (Paris, 1907).}

STOLITSA, Z. I., *Razvitie v detyakh zhizneradostnosti i bor'ba s pessimizmom* (St Petersburg and Moscow: tovarishchestvo M. O. Vol'f, 1912).

SVETOZARSKAYA, K. K., *Zhizn' v svete, doma i pri dvore* (St Petersburg: npg, 1890). 'Biblioteka prakticheskikh svedenii'.

TOLSTOI, L. N., *Kalendar' s poslovitsami na 1887 god* (Moscow: Posrednik, 1886) (*PSS* xl).

——, *Mysli mudrykh lyudei na kazhdyi den' sobrany L. N. Tolstym* (Moscow: Posrednik, 1903) (*PSS* xl).

——, *Odumaites'!* (St Petersburg: Obnovlenie, 1906) (*PSS* xxxvi).

——, *Kak osvobodit'sya rabochemu narodu? Pis'mo k krest'yaninu* (St Petersburg: Obnovlenie, 1906) (*PSS* xc).

——, *Na kazhdyi den'* (Moscow: Posrednik, 1909) (*PSS* xliii).

——, *Gde vykhod?* (St Petersburg: Obnovlenie, 1917) (*PSS* xxxiv).

UKHOV, V., *Rukovodstvo k pedagogicheskoi i gigienicheskoi gimnastike po sisteme shvedskogo gimnaziarkha Linga* (St Petersburg: tip. Zamyslovskogo i Bobyleva, 1872).

VOSKRESENSKAYA, S. I., *Drug khozyaiki* (St Petersburg: A. A. Kaspari, 1909).

V–v, M., *Kak provodit' leto na dache: Dachnaya dietetika* (St Petersburg: tip. tovarishchestva Elektro-tip. N. Ya Stoikovoi, 1909).

ZARINA, M. M., *Uchebnik kulinarii* (Moscow: Moskovskaya gubernskaya tip., 1910).

ZOLOTAREV, L. A., *Bor'ba s len'yu: Populyarno-nauchnyi ocherk* (Moscow: tip.-litografiya tovarishchestva I. N. Kushnarev i Ko., 1907).

1917–1953

ADOV, A., *Uchebnik lyubvi: dlya vzroslykh. Poeziya i praktika lyubvi* (Berlin: npg, 1924).

AL'TGAUZEN, N. F. and STELITSKY, S. A. (eds.), *Besedy s devushkami o materinstve* (Moscow: Gosudarstvennoe meditsinskoe izdatel'stvo, 1929).

——, *Otets i rebenok* (Moscow: Gosudarstvennoe meditsinskoe izdatel'stvo, 1929). ('Okhrana materinstva i mladenchestva' series).

Anon., *Nastavlenie dlya khoroshego i zdorovogo pitaniya (100 poleznykh retseptov dlya prigotovleniya pishchi. Gigiena)* (Petrograd: self-published, 1918).

ARKHANGEL'SKY, B. A., and SPERANSKY, G. N., *Mat' i ditya: Shkola molodoi materi* (Moscow: Medgiz, 1951).

BABINA, A., *Kak organizovat' dosug detei* (Moscow: Rabotnik prosveshcheniya, 1929).

BOIKO, G. P., *Stennaya gazeta i boevoi listok podrazdeleniya. V pomoshch' redkollegiyam stennykh gazet, voenkoram, aktivu* (Moscow: Voenizdat, 1949).

BRUK, G. YA., *Chto nado znat' krest'yaninu, otpravlyayushchemusya na rabotu v gorod* (Moscow and Leningrad: Meditsynskoe izdatel'stvo, 1930).

CHARNYI, M., *Gazeta na stene* (Ekaterinburg: Uralkniga, 1924).

Demobilizovannym ryadovym i serzhantam Krasnoi Armii (Moscow: Voenizdat, 1945; repr. 1945 and 1946).

CHUNIKHIN, V. M., *Kak imet' krasivye ruki: manikyur i pedikyur: Kak nado i ne nado ikh delat': Rukovodstvo i samouchitel'* (Kharbin: N. P. Sinitsyna, n.d.: c.1930). 'Vrachebno-kosmeticheskaya biblioteka'.

DOKUNIN, V., *Kak rabotat' rabkoru* (Moscow: Pravda, 1925).

Domovodstvo: Khrestomatiya (Moscow and Leningrad: Glavpolitprosvet /Molodaya gvardiya, 1929). ('V pomoshch' krest'yanke-khozyaike' series).

FRONSHTEIN, R. M., *Onanizm* (Moscow and Leningrad: Meditsynskoe izda-tel'stvo, 1930).

GASTEV, A., *Trudovye ustanovki* (Moscow and Leningrad: Tsentral'nyi institut truda, 1924).

——, *Kak nado rabotat'* (2nd edn.; Moscow: VTsSPS, 1926).

Gimnastika po radio: Kompleksy uprazhnenii (Moscow: Vechernyaya Moskva, 1946).

GOL'DFAIL', L. G., *Lechenie vodoi doma, na kurorte i v lechebnom uchrezhdenii* (Moscow and Leningrad: Meditsynskoe izdatel'stvo, 1930).

GOLOMB, YA. D., *Polovoe vozderzhanie: za i protiv. Chto dolzhen znat' kazhdyi o sovremennom sostoyanii voprosa* (2nd edn.; Odessa: Svetoch, 1927).

GORELIK, B. E., *Kak organizovat' rabotu kolkhoznoi stennoi gazety* (Moscow: Sotsialisticheskoe zemledelie, 1946).

GORINEVSKY, V. V., *Remont i zakalivanie organizma* (Moscow: Trud i kniga, 1925).

GUREVICH, A., A. SVETLOVA, M. SOKOLOVA and M. YANCHEVSKAYA, *Kul'tura rechi v obraztsakh i zadaniyakh: Rabochaya kniga dlya shkol II-oi stepeni, rabkorov, komvuzov, partshkol i pedtekhnikumov. S prilozheniem spravochnika po rasstanovke znakov prepinaniya* (Moscow: Brokgauz–Efron, 1929).

Kak i o chem pisat' v gazetu? (Moscow: Pravda, 1928).

Kruzhok domovodstva v izbe-chital'ne (Moscow, 1925).

KALININ, M., *O kommunisticheskom vospitanii* (Leningrad: Lenizdat, 1947).

KAMBON, ZH., *Diplomat. Perevod s frantsuzskogo pod redaktsiei i s predisloviem A. A. Troyanovskogo* (Moscow: Gospolitizdat/Krasnyi proletarii, 1946). {Cambon, Jules, *Le Diplomate* (Paris, 1926).}

KATSENEL'SON, I. S. *Sovety materyam* (3rd edn., Leningrad: Lenigradskaya pravda, 1930). 'Biblioteka zhurnala *Gigiena i zdorov'ya rabochei i krest'yanskoi sem'i*'.

KEKCHEEV, K. KH. *Gigiena umstrennogo truda* (Moscow: Krasnyi proletarii, 1948).

KERZHENTSEV, P., *Kak vesti sobraniya* (Petrograd: Petrogradskii sovet rabochikh i krest'yanskikh deputatov, 1919).

——, *Organizui samogo sebya!* (Moscow: Molodaya gvardiya, 1925).

KHERSONSKAYA, E., *Molodym propagandistam i agitatoram* (Moscow: Gosizdat, 1920).

KHRISANFOV, N. E. and TRAKHTMAN, L. B., *Pamyatka turista: gigiena i samokontrol'* (Moscow: Profizdat, 1951).

Kniga o vkusnoi i zdorovoi pishche (Moscow: Pishchepromizdat, 1939: repr. 1946, 1948, 1952).

KORABLEV, N. V., *Ezhednevnaya gimnastika dlya lyudei umstvennogo truda* (2nd edn., Moscow: Fizkul'tura i sport, 1950).

——, *Fizicheskaya kul'tura i zdorov'e* (Moscow: Fizkul'tura i sport, 1953).

KREPS, V. M., and ERBERG, K. A., *Praktika oratorskoi rechi* (Leningrad: Institut Agitatsii imeni Volodarskogo, 1931).

KRUPSKAYA, N. N., *Kakie znaniya nuzhny molodomu rabochemu, krest'yaninu, krasnoarmeitsu* (Moscow: izd. TsKRKSM, 1922).

——, *O samoobrazovanii: Sbornik stat'ei* (Moscow: Molodaya gvardiya, 1936), 10–14.

Kruzhok domovodstva v izbe-chital'ne (Moscow: Doloi negramotnost', 1925).

Kul'tura obsluzhivaniya passazhirov (Smolensk: Bol'shevistskii put', 1950).

LILINA, Z., *Roditeli, uchites' vospityvat' svoikh detei!* (Moscow: Narkompros/ Rabotnik prosveshcheniya, 1929).

MAKARENKO, A. A., *Kniga dlya roditelei* (Moscow: Khudozhestvennaya literatura, 1937).

——, *Besedy s roditelyami* (Stalingrad: Obshchee knigoizdatel'stvo, 1941).

MAYAKOVSKY, V. V., *Kak delat' stikhi* (Moscow: Ogonek, 1927).

MENDEL'SON, A. L., *Ob ukreplenii pamyati* (4th edn., Leningrad: Leningradskaya pravda, 1930). 'Biblioteka zhurnala *Gigiena i zdorov'ya*'.

——, *Onanizm i bor'ba s nim* (1924: 8th edn., Leningrad: Leningradskaya pravda, 1930). ('Biblioteka zhurnala *Gigiena i zdorov'ya*' series.)

——, *Zastenchivost' i bor'ba s neyu* (1928: 4th edn., Leningrad: Leningradskaya pravda, 1930).

MEREZHKOVSKAYA, O., *Sovety khozyaikam: Kulinariya* (Paris: npg, *c.*1935).

MIRTOV, A. V., *Kak chitat' knigu* (Bakhmut: Rabochii Donbassa, 1924).

——, *Umen'e govorit' publichno* (Moscow: Aktsiznoe izdatel'skoe obshchestvo, 1925).

MONTESSORI, M., *Metod nauchnoi pedagogiki, primenyaemyi k detskomu vospitaniyu v Domakh rebenka*, trans. I. M. Solov'ev (Moscow: Zadruga, 1920). {Montessori, Maria, *Il metodo della pedagogia scientifica applicato all'educazione infantile nelle case dei bambini* (Rome, 1913).}

MURALEVICH, V. S., *Remont chelovecheskoi mashiny. Bolezni, starost' i bor'ba s nimi* (Moscow and Leningrad: Molodaya gvardiya, 1927).

PETROV, A. A., *Kak rabotat' nad dokladom* (Moscow and Leningrad: Gosizdat, 1929).

PETRYAK, V., *Pechat' komsomol'skikh yacheek* (Moscow: Novaya Moskva, 1924).

PILATSKAYA, N., and ZUEV, A., *Kruzhok rabkorov i stennaya gazeta* (Moscow: Pravda, 1925).

PISAREV, P. A., *Organizatsiya i tekhnika raboty ofitsianta* (Moscow: Gostorgizdat, 1949).

PLOTNIKOV, B. S., *Deshevoe dachnoe stroitel'stvo* (Moscow: Tsentrozhilsoyuz, 1930).

POGREBETSKY, M., *V pomoshch' turistu* (Khar'kov: Ukraïns'kii robitnik, 1935).

POLOTSKAYA, N., and DOKUNIN, V., *Redkollegiya stennoi gazety i kruzhok rabkorov* (Moscow: Pravda, 1928).

PRIMAKOVSKY, A., *Kak rabotat' s knigoi* (Moscow: Molodaya gvardiya, 1951). ('Bibliotechka komsomol'skogo propagandista' series.)

[PROKLITOV, S. A. *et al.*], *Drug rabotnitsy: Spravochnik dlya zhenshchin* (Moscow: Golos tekstilei, 1929).

Rabkor i gazeta (2nd edn.; Perm': Zvezda, 1924).

Rabkor i stennaya gazeta (Moscow: Moskovskii komitet RKP(b)/Novaya Moskva, 1924).

Rabochii fakul'tet na domu: podgotovitel'nyi kurs (Moscow: Gosizdat, 1926).

ROZHITSYN, V., *Kak vystupat' na sobranii s dokladami i rechami* (Khar'kov: Proletarii, 1928).

RUBAKIN, N. A., *Kak i s kakoi tsel'yu chitat' knigu* (Petersburg and Moscow: Kooperativnoe izdatel'stvo, 1922).

RUBAKIN, N. A., *Pis'ma k chitatelyam o samoobrazovanii: Kak nachinayushchie chitateli dolzhny pristupat' k nemu i kak vesti ego. Tseli i sposoby samoobrazovatel'noi raboty* (3rd edn.; New York: Gruppa russkikh chitatelei, 1923).

RYABOV, V. N., *Kakim dolzhen byt' blagoustroennoe selo* (Moscow: Moskovskii bol'shevik, 1947).

Samoobrazovanie putem chitki belletristiki: Chto chitat' vo vremya otpuska (Leningrad: Vasileostrovskii raikom, 1929).

SATOU, E., *Rukovodstvo po diplomaticheskoi praktike* (2nd edn., Moscow: Gospolitizdat/Krasnyi proletarii, 1947). {Satow, E., *A Guide to Diplomatic Practice* (2nd rev. edn.; 2 vols., London, 1922).}

SEMASHKO, N. A., *Iskusstvo odevat'sya* (Moscow and Leningrad: Gosizdat, 1927).

SARKIZOV-SERAZINI, I. M. *Lechites' solntsem!* (4th edn., Moscow and Leningrad: Zemlya i fabrika, 1927).

SHENGELI, G. A., *Kak pisat' stat'i, stikhi i rasskazy* (Moscow: Pravda/Bednota, 1926).

——, *Shkola pisatelya: osnovy literaturnoi tekhniki* (Moscow: Vserossiiskii Soyuz poetov, 1929).

TOPCHAN, P., *Den' za dnem. Opyt ezhednevnoi stennoi gazety "Montazhnik"* (Moscow: Moskovskii rabochii, 1946).

TOPORKOV, A. K., *Kak stat' kul'turnym* (Moscow: Rabotnik prosveshcheniya, 1929).

TSYPLENKOV, N. P., *Povarennaya kniga: 200 blyud dlya domashnego stola* (Moscow: Gostorgizdat, 1939).

——, *Obsluzhivanie v restorane* (Moscow: Gostorgizdat, 1945).

Turizm zimoi (Moscow: Tsentral'nyi sovet Obshchestvo Proletarskogo turizma i ekskursii, 1935).

UL'YANOV, L. D., *Odezhda i zdorov'e* (Khar'kov: Nauchnaya mysl', 1929).

Ustav voennoi sluzhby Raboche-Krest'yanskoi Krasnoi Armii (Petrograd, 1922).

UVAROVA, E. G. *Sputnik domashnei khozyaiki: 1000 kulinarnykh retseptov s ukazaniem kak gotovit' na primuse* (Leningrad: self-published, 1927).

V pomoshch' stengazete: Lektsii, opublikovannye v zhurnale "Raboche-krest'yanskii korrespondent" za 1935 i 1936 gg. (Pyatigorsk: Severo-kavkazskii bol'shevik, 1937).

VINOKUR, G., *Kul'tura yazyka: ocherki lingvisticheskoi tekhnologii* (1925: 2nd edn.; Moscow: Federatsiya, 1929).

Za zdorovoe zhilishche! (Leningrad: Pervaya tip. Gizlegproma, 1946).

ZARINA, M. M., *Uchebnik kulinarii* (Moscow: Skoropechatnya A. A. Levenson, 1918).

——, *Domovodstvo: pishcha, zhilishche, odezhda* (Moscow: Gosizdat, 1928). ('Biblioteka rabotnitsy i krest'yanki' series.)

——, *Uchis' khorosho stryapat'! (V pomoshch' khozyaike-krest'yanke)* (Moscow: Krest'yanskaya gazeta, 1928).

——, *Organizuite svoe domashnee khozyaistvo* (Moscow and Leningrad: Mospoligraf, 1929).

——, *Za obshchim stolom* (5th edn.; Moscow and Leningrad: Krest'yanskaya gazeta, 1933).

ZUEV-INSAROV, D. M., *Pocherk i lichnost'* (Moscow: self-published, 1929).

1954–1988

AASAMAA, I., *Kak sebya vesti* (4th edn.; Tallinn: Valgus, 1974).

ALESHINA, L., *O vezhlivosti, o takte i delikatnosti* (Leningrad: Lenizdat, 1975: repr. 1981, 1986, 1990).

ANTONOVA, S. (comp.), *Uchites' vlastvovat' soboyu* (Moscow: Molodaya gvardiya, 1975). 'Kompas'.

BARDIN, S. M., *Pogovorim o skromnosti* (Moscow: Sovetskaya Rossiya, 1959).

BLNDEROVA, V., *Synovnii dolg: Ocherki o sem'e* (Moscow: Gospolitizdat, 1959).

BENEZE, ZH., *et al.* [12 names listed], *Muzhchina u sebya doma* (Moscow: Legkaya industriya, 1980).

BLINOV, G. M., and DANYUSHEVSKY, B. L., *Skazhi sebe 'net!'* (Moscow: Molodaya gvardiya, 1973).

BUSHELEVA, B. V. *Pogovorim o vospitannosti* (Moscow: Prosveshchenie, 1980).

Bytovye sovety (Kiev: Ukrainizdat, 1958).

CHESTERFILD, FILIPP, *Pis'ma k synu. Maksimy. Kharaktery* (Moscow: Nauka, 1978). {Chesterfield, Philip D. S., *The Letters of Philip Dormer Stanhope, Earl of Chesterfield, with the Characters*, ed. J. Broadshaw, 3 vols. (London, 1905).

CHUKOVSKY, K. I., *Zhivoi kak zhizn'* (2nd edn.; Moscow: Molodaya gvardiya, 1963).

DOLININA, N., *Chelovek—lyudyam* (Moscow: Moskovskii rabochii, 1961). 'Besedy o nravstvennosti'.

Domovodstvo (1957: 4th edn., Moscow: Kolos, 1965).

DOROKHOV, A., *Eto ne melochi!* (Moscow: Politizdat, 1961).

——, *Eto stoit zapomnit'* (2nd edn.; Moscow: Detskaya literatura, 1961).

——, *Kak sebya vesti* (Moscow: Prosveshchenie, 1966).

——, *Eto stoit zapomnit'. Kniga o tom, kak sebya vesti, chtoby i tebe i drugim bylo luchshe i priyatnee zhit'* (Moscow: Detgiz, 1961).

——, *Estetika povedeniya* (Moscow: Shkol'naya biblioteka, 1963).

EMEL'YANOVA, K. L., *Pervyi v strane* (Leningrad: Lenizdat, 1964).

Etiket i takt sotrudnika militsii. Uchebnoe posobie (Moscow: Akademiya MVD SSSR, 1977).

Etiquette: After Emily Post, ed. and trans. E. Gluskina (Moscow: Institut mezhdunarodnykh otnoshenii, 1961).

FEDOROVA, N. V., *300 poleznykh sovetov po domovodstvu* (Leningrad: Lenizdat, 1958).

GASTEV, A., *Kak nado rabotat'* (Moscow: Ekonomika, 1966).

GRIGOR'EV, P. YA., and SEMENOVA, L. N., *Sem'ya za obedennym stolom* (Moscow: Znanie, 1960).

IVANCHENKO, V., *Tainy russkogo zakala* (Moscow: Molodaya gvardiya, 1985).

Kalendar' dlya zhenshchin (Moscow: Politizdat, 1980).

Kalendar' dlya zhenshchin na 1982 god (Moscow, 1980).

KASSIL', LEV, *Delo vkusa: Zametki pisatelya* (2nd edn.; Moscow: Iskusstvo, 1964).

KHODAKOV, M., *Kak ne nado sebya vesti (naedine s samim soboi)* (Moscow: Molodaya gvardiya, 1975).

Kniga o vkusnoi i zdorovoi pishche (Moscow: Pishchepromizdat, 1953: repr. 1954, 1961 etc.).

Kniga poleznykh sovetov (Minsk: Gosizdat BSSR, 1958).

KOLESOV, V. V., *Kul'tura rechi—kul'tura povedeniya* (Leningrad: Lenizdat, 1988).

Kratkaya entsiklopediya domashnego khozyaistva (2 vols.; Moscow: Sovetskaya entsiklopediya, 1959; repr. 1962 and 1966).

Kul'tura zhilogo inter'era (Moscow: Iskusstvo, 1966).

KURENNOV, P. M., *Russkii Narodnyi Lechebnik [. . .] i stat'i o lechenii golodom* (New York: npg, 1955).

LIKHACHEV, D. S., *Pis'ma o dobrom i prekrasnom* (Leningrad: Detskaya literatura, 1985).

LISITSYN, N. A., *Kak zhivesh', mama?* (Voronezh: Tsentral'no-chernozemnoe izdatel'stvo, 1965).

MOLOCHKOV, F. F., *Diplomaticheskii protokol i diplomaticheskaya praktika* (2nd edn., Moscow: Mezhdunarodnye otnosheniya, 1979).

NIKIFOROV, D. S., and BORUNKOV, A. F., *Diplomaticheskii protokol v SSSR: printsipy, normy, praktika* (Moscow: Mezhdunarodnye otnosheniya, 1985).

Odezhda dlya molodykh, comp. N. A. Golikova (Moscow: Molodaya gvardiya, 1959).

OSIPOV, V., *Kniga v vashem dome* (Moscow: Kniga, 1967).

Osnovy kul'tury rechi: khrestomatiya, ed. L. I. Skvortsov (Moscow: Vysshaya shkola, 1984).

Poleznye sovety (Moscow: Moskovskii rabochii, 1959).

Poleznye sovety (Yuzhnosakhalinsk: Yuzhnosakhalinskoe knizhnoe izdatel'stvo, 1960).

Poleznye sovety voinu (3rd edn.; Moscow: Voenizdat, 1976).

PRONSKY, B. N. [as Timofeev, B.], *Pravil'no li my govorim? Zapiski pisatelya* (2nd edn.; Leningrad: Leninizdat, 1963).

RAZUMNY, V., *O khoroshem khudozhestvennom vkuse* (Moscow: Politicheskaya literatura, 1961). ('Populyarnaya bibliotechka po estetike' series.)

RUBAKIN, N. A., *Kak zanimat'sya samoobrazovaniem* (Moscow: Sovetskaya Rossiya, 1962).

RUNOVA, I. S., *S meshchanstvom nado borot'sya* (Leningrad: Lenizdat, 1962). 'Besedy o moral'nom kodekse'.

Semeinoe vospitanie—slovar' dlya roditelei (Moscow: Prosveshchenie/Akademiya politicheskikh nauk SSSR, 1967).

SHENKMAN, S. B., *My—muzhchiny* (2nd edn., Moscow: Fizkul'tura i sport, 1980).

SMOLKA, K., *Pravila khoroshego tona*, (Moscow: Progress, 1980).

Sovety po domovodstvu (Murmansk, 1959).

SPOK, B., *Rebenok i ukhod za nim* (Moscow: Progress, 1970). {Spock, B., *Baby and Child Care* (new and enlarged edn.; New York, 1959).}

——, *Razgovor s mater'yu* (Moscow: Progress, 1987). {Spock, B., *Dr Spock Talks with Mothers: Growth and Guidance* (New York, 1962).}

STROGOV, N. I., *Kul'tura obsluzhivaniya pokupatelei* (Moscow: Tsentrosoyuz, 1962).

SUKHOMLINSKY, V. A., *Pis'ma k synu* (Moscow: Prosveshchenie, 1979).

——, *On Education*, trans. K. Judelson (Moscow: Progress, 1977).

——, *Rozhdenie grazhdanina* (3rd edn.; Moscow: Molodaya gvardiya, 1979).

——, *Kniga o lyubvi* (Moscow: Molodaya gvardiya, 1982).

SVETOZARSKAYA, K., *Zhizn' v svete, doma i pri dvore* (Moscow: Ekomak, 1990: repr. of St Petersburg, 1890 edn.).

SYSENKO, V. A., *Molodezh' vstupaet v brak* (Moscow: Mysl', 1986).

——, V. A., *Supruzheskie konflikty* (2nd edn.; Moscow: Mysl', 1989).

Tysyacha sovetov 'na zdorov'e' (Moscow: Sovetskaya Rossiya, 1971).

USPENSKY, L. V., *Kul'tura rechi* (Moscow: Znanie, 1976).

Za novye obryady, obychai, traditsii (Perm': Knizhnoe izdatel'stvo, 1964).

VAIL', PETR, and GENIS, ALEKSANDR, *Russkaya kukhnya v izgnanii* (Los Angeles: Al'manakh, 1987).

VLADIN, V., and KAPUSTIN, D., *Garmoniya semeinykh otnoshenii* (1988: reprinted Petrozavodsk: Kareliya, 1991).

ZENEVICH, G. V., *Vrednaya privychka ili bolezn'?* (2nd edn.; Leningrad, Meditsyna, 1972).

1989–1998

Anon., *Pravila svetskoi zhizni i etiketa: Khoroshii ton* (Moscow: Ripol, 1990: repr. of St Petersburg, 1889 edn.).

BEKLASHOV, D. V., *Manery i povedenie delovogo cheloveka. Delovoi chelovek, kakim on dolzhen byt'* (Novyi Urengoi: Tyumenburgaz, 1993).

BORUNKOV, A. F., *Diplomaticheskii protokol v Rossii i diplomaticheskii etiket* (Moscow: Mezhdunarodnye otnosheniya, 1993).

——, *Diplomaticheskii protokol v Rossii* (Moscow; Mezhdunarodnye otnosheniya, 1999).

CHINENNYI, A. I., and STOYAN, T. A., *Etiket na vse sluchai zhizni* (Moscow: Akalis/ Assotsiatsiya avtorov i izdatelei, 1996).

Chto dolzhen znat' kazhdyi, prikhodyashchii v pravoslavnyi khram (Moscow: Sretenskii monastyr', 1999).

Delaite eto pravil'no: pokhorony (Moscow: Bukmen, 1996). 'Delaite eto pravil'no' series.

Delaite eto pravil'no: svad'ba (Moscow: Bukmen, 1996). 'Delaite eto pravil'no' series.

Entsiklopediya dlya malen'kikh printsess (St Petersburg: Diamant, 1996).

Etiket i my, comp. N. M. Goncharova (Moscow: MK-Servis, 1993).

Etiket: Umen'e zhit' i vesti sebya doma v sem'e i v obshchestve, comp. Nikolaeva and Petrov (Moscow: Tsitadel'-triada, 1995).

GOGOL', N. V., *Vybrannye mesta iz perepiski s druz'yami* (repr. Moscow: Patriot, 1993).

GUSEV, V. G., *Lyubitel'skaya okhota* (Moscow: Tsitadel', 1997).

Kak ne stat' zhertvoi prestupleniya: Sovety professionalov (Leningrad: Leningradskaya assotsiatsiya rabotnikov organov vnutrennikh del, 1991).

Kak vesti sebya na kladbishche (Moscow: Sretenskii monastyr', 1999).

KARNEGI, Deil, *Kak zavoevyvat' druzei i okazyvat' vliyanie na lyudei. Kak vyrabatyvat' uverennost' v sebe i vliyat' na lyudei, vystupaya publichno. Kak perestat' bespokoit'sya i nachat' zhit'* (Moscow: Progress, 1989). {Carnegie, Dale, *How to Win Friends and Influence People* (New York, 1937).}

——, *Kak zavoevyvat' druzei i okazyvat' vliyanie na lyudei. Kak perestat' bespokoit'sya i nachat'sya zhit'. Doroti Karnegi, Kak pomoch' vashemu muzhu dostich' uspekha* (Kemerovo: Knizhnoe izdatel'stvo, 1990). {A trans. of *How to Win Friends . . .* (see above), plus Carnegie, Dorothy, *How to Help Your Husband Get Ahead in His Business and Social Life* (New York, 1954).}

KHOLLANDER, Ks., *Kak stat' seksual'noi zhenshchiny* (Moscow: LADS, 1990). {Abridged trans. of Hollander, Xaviera, *Xaviera on the Best Part of a Man* (London, 1975).}

KOMFORT, A., A., *Radost' seksa* (Moscow: Novosti, 1991). {Comfort, Alex, *The Joy of Sex* (2nd edn.; London, 1989).}

KOZLOV, N., *Kak otnosit'sya k sebe i lyudyam, ili Prakticheskaya psikhologiya na kazhdyi den'* (Moscow: Novaya shkola, 1996).

Kto zashchishchaet zhenshchin: Sbornik materialov i publikatsii (Moscow, 1996).

MAKSIMOVSKY, M., *Etiket delovogo cheloveka* (Moscow: Didakt, 1994).

MAL'SAGOV, A., *Pritchi o gorskom etikete* (Nal'chik: El'brus, 1989).

Muzhchina v dome, comp. V. Verzhbovich, S. Ivanov, and Yu. Sidorov (Ivanovo: Infokom, 1991).

MOLOKHOVETS, E. *Podarok molodym khozyaikam* (St Petersburg: Diamant, 1999).

NIKIFOROVA, M. I., and KAGANOVSKAYA, O. N., *Domovodstvo: Izdanie dlya dosuga* (2nd edn.; Moscow: Kolos, 1998).

PARKINSON, S. N., *Zakony Parkinsona* (Moscow: Progress, 1989). {Parkinson, C. N., *Parkinson's Law, or the Pursuit of Progress* (London, 1957).}

Poleznye sovety po gostepriimstvu, etiketu i ratsional'nomu pitaniyu po BREGGU i dr. na vse sluchai zhizni. (Metodicheskoe posobie) (Kiev: Uchebno-metodicheskii tsentr 'Etiket', 1991).

ROSSITER, F. M., *Vse o sekse* (Moscow: npg, 1989). {Rossiter, F. M., *The Torch of Life: A Key to Sex Harmony* (New York, 1925).}

RUKAVCHUK, L. N. (ed.), *Entsiklopediya etiketa* (St Petersburg: Ekspress/M.i M., 1996).

Shkola etiketa: poucheniya na vsyakii sluchai, comp. L. S. Likhacheva (Ekaterinburg: Sredne-Ural'skoe knizhnoe izdatel'stvo, 1996).

STRIT, R. *Tekhnika sovremennogo seksa* (Riga: Avers, 1990). {Abridged trans. of Street, Robert, *Modern Sex Techniques* (New York, 1955).}

TROFIMENKO, V. P. and VOLGIN, A. N. *Pogovorim ob etikete* (Moscow: Moskovskaya pravda, 1991)

Ukrashaem okna: sorok pyat' stilei opisannykh shag za shagom (Moscow: Trien, 1997). {*Arts and Crafts for Home Decorating*, vol. 3, New York, 1994.}.

VANDERBIL'T, E., *Etiket* (2 vols.; Moscow: Avial', 1995). {Vanderbilt, Amy, *Amy Vanderbilt's New Complete Book of Etiquette: The Guide to Gracious Living* (New York, 1963).}

VENEDIKTOVA, V. I., *O delovoi etike i etikete* (Moscow: fond 'Pravovaya kul'tura', 1994).

VERZHBOVICH, V., IVANOV, S., and SIDOROV, YU., *Muzhchina v dome* (Tver': Terminal, 1991).

YAGODINSKY, V. N., *Kak sebya vesti: Prakticheskii kurs kul'turnogo povedeniya* (Moscow: Znanie, 1991).

Zhenskaya magiya (Moscow: Institut gendernykh issledovanii, 1990).

Index of Names and Places

Index of Subjects